ACCOUNTANCY
QUESTIONS AND KEY

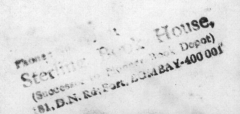

ACCOUNTANCY
QUESTIONS
AND KEY

Questions and Answers on accounts
to supplement the textbook

WILLIAM PICKLES
B COM FCA FRSA

*Late Senior Lecturer in Accountancy and Allied Subjects for the
Professional Accountants' Examination Course at the
Municipal High School of Commerce, Manchester
(now College of Commerce)*

Fourth Edition
by
JAMES L LAFFERTY
CA ATII

*Formerly Director and Vice-Principal,
The School of Accountancy and Business Studies
of Glasgow and London*

THE ENGLISH LANGUAGE BOOK SOCIETY
AND
PITMAN PUBLISHING

PITMAN PUBLISHING LIMITED
39 Parker Street, London WC2B 5PB

ELBS Edition first published 1964
Fourth Edition 1974
Reprinted 1966, 1968, ELBS Edition of Fourth Edition 1974
Reprinted 1977

Reproduced and printed by photolithography and bound in
Great Britain at The Pitman Press, Bath

ISBN 0 273 00836 6

Preface to the Fourth Edition

THIS EDITION, despite extensive revision, preserves the essential features and aims of the previous editions by Mr. William Pickles, the original author.

The revision work entailed re-arrangement of chapters to correspond with those of the fourth edition of *Accountancy*; rounding off figures throughout to the nearest £ or decimalizing where considered more appropriate; eliminating all obsolete data; replacing all out-dated legislation; presenting final accounts, in a number of cases, in vertical form to conform with modern accounting practice; and introducing a considerable number of new questions and answers, mainly on management accounting.

It is hoped that this new edition will continue to serve the needs of the modern student.

JAMES L. LAFFERTY

Preface to the First Edition

THIS KEY has been prepared in an endeavour to assist tutors, lecturers, and students in checking up answers to the exercises set out in the work *Accountancy*.

There is abundant evidence to prove that students as a whole have a pronounced tendency to neglect—in many cases deliberately to shirk—a most important part of their studies, viz. the working of illustrations. In order that the principles learned in a textbook should be firmly implanted in their minds, as well as the ability to *apply* those principles, students must of necessity spend a considerable proportion of their time working out problems of the type most likely to be presented to them in the examination hall; no mere re-reading of illustrations, nor the cursory, indolent procedure of "ticking-up" worked problems, will ensure that firm grasp and mastery of examination technique so essential in the professional accountants' examinations. Students are strongly recommended to attempt each problem, always striving to increase their speed, after which (and not *before*) their worked answers should be compared with the Key. On more occasions than one it will be necessary for students to restrain themselves from taking the line of least resistance, which generally assumes the form of having a "peep" at the Key.

Students will be wise in resisting to the uttermost, and at all times, such temptations, for their reward will, in the long run, be a steady growth of confidence and ability. The serviceability of the Key, then, depends very materially upon the judicious use to which it is put, and its abuse, it is enjoined, should most rigorously be avoided. In short, the purpose of the Key is to check and guide; not to afford a means of enabling students to evade the concentration and labour entailed in examination preparation.

The disciplinary effect of effort and result, important in study and yet more important in professional life, will, it is hoped, never be lost sight of by the presence (too near at hand) of the Key.

There is no objection to students preparing answers in draft form and employing reasonable abbreviations, but it is necessary that the answers contain all the essential aasumptions, points, comments, and observations. In this connection it cannot be too often reiterated that mere quantitative, as distinct from qualitative, output of students will not gain success, so that where necessary matters of mere detail must be subordinated to those of principle.

Wherever thought useful to students notes have been appended, and in several instances an answer more complete than is called for by the question has been additionally supplied, so as to enable students to obtain a clear perspective of the problem set for their elucidation.

As will be seen, almost all the questions have been taken from the recent examinations of the various bodies of professional accountants.

My thanks are due to Mr. C. E. Ruddin, B.A. (Com.), A.C.A., for his assistance in preparing the Key.

WILLIAM PICKLES

Contents

CHAPTER I

BOOK-KEEPING TO THE TRIAL BALANCE

1. Define Double Entry Book-keeping.

2. Classify the following under the headings of Personal, Real, and Nominal Accounts, and state on which side of the ledger you would expect to find the balances.

      (i) B. Robot (a supplier).   (iv) Bank Overdraft.
      (ii) Rates.   (v) Stock.
      (iii) Insurance.   (vi) Plant.

3. On 1st January R. Brick bought goods from B. Pitt value £600, less 33⅓ per cent trade discount. On the same day R. Brick returned half the goods and sent a cheque for the balance, less 5 per cent cash discount. Show how this transaction will be dealt with in the books of R. Brick.

4. From the following information prepare the ledger account of B. Wise in the books of J. Dixon, and bring down the balance on 31st January.

B. Wise—

Jan. 1. Purchased goods on credit for £320, less 25 per cent trade discount.
    4. Paid £150 on account.
    6. Purchased goods on credit for £200, less 25 per cent trade discount.
  10. Returned half the goods purchased on 6th January as damaged.
  12. Paid cheque £85, discount allowed £5.
  15. Purchased goods for cash £20.
  20. Purchased goods on credit for £100, less 20 per cent trade discount.
  25. Paid cheque £85, discount allowed £5.

5. A. Borker commenced business with the following assets: Cash in Hand, £4; Cash at Bank, £150; Stock, £400; Buildings, £1,000; Fixtures, £90; Debtors, £10; Machinery, £300. His liabilities were: Bills Payable, £350; Creditors, £75; Loan from A. Mann, £150.

Prepare opening Journal entries.

6. Journalize the following transactions in the books of T. Street—

(1) Bought Goods on credit from A. Text for £200.
(2) Goods returned from B. Jones, £25.
(3) Paid Carriage Inwards, £5.
(4) Cheque £70, previously received from A. Wood in settlement of a debt of £75, now returned dishonoured.
(5) Paid Insurance, £10.
(6) Sale of Typewriter for £5.
(7) £15 owing by M. Stone written off as a bad debt.
(8) Drew three months Bill of Exchange on A. Rose for £100.
(9) Sold Goods, £40, to N. Town on credit.

7. In what Ledger or other accounts, and upon which side of such accounts, would you expect to find the following?—

(a) £500 paid for new machinery.
(b) £170 received from J. Robinson in full settlement of his account of £172·63.
(c) £600 received from an Insurance Company in settlement of a claim for damages to premises by fire.
(d) £75 received for the sale of old Motor Van.
(e) £250 paid to J. Fitter in full settlement of an account due to him three months hence of £260·75.   (R.S.A.)

8. On 16th May, 19.., E. Short bought from G. Long 10 doz. pairs of blankets at £5·25 per pair, subject to 10 per cent trade discount and 5 per cent discount for cash within fourteen days. On 18th May, E. Short returned 20 pairs of blankets and on 27th May sent a cheque to settle his account. Pass these transactions through the proper subsidiary books of E. Short, and show G. Long's account in the ledger.   (R.S.A.)

9. What is a Trial Balance? Give six reasons why the Trial Balance may be out of balance.

10. (*a*) What types of errors may not be disclosed by the Trial Balance?

(*b*) State on what side of the Trial Balance you would expect to find the following balances, giving reasons for your answer—

1. Capital Account.	4. Bills Payable.
2. Purchases.	5. Bank Overdraft.
3. Returns Inwards.	6. Drawings.

11. The following balances were extracted from the books of a trader and you are asked to prepare a Trial Balance as at 31st December, 19..—

	£
Capital	3,000
Premises	1,500
Fixtures	500
Plant and Machinery	400
Sales	10,500
Purchases	7,640
Returns Inwards	150
Returns Outwards	70
Carriage Inwards	40
Carriage Outwards	75
Discounts Received	175
Discounts Allowed	240
Wages	730
Insurance and Rates	135
Rent Receivable	110
General Expenses	325
Creditors	1,224
Debtors	3,420
Drawings	300
Bills Payable	100
Cash in Hand	12
Bank Overdraft	288

12. B. Blank, a client of yours, with whom book-keeping is not a strong point, asks you to audit his accounts for the year ended 31st December, upon which date his closing stock was valued at £574.

As a basis for your audit, Blank furnishes you with the following statement—

TRIAL BALANCE 31ST DECEMBER	Dr.	Cr.
	£	£
B. Blank, Capital		1,556
„ Drawings	564	
Leasehold Premises	741	
Sales		2,756
Due from Customers		530
Purchases	1,268	
Purchases Returns	264	
Loan from Bank		250
Creditors	528	
Trade and Office Expenses	784	
Cash at Bank	142	
Bill Payable	100	
Salaries and Wages	598	
Stock (1st January)		264
Rent, Rates, etc.	465	
Sales Returns		98
	£5,454	£5,454

If you do not approve this statement, amend it.   (*C.A. Inter.*)

13. The following Trial Balance was extracted from the books of J. Cooper, a trader, on 19th March, 19..—

TRIAL BALANCE, 19TH MARCH, 19..

	Dr. £	Cr. £
Capital (1st April, 19..)		3,000
Drawings	330	
Freehold Property	1,200	
Furniture and Fittings	150	
Stock (1st April, 19..)	1,436	
Sales		8,041
Returns Inwards	159	
Purchases	6,735	
Returns Outwards		252
Office Expenses	510	
Bad Debts	131	
Carriage Outwards	159	
Carriage Inwards	145	
Salaries and Commission	455	
Discount		15
F. Drake	74	
W. Wright	33	
H. Nelson		318
C. Blake		152
Cash	37	
Bank	224	
	£11,778	£11,778

Post the above balances direct to the appropriate accounts in the Ledger, then pass thereto, through the proper subsidiary books, the following transactions—

19..

Mar. 21. Received from F. Drake a cheque for the amount of his account. The cheque was paid into bank.
  22. Sold goods on credit to G. Cook, £94.
  23. Bought goods by cheque, £82.
    Received a first and final dividend of 33⅓ per cent from W. Wright, the balance being irrecoverable. The cheque was paid into bank.
  24. Sold goods on credit to F. Drake, £154, and paid £5 out of cash for carriage on these goods.
    Paid salaries and commission in cash, £23.
  29. Paid H. Nelson, £100 on account by cheque.
  30. Drew and cashed a cheque for £50, and paid in cash Office Expenses £16, and Private Expenses £30.
    Sent a Credit Note for £25 to F. Drake for goods returned.
  31. Cash Sales, £36. (Not banked.)
Extract a Trial Balance as on 31st March, 19... (*R.S.A.*)

14. A had the following balances in his Ledger at 1st January, 19..—

		£
Capital		4,750
Debtors—		
T. Green	£100	
W. Cox	300	
J. Cooper & Co.	150	
A. Black	250	
		800
Creditors—		
F. Flint	£650	
J. Smith	150	
		800

Sold on credit ⟷ Bank
sold on cheque = Cash

	£
Stock	2,000
Motor Vans	2,000
Fire Insurance (£200) paid in advance to 31st March, 19..	50
Rent owing, due 25th December, 19.., for Premises occupied by A.	200
Post-dated Cheque given by J. Cooper & Co. due 7th January, 19..	150
Cash at Bank	750

You are required to open Ledger Accounts recording the above, and to pass the following transactions through the proper books to the Ledger and extract a Trial Balance. No Journal entries are required: all moneys received are banked immediately.

19..

Jan. 1. Drew and cashed cheque for petty cash purposes £5.

Paid rent £200 by cheque.

Sold W. Cox 240 yds. of linoleum at 60p a yard *less* trade discount 8⅓ per cent.

2. Paid Flint by cheque his account of £350 subject to £13 cash discount.

Drew and cashed cheque for petty cash purposes £15.

Paid out of petty cash, wages £12, postages £4, telephone £3.

4. Received from Black & Co. £50 on account.

Bought on credit from F. Flint & Co. 360 yds. of cloth at 20p a yard.

5. Paid Mobile & Co. £23 for sundry motor accessories.

W. Cox paid £250 on account.

6. Black & Co. paid their account *less* 2½ per cent discount.

7. Allowed £5 for damaged goods by J. Smith & Co.

Paid by cheque J. Smith & Co. their account *less* £3 discount.

J. Cooper & Co. post-dated cheque dishonoured. They gave two new post-dated cheques of £150 each due 1 month and 2 months respectively.

Received from the trustee in the bankruptcy of T. Green a first and final dividend of 25 per cent.

CHAPTER II

BANK RECONCILIATION STATEMENTS AND PETTY CASH

1. F. Smith's Cash Book showed a balance of cash at bank of £327·95 on 31st December, 19... His Bank Statement showed an overdraft of £267·89 on that date. The difference arose as follows—

A cheque for £32·94, drawn by F. Smith, had not been presented for payment; £616·45, received on 31st December, was not credited by the bank until 1st January, 19..; the bank had charged him with £12·33 interest, which was not entered in the Cash Book.

Prepare the Reconciliation Statement.

(R.S.A.)

2. From the following particulars prepare a Statement showing how the difference between the Cash Book Balance and the Bank Statement Balance is reconciled—

	£
Bank Statement Balance—30th June, 19.. . . .	1,401·63
Cash Book Balance—30th June, 19.. . . .	557·50

Cheques drawn prior to 30th June, 19.., but not presented until after that date—

	£
P.	29·20
Q.	801·17
R.	5·74
S.	132·32

	£
Country cheques paid into the Bank on 30th June, 19.., not collected until 2nd July, 19..	116·19
Bank Charges and Interest to 30th June, 19.., not entered in the Cash Book	8·11

(R.S.A.)

3. From the following particulars, prepare a Bank Reconciliation Statement as at 31st January, 19..—

	£
Bank Statement Balance overdrawn . . .	539·83
Cash Book Balance in hand	1,257·47

The following amounts have not been entered in the Cash Book—

	£
Commission . . .	2·53
Interest allowed .	18·63

A cheque received from the London Branch (£2,500) had not been entered as at 31st January, 19...

The following cheques have not been presented for payment—

£	£
100·11	92·42
89·63	113·58
247·75	43·11

4. A firm runs three banking accounts: Current, Deposit, and Customs Duties Account.

Prepare the Bank Reconciliation from the following particulars—

	£
Current Account—Bank Statement Balance in hand . . .	1·34
Cash Book Balance overdrawn . . .	812·94

5

During the period, Commissions £5·50 and Interest £13·57 have been charged, but have not been entered in the Cash Book.

No account has been taken of the following transfers—

	£
Current Account to Customs Duties Account . . .	2,500·00
Current Account to Deposit Account	2,000·00
Deposit Account to Current Account	5,450·00
Customs Duties Account to Current Account . .	1,088·68

The following cheques had not been presented—

£	£
102·28	150·00
50·00	

The lodgments not cleared amounted to £1,507·61.

5. Rule a Petty Cash Book with four analysis columns for Postages and Stationery, Travelling Expenses, Carriage, and Office Expenses; and enter up the following transactions. The book is kept on the imprest system, the amount of the imprest being £20.

19..

Jan. 4. Petty Cash in hand, £2·50.
       Received Cash to make up the imprest.
       Bought Stamps, £1·50.
   5. Paid Railway Fares, 20p, and Bus Fares, 25p.
       Telegrams, 46p.
       Bought Shorthand Notebooks for office, 55p.
   6. Paid Carriage on Small Parcels, 27p.
       Paid Bus Fares, 12p; and Railway Fares, 25p.
       Bought Envelopes, £1·15.
   8. Paid for Repairs to Typewriter, £4·22.
       Paid Carrier's Account for December, £1·84.
   9. Paid Office Cleaner, 60p.

Balance the Petty Cash Book as on 9th January, 19.., and bring down the balance.

(*R.S.A.*)

6. The following facts relate to the business of X, a client of yours who requires you to reconcile his Bank Statement balance with his Cash Book balance—

			£
Balance as per Bank Statement (in favour) .	.	*Dr.*	60
Balance as per Cash Book (overdrawn) .	.	*Cr.*	80
Unpresented Cheques	.	.	144
Uncredited Cheques	.	.	26

In addition you ascertain the following—

(1) A cheque for £20 paid to J. Jones has been entered in error in the Cash column.
(2) Bank commission of £8 has not been entered in the Cash Book.
(3) The debit side of the Cash Book (Bank column) has been undercast £50.

7. During an interim audit at 31st December, 19.4 (final accounts made up to a later date), you are instructed by your principal to reconcile the bank balance shown in the books of account with the balance shown in the Bank Statement. From the following particulars, prepare a Reconciliation Statement—

Balance per Bank Statement, 31st December, 19.4, overdrawn £1,026·64. Cheques drawn on 31st December, but not cleared till January, 19.5: £12, £1,021·14, £98·12, and £112·80.

Bank overdraft interest, 20th December, 19.4, not entered in Cash Book, £151·06.

Sum received on 30th December, 19.4, but not lodged in bank till 3rd January, 19.5, £2,100.

Cheque book, £0·25, November, 19.4, entered in the Cash Book twice in error and another cheque book debited in Bank Statement in August, 19.4, £1, not entered in the Cash Book.

Bill Receivable due on 29th December, 19.4, was passed to the Bank for collection on 28th December, 19.4, and was entered in the Cash Book forthwith, whereas the proceeds were not credited in the Bank Statement till 1st January, 19.5, £250.

Chamber of Commerce subscription paid by bankers' order on 1st December, 19.4, had not been entered in the Cash Book—£4·20.

Note. Assume that you do not alter the Cash Book balance at 31st December, 19.4, all correcting entries being made in January, 19.5. (*C.A. Inter.*)

8. A operated on two separate banking accounts, described as No. 1 and No. 2.

At 31st December, 19.9, the balances at bank, per Bank Sheets, were No. 1 £809 and No. 2 £2,009; whilst the bank balances in A's books at the same date were debit balances against the bank, No. 1 £85 and No. 2 £3,094.

The differences arose by reason of the following—

(1) Cheques lodged but not yet credited, £200 and £140 for No. 1 and No. 2 respectively.

(2) Cheque £20 paid in to No. 2 dishonoured, the entry therefor not having been made in A's books.

(3) A cheque from D. & Co. £22 remitted direct to No. 1 not entered in A's books.

(4) A draft paid into No. 2 for A£20 and entered in A's books as £20. (Rate of Exchange £125 Australian to £100 Sterling.)

(5) Cheque paid out for £73 intended to be a No. 1 cheque and entered in Cash Book as such, but in error signed as a No. 2 cheque.

(6) Cheque for £32 drawn on No. 2 inadvertently entered in the Cash Book as No. 1.

(7) A transfer of £1,000 out of No. 1 into No. 2 entered, but transfer instructions to bank overlooked.

(8) A periodic payment of £10 under standing order ex No. 2 not entered in Cash Book.

(9) A cheque drawn on No. 2 entered in correct account in the Cash Book but as £12 instead of the correct amount of £21.

(10) Bank Charges of £3 and £4 for No. 1 and No. 2 respectively not entered in Cash Book.

(11) Cheque received £200 for No. 2, and paid into No. 2, incorrectly entered in the Cash Book as No. 1.

(12) Cheque received and paid in to correct account No. 2, £18 entered as £17.

(13) There are no unpresented cheques, except £6, No. 2 account.

Prepare Bank Reconciliation Statement after adjusting bank balances, as required, in A's Cash Book.

9. According to an Estate Cash Book which you are examining, the balances in the bank on 30th June, 19.., to the credit of Henry Smithson, deceased, were £1,600 on Income Account and £4,941 on Capital Account. All capital sums are paid into or withdrawn from a Deposit Account. The Bank Statements show balances differing from those in the Cash Book. On investigation you find that—

(1) Dividends amounting to £141 entered in the Cash Book were not paid into the bank till 1st July, 19.. (the following day).

(2) Cheques amounting to £400, being payments of £400 to beneficiaries on account of income, were not presented to the bank till after 1st July, 19...

(3) Interest of £9 to 30th June, 19.., credited by the bank to the Deposit Account had not been entered in the Cash Book.

(4) A cheque for £10 for Professional Charges had been drawn in error on the Deposit Account instead of the Current Account.

(5) A cheque for £110 for Funeral Expenses had been entered in error in the Cash Book as £100 (although posted to the correct account).

You are required—

(*a*) to make the necessary adjustments in the Cash Book for the purpose of preparing Estate Accounts at 30th June, 19.., and

(*b*) to prepare a statement reconciling the adjusted Cash Book balances with the balances shown in the Bank Statement.

CHAPTER III

ARITHMETIC OF ACCOUNTANCY

1. An article is sold for £180, the gross profit being 20 per cent on cost. What is the cost price?

2. An article costs £180 and is sold at a gross profit of 20 per cent on selling price. What is the selling price?

3. A firm which dispatches its goods in returnable packages, values the packages at Balance Sheet dates at cost less 25 per cent. Packages are invoiced to customers at cost plus 50 per cent, and full credit is given on return. From the following information compute the value of packages in customers' hands for the Balance Sheet at the end of the year—

	£
Opening stock at Balance Sheet value	180
Packages sent out during the year at invoice price	2,200
Returns during the year at invoice price	1,600

4. A, B, C, and D are partners sharing profits in the ratio of 5:2:2:1. If the profit is £1,500, how much does each receive? A dies and the remaining partners continue in the same profit-sharing ratio. Assuming the same profit, how much does each receive?

5. Sales for the year are £15,500. Average sales for the last five months of the year (August to December) are four times the average for the first three months and twice the average for the four months April to July. Of these latter four months, June sales are five times the average of the other three months. How much are the June sales?

6. A invests £5,000 in the purchase of 4 per cent Stock at 80, which he sells at 85. With the proceeds he buys 5 per cent Stock at 95, which he holds until redemption date, the Stock being redeemed ten years later at 102. Ignoring expenses, what sum (to the nearest £) is finally realized? What is (a) the flat yield and (b) the redemption yield on the 5 per cent Stock?

7. A contractor, when estimating the price of a contract, adds to the actual costs to be incurred a sum to cover contingencies representing 5 per cent of the *total* costs (i.e. including the addition for contingencies). To the total costs he adds 20 per cent of the contract price as his profit. If the actual costs to be incurred are £1,900, what is the contract price?

8. A Ltd., who has bought the business of X Ltd., arranges to collect the latter company's book debts subject to (a) any bad debts properly incurred, (b) 5 per cent cash discount, and (c) a collecting commission of 3¾ per cent of the net cash collected.

Bad debts properly incurred are agreed between A Ltd. and X Ltd. at 2 per cent of the total book debts.

The final sum remitted to X Ltd. by A Ltd. was £89,608·75. Calculate the amount of the book debts.

9. A manager is entitled (in addition to his normal remuneration) to a percentage of net profit (such percentage to be charged in arriving at the net profit).

The arrangement is that—

> First £2,000 of the net profit to be ignored.
> Next £2,000 of the net profit to carry 10 per cent Commission.
> Next £2,000 of the net profit to carry 15 per cent Commission.
> Next £2,000 of the net profit to carry 20 per cent Commission.

Assuming that the profit (as agreed) *before* computing the manager's percentage is £7,700, compute the amount due to the manager.

10. A contractor is engaged on a contract, upon which he estimates that the Cost of Materials, Labour and Depreciation of Plant and Overheads will be £3,000.

Based on previous experience he estimates that 10 per cent of *total* cost must be provided for to cover extras, claims, and contingencies.

The manager (in addition to his normal remuneration) is entitled to 10 per cent of the net profit after charging such percentage.

The estimated profit is 16⅔ per cent of contract price. Compute the estimated contract price.

11. A carries on business and earns a profit of 33⅓ per cent on Cost: and his selling expenses are 10 per cent of Sales. His standing charges are £1,500 per annum. Ascertain the sales required to "break even," that is, to cover exactly the standing charges.

12. A is entitled to a commission made up of two parts, viz. (*a*) 5 per cent on Sales and (*b*) 10 per cent the *excess* of Sales over the Cost of Sales, such cost to include the *total* commission payable.

	£
The goods cost (excluding commission) . .	4,000
Sales (¾ of the goods)	4,800

Calculate commission payable to A.

CHAPTER IV

ACCOUNTS CURRENT AND AVERAGE DUE DATE

1. A. N. Drew has withdrawn on account of profits for half-year ended 31st December the undermentioned amounts—July 18, £500; Aug. 12, £600; Nov. 16, £800.
Find the average date and calculate the interest at 5 per cent.

2. James Smith, a merchant, purchased goods from L. Ross, the due dates for payment in cash being as follows—

March 15	. .	£220	. .	Due 18th April
April 21	. .	£125	. .	Due 24th May
27	. .	£200	. .	Due 30th June
May 15	. .	£350	. .	Due 18th July

L. Ross agreed to draw a bill for the total amount due on the average due date, and you are required to ascertain this date.   (*C.A. Inter.*)

3. A purchases goods from B as follows—July 4, £364; July 30, £523; Sept. 10, £462.
Goods were to be drawn for at three months from average date.
What is the average date?   (*C.A. Inter.*)

4. From the following particulars make up an Account Current to be rendered by F. K. Johnson to L. M. Gibson at 31st December, reckoning interest at 5 per cent per annum—

June 30. Balance owing by Gibson, £513·86.
July 17. Goods sold to Gibson, £40..
Aug. 1. Cash received of Gibson, £500.
19. Goods sold to Gibson, £720·67.
30. Goods sold to Gibson, £15.
Sept. 1. Cash received of Gibson, £400.
Gibson accepted Johnson's draft at 3 months' date for £300.
Oct. 22. Goods bought of Gibson, £20.
Nov. 12. Goods sold to Gibson, £13·90.
Dec. 14. Cash received of Gibson, £50.   (*C.A. Inter.*)

5. From the following information prepare Account Current to be rendered by M. Side to V. Park up to 31st December. Interest to be calculated on the product system at the rate of 5 per cent per annum.

		£
July	2. Goods sold to V. Park	400
	10. Received Sight Draft from Park . . .	200
Aug.	1. Paid Cash on behalf of Park . . .	1,400
Sept.	1. Received Goods from Park	1,500
Oct.	1. Supplied Goods to Park	1,000
	15. Received Cash from Park	800
Nov.	15. Received Goods from Park	1,600
Dec.	1. Accepted Bill at 2 months	1,000
	15. Remitted Cash to Park	300

6. R. U. Dinn, a customer at the Western Bank, had the following transactions for the half-year to 31st December.
Debit balance at 1st July, £200.

He paid in the following amounts—

		£			£
July 15	. .	340	Sept. 30	. .	20
Aug. 15	. .	120	Nov. 30	. .	170
31	. .	50	Dec. 15	. .	290
Sept. 15	. .	60	31	. .	110

He drew out—

	£		£
July 31 . .	40	Oct. 31 . .	240
Aug. 31 . .	70	Nov. 30 . .	110
Sept. 30 . .	180	Dec. 31 . .	80

You are required to show the account of R. U. Dinn in the books of the Bank, taking into account the following facts—

(1) 1 per cent interest is allowed on credit balances.
(2) 5 per cent interest is charged on debit balances.
(3) Commission at the rate of 10p per £100 on payments into Bank.

[*Note.* Interest is not at present allowed on current account balances with banks in this country.]

CHAPTER V

TRADING AND PROFIT AND LOSS ACCOUNT—
BALANCE SHEET

1. (a) What do you understand by a "Profit and Loss Account"?
(b) Explain the difference between a Profit and Loss Account and a Trading Account.
(*R.S.A.*)

2. G. Stevens is a silk merchant. Show his Journal entries to record the following transactions—
19..
Dec. 18. Bought on credit, from the Acme Manufacturing Co., a Filing Cabinet value £20.
31. Rent for December quarter, £50, due, but not paid. (*R.S.A.*)

3. On 1st January, 19.9, A. Tennant took over a shop at a rental of £240 per annum, payable quarterly. He sent a cheque to the landlord for a quarter's rent on each of the following dates—
3rd April, 19.9; 2nd July, 19.9; 1st October, 19.9; and 5th January, 19.0. You are required to show the entries in A. Tennant's Rent Account up to 5th January, 19.0, Profit and Loss Account for the year ended 31st December, 19.9; and Balance Sheet on 31st December, 19.9.

4. The books of Blanks were closed on the 31st December, 19... At that date—
(a) £98 was owing for three days' Factory Wages;
(b) a credit note for goods returned (£17) to George Dickson on 28th December had not been passed through the books; and
(c) £21 of the Fire Insurance Premium debited to the Insurance Account covered a portion of the following year.
Show how you would record these matters in Blanks' Ledger. (*R.S.A.*)

5. From the following particulars give the Telephone Account for 19.6, as it would appear in the Nominal Ledger—

19.6		£	£
Jan. 15. Cash paid for Rent to 31st March, 19.6	. .	5·00	
Cash paid for Calls to 31st December, 19.5	.	12·00	
			17·00
Apr. 16. Cash paid for Rent to 30th June, 19.6	. .	5·00	
Cash paid for Calls to 31st March, 19.6	.	16·27	
			21·27
July 12. Cash paid for Rent to 30th Sept., 19.6	. .	5·00	
Cash paid for Calls to 30th June, 19.6	. .	15·33	
			20·33
Oct. 15. Cash paid for Rent to 31st Dec., 19.6	. .	5·00	
Cash paid for Calls to 30th Sept., 19.6	. .	14·16	
			19·16

The charge for calls to 31st December, 19.6 was £14·17; this was paid on 17th January, 19.7. (*R.S.A.*)

6. The following is the Trial Balance of B. Hinder on 30th September, 19...

	£	£
Freehold Land and Buildings	5,500	
Plant and Machinery	2,675	
Stock, 31st March, 19..	8,345	
Sales		41,567
Purchases	25,467	
Carried forward	£41,987	£41,567

12

	£	£
Brought forward	41,987	41,567
Carriage	945	
Wages	2,454	
Bad Debts	450	
Provision for Bad Debts		1,350
Debtors	10,891	
Creditors		4,908
Discounts	1,647	1,476
Furniture	384	
Capital—B. Hinder		19,972
General Expenses	2,676	
Bank	3,749	
Rates	375	
Drawings—B. Hinder	3,715	
	£69,273	£69,273

The Stock at 30th September, 19.., was £8,840.

Depreciation on Plant and Machinery to be provided for at the rate of 10 per cent per annum.

Provide 5 per cent on Debtors for further Bad Debts and Doubtful Debts.

The value of unexpired insurances is £125.

The rates for the year are £1,000, the Trial Balance figure being the actual cash paid.

Prepare a Trading and Profit and Loss Account for the six months to 30th September, 19.., and a Balance Sheet at that date.

7. Owing to the illness of his book-keeper, I. Kneadem asks you to prepare his Accounts as at 31st December, 19.9.

Show with explanatory narratives the Journal entries necessary in respect of the following—

(1) Stock on hand at 31st December, 19.9, £9,327.

(2) Depreciation of Plant and Machinery at 6¼ per cent.

Value of Plant and Machinery per Balance Sheet at 31st December, 19.9, £17,764. Machine included in Balance Sheet at 31st December, 19.8, at £164, sold on 30th June, 19.9, for £56.

(3) Bad Debt Provision to be 5 per cent on Debtors at 31st December, 19.9, £12,345. Provision at 31st December, 19.8, was £575; and during year to 31st December, 19.9, Bad Debts amounting to £185 were written off thereto.

(4) Difference in balance at 31st December, 19.9, £4 (credits exceeding debits by this amount), to be kept in suspense.

(5) Debit balance on Suspense Account, £9, representing difference in balance at 31st December, 19.8, now found to be due to a sale of £110, having been debited to a customer's account as £101.   (*C.A. Final.*)

8. The following Trial Balance has been drawn up from the books of a farmer, effect having been given to Stocks and Outstandings, as at 28th November, 19.6—

	£	£
Cattle		595
Horses		117
Hens		217
Straw and Hay		13
Oats		102
Wheat	27	
Manures	185	
Vegetables		402
Sundries		156
Feeding Stuffs	141	
Carried forward	£353	£1,602

	£	£
Brought forward	353	1,602
Grazing		10
Stocks	401	
Debtors	75	
Creditors		252
Cash on Hand	13	
Cash in Bank	274	
Wages	1,084	
Rent and Taxes	258	
Carriage	27	
Heating and Lighting	202	
Postages	11	
Implements as at 29th November, 19.5	259	
Implements (additions during year)	70	
Repairs to Property	108	
Horse Expenses	25	
Insurance	139	
Implements Upkeep	113	
Sundries	12	
Capital		1,560
	£3,424	£3,424

Prepare Balance Sheet as at 28th November, 19.6, with relative Profit and Loss Account for year ending that date. Allow Depreciation of £33 off Implements.

When preparing the accounts, the following adjustments must be taken into account—

(1) Included in the Debtors is an amount of £10 in respect of a bankrupt whose estate is expected to realize not more than 20p in the £.

(2) Included in the Creditors are the following accounts owing by the proprietor—

	£				£
Tailor	.	.	.	30	Wines 12

These items have been debited to Rent and Taxes Account.

(3) Drawings amounting to £650 are included in Wages.
(4) Vegetables to the value of £80 have been consumed by the proprietor.
(5) Vegetables to the value of £50 have been consumed by the farm labourer.
(6) The following amounts are in respect of the proprietor's dwelling-house—

	£			£
Rent 125	Heating 101
Repairs 63	Insurance . . . 10

9. The following balances at 30th September, 19.8, have been extracted from the books of Well, trading as a coal merchant—

	£
Petty Cash	47
Sundry Creditors	5,102
Sundry Debtors	6,717
Bank Overdraft	2,198
Well—Capital	2,405
Stock-in-trade, 1st October, 19.7	394
Furniture, Fittings, and Fixtures	160
Wagons	886
Drawings	1,907
Motor-car	475
Provision for Bad Debts	86
Purchases of Coal and Coke	26,805
Sales of Coal and Coke	47,102
Wagon Hire Earned	84
Cartage Earnings	219
Purchase Returns	5
Carriage and Cartage Inwards	8,531

	£
Carriage and Cartage Outwards	4,254
Wagon Hire	198
Commission on Sales	210
Rent, Rates, Taxes and Insurance	303
Telephone Rent and Calls	66
Legal and Professional Charges	127
Salaries and Wages	3,589
Motor-running Expenses	152
Trade Expenses	868
Interest on Bank Overdraft and Bank Charges	45
Discounts Allowed	53
Travelling Expenses	924
Sack Hire	131
Bad Debts Recovered	17
Wagon Repairs	476

The Stock at 30th September, 19.8 is valued by Well at £932.

You are required to prepare a Trading and Profit and Loss Account for the year ended 30th September, 19.8 and a Balance Sheet as at that date after taking into consideration—

(a) The Provision for Bad Debts is to be increased by £103.
(b) Outstanding amounts of £42 Audit Fee and £65 Rent have not been brought into the books.
(c) Fire Insurance Premium of £16 has been paid to 24th June, 19.9.
(d) Depreciation is to be charged as follows—

Wagons, 5 per cent per annum.
Motor-car, 20 per cent per annum.
Furniture, etc., 2½ per cent per annum.   (R.S.A.)

10. From the following information prepare in columnar form Trading Account, Profit and Loss Account, and Balance Sheet at 31st December, 19. .—

	£
Discounts	1,200
Carriage Inwards	2,300
Rates, Taxes, etc.	2,200
Delivery Vans	6,000
Stock, Opening	26,600
Purchases	49,300
Salaries and Wages	52,200
Heating, Lighting and Cleaning	2,520
Buildings and Plant	80,000
Goodwill	6,700
Debtors	16,020
Advertising	3,300
Bad Debts	1,020
Cash	720
Loan Interest—Half-year to 30th June at 8 per cent p.a.. . .	3,200
Drawings	2,000
Bank Charges	1,640
Capital—M. Dore	1,640
Loan	80,000
Bank Overdraft	15,280
Creditors	9,620
Sales	150,380

Write off depreciation: Buildings and Plant, 10 per cent; Delivery Vans, 25 per cent. Allow 2½ per cent on Debtors for Discount and provide £860 for Bad Debts. Closing Stock £14,300.

11. When preparing the accounts of a firm of builders for the year ended 31st December, 19.9, you find that the following matters require to be dealt with—

(*a*) A motor-car which cost £360 some years ago was sold on 31st May, 19.9, for £60. Depreciation at the rate of 20 per cent per annum on the diminishing balance had been regularly written off, and at 1st January, 19.9, the car stood in the books at £110. On 1st May, 19.9, a new car was purchased for £300.

(*b*) The firm's premises are held on a twenty-one years' lease, which expires at the end of 19.5. The original cost was £3,150, and the asset had been written down to £1,050 at 31st December, 19.8, by an annual transfer of £150 to Profit and Loss. On 30th June, 19.9, the firm purchased the lease of adjoining premises, also expiring at the end of 19.5, at a cost of £975. The necessary alterations were carried out by the firm's own workmen at a cost of £125 for materials and £148 for labour, but no adjustment in respect of this work had been made.

Show the Car Account and Leasehold Premises Account as they should appear after the closing of the books to 31st December, 19.9. (*R.S.A. Advanced.*)

12. A. Street is in business as a stationer. The understated balances were extracted from his books as on 31st December, 19... You are required to prepare Trading and Profit and Loss Account for the year ended 31st December, and a Balance Sheet at that date—

	£	£
Capital .		16,000
Drawings .	2,000	
Purchases *less* Returns .	7,805	
Rates and Taxes .	194	
Salaries .	806	
Lighting and Heating .	82	
Electric Power .	192	
Travellers' Commission .	207	
Insurance .	103	
Advertising .	107	
Sales *less* Returns .		17,040
Bad Debts written off .	31	
Discounts (Balance) .		48
General Expenses .	302	
Postages, Telephone, etc. .	111	
Carriage .	377	
Stock-in-trade (Opening) .	3,080	
Wages .	3,981	
Freehold Land and Buildings .	7,920	
Plant and Machinery .	2,017	
Furniture and Fittings .	189	
Sundry Debtors .	3,040	
Sundry Creditors .		2,091
Cash in Bank .	2,635	
	£35,179	£35,179

When preparing these accounts it is necessary to take the following matters into consideration—

(*a*) Provide 2½ per cent for Discount on Debtors and create a Bad Debt Provision of 10 per cent.

(*b*) Depreciation of 10 per cent is to be written off Plant and Machinery and 5 per cent off Furniture, etc.

(*c*) Stock-in-trade as on 31st December was valued at £4,380.

(*d*) Wages owing at 31st December amounted to £250.

(*e*) Insurance paid in advance amounted to £10.

(*f*) Included in Debtors is £300 owing by Stone; included in the Creditors is £100 owing to Stone.

(*g*) Plant which stood at £500 in the books on 1st January was disposed of for £190 in part exchange for a new Machine costing £420. A net invoice of £230 was passed through Purchase Day Book.

(*h*) Purchase invoices amounting to £120 had been omitted from the books.

(*i*) A new sign costing £50 was included in Advertising.

(*j*) The debits for two dishonoured cheques for £30 and £20 respectively had not been entered in the Cash Book. In the case of the second cheque for £20, it was expected that the Debtor would be in a position to pay a dividend of 75p in the £.

(*k*) Private purchases amounting to £120 had been included in the Purchase Day Book.

13. X purchased a business on 1st January, 19. . for £2,000 from Y. The assets acquired by X were as follows—

	£
Fixtures . . .	400
Debtors . . .	1,200
Stock	350

The liabilities were—

Creditors . . .	250

In order to provide for the above, and to provide working capital, X brought in £3,000.

From this information and from the following details prepare a Trading and Profit and Loss Account and Balance Sheet for the year to 31st December, 19. .—

	£	£
Stock	350	
Debtors	1,920	
Purchases	8,120	
Sales		9,280
Wages	720	
General Expenses . . .	517	
Fixtures	400	
Goodwill	300	
Bank Overdraft . . .		170
Capital		3,000
Drawings	513	
Creditors		390
	£12,840	£12,840

The value of the stock at the 31st December, 19. . was £495.

Investment Income of £45 was included in the Sales figure of £9,280.

14. A business prepares accounts annually to 31st October, and stocktaking takes place during the following week-end.

In 19. ., 31st October fell on a Wednesday, stocktaking commenced on 3rd November, and the value of stock then actually on the premises was found to be £15,918. You ascertain the following additional facts—

(1) Goods outwards are entered in the Sales Journal as on the day of dispatch.

(2) Goods inwards are entered in the Purchases Journal as on the date of the invoice.

(3) Sales during the period 1st–3rd November, as shown by the Sales Journal and the Cash Sales Book, amounted to £195.

(4) Purchases during the same period as shown by the Purchases Journal amounted to £151, but, of these, goods to the value of £53 were not received until after 3rd November.

(5) Goods invoiced during October and not received until November totalled £160. Of these, goods to the value of £130 were actually received during the period 1st–3rd November and £29 after 3rd November.

(6) The average ratio of gross profit to turnover is 28 per cent.

You are instructed to ascertain the value of the stock as on 31st October for inclusion in the year's accounts. (*C.A. Inter.*)

15. On 1st April, 19.9, H Ltd., whose financial year ends on 30th June, took out a policy with Insurers Ltd., to cover employers' liability for the year to 31st March, 19.0.

The premium was at the rate of £1 per cent of wages paid during the year covered. On the taking out of the policy there was payable an amount calculated at that rate on the wages paid for the year to 31st March, 19.9; adjustment to the actual premium was to be effected by a balance payment to or by Insurers Ltd., on 7th April, 19.0.

On 1st April, 19.0, the insurance was renewed for a further year, the premium being raised to £1·50 per cent of wages paid for the year covered, and the amount payable on the renewal of the policy was based on the wages for the year to 31st March, 19.0.

Wages paid were as follows—

	£
Year ended 31st March, 19.9	100,000
Three months ended 30th June, 19.9	20,000
Nine months ended 31st March, 19.0	70,000
Three months ended 30th June, 19.0	30,000

Set out in Journal form the entries necessary to record the transactions and the appropriate closing entries at 30th June, 19.9 and 19.0, in the books of H Ltd.

(Adapted from C. A. Final.)

CHAPTER VI

BILLS OF EXCHANGE

1. Draft the ruling of a Bills Payable Book and enter therein the following—

Two months' bill accepted on 1st July (due 1st September) drawn by Tyre; payable to himself.

Four months' bill for £400 accepted on 1st August (due 1st December) drawn by Spoule; payable to Carr.

2. G drew a three months' bill upon H for £500 for value received. The bill was accepted by H and discounted by G, the discount charges being £5. The bill was dishonoured, and seven days after the due date of the old bill H accepted a new bill at two months for the amount due by him, plus interest at 7 per cent per annum plus discount charges. Write up the necessary accounts to record these transactions in the books of both parties.

3. What do you understand by the following—

(a) An Inland Bill.

(b) A Foreign Bill.

(c) An Accommodation Bill.

(d) Retiring a Bill?

4. F. Smith and J. Jones each agree to draw on the other on 1st July a Bill of Exchange at four months for £600, and to discount the other's bill, each meeting his own bill when it falls due, and paying the expenses of discounting the other's bill. Both bills are accepted, and are discounted at 5 per cent. Smith meets his own acceptance at maturity, but Jones's acceptance is dishonoured, and Smith, the drawer, is called upon to take it up. Expenses charged by the bank on the dishonoured bill amount to 35p. Jones accepts a new bill drawn by Smith at three months for the amount due to the latter, plus interest at 5 per cent. This bill is met by Jones at maturity.

Show the entries in Smith's books recording the above transactions.

5. Smith had accepted bills payable to Robinson as follows—

5th February,	for £300 at 4 months.
15th February,	for £500 at 3 months.
19th March,	for £600 at 6 months.
8th April,	for £500 at 3 months.

On 1st May it was agreed that these bills should be withdrawn, and that Smith should accept on that day two bills, one for £1,000 due in four months, and the other, for the balance, due in six months.

Calculate the amount of the second bill, taking interest at 5 per cent per annum.

(*R.S.A. Advanced.*)

6. A owes B £850, and on 1st January B draws a three months' bill which A returns, having accepted it in full settlement. B discounts the bill with his bankers for £10; at its due date the bill is met by A.

Show the Journal entries in the books of B.

7. On 1st June Schofield owes Walkden £2,000, and he accepts two bills of equal amounts due respectively in two and four months. The first bill is met in due course by Schofield; the second bill is discounted by Walkden (charge £4) and is met in due course.

Write up the Ledger accounts of Walkden.

8. X accepts a bill for the accommodation of Y, in return for which Y accepts a bill in favour of X, both bills being for three months and for sums of £800. X's bill only is discounted.

Write up the above transactions in the books of both parties.

9. On 1st January Moss & Co. draw a bill upon Saul Bros. for £1,000 at two months, in respect of goods supplied. The bill is accepted payable at L.C. & M. Bank. The drawers discount the bill which upon maturity is presented and dishonoured. Assume the due date to fall on a Saturday.

(a) Draw the bill in the usual form.

(b) Record the necessary entries in—

   (1) The books of Moss & Co.
   (2) The books of Saul Bros.

(c) Record the further entries upon the bill being dishonoured.

10. On 1st February, 19. ., John Cubley received from one of his customers a bill at three months for £600. He discounted it the same day with his bankers at 6 per cent per annum. When the bill became due it was dishonoured and John Cubley received from the debtor a cheque for £200, which he paid into the bank that day, and a further bill, dated 5th May, 19. ., at three months for £400. On 6th May, 19. ., John Cubley discounted the second bill with his bankers on the same terms as the first.

Give the entries in the books of the bank relating to these transactions.

(*C.A. Final.*)

11. A. Baker owes W. Flour £1,000, subject to a discount of 2½ per cent, and he has a contra account against the latter of £600, subject to a deduction for defective goods of £15. A settlement of the balance of accounts is agreed upon by means of a three months' bill. The bill is discounted one month previous to maturity at 5 per cent per annum.

Show these transactions as they will appear in the books of W. Flour.

12. V. R. & Co. draw a bill for £5,000 at three months dated 1st October, which H. V. & Co. accept. V. R. & Co. discount the bill on the same date and remit the proceeds, less discounting charges amounting to £62·50, to H. V. & Co. When the bill falls due H. V. & Co. are unable to meet it, and V. R. & Co. send that company a cheque to take up the bill. Give the necessary entries in the books of both concerns to record these transactions. (*C.A. Inter.*)

13. Amongst the Ledger balances of a company carrying on business as shippers, there appeared the following on 31st March—

Bills Receivable	£8,620
Export Bank, Ltd.: Advances on Bills Account . .	£6,535
Special Margins Account . .	£816

The under-mentioned transactions took place—

April 3. Received of Export Bank Ltd., £26·50, being balance of proceeds of Bill No. 308 for £150, a sum of £3·50 having been charged for interest on the advance.

   12. Advice from Export Bank Ltd., of payment of Bill No. 320 for £200, which had been advanced against in full. The bank sent a debit note for interest for £4·75, and a cheque was sent for this.

   15. Advice from the company's own bankers of the receipt of £185, being proceeds of Bill No. 312 for that amount, sent to them for collection.

   20. Advice from Export Bank Ltd., that X Y of Bombay had refused to take delivery of goods relating to Bill No. 316 for £125, and that the documents had been handed over to the company's agents. The bank claimed repayment of their advance of £100, plus interest £4·10, and a remittance was sent to them accordingly.

   30. Export Bank Ltd., advised having received £350, being payment in full of Bill No. 324. They deducted their advance of £280, plus interest £6·25, and placed the balance to the credit of the company's Special Margins Account.

May 20. Received from the Bombay agent a remittance for £70, being the net proceeds of the sale by him of the goods originally sold to X Y, a claim for the shortfall, plus an amount of £10 for warehousing the goods prior to the sale having been made.

23. Advice from Export Bank Ltd., of the receipt by them of £55, being payment on account, against partial delivery, of Bill No. 317 for £165, upon which they had made an advance of 80 per cent.

The company's own bankers were the Empire Bank Ltd. All amounts received were paid to the credit of the company's account there, and all payments made by cheque.

Show—by means of Ledger accounts—how the foregoing transactions would be entered in the books of the company, and bring down the balances on the various accounts.   (*C.A. Final.*)

14. (*a*) Rosenkranz of New York forwarded a consignment of goods to Johnson & Co., of London, on 18th July, 19.0, drawing on the consignees, a three months' bill for £3,500 representing 80 per cent of the invoice value; Johnson & Co. drawing a cheque on their bankers on 21st October, 19.0, to meet the above bill.

(*b*) In order to finance the above transaction, Johnson & Co. on 20th October drew a bill for three months on Trade Bank for £3,500, discounting this bill with Trade Bank, the latter holding the documents of the consignment as security. The discounting charge was £50·50 and the commission was ½ per cent. Johnson & Co. received a cheque for the balance, which they paid into their bank.

On 23rd January, 19.1, the above-mentioned bill (*b*) was retired, Johnson & Co. furnishing a cheque to meet it, whereupon they drew a new bill for three months for £4,000 on Trade Bank, putting up additional security. This bill was discounted by Trade Bank, same rate of commission as before, discounting charges being £50. Johnson & Co. received a cheque for the balance and banked it. Show the Ledger entries in Johnson & Co.'s books (relating to the bill transactions).   (*C.A. Final.*)

15. X, carrying on business as exporters, send the following bills to the Credit Bank Ltd., against which are advances, thus—

					Bill £			Advance £
No. 300	.	.	.	.	150	.	.	120
No. 301	.	.	.	.	185	.	.	*nil*
No. 302	.	.	.	.	125	.	.	100
No. 303	.	.	.	.	200	.	.	200
No. 304	.	.	.	.	350	.	.	280
No. 305	.	.	.	.	165	.	.	130
No. 306	.	.	.	.	100	.	.	60

At 31st December, Year 9, the following bills have been dealt with in order of date—

No. 300. The balance of proceeds remitted for £26, £4 being interest.

No. 303. A debit note is received for interest, £5.

No. 301. Bill duly met.

No. 302. The customer of X refused to accept delivery, the documents being handed over to X's agent abroad. The Credit Bank sends a debit note for £104.

The balances are to be brought down as at 31st December, Year 9.

The transactions relating to the above in Year 10 are in order of date—

No. 304. The balance due to X, less interest of £6, is placed to the credit of X's Special Loan Account.

No. 305. The customer of X refused to take the goods unless an allowance were made to cover exchange of £12. This was agreed upon, and the Credit Bank remitted £18, the balance, after the above allowance, cable expenses of £2, interest £3.

No. 306. The customer took partial delivery and Credit Bank remitted £22, being the cash received on the bill, less an appropriation of £30 in respect of the advance, and interest, £1.

Show accounts for Year 9 and Year 10 relating to the above transactions.

(*Adapted from C.A. Final.*)

CHAPTER VII

DEPRECIATION, RESERVES AND PROVISIONS

1. What is meant by the term "Depreciation"? Give three examples of its application.
(*C.A. Inter.*)

2. What considerations should govern the amount to be provided (if any) for the depreciation or diminution in value of the following assets appearing in a Balance Sheet: (1) Goodwill; (2) Leasehold Land and Works erected thereon; (3) Fixed Machinery and Plant, including Engine Power; (4) Loose Tools; (5) Book Debts; (6) Investments in gilt-edged and other securities; (7) amount expended on partly completed contracts? (*C.A. Inter.*)

3. Soleil d'Or possessed leasehold works, the Ledger Account of which stood in the books as follows—

Dr.   LEASEHOLD WORKS   *Cr.*

19..		£	19..		£
Jan. 1	To Cost of Lease	10,000	Dec. 31	By Depreciation transferred to Profit and Loss Account	500
Dec. 31	,, Additions during year	1,400		,, Balance c/d	11,278
	,, Repairs during year	378			
		£11,778			£11,778

The lease was dated 31st December previous, and was for fifteen years. The lessees were liable for dilapidations.

Do you approve of the above method of setting out the concern's position in regard to this lease? If not, how would you amend it? (*C.I.S. Final.*)

4. The following assets appeared in the Balance Sheet of a limited company. You are required to say whether the provisions made for depreciation appear to be adequate.

	£	£
FREEHOLD LAND AND BUILDINGS AT COST		63,580

30 years ago the land cost £40,000 and the buildings cost £20,000. The balance represents the cost of additions to buildings since that date.

PATENT ACCOUNT—

	£	£
Balance as per last Balance Sheet	9,876	
Less written off	2,000	
		7,876

£5,000 of this item represents the original purchase price of the patent, and the balance (£4,876) represents the cost of experiments. The patent was granted 20 years ago. The experience resulting from the experiments has rendered the original specification of little value.

LOOSE TOOLS—

	£	£
Balance as per last Balance Sheet	6,000	
Additions during the year	500	
	6,500	
Less Depreciation (10 per cent)	650	
		5,850

The great majority of these tools are made by the company's staff. The Asset Account is debited with the cost of materials and labour. Depreciation at 10 per cent is written off the final balance of the account each year.

22

PATTERNS—	£	£
Balance as per last Balance Sheet	4,500	
Additions during the year	500	
	5,000	
Less Depreciation (10 per cent).	500	
		4,500

These patterns are constructed of wood and are made by the company's staff, the cost of materials and labour being debited to the Asset Account. Half the patterns are in constant use, the remainder being employed with varying degrees of frequency.

If the information given above is inadequate, state in what directions you would require it to be amplified.   (*C.A. Final.*)

5. The following paragraph occurs in a company's annual report: "Owing to the serious falling off in the profits of the Company, your Directors recommend that no depreciation be written off this year." Give your views on this policy. (*C.I.S. Inter.*)

6. Define Reserve; Reserve Fund; Sinking Fund; Reserve Account; Depreciation Fund; Provision.

7. The value of a lease which has five years to run is £500. Show the working of a Sinking Fund on a 5 per cent basis in the books of a business, having regard to the fact that 0·180975 of a pound annually invested at 5 per cent compound interest will amount to £1 at the end of five years.   (*C.A. Final.*)

8. A trading company takes out a Capital Redemption Policy with an insurance company to provide for a wasting asset, paying £70 per annum premium. The premium is to be provided out of revenue. Give examples showing the entries to be made in the books of the trading company (1) annually and (2) upon payment of the capital sum by the insurance company.   (*C.A. Inter.*)

9. A trading company takes out an Assets Amortization Policy with an insurance company, paying a premium of £100 annually. An Asset Account is to be opened and the surrender value to be brought down each year. The surrender values for the first three years were: (1) nil; (2) £85; (3) £180. Write up the Policy Account in the books of the company.

10. Ought the amounts put aside by directors, out of profits, to the credit of a "Reserve Fund" to be necessarily invested in interest-bearing securities? If they be so invested, to what account would you credit the interest received on the investments?
                                        (*C.A. Inter.*)

11. What is a secret reserve? Enumerate two methods employed by bankers in order to create secret reserves, and criticize the practice from the point of view of the bank's customers.   (*C.I.S. Final.*)

12. A factory contains a quantity of Plant and Machinery, depreciation on the whole of which is provided by the "straight-line" method at the rate of 10 per cent per annum. A full year's depreciation is provided at the end of each year on all plant not already completely written off or sold, including any plant purchased during the year in question, notwithstanding that such plant may have been in use for less than a full year. Any profit or loss which may result from sales is transferred to Profit and Loss Account at the end of the year. Accounts are prepared annually to 31st December.

The balance standing on the Plant and Machinery Account at 31st December, Year 88, after writing off depreciation for that year, was £19,515, and subsidiary records showed that the cost of plant then on hand was made up as follows—

				£
Items bought in Year 78 (or earlier)				5,800
,, ,, ,, Year 79				3,100
,, ,, ,, Year 80				1,700
,, ,, ,, Year 81 (or later)				25,200
				£35,800

During Year 89 new plant was bought at a cost of £2,950, and one machine which had cost £550 in Year 77 was sold as scrap for £35.

During Year 90 there were additions costing £1,800, and a machine which had cost £700 in Year 86 was sold for £350.

You are required to write up Plant and Machinery Account for Year 89 and Year 90. All calculations to be shown. (*C.A. Inter.*)

13. On 1st January, 19.9, Robertson & Co. began to operate lorries in connection with their business. Depreciation was provided at the rate of 20 per cent per annum on their net book value at the commencement of each year. When a lorry was replaced, the "trade-in" price of the old lorry was deducted from the cost of the new lorry and the net amount capitalized.

The Lorries Account appears in the books thus—

Dr.   *Cr.*

		£			£
19.9			19.9		
Jan. 1	To Lorry No. 1	1,000	Dec. 31	By Depreciation	200
July 1	,, Lorry No. 2	1,400		,, Balance	2,200
		£2,400			£2,400
19.0			19.0		
Jan. 1	To Balance	2,200	Dec. 31	By Depreciation	440
				,, Balance	1,760
		£2,200			£2,200
19.1			19.1		
Jan. 1	To Balance	1,760	Dec. 31	By Depreciation	352
Apr. 1	,, Lorry No. 3	800		,, Balance	2,808
Oct. 1	,, Lorry No. 4	600			
		£3,160			£3,160
19.2					
Jan. 1	To Balance	2,808			

Robertson & Co. agreed that this method was misleading and they decided that the account should be reconstructed so as to provide depreciation at the rate of 20 per cent per annum on cost as from the date of purchase, also that a separate account should be opened for the provision of depreciation.

You ascertain that the "trade-in" price of Lorry No. 1, which was replaced by Lorry No. 3, was £800 and that of Lorry No. 2, which was replaced by Lorry No. 4, was £500.

You are required—

(*a*) to draw up the reconstructed Lorries Account and the Provision for Depreciation of Lorries Account on the agreed lines, and

(*b*) to draft the journal entry to correct the balances on the ledger as on 31st December, 19.1.

CHAPTER VIII

CAPITAL AND REVENUE EXPENDITURE

1. State the considerations which would guide you in deciding whether any particular item should be regarded as of a "capital" or of a "revenue" nature. *(L.C.C.)*

2. Explain the basic principles which would guide you in allocating expenditure as between capital and revenue. Illustrate your answer by reference to the two assets given below, describing expenditure upon them, and allocating it as between capital and revenue: printing machine; motor vans. *(L.C.C.)*

3. In auditing the Profit and Loss Account of a Mining Company, you find large sums included therein under the head of "Prospecting and Development Account," and you are informed that these consist of moneys spent in sinking shafts and driving levels during the year under review, some of which shafts and levels have been productive and others not. Do you consider that this expenditure is properly chargeable to profit and loss? *(C.A. Inter.)*

4. An old building, which originally cost, and stands in the books at, £10,500, is pulled down and a new one erected in its place; £50 worth of material out of the old building is sold and £200 worth is used on the new building. In addition to this, £22,250 is expended under a contract for its construction; £600 had been set aside by the firm for the depreciation on the old building, and is now appropriated. What addition to the Capital Account will legitimately arise out of the rebuilding, and how much of it will be borne by profit and loss? *(C.A. Inter.)*

5. A firm spends a large sum on advertising in order to form a business. Assuming that the expenditure thereon decreases annually until, in the seventh year, it reaches a point representing a normal cost under this head, how would you expect the amounts to be treated in the firm's Balance Sheet? In your reply, let £14,000 be the expenditure of the first year and decrease £2,000 annually. *(C.A. Inter.)*

6. The following items are included in the Balance Sheet of a company under the head of Works and Plant: Wages, £13,712; salary of engineer, £2,500; two-thirds of salary of secretary, 1¾ years, £1,400; one-half directors' fees, 1¾ years, £1,000; interest on bank loan, £327; law costs, £832. Do you see anything objectionable, and if so, what, in these items being treated as capital outlay? *(C.A. Final.)*

7. Would you consider the following chargeable to capital expenditure or revenue?: (a) premium given for a lease; (b) costs attending a mortgage; (c) commission on issue of debenture bonds; (d) commission on issue of debenture stock; (e) accrued dividend or interest included in the cost price of an investment. *(C.A. Final.)*

8. A limited company, formed to acquire and work certain patent rights which cost them £6,000, erect a factory for the manufacture of their patented articles.
Leasehold buildings (99 years) cost £4,000; motive-power plant, gearing, and shafting, £3,000; and loose machinery, £5,000. They embark upon an advertising campaign on which they lay out in the first year £10,000, which is considerably in excess of the amount they expect to spend in each subsequent year. In the same period it cost them £500 to defend and defeat an action for alleged infringement of patent rights brought against them by a rival company, and they sold the foreign rights of their patent for £5,000.
Explain how the above matters should be dealt with in the company's accounts, and indicate on what basis provision should be made for writing off the above-named expenditure. *(C.A. Inter.)*

9. A local authority, owning an omnibus undertaking, repays indebtedness by means of sinking funds. The debt created relates to (1) payment for goodwill of a former undertaking purchased; (2) expenditure upon land, freehold and leasehold, and buildings; (3) buses and plant.
To what extent may the annual contributions to the sinking funds be said to be the equivalent of depreciation? *(C.A. Final.)*

10. As one of the conditions of a debenture trust deed, A Ltd. took out a Leasehold Redemption Policy for £237,000 on 30th June, 19.5, the annual premium of £6,005 to be charged to Profit and Loss Account. The policy has not appeared in the Balance Sheets in the past.

The surrender value of the policy on 30th June, 19.9 was £30,134, and, in the year following, 30th June, 19.0, £37,250.

(*a*) Give in Journal form the entries that would be necessary to convert the hidden reserve into an open reserve and to record the transactions of the year to 30th June, 19.0.

(*b*) Set out the entries that should appear in the Balance Sheet as on 30th June, 19.0.   (*C.A. Final.*)

11. In 19.5, Bricks Ltd. built a new kiln at their Apex brickyard. The work was carried out with the company's own labour and materials, and the expenditure thereon was included in the Apex Brickyard Account. The following is a summary of that account for the years ended 31st December, 19.4 and 19.5, in the company's books—

	19.4		19.5			19.4		19.5	
	Bricks		Bricks			Bricks		Bricks	
		£		£			£		£
Stock, 1st Jan.	200,000	350	100,000	175	Sales .	2,550,000	5,100	2,050,000	4,305
Wages .		2,500		4,255	Bricks				
Stores, Fuel,					spoiled .	50,000		50,000	
etc. .		1,000		3,800	Bricks used				
Salaries. .		300		500	for new				
Head Office					kiln . .			950,000	
and Sundry					Stock, 31st				
Exps. .		475		730	Dec. .	100,000	175	150,000	270
Profit . .		650			Balance .				4,885
		£5,275		£9,460			£5,275		£9,460

Examination revealed—

(*a*) That no particulars had been kept of wages spent on building; men had worked part of their time digging clay and watering in the kilns, and part on the building of the new kiln.

(*b*) That the wages cost per 1,000 bricks (including bricks spoiled) was higher by 5 per cent in 19.5 than in 19.4.

(*c*) That, in 19.5, £150 of the salaries, £2,500 of the stores, etc., and £150 of the head office expenses were attributable to the new kiln.

(*d*) That Employers' Liability Insurance at a premium of 50p per cent of wages was included in Sundry Expenses.

Construct the Bricks Ltd. Brickyard Account for 19.5, duly adjusted, and show the amounts chargeable to capital expenditure and/or elsewhere in respect of the new kiln.

(*Adapted from C.A. Final.*)

CHAPTER IX

CONTAINERS, GOODS ON APPROVAL, C.O.D., VOYAGE ACCOUNTS

1. Show Cases Stock and Cases Trading Accounts in respect of the following transactions for the year to 31st December, 19..—

	£
Opening Stock (cost 15p each):	
In warehouse	4,000
In customers' hands (all returnable)	8,000
Purchases during the year at 25p each	5,000
Sent to customers during the year	6,400
Returned by customers	4,600
Sold for scrap (for £5)	160
Closing Stock in customers' hands (all returnable)	3,800

Cases are valued in the books at cost and are charged out to customers at 37½p each, and credited at 25p each if returned within a stipulated time.

2. A firm carrying on business as stoneware manufacturers make their own packing cases, which are charged to customers at 100 per cent on cost, but are returnable, full credit then being given. The following are the items relating thereto in respect of the year ended 31st December, 19.8—

	£
Stock of cases in the factory at 1st January, 19.8	596
Cases in the hands of customers as per Ledger Balances at 1st January, 19.8	840
Cases charged to customers	3,140
Materials used	38
Wages paid for making and repairing cases	156
Cases returned by customers	3,260
Cases kept by (i.e. sold to) customers	140
Stock of cases in the factory at 31st December, 19.8 . . .	280

Cases in the hands of customers are valued at cost, less 20 per cent.

You are required to write up Cases Stock and Cases Reserve Accounts in respect of the foregoing items in the books of the firm, and to state how the balances remaining would be dealt with in the Balance Sheet at 31st December, 19.7 and 19.8.

3. During the year ended 31st December, 19.8 (the first year's trading), 4,000 Cases were purchased at £1, to be sent to customers charged out at £1·50 each and, subject to certain conditions, returnable at that price. 1,800 Cases had been so sent out and 1,200 returned in the ordinary way. None had been retained permanently and the remainder are assumed to be returned in due course. Write up Cases Control Account, Cases Stock Account, and Cases Profit Suspense Account. Ignore date column.

4. The following are the transactions of the business (continuing the preceding question) in its second year, prices remaining unchanged.

Cases sent out to customers numbered 1,600 and 2,000, were returned. There were 40 now not returnable, but these had been paid for by the customers (and no allowance given to them). A further 30 cases were in inferior condition and sold as scrap for £5 before the year end. Another 100 were found to be slightly damaged and before the year end were repaired at an average cost of 35p each. Write up the accounts as employed in the previous illustration.

5. The M.V. *Mary Rose*, a tramp vessel of 3,048 tons net register, is requisitioned by the Department of Trade and Industry and managed for the Department by her owners.

The terms of requisition are that, in consideration of a monthly rate of hire, the vessel is maintained at the Department's disposal in full running order by the owners, who bear all charges, such as insurance, repairs, stores, crew's wages, and expenses necessary to do this (i.e. similar to an ordinary time charter).

Voyage No. 5 commenced at Swansea on 15th June, 19.., the managers having arranged for a full cargo of anthracite to Montreal and a return run with grain to Liverpool, discharge being completed on 30th September, 19...

From the following details, select the relevant items and prepare an account showing the balance due to or from the Department. (Foreign currency to be ignored.)

At Swansea—

Took bunkers, 30,000 gallons at 40p per gallon
Managers' Fittage (Commission) thereon, 50p per 100 gallons
Agents' Disbursements—   £

Dock Dues, Pilotage, Towage, etc.	806
Trimming Cargo	408
Trimming Bunkers	175
Cash to Captain for advances to Crew	800
	£2,189

At Montreal—
Agents' Disbursements—   £

Dock Dues, Pilotage, Towage, etc.	910
Towage, Boatmen, etc., to and from dry dock	130
Dry-docking and Repairs	2,050
Provisions and Stores	1,263
Discharging Anthracite (payable by receivers).	
Cleaning Holds	240
Doctor attending Crew	20
Loading Grain	734
	£5,347

At Liverpool—
Agents' Disbursements—   £

Dock Dues, Pilotage, Towage, etc.	718
Discharging Grain	450
Cash to Captain to pay off Crew (including overtime *re* cargo work, £856)	3,053
	£4,221

Received freight on anthracite, 8,000 tons at £4, less 2 per cent Address commission and one-third of 5 per cent brokerage.

Managers' commission on above at 1 per cent.
Received freight on grain, 7,000 tons at £3.

6. A, who keeps a special set of books for this type of business, sends out goods on sale or return as follows—

		£		
Jan.	1. B	50	Jan.	4. All retained.
	9. C	25		10. Returned £15, retained £10.
	16. D	70		19. All retained.
	23. C	25		25. All returned.
	30. B	40		⎧ No intimation received as
	31. E	50		⎨ to sale and goods not yet
				⎩ returned.

Show Journals and Ledger Accounts (only B's personal account is required). What does the balance on the Goods on Sale or Return Total Account represent?

7. A sends out the following goods C.O.D. during the month of December—

						Price	Postage and C.O.D. Fees	
						£	p	
Dec.	1	B	.	.	.	10	28	Cash received, Dec. 6
	3	C	.	.	.	3	10	Cash received, Dec. 7
	7	D	.	.	.	5	12	Goods returned, Dec. 14
	15	E	.	.	.	7	14	Cash received, Dec. 22
	30	F	.	.	.	10	24	Outstanding

A charges postage and fees to his customers. Show how these transactions should be dealt with in A's books.

CHAPTER X

SELF-BALANCING LEDGERS AND SECTIONAL BALANCING

1. A company keeps its Ledgers upon the self-balancing principle. You are required to describe the operation of this system and its advantages, illustrating your answer with *pro forma* examples and explaining the source of the entries made by you.

(*C.I.S.*)

2. The following details were extracted from the books of a company for the six months ended 30th June, 19.. —

		£
19..		
Jan. 1.	Sales Ledger balances total	37,262
	Provision for Doubtful Debts	2,500
June 30.	Sales	73,127
	Returns from Customers	741
	Cash received from Customers	70,813
	Cheques dishonoured	289
	Bills accepted by Customers	2,690
	Bills dishonoured	360
	Bad Debts written off	632
	Interest on Customers' Overdue Accounts	68
	Carriage charged to Customers	120
	Cash Discount allowed	1,782
	Bad Debts, previously written off, recovered	121

Prepare an Account to show the aggregate Sales Ledger Balances outstanding on that date. (*C.A. Inter.*)

3. The following details were extracted from the books of a company for the six months ended 31st March, 19.8—

	£
Debtors' Balances total 1st October, 19.7	1,926
Suppliers' Balances total 1st October, 19.7	1,215
Cash paid to Suppliers	7,613
Cash received from Debtors	12,993
Purchases	8,848
Discount received	285
Bad Debts written off	55
Sales Returns	93
Purchases Returns	182
Interest charged to Debtors	5
Debtors' Cheques dishonoured	76
Discount allowed	356
Bills Payable accepted (including Renewals)	890
Bills Payable withdrawn upon renewal	200
Interest on Bills Payable renewed	2
Sales	13,308

The totals of the Balances extracted from the Trade Ledgers on 31st March, 19.8, were—

	£
Sales Ledger	1,807
Bought Ledger	1,290

Are these totals in accordance with the above details? Show your workings.

(*C.A. Inter.*)

4. You are consulted by Wm. Baird, who requests you to re-organize his book-keeping system.

30

At 30th June, 19.4, his Balance Sheet was as follows—

	£			£
Trade Creditors	2,359	Buildings		900
Loan Creditor	1,000	Furniture and Fittings . . .		140
Capital	1,586	Stock-in-trade		1,582
		Bills Receivable . . .		295
		Sundry Debtors . .	£1,670	
		Less Bad Debts		
		Provision . .	100	
				1,570
		Cash at Bank . .	419	
		Cash in Hand . .	39	
				458
	£4,945			£4,945

From the books and accounts you obtain the following information—

	£
Sales for year to 30th June, 19.5	4,750
Purchases to 30th June, 19.5	3,166
Cash from Debtors to 30th June, 19.5	4,199
Cash paid to Creditors to 30th June, 19.5	4,213
Discount Allowed to 30th June, 19.5	182
Discount Received to 30th June, 19.5	153
Wm. Baird's Drawings to 30th June, 19.5	433
Loan Interest paid to 30th June, 19.5	38
General Expenses paid to 30th June, 19.5	397
Returns (Inward) during year to 30th June, 19.5 . . .	113
Returns (Outward) during year to 30th June, 19.5 . . .	59
Bills Receivable met during year to 30th June, 19.5 . . .	355
Bills Receivable granted by Debtors during year to 30th June, 19.5 .	110
Bank—Drawn during year to 30th June, 19.5	5,276
Bank—Lodged during year to 30th June, 19.5	4,545
Stock on hand as at 30th June, 19.5	1,773

You advise that the Sales, Purchases and Private (or General) Ledgers be made self-balancing, and you put them on this basis for year ended 30th June, 19.5.

You are required to show the Private (or General) Ledger Trial Balance as at 30th June, 19.5, and also as at 1st July, 19.5, the commencement of next financial year. Show any working accounts which you consider necessary to support your answer.

CHAPTER XI

SINGLE ENTRY

1.

BALANCE SHEET

	£		£
Creditors	721	Freehold Premises . . .	1,560
Capital	3,150	Machinery and Plant . .	420
		Stock	876
		Debtors	982
		Cash	33
	£3,871		**£3,871**

The above is a copy of Samuel Wood's Balance Sheet as on the 31st December, 19.4. The only books kept are a Cash Book and a Ledger. The following is a summary of his receipts and payments for the year ended 31st December, 19.5—

Receipts	£	Payments	£
Cash on account of Credit Sales	4,276	Creditors for Goods purchased	3,954
Cash Sales . . .	1,863	Wages	743
Capital paid in . .	200	General Expenses . .	627
		Additions to Machinery .	160
		Drawings . . .	536
	£6,339		**£6,020**

On 31st December, 19.5, the amount due to Creditors was £816, and the Debtors and Stock amounted to £918 and £854 respectively. You are required to prepare Trading and Profit and Loss Account for the year ended 31st December, 19.5, and a Balance Sheet as on that date, after making adjustments in respect of the following—

(a) Depreciation of 10 per cent is to be written off the Machinery and Plant, including additions during the year.

(b) £150 is to be provided for Bad Debts.

(c) The sum of £38 for goods supplied to the proprietor was included in the Debtors' balances at 31st December, 19.5.   (R.S.A.)

2. The books of F. A. Miller, a shopkeeper, are kept by single entry. He has submitted accounts for the purposes of Income Tax showing the following profits—

						£
Year ended 31st December, 19.4		.	.	.		735
,,	,,	,,	,,	19.5	. . .	740
,,	,,	,,	,,	19.6	. . .	787
,,	,,	,,	,,	19.7	. . .	1,375
,,	,,	,,	,,	19.8	. . .	1,214
,,	,,	,,	,,	19.9	. . .	926

The Inspector of Taxes is not satisfied as to the accuracy of the accounts submitted. You are instructed to assist in establishing their correctness, and for that purpose you are supplied with the following information—

(a) Business Liabilities and Assets at 31st December, 19.3 were: Creditors, £732; Debtors, £145; Cash at Bank and in Hand, £947; Stock, £542.

(b) Miller owed his brother, K. T. Miller, £400 on 31st December, 19.3. On 15th February, 19.6, he repaid this amount, and on 1st January, 19.9, he lent K. T. Miller £300.

32

(c) Miller owns a house which he purchased in 19.1 for £2,000 and a car which he purchased in 19.5 for £750. In 19.8 he bought £1,000 X Ltd. Stock for £750.

(d) In 19.9 £300 was stolen from his private house. (He was not insured against theft.)

(e) Miller estimates that his living expenses have been: 19.4, £300; 19.5, £400; 19.6, £600; 19.7, 19.8 and 19.9, £700 per annum (exclusive of amount stolen).

(f) On 31st December, 19.9, the business Liabilities and Assets were: Creditors, £840; Debtors, £592; Cash at Bank and in Hand, £1,945; Stock, £674.

From the information submitted prepare a statement showing the increase of capital over the period as a whole, and its relation to the total of the profits stated.

(C.A. Inter.)

3. P. Smithson is a trader, some years established, who keeps his books on a "single entry" basis. He keeps a Cash Book, Purchases and Sales Journals (not cast), and a Ledger in which are personal accounts only, the latter being posted up from the foregoing.

The Inspector of Taxes having required the production of a proper Profit and Loss Account for the year recently completed, together with a Balance Sheet as on the closing date, Smithson asks you to complete the double entry for him for the period in question and to prepare the accounts.

State, shortly and concisely, what steps you would have to take in order to carry out this request, and outline your procedure up to the point of obtaining a Trial Balance.

(L.C.C.)

4. I. Rally was a retail tobacconist and also resided on the premises. He had not kept his books on the double-entry principle nor had he balanced his Cash Book, but you are able to ascertain the following particulars—

	1st January, 19..	31st December, 19..
	£	£
Cash in Hand	3	5
Cash at Bank	100	150
Sundry Debtors	175	250
Sundry Creditors	341	374
War Loan	625	625
Stock-in-trade	250	187

Transactions during 19..—

Salaries	150
General Trade Charges	350
Stationery and Wrapping Paper	87
Rent and Rates	70
Lighting, etc.	25
Cash Receipts	3,125
Payments through Bank and by Cash for Goods	2,000
Payments into Bank—Business	1,875
Payments into Bank—Personal	25
Payments out of Bank—Business	1,525
Payments out of Bank—Personal	325
Personal Cash Payments	91
Stock taken for Personal Use	14

You are required to prepare accounts for the year ended 31st December, 19..., and Balance Sheet at the latter date.

5. What do you understand by single entry? What are its disadvantages?

6. State briefly how you would convert a set of books from single entry to double entry.

7. A client (credit and ready-money business) who has kept his books on single entry now desires to keep them on a complete double-entry system under your

instructions and supervision. Set out clearly and fully the instructions you would give your client, bearing in mind that he has not any knowledge of double-entry book-keeping.   (*C.A. Inter.*)

8. A retail tradesman asks you to prepare accounts of his business for the year ended 31st December, and on investigation you find that while records of business takings and payments have been kept, they have not been reconciled with the cash in hand. From time to time cash has been paid into a banking account, and cheques thereon have been drawn both for business and private purposes.

From the following information obtained from the records and from your client, prepare accounts at 31st December, allowing for the fact that he lives with his family over the business premises. No record has been kept of amounts taken from cash for living and personal expenses, and a difference in the cash amounting to £365 is treated as private expenditure.

	£
Cash paid into Bank	7,500
Private Dividends paid into Bank	100
Private Payments out of Bank	1,300
Business Payments out of Bank	6,100
Cash Takings	12,500
Payments for Goods by Cash and Cheque	8,000
Wages	2,000
Delivery Expenses	350
Rents and Rates	100
Lighting and Heating	50
General Expenses	230

The Assets and Liabilities at the beginning and end of the period are as follows—

	Opening	Closing
	£	£
Stock	1,000	750
Bank Balance	400	600
Cash in Hand	15	20
Trade Debtors	700	1,000
Trade Creditors	1,365	1,500
Investments	2,500	2,500

9. Mrs. Agnes Jones, who had carried on a small grocery concern, in the management of which she was assisted by her daughter Mary, transferred the business to the latter as at 31st March, 19.4.

The Balance Sheet at date of transfer was as follows—

		£			£
Capital Account	. . .	164	Stock	.	305
Sundry Creditors	. . .	193	Sundry Debtors	. .	30
			Cash in Hand	. .	22
		£357			£357

Mary took over the business exactly on the basis of the above Balance Sheet, no cash payment being involved.

Given the following further information, draft Balance Sheet at 31st March, 19.5—

	£
Sundry Creditors, 31st March, 19.5	181
Stock, 31st March, 19.5	297
Cash, 31st March, 19.5	13
Sundry Debtors, 31st March, 19.5	35
Profit for year to 31st March, 19.5 (arrived at after wages of £12 per week to Miss Jones have been charged)	484
Drawn by Miss Jones during year to 31st March, 19.5, against profits	1,108

CHAPTER XII

RECEIPTS AND PAYMENTS, AND INCOME AND EXPENDITURE ACCOUNTS

1. The following particulars relate to a retired Army officer who asks you to prepare an Income and Expenditure Account for the year ended 31st December, 19.., and a Balance Sheet at that date.

	£
Investments purchased during the year	625
Investments sold during the year	750
Investments held at 31st December, 19.., on which dividends have been received at 5 per cent (tax free) during the year	4,500
Mortgages at 7 per cent on which interest has been received during the year	5,000
Directors' Fees (received after P.A.Y.E. at the standard rate)	650
Household Furniture, etc., at 1st January, 19..	1,000
Cash at Bank on Deposit Account at 1st January, 19..	1,500
£375 and Interest £60 has been withdrawn during the year	
Cash at Bank on Current Account at 1st January, 19..	160
Cash at Bank on Current Account at 31st December, 19..	150
Paid in respect of Action for Damages and Law Costs	444

Depreciate Furniture, etc., by 10 per cent.

Any balance not accounted for to be regarded as Personal Expenditure.

Assume Income Tax at 40 per cent.

2. Enumerate the main differences between an Income and Expenditure Account and Receipts and Payments Account.

3. From the following balances extracted from the books of the Bachelors' Club as at 30th April, 19.., prepare Revenue Account for the year ended that date—

	£	£
Mortgage Interest	820	
Debenture Interest	755	
Rates, Taxes and Insurance	1,925	
Subscription and Entry Moneys		11,311
Wages	5,721	
Heat, Light and Power	1,303	
Laundry	1,008	
Newspapers	280	
Telephone	35	
Printing and Stationery	381	
Books and Binding	131	
Management Expenses	1,003	
Postages and Miscellaneous Expenses	601	
Stocks as at 1st May, 19..—		
Wines and Spirits	£887	
Mineral Waters, etc.	125	
Cigars	73	
Provisions	310	
	1,395	
Wines and Spirits	7,985	9,751
Mineral Waters, etc.	1,125	1,511
Cigars	657	784
Provisions	5,892	7,235
Billiards		282
Bedrooms		991
Repairs and Renewals	1,738	
Deposit Receipt Interest		165

The Stocks on Hand at 30th April, 19.., are Wines and Spirits, £973; Mineral Waters, £142; Cigars, £81; Provisions, £204. During the year certain alterations to the buildings were carried out at a cost of £1,150, which falls to be written off against Revenue.

4. The balances on the books of the Serf Club at 31st March, 19.8, were as follows—

	£
Furniture at 31st March, 19.7	84
Furniture Additions, 31st March, 19.8	54
Fixtures and Fittings, 31st March, 19.7	29
Billiard Table and Accessories, 31st March, 19.7	89
China, Glass, Cutlery, and Linen, 31st March, 19.7	20
Stock in Restaurant, 31st March, 19.7	4
Stock in Bar, 31st March, 19.7	36
Restaurant Takings	1,616
Bar Takings	1,305
Billiard Takings	256
Subscriptions from Members	315
Interest on Deposit	8
Purchases for Restaurant	1,078
Purchases for Bar	822
Rent and Rates	349
Wages	623
Repairs and Renewals of China, Glass, etc.	179
Fuel and Light	175
Sundry Expenses	134
Cash in Hand, 31st March, 19.8	13
Bank Balance, 31st March, 19.8	91
Bank Deposit, 31st March, 19.8	283
Debtors, 31st March, 19.8	74
Creditors, 31st March, 19.8	175
Balance on Income and Expenditure Account, 31st March, 19.7	462

You are required to prepare separate Trading Accounts for the Restaurant and Bar and Income and Expenditure Account for the year to 31st March, 19.8, together with Balance Sheet at that date, after making adjustments for the following—

The cost of maintenance of staff is estimated at £275, of which £250 is to be credited to Restaurant and £25 to the Bar.

Stocks at 31st March, 19.8: Restaurant, £3; Bar, £29. Depreciation: Furniture, 10 per cent; Fixtures, 5 per cent; Billiard Table and Accessories, 15 per cent.

5. From the following Receipts and Payments Account of a charitable institution and the subjoined information, prepare General Income and Expenditure Account for the year ended 31st December, 19...

RECEIPTS AND PAYMENTS ACCOUNT

19..			£	19..			£
Jan. 1	To Balance—			Dec. 31	By Payments to Pensioners		1,265
		Cash on Deposit	500		,, Rent, three-quarters paid		75
		Cash on Current Account	116		,, Office Expenses and Salaries		275
		Cash in Hand	7		,, Collectors' Commission		37
Dec. 31	,, Donations and Subscriptions		1,272		,, Printing Year Book		26
	,, Legacies		400		,, Postages		18
	,, Special Fund Donations		170		,, Gratuities from Special Fund		143
	,, Interest on Investments		135		,, Investment in £300 Birming-		
	,, Interest on Deposit		24		ham 3 per cent Stock		300
					,, Balance—		
					Cash on Deposit		400
					Cash on Current Account		73
					Cash in Hand		12
			£2,624				£2,624

The committee of management resolve that one-half of the legacies received shall be treated as income, the remainder being capital, and that the "Special Fund" should be separated from the General Funds. A quarter's rent was unpaid at 31st December, 19... Sundry persons owed £15 for advertisements in the Year Book.

(C.A. Inter.)

6. The following Statement of Accounts of the Blankshire Benevolent Charity was submitted as shown for adoption at the annual meeting. You are invited to criticize it and make such alterations as you think necessary.

STATEMENT OF ACCOUNTS FOR THE YEAR ENDED 30TH JUNE, 19..

Receipts	£	*Expenditure*	£
To Balance	457	By Annuities	805
„ Interest on Investments	418	„ Salary—	
„ Donations	383	Secretary	75
„ Special Appeal	182	Treasurer	75
„ Rent Received	84	„ Incidentals	4
„ Bank Interest	18	„ Printing	18
„ Amount, Bank, in error	1	„ Chief Rent	105
		„ Law Charges	9
		„ Bank Commission	8
		„ Sundries	8
		„ Balance in Bank	499
	£1,606		£1,606

PRESENT FUNDS

	£
6 per cent Treasury Stock	1,168
5 per cent British Transport Stock	1,255
4 per cent Consols	923
7 per cent Manchester Corporation Stock	514
8 per cent Blackpool Corporation Stock	500
7½ per cent Stockport Corporation Stock	2,500
Mortgages at 8 per cent	3,300
	£10,162

Audited and found correct.

HERBERT TRUSTEM.

The securities upon which the present funds of the institution are invested were produced to and examined by us, and we certify that they are in perfect order and in safe custody.

W. T. SUPPLETON, *Chairman.*
J. UNION, *Vice-Chairman.*

7. The following balances are extracted from the Private Ledger of A. N. Investor as at 30th June, 19.6—

	£
Sundry Investments	155,000
Profits on Realization of Investments	15,500
Losses on Realization of Investments	23,000
Provision for Depreciation of Investments (as at 1st July, 19.5)	24,000
Dividends and Interest Received (Net)	7,600
Capital (as at 1st July, 19.5)	159,760
Drawings	8,500
Provision for Tax Liability outstanding	1,500
Properties	14,000

Rents Received	1,600
Outgoings *re* Properties	230
Sundry Debtors for Rents	450
Sundry Creditors	500
Deposit Interest Received	220
Cash at Bank (Current Account)	4,500
Cash at Bank (Deposit Account)	5,000

The market value of the investments at 30th June, 19.6, was £124,000 and the provision is to be increased to cover the full depreciation.

The liability for outstanding tax has been agreed at £1,200. Provide for £950 on current profit. Prepare a Trial Balance and draw up an Income and Expenditure Account for the twelve months to 30th June, 19.6, together with a Balance Sheet as at that date.

8. The account set out below has been submitted to you for audit. If you do not approve of it, criticize and amend it.

LOAMSHIRE ENTOMOLOGICAL SOCIETY
INCOME AND EXPENDITURE ACCOUNT, 31ST DECEMBER, 19..

		£			£
To Entrance Fees (60 at £30) . .		1,800	By Salaries and Wages . . .		1,675
„ Fees for Life Membership (10 at			„ Secretary's Salary		850
£52)		520	„ Rent, Rates, etc. . . .		1,264
„ Annual Subscriptions .	£1,564		„ Printing and Postages . .		136
„ Annual Subscriptions			„ Repairs to Premises . .		324
paid in advance . .	65		„ Interest on Bank Loan . .		57
		1,629	„ Balance carried down . .		1,061
„ Interest on Treasury Stock . .		120			
„ Sundry Receipts . . .		62			
„ Balance from last year . .		1,236			
		£5,367			£5,367
To Balance brought down . .		970			

Treasurer's Notes. Subscriptions in arrear, £121; sundry tradesmen's bills, £42 were outstanding at 31st December, but have since been paid. The Secretary's salary, though sanctioned by the committee, has not yet been paid. The Treasury Stock purchased several years ago cost £1,970. The lease (sixteen years to run) cost £2,124. Bank Loan secured on premises remains at £1,000.   (*Adapted from C.A. Inter.*)

CHAPTER XIII

TABULAR BOOK-KEEPING

1. What do you understand by Tabular book-keeping? What are its advantages and disadvantages?

2. Sketch the system of Book-keeping and Accounts you would recommend for an hotel.

3. From the following particulars prepare Rental Ledger for the year ended 24th June, 19.8. The rents stated are yearly, being payable half-yearly, at Christmas and Midsummer.

3 Spring Road—A. Butcher, £40—arrears at Midsummer, 19.7, £15; paid at Christmas, 19.7, £30; nothing at Midsummer, 19.8.
5 Spring Road—H. Sadler, £35.
7 Spring Road—P. Baker, £42.
9 Spring Road—R. Merchant, £50.
Garage—A. Driver, £20—let from Christmas, 19.7; unlet previously.
Flower Farm—J. Handcock, £190—Interest on Improvements,. £5; Christmas, 19.7, paid in full; Midsummer, 19.8, paid £80 only.
Croft—C. Toiler, £10.
Stable and Garage—M. Dealer, £18. Arrears at Midsummer, 19.7, £6, paid with Christmas, 19.7, rent.
Fenhead Farm—G. Digger, £210.

4. Prepare a form of a Columnar Ledger suitable for use in a small hotel and enter the following details therein—
Tuesday, 17th January: visitors' accounts—J. Hughes (Room 1): balance from previous day, £3·25; apartments, £1·50; breakfast, 50p; lunch, 75p; dinner, £1; wines, 75p; spirits, 52p; cigars, 25p; postages, 5p; laundry, 43p; F. J. Griffiths (Room 5): apartments, £1·25; breakfast, 50p; tea, 20p; supper, 25p; liqueurs, 35p; minerals, 8p; bath, 15p; newspapers, 12p; J. E. Elliott (Room 3): balance from previous day, £4·72; breakfast, 50p; cigarettes, 32p; cash received in settlement of bill, £5·54. *(L.C.C.)*

5. A property company owns a number of buildings which are mainly let out in suites of offices.
The rents are collected and outgoings paid by a firm of estate agents, who render quarterly accounts for each building (sometimes supplemented by interim accounts) with a cheque for the balance in their hands.
Describe a book through which the agents' statements may be incorporated in the company's accountancy system, illustrating your description with rulings. *(C.A. Inter.)*

CHAPTER XIV

CORRECTION OF ERRORS

1. The book-keeper employed by John Horton handed you a trial balance which included on the debit side an item "Suspense Account, £97·41." He stated that this was the difference between the two sides of the trial balance which he could not trace. On investigation you find that the difference is caused by the following errors—

(a) The Sales Journal has been over-cast on page 87 by £100.

(b) The Returns Outwards for November, amounting to £30·58, have been posted to personal accounts only.

(c) A cheque for £70·32 received from Barton Bros. has been posted to their Sales Ledger Account as £73·20.

(d) A first and final dividend amounting to £1·36 received from the trustee in bankruptcy of Hubert Wilkins has not been posted to the Sales Ledger Account. The full amount of the debt (£19) has been written off as bad during the year.

(e) A cheque for £13·24 paid to J. Smithson for goods supplied has been posted to his credit in the Sales Ledger.

Show the entries (journal or ledger) which are necessary to correct the above errors.

(R.S.A. Advanced.)

2. The following errors are discovered in the books of a business concern—

(a) £152·50 paid for new office furniture has been charged to Office Expenses.

(b) £39·18, representing a monthly total of discounts allowed to debtors, has been posted from the debit side of the cash book to the *credit* of Discount Account.

(c) An entry of £10, representing the retail value of goods returned to X & Co., wholesalers, has been made in the Returns Outwards Book and posted. The amount should have been £7, the invoiced value of the goods in question.

Show the entries necessary to correct these errors. The original wrong entries are not to be deleted. Subject to this restriction, make the corrections in whatever form you consider most appropriate. *(R.S.A. Stage II.)*

3. A.B. & Co. closed their books on 31st December. As on that date you find that—

(a) Materials from store (£318) and wages (£158) had been used in making loose tools for use in the Company's factory, but no entries had been made in the books.

(b) £56 (debited to Wages Account) had been paid in weekly instalments to an injured workman pending the settlement of a claim against the Accident Assurance Co. Ltd.

(c) Goods (£21), purchased from J. B. Robinson on 28th December, had been entered in the Purchases Journal and credited to him, but were not delivered until 5th January.

(d) Goods (cost price £1,287; minimum sale price £1,487) had been consigned to Australia, but were still unsold.

How should the above matters be dealt with in the Company's books? If, in your opinion, any adjusting entries are necessary, submit them. *(C.A. Inter.)*

4. A trader's book-keeper has agreed a Trial Balance and drafted the Trading and Profit and Loss Account and the Balance Sheet. You discover the following errors—

(1) Sales on Appro. amounting to £100 have been included in the Sales Account; £75 of these goods were returned. No record of the return was made in the books, but the returned goods were included in Stock at their cost price of £50.

(2) A cheque for £250 received for a loss of stock sustained by fire has been paid by the proprietor into his private bank account and not recorded in the business books.

(3) Purchased goods amounting to £200 are included in Stock, but the invoice was dated forward and is not entered for the period under review.

(4) There were three compensating errors, viz. Discounts received were undercast £5, Debit side of a Sales Ledger Account was overcast £10, and a payment of £15 for Legal Expenses had not been posted from the Cash Book.

State the effect of each of these errors, and summarize the alterations to be made in the Accounts as originally drafted.

5. The book-keeper of a firm, having been unable to agree the Trial Balance at 31st January, raised a Suspense Account, in which he entered the amount he was out of balance.

He then prepared a draft Balance Sheet into which he carried the amount of the Suspense Account.

The following errors were subsequently discovered in the books and duly rectified, thus balancing the books, the Suspense Account being adjusted accordingly—

(a) The addition of the analysis column in the tabular Purchase Journal posted to Goods Purchased for Re-sale Account was found to be £15 short, though the addition of the total column was correct.

(b) Goods bought from a supplier amounting to £5·25 had been posted to the credit of his account as £55.

(c) A dishonoured Bill of Exchange receivable for £200, returned by the firm's bank, had been credited to the Bank Account and debited to Bills Receivable Account.

(d) An item of £10·50 entered in the Sales Returns Book had been posted to the debit of the customer who returned the goods.

(e) Sundry items of Plant sold amounting to £300 had been entered in the Sales Day Book, the total of which book had been posted to the credit of Sales Account.

(f) An amount of £60 owing by a customer had been omitted from the Schedule of Sundry Debtors.

(g) Discounts amounting to £2·25 allowed to a customer had been duly entered in his account but not posted to Discount Account.

(h) An amount of £45, being rates treated as paid in advance in the previous year, had not been brought forward as a balance on the Rates Account.

(1) Show the Suspense Account as raised by the book-keeper with the adjusting entries you would find it necessary to make therein; and

(2) Explain what effect any of the above-mentioned errors would have on the profit shown in the Accounts if not rectified.

Assume the Purchase and Sales Ledgers to be Self-Balancing.

(Adapted from C.A. Inter.)

6. At 31st December, 19.7, there was a difference in the books of N. Bilston of £38·57, the Credit column of the Trial Balance exceeding the Debit column by this amount. The difference was placed to a Suspense Account. During the next year the following errors—affecting the 19.7 accounts—were discovered. Make the entries in the Suspense Account necessary to close it before taking out a Trial Balance at 31st December, 19.8—

(a) Bank Balance £576·66 was included in the Trial Balance as £567·66.

(b) A Credit Balance on J. Jones's account in the Bought Ledger of £79·45 was extracted as £70·45.

(c) The Debit and Credit sides of the Salaries Account in the Nominal Ledger were found added up (correctly) to £560 and £550 respectively.

(d) When making a Schedule of Debtors at 31st December, 19.7, an item of £30·01 owing by S. Minett had been omitted.

(e) £21·60 had been charged to R. Foley, the correct amount as appearing in the Sales Day Book being £20·16.

7. The net total of the balances as on 31st December, 19.8, shown by a Sales Ledger was £1,464 which did not agree with the balance on the relevant Control Account.

The difference was found to be due to the following errors, after correction of which the books balanced and the amended balance on the Sales Ledger Control Account agreed with the corrected list of Sales Ledger balances.

(1) Bad Debts totalling £20 were written off during 19.8, but not adjusted in the Control Account.

(2) The total of the Discounts Allowed column in the Cash Book for the month of April, 19.8, totalling £36, was not posted.

(3) A debit balance of £14 on B's account was omitted from the list of balances.

(4) In May, 19.8, C paid £39, being a net amount after deduction of 2½ per cent cash discount against a debit balance of his account £30. It was found that the posting of an invoice for £10 to his account from the Sales Journal had been missed, and that no entry had been made in respect of the discount allowed.

(5) No adjustments had been made in the Control Account in respect of a direct transfer of £25 from D's account in the Sales Ledger, to the debit of his account in the Bought Ledger.

(6) A credit balance of £42 on E's account represented the payment of an invoice which had, in error, been omitted from the books. No discount was allowed on this item.

You are required—

(a) to explain, in respect of each of the items given, the steps necessary to correct the records; and

(b) to show the Control Account as corrected commencing with the balance before the correction of the errors. (*C.A. Inter.*)

CHAPTER XV

ROYALTY ACCOUNTS

1. What do you understand by the following terms?

(a) Mineral Rent.   (c) Minimum Rent.
(b) Surface Rent.   (d) Rack Rent.   (*C.A. Inter.*)

2. What is meant by "Power to recoup shortworkings over a term of years"?

3. As from 1st January, 19.., the Universal Mining Co. took a lease of a mine at a royalty of 5p per ton of ore raised, the dead rent being £300 per annum, with the right to recoup short workings out of subsequent surplus royalties within a period of five years. In the first five years the amounts of ore raised were as follows—

1st year	. .	2,800 tons	4th year	. .	8,500 tons
2nd year	. .	5,500 tons	5th year	. .	9,500 tons
3rd year	. .	7,500 tons			

All payments were made when due. Prepare Owner's Account, Minimum Rent Account, Royalty Account, and Short Workings Account for the five years as they should appear in the Mining Co.'s books.

4. Show your understanding of each of the following Journal Entries in the books of the Alpha Mining Co. Ltd. (whose mineral leases all provide for royalties at 2½p a ton and half-yearly payments), by setting out suitable narrative.

				£	£
(a) Dec. 31	Sundries—		*Dr.*		
	To A. YOUNG				1,500
	Short workings			500	
	Royalties			1,000	
(b) Dec. 31	Royalties		*Dr.*	1,200	
	To C. WOODLEY				1,200
(c) Dec. 31	C. WOODLEY		*Dr.*	600	
	To Short workings				600
(d) Dec. 31	Profit & Loss Account		*Dr.*	3,900	
	To Sundries—				
	Short workings				1,700
	Royalties				2,200

(*C.A. Final.*)

5. A B Co. Ltd. hold a lease of minerals from R S for a period of 40 years from 1st January, 19.4, under this lease there is payable a royalty of 2½p a ton merging in a minimum rent of £1,000 a year, payable half-yearly on 30th June and 31st December. They granted a sub-lease for 20 years from 1st July, 19.4, to X Y Co. Ltd., of one-half of the area for a royalty of 3¾p a ton merging in a minimum rent of £750 a year payable half-yearly on 30th June and 31st December. A B Co. Ltd. are entitled under the lease from R S to recoup short workings out of subsequent excess workings throughout the term of the lease, but the sub-lease only allows X Y Co. Ltd. to recoup short workings out of excess workings in any of the three half-years immediately following that in which the short workings accrued. Minerals were worked as follows—

						Combined Total	By X Y Co. Ltd.
Half-year ended 30th June, 19.4	.	.	.	.	5,000 tons	——
„	„	31st Dec., 19.4	.	.	.	5,000 tons	5,000 tons
„	„	30th June, 19.5	.	.	.	20,000 tons	6,000 tons
„	„	31st Dec., 19.5	.	.	.	30,000 tons	6,000 tons
„	„	30th June, 19.6	.	.	.	25,000 tons	12,000 tons

Show the Royalties Account and the Short Workings Accounts under the lease from R S and the sub-lease to X Y Co. Ltd. in the books of A B Co. Ltd., which are balanced yearly on 30th June.   (*C.A. Final.*)

6. The R Mining Co. Ltd. leased a property from A at a royalty of $7\frac{1}{2}$p per ton, with a minimum rent of £2,000 per annum. Each year's excess of minimum rent over royalties is recoverable out of the royalties of the next five years. In the event of a strike and the minimum rental not being reached, the lease provided that the actual royalties earned for the year discharged all rental obligations for that year.

The results of the working were as follows: First year of the Company, ended 31st December, 19.5, actual royalties, nil; year ended 31st December, 19.6, actual royalties, £650; year ended 31st December, 19.7, actual royalties, £1,850; year ended 31st December, 19.8, actual royalties, £2,250; year ended 31st December, 19.9, £2,800; year ended 31st December, 19.0, £3,500; year ended 31st December, 19.1 (strike), actual royalties, £1,900; year ended 31st December, 19.2 actual royalties, £3,000.

Write up the Minimum Rent Account and the Royalties Account, showing the amount charged to Profit and Loss Account each year.   (*C.A. Final.*)

CHAPTER XVI

JOINT VENTURE ACCOUNTS

1. Andrew Stewart, of London, and John Williams, of Cardiff, entered into a joint venture to sell oil. They agreed that profits or losses should be divided equally, but that 6 per cent interest should be charged on all transactions.

Williams purchased oil on 1st November, 19.., to the value of £1,250 and accepted a bill drawn on him by the seller, payable in 5 months, for the amount due; he paid on 1st November, 19.., £30 freight and carriage. The consignment was sold by Stewart for £1,550 and payment was received by him as follows—

1st February, 19..	.	.	£600	1st April, 19...	.	.	£950

Expenses in connection with the venture were paid by Stewart on 1st April, 19.., amounting to £35, and on 1st May he paid Williams the amount due to him.

You are required to show the Joint Account in the books of both parties, together with the Joint Venture Account. (Calculations in respect of interest may be made in months.)

2. Adams and Bell were art dealers who agreed to purchase certain pictures on joint account, the arrangement being that the party effecting the sale was to be allowed a commission of 5 per cent on the amount realized, the remaining profit being divided equally.

On 25th June, 19.., Adams bought three pictures for £1,600 and Bell purchased two others for £1,350. Expenses of £35 were incurred, of which Adams paid £25 and Bell £10.

On 17th July, Adams sold one of the pictures for £630, and on 25th July forwarded another picture to Bell, the cost of carriage and insurance (paid by Adams) being £7·80. Bell sold this picture on 5th August for £756, and on the same day sent Adams a cheque for the amount realized, less 5 per cent. The pictures purchased by Bell were sold by him on 10th and 29th July for £892·50 and £819 respectively.

At 30th September the remaining picture was still unsold, and it was arranged that Adams should take this over for £400. On 5th October the amount due from one party to the other was settled by cheque.

Prepare a general statement showing the result of the venture and write up the Joint Account as it would appear in the books of Adams. *(R.S.A.)*

3. Green of London, and Brown of Bombay, entered into a joint venture in regard to a consignment of transistor radios to be sent from London for sale in India; profits to be shared equally. The transactions were as follows—

On 15th April, 19.., Green bought 1,000 transistors at the rate of £1,250 per hundred, subject to 30 per cent trade discount. On the same day he paid freight and insurance charges amounting to £565·60, and drew a bill of exchange on Brown payable one month after sight for 140,000 rupees, discounting this with the Chartered Bank of India for £7,371·53.

Brown received the consignment on 20th June. On 24th June he paid landing and warehouse charges amounting to 1,475 rupees, and on 29th June he sold the whole consignment for 224,000 rupees and paid the bill of exchange under discount, the discount amounting to 325 rupees.

Green paid petty and incidental expenses amounting to £17·25 and Brown paid 340 rupees, and on 4th July Brown sent Green a draft in final settlement.

You are required to draw up accounts, ignoring interest as between Green and Brown, showing how these transactions would be recorded in the books of each party, discount being treated as divisible jointly and 100 rupees being taken as worth £5·35.

(L.C.C.)

4. Kahla and Bateman agreed to enter upon a joint venture to promote and underwrite a public issue of shares in connection with a limited company to be called the No Good Finance Corporation Ltd.

45

The company was formed and duly registered on 1st January, 19.., with a Share Capital of £280,000 divided into 125,000 6 per cent Cum. Preference Shares of £1 each, and 155,000 Ordinary Shares of £1 each. It was agreed between the partners that they should share the Profits or Losses of the venture 3:2.

Kahla and Bateman contracted with the Company—

(1) To bear all expenses of registration of the company.

(2) To bear all expenses of the public issue of the Preference Share Capital except the underwriting commission due to them.

(3) To underwrite the whole of the issue.

The consideration for such services comprises an allotment to the partners of 15,000 £1 Ordinary Shares as fully paid at par and an underwriting commission of 2½p per share in connection with the Preference issue. The Ordinary Shares were duly allotted to the partners on 2nd January, 19.., and the underwriting commission was paid to them on 15th March, 19...

As between themselves the partners agreed to finance the partnership as follows—

Kahla provided the cash necessary to meet the expenditure entailed by the public issue as follows—

			£
19..			
Feb.	1.	Printing and Dispatch of Prospectuses . . .	350
		Advertising Prospectus	3,000
	26.	Professional Charges re Expert Reports and Valuations	750
Mar.	1.	Printing Allotment Letters and Share Certificates .	45
	5.	Solicitor's Charges re Prospectus and Public Issue of Capital.	525
		Brokerage of 1¼p per share on 75,000 Preference Shares	937½

Bateman provided cash for all other expenses as follows—

			£
19..			
Jan.	1.	Capital Duty.	1,400
		Solicitor's Charges re Formation of Company . .	105
		Printing Memorandum and Articles. . . .	35
	20.	Printing Books of Account and Statutory Books .	95
Mar.	31.	Office Rent and Rates to 31st March, 19.. .	50
		Salaries of Office Staff to 31st March, 19.. . .	250
		Sundry Petty Cash Expenditure to 31st March, 19...	35

The issue of Preference Shares was under-subscribed by the public and Kahla and Bateman were called upon, under the terms of their Underwriting Agreement, to take up the balance of 5,000 Preference Shares, in respect of which on 1st March, 19.., Kahla provided cash for the payment for 3,000 of the shares and Bateman paid for the balance. A pool was then formed through which the 5,000 Preference Shares and 15,000 Ordinary Shares held by the partners were sold at average prices of 90p and 95p each respectively.

The pool expenses were met by a charge of 5p per share in respect of these sales, settlement of the transaction being effected on 31st March, 19...

Separate books of account having been kept in respect of the partnership business, prepare the usual accounts showing the Profit or Loss on the partnership and the position of the partners in relation to their respective capitals for the period of the venture which terminated on 31st March, 19.., on which date both partners' capitals were paid out.

5. A and B enter into joint transactions for the purchase and sale of shares. On 30th September, 19.., A buys for the joint account the following—

	£
200 £1 Ordinary Shares in A.B. Plantations Ltd., cost . .	384
200 £1 Ordinary Shares in X.Y. Tobacco Co. Ltd., cost . . .	757
40 £1 Ordinary Shares in Z. Insurance Co. Ltd., cost . .	733
	£1,874

The first and second of these are registered in the name of A, the third in that of the Broker, who (on this security) lends £700 with interest at 7¼ per cent per annum. The balance of the cost is found equally by A and B.

Dividends received are—

A.B. Plantations Ltd., 15th November, 19..—25 per cent (actual), *less* tax, and Bonus of one fully-paid share for every two held.

X.Y. Tobacco Co. Ltd., 12th October, 19..—5 per cent (actual), *less* tax; 12th January, 19..—9 per cent (actual), *less* tax.

Z. Insurance Co. Ltd., 10th November, 19..—55p per share, *less* tax.

On 15th December, 19.., the shares in the X.Y. Tobacco Co. Ltd. are transferred to the Broker as additional security.

On 20th January, 19.., 100 shares in the same Company are sold, realizing £348·25 net, and on 31st January, 19.., the Broker renders his account, remitting cheques to A and B, in equal shares, for the balance in his hands, irrespective of the loan, which is continued.

Show (as in the books of A) the Ledger Accounts recording these transactions made up to 31st March, 19... Assume income tax at 40 per cent.   (*C.A. Final.*)

6. On 1st January, 19.., A B, a London merchant, arranged with C D Ltd. also of London, to join him in executing an order he had received from X Y, of Lisbon, for goods which could be purchased advantageously in Stockholm. C D Ltd. were to carry through the business in A B's name, and to pay him one-half of the profit, taking the escudos rate at 86 and the kronor rate at 14·25, and charging A B with £25 for office expenses.

The goods were bought from S T, Stockholm, for 56,600 kronor and paid for by C D Ltd., on 6th January, when the rate was 14·15. On 13th January, when the rate was 14·40, C D Ltd. remitted freight and both charges amounting to 10,800 kronor.

On 6th January the goods were invoiced to X Y for 484,000 escudos, and a draft was received in due course in payment for 457,600 escudos, the difference being a deduction for damage claimed by X Y, which was allowed.

The proceeds of the draft were credited to C D Ltd., by their bankers on 20th January at the rate of 88; and on 3rd February they were also credited at the rate of 14·59 with the proceeds of a draft for 4,377 kronor received from the carriers in settlement of a claim for the damage to the goods.

A B was paid his share of the profit on 4th February.

Write up the Joint Venture Account in the books of C D Ltd., and show how you arrive at A B's share of the profit.   (*C.A. Final.*)

7. Tower and Castle entered into a joint venture to buy and sell a quantity of briar pipes. It was agreed that Tower should receive a commission of two per cent on all sales, in consideration for which he was to bear all losses from bad debts. Subject to this arrangement, profits and losses were to be shared equally.

On 2nd January, 19.4, Tower purchased goods for £6,800 for which he paid £4,800 in cash, and accepted bills of exchange for £800 and £1,200.

On 3rd January, Tower sent to Castle goods which had cost £2,750, and Castle paid £3,500 to Tower.

On 9th January, Tower sold goods to Brown for £420 and to Green for £250 and they accepted bills of exchange for the amounts respectively due from them. Tower endorsed both these bills over to Castle, who discounted them. (Ignore discounting charges.)

On 3rd February, Tower sold goods for £1,800. On delivery the customer rejected goods invoiced at £90, and these goods were collected by Castle, who sold them to another customer for £110.

On 11th February, Brown met his bill, but Green's bill was dishonoured. Green was insolvent, with no assets.

On 5th March, Castle paid the bill for £800 which had been accepted by Tower, and Tower paid the second bill, £1,200.

During March, 19.4, Tower sold the remainder of the goods in his possession for £2,910, and Castle's sales amounted to £3,400. Bad debts (apart from the amount due from Green) were £42, of which £30 was in respect of sales by Tower, and £12 was in respect of sales by Castle.

On 30th April, 19.4, the venture was closed. Castle took over the stock in his possession at a valuation of £500, and the sum required to settle accounts between the venturers was paid by the party accountable.

You are required to show—

(a) the accounts which would appear in the books of Tower and Castle respectively to record the joint venture, and

(b) a memorandum Joint Venture account, showing the net profit.

(*C.A. Final.*)

8. A and B enter into a joint venture in respect of a consignment of 100 articles each costing £10.

A supplies such goods and sends them to B for sale, paying carriage thereon £20.

B is to have commission of 10 per cent on sales and the profit divided in the ratio of 2:1.

It is found that 10 articles are below standard, and it is agreed that A will take them back and sell them as his own goods, without commission, and loss thereon being borne solely by A. It is further agreed that at the same time 5 articles be returned to A as he is in a position to effect a sale (on account of the joint venture) at £18 each, being a better price than what B could get. B sells the remaining articles (*less* 3 taken over by him at an agreed figure of £11 each) at £14 each. The carriage on the goods returned by B to A is £4, and it is agreed that £2 thereof relates to the cost of returning the 10 articles and to be borne by A.

Show the accounts of A in B's books, B in A's books and Memorandum Joint Venture.

9. Jasper and Mortimer Rhode entered into a joint venture for the sale of caravans and accessories. They agreed to share profits and losses as 3:2.

A hall was hired for a period of 12 days at a charge of £60 inclusive of lighting, cleaning, etc., and to encourage public attendance it was decided to award a prize, in the form of accessories, for the most accurate forecast of the total numbers visiting the display.

Fully equipped caravans were delivered to the hall by Jasper Rhode from his stock as follows—

	£
5 Rhode "Major" at cost £600	3,000
6 Rhode "Rider" at cost £400	2,400
5 Rhode "Minor" at cost £240	1,200

Mortimer Rhode exhibited a variety of accessories which were supplied by Nu-Homes Ltd., and invoiced to him on sale or return terms at £470.

Other expenses incurred were—

Paid by Jasper Rhode—

	£
Attendant's wages	48
Advertising	30
Transport	10

Paid by Mortimer Rhode—

	£
Hire of Hall	60
Insurance—Fire and Public Liability	12
Transport	5

Sales were made partly for cash, and partly on extended terms, the outstanding balances arising out of the latter being taken over by Jasper Rhode.

Such sales were—

Cash—

	£
1 Rhode "Major"	750
1 Rhode "Rider"	500
Accessories	450

Extended Terms—

						Selling Price £	Cash Deposits (20 per cent) £
4 Rhode "Major"	.	.	.	.	.	3,000	600
4 Rhode "Rider"	.	.	.	.	.	2,000	400
5 Rhode "Minor"	.	.	.	.	.	1,500	300

The whole of the cash thus received was paid into a joint bank account.

The prize in the form of accessories was duly awarded at a cost to the organizers of £50.

Subsequently the remaining accessories (invoiced at £120) were returned to Nu-Homes Ltd., with a cheque, drawn on the joint bank account, for the balance due.

The caravan unsold was taken back by Jasper Rhode at cost less 5 per cent.

The joint bank account was closed.

You are required—

(a) to make appropriate records of the foregoing transactions in the books of each party;

(b) to draw up the accounts of the joint venture.

CHAPTER XVII

CONSIGNMENT ACCOUNTS

1. R. Uprichard, of Cape Town, received 10 cases of hardware from G. McArthur & Co., of London. In connection with this consignment he paid: Dock and landing charges, £3·98; warehouse charges, £2·20; insurance, £3·38; and cartage, £1·99.

On 15th January, 19.., he sold 8 cases of goods at £42 per case, less 5 per cent cash discount, and on 19th February he sold the balance of the consignment at £43·53 per case net. Uprichard was entitled to 2½ per cent commission and 1 per cent *del credere* on gross proceeds of all sales. He remitted the amount due to G. McArthur & Co. on 21st February, 19...

Prepare the Account Sales sent by Uprichard to McArthur & Co.   (*R.S.A.*)

2. X & Co. Ltd. of London, consigned to their Agent A B in Jamaica, on 10th January, 19.., a shipment of boots, paying £40 for carriage and freight and £25 insurance. The goods cost £625 and a *pro forma* invoice for £700 was sent to the Agent on the above-named date, along with a draft at 3 months for £400. The draft was accepted by him and received back in London on 4th February, 19... On arrival of the goods in Jamaica it was found that, owing to faulty packing, boots which cost £20 were unsaleable, in respect of which there was no valid claim against the Underwriters.

On 28th January, 19.., A B advised his Principals that he had sold a portion of the shipment for £150 on credit. He sold the remainder on credit for £590 on 20th February, 19.., and on that date he forwarded to X & Co. Ltd., an Account Sales along with an acceptance at 2 months for the balance due by him (including an agreed figure of £5 for interest due to X & Co.), these documents being received by X & Co. on 2nd March, 19... A B's expenses in connection with the consignment were £15 and he was entitled to commission at the rate of 5 per cent on sales.

Show by means of ledger accounts how the foregoing transactions would be recorded in X & Co.'s books of account.   (*C.A. Inter.*)

3. On 15th April, 19.., Boyd, Walker & Co., Liverpool, consigned to Jones & Ware, Bombay, 100 cases of cotton goods and invoiced same at £21·26 per case, the cost price.

Boyd, Walker & Co. paid the following charges—

					£
Insurance	.	.	.	.	35·50
Freight, etc.	.	.	.	.	86·75

The goods arrived on 31st May, 19.., and Jones & Ware paid the landing charges, amounting to 415 rupees. They also met the cost of storing and insuring the goods at 1 rupee per case per month.

Jones & Ware ascertained that two cases had been lost in transit and informed Boyd, Walker & Co., who, having made the necessary claim, recovered on 15th August, 19.., £44, the insured value of the two cases.

On 16th June, 19.., Jones & Ware sold 80 cases for cash at 530 rupees per case, and next day remitted sight draft for 37,500 rupees at £5·365 per 100 rupees, which was received by Boyd, Walker & Co. on 18th July, 19...

Jones & Ware disposed of the remaining cases on 15th August, 19.., at 500 rupees per case, and next day remitted the balance due by draft at £5·35 per 100 rupees, after deduction of commission at 2½ per cent on Sales.

Show the Consignment Account as at 31st July, 19.. (the end of Boyd, Walker & Co.'s financial year), and also the account with Jones & Ware.

Expenses at Bombay to be calculated at £5·35 per 100 rupees.

4. A firm whose business consists of shipping goods on consignment to Agents abroad, debits the agents through the Sales Book with the approximate net proceeds expected at the time of consignment, any necessary adjustment being made on the receipt of Account Sales.

Given the following particulars, frame the necessary adjusting Journal Entries, and show how the open shipments would appear in the firm's Balance Sheet as at 31st December, 19...

19..

Aug. 31. Goods costing £925 consigned to A B, Bombay; approximate net proceeds expected, £1,150.

Dec. 2. Account Sales received from A B showing net proceeds of consignment, £1,114·50.

Sept. 12. Goods costing £350 consigned to X Y, Cape Town; approximate net proceeds expected, £435.

Dec. 23. Account Sales received from X Y showing net proceeds of consignment, £441·75.

Oct. 1. Goods costing £822 consigned to R S, Cape Town; approximate net proceeds expected, £941.

Oct. 10. Goods costing £1,145, consigned to M N, Lisbon; approximate net proceeds expected, £1,284.

5. Midland Motors Ltd. consign to their Selling Agents in Bombay two cars costing £600 for sale on the basis of 8 per cent plus 2 per cent *del credere* commission, the Agents to pay all landing charges in Bombay (these amounted to Rs. 650). The consignor paid £175 for cartage, freight and insurance.

The Agents sold one car for Rs. 6,500 and remitted Rs. 5,200 on account. The second car was sold for Rs. 7,150, but Rs. 1,300 was not paid, and became a bad debt.

Prepare an Account Sales to accompany the Agent's remittance to balance and open the necessary ledger accounts in the books of both the consignor and consignee to record the transaction (rupees at 13 to the £).

6. A London firm of shippers dealing with Eastern markets send out goods on consignment to Agents abroad.

How would you advise them to arrange their book-keeping records in regard to the consignments?

Having in view the fact that in some cases considerable periods elapse between the dispatch of the goods and their realization by sale, explain how outstanding consignments should be dealt with when preparing the annual accounts of the firm.

(*C.A. Inter.*)

7. Dickens in London consigns to Jones in Gibraltar goods to the value of £3,000 (cost £2,000), paying Freight and Insurance of £200, and draws a bill on Jones for £2,000 at sixty days.

Nine-tenths of the consignment was sold by Jones for £3,500, and expenses of £200 were incurred. Jones is also entitled to a commission of 10 per cent on Sales.

Jones remitted to Dickens the net amount held for his account by means of a sight draft.

Show by means of Journal entries how the above transactions would be recorded in the books of both Dickens and Jones.

CHAPTER XVIII

DEPARTMENTAL ACCOUNTS

1. The following particulars are taken from the books of the Elizabeth Garage Co., from which you are required to prepare a departmental Trading Account and a General Profit and Loss Account for the year ended 31st December, 19..—

	£
Sales of Motor-cars	29,500
Purchases of Motor-cars (for re-sale)	25,000
Carriage on Cars Sold	230
Hire of Cars, viz. Charges to Customers	810
Repairing Charges (to Customers)	1,900
Expenses—Hire Cars	450
Fixtures and Fittings	150
Petrol, Oil, etc., Sales	1,950
Loose Plant and Tools	450
Salaries	1,020
Profit and Loss Account, Cr. Balance, 1st January, 19..	1,300
Loan Interest	250
Sundry Debtors	5,800
Bad Debts written off	100
Petrol, Oil, etc., used	1,250
Garage Rents received	180
Stock of Hire Cars	1,300
Accessories (Tubes, Tyres, etc.) used	4,700
Stock of Accessories (Tubes, Tyres, etc.) at 31st December, 19..	750
Repairs to Plant, etc.	54
Sundry Receipts (Cleaning Cars, Charging Batteries, etc.)	330
Bad Debts Provision at 1st January, 19...	240
Cost of Repairs to Cars (Materials, Wages, etc.)	1,750
Yard Wages	310
Sales of Accessories (Tubes, Tyres, etc.)	5,470

The following provisions are to be made: for bad debts, 5 per cent on debtors; depreciate loose plant and tools by 20 per cent; fixtures and fittings, 5 per cent; and hire cars, 20 per cent. The manager is entitled to a commission of 5 per cent after charging this commission.

2. On 30th June, 19.., the Balance Sheet of Young & Zero was as follows—

	£		£
Sundry Creditors	10,000	Cash at Bank	5,000
Partners' Current Accounts	5,000	Sundry Debtors	15,000
Partners' Capital Accounts	25,000	Stock-in-trade	7,500
		Fixtures, Fittings, etc.	2,500
		Machinery and Plant	10,000
	£40,000		£40,000

There are four departments in connection with the business, namely, Mail, Town, Country, and Foreign; and while it is not practicable for the stock to be taken until 31st December, 19.., interim account is required at 30th September, 19...

From the following particulars you are required to prepare the four departmental accounts and afterwards to draw up a General Trial Balance—

Department	Stock-in-Trade	Purchases	Sales	Departmental Charges
Mail	£2,500	£3,000	£6,000	£1,000
Town	£3,500	£2,500	£3,500	£750
Country	£1,000	£2,000	£3,000	£350
Foreign	£500	£1,000	£500	£300

The rate of profit on Sales in each department is to be taken as: Mail, 40; Town, 30; Country, 25; and Foreign, 20 per cent respectively.

The general, or indirect, expenses are £1,000; partners' drawings, £1,000; interest on capital, 5 per cent per annum. Depreciate machinery and plant at the rate of 20 per cent per annum and fixtures and fittings at the rate of 10 per cent per annum.

The debtors at 30th September, 19.., amount to £8,500 and the creditors to £7,506, while the cash at bank is £9,100, which is arrived at as follows—

	£	£
Balance	5,000	
Sundry Debtors	19,500	
		24,500
Sundry Creditors	10,994	
Direct Expenses	2,400	
Indirect Expenses	1,000	
Drawings	1,000	
Interest on Loan	6	
		15,400
		£9,100

3. An hotel proprietor's books show the following balances on 31st December, 19..—

	£
Capital—Credit Balance on 1st January, 19..	18,895
Drawings.	2,500
Freehold Premises	15,600
Furniture and Fittings	2,978
Glass and China	367
Linen	280
Cutlery and Plate	130
Rates, Taxes, and Insurance	571
Salaries	800
Wages	1,435
Stocks on 1st January, 19..—	
Wines, £413; Spirits, £126; Beers, £55 . . .	594
Minerals, £49; Cigars and Cigarettes, £38 . . .	87
Sundry Provisions and Stores, £61; Solid Fuel, £50 . .	111
Purchases—	
Meat, £1,209; Fish and Poultry, £1,320 . . .	2,529
Sundry Provisions and Stores, £1,740; Wines, £627 . .	2,367
Spirits, £730; Beers, £384	1,114
Minerals, £350; Cigars and Cigarettes, £80 . . .	430
Laundry	317
Heating	720
Electric Light	376
General Expenses	570
Sales—	
Wines, £1,290; Spirits, £1,445; Beers, £621 . . .	3,356
Minerals, £720; Cigars, and Cigarettes, £130 . . .	850
Meals	7,943
Rooms	3,125
Fires in Bedrooms	194
Washing Charged	73
Repairs, Renewals, and Depreciation—	
Premises, £116; Furniture and Fittings, £220 . . .	336
Glass and China, £203; Linen, £130 . . .	333
Cutlery and Plate.	69
Cash Book—Debit Balances: Bank	716
In hand	73
Visitors' Accounts unpaid	163
Sundry Creditors	1,130

Stocks on 31st December, 19.., were valued as follows—

Wines, £399; Spirits, £111; Beers, £58; Minerals, £119; Cigars and Cigarettes, £23; Sundry Provisions and Stores, £47; Coal, £33.

All other necessary adjustments have been already made. Prepare Accounts for the year ended 31st December, 19.., and Balance Sheet as on that date. (*C.A. Final.*)

4. The following Trial Balance for the year ended 30th June, 19.., was extracted from the books of Black.

	£	£
Capital on 1st July, 19..—		
A. Black		10,000
Drawings—		
A. Black	2,000	
Stock 1st July, 19..—		
Department A	1,140	
Department B	980	
Purchases—		
Department A	3,960	
Department B	3,740	
Sales—		
Department A		7,400
Department B		6,630
Inter-departmental Transfers—		
Department A		250
Department B	250	
Returns Inwards—		
Department A	350	
Department B	280	
Wages and Salaries	1,650	
Advertising and Catalogues	870	
Dividends on Shares in X Y & Co. Ltd.		105
Shares in X Y & Co. Ltd.	2,300	
Sundry Debtors	4,920	
Sundry Creditors		2,974
Carriage Inwards	240	
Rent, Rates, Taxes, and Lighting	1,830	
Furniture and Fixtures	1,500	
Sundry Expenses, including Printing, Stationery, Commission, Postage, Telephone, Insurance, etc.	740	
Bank Balance	684	
Provision for Bad and Doubtful Debts as on 1st July, 19..		75
	£27,434	£27,434

You are required to prepare Departmental Trading and Profit and Loss Accounts and a Balance Sheet, after making the following adjustments—

(1) Write off bad debts amounting to £120, and thereafter increase the provision for doubtful debts to 5 per cent of the book debts outstanding.

(2) Provide £40 for Stationery and Telephone Accounts, owing 30th June, 19...

(3) Depreciate furniture and fixtures by 10 per cent per annum.

(4) The value of the stocks on hand on 30th June, 19.., was: Department A, £2,960; Department, B, £1,700.

(5) Catalogues in hand were valued at £60.

(6) Inter-departmental transfers were made at cost price.

(7) All expenses are to be allocated between the departments in the proportions: A Department, two-thirds; B Department, one-third. (*C.A. Inter.*)

5. Art Sales Ltd. is a public company having an authorized and issued share capital of £150,000, divided into 25,000 6 per cent preference shares and 125,000 ordinary shares, all of £1 each. On 1st July, 19.., there were also in issue £55,000 (nominal) of 5 per cent debentures, the balance of an issue made several years ago at a price of 90 per cent, £5,000 of which were repayable annually at par on 31st December.

A further £5,000 was duly paid off on 31st December, 19.., and half-yearly interest payments on the amounts outstanding were made on 31st December, 19.., and 30th June, following.

The business of the company is carried on in two departments, which trade respectively in pictures and pottery, but there is no hard-and-fast division between the personnel of the two departments, nor is any analysis of the trade expenses made except so far as is indicated in the balances below. A small workshop, however, is concerned solely with the renovation and framing of pictures.

The balances standing in the books of the company, as on 30th June, 19.., in addition to those disclosed by the foregoing information, were as follows—

	£
Debenture Redemption Fund, 1/7/19...	25,000
Debenture Discount 1/7/19..	3,000
Purchases—	
Pictures .	97,028
Pottery .	52,318
Sales—	
Pictures .	118,416
Pottery .	38,557
Salaries and Wages—	
Workshop .	525
Shop and Office	4,472
Directors' Fees .	600
Commissions Received (Pictures, £3,231; Pottery, £597)	3,828
Commissions Paid (Pictures, £1,074; Pottery, £238)	1,312
Rent and Rates .	7,300
Heating, Lighting, and Insurance .	817
Workshop Expenses .	293
Advertising .	2,954
Lease Account, 1/7/19..	19,200
Stock, 1/7/19.. (Pictures, £94,427; Pottery, £33,155)	127,582
Fixtures and Fittings, 1/7/19..	3,100
Fixtures and Fittings purchased during year .	260
Trade Creditors .	15,191
Sundry Debtors .	53,600
Cash at Bank .	7,374
Cash in Hand .	219
Office and Trade Expenses .	1,318
Profit and Loss Account, 1/7/19.. (Cr.)	2,337
Interim Dividend on Preference Shares .	750
Packing Materials and Carriage .	881
Goodwill .	15,000
Art Catalogues, 1/7/19.. (390 valued at 30p each) .	117
Repairs to Buildings .	164
Bad Debts written off, less Provision 1/7/19..	212
Travelling Expenses .	308

You are required to prepare a Trading and Profit and Loss Account (in departmental form) for the year ended 30th June, 19.., and a Balance Sheet as on that date.

In preparing these accounts, regard is to be had to the following information and instructions—

(a) The stock-in-trade as on 30th June, 19.., was valued as follows: Pictures, £99,683; pottery, £54,318. Packing materials not used were valued at £37.

(b) During the year 210 of the art catalogues were distributed to dealers and customers (no entry having been passed through the books) and it was decided to value the remainder at 25p each.

(c) A further £5,000 is to be appropriated to the Debenture Redemption Fund.

(d) The provision for bad and doubtful debts is to be made equal to 1 per cent of the sundry debtors.

(e) Provision is to be made for the following outstanding amounts: Heating and lighting, £107; office expenses, £22; and advertising, £146. The last payment of rates, amounting to £624, was in respect of the half-year to 30th September, in advance.

(*f*) £1,000 is to be written off the Debenture Discount Account, and one-eighth off the Lease Account; the fixtures and fittings are to be depreciated 7½ per cent.

(*g*) Expenditure not directly apportioned is to be allocated three-quarters to the picture department and one-quarter to the pottery department.

(*h*) Tax is to be ignored.   (*L.C.C.*)

[*Students may prefer to defer dealing with this question until Ch. XXIII has been studied.*]

6. Flash Ltd. generate their own electricity and arrange with Splash Ltd. to use their water supply, which they get by pumping operations, the electricity therefor being supplied by Flash Ltd., each mutually agreeing to supply at cost.

The cost of generating electricity (*excluding* the charge made for the use of the water supply) is £500; and the cost of the water pumping (*excluding* the charge made for the use of electricity) is £200.

It is revealed that the total units of electricity generated are 500,000, utilized as follows—

Generating	100,000
Factory	300,000
Sold to Splash Ltd.	100,000

In regard to the quantity of water pumped, the allocation is: Factory, three-fifths; sold to Flash Ltd., two-fifths.

From the foregoing, prepare statements showing (*a*) the total cost of electricity generated by Flash Ltd., and (*b*) the total cost of water pumped by Splash Ltd.

7. Horace Cope is in business and has two selling lines, manufactured by his own factory, its two sections A and B and the Office being on separate floors of the factory building. In addition, a part of the factory building comprises the Boiler Room.

The goods, subject to the next paragraph, all go to the retail shops on the basis of Factory Cost, plus 20 per cent.

Part of the manufactured goods of A are required by B as Raw Material and vice versa. The transfer basis is Cost. A transfers one-fifth of its output to B: and B one-tenth to A.

From the following information you are required to prepare Departmental Statement showing Cost and Profit for the year ended 31st December, 19... Ignore Tax.

		£	£	£
Raw Materials used—				
A	. . . .	38,258		
B	. . . .	21,365		
			59,623	
Direct Wages—				
A	. . . .	21,062		
Overhead Charges—	. . . .			
B	. . . .	18,043	39,105	
				98,728
Indirect Wages—				
A	. . . . . .	12,000		
B	. . . . . .	5,200		
Boilermen .	. . . . .	1,700		
Cost Office	. . . . .	1,100		
			20,000	
Depreciation—				
A . . .	45 per cent			
B . . .	30 per cent			
Boilers . .	20 per cent			
Office Machinery .	5 per cent			
	100 per cent	2,000		
Buildings		400		
			2,400	
	Carried forward		£22,400	£98,728

		£	£	£
	Brought forward		22,400	98,728
Rent and Rates Factory			1,000	
Insurance—				
A, B and Boilers		285		
Buildings		200		
Office (Machinery)		5		
			490	
Repairs—				
A, B and Boilers		2,850		
Office Machinery		90		
Buildings		1,500		
			4,440	
Coal and Water			2,311	
Printing, Postage, etc. (all Office) . . .			201	
Cleaning Materials—				
A, B and Boilers		190		
Buildings		240	430	
				31,272
				£130,000

Allocate (1) Repairs (2) Insurance (except Office Machinery £5) and (3) Cleaning Materials on the same basis as depreciation.

The floor space is occupied as to A 50 per cent; B 30 per cent; Boiler Room 10 per cent and Cost Office 10 per cent.

The Boiler Room provides Power, Heat and Light.

The Power consumption is in the ratio of A2, B1, whilst the space heat and light £200 is allocated to *all four departments* on a floor-space basis.

The cost of services rendered by the Cost Office is to be charged equally to A and B.

For the purpose of the allocation the amount of £8, the estimated water charge for A, B and Office, is to be ignored.

8. Harry Coate has a factory in which there are two distinct sections.

After dealing with the various allocations (on lines similar to the preceding question) the cost to Department A is £3,000 and to Department B £1,000, subject to the following matters which have not been brought into account—

Department A—
   (i) Supplies one-fifth of its production to B at cost.
   (ii) Supplies the selling departments the whole of its output, after (i) at invoice price of cost plus 16⅔ per cent profit on the selling department *selling* price.
   (iii) The Manager is entitled to a commission of 10 per cent of the profit to his department, such commission to be included in the cost for the purposes of (i) (ii) (iii), that is, the commission is to be regarded as an addition to the cost of £3,000, the cost before dealing with (*a*) transfer from B and (*b*) Commission to Manager of A.

Department B—
   (i) Supplies one-sixth of its production to A at cost.
   (ii) As above.
   (iii) As above, except that the Manager of B takes 20 per cent commission (as compared with 10 per cent to the Manager of Department A).

Show Statement of Cost and Profit to each Department.

9. Orchard carries on trade as a fruit grower and as a canner. On 31st December, 19.8, the Trial Balance extracted from his books was as follows—

	Dr.	Cr.
	£	£
Orchard—		
Capital Account (1st January, 19.8)		13,500
Drawings Account.	1,200	
Freehold Land and Premises at cost . . .	14,900	
Freehold Land and Premises sales during year . . .		800
Carried forward	£16,100	£14,300

	Dr. £	Cr. £
Brought forward	16,100	14,300
Plant and Machinery at cost—		
Farm	1,900	
Cannery	4,800	
Purchases of plant and machinery *less* sales during the year	500	
Provision for depreciation—		
Farm		1,000
Cannery		1,640
Fruit Trees and Bushes at cost	800	
Stock, 1st January, 19.8—		
Farm	400	
Cannery	1,650	
Loan at 6 per cent (interest payable 31st March and 30th September)		8,000
Balance at bank	864	
Sales Ledger balances	642	
Bought Ledger balances—		
Farm		200
Cannery		740
Purchases—		
Farm	250	
Cannery	1,210	
Wages—		
Farm	1,600	
Cannery	2,400	
Sales—		
Farm		530
Cannery		9,950
Trade Expenses	920	
Administration and Motor Expenses (including loan interest to 30th September, 19.8)	584	
Repairs—		
Farm	80	
Cannery	360	
Salaries	1,400	
	£36,460	£36,460

You are instructed to prepare the accounts and are given further information as follows—

(1) Provision is to be made for depreciation for the year of Plant and Machinery on cost at the end of the year at the rate of 10 per cent in the case of the Farm and 7½ per cent in the case of the Cannery.

(2) During the year a tractor, included in Farm Plant and Machinery at a cost of £600, and in respect of which depreciation of £500 had been provided, was sold for £300 and was replaced by a new tractor costing £800.

(3) Fruit to the value of £2,200 was supplied by the Farm to the Cannery.

(4) Stocks on hand on 31st December, 19.8, were valued as follows—

	£
Farm	300
Cannery	1,720

(5) Amounts owing, *excluding* loan interest accrued due, at the end of the year were—

Purchases—	£
Cannery (included in stock but not entered in the books)	140
Trade Expenses	80

(6) Bought Ledger balances at the end of the year included £320 for cans supplied. Since the books were closed the supplier agreed to allow £160 as the cans were

sub-standard. This allowance had been taken into account in valuing the stock on 31st December, 19.8.

(7) All expenses, except where otherwise indicated, are to be apportioned on the basis: Farm one-fourth, Cannery three-fourths.

(8) Orchard is to be charged £2 per week for expenses incurred on his private car.

(9) Freehold land, sold for £800, had cost £350.

(10) Pippin, the manager of the Cannery, is to be credited with 5 per cent of the Cannery profits, *after* charging his commission.

You are required to prepare—

(a) Trading and Profit and Loss Accounts showing, separately, the net profit or loss of the Farm and of the Cannery for the year ended 31st December, 19.8, and

(b) Balance Sheet as on that date.

Ignore taxation. (*C.A. Inter.*)

CHAPTER XIX

BRANCH ACCOUNTS

1. An English company, having a branch in France and a branch in Brazil, converts the Trial Balances received from the branches as on 31st December, 19.., into sterling at the exchange rates ruling on that day, and incorporates the figures so arrived at in the head office books.

Do you consider the method adopted to be correct? If not, suggest an alternative.

(R.S.A.)

2. A British company owns a plantation in South America, where the currency is subject to considerable fluctuations. As the major portion of the produce is disposed of in the United Kingdom, periodical remittances have to be made from London to meet the current expenses. At the end of the company's year a Trial Balance in the foreign currency is forwarded by the manager of the plantation to the head office in London.

State in detail how this Trial Balance should be converted into sterling when the annual accounts of the company are prepared.

(R.S.A.)

3. The Seaton Trading Co. Ltd., of Liverpool, established a factory in India. The company remitted to its Indian factory during the year 19.. cash amounting to £7,500, and the manager in India drew bills on the company during the year for £2,500, which were accepted.

At 31st December, 19.., it was ascertained that the Indian factory had made a loss of the equivalent of £1,800, and this was transferred to the Liverpool office.

Give the entries in the Liverpool books necessary to record these transactions.

4. Some of the goods purchased by L. & Co. are obtained from Italy, and invoices are received in currency (lire). As book-keeper to the firm, state how you would record (*a*) the invoices, and (*b*) the remittances to the creditors; and mention three methods by which payment could be made.

(R.S.A.)

5. A limited company has its head office in London and a branch in Birmingham. The head office supplies the branch with all its goods, which are charged out at cost, plus 10 per cent to cover the cost of handling.

The branch sales are for cash, and no provision is made in the system of book-keeping for credit sales at the branch, but in actual practice limited credit is given in a few selected cases. All takings are paid into the bank for the credit of head office.

Show how the following items relating to the branch would appear in the head office ledger, and close off the accounts concerned—

	£
Stock, 1st January, 19.. (at cost to Branch)	2,200
Cash received during the year	20,000
Debtors, 1st January, 19..	80
Goods from Head Office during the year	14,000
Debtors, 31st December, 19..	100
Stock, 31st December, 19.. (at cost to Branch) . . .	1,980

6. The Upsilon Stores Ltd. invoice goods to their various branches at cost, and the branches sell on credit as well as for cash. From the following details relating to the Leicester Branch, show the Branch Goods, Expenses, Debtors and Profit and Loss Accounts in the head office books—

	£
Debtors, 1st January	2,620
Debtors, 31st December	3,310
Stock, 1st January	1,500
Stock, 31st December	1,390
Goods received from Head Office	5,080
Goods returned to Head Office	70
Cash Sales	3,350
Credit Sales	6,000
Allowances to Customers	32

Returns from Customers	. . . . .	58
Discounts allowed to Customers	. . . .	240
Bad Debts	. . . .	60
Cash received on Ledger Accounts	. . .	4,920
Rent, Rates, etc.	. . . . . .	180
Wages and Salaries	. . . . .	600
General Trade Charges	. . . . .	130

7. A merchant grocer has retail branch shops at Henley, Kingston, and Sutton, and these branch establishments are supplied from the head office and pay daily to the latter the cash which they receive.

All expenses, including salaries, are paid by cheques from the head office. Each branch has its own Sales Ledger, and makes a weekly return of cash received and trade done. The following particulars relate to the half-year ended 30th June, 19.., and have been obtained from the returns made by the branches and the head office books.

	Henley	Kingston	Sutton
	£	£	£
Book Debts, 1st January	2,100	1,660	640
Stock, 1st January	1,400	1,280	1,290
Sales—Credit	6,409	6,815	4,701
Returns and Allowances (Sales) . . .	51	54	64
Sales—Cash	3,011	4,718	1,633
Cash re Ledger Accounts	6,240	6,601	4,803
Bad Debts	79	62	—
Rent and Rates	304	581	262
Book Debts, 30th June	2,139	1,758	474
Stock, 30th June	1,675	1,015	1,405
Salaries and Expenses	1,604	2,659	1,240
Goods received from Head Office . . .	5,998	7,602	5,438

Set out the accounts of the three branches as they will appear in the head office books, showing the profit or loss for the period, and also prepare the Trading and Profit and Loss Account for each branch.

8. A retail business having its head office in London has a branch at Ipswich, where a complete set of double entry books is kept. All purchases are made in London and stock required by the Ipswich branch is invoiced to them by London at selling price less 20 per cent, the local manager being entitled to a commission equal to one-half of the net profit earned by the Ipswich branch on the basis of such invoice price.

The following are the Trial Balances extracted from the London and Ipswich books respectively as on 31st March, 19..—

	London		Ipswich	
	Dr.	Cr.	Dr.	Cr.
	£	£	£	£
Capital		20,000		
Sundry Creditors		931		27
Goodwill	1,000			
Cash	1,793		49	
Sundry Debtors	3,973		1,438	
Stock, 1/4/19.., at cost—				
At London	11,482			
At Ipswich	1,431			
Stock at Ipswich, 1/4/19.., as *invoiced* .			1,792	1,792
Purchases	28,724			
Goods invoiced during year . . .		7,715	7,715	
Salaries and Wages	2,280		846	
Rent and Rates	743		212	
Sundry Expenses	656		157	
Ipswich Adjustment Account . . .	2,947			
London Adjustment Account . . .				2,847
Sales		25,331		9,575
Furniture and Fittings, 1/4/19.. . .	740		240	
	£55,769	£55,769	£12,449	£12,449

You are required to prepare the Profit and Loss Account of the business for the year ended 31st March, 19.. (showing the profit made in each town separately), and the Balance Sheet as on that date.

The furniture and fittings are to be depreciated 5 per cent. The cost price of the goods invoiced to Ipswich during the year was £6,305. The stock on hand on 31st March, 19.., at London was valued at £15,427, and at Ipswich at £1,542 at cost and £1,847 at invoice price. The difference between the adjustment accounts is due to a remittance of £100 in transit.   (L.C.C.)

9. Weston & Sons, whose head office is in London, have a branch at Liverpool at which a complete set of books is kept. At the close of the financial year on 31st March, 19.., the following summary of the transactions between the head office and branch was extracted from the London books—

		£
Balance due by Branch at 1st April, 19..	. . .	18,750
Cash received from Branch .	. . .	29,800
Goods returned by Branch .	. . .	423
Goods supplied to Branch .	. . .	22,025
Expenses paid on behalf of Branch	. . .	5,832

On 15th April, 19.., the Branch Profit and Loss Account was received, and showed a net profit of £3,476.

Show the above items as they would appear in the head office Ledger after the accounts for the year were completed. What does the balance of the account represent, and how can it be proved?   (R.S.A.)

10. The branches of a multiple shop company are supplied from the head office with goods at cost. The branches pay wages and minor items of petty cash, but otherwise all expenses are paid by the head office.

From the weekly returns of the branches, the following summaries are prepared—

CASH ACCOUNT (BRANCHES), YEAR 19..

19..		£	19..		£
Jan. 1.	To Balance . .	1,200	Dec. 31.	By Cash Purchases	4,360
Dec. 31.	„ Cash Sales .	413,680		„ Wages . .	112,500
	„ Cash on Ledger			„ Expenses .	2,320
	Accounts .	12,350		„ Amounts	
				Banked .	306,550
				„ Balance. .	1,500
		£427,230			£427,230
	To Balance . .	1,500			

DEBTORS' ACCOUNT (BRANCHES), YEAR 19..

19..		£	19..		£
Jan. 1.	To Balance . .	890	Dec. 31.	By Cash received .	12,350
Dec. 31.	„ Sales . .	14,350		„ Allowances .	480
				„ Balance. .	2,410
		£15,240			£15,240
	To Balance . .	2,410			

Branches Current Account (in head office books) appears in summarized form as follows—

19..		£	£	19..		£
Jan. 1.	To Balance—			Jan. 1.	By Balance—	
	Cash	1,200			Rent and Rates	4,340
	Debts	890		Dec. 31.	„ Bank . .	306,550
	Stock	16,380			„ Balance . .	60
	Fittings	10,000				
			28,470			
Carried forward . .			£28,470	*Carried forward* . .		£310,950

	£		£
Brought forward . .	28,470	*Brought forward* . .	310,950
Dec. 31. To Goods . .	226,500		
„ Cash—			
Rent and			
Rates .	20,200		
Salaries .	32,300		
Sundry			
Expenses .	2,480		
Fittings .	1,000		
	£310,950		£310,950
To Balance . .	60		

On 31st December, 19.., stock at the branches was £20,400; liabilities were, for rent and rates, £6,320; and for salaries, £1,000.

Prepare statement of branches trading for the year 19.. (writing off 10 per cent on fittings) and complete the Current Account.   (*C.A. Final.*)

11. A trading company has its head office in London and a trading branch at Bombay.

The following is a list of balances on the Bombay books at 31st December, 19.. (when the first year's trading ended)—

	Rupees
London Account	208,000
Sales	225,676
Purchases	261,604
Wages and Salaries	43,868
Freight and Insurance	26,608
General Expenses	31,248
Bank Account—debit Balance.	12,641
Cash in hand	1,563
Sundry Debtors	106,462
Sundry Creditors	50,318

Stocks at Bombay on 31st December, 19.., were valued at 148,500 rupees.

The balance of the London Account represents remittances to Bombay as follows—

8th January.	.	.	.	.64,000 rupees, purchased at £6·56¼ per 100
6th April .	.	.	.	.96,000 rupees, purchased at £6·04⅙ per 100
17th August .	.	.	.	.48,000 rupees, purchased at £6·45⅝ per 100

The average rate of exchange for the year was £6·66⅔ per 100, and the rate on 31st December, 19.., £6·25 per 100. Journalize the closing entries of the Bombay books, and show the Bombay Branch Account in the London books from 1st January, 19.., to 31st December, 19...

What does the balance on the latter date represent?   (*C.A. Final.*)

12. Wood Bros., timber importers, Hull, send the following cash remittances during 19.. to their buying agents in Copenhagen—

19..				£	Realizing in Kroner
15th January	.	.	.	4,000	73,000
20th February	.	.	.	6,000	103,000
28th April .	.	.	.	20,000	340,000
10th June .	.	.	.	30,000	510,000
31st August	.	.	.	10,000	180,000
				£70,000	1,206,000

The agents rendered a Cash Account as follows on 31st October, 19..—

	Kr.	Kr.
Received from Hull		1,206,000
Paid for May Shipment . . .	252,000	
Paid for June Shipment . . .	180,000	
Paid for July Shipment. . . .	216,000	
Paid for August Shipment . . .	324,000	
Paid for Carriage on May Shipment .	90,000	
Paid for Shipping Charges on June Ship-		
ment	72,000	
Balance on hand, 31st October, 19.. .	72,000	
	1,206,000	1,206,000

Wood Bros. paid freight and insurance on each of the shipments—May, £7,000; June, £1,000; July, £6,000; August, £9,000. The timber is sold for cash and realized as under—

	£
May Shipment	24,280
June Shipment	12,200
July Shipment. . . .	26,240
August Shipment	37,360

Open Ledger Accounts in the books of Wood Bros. and enter the foregoing transactions. The buying agents are entitled to a buying commission of 2 per cent on the cost price of timber purchased by them, and also 10 per cent on the net profit on each shipment. Assume an average rate of exchange of 18 kroner to the £1.

13. TRIAL BALANCE, 30TH JUNE, 19..

	Fcs.	Fcs.
Head Office Account, 1st January, 19.. . . .		451,373
Remittances to Head Office	236,062	
Fixtures and Fittings	26,040	
Sundry Debtors	171,288	
Stock, 1st January, 19..	87,365	
Sundry Creditors		57,828
Purchases	186,989	
Sales.		270,738
Cash Discount allowed	4,183	
Cash Discount received		5,429
Salaries	46,369	
Rent and Rates	20,826	
Bad Debts written off	2,403	
Cash in hand	3,843	
	785,368	785,368

Stock, 30th June, 19.., fcs. 91,863.

The above is a Trial Balance sent from the Branch of a London Company. In the London books the Branch balance on 1st January, 19.., was £5,218; and on 30th June, 19.., the Remittance Account balance was £2,641; there was no cash in transit.

The rates of exchange were as follows—

1st January, 86½; 30th June, 91½. At the time of purchase of the fixtures the rate was 124.

How would you deal with the above details in order to show the Branch results of trading and incorporate them in the London books? What percentage of gross profit to sales do the branch results show? (C.A. Inter.)

14. Ray & Co., London, have a Branch to which they supply goods for sale. The book-keeping of the business is worked on a fixed exchange of 25 fr. to the £, all profits and losses on exchange being recorded in the London books.

On 14th February the London office sent to the Branch goods invoiced at £1,000. The Branch on 16th February remitted to London a cheque for £1,000 drawn by the local Société Générale on the Société Générale, London, for which the Branch had paid, at the rate of the day, 25·125 fr.

(a) Show the entries that would be made in the London books if a fixed exchange of 25·25 fr. to the £ were used in the business instead of an exchange of 25 fr. to the £.

(b) Show the entries in the London books for the above transactions.

15. The following is the Trial Balance of Woodvill & Co. Ltd. at 31st December, 19..—

	Head Office Dr. £	Head Office Cr. £	Branch Dr. £	Branch Cr. £
Share Capital, authorized and issued:				
50,000 Shares of £1 each, fully paid		50,000		
Branch Fixtures	600			
Head Office Remittances			21,266	
Purchases	49,218			
Goods to Branch		25,092		
Head Office Stock, 1st January	9,846			
Branch Office Stock, 1st January (at wholesale price)	5,844			
Head Office Fixed Assets	49,266			
Trade Debtors	17,280		1,425	
Head Office				1,190
Sales		74,562		24,042
Branch Purchases	25,092			
Trade Creditors		6,080		
Branch Remittances		21,266		
Cash at Bank	18,210		200	
Cash on hand	50		10	
Profit and Loss Account		25,400		
Branch	1,190			
Sundry Expenses: Head Office	26,584			
Sundry Expenses: Branch	1,168		2,331	
Branch Stock Adjustment Account		1,948		
	£204,348	£204,348	£25,232	£25,232

Head Office supplies the Branch with all the goods required, and these are charged out at retail selling price, which is cost plus 100 per cent. At the end of the year an adjustment is made to reduce the price charged to the wholesale price, which is cost plus 50 per cent.

Books are kept at the Branch to record sales and certain cash transactions. All cash received by the Branch is paid to the Bank for credit of Head Office, but the Branch has a local bank account, worked on an imprest, for the payment of sundry expenses, the remittances being made monthly by Head Office.

The values of the Stocks on hand at 31st December, 19.., were: Head Office, £9,460 and Branch (at retail selling price), £9,200.

From the above, prepare a columnar Trading and Profit and Loss Account for the year ended 31st December, 19.., and Balance Sheet as on that date. Ignore taxation.

(C.A. Final.)

16. Marketers Ltd. has a Head Office and a number of retail branches which are supplied by Head Office at cost price. The accounts are kept at Head Office, from which all expenses are paid other than wages and petty cash. These are paid by the Branches, which send in weekly reports to Head Office.

The books showed the following balances on 1st January, 19.9—

	£
Cash in hand at Branches	700
Sundry Debtors at Branches	1,300
Stock on hand at Branches	24,500
Fixtures at Branches	12,000
Rates and Insurance in advance (Branches)	900

The transactions relating to the Branches for the year ended 31st December, 19.9, are embodied in the undermentioned figures—

	£
Cash Sales at Branches	620,740
Credit Sales at Branches	21,500
Cash received from credit customers	18,600
Remittances to Head Office (paid to Bank)	460,150
Goods sent to Branches (*less* Returns)	340,000
Allowances to customers	715
Payments by Head Office—	
Rent, Rates, and Insurance	30,180
Salaries	47,000
Sundry Expenses	5,180
Additional Fixtures (purchased 1st October, 19.9)	800
Payments by Branches—	
Wages	169,000
Cash Purchases	5,000
Petty Cash	3,500

The Stock at the Branches on 31st December, 19.9, was valued at £31,000, and on that date payments in advance in respect of Branches' Rates and Insurance amounted to £1,050. Debts amounting to £120 were written off as bad: Fixtures were depreciated at the rate of 20 per cent per annum.

You are required to—

(a) Prepare the Branches Trading and Profit and Loss Account for the year ended 31st December, 19.9.

(b) Show the relevant accounts in the Head Office books.

17. X Ltd. commenced business on 1st January, 19... It has a Head Office and a Branch. Goods are supplied by the Head Office and charged to the Branch at selling price, *less* 20 per cent. The company sells to its customers at a profit of 100 per cent on cost.

From the following particulars prepare the Trading Accounts of the Head Office and Branch for the first year of business, and show the provision for unrealized profit on Head Office goods at Branch. It can be assumed that there are no stock deficiencies.

	Head Office £	Branch £
Purchases	20,000	
Sales	17,000	5,000
Goods to Branch	8,000	
Goods from Head Office		8,000

(*Institute of Company Accountants' Final.*)

18. A company has two branch retail shops, P and Q, each with a separate manager. The ratio of Gross Profit to selling price is constant at each shop at 25 per cent throughout the year to 31st December, 19...

Each Branch Manager is entitled to a commission of 10 per cent of the net profit earned by his Branch, calculated before charging his commission, but subject to a deduction from such commission equal to 25 per cent of any ascertained deficiency of Branch Stock. All goods were supplied to Branches by Head Office.

From the undermentioned figures, calculate the commission due to each manager for the year to 31st December, 19... Ignore taxation.

	Branch P £	Branch Q £
Stocks at 1st January, 19.., at cost	9,342	6,242
Goods to Branches at cost	36,210	21,740
Sales	45,160	29,280
Manager's Commission paid on account	300	200
Chargeable Expenses	6,140	4,510
Stocks at 31st December, 19.., at selling price	15,416	7,976

(*Adapted from C.A. Inter.*)

19. The balances in the books of J. Potts at 31st March, 19.5, were—

	Dr. £	Cr. £
Sundry Assets	184,328	
Cash at Bank	25,217	
Debtors	82,506	
Stock as valued 31st March, 19.5. . . .	100,500	
Eastern Branch: Goods Account . . .	22,030	
Remittance Account . .		14,500
Drawings	20,000	
Trading Profit		67,109
Sundry Expenses	10,881	
Sundry Creditors and accruals . . .		134,906
Capital		228,947
	£445,462	£445,462

During the year Potts opened an Eastern branch. Goods are invoiced to the Branch at cost plus 25 per cent. The Branch converts Head Office invoices into local currency at a fixed exchange rate of 80. The Branch Trial Balance and Stocks as certified by the local manager as at 31st March, 19.5, were—

	Dr. Ficals	Cr. Ficals
Balance at Bank	183,400	
Creditors		117,900
Debtors	388,800	
Local Expenses	377,100	
Head Office: Goods Account . .		1,762,400
Remittance Account . .	1,345,000	
Purchases and Import Duties . . .	2,651,400	
Sales.		3,065,400
	F. 4,945,700	F. 4,945,700

Stocks: Goods ex Head Office, F. 522,800; locally purchased, F. 136,800; and import duties, F. 29,700—total, F. 689,300.

A remittance of F. 297,000 was in transit on 31st March, 19.5, subsequently realizing £3,000. The average exchange rate during the period was 90 and the closing rate 100.

You are required—

(a) to prepare the final adjusted Trial Balance of the Eastern Branch, with conversions to sterling to show the figures to be incorporated in the accounts of Potts;

(b) to show the Eastern Branch account in the Head Office books; and

(c) to prepare abridged Balance Sheet and Profit and Loss Account as on 31st March, 19.5, all questions of tax and further analysis of assets and expenses to be ignored. (Adapted from C.A. Final.)

20. The London-Lyria Trading Co. Ltd. began to build a branch in Lyria on 1st January. The building was completed on 30th June and paid for on that date by the remittance of £10,000 from London. On the same date the Branch received from Head Office goods invoiced at £2,000 and commenced to trade.

On 30th September, Head Office sent further goods invoiced at £1,500, but these were returned as unsuitable. Damage amounting to £500 was done to the goods in returning and Head Office decided that the loss should be charged to Lyria, but no entry was made at the time in the Lyrian books.

Lyria sent Head Office remittances of 248,750 lyras on 30th September and 240,000 lyras on 22nd December, the latter reaching London after 31st December.

From the following balances, prepare the company's Balance Sheet as on 31st

December and accounts for the year. Stocks in London were valued at £22,500 and in Lyria at 37,000 lyras. Assume exchange rates as follows—

Year.		Average 185 lyras to the £
Half-year to 31st December.	. . .	„ 180 „
On 30th June	. . . . .	„ 200 „
On 30th September	. . . . .	„ 199 „
On 22nd December	. . . . .	„ 192 „
On 31st December	. . . . .	„ 185 „

BALANCES ON 31ST DECEMBER

	London £	Lyria Lyras
Capital	125,000	
Sundry Creditors	25,000	27,750
	Lyras	
Head Office	2,400,000	
Less remitted	488,750	
		1,911,250
Sales	120,000	900,000
Goods sent to Lyria, *less* returned	2,500	
Buildings	80,000	2,000,000
Sundry Debtors	40,250	18,500
Bank Balances	26,000	55,500
	£	
Lyria Branch	12,000	
Damage to Goods in Transit . . .	500	
	12,500	
Less remitted	1,250	
	11,250	
Purchases	80,000	180,000
Goods from Head Office		400,000
Rent for *Full* Year		18,500
Trade Salaries and Expenses	25,000	166,500
Stock	10,000	

(C.A. Final.)

21. The following balances appear in the Trial Balances of Leeds (Head Office) and Liverpool (Branch) at 30th June, 19.9—

	Leeds £	Liverpool £
Debit balances—		
Current Account with Liverpool . . .	19,624	
Stock-in-trade 30th June, 19.9—		
Leeds	8,273	
Liverpool (at invoiced prices) . . .		3,525
Credit balances—		
Current Account with Leeds		18,629
Branch Stock Suspense Account . . .	246	

The balance on Branch Stock Suspense Account was equivalent at 30th June, 19.8, to the 25 per cent addition to cost included in the branch Stock-in-trade in the branch books. This balance requires adjustment to the appropriate amount at 30th June, 19.9.

There are goods in transit from Leeds to Liverpool invoiced at the usual percentage load on cost of £636 not having been dealt with in the Liverpool books; whilst a remittance of £200 on 30th June, 19.9, from Liverpool to Leeds has not been dealt with in the Leeds books.

Draft the Journal entries necessary to adjust the above matters and show the Stock item in the combined Balance Sheet.

22. Arcady Ltd. conduct their business as wholesalers and retailers from their head office and warehouse in London and from a foreign branch office and warehouse in Utopia.

Trial Balances extracted from the company's two sets of books as on 30th September, 19.9, are as follows—

	London Books		Utopia Books	
	£	£	Topas	Topas
Utopia Branch Account . . .	23,410			
Balances at banks and cash in hand .	26,600		7,000	
Sales (including internal) . . .		790,000		311,800
Purchases (including internal) . .	620,000		216,800	
Stocks on 1st October, 19.8, in warehouses and in transit, at invoiced prices	64,983		41,250	
Plant and Vehicles	34,800		14,000	
Plant and Vehicles—provision for depreciation on 1st October, 19.8 .		17,800		9,400
Wages, salaries, rent and working expenses	145,000		48,400	
Directors' remuneration . . .	10,500			
Stock Reserve on 1st October, 19.8 .		9,305		
Carriage, insurance and freight . .	8,025		2,800	
Profit and Loss Account—balance on 1st October, 19.8 . . .		34,500		
Debtors and Creditors . . .	82,000	78,713	48,500	28,800
Head Office Account. . . .				28,750
Ordinary Shares of £1 each issued and fully paid		85,000		
	£1,015,318	£1,015,318	378,750	378,750

The following additional information is relevant—

(1) During the year, the branch bought and paid for goods in Utopia to the value of 40,000 Topas, of which goods costing 11,000 Topas remained in stock on 30th September, 19.9. There had been no local purchases by the branch in the previous year.

(2) With the above exception, head office purchased all goods and those sent to the branch in any year were invoiced at cost plus 10 per cent. This addition was made up of 8 per cent for insurance, freight and other expenses and 2 per cent profit.

(3) On 30th September, 19.9, stock in both warehouses was valued at invoiced prices as follows—

London warehouse £52,000
Utopia warehouse . . . . 33,000 Topas

These values are to be used for the Trading Accounts, any adjustments necessary to eliminate profit therefrom being made in the Profit and Loss Account and Stock Reserve Account. In addition, it has been decided that there is to be transferred as an appropriation a sum sufficient to make the Stock Reserve on 30th September, 19.9, equal to 12 per cent of the stock as valued in the Trading Accounts.

(4) In the London warehouse there were goods, of which the cost was £1,700, awaiting shipment to Utopia. These were not included in the London stock, but had been invoiced to Utopia on 29th September, 19.9, at £1,870. No expenses had yet been incurred on these goods.

(5) Plant and Vehicles are stated at cost except that, on 30th September, 19.9, Utopia branch sold for 800 Topas a lorry bought for 600 Topas in October, 19.6, and the proceeds of sale had been credited to Plant and Vehicles Account. It is the Company's practice to provide annually for depreciation on Plant and Vehicles at 10 per cent of original cost, and such provision is to be made on the cost of Plant and Vehicles (all of which are at least three years old) remaining on the books on 30th September, 19.9.

(6) Provision is to be made for a commission to the Utopia manager of ½ per cent on collections in the year from debtors. Utopia debtors on 1st October, 19.8, amounted to 56,700 Topas.

(7) Provision is to be made for a dividend of 10 per cent on the Ordinary shares. Exchange rates were as follows—

		£
From 1st January, 19.0, to 29th September, 19.8 . .	1,000 Topas =	750
On 30th September, 19.8	1,000 Topas =	800
Average during the year ended 30th September, 19.9.	1,000 Topas =	825
On 30th September, 19.9	1,000 Topas =	850

You are required to prepare in sterling—

(a) Trial Balance of Utopia branch as on 30th September, 19.9, after making all adjustments which should be made in the branch books by reason of the information given above; and

(b) for the year ended 30th September, 19.9—

    (i) Trading Accounts (in columnar form) of London and Utopia, and
    (ii) the Company's Profit and Loss and Appropriation Accounts.

(C.A. Final.)

23. Distributors Ltd. sell proprietary goods which are purchased from manufacturers at 66⅔ per cent of the fixed retail selling prices. Wholesale sales are made through head office, and all retail sales are made through branches, of which only that in Dublin maintains its own accounts.

Goods sent to Dublin are charged to that branch at cost price (the branch also makes certain direct purchases) but goods sent to the English branches are charged to a Branches Control Account at selling price.

Memorandum records only are maintained at the English branches and the Control Account at head office is credited with all expenditure defrayed by them locally and with cash banked by them.

The following are the Trial Balances as on 31st March, 19.6—

	Head Office Dr. £	Head Office Cr. £	Dublin Branch Dr. £	Dublin Branch Cr. £
Share Capital		40,000		
Profit and Loss Account 1st April, 19.5		4,253		
Sundry Assets and Liabilities . .	35,874	16,137	4,985	1,144
Expenses	25,535		5,000	
Dublin Current Account . .	287			
Head Office Current Account . .				363
English Branches Control Account .	18,884			
Purchases and Transfer . . .	127,720		21,838	
Goods sent to English Branches at selling price		105,630		
Goods sent to Dublin . . .		12,000		
Wholesale Sales		59,980		
Stocks at 1st April, 19.5 . .	19,500		1,970	
Stocks at Branches (Cost) . .	10,200			
Dublin Branch Sales . . .				33,012
	£238,000	£238,000	£34,156	£34,156

Goods invoiced to Dublin on 30th March, 19.6, were lost in transit, and head office subsequently claimed and received from the carriers the cost thereof (£200) and no entry had been made of this claim. A remittance of £450 had been sent from Dublin on the 31st March, 19.6, and was received at head office two days later.

Stocks at 31st March, 19.6, at cost, amounted to £25,000 at the head office and to £2,800 at the Dublin branch. As shown by returns and inventories the Control Account for the English branches as on 31st March, 19.6, was represented by cash floats £150, debtors £3,284, and stocks £15,270, the difference being due to certain stock shortages.

A debt of £40, included in the above Branch Debtors, is to be written off as irrecoverable.

You are required to prepare—

(a) the Trading and Profit and Loss Accounts of the Company for the year ended 31st March, 19.6 (without differentiating between the various sections of the Company's business); and

(b) The final Trial Balances after preparing the accounts required in (a) above.

Ignore Taxation and Directors' Fees. Workings may be shown in marginal insets.

(Adapted from C.A. Final.)

24. H. Ltd. commence business on 1st January, and open a branch.

Goods are all sold at a fixed price to cover cost plus 25 per cent thereon.

During the first year all the goods were purchased at head office (i.e. no local purchases by branch) amounting to £11,000. The goods were sent to the branch at selling price *less* 5 per cent, head office taking credit for the remainder of the profit of the branch. There was no wastage or leakage of stock.

From the following information, show the Trading Accounts of head office and branch for the year ended 31st December, expenses to be ignored. In addition, show the Trading Account as a whole unit.

Head Office: Purchases £11,000; Cash Sales £2,000; receipts from debtors £6,100; closing debtors £400; closing stock £1,000 at cost.

Branch: Sales (all Cash) £3,000; closing stock at "invoice" price to branch £950.

25. X has a branch, and all goods are sent thereto at cost plus 25 per cent. The accounting is done at head office.

In the first year, the branch received goods from head office costing £8,000. During the year the branch sent back to head office goods at internal invoice price of £500.

Some of the goods sold to customers by the branch were unsatisfactory, and the customers complained and sent the goods in question, amounting to £50, *direct* to head office.

During the year remittances to head office were £5,000, closing cash balance at branch £1,010, and closing branch debtors £2,340.

The branch deals only with goods sent from head office. There are no discounts or bad debts and no stock differences.

Ignoring expenses, show the essential entries in the head office books by four alternative methods.

CHAPTER XX

HIRE PURCHASE ACCOUNTS

1. Assume the cash price of a machine which is to be acquired under hire purchase is £800. The hire-purchase price is to be settled by an initial deposit of £200 and six equal half-yearly instalments with interest at 6 per cent per annum, calculated with half-yearly rests. Given that the present value of an annuity of £1 for six years is £5·4172, what is the amount of each instalment?

2. A man bought a machine by hire purchase. He paid £600 down, £640 at the end of the first year, £890 at the end of the second year, and £880 at the end of the third year. The interest on the cash price is 10 per cent per annum and depreciation is charged at 5 per cent per annum.

Write up the books of the purchaser and seller.

3. A buys by hire purchase machines amounting to £3,000, the yearly payments being £900, with interest at 10 per cent per annum. In the first and second years he pays as agreed, but in the third year finds himself in difficulties. The seller agrees to take back one-third of the machinery, provided that the buyer pays his half-yearly interest, and the machinery is to be taken as having depreciated 15 per cent per annum with yearly rests. A then duly discharges his obligations (including interest thereon) to the end of the year for the other machines. In his books he has charged depreciation at 10 per cent per annum with yearly rests.

Write up the books of seller and buyer.

4. On 1st January, 19.4, Tallboy & Co. Ltd. took delivery, from Plain Vans Ltd., of five vans on a hire purchase system, £200 being paid on delivery and the balance in five instalments of £300 each, payable annually on 31st December. The vendors charge 5 per cent per annum interest on yearly balances. The cash value of the five vans was £1,500.

How should the details of this transaction be entered in the books of the vendor company?

Show the Ledger Accounts in the vendor's books for the five years to 31st December, 19.8.

(Calculations may be made to the nearest £.) *(C.A. Inter.)*

5. The D.P.F. Mining Co. Ltd. agreed to purchase wagons on the hire purchase system for £4,600; £600 was paid when the wagons were delivered on 1st January, 19.., and the balance was to be paid by annual instalments of £800, plus interest at 5 per cent per annum.

Draft the various Ledger Accounts in the books of the Mining Company, showing the details—to completion—of this transaction.

The Mining Company depreciates the wagons each year by 10 per cent on the original cost.

6. From the following details set out the Hire Purchase Account in the books of a trader who sells numbers of articles of comparatively small value daily on the hire purchase system, showing his profit on this department of the business for the year ended 31st December, 19... For the purpose of charging his hire purchase customers, he adds 60 per cent to the cost price of the goods.

			£
19..			
Jan. 1.	Stock in customers' hands at selling price		1,620
Dec. 31.	Sales of hire purchase goods during year at selling price .		6,534
	Cash received from hire purchases at selling price . .		2,100
	Stock in customers' hands at selling price		5,674

7. X, Y, and Z are partners in a printing business, and share profits and losses equally. Owing to an increase in business it is proposed to purchase a linotype printing machine, and a quotation is submitted by the R Co. Ltd. (who manufacture the type of machinery required), which provides as follows: (a) That the R Co. Ltd. supply a new linotype for an immediate cash payment of £866, or as an alternative that they supply a machine on the hire purchase system by payment of five yearly instalments of £200 each, the first instalment to be discharged twelve months after the machine is installed, and interest at the rate of 5 per cent per annum be charged on the yearly balance outstanding and calculated on the cash price of the machine.

Z, however, is willing, if his co-partners agree, to loan the whole of the £866 to the firm, on the following terms: That the loan be discharged by half-yearly instalments of £100 and interest at the rate of 4 per cent per annum, on the half-yearly balances, be credited to the Loan Account.

State which of the two courses you would advise the firm to adopt.

8. A mining company hires 100 wagons on the deferred purchase system, over a term of seven years, the rent being payable by quarterly instalments of £200 with an addition for repairs of £2 per wagon per annum.

Assuming the wagon company's charge for interest to be 5 per cent per annum make Journal entries for the first year necessary to apportion payments between Capital and Revenue.

9. On 1st April, 19.6, the Imperial Hotel ordered furniture from Universal Stores to the value of £2,500, and entered into a Hire Purchase agreement to pay eight quarterly instalments of £330, the first payment to be made on 30th June, 19.6. The *rate* of interest may be taken at 5 per cent per annum, with quarterly rests, and the furniture is to be depreciated at 5 per cent per annum on the diminishing balance.

Show the Furniture Account and the Account of the Universal Stores in the Hotel books for the two years ended 31st March, 19.8.

10. On 1st January, 19.4, A Ltd. acquired a machine of which the cash price was £644·75. The purchase of the machine was financed by the X Discount Society Ltd. to whom £100 was payable by A Ltd. on 1st January, 19.4, and instalments (including interest) of £200 on 31st December, 19.4, 19.5, and 19.6 respectively.

The rate of interest was 5 per cent per annum.

On 1st January, 19.6, the machine was sold for £500, and the Discount Society's debt was discharged on that date.

Show the accounts of the Discount Society and the machine in A Ltd.'s Ledger, writing off depreciation at 10 per cent per annum on the diminishing balance.

11. X sells goods both for cash and on hire purchase, the latter being 25 per cent more than the cash retail terms. The Trial Balance at 31st December, 19.8, is—

	£	£
Creditors		16,600
Sales—		
Cash		11,600
Hire Purchase		48,400
X Capital		20,000
Purchases	34,400	
Stock, 1st January, 19.8	6,900	
Cash at Bank	2,000	
Instalments Receivable Account . . .	41,200	
General Expenses	12,100	
	£96,600	£96,600

Closing Stock £12,900.

The Instalments Receivable Account is made up of pre-19.8 Sales balances of £3,000 and those in respect of the current year £38,200.

During the year X took repossession of the goods in the hands of defaulters (current year transactions) whose debit balances were £3,600 (not yet written off). Some of these goods were sold for cash £1,200 and included in Cash Sales, and the remainder included in the Closing Stock at £2,300 but were estimated to be worth only £1,500.

Previously credit had been taken in full on the hire purchase transactions as and when the goods were delivered (i.e. as Cash Sales), but it is now decided to take profit only proportionate to instalments received, and accordingly to adjust the position in respect of previous years' transactions in addition to those of the current year. Prepare final accounts (tax to be ignored), taking the rate of gross profit for previous years as 40 per cent.

12. A commenced business as a retailer on 1st January, selling electrical equipment both for cash and on hire purchase, the latter being the cash retail price plus 12½ per cent thereon. The following are the relevant details—

Goods purchased £11,000; closing stock at cost £3,800.

Cash Sales £2,400 and deliveries to customers on hire purchase £6,300.

There are no sales on credit, except on hire purchase terms.

The receipts from debtors are £4,500; there are no repossessions, discounts allowances or bad debts.

A treats the hire purchase deliveries as sales and provides for unearned profit on unpaid instalments based on the gross profit arising on hire purchase transactions, no separate account being taken of any part of the hire purchase price which covers interest.

Prepare the Trading Account for the year ended 31st December, showing the respective rates of gross profit on Cash Sales and Hire Purchase Sales.

13. A. Webb commenced business on 1st July, 19.8. During the year ended 30th June, 19.9, purchases amounted to £5,400 and ordinary sales £6,200. In addition, the following sales were made under hire purchase arrangements—

Article	Cost	Sale Price	Deposit Paid	Monthly Instalments	No. of Instalments Paid in year 19.8–19.9
	£	£	£		
Television Set .	60	90	10	20 of £4	8
Washing Machine	80	120	12	12 of £9	2
Refrigerator .	70	100	10	18 of £5	4

Instalments on the refrigerator could not be kept up and it was returned on 28th June, 19.9.

Stock-in-trade at 30th June, 19.9, excluding the returned refrigerator, amounted to £700.

Prepare the Hire Purchase Trading Account, Memorandum Hire Purchase Debtors Account, and the General Trading Account for the year ended 30th June, 19.9.

14. Contrivances Ltd. commenced business on 1st January, 19.2.

The company sold television sets of a uniform type, which cost £60 each, for a cash price of £82·06⅔ each, and also on hire purchase terms, which at the time required an initial deposit of £30, followed by two instalments of £30 each on the first and second anniversaries of the date of the contract. The total price of £90 included compound interest at 10 per cent per annum on the reducing balance (with yearly rests) of the normal cash selling price.

The company also sold bicycles of a uniform type on hire purchase terms only, which required an initial deposit of £3, followed by twelve quarterly instalments of £1 each over a period of three years. The cost of the bicycles was £9 each.

The following Trial Balance was extracted as on 31st December, 19.2—

	£	£
Issued share capital		100,000
Balance at Bank	24,200	
Creditors		17,969
Salaries and general expenses	20,000	
Cash Sales		1,231
Purchases—		
Television sets	30,900	
Bicycles	117,900	
Hire Purchase Sales: Television sets (£90 each) . .		40,500
Cash collected from hire purchasers of bicycles . . .		60,300
Debtors	27,000	
	£220,000	£220,000

It was decided to take credit, in the annual accounts, for the normal gross profit (excluding interest) on television sets delivered to customers, and to apportion the interest on a time basis. Sales of television sets were evenly spread throughout the year.

During 19.2, 12,100 bicycles were sold. On 31st December, 19.2, the company retook possession of 100 bicycles from customers who had paid the initial deposits only and had failed to pay subsequent instalments.

In view of the large number of transactions in bicycles and the difficulty of apportioning the interest, it was decided to adopt, for this section of the business, the alternative method of taking credit for the profit (including interest) on bicycles only in proportion to the cash collected. The repossessed bicycles were taken back into stock at £7 each.

You are required to prepare—

(a) for the year ended December 31st, 19.2—
    (i) Television Trading Account;
    (ii) Bicycle Trading Account;
    (iii) Profit and Loss Account; and
(b) the Balance Sheet as on 31st December, 19.2.

You are not expected to consider the requirements of the Companies Acts 1948 and 1967. Ignore taxation.

CHAPTER XXI

INCOME TAX IN RELATION TO ACCOUNTS

1. Write up the undermentioned transactions of A for the year to 5th April, 19.4. Close off the accounts at that date, after making full provision for income tax, on the assumption that A is liable at 40 per cent only—

19.3
June   1. Received interest on £400 3½ per cent War Loan (recently acquired).
Sept. 29. Received first half-year's rent to date, £126.
Dec.   1. Received interest on £400 3½ per cent War Loan.
    19.4
Jan.   1. Paid Schedule A tax on rented premises £61.
       3. Paid first instalment of Schedule D, Case I tax (liability for 19.3–19.4 is £700).
Mar.   1. Paid year's interest on loan of £1,000 at 8 per cent per annum.
     25. Received half-year's rent to date, £126.
     31. Received dividend, £550 (net).

2. The following particulars, extracted from the books of Bleddry Ltd. at 31st December, 19.6, relate to taxation and taxed payments and receipts—

	£	£
Corporation Tax (Provision—year ended 31/12/19.5). .		10,200
Dividend from trade investment in Transfusion Ltd. received net 21/9/19.6		210
Loan Interest received net 5/7/19.6		153
Section 53 tax paid	160	
Interim Ordinary Dividend of 10 per cent paid net 15/8/19.6	1,200	
Debenture Interest paid net on due dates		
Half-year to 15/6/19.6 . . . . £360		
Half-year to 15/12/19.6 360		
	720	

Corporation Tax for the year ended 31/12/19.5 has been agreed at £10,400. Provide £12,500 for Corporation Tax on current profits.

Provide for a final ordinary dividend of 5 per cent gross.

Assuming a standard rate of Income Tax of 40 per cent show how the relevant accounts should appear in the books of Bleddry Ltd. and show also relative extracts from the published accounts at 31st December, 19.6.

3. In respect of long-term Capital Gains Tax—

    (*a*) What items of expenditure are deductible in computing liability?
    (*b*) What is the basis of assessment in respect of individuals?

4. Describe briefly the system of Value Added Tax (VAT) as operated in the United Kingdom.

CHAPTER XXII

PARTNERSHIP ACCOUNTS

1. X, Y, and Z were in partnership, X and Y sharing profits in the proportion of three to one, and Z receiving a salary of £2,500, plus 5 per cent of the profit after charging his salary and his 5 per cent of the profit, or one-seventh of the profit of the firm, whichever is the larger. Any excess of the latter over the former is, under the partnership agreement, to be charged to X.

The profit for the year ended 31st December, 19.., was £28,700 after charging interest on capital and Z's salary.

You are required to show the distribution of the profit between the partners.

(C.A. Final.)

2. X, Y, and Z are in partnership, and throughout the year 19.. their Capital Accounts (entitled to interest at 5 per cent per annum) have remained unchanged at £6,000, £4,000, and £3,000 respectively. The firm's books have been written up to 31st December, 19.., but no closing entries or adjustments made.

Set out, in Journal form, the entries necessary to adjust the following matters—

(a) The year's interest on capital due to the partners.

(b) Goods valued at £67·50 (at cost) which have been taken from stock by X for his own use, no entry in connection therewith having been passed through the books.

(c) An amount of £137·65 included in the Wages Account, representing wages paid to workmen in respect of time spent in repairing the firm's own machinery.

(R.S.A.)

3. C. Testout was a partner in a manufacturing firm. On 1st January, 19.., the following balances stood to his credit—

Capital Account, £6,000; Current Account, £3,128.

During the year he withdrew goods (£71) from the firm. His drawings, in cash, were as follows—

1st June, £50; 1st August, £70; 1st October, £75; 1st December, £50.

Interest at 5 per cent per annum was allowed on capital and chargeable on cash drawings.

Prepare Testout's Current Account as it would appear in the firm's books on 31st December, 19... *(R.S.A.)*

4. A, B, and C were in partnership, sharing profits four-sevenths, two-sevenths, and one-seventh respectively, it being provided that in no year should C's share be less than £750.

The profits for the year 19.. amounted to £2,821.

You are required to show the appropriation as between the partners.

(R.S.A.)

5. Explain why, where persons are trading in partnership, it is customary to credit each partner with interest on his capital before the balance of profit is ascertained and divided.

If there is any particular case where you consider such a provision might equitably be dispensed with, describe it and state shortly your reason for making this exception to the general rule. *(R.S.A.)*

6. White, Green, and Brown are partners in the firm of Black & Co. Proper accounts have not been kept, and you were asked to prepare statements showing the position of the partners as on 30th June, 19...

After investigation you ascertain that the capitals of the partners as on 1st January, 19.., were as follows—

White, £3,000; Green, £2,520; Brown, £1,500; and that at 30th June, 19.., their assets amounted to £23,625, and their liabilities to £16,649. During the half-year ended 30th June, 19.., the partners had drawn out the following sums: White, £603; Green, £410; Brown, £300. The trading results were divisible as follows: White, five-tenths; Green, three-tenths; Brown, two-tenths.

You are required to prepare statements showing how the profits for the half-year, after allowing for interest on capital at 5 per cent per annum, should be divided; also the partners' capital accounts for the same period.

7. After the accounts of a partnership have been prepared, it is discovered that for the years 19.7, 19.8, and 19.9 interest has been credited upon Partners' Capital Accounts at 5 per cent per annum, although no provision is made for interest in the partnership agreement. The amounts involved are—

	19.7	19.8	19.9
A . . .	£325	£350	£360
B . . .	210	200	215
C . . .	90	110	110

You are required to put through an adjusting entry as on 1st January, 19.1, assuming that the profits are shared in the following proportions—

$$19.7 . . .A \tfrac{1}{2} \quad B \tfrac{3}{10} \quad C \tfrac{1}{5}$$
$$19.8 . . .A \tfrac{2}{5} \quad B \tfrac{2}{5} \quad C \tfrac{1}{5}$$
$$19.9 . . .A \tfrac{3}{10} \quad B \tfrac{2}{5} \quad C \tfrac{3}{10}$$

You are not required to calculate compound interest on the adjustments.

(*C.A. Final.*)

8. A, B, and C were partners, and the partnership agreement provided that the accounts should be made up annually to 31st December, and that the profits should be divided as follows—

The first £6,000	$A\tfrac{1}{3}$	$B\tfrac{1}{3}$	$C\tfrac{1}{3}$
The next £8,000	$A\tfrac{1}{2}$	$B\tfrac{3}{8}$	$C\tfrac{1}{8}$
The remainder	$A\tfrac{4}{9}$	$B\tfrac{1}{3}$	$C\tfrac{2}{9}$

On 1st January, 19.., the partners agreed that the accounts should in future be made up to 31st August in each year, the scheme for the division of profits to remain unaltered.

Accounts were prepared for the eight months ended 31st August, 19.., and the profits available for distribution were £13,800. The partners could not agree as to the apportionment of these profits, and you were asked to decide the proper division.

Prepare a statement showing how you would divide this £13,800, bearing in mind that the yearly profits have for the past four years been in excess of £14,000.

9. A, B, and C were partners during the three years ended 31st December, 19.4, sharing profits as follows—

	A	B	C
19.2	$\tfrac{1}{2}$	$\tfrac{1}{4}$	$\tfrac{1}{4}$
19.3 . . .	$\tfrac{2}{3}$	$\tfrac{1}{6}$	$\tfrac{1}{6}$
19.4 . . .	$\tfrac{3}{4}$	$\tfrac{1}{8}$	$\tfrac{1}{8}$

On 1st January, 19.5, it was mutually agreed that interest on capital at the rate of 6 per cent per annum should be credited to each partner in respect of the three past years, the partners' balances on 1st January, 19.2, being as follows—

	£
A	1,000
B	500
C	500

Assume that net trading results were as follows—

		£
19.2	Profit. .	1,500
19.3	Loss . .	450
19.4	Profit. .	600

Show one Journal entry giving effect to the partners' decision.

10. George Southern and Hugh Weston, carrying on business in partnership, prepared their annual accounts at 31st December, 19.8.

At that date, the Capital Accounts were as follows—

Southern £5,500, Weston £1,650,

profits or losses being shared in the same proportion.

The balances on Partners' Current Accounts at 31st December, 19.8, were—

Southern, credit £450, Weston, debit £125.

As from 1st January, 19.9, it was agreed that profits or losses should be shared thus—

Southern $\frac{2}{3}$, Weston $\frac{1}{3}$,

and that the Capital Accounts should be adjusted accordingly. Weston, in view of his share of profits having been increased, was to credit Southern (by three equal annual instalments commencing on 1st January, 19.9) for the goodwill of such increased share, with three years' purchase of the increased proportion based on the average of the profits for the five years ended 31st December, 19.8, as follows—

		£
Year ended 31st December, 19.4	. . . . .	2,001
„ „ „ „ 19.5	. . . . .	1,892
„ „ „ „ 19.6	. . . . .	1,733
„ „ „ „ 19.7	. . . . .	1,998
„ „ „ „ 19.8	. . . . .	2,126

Southern drew £300 and Weston £150 on 31st March, 30th June, 30th September, and 31st December, 19.9.

On the footing that Interest at 5 per cent per annum is to be calculated on Capital and Current Accounts, show (a) the Appropriation of Profits Account for the year ended 31st December, 19.9, the profit for that year, before allowing for interest as above, amounting to £2,286; and (b) the Partners' Capital and Current Accounts as adjusted at 31st December, 19.9.

11. Black and White are partners sharing profits in proportion to their capitals. At the close of their financial year on 30th September, 19.8, the following balances stood to the credit of the partners—

Capital Accounts .	.	.	Black, £20,000	White, £5,000
Current Accounts	.	.	Black, £1,060	White, £2,800

The partnership deed provides—

(a) That White shall be credited with a partnership salary of £1,000 per annum for managing the business.

(b) That White shall be entitled to 10 per cent of the net profits after charging his salary, and Interest on Capital, Current Accounts, and drawings.

(c) Interest at 5 per cent per annum to be allowed on Capital and Current Accounts.

The partners' drawings were: Black, £10,000; and White, £3,000, on which the following amounts for Interest are to be charged: Black, £330; White, £80.

In addition to the entries necessary to record the above particulars, the following balances were extracted from the books of the firm as on 30th September, 19.8—

	£
Freehold Premises	15,000
Sundry Creditors	24,150
Advertising	4,339
Office Salaries	2,189
Sundry Debtors	16,020
Office Expenses	622
Insurance	364
Delivery Expenses	2,203
Stock, 30th September, 19.8	21,069
Provision for Bad Debts, 1st October, 19.7 . . .	600

Trading Account *Cr.* Balance	34,628
Machinery and Plant, 1st October, 19.7 . . .	13,280
Machinery additions during the year . . .	1,560
Motor Lorries	900
Factory Expenses paid in advance	70
Cash at Bank	2,841
Cash in Hand	31
Mortgage on Freehold Premises at 6 per cent per annum .	10,000
Office Furniture	300
Patents	4,000
Mortgage Interest	450

You are required to prepare a Profit and Loss Account for the year ended 30th September, 19.8, and a Balance Sheet as on that date.

When preparing the above accounts the following matters are to be taken into consideration regarding which no entries had been made in the books—

(a) Depreciation to be provided as follows—

Plant, old balance, 10 per cent per annum; Plant, additions, 25 per cent; Office Furniture, 10 per cent per annum; Patents, 10 per cent per annum.

(b) Motor vans were valued at 30th September, 19.8, at £800.

(c) The Provision for Bad Debts is to be made up to 5 per cent on the Sundry Debtors.

(d) Interest on the mortgage has been paid to 30th June, 19.8. (Tax need not be dealt with.)

(e) The following amounts are to be carried forward to next year—

Insurance, £62; Advertising, £878.

(f) Office Salaries £69 were owing at 30th September, 19.8.   (*C.A. Inter.*)

12. A, B, and C were partners in a firm of insurance brokers, dividing profits as to A, one-half; B, one-third; and C, one-sixth. The balances on their books as at 31st December, 19.., were as follows—

		£
Brokerage		44,000
Bank Interest received		1,300
Salaries		12,500
Rent		3,500
Stationery and Printing		1,250
Accountancy Charges and Audit Fee . . .		815
Subscriptions to Lloyd's		2,530
Travelling Expenses		350
Sundry Office Expenses		400
Cash at Bank		18,000
Cash in Hand		55
Debtors		65,000
Creditors		75,000
Investments at cost		20,100
Capital Account—A	*Cr.*	1,200
B	*Cr.*	800
C	*Cr.*	400
Current Account—A	*Dr.*	600
B	*Dr.*	400
C	*Dr.*	200

Prepare Profit and Loss Account for the twelve months to 31st December, 19.., and Balance Sheet as at that date, after bringing into account the following adjustments—

(a) Outstanding creditors; Stationery, £35; Sundry Office Expenses, £120.

(b) C is to be credited with a partnership salary of £3,000.

(c) Interest on capital at 5 per cent to be allowed for the full year; no interest on current account.

(d) Amongst the "Debtors" is an amount of £1,500, which is really owing by A.

(e) 1¼ per cent on debtors to go to Bad Debt Provision.

(f) Mrs. X, widow of a former partner, is entitled to one-twentieth of the profit after making the foregoing adjustments.

(g) 7½ per cent of the ultimate balance available for the partners to be transferred to a General Reserve Account.

13. A and B are partners, and commenced business on 1st January, 19.2, with capitals of £15,000 and £10,000 respectively. The capitals remain fixed and carry interest at 5 per cent per annum. Profits are shared in proportion to their capitals.

C, their manager, joined them on 1st January, 19.2, at a salary of £1,600 per annum plus a bonus of 5 per cent of the profits, which, subject to this charge and interest on capital, would be divisible between A and B. On his appointment, C deposited as security £5,000, carrying interest at 6 per cent per annum.

At the end of 19.4 it was agreed that C should be treated as a partner from 1st January, 19.2, his deposit entitling him to one-fourth of the profits and carrying 5 per cent interest instead of the 6 per cent he had received. It was also agreed that the new arrangement should not result in C's share for any year being less than he had received under the original terms.

The profits before providing for C's bonus and interest on capital or giving effect to the new arrangement were—

19.2, £8,000; 19.3, £10,000; 19.4, £14,000.

Show by Journal entry, with explanatory computation, the adjustment necessary to give effect to the new arrangement. (*C.A. Inter.*)

14. On 1st April, 19.., the Balance Sheet of Field and Paddock, who were in partnership sharing profits and losses as to three-fifths and two-fifths respectively, showed that Field's capital was £6,000 and Paddock's capital £4,000, while the Sundry Creditors amounted to £2,500.

At 31st March, 19.., the following details show their position—

	£
Sundry Creditors	2,749
Sundry Debtors	7,600
Cash at Bank	900
Stock-in-trade	5,100
Fixtures and Fittings	230
Motor Vans	590

The drawings of the partners during the year had been: Field, £1,800; and Paddock, £1,000.

Prepare a statement showing the Profit or Loss for the year ended 31st March, 19.., and draw up a Statement of Affairs at the latter date. Partners are entitled to 5 per cent interest on their capitals before dividing profits. Depreciate Motor Vans by 20 per cent; Fixtures, etc., by 10 per cent; and provide £300 for bad debts.

15. On 31st December, 19.., three partners had the following amounts at the credit of their Capital Accounts: A, £5,000; B, £3,000; C, £2,000.

On 1st January, 19.., they had to the credit of their Drawing Accounts: A, £750; B, £500; C, £400.

Profits are divided in the same proportion as the capital up to £6,000. Above that amount A gets 25 per cent; B, 35 per cent; and C, 40 per cent.

A drew during the year 19.., £2,500; B drew £2,000; C drew £1,500.

The profits for 19.. amounted to £3,000 before charging interest on capital (to which all are entitled) at 6 per cent.

Give the Drawings Account of each partner on 31st December, 19.., interest on drawings to be ignored. (*C.A. Inter.*)

16. A and B, solicitors, are partners in the firm of A B & Co., sharing profits in the proportions of two-fifths to A and three-fifths to B.

On 1st July, 19.., they took over the practice of D, who had died, and agreed to pay the widow £100 for Furniture, to collect outstanding debts on a 5 per cent commission basis, and to pay her one-third of the profit costs of all work arising from the practice of D for a period of three years.

The Trial Balance of the firm at 30th June, following, was as follows—

	£	£
Estimate of Costs not made up at 1st July, 19..	2,000	
Bills of Costs rendered. A B & Co..		6,000
Bills of Costs rendered. D		1,500
Clients' Disbursements. A B & Co..	1,040	
Clients' Disbursements. D	600	
Office Expenses	870	
Salaries	1,430	
Depreciation of Furniture	60	
Bills of Costs not paid	900	
Sundry Debtors	1,300	
Sundry Creditors		670
Amounts due to Clients		1,185
Amount due to Widow for Furniture		100
Debts collected on behalf of Widow		900
Library and Furniture	540	
Balance at Bank—Firm's Account	1,780	
Balance at Bank—Clients' Account	1,210	
Capital—A		2,480
Capital—B		1,920
Drawings—A	1,125	
Drawings—B	1,250	
Payments on Account to D's Widow	650	
	£14,755	£14,755

You are required to prepare Costs, Profit and Loss, and Appropriation Accounts for the year ended 30th June, 19.., and Balance Sheet, after making provision for the following—

Bills of Costs not made up at 30th June, 19.., are estimated at £2,200 for A B & Co. and £1,050 for D, Disbursements of £200 and £110, respectively, being included in those figures.

Interest on Capital at 5 per cent per annum.

17. Costello & Bryant were in partnership sharing profits three-fourths and one-fourth respectively. On 1st April, 19.., they agree to admit their Manager, Black, as a partner with a fifth-share of the profits. It is agreed that any excess over his former remuneration to which Black became entitled as a partner is to be borne by Costello. Black has previously been in receipt of a salary of £2,000 per annum together with a commission of 5 per cent of the net profits *after* charging such salary and commission.

The profits for the year ended 31st March, 19.., were £14,390. Prepare a statement showing how this would be divided between the partners.

18. Collins and Dickson, who are equal partners, contemplate admitting Perkins into partnership. The existing partners require compensation for the admission of Perkins as a partner, but the latter is unable to raise any cash in excess of the agreed Capital of £2,000 which he is bringing into the business.

Suggest a method by which the existing partners can obtain the compensation they desire in these circumstances.

Give the entries you would make to carry out your suggestion.   (*C.A. Inter.*)

19. A. Alver carried on the business of a retail boot and shoe merchant, having several branch shops. On 1st January, 19.., he decided to admit C. Clifton, the senior of his branch managers, into partnership. At this date A. Alver's capital was £8,000. He considered his premises were worth at least £2,000 more than the figure

stated in the Balance Sheet, and this sum he placed to the credit of C. Clifton's Capital Account, but stipulated that his drawings should not exceed £520 per annum until his (C. Clifton's) Capital Account amounted to £4,000.

Interest on Capital to be allowed at 5 per cent per annum, after charging which the net profit was to be divided as to A. Alver ⅔ths and C. Clifton ⅓th.

The net profit before charging interest for the year ended 31st December, 19.., amounted to £4,500, and the drawings of the partners were: A. Alver £1,900, C. Clifton £490.

Show Appropriation Account and Partners' Capital and Current Accounts.

20. Byron & Scott, who carried on business as provision merchants, were partners sharing Profits and Losses as to Byron two-thirds and Scott one-third. On 1st January, 19.., it was proposed to admit Dumas as a partner on the following terms: That in addition to bringing into the business £5,000 capital, he should pay £3,000 to Byron and Scott for his share of the Goodwill, and in consideration thereof he should receive one-fifth share of the profits. During the negotiations, however, circumstances arose which prevented Dumas from raising the £3,000, and he submits the following tentative propositions for consideration—

(1) That a Goodwill Account for £12,000 be opened, and that this sum be credited to Byron and Scott as to two-thirds and one-third respectively.

(2) That a Loan Account in the name of Dumas be debited with £3,000 and credited to Byron and Scott in their correct proportions, such loan to be repaid out of Dumas's share of profit.

(3) That a Policy on the Joint Lives of the Partners be taken out for £18,000, the annual premiums being charged to Profit and Loss Account. State briefly which suggestion, if any, of (1), (2), or (3) you consider equitable.

21. P. B. Robinson was in business as a grocer, and on 31st March, 19.., his financial position was as follows—

	£		£
Trade Creditors	480	Cash	10
Bank Overdraft	1,200	Trade Debtors	1,600
Capital	960	Stock.	880
		Motor Van	150
	£2,640		£2,640

P. B. Robinson contemplates taking his manager, R. Bell, as a partner. It has been suggested that the manager be invited to join Robinson on any of the following three alternatives—

(a) That P. B. Robinson should be credited with £800 for goodwill and that R. Bell should bring in cash equal to half Robinson's capital.

(b) That R. Bell should pay P. B. Robinson £400 as a premium and in addition bring in cash equal to half Robinson's capital.

(c) That R. Bell should bring in £480 as capital and that P. B. Robinson should draw out £300 to be treated as "Goodwill."

You are required (1) to draft Balance Sheets based on each of the above plans showing how the accounts would appear if any of them were adopted; (2) to state which alternative you would advise Bell to adopt, bearing in mind that it is proposed that profits should be divided: Robinson, two-thirds, Bell, one-third.

22. Axe was in practice as a certified accountant, and on 31st December, 19.6, his position was as follows—

	£
Cash at Bank	590
Sundry Debtors	1,420
Furniture, Office Appliances, etc.	380
Estimated Value of Uncompleted Work	410
Sundry Creditors	100

For the past three years Coe had been his managing clerk, and, as from 1st January, 19.7, Axe agreed to take him into partnership on the following terms: Coe is to introduce capital equal to one-third of the amount shown as being Axe's capital at 31st December, 19.6; he is to pay Axe a premium equal to three years' purchase of a quarter share of the net profits based on the average for the last three years. The net profits for the three years were—

		£
Year ended 31st December, 19.4	. . .	5,800
„ „ „ „ 19.5	. . .	5,400
„ „ „ „ 19.6	. . .	5,600

Further, Axe guaranteed that Coe's share of the profits should not be less than such quarter based on the average of the years in question. The partners are to receive 5 per cent interest on capital before distributing profits, viz. Axe three-quarters and Coe one-quarter.

(a) Set out the opening Balance Sheet of the new firm.

(b) Set out an account showing the distribution of the profits at 31st December, 19.7, these amounting to £5,230, before charging interest on Capital.

23. Red, White, and Blue are in partnership, sharing profits in the proportion of 4, 3 and 2 respectively.

The partnership deed provides that the goodwill of the firm shall be equal to $2\frac{1}{2}$ times the average profits of the four years to the date of change, and that the consideration for the changes in the partners' shares is to be calculated on this basis, but no entries are to be made in the firm's books in respect of goodwill. Profits of the firm have been: 19.5 £25,000; 19.6 £30,000; 19.7 £28,000; 19.8 £43,000.

It was agreed that—

(1) As on 31st December, 19.8, White and Blue should each acquire from Red an additional one-ninth share in the firm, and

(2) As on 1st January, 19.9, Red's son Pink should be admitted into the partnership on the following terms: his share to be one-seventh, of which a proportion, calculated to produce £2,750 per annum on the basis of the past profits set out above, is ceded to him by his father; the balance to be purchased by him (Pink) from White and Blue in the proportions equal to their respective shares as they were immediately prior to the admission of Pink.

(3) On 31st December, 19.9, Red retires and the continuing partners agree to acquire Red's share of goodwill in such proportions as will make them equal owners of the goodwill of the firm, the amount of goodwill remaining unchanged and the item of goodwill not to be brought into the books as an asset.

You are required—

(a) to set out the Journal entries necessary to record the foregoing matters in the books of the firm, and

(b) to set out the revised proportions in which the partners share, following the admission of Pink and the retirement of Red.

24. Culme and Burr are in partnership in a manufacturing business, sharing profits and losses as to Culme two-thirds and Burr one-third. As from 1st July, 19. ., they agree to admit Land as a partner, Culme to become a limited partner, his capital to be £5,000, and the shares of the partners in the new firm to be Culme one-fourth, Burr three-eighths, and Land three-eighths, the two latter being general partners. Land is to contribute a sum of £3,750 as his capital in the concern.

The Balance Sheet of Culme and Burr at 30th June, 19. ., was as follows—

Capitals—		£	£		£
Culme	.	£6,250		Cash at Bank . . .	630
Burr	.	3,750		Stock-in-trade . .	5,000
			10,000	Sundry Debtors . .	3,120
Sundry Creditors	. . .		5,000	Machinery and Plant .	2,500
				Freehold Premises . .	3,750
			£15,000		£15,000

It is agreed that the new firm shall assume the liabilities of Culme and Burr and that the assets shall be taken over at the following figures—

Stock-in-trade, £4,687.
Machinery and Plant, £1,875.
Freehold Premises, £4,375.
10 per cent to be deducted from Sundry Debtors.

It is further agreed that Culme is to be charged with any loss arising from the acquisition of the assets by the new firm.
On 1st July, 19.., Land paid in his capital.
Give the journal entries necessary to open the new firm's books and also set out the Balance Sheet on 1st July, 19...

25. A, B & C were in partnership sharing profits as to A one-half, B one-third, and C one-sixth. As from 1st January, 19.., they admitted D into partnership on the following terms—

D to have a one-sixth share, which he purchased entirely from A, paying A £4,000 for that share of Goodwill. Of this amount A retained £3,000 and put the balance in the firm as additional capital. D also brought £2,500 capital into the firm. It was further agreed that Investments should be reduced to their market value, viz. £1,800, and that Plant should be reduced to £2,900.
The Balance Sheet of the old firm at 31st December, previous, was as follows—

	£		£
Creditors . . .	10,500	Cash at Bank . . .	4,000
Capital—		Debtors . . .	6,000
A	6,000	Stock	5,000
B	4,000	Investments at Cost . .	3,000
C	2,000	Furniture and Fittings .	1,000
		Plant	3,500
	£22,500		£22,500

The Profits for the year 19.. were £12,000, and the Drawings: A, £3,000; B, £3,000; C, £1,500; D, £1,500.
You are required to journalize the opening adjustments, prepare the opening Balance Sheet of the new firm on 1st January, 19.., and the Capital Account of each partner as at 31st December, 19...

26. P and Q are in partnership with Capitals of £4,000 and £2,000 respectively; profits and losses are shared in proportion to their Capitals, after charging interest on Capital at 5 per cent per annum and a partnership salary of £1,400 to Q. P desires to retire from full active work in the partnership as from 1st January, 19... It is accordingly agreed that—

(a) Q shall in future be entitled to a partnership salary of £1,800 per annum.
(b) Interest is to be allowed on Capital at 5 per cent per annum.
(c) R, a departmental manager, shall be introduced as a partner, without Capital as from 1st January, 19.., with a salary of £1,750 per annum, the excess over £1,400 (his former salary as manager) being chargeable against P and not against the firm's profits before division.
(d) R shall also be entitled to 5 per cent of the profits after charging Interest on Capital and Partnership salaries.
(e) The balance of Profits is to be divided as to three-fifths to P, and two-fifths to Q.

The Profits for the year ended 31st December, 19.., were £13,200 before charging Interest on Capital or Partnership salaries.
You are required to show the division between the partners. (*C.A. Inter.*)

27. The Balance Sheet of A. and B. Dun as at 30th November, 19.., is—

		£			£
Creditors	. . .	6,700	Buildings		6,000
General Reserve	. .	1,300	Machinery and Plant	.	3,000
Capital—			Furniture and Fittings	.	400
A. Dun.	. . £8,400		Stocks		4,100
B. Dun	. . 4,250		Debtors		6,200
		12,650	Cash in Bank . . .		900
			Cash on Hand . . .		50
		£20,650			£20,650

The profits are divisible, two-thirds to A. Dun and one-third to B. Dun. A new partner, C. Dun, is admitted on payment of £3,500 Capital and £2,000 for Goodwill, which is to remain in the business. The Stock, on being revalued, shows an increase of £900, at which figure the new partnership takes same over. It is agreed that Buildings shall be depreciated 5 per cent, Machinery and Plant 10 per cent, and a provision of £200 made for Doubtful Debts, otherwise the figures in the above Balance Sheet remain.

Prepare Journal Entries showing the necessary adjustments, and draw up a Balance Sheet of the new partnership as at 1st December, 19... Workings to nearest £.

28. On 1st January, 19.2, C and P commenced business as owners of property, sharing profits and losses in the proportions C two-thirds and P one-third.

The property was let at rents amounting to £1,000 per calendar month, rates, repairs and insurance being borne by the owners. The management of the property was entrusted to an agent, at a commission of 7½ per cent of the gross rents collected. Only the amounts actually *received* from the agent during 19.2 were brought into the firm's books and no account was taken of any outstandings.

On 1st January, 19.3, T was admitted as a partner. It was agreed that he should contribute £20,000 as capital and that he should pay £1,500 for a quarter share of the goodwill. No Goodwill Account is to be raised in the books. It was also agreed that the accounts for the period prior to T's admission should be amended to an income and expenditure basis by adjusting entries as on 31st December, 19.2, through the partners' Capital Accounts. Apart from the entry for the cash paid in by T, no entries for any of the matters mentioned in this paragraph were made in 19.3.

It was further agreed that profits and losses should be shared in the proportions C, one-half, and P and T one-quarter each: that, for the year 19.3, interest should be allowed at 5 per cent on the adjusted balances on capital accounts as on 1st January, 19.3, and that no partners' current accounts should be opened.

The following Trial Balance was extracted as on 31st December, 19.3—

	£	£
Capital accounts Balances on 31st December, 19.2—		
C		30,000
P		23,000
Amount paid in by T		21,500
Drawings (£2,000 for each partner)	6,000	
Property, at cost	70,000	
Rents (net receipts from agent)		4,815
Insurances (for year to 31st December, 19.3) . .	131	
General expenses	200	
Balance at bank	2,984	
	£79,315	£79,315

On 31st December, 19.3, it was agreed to equate the capitals to profit ratios by a cash adjustment. (The resultant capitals to be rounded off to the nearest £10.)

The following is a copy of the personal account of the partnership for the year 19.3, as it appeared in the books of the agent—

	£			£
Balance on 31st December, 19.2—			Rents for 12 months to 30th November, 19.3 . .	12,000
Rates for 6 months to 31st March, 19.3 .	1,540			
Commission on rents for November, 19.2	75			
	1,615			
Less Rents for November, 19.2 . .	1,000			
		615		
Repairs (all 19.3) . . .		1,480		
Commission . . .		900		
Rates for year to 31st March, 19.4 . . .		3,120		
Cash paid to partnership .		4,815		
Balance, 31st December, 19.3, carried down . . .		1,070		
		£12,000		£12,000
			Balance, brought down .	1,070

You are required to show—

(a) the Partners' Capital Accounts in columnar form commencing with the balances shown in the Trial Balance as on 31st December, 19.3, and incorporating the adjustments to be made as on 31st December, 19.2, and

(b) the Balance Sheet as on 31st December, 19.3, and the Profit and Loss Account for the year ended on that date.

Ignore taxation and depreciation.

29. A, B, and C share profits in the ratio of 6:3:1, the capitals being £9,000, £6,000, and £3,000 respectively.

The partnership agreement provides for—

(1) B and C to receive salaries of £2,600 and £2,800 per annum respectively.

(2) Interest on Drawings of 5 per cent on the excess of a partner's drawings (excluding those on account of salary due to him) over his share of profit for the year before taking into account interest under this clause, to be debited to such partner (conversely for a deficiency).

(3) From B's share of profit is to be deducted £100 annually, representing benefits in kind received by him from the firm, this adjustment to be made without affecting Clause 2.

The net trading profit for the year ended 31st December, 19.9, is £12,000 after charging salaries per (1) above but before charging items in (2) and (3). After closing off the Profit and Loss Account (representing net trading profit) it was discovered that a sale of a motor vehicle for £800 had been incorrectly credited to Sales, and the purchase of the replacing vehicle costing £1,600 debited to Purchases. The former vehicle had cost £1,200 and the provision for depreciation was £600, the rate of depreciation being 10 per cent per annum based on the cost at the end of the year. (This is the only motor vehicle used by the firm.) No depreciation on the new vehicle has been provided for.

The Drawings Accounts are (including full partnership salaries paid): A, £5,800; B, £6,000; and C, £4,600, as per the Trial Balance [i.e. although the partners A and B have been debited with their salaries paid, no credits to them therefor have been made].

Prepare Appropriation Account, showing the division of the final profit of the firm for the year ended 31st December, 19.9. Ignore interest on Capital, and Taxation. Calculate to the nearest £. (Adapted from C.A. Inter.)

30. The partners of Lock & Co. share profits equally and the following is their Balance Sheet at 31st December, 19..—

	£		£
Creditors	5,000	Freehold Premises	2,000
Capitals—		Fixtures and Fittings	500
J. Lock	3,000	Stock	3,500
F. Lock	2,000	Debtors	2,700
		Bank and Cash Balances	1,300
	£10,000		£10,000

They agree to admit A. Key into equal partnership on payment of £2,000 for Goodwill and to credit him with the following assets brought in: Goodwill, £500; Furniture, £100; Stock, £1,500; Debtors, £400. It is further agreed that the Freehold Premises shall be revalued at £3,000 and that J. and F. Lock shall withdraw cash so as to leave all the Capitals equal.

Prepare Journal entries for the necessary adjustments in the books and draw up Balance Sheet of the new firm at 1st January, assuming that all transactions have been completed.

31. W, X, and Y are partners. They admit Z as a partner and guarantee that his share of profits shall not be less than £2,000 per annum. Profits are to be shared in the proportions of four-twelfths to W, three-twelfths to X, three-twelfths to Y, and two-twelfths to Z. The total profits for the year were £9,600. Prepare the Appropriation Account showing the division of the profits for the year.

32. Brown and Green, carrying on business in partnership, admitted White on the basis of equal division of profits. White did not introduce any capital, and in the event of dissolution has no interest in the Goodwill.

On 1st February, 19.., the partnership was formally dissolved, and as from that date the business was sold as a going concern to Black & Co. for £45,000 in cash. Of this sum £24,000 was in respect of property, plant, and machinery. The Balance Sheet of Brown, Green, and White on 1st February, 19.., was as follows—

	£		£
Creditors	4,500	Freehold Property, Plant and	
Capitals—		Machinery	18,000
Brown	15,000	Debtors	11,000
Green	15,000	Stock-in-trade	7,000
Current Accounts—		Cash	600
Brown	400		
Green	800		
White	900		
	£36,600		£36,600

You are required to draw up the final accounts on the dissolution of the partnership.

33. On 1st January, 19.., A took B into partnership. A's books were kept by single entry, and the following statement as on the above date showed his position as follows—

	£		£
Sundry Creditors	1,600	Sundry Debtors	2,500
A's Capital	2,600	Stock-in-trade	1,000
		Fixtures and Fittings	500
		Cash at Bank and in Hand	200
	£4,200		£4,200

It was agreed that B should not draw on account of profits more than £2,250 per annum until he had paid to A a premium of £400 out of his share of profits in excess of £2,250, A's capital was to be £2,600, as shown above, the new firm taking over the assets and discharging the liabilities. B was to bring in £500, which he did on 1st

January. The partners were to receive 5 per cent interest on their capitals and the profits or losses were to be divided, A two-thirds and B one-third. A's drawings were: year (a), £3,600; year (b), £3,540; year (c), £3,580; B drew £2,250 each year.

The position (apart from capital) on 31st December, years (a), (b), and (c), was as follows—

	(a) £	(b) £	(c) £
Assets	6,000	7,300	8,400
Liabilities	1,750	1,500	1,600

Amounts due from B to A in respect of premium were to be transferred from his Capital to A's Capital Account.

Make out a statement showing the profit or loss for each year and write up the partner's Capital Accounts.

Also show the position between A and B as regards the premium.

34. A, B, and C who were in partnership without any definite agreement decide to dissolve partnership. They prepare the following Balance Sheet and request you to close the affairs of the firm.

BALANCE SHEET, 31ST DEC., 19..

	£	£		£
Capitals—			Sundry Assets . . .	12,600
A	6,000		Profit and Loss Account (bal-	
B . . .	3,000		ance)	2,800
	9,000			
C . . .	900			
		8,100		
Loan: A (advanced 1st Jan. 19..)		1,000		
Sundry Creditors . . .		6,300		
		£15,400		£15,400

The Assets realize £8,700 and the Expenses of Realization amount to £270. You ascertain that the balance of the Profit and Loss Account is prior to charging any interest.

You are required to close the books of the firm assuming that C is insolvent and unable to contribute anything towards his deficit, and that A and B are willing and able to pay in such cash as may be required from them. (*C.A. Final.*)

35. A, B, and C were in partnership sharing profits four-ninths, three-ninths, and two-ninths. It was agreed that in the event of the retirement of a partner, the remaining partners should take over, in equal proportions, his share of the property and goodwill, the consideration to be an annuity (payable out of business profits) of £100 in respect of each of his one-ninth shares. A retired from the firm on 31st December, 19.., his capital including his share of goodwill being then £3,600. How would you suggest that the transaction should be dealt with in the books of the firm, and how would you deal with A's annuity for the year following? (*C.A. Final.*)

36. X and Y who are equal partners in a manufacturing business agreed to dissolve partnership and to realize their business as at 30th June, 19... On that date their Balance Sheet was as follows—

	£		£
Capitals—		Sundry Assets . . .	5,150
X	3,000	Cash	850
Y	700		
Sundry Creditors . . .	2,300		
	£6,000		£6,000

The expenses of the realization which were paid in cash amounted to £270, and Sundry Assets realized £3,920. You are required to show fully the result of the realization which was concluded on 16th August. Under the partnership articles in event of there being any deficiency on the Capital Account of either partner, the amount of such deficiency is to be at once made good in cash.   *(L.C.C.)*

37. A, B, and C are equal partners in a Solicitor's practice, their Capitals being £1,000 each. Their accounts have been prepared on a cash basis at 31st March in each year and the profits for the past two years have been £4,500 and £6,000. A decides to retire and it is agreed to assess his Goodwill at his share of the profits for the two years and to pay his share of the fees subsequently to be received for work done whilst he was in the business. B and C agree to pay A £250 per quarter with interest at 5 per cent per annum on outstanding balances and they arrange between themselves that payment of A's Capital and Goodwill shall be made out of their profits.

A year after the dissolution the total profits are £7,000, of which £3,000 represents all the fees earned prior thereto. Prepare an Appropriation Account showing the distribution of the profits of the new partnership, also the accounts of A, B, and C, and a Balance Sheet assuming that the partnership assets, apart from Goodwill and Cash, remain the same. Ignore tax. Workings to nearest £.

38. Devon, Dorset, and Poole dissolved partnership, and the realization of their assets resulted in a deficiency of £1,800. The partners' Capital Accounts stood as follows: Devon, £9,000; Dorset, £1,500; while Poole's Capital Account was in debit to the extent of £900. Poole being unable to contribute towards the deficiency, prepare necessary ledger accounts, showing how the available cash should be allocated as between Devon and Dorset. The partners shared Profits and Losses equally.

39. H. and M. decided to cease business and dissolve their partnership as at 30th June. Their Balance Sheet as at that date was as follows—

	£		£
Creditors	2,400	Sundry Debtors . . .	7,000
Reserve	1,500	Fixtures and Furniture. .	450
Current Account M . . .	350	Stock . . .	4,300
Capital H.	5,600	Current Account H. . .	250
Capital M.	4,000	Cash at Bank . . .	1,850
	£13,850		£13,850

They share profits as to seven-twelfths to H and five-twelfths to M. Debtors realized 89 per cent of the book value. Fixtures and Furniture, £315. Stock was sold at a discount of 17½ per cent. Creditors were paid at £2,700, there having been an error in the Balance Sheet, and the realization expenses amounted to £580. Prepare the necessary accounts to show the result of the realization.

40. Using imaginary figures, prepare (*a*) Realization Account, (*b*) Cash Account, (*c*) Partners' Capital Accounts, illustrating the ruling in *Garner* v. *Murray*, assuming that there are three partners, sharing Profits and Losses equally, and that the balances of their Capital Accounts were as follows—

	X	Y	Z
1st year.	£	£	£
1 Jan. (date of commencement of Partnership) .	1,000	800	600
2nd year.			
1 Jan.	1,200	950	750
3rd year.			
1 Jan. (date of dissolution of Partnership) . .	900	600	500

41. Geoffrey Fay and Godfrey Fry were equal partners. The first named died on 29th June, 19... The financial year of the firm ended 30th June. Upon accounts being taken the partners' accounts were as follows—

	£
Fay—Capital	16,000
Current Account *Cr.*	1,924
Fry—Capital	14,000
Current Account *Cr.*	1,704

It was agreed with Fay's executor that Goodwill should now be brought into account at the figure of £6,000 and that the assets should be revalued as follows—

	£
Reduce Plant and Machinery by	1,000
Reduce Provision for Bad Debts by	400
Increase value of Stock by	700
Increase value of Freehold Property by	1,340
Write out of the books Patents account standing at . . .	600

Prepare partners' accounts as they would now appear.

42. Alton, Bowers and Crann became partners on 1st January, 19.6, but did not execute an express agreement. Crann brought in no capital, but Alton introduced £11,250 and Bowers £5,250. More cash being necessary, Crann lent to the firm on 30th June, 19.6, the sum of £7,500 at 5 per cent interest. The trading results, before charging interest, were—

	£
Year ended 31st December, 19.6—Profit	3,824
Year ended 31st December, 19.7—Loss	1,344

Each partner drew £750 on account during 19.6 and 19.7.

On 31st December, 19.7, Alton died, and it was decided to dissolve the partnership immediately, the position then being—

Amount due to Sundry Creditors, £2,512.

Assets, standing at £24,492, realized £14,100 net.

Prepare accounts showing the result of the winding-up.

43. X, Y and Z carried on business as Iron Founders, sharing profits three-twelfths, four-twelfths, and five-twelfths respectively. They decided to dissolve partnership as on 1st June, 19.. and agreed that a sale of the assets should not be forced but that they should be realized gradually. As the realization was not likely to be completed for over a year and as the partners wished the receipts from sales to be dealt with *as and when received*, you are asked to prepare a scheme for the distribution of the money so that the amounts received by each partner would be equitable as between themselves.

The following was the Balance Sheet as at the date of dissolution—

	£		£
Creditors . . .	10,000	Sundry Assets . . .	38,000
Loan X	6,000		
Z	4,000		
Capital—X . . .	10,000		
Y . . .	6,000		
Z . . .	2,000		
	£38,000		£38,000

The amounts received from the gradual realization of the assets were as follows—

	£		£
1st Instalment . .	5,000	2nd Instalment . . .	10,000
3rd Instalment .	5,000	4th Instalment . . .	1,000
5th Instalment . .	4,400	6th Instalment . . .	600

Draw up a detailed memorandum showing the basis of the distribution of each of the instalments received, bearing in mind that the final results are *not* yet known nor likely to be known for some considerable time.

44. A, B, and C were in partnership sharing profits in the proportions of four-sevenths, two-sevenths, and one-seventh respectively.

Their partnership agreement provided that, on the death or retirement of a partner, the partnership position should be reviewed for the purpose of arriving at the amount to be paid to a retiring partner or to his representatives, if deceased. For the purposes of this review, Goodwill, for which no figure appeared in the Balance Sheet of the firm, was to be estimated at two years' purchase of the average profits of the four years preceding death or retirement.

C retired from the firm on 31st December, 19.7, when, for the purposes of arriving at the amount to be paid out to him, the following were to be taken into consideration, and the requisite entries were put through the books—

(a) Capital expenditure of £400 had been charged to Revenue in 19.4. This was to be written back and depreciation written off at the rate of 10 per cent per annum for three years from the diminishing balance.

(b) Plant and Fixtures were revalued at a figure £250 in excess of the book figure.

(c) A Provision for Bad Debts amounting to £460 was to be made.

(d) The capitalized value of pensions payable to ex-employees was £1,560. The pensions had been charged to revenue as and when paid.

(e) C's share of the 19.7–19.8 Income Tax liability was £56. It was agreed that he should be charged with three-quarters of this.

(i) Prepare an account, showing the amount to be credited or debited to C as a result of the above, assuming that the profits of the firm (upon which Goodwill was to be calculated) for the four years preceding his retirement were—

19.4 £3,245, 19.5 £2,786, 19.6 £2,840, 19.7 £1,945.

(ii) The remaining partners agreed to share profits in the same relative proportions as before and to write back the entries made in respect of Goodwill and the capital value of the pensions. What entries would be necessary to give effect to this?

(C.A. Final.)

45. Jones, Smith and Brown are in partnership, sharing profits and losses equally. At 30th June, 19.., the firm's Balance Sheet was as under—

	£		£
Sundry Creditors . .	17,000	Cash	150
Capital—		Sundry Debtors . . .	13,500
Jones	6,000	Stock	5,050
Smith	2,000	Machinery and Plant . .	7,000
Brown	1,000	Current Accounts—	
Current Account—		Smith	500
Jones	1,700	Brown	1,500
	£27,700		£27,700

As a result of general industrial depression, combined with pressure on the part of certain creditors, it was decided to sell the business and wind up the firm. The Machinery, Plant, Stock, and Debtors were acquired by a Limited Company for £17,450 in cash.

Show the entries in the firm's books recording the realization of the assets and the distribution of the proceeds, assuming that Brown proved to be insolvent and could not meet his liability to the firm.

46. Under a Partnership Agreement between N, O, and P it was provided that on the death of a partner the survivors should purchase his share in their own respective proportions on the following terms: Deceased's share of Goodwill to be reckoned at two years' purchase of his share of profits on average of previous four years' completed accounts; total amount, including capital and current account balances, to be paid by survivors in four equal instalments at 6, 12, 18, and 24 months after death, with interest on outstanding balance at 5 per cent from date of death.

The profits were shared as to N nine-sixteenths, O four-sixteenths, and P three-sixteenths.

N died on 30th June, 19.6.

Accounts were drawn up each year at 31st December, and the essential figures were as follows—

Firm's Profits: 19.2, £8,800; 19.3, £7,040; 19.4, £5,520; 19.5, £2,176.

Capital Accounts at date of death: N, £3,600; O, £1,600; P, £1,200.

N's Current Account at date of death, after crediting profits to that date, showed a debit of £450.

Set out in account form the amount payable to N's Estate at the end of each half-year, showing proportions to be provided by the surviving partners. (Ignore income tax.) Workings to nearest £.

47. X, Y, and Z are partners sharing profits and losses in equal proportions. Upon a dissolution of the partnership, and after realization of the assets, the position is as follows—

	£
Capital X	6,000 *Cr.*
Capital Y	4,000 *Cr.*
Capital Z	2,000 *Dr.*
Cash at Bank	5,000

Z is unable to contribute anything either in respect of his capital account or in respect of the firm's deficiency. Raise accounts showing the position.

48. The partnership agreement of P and Q provides that—

(*a*) Profits and losses shall be shared equally.

(*b*) Interest at 5 per cent per annum is to be allowed on Capitals, but no interest is to be charged on drawings.

(*c*) On the death of one of the partners—

(i) The survivor shall pay out the interest of the deceased partner and purchase his share.

(ii) The purchase price of the Goodwill shall be the profits of the preceding three completed years.

(iii) Assets are to be taken at the date of death at their book value. P died on 31st March, 19...

The Stock on that date was valued at £2,874.
The following Trial Balance was extracted from the books as at the date of death—

	£	£
P Capital		4,000
Q Capital		2,000
P Drawings	2,450	
Q Drawings	2,350	
Salaries	8,755	
Rent and Rates	1,263	
Purchases	21,470	
Stock (30th September, 19..)	2,749	
Travellers' Commission and Expenses	580	
Wages	6,636	
Sales		44,384
Sales Returns	49	
Sundry Debtors	2,640	
Cash at Bank	552	
Furniture and Fittings	200	
Sundry Creditors		1,800
General Expenses	375	
Discount Account (balance)		35
Plant and Machinery	2,150	
	£52,219	£52,219

The profits of the preceding three completed years to 30th September, were: £3,100, £2,640, and £2,460.

Prepare the necessary accounts to produce to the Executors of P, showing the amount due to his Estate. (*C.A. Inter.*)

49. A, B, and C were partners. C retired, and took no steps to free himself from partnership liabilities. His capital on retirement was £10,000. He received half in cash and left the other half as a loan at a minimum rate of interest of 5 per cent, a higher rate on a sliding scale to be paid dependent on profits. The firm failed. The creditors whose claims existed when C retired amounted to £10,000, and there are claims subsequently contracted of £5,000. Do you consider C is liable for either or both classes of creditors? Give reasons for your answer.   (*C.A. Inter.*)

50. B and C were partners, sharing profits and losses equally. The partnership deed provided that in the event of a partner's death no sum should be payable to his estate for goodwill, but in lieu thereof a life annuity of £3,600 a year should be paid to his widow in equal half-yearly sums, the first payment to be made six months from his death.

C having died, you are asked to suggest alternative methods of providing for the annuity in the books of the firm, drafting the necessary entries for the first year in each case. Assume Income Tax at 40 per cent.   (*C.A. Final.*)

51. Two partners, viz. L. Moor and M. Lane, assured their lives jointly for £10,000 at an annual premium of £400 for the purpose of providing funds for repayment of their share of the capital and goodwill in the event of death, the premium being charged to the firm's Profit and Loss Account each December. Under the partnership deed the representatives of a deceased partner are to be paid his capital *as shown by the last Balance Sheet* plus interest at 5 per cent per annum to date of death and also his share of profits to date of death, such to date of death being calculated according to the profits of the preceding year. Further, they are to be paid his share of the goodwill, this to be calculated at two years' purchase of his average net profits of the last three years before charging the insurance premium.

The accounts of the partnership were regularly made up to the 31st December in each year, and the partners shared profits and losses as to L. Moor five-eighths and M. Lane three-eighths. M. Lane died on the 30th April, 19... After charging the insurance premiums the net profits for the last three years were £2,800, £3,200, and £2,712. The last Balance Sheet showed M. Lane's capital to be £3,600; his drawings to date of death amounted to £570. You are required to make the necessary adjustments and prepare M. Lane's account, showing the amount due to his personal representatives.

52. W. Edgar and R. Ward commenced business in partnership, as from 1st January, 19.., their capitals at that date being, Edgar, £10,600, and Ward, £7,950.

Interest on capital was to be allowed at 5 per cent, and profits or losses were to be divisible in proportion to the capitals.

To provide funds for the payment to his representatives in the event of a partner's death, Edgar and Ward, on 1st January, 19.., made the following arrangements regarding life insurance—

(*a*) Each partner's life was insured for the amount at credit of his Capital Account, the premiums being charged to Profit and Loss Account.

(*b*) Each insured his partner's life for the amount at credit of his (the partner's) Capital Account, the premiums being charged to the respective Drawings Accounts.

(*c*) A joint life insurance was effected for the combined total of the Capital Accounts, the premiums being charged to Profit and Loss Account.

The premium rates were as follows—

Edgar £3 per cent, Ward £2 per cent, and for the joint lives £4 per cent.

Edgar died on 30th September, 19...

Show the Capital and Drawings Accounts of each partner, as finally adjusted after Edgar's representatives have been paid out, on the footing that the trading profit for period to 30th September, 19.. (before providing for interest on capital or life assurance premiums) amounted to £2,850, and that each partner had drawn £75 cash on the 15th of each month.

53. A and B, who were partners, trading under the name of the Tea Trading Co., and X and Y, who were partners, trading under the name of the Cocoa Trading

Co., decided to amalgamate as on 1st April, 19... Their Balance Sheets were as follows—

A AND B

	£		£
Creditors . . .	1,000	Premises	1,800
Reserve	2,000	Stock.	3,000
Capitals—		Debtors	1,200
A . . . £3,000		Investment	2,000
B . . . 2,000			
	5,000		
	£8,000		£8,000

A and B share profits in proportion to capitals.

X AND Y

	£		£
Bank Loan . . .	800	Goodwill	1,000
Creditors . . .	2,200	Stock.	2,600
Capitals—		Debtors	2,400
X . . . £1,500			
Y . . . 1,500			
	3,000		
	£6,000		£6,000

X and Y share profits equally.

The terms of the amalgamation provide *inter alia* that—

(1) A new firm to be called the Cash Trading Co., consisting of A, B, X, and Y as partners, should be formed, and that the partners should share profits or losses in the same ratio as their capitals in the new firm after all adjustments had been made.

(2) The premises owned by A and B should be taken over by the new firm at a valuation of £2,300.

(3) The goodwill appearing on the Balance Sheet of X and Y was worthless.

(4) After the above adjustments have been made, that X and Y should each bring in an additional capital in the new firm, £500.

On the assumption that the above transactions were duly completed on 1st April, 19.., you are required to show the Journal entries necessary to close the books of A and B and the books of X and Y. Show also the Journal entries required to open the books of the new firm.

54. On 30th April, 19.., Ernest Jackson, who carried on business as a grocer, decided to accept an offer to combine his business with that of Thomas and Richard Parker, trading as Parker Bros. The agreement provided that Jackson was to be entitled to one-fifth of the net profits of the whole business, and was to contribute £1,000 as capital. If the net assets of his business were less than this amount, he was to make up the difference in cash.

His Balance Sheet at 30th April, 19.., was as follows—

	£		£
Sundry Creditors . . .	340	Fixtures and Fittings . .	190
Capital	962	Motor Van	120
		Stock.	464
		Sundry Debtors	478
		Cash at Bank	50
	£1,302		£1,302

The values placed upon the Fixtures, Fittings and Stock were agreed to, but it was decided that the Motor Van should be taken over at £90 and that a Bad Debts Provision of £22 should be created. The amount due by Jackson was paid into the new firm's account.

You are required to show in the books of the new firm the journal entry or entries recording the taking over of Jackson's business, and to state how the first year's profit of £2,200 is to be divided, Thomas Parker being entitled to five-eighths and Richard Parker to three-eighths of the balance of profits of the combined business.

(*R.S.A. Advanced.*)

55. William Brookshaw carried on business as a potato merchant, and on 31st January, 19.., owing to trade depression, he was compelled to call his creditors together. After considerable controversy it was agreed by the whole of the creditors (with the exception of three whose combined debts amounted to £43) that the business should be sold to Messrs. Smith and Johnson for a sum which would provide a composition of 75p in the £, on the debts of the ordinary creditors, and also discharge fully the preferential creditors. The assets and liabilities were duly assigned on 2nd February, 19.., and it was agreed that the purchase consideration should be discharged by an immediate cash payment of £10,000, and the balance on 31st March, 19... The Balance Sheet of Brookshaw showed the following position—

BALANCE SHEET, 2ND FEBRUARY, 19..

	£		£
Trade Creditors . .	34,624	Cash at Bank . . .	465
Preferential Creditors .	532	Sundry Debtors . . .	15,650
		Stock-in-trade . . .	5,875
		Motor Vehicles . . .	2,570
		Fixtures and Fittings . .	650
		Leasehold Premises . .	4,600
		W. Brookshaw—	
		Capital Account . .	5,346
	£35,156		£35,156

The new firm decided to revalue the assets taken over, as follows—

	£
Motor Vehicles	2,000
Fixtures and Fittings	500
Stock	5,250

It was also decided to create a Provision for Bad Debts amounting to £1,500.

You are required to show the opening Journal entries in the books of the firm, assuming that the legal expenses, in connection with the assignment of the business, amounted to £100, and that the sum of £6,000 each was paid into the firm's Banking Account by Smith and Johnson. The deposit of £10,000 was duly paid to the creditors on the 2nd February, 19... What are the rights, if any, of the dissenting creditors?

56. William Blake, a wholesale merchant, found himself in financial difficulties and called a meeting of creditors, with the result that it was arranged for him to assign all his assets and liabilities to a syndicate of nine creditors who undertook to advance £1,000 each for the purpose of paying a composition of 37½p in the £ and providing funds for the business to be carried on by the syndicate. All the creditors agreed to the foregoing arrangements.

The position of the business according to the books at 1st June—the date of the assignment—was—

BALANCE SHEET

	£		£
Trade Creditors . .	22,896	Leasehold Premises . .	3,250
Creditors for Rates and Wages		Furniture, Fixtures, and Fittings	565
(payable in full) . .	133	Stock-in-trade . . .	4,325
		Sundry Debtors . . .	2,160
		Cash in Bank . . .	35
		Cash on Hand . . .	10
		W. Blake—	
		Capital Account . .	12,684
	£23,029		£23,029

Furniture, etc., were to be revalued at £300, the stock-in-trade at £4,000, and a provision of £250 was made in respect of bad debts.

Show the opening entries in the books of the syndicate and prepare Balance Sheet as at 2nd June, assuming that the members thereof have each paid the amount agreed.

57. A, B, and C are partners in X & Co., boot dealers. The firm controls three shops, and each partner undertakes the management of one of these. C, in addition, manages a Repair Department, occupied entirely with work for the retail branches of the business.

The profits of each department are separately ascertained, and are subject to a charge for interest of $7\frac{1}{2}$ per cent per annum on loan and partners' capital employed. The profits of Repair Department are in addition chargeable with a payment of £400 per annum in favour of C.

The profits, subject to interest and C's payment as stated, are apportionable thus—

Repair Department: allocable to shops in proportion of their respective shares in turnover of this department.

Shops: including transfer from Repair Department, 90 per cent to individual partners having control of each respectively, 10 per cent to a general pool.

General Pool: A, one-half; B, one-third; C, one-sixth.

For the year 19.., Repair Department shows profits, prior to charge for interest and C's payment, of £825. Turnover with shops has been A, £5,500; B, £3,000; C, £1,500. For the same period, profits of shops, prior to charge for interest, are A, £6,400; B, £5,605; C, £4,200.

Interest has been paid on loans of £10,000, and the partners are entitled to interest on their capital, A, £10,000; B, £7,000; C, £5,000. Loan and partners' capital is employed by A, £14,000; B, £9,000; C, £6,000; Repair Department, £3,000.

Prepare, for year 19.., accounts showing allocation of interest and apportionment of profits. (*C.A. Final.*)

58. Johnson admits Williamson into partnership on 1st January. The agreement provides—

(1) Williamson is to introduce cash capital, £5,000.

(2) Johnson is to credit his own account with goodwill, £6,000.

(3) Goodwill Account to be created for £6,000.

(4) Profits and losses to be dealt with in the ratio of 3:2, after *payment* of £2,300 per annum to Johnson, and an appropriation of one-seventh of the *final net* divisible profits for the purpose of a Staff Thrift Fund, and interest on capital at 5 per cent per annum.

(5) Cash withdrawals free of interest are to be restricted to £2,700 and £2,500 per annum for Johnson and Williamson respectively. No interest to be charged on *cash* drawings unless they exceed the above stipulated amounts, such excess being charged at 10 per cent per annum.

Johnson withdrew cash as follows—

	£
1st March	1,500
1st September	750
1st October	650

Williamson withdrew cash £170 at the end of each month, commencing 31st January.
In addition to the balances arising out of the above, the following balances appear
in the books of the firm on 31st December, 19..—

	£
Agents' Deposits	260
Johnson (Capital at 31st December prior to Williamson's admission)	8,000
Premises at Cost	9,440
Fixtures	1,000
Stock (1st January)	3,100
Purchases	35,200
Sales	47,180
Sales Returns	2,460
Wages and Salaries	8,120
Rates and Insurance	1,720
General Expenses	937
Debtors	15,160
Creditors	8,130
Advertising (all incurred since 1st January)	1,080
Cash in Bank	1,450
Bills Receivable	500
Bad Debts	572
Bank Interest (Cr.)	40
Discounts Net (Dr.)	631

Adjustments required—

1. Depreciation of fixtures 10 per cent.
2. Purchases invoices (goods bought having been included in stock) £516 omitted
inadvertently.
3. Rates accruing £300. Rates for half-year ended 31st March next of £420 paid on
2nd December.
4. Part of premises are sublet to X on 1st October at £240 per annum *plus* one-tenth
rates, payable half-yearly, 31st March and 30th September.
[No entry yet made in books for Sublet Rent and Rates.]
5. Carry forward 20 per cent of net advertising expenditure.
6. Included in debtors are Johnson £140, Williamson £220, for goods charged at
cost and included in sales.
7. An allowance of £80 without interest to be made to Williamson for agreed
expenditure incurred privately on behalf of the firm.
8. Closing Stocks—

	£	
Goods	4,952	
Advertising matter at cost	250	(Estimated worth 60 per cent of cost.)

9. Create provisions for—

Bad Debts	.5 per cent of Trade Debtors.
Discounts	.2½ per cent of estimated good Trade Debts.

Prepare Trial Balance at 31st December; Trading and Profit and Loss Account
for the year ended, and Balance Sheet as at, 31st December.
In addition, prepare a Rough Adjustment Sheet connecting the Trial Balance with
the final figures.   (*Adapted from C.A. Inter.*)

59. X and Y carried on the business of X, Y & Co. as equal partners. It was agreed
that X should retire on 31st December, 19.8, and that his son Z should join Y in
partnership on 1st January, 19.9, and should be entitled to one-third of the profits of
the firm, the style of the firm remaining unchanged.
The balances in the firm's books on 31st December, 19.8, were as follows—

	£		£
Sundry Creditors	980	Goodwill	1,000
Capitals—		Freehold Premises	2,070
X	3,400	Furniture	1,420
Y	2,820	Sundry Debtors	1,610
		Balance at Bank	1,100
	£7,200		£7,200

For the purposes of X's retirement and Z's admission, Goodwill was written up to £2,200 and Freehold Premises to £2,400. Other terms agreed were that enough money should be introduced to enable X to be paid out and leave £1,000 cash for working capital, and that Y and Z should respectively provide such sums as would make their capitals proportionate to their shares of profit. X agreed to make Z a gift by transfer from his capital account, of half the amount which Z had to provide.

Y and Z paid in the cash due from them on 7th January, 19.9, and the amount due to X was paid out the same day.

Set out Journal entries, with full explanatory narrative to record the above transactions (including cash transactions) in the firm's books.

(Adapted from C.A. Final.)

60. A and B are partners sharing profits in the ratio of 3:2. They decide to admit C as a partner on the basis that the latter pays in to the firm cash £3,000, of which £1,000 is to be premium on his admission to a quarter share, the ratios between A and B to be 2:1.

On the other hand, C brings into the business his Goodwill, to be run as a separate unit, and the profit-sharing to be: A, B, and C—3:2:5. The Goodwill is agreed at £1,600.

Show entries required to give effect to the above arrangements.

61. A and B are in partnership, and on 31st August, 19.7, B retires from the firm. The profit ratio 3:2, after providing for interest on capital at 5 per cent per annum and A and B's annual salaries of £2,700 and £2,400.

The partners agree that, pending settlement on 1st January, 19.8, B shall be credited with interest at 8 per cent per annum on the balance of his account, after crediting him with his *share* of Goodwill (which was valued at £1,250). On 31st December, 19.7, a payment of £500 was made to B.

All profits to the 31st December, 19.6, had been withdrawn.

Depreciation is to be written off Fixtures, £100, and Stock at 31st December, 19.7, was valued at £1,000.

The partnership books were not closed off at the date of B's retirement, and it was agreed that the accounts for the year ended 31st December, 19.7, be taken as the basis for the settlement and apportioned on a time basis.

B had been paid the *whole* of his year's salary, but the overpayment, as well as the partners' drawings, are to be ignored so far as interest on capital is concerned.

You are required to prepare accounts for the year ended 31st December, 19.7, and to write up B's Loan Account from the following balances—

	£	£
Stock	1,500	
Office Salaries	4,000	
Debtors and Creditors	1,697	750
General Expenses	660	
B—Loan	500	
A—Salary	2,700	
B—Salary	2,400	
Bad Debts written off Aug., 19.7	20	
Bad Debts Provision (at 31st Dec., 19.6)		200
Decoration (paid for in May, 19.7, work done Dec., 19.6)	219	
Bank	806	
Fixtures	800	
Repairs (£17 in respect of Dec., 19.7)	168	
Stock Reserve		420
Purchases and Sales	18,000	30,000
A's Drawings and Capital	1,600	2,800
B's Drawings and Capital	1,300	2,200
	£36,370	£36,370

The Bad Debts Provision was no longer required at 31st August, 19.7. Ignore tax.

62. Towns and Field, who shared profits in the proportion of two-thirds and one-third respectively, were in partnership as estate agents in London, and Willett, who carried on a similar business in Folkestone, acted as their local agent.

The two concerns amalgamated as from 1st October, 19.., on which date their Balance Sheets were as under—

TOWNS AND FIELD

	£		£
Creditors—		Furniture	120
Clients . .	£2,200	Debtors	3,850
Sundry Expenses .	700	Bank Balance . . .	2,780
	2,900	Bank Balance ("C" account).	2,500
Capitals—		Cash in hand . . .	50
Towns . . .	£3,800		
Field . . .	2,600		
	6,400		
	£9,300		£9,300

WILLETT

	£		£
Creditors—		Furniture	100
Clients . .	£1,600	Debtors for Disbursements .	820
Sundry Expenses .	250	Bank Balance . . .	1,600
	1,850	Bank Balance ("C" account) .	1,940
Capital	2,650	Cash in hand . . .	40
	£4,500		£4,500

In the case of Towns and Field, credit had been taken for commission and fees earned, but Willett had kept his accounts on a cash basis.

The terms relating to the amalgamation and the new partnership were—

(*a*) Towns and Field were to manage the London office and Willett was to be in charge of the Folkestone office.

(*b*) The goodwill of Towns and Field was valued at £6,000 and that of Willett at £3,600. (No Goodwill Account was raised, but the necessary adjustments relating thereto, on the basis of the profit-sharing ratios, were dealt with in the Capital Accounts. As between Towns and Field, no adjustment was required.)

(*c*) Profits and losses were to be divided as follows—

	Towns	Field	Willett
London	One-half	Three-tenths	One-fifth
Folkestone . . .	Three-tenths	One-fifth	One-half

(*d*) Prior to amalgamation, the value of the Furniture, in each case, was reduced by 50 per cent.

(*e*) Commission and fees received at Folkestone after 1st October, 19.., for work done prior to that date were to be credited to Willett.

(*f*) Interest on capital was to be allowed at 5 per cent per annum.

(*g*) Provision was made for the following annual salaries—

Towns, £800; Field, £600; Willett, £600.

(*h*) Commission amounting to £300, due by Towns and Field to Willett on 18th October, 19.., was to be transferred to Willett's Capital Account.

The figures relating to the transactions of the firm for the year to 30th September, 19.., were—

	London Dr. £	London Cr. £	Folkestone Dr. £	Folkestone Cr. £
Commission and Fees charged		9,477		5,265
Commission and Fees charged (pre-amalgamation)				620
Partners' Drawings—				
Towns	1,200			
Field	1,000			
Willett			1,300	
Staff Salaries and Office Expenses	5,820		3,540	
Debtors	3,710		1,685	
Creditors—Clients		1,830		1,520
Expenses		450		230
Bank Balances—				
Office Accounts	4,367		1,960	
"C" Accounts	2,190		1,660	
Cash	50		40	

A separate set of books was kept at each office, but the annual accounts and Willett's Capital Account appeared in the London books. The interest on the latter was to be charged against the Folkestone business.

From the foregoing information you are required—

(a) To make the necessary adjustments consequent upon the amalgamation.

(b) To prepare, in columnar form, a Profit and Loss Account for the year to 30th September, 19.., and a Balance Sheet as on that date.

(c) To show the Partners' Capital Accounts and the Folkestone Office Account in the London books. (*C.A. Final.*)

63. Todd & Bond were partners in business, their agreement containing the following provisions regarding the sharing of profits and losses—

(a) After providing for (i) interest on capital at 5 per cent per annum, and (ii) equal salaries amounting together to one-third of the remaining surplus, profits and losses were to be divided equally.

(b) If the accounts showed a net loss, but a surplus for allocation before providing for interest on capital and salaries, Todd was to bear the *lesser* of (i) the whole net loss or (ii) such proportion of same as would make his share of the surplus for allocation at least one-third, but in no case was he to bear less than one-half of the net loss as provided in (a).

The Partners' Capitals were as follows—

	Todd £	Bond £
31st December, 19.6	10,000	11,000
31st December, 19.7	10,400	11,200

The trading results, before providing for interest on capital and salaries, were as undernoted—

	£
Year ended 31st December, 19.7—Profit	1,395
Year ended 31st December, 19.8—Profit	837

Prepare statement showing the allocations in each of the two years ended 31st December, 19.7 and 19.8.

64. A, B and C have been in partnership since 1st July, 19.2.

C received a fixed and guaranteed share of profits of £500 per annum, and the balance of profits and losses was divisible between A and B in the proportions of three-fifths and two-fifths respectively.

On 1st July, 19.7, A and B mutually agreed with C that he should be entitled to a one-tenth share in the partnership, and C paid the sum of £100 into the partnership funds on that date for his share of the goodwill.

The partners decided to dissolve the partnership on 30th June, 19.8, as B had disclosed (prior to that date) that he had been responsible for the following irregularities—

(1) The value of stock on hand on 30th June, 19.7, had been inflated by B by £500 to cover goods (at their cost price) removed and sold by him personally for £400. All the partners agreed that the stock should have realized £600. The stock on hand at 30th June, 19.8, was valued correctly at £3,575.

(2) Cheques received from old debtors in June, 19.8, amounting to £300 (and in respect of which no discount was allowable) had been omitted from the books of account and appropriated by B for his own use.

The Balance Sheet at 30th June, 19.8, as approved by the partners before making the adjustments necessary on the disclosure of B's irregularities, was—

		£				£
Trade Creditors	£4,000		Sundry Fixed Assets	.	.	500
Less Discount Provision			Stocks on hand	.	.	3,575
at 2½ per cent	100		Trade Debtors	.	£7,800	
		3,900	Less Discount Provision			
Bank Overdraft	. .	200	at 5 per cent.	.	390	
Partners' Capitals—						7,410
A . . .	£7,020		Cash in hand	.	.	155
B . . .	450					
C . . .	70					
		7,540				
		£11,640				£11,640

The Goodwill and other assets (except cash) were taken over by A for £12,000.

Final settlement was made on 31st July, 19.8, B having agreed to make good the amount due by him to the partnership. The creditors were also paid off on that date, discount being allowed as per provision.

You are required to close the books of the partnership. Only the accounting aspect of B's irregularities need be considered.   (*Adapted from C.A. Final.*)

65. A and B are in partnership sharing equally, A managing the Aberdare Branch and B the Birmingham Branch.

On 1st July they admit C as a partner, who pays in £2,500, of which £500 is premium, the ratio of profit sharing to be 3:2:1.

On 30th November they decide to form a limited company to operate as and from 30th September, of which the sole shareholders are to be A, B, and C.

The purchase consideration is £15,000 in shares of £1 each fully paid, to be allotted in profit ratio subject to a cash adjustment. The expenses of formation are £120.

It was decided to utilize the old partnership books. No adjustments have been made to any of the accounts arising out of the above, and no accounts have been drawn up during the year.

It was agreed to take the gross profit as being earned evenly over the period. All sales are for cash.

From the following balances prepare final accounts for the year ended 31st December—

	£
Closing Stock	4,380
Preliminary Expenses	120
Gross Profit	4,800
Expenses apportionable on a time basis	600
Expenses solely referable to Jan. 1–June 30	300
Expenses solely referable to July 1–Sept. 30	360
Expenses solely referable to Oct. 1–Nov. 30	180
Expenses solely referable to Dec. 1–Dec. 31	100

Cash on hand	20
Cash at Bank	2,280
Other Assets	4,800
Goodwill per last Balance Sheet	1,000
Creditors	780
Capitals: A	4,200
B	3,000
C	2,500
Drawings: A	550
B	440
C	150

Drawings are made regularly at the end of each month till 30th November. There is no interest on capital or drawings. At 30th September the total assets, including goodwill £1,000 and stock £3,500, were £11,776 and creditors £370.

(Institute of Company Accountants' Final.)

66. Hill, Fell, and Mount were in partnership, sharing profits and losses as to one-half, one-quarter, and one-quarter respectively. The partners received no salary and no account is to be taken of interest on capital. The capital accounts have been kept on a current account basis.

The Balance Sheet of the partnership as on 31st December, 19.6, was as follows—

		£			£
Sundry Creditors	. .	2,970	Buildings		2,000
Partners' Capitals—	.	.	Plant		1,000
Hill . . .	£1,400		Stock		600
Fell . . .	300		Debtors		750
Mount . .	600		Cash and Bank Balances	.	920
		2,300			
		£5,270			£5,270

An offer made by Peaks Ltd. (a public company), to take over as on 30th June, 19.7, the then remaining assets (excluding cash and bank balances) and liabilities of the partnership was accepted by the partners on 20th June, 19.7. The purchase consideration was to be settled by the issue of 800 5 per cent Preference Shares of £1 each (market price 112½p) and 2,600 Ordinary Shares of 25p (market price 30p). The respective market price of the shares remained constant throughout 19.7.

The completion of the contract for sale was to take place on 1st July, 19.7, on which date the purchase consideration was duly received by the partners.

During the half-year to 30th June, 19.7, Fell got into financial difficulties unknown to his partners and lost all his private assets other than his share in the partnership.

After providing £200 for depreciation of plant and writing off debts of £300, which proved to be irrecoverable, the profit for the half-year was £160.

The partners' drawings during the half-year had been as follows: Hill, £520; Fell, £930; and Mount, £250.

The cash and bank balances on 30th June, 19.7, amounted to £160, and by mutual agreement this sum was paid on that day to Mount in reduction of his capital.

You are required—

  (a) to close the books of the partnership on 30th June, 19.7; and
  (b) to show the division of the shares between the partners.

(C.A. Final.)

67. Salmon and Rose have been carrying on a retail business in partnership, sharing profits equally.

As on 1st October, 19.7, the firm absorbed the business of White, who thereupon became a partner on the following terms—

(1) The firm took over White's assets at the following agreed valuations—

	£
Goodwill	1,240
Furniture	630
Motors	920
Stock	4,040
Debtors (Book Value £910) . . .	890
	£7,720

Any profit or loss which might arise on the subsequent realization of the debtors was to accrue to the firm.

(2) The firm undertook to pay White's creditors (£360) and White was to pay in sufficient cash to make his capital up to £7,500.

(3) The old firm's Goodwill Account, which on 30th September, 19.7, stood in the books at £2,000, was to be written up to £3,100 before White's admission.

(4) The profit is to be divided between Salmon, Rose, and White in the proportions of 2, 3, and 2 respectively, and in consideration of the transfer from Salmon to Rose of the portion of the old firm's goodwill (implied by the alteration of the profit-sharing ratio), their capitals are to be credited and debited respectively with the amount in question.

In order to balance his books, the firm's book-keeper credited White with the cash paid in by him in accordance with clause (2) above and the full book value of the debtors taken over, less the creditors, but he made no further entry whatever regarding the foregoing matters.

At 30th September, 19.7, the capitals of Salmon and Rose, before any adjustments had been made, were £9,240 and £3,860; and the balance of White's account, after the book-keeper had made the above entries, was £690.

You are required to write up the capital accounts to give effect to the above arrangements.   (*Adapted from C.A. Inter.*)

68. Radman and Ingleton are in partnership as wholesale clothiers, sharing profits and losses in the proportion of three-quarters and one-quarter respectively. The partnership deed provides that interest on capital shall be allowed at 5 per cent per annum, and that Radman shall be entitled to a salary of £2,800 and Ingleton of £2,700 per annum.

The following is the Balance Sheet of the firm as on 30th April—

	£		£
Trade Creditors . .	4,600	Bank Balance . . .	2,900
Loan Creditors . .	2,000	Trade Debtors . . .	6,500
Capitals: Radman . .	9,100	Stock on hand . . .	7,400
Ingleton . .	5,700	Machinery	3,800
		Fixtures . . .	800
	£21,400		£21,400

The partnership deed expired on that date, and it had been agreed that the provisions relating to interest and salaries should continue, but that for the future the shares should be: Radman, four-sevenths; Ingleton, three-sevenths.

Instead of renewing the partnership as such, it is decided to convert the concern into a private limited company on the understanding that the relative positions of the partners on the new basis shall be preserved.

Prior to the conversion, Ingleton is to introduce cash to enable the loan creditors to be paid out.

The book value of Machinery is to be increased to £5,000, but the remaining assets are to be taken over at the values shown. The present capital is sufficient for the requirements of the business.

Goodwill is agreed at £5,600.

You are required to—

(a) submit your recommendations to carry out the desired arrangements;
(b) close the books of the firm; and
(c) show the commencing Balance Sheet of the new company.

The question of the preliminary expenses of the company and realization expenses of the firm may be ignored. *(C.A. Final.)*

69. On 30th April, 19.., Hamer and Grace agree to purchase the business then carried on by Brydon. The Balance Sheet of the business at that date was as set out below—

	£		£
Trade Creditors . .	3,250	Fixed Assets . . .	2,100
Capital Account (Brydon) .	11,000	Stocks	4,850
		Trade Debtors . . .	6,150
		Cash and Bank Balances .	1,150
	£14,250		£14,250

It was agreed that Brydon should retain the cash and bank balances, and that the remaining assets, subject to the liabilities, should be sold for £12,000.

Hamer and Grace were unable to finance the purchase immediately, and Brydon carried on the business as their agent until 31st July, 19.. (the same year), when the purchase price and the balance due by the purchasers on current account were paid over. For this service, Brydon charged a salary of £300 and interest on the purchase money (but not on the cash and bank balances) at the rate of 5 per cent per annum.

Control and Suspense Accounts for debtors and creditors were maintained by Brydon throughout the agency period. Hamer and Grace dealt with the debtors and creditors outstanding on 31st July, 19...

The following is a summary of the transactions, other than those referred to above, during the three months ended 31st July, 19..—

	£
Cash paid: Expenses	4,000
Trade Creditors	9,000
Brydon (on account of £1,150)	1,000
Cash received: Trade Debtors.	12,800
Sales, *less* Returns	10,100
Purchases, *less* Returns	8,900
Discounts received.	270
Discounts allowed	350

You are required to write up the books of Brydon to 31st July, 19.., on which date they were closed. Ignore taxation. Journal entries are not required. *(C.A. Final.)*

CHAPTER XXIII

LIMITED COMPANY ACCOUNTS

1. Prepare "Statutory Report" from the following figures. Receipts: on allotment of 50,000 shares of £10 each, £137,000; proceeds, sale of old building material removed from freehold, £1,742; advanced on mortgage, £47,000; received in respect of allotment of debenture stock (75 per cent of £100,000), £75,000. Payments: purchase of freehold, £205,000; paid builders on account, £12,600; paid for stock in bond, £24,350; paid salaries, £247; office and petty expenses, £147; preliminary expenses to date, £2,471. (*C.A. Inter.*)

2. Walter Hope, of "Yarborough," Wynott Avenue Deal, applied on 5th January, 19.., for 800 ordinary shares, of £1 each, in Wellspun Yarn Ltd., remitting the amount due on application, 12½p per share. On 9th January he received a letter of allotment No. 18 for 800 shares, numbered 7,021 to 7,820. The amount due on allotment, 37½p per share, was remitted to the company on 12th January.

On the 18th of March he purchased 700 further shares, 50p paid, at 62½p per share, and transfer No. 33 for 700 shares, numbered 651 to 1,350, was duly completed on 25th March.

Prepare a folio ruling for the ordinary share register of members of the company, and record the above particulars therein, so far as they relate to Hope.

(*C.A. Inter.*)

3. Prepare from the particulars given below the statutory report—

Total number of shares allotted is 41,044 of £1 each, 33,000 issued as fully paid to the vendor; on the remaining 8,044, 5,500 have been paid up, but in respect of the balance although they have been allotted by the directors, no cash has been received by the company.

The company was entitled to commence business on 3rd August, 19...

The report to be dated 13th October, 19...

The following payments have been made: £1,000 to vendor; £200 for preliminary expenses; £750 for plant purchased; £315 wages and salaries; £75 rent of warehouse; £80 fittings and fixtures.

4. The directors of Whites Ltd. resolved on 1st May, 19.., that 2,000 ordinary shares of £1 each, 75p paid up, be forfeited for non-payment of the final call of 25p.

On 10th June, 19.., 1,000 of the shares were reissued as fully paid for 60p per share.

Show the Journal entries required to give effect to the foregoing, and state what the resultant balance on Forfeited Shares Account represents.

5. The Decoy Trading Co. Ltd. was registered with a nominal capital of £20,000 in shares of £1 each, 10,000 of which were issued payable as to 12½p on application, 12½p on allotment, 25p payable three months after allotment, and the balance to be called up as required. All moneys up to allotment were duly received, but as regards the call of 25p per share, a shareholder having 100 shares did not pay the amount due. Another shareholder who was allotted 50 shares paid them up in full.

Give the entries in the books of the company recording the above transactions and show how the capital should appear on the Balance Sheet.

6. A prospectus issued by a company invited applications for 200,000 shares of £1 each, payable 12½p per share on application, 12½p on allotment, 37½p three months after allotment, and 37½p six months after allotment; the vendor was to receive 20,000 fully paid shares as part payment of the purchase consideration of £160,000, made up as follows: land and buildings £60,000, plant £35,000, stock-in-trade £45,000, goodwill £20,000.

The offer was oversubscribed by 20,000 shares, and the amount due on allotment was received in full. £72,500 and £72,000 were received on first and second calls respectively.

Show the accounts concerned after opening the books, recording the above receipts on account of capital, and paying the balance of the purchase consideration to the vendor.

(Journal entries are not to be shown.) *(C.A. Inter.)*

7. Under the terms of a prospectus issued by North & South Ltd., the following applications for ordinary shares of £1 each were received with the deposit of 5p per share in each case—

John East, Southampton	100 shares
William West, Cardiff.	500 ,,
Robert Right, Leeds	2,000 ,,
Thomas Left, London.	5,000 ,,
Henry Centre, Liverpool	6,000 ,,
Richard Radius, Manchester	50 ,,

Allotments were made as follows—

On applications for 500 shares or less: in full.
On applications for more than 500 but not more than 3,000 shares: 25 per cent.
On applications for more than 3,000 shares: 10 per cent.
The amount payable on allotment was 25p per share.

Write up the application and allotment list with the necessary particulars for the issue of allotment letters, giving all the columns you deem necessary with proper headings.

8. A private limited company, being in need of further capital, issued debentures to the amount of £20,000. One of the directors took up £5,000 at a premium of £2 per cent; a friend of his subscribed for £5,000 at a premium of £1 per cent, while £10,000 was issued to the company's bankers by way of collateral security for a loan of £6,000. Show how these transactions would appear in the company's Balance Sheet.

9. Under its articles of association a company has power to apply profits in the purchase of its debenture stock. On 1st January, 19.., the credit balance of Profit and Loss Account was £27,000, the debentures issued and outstanding amounted to £43,000 and the cash balance was £22,000. The directors decided to purchase and cancel debenture stock, and on 1st January expended £16,000 for that purpose. The purchase price, inclusive of all charges, was £92 per £100 nominal.

Write up the accounts affected by these transactions. *(C.A. Inter.)*

10. A company took power in its articles of association to purchase out of profits its own debentures in the open market for cancellation.

On 31st December, 19.., the debentures outstanding amounted to £25,000 in debentures of £50 each, and there stood to the credit of Debenture Redemption Reserve Account a sum of £6,000, which had been provided out of profits of past years.

In January following the directors decided to utilize this reserve (the cash being available) in the purchase of its own debentures, and they bought these at an average price of £48 per debenture.

Show how this transaction should be recorded in the company's books, ignoring any question of charges or expenses. *(R.S.A.)*

11. Explain what is meant by the issue of debentures (a) at a premium, (b) at a discount.

In February, 19.., Universal Stores Ltd. offered for subscription 1,000 7 per cent Debentures of £100 each at the issue price of 94, payable £5 per Debenture on application, £50 on allotment, and the balance on 1st May, 19... Interest was to be payable half-yearly, on 30th June and 31st December, the first coupon, payable on 30th June, 19.., being for 2 per cent. The issue was fully taken up.

Set out any items relating to the above which should appear in the company's Profit and Loss Account for the year ended 31st December, 19.., or the accompanying Balance Sheet, assuming that half the discount is written off.

12. On 1st January, Year 6, a limited company issued 200 debentures of £100 each at a discount of 5 per cent.

The debentures were repayable at par on 31st December, Year 15, and in accordance with the terms of issue an accumulating sinking fund was created by the setting aside out of profits of an equal sum at 31st December in each year, the same being invested at compound interest.

Taking the annual amount thus set aside to be £1,590 and the rate of interest received on investment 5 per cent per annum—

(a) Set out the Sinking Fund Account and the Investment Account as they would appear in the company's books for the five years ended 31st December, Year 10, and show how the particulars as to the debenture and relative accounts will appear on the company's Balance Sheet on that date.

(b) Explain how the various accounts will be adjusted assuming that repayment of the debentures takes place on the due date.

Note. Income tax to be ignored. (*C.A. Inter.*)

13. The National Greyhound Syndicate Ltd. was incorporated on the 30th of September, 19.2, with a nominal capital of £50,000 and £10,000 first mortgage debenture stock. At the conclusion of the first year's trading, the directors, with the consent of the company and debenture stock holders, resolved to redeem the stock in the open market, from time to time, as the opportunity occurred, and it was decided to allocate one-third of the company's annual net profits as from the inception of the company for this specific purpose. The profits of the company were as follows—

						£
Year ended 30th September, 19.3.	.	.	.	.	850
„ „ „ „ 19.4.	.	.	.	.	1,350
„ „ „ „ 19.5.	.	.	.	.	950
„ „ „ „ 19.6.	.	.	.	.	1,275

Assume that the whole of the third share of profits was utilized in redeeming stock and that the various prices at which the stock was purchased for cancellation (based on weighted averages) were as follows—

19.3–.4. 77½ per cent of the nominal value.
19.4–.5. 80 „ „ „ „
19.5–.6. 85 „ „ „ „
19.6–.7. 90 „ „ „ „

You are required to submit—

(a) Debenture Stock Account.
(b) Debenture Stock Redemption Account.
(c) Reserve Account.
(d) Balance Sheet entries as at 30th September, 19.7, giving effect to the above decisions of the board, assuming that no dividends have been declared since the inception of the company.

14. The Soft Wood Co. Ltd. issued on 1st April, 19.1, £100,000 of second debentures at 5½ per cent, on condition that before paying, or providing for payment of any dividend on any shares or stock, the company should pay to the trustees for the debenture holders (immediately on the ascertainment of the result of the trading for the company's financial year which ends on 31st March), one-fourth part of the amount, if any, which might then otherwise be applied in payment of dividend on such shares or stock.

The company made a profit for the year ended 31st March, 19.2, of £14,500 and there was £1,500 brought forward from the previous year.

Draft the Journal entry necessary to make the company's Ledger show the liability to the trustees, and show how the items affected should appear on the Balance Sheet of the company. Ignore tax. (*C.A. Inter.*)

15. A company owned a mine which cost £40,000. They borrowed £25,000 on debentures at a discount of 5 per cent. It was agreed that until full repayment of this loan a Depletion Fund should be set aside to the extent of 5p a ton on every ton of ore raised and invested in "outside" securities. The company estimated that the true depletion was 3½p a ton.

During the first year the output was 120,000 tons and the fund was created and the necessary investment made on the last day of the financial year. The Profit and Loss Account for the first year before providing for the above was £8,200. Ignore interest.

Show Profit and Loss Account and (so far as relates to the above) the Balance Sheet.

16. On 30th June, 19.., the following balances stood in the books of a company—

	£
Four per cent First Mortgage Debenture Stock .	100,000
Debenture Redemption Fund	106,540
Debenture Redemption Fund Investments—	
£35,000 3 per cent British Electricity Stock . .	35,630
£40,000 5 per cent Exchequer Loan . . .	32,034
£30,000 4 per cent Consolidated Loan . . .	30,855
£8,000 3½ per cent Conversion Loan . . .	8,021

On the same day the investments were sold: Electricity Stock at 90, the 5 per cent Exchequer Loan at 91, the 4 per cent Consolidated Loan at 43, and the 3½ per cent Conversion Loan at 38. On 1st July the debentures were redeemed at a premium of 5 per cent.

Write up the accounts concerned (other than the Cash Account), bringing down the balances, if any, after the above transactions have been completed, and stating how such balances should be dealt with in the next Balance Sheet of the company.

(No Journal entries are required and brokers' charges may be ignored.)

(C.A. Inter.)

17. Make the necessary entries in Journal form to record the following transactions in the books of account of a limited company—

(1) 1st January, 19... The company purchased from vendors plant and machinery valued at £5,000, stock-in-trade valued at £2,500, and patent rights valued at £3,000.

(2) 10th January, 19... The company allotted to vendors in part payment of purchase of these assets, 800 fully paid ordinary shares of £10 each and issued 25 mortgage debentures of £100 each in satisfaction of the balance of purchase money.

(3) 15th January, 19... The company allotted to applicants 1,000 ordinary shares of £10 each, having received on same date £2 per share, the amount payable on application and allotment.

(4) 15th February, 19... First call of £2 per share made on 1,000 ordinary shares.

(5) 20th February, 19... Payment of first call received in full.

(6) 1st March, 19... The company received £2,500 in respect of book debts due to vendors, agreed to be collected on their behalf. Vendors agreed to accept thirty mortgage debentures of £100 each in payment thereof, and these debentures were issued to them on this date.

(7) 1st April, 19... Certain shareholders being desirous of paying up the balance due on their shares pending further calls, the company agreed to allow them 5 per cent per annum interest on the calls paid in advance. £3,000 was received on this date from shareholders under this arrangement.

(8) 15th April, 19... The company applied the sum of £2,300 in redeeming twenty debentures of £100 each at a premium of 10 per cent with £100 interest thereon to date of redemption.

In addition to the entries in the books of account, state briefly what other entries must be made in the records of the company in respect of the above transactions.

(C.A. Final.)

18. On 31st December, 19.., the North and South Iron Foundry Ltd. had ordinary share capital, authorized and fully subscribed, of £200,000 in shares of £10 each, and a general reserve of £150,000. During 19.. the capital was increased by £100,000 in new shares of £1 each, and the original shares were converted into shares of £1 each. Resolutions were duly passed whereby £100,000 of the reserve was distributed to the ordinary shareholders as bonus, and was applied in satisfaction of new shares issued to the shareholders at par. Set out the Journal entries and the accounts in full recording the foregoing transactions, and the information, in respect thereof, which should appear on the Balance Sheet of the company as on 31st December, 19... *(C.A. Final.)*

19. The following is a summarized Balance Sheet of Communications Ltd. at 30th June, 19..—

	£		£
Capital Issued and Fully Paid—		Sundry Assets. . . .	200,000
100,000 Ordinary £1 Shares	100,000	Bank Balance. . . .	85,000
50,000 Redeemable Prefer-			
ence £1 Shares . .	50,000		
Profit and Loss Account .	60,000		
Sundry Creditors . . .	75,000		
	£285,000		£285,000

Under powers contained in the articles of association, the company resolves to redeem the preference shares out of profits at a premium of 10p per share in accordance with Section 58 of the Companies Act, 1948.

Prepare the Ledger Accounts necessary for recording the transactions, and a summarized Balance Sheet showing the position on completion of the redemption.

20. The directors of a company contemplate making an issue of redeemable preference shares and ask your advice upon the following points—

(*a*) The procedure necessary before making the issue.

(*b*) The entries you would require in the books and the Balance Sheet when the issue is made.

(*c*) How redemption can, in due course, be effected.

(*d*) When redemption is made what effect will it have on the Balance Sheet of the company?

(*e*) Can redemption be made from the proceeds of another issue of shares and, if so, will additional duty be payable on the new issue?

State briefly your answers to these questions.   (*C.A. Inter.*)

21. A, B, and C, being in partnership, sharing profits in the proportions of four-ninths, three-ninths, and two-ninths respectively, agreed to sell their business as a going concern to a company in consideration of 18,000 fully paid ordinary shares of £1 each which had a market value at the date of sale of £1·25 per share.

The net value of the assets of the partnership which passed to the company was agreed at £21,500, and this amount was represented by the partners' Capital Accounts as follows—

A, £8,350; B, £7,000; C, £5,900.

Prepare a statement showing how, in your opinion, the shares should be divided, taking into consideration their market value.   (*C.A. Final.*)

22. A, B, and C are in partnership, sharing profits in the proportion 5, 3, and 2 respectively, and the firm's Balance Sheet as on 31st March, 19.., was as follows—

	£	£		£
Capitals—			Assets	98,238
A . . .	40,000		Cash	2,939
B . . .	30,000			
C . . .	18,000			
		88,000		
Current Accounts—.				
A . . .	3,190			
B . . .	1,173			
C . . .	841			
		5,204		
Creditors . . .		7,973		
		£101,177		£101,177

As on 1st April, 19.., the business was sold to a limited company on the following terms—

(1) The partners were to withdraw £1,704 in cash. Of this A took £1,190, B £173, and C £341.

(2) The company was to take over the assets, and the balance of the cash, and the liabilities, in consideration for a sum of £100,000, to be satisfied by the issue to the partners of £15,000 5 per cent debentures, £36,500 in 7 per cent preference shares, and £48,500 in ordinary shares.

(3) As between themselves, the partners agreed that the purchase consideration should be divided as follows—

Debentures: A £10,000, and B £5,000.
Preference shares in the proportion of their original Capital Accounts after deducting amounts satisfied by the issue of debentures.

Set out the accounts showing the dissolution of the partnership and showing how the shares were divided between the partners. (*L.C.C.*)

23. The following Balance Sheet shows the position of John Thynne & Co. Ltd. at 31st October, 19.., when it was decided to dispose of the business as a going concern to the Hayden Manufacturing Co. Ltd.

BALANCE SHEET AT 31ST OCTOBER, 19..

	£			£
Capital and Surplus—		*Fixed Assets—*		
Share Capital:		Freehold Land and Buildings .		58,000
Authorized:		Leasehold Property . .		7,000
100,000 Ordinary Shares of £1		Plant and Machinery . .		51,500
each	100,000	Motor Vehicles . .		3,400
		Fixtures and Fittings . .		750
Issued:		Loose Tools . . .		6,800
99,750 Ordinary Shares		Patterns . . .		900
of £1 each, fully paid . .	99,750	Patents and Trade-marks . .		1,200
Revenue Reserves:		Goodwill		15,000
General . . £10,000				
Profit and Loss Account 25,000				144,550
	35,000	*Current Assets—*		
		Stock . . 27,500		
	134,750	Debtors . . 35,000		
Current Liabilities and Provi-		Investments . . 10,500		
sions—		Cash . . 100		
Bank Overdraft . . £18,050				73,100
Loan . . . 20,000				
Creditors . . 34,500				
Bills Payable . 6,350				
Superannuation Fund . 4,000				
	82,900			
	£217,650			£217,650

The vendor company agrees to sell the assets on the basis of the above Balance Sheet, subject to the following increases—

Plant and Machinery.	.	.	.	.	25 per cent	
Stock	.	.	.	.	20	,,
Motor Vehicles.	.	.	.	.	10	,,
Loose Tools	.	.	.	.	30	,,

The item Goodwill was to be eliminated, and the investments were to be taken over at market price, namely, £9,000.

The liabilities were assumed at their book value.

The purchase consideration was discharged by the issue of 50,000 ordinary shares of £1 each at £1·50 per share, £25,000 5 per cent debentures, and the balance in cash.

Show the Journal entries necessary to give effect to the above scheme in the purchasing company's books.

24. On 1st January, 19. ., a company with a nominal capital of £100,000 in ordinary shares of £1 each was formed to take over the business and assets of Richard Best & Sons at the following valuation—

	£
Leasehold Land and Premises	20,000
Goodwill	25,000
Books Debts (guaranteed by the Vendors)	8,000
Stock	7,000

There were no amounts owing to creditors.

The public subscribed for £23,500 of the capital. The vendors took £8,500 of the purchase money in cash and the remainder in fully paid shares; 150 shares belonging to the public were forfeited for non-payment of the two last calls of 25p each, 50p per share having been paid thereon.

At the end of the first year the figures extracted from the company's books were as under—

	£
Purchases	37,500
Sales.	49,000
Discounts Received	475
Discounts Allowed (of which £135 was in respect of Debts taken over by the Company)	900
Trade Expenses	1,300
Advertising	2,500
Wages	3,700
Salaries	1,000
Rent.	600
Rates	250
Directors' Fees	400
Trade Debtors	13,150
Trade Creditors	6,000
Cash in Hand	4,400
Machinery Purchased	10,000
Interim Dividend paid	1,850
Bad Debts (of which £350 was in respect of Debts taken over by the Company)	850
Stock	12,400

Write off £400 from Leasehold Land and Premises Account and prepare the company's Balance Sheet as at 31st December, 19. ., and Trading and Profit and Loss Account for the year (not for publication).   (*C.I.S. Inter.*)

25. The partners of a private firm decide to form their business into a limited company. The assets stand in the firm's books as follows—

	£
Land and Buildings at Cost	7,000
Plant and Machinery, *less* Depreciation . .	5,000
Stock-in-trade at Cost Price	3,000
	£15,000

These assets are sold to the company for £12,000, and the following accounts are opened in the books of the new company in respect thereof—

	£
Land and Buildings	6,000
Plant and Machinery.	4,000
Stock	2,000
	£12,000

At the end of the first year's trading one-half of the old stock in still unsold, and is included in stock on the basis of its original cost price, the new stock on hand being valued on a similar basis. The profit for the year, after providing for depreciation on plant and machinery, is £1,500, which the directors recommend to be distributed as dividend.

From the information before you, what observations, if any, would you make on these accounts? (*C.A. Final.*)

26. H. Jones, J. Baird, and R. Woods, who carried on the same class of business, decided to combine and form a private limited company, the various assets and liabilities being taken over by the company as at 1st January, 19...

The capital of the company was to be £120,000 in £1 shares, all of which were to be issued, fully paid, to the three vendors in proportion to the interests handed over. As at 31st December previous the various assets and liabilities were as follows—

H. JONES. Stock, £10,845; sundry debtors, £16,050; bills receivable, £4,746; cash at bank, £2,685; sundry creditors, £9,000; bills payable, £6,000.

J. BAIRD. Stock, £14,593; sundry debtors, £27,740; bills receivable, £4,750; bank overdraft, £3,870; sundry creditors, £17,445.

R. WOODS. Stock, £24,000; sundry debtors, £53,282; cash at bank, £18,630; sundry creditors, £46,146; bills payable, £17,556; reserve fund, £15,000.

(*a*) Draft the opening Journal entries for the limited company, and
(*b*) Prepare Balance Sheet as at 1st January, 19.., preliminary expenses, etc., £1,500 having been paid.

27. A limited company is formed to purchase an existing business with a nominal capital of £200,000, one-half in ordinary and one-half in 5 per cent preference shares of £1 each. 6,000 of the ordinary shares are issued at a premium of 25p per share, the preference shares being all issued at par, 25p per share being payable on application and 50p on allotment in each case. £20,000 6 per cent debentures are underwritten at 98 per cent. On account of the purchase money of £54,000 a sum of £8,000 is paid in discharge of the liabilities of the vendor, and the following assets taken over—

Stock-in-trade £12,000, book debts £20,000, machinery and plant £6,000.

Journalize the entries necessary for recording the purchase in the books of the company. (*C.A. Inter.*)

28. The Trial Balance at 31st December, 19.., of a company contained the following—

	£
10,000 6 per cent Preference Shares of £1 each, fully paid	10,000
Preference Dividend for the year	480

Assuming income tax at 40 per cent, state the correcting entry which would appear to be required.

29. On 1st April, 19.., Marie & Bright Ltd. was incorporated for the purpose of taking over, and carrying on, a business as from that date.

For the year ended 31st December the total turnover amounted to £50,000, namely, from 1st January to 31st March £10,000, and £40,000 for the remaining nine months of the year.

The accounts for the whole year showed a gross profit of £15,000 and a total expenditure for the year of £9,900. The expenditure included directors' fees amounting to £300.

What portion of the profit should be regarded as being earned prior to incorporation, taking turnover as a basis, and what is the amount of the profit subsequent to incorporation?

30. Submit a Balance Sheet as at 31st December, Year 6, of A B C Ltd., a manufacturing public company, showing how the following matters should be recorded—

Authorized and issued capital 200,000 (£1) ordinary shares; 120,000 (£1) 5 per cent redeemable preference shares; redeemable by annual drawings of 10,000 shares at a premium of 25p per share on 30th November in each year, the yearly dividend being paid on that date. First drawing November, Year 6.

Profit and loss balance to credit at 1st January, Year 6, £150,000.

Profit on trading for year is £60,000.

The company had applied for and had been allotted 99,000 ordinary shares of £1 each out of a total capitalization of 100,000 shares in L M N Ltd., and 50p per share had been called and paid. A B C Ltd. had also advanced on loan at short notice to L M N Ltd., £15,000. Stocks and shares held by A B C Ltd. prior to the aforementioned purchase had cost £175,000 and were quoted on the Stock Exchange at £155,000.

During the year certain shares had been sold at a profit of £18,000.

General reserve at 1st January, Year 6, was £82,000.

The difference between the two sides of the Balance Sheet after recording the above items represents the net difference between the other assets and liabilities and may be entered as one sum on the Balance Sheet.

31. The books of the Alpha Beta Mining Co. Ltd. on 30th June, 19.., contained the undermentioned balances—

	£
Capital (Authorized and Issued) in Shares of £1 each . . .	600,000
Reserve Fund	24,314
Profit and Loss—Undivided Profit at 1st July, 19.. . . .	18,078
Sundry Creditors	73,210
Sales of Ore	524,004
Leasehold Mine, Plant, Machinery, etc., at cost . . .	600,000
New Works Expenditure	11,416
Sundry Debtors	77,970
Bills Receivable	7,404
Cash at Bank and in Hand	15,358
Investments at cost	15,480
Ore Stock, 1st July, 19..	1,749
Interim Dividend, 1st January, 19..	45,000
Wages	263,647
Rents and Royalties	35,791
Wood, Stores, etc.	52,044
Power Expenses	19,752
Wagon Hire, Freight, and Carriage	56,224
Surface Damages	1,340
Discounts and Allowances	13,396
Salaries	5,499
Directors' and Auditors' Fees and Law Charges . . .	3,954
Rates and Insurance	8,051
General Office Expenses	3,741
Subscriptions and Donations	1,790

You are asked to prepare Trading and Profit and Loss Account for the year ended and Balance Sheet as at 30th June, 19...

Note. Stock of ore on hand at 30th June, 19.., was valued at £2,531.

32. Square Deals Ltd. has an authorized share capital of £1,000,000, divided into 250,000 6 per cent cumulative preference shares of £1,700,000 ordinary shares of £1, and 200,000 deferred shares of 25p. On 31st March, 19.6, there had been issued 200,000 of the preference shares (all fully paid), 550,000 of the ordinary shares (400,000 fully paid and 150,000 on which 50p had been called up, but a call of 25p was outstanding on 600 of the latter) and all the deferred shares (fully paid).

The accounts for the year to 31st March, 19.6, showed a disposable balance, after deducting the interim dividends paid, of £68,178, which was dealt with as follows—

(a) £25,000 was transferred to general reserve, which previously stood at £125,000.

(b) Six months final dividend was paid on the preference shares, a final dividend of 6 per cent on the ordinary shares, calculated on the amounts called up, and a dividend for the year of 10 per cent on the deferred shares.

(c) The balance was carried forward.

In November, 19.6, the directors declared interim dividends of 3 per cent on the preference shares and 4 per cent on the ordinary shares, calculated on the amounts called up.

Interest on calls in arrear was payable at the rate of 10 per cent per annum. In the accounts to 31st March, 19.6, the amount of such interest outstanding was calculated and brought into account, being for two years on the 25p call on 600 shares. On 1st December, 19.6, the calls in arrear were paid up with interest to date.

In addition to the balances disclosed by the above information, the following were standing on the company's books as on 31st March, 19.7—

BALANCES

	£
Trade Debtors	95,347
Trade Creditors	14,748
Leasehold Property at cost	240,150
Leasehold Redemption Fund, 31st March, 19.6 . . .	34,720
Leasehold Redemption Fund Policy, 31st March, 19.6 . .	34,720
Premiums paid on above during year	4,500
Machinery and Plant, 31st March, 19.6 (cost £190,000) . .	124,800
Machinery and Plant bought during year	6,300
Patents and Trade Marks at cost	230,000
Vans, Lorries, and Cars, 31st March, 19.6 (cost £10,000) . .	7,250
Van sold during year (book value £580; cost £1,000) . . .	423
Bank Overdraft (secured).	12,371
Loose Tools, 31st March, 19.6, plus Purchases . . .	1,742
Stock, 31st March, 19.6	242,393
Cash in Hand.	419
Purchases, less Returns	326,623
Sales, less Returns	590,105
Directors' Remuneration	15,000
Factory Power and Expenses	15,663
Office and Showroom Expenses	3,592
Salaries and Wages, Factory	132,646
Salaries and Wages, Office and Showroom. . . .	6,375
Travellers' Salaries and Commission	10,974
Heating and Lighting	1,868
Discount (Cr. Balance)	2,332
Transfer Fees	34
Provision for Bad Debts, 31st March, 19.6 . . .	1,750
Advertising	9,347
Legal Expenses and Audit Fee (£500 not fixed at General Meeting)	612
Corporation Tax (Cr. balance)	150

You are required to prepare the company's Manufacturing and Profit and Loss Accounts for the year ended 31st March, 19.7, and a Profit and Loss Account for the year and Balance Sheet for publication purposes. In preparing these accounts the following information and instructions are to be taken into account—

(a) The stock-in-trade on hand at 31st March, 19.7, was valued at £238,689, the loose tools at £1,375, and the vans, lorries, and cars at £5,730.

(b) The managing director is entitled to a commission equal to 5 per cent of the net profit (calculated to the nearest £).

(c) The bad debts provision is to be made up to £2,000.

(d) The Heating and Lighting is to be apportioned, four-fifths to the factory, and one-fifth to the office and showroom.

(e) The old plant and machinery is to be depreciated 10 per cent (on book value) and the new 4 per cent.

(f) Factory wages were accrued and unpaid amounting to £123, and heating and lighting £272.

(g) The surrender value of the policy at 31st March, 19.7, was £39,521.

(h) £750 of the expenditure on advertising is to be carried forward.

(i) Provide for £8,000 Corporation Tax on current year's profit.

(j) There are three directors of Square Deals Ltd. The amount shown in respect of Directors' Remuneration comprises:

	Fees £	Salary £	Total £
G. High—Chairman	500	7,000	7,500
N. Control—Managing Director . . .	300	3,800	4,100
B. Low—Director	100	3,300	3,400
	£900	£14,100	£15,000

(k) The directors recommend the following:

(i) Transfer from general reserve of £20,000.

(ii) Payment of the six months final dividend of 4 per cent on the ordinary shares, calculated on the amount called up, and a dividend for the year of 10 per cent on the deferred shares.

(iii) The balance to be carried forward.

Assume Income Tax at 40 per cent.

(l) The leasehold property is occupied under a lease which has less than 50 years to run.   (L.C.C.)

33. The directors of Givortake Ltd. ask you to prepare the Balance Sheet as on 31st December, 19.4, and Profit and Loss Account for the year ended on that date, in a form suitable for presentation to the members at the annual general meeting.

The balances on the books after the Trading Account are as follows—

Debits	£	Debits—(contd.)	£
SubsidiaryCo.,CurrentAccount	6,500	Balance at Bankers . . .	88,250
Investments in Subsidiary Co. at cost—		Freehold Properties at cost .	500,000
Shares £50,000, 5% Debentures £20,000 . . .	70,000	Plant and Machinery at cost (£300,000), less depreciation .	200,000
Other Investments at cost—		*Credits*	
Extras Ltd., 10,000 Ordinary Shares of £1 each, 75p paid	5,000	Shares issued—	
Imports Ltd., 5,000 Ordinary Shares of £1 each, fully paid	5,000	Preference (300,000) . .	300,000
		Ordinary (300,000) . .	300,000
Stock (as valued by the directors)	81,650	Profit and Loss Account . .	45,000
Preference Dividend paid for half-year to 30th June, 19.4 (Gross)	9,000	Provision for Depreciation of Freehold Properties . .	70,000
Debenture Interest paid for half-year to 30th June, 19.4 (Gross)	5,000	5% Debentures, secured by a floating charge on all the assets	200,000
Tax Reserve Certificates .	12,500	Trade Creditors . . .	40,500
Trade Debtors . . .	105,800	Trading Account balance .	100,000
		Interest on Investments (Gross)	2,000
		Taxation Account . . .	31,200

The authorized capital of £800,000 (400,000 6 per cent cumulative preference and 400,000 ordinary shares) was increased during the year by the creation of 25,000 deferred shares of £1 each, following an agreement between the company and Exploiters Ltd., whereby the latter waived certain prospective rights against the company. The agreement was dated 16th December, and the shares were allotted, credited as fully paid up, on that date.

The managing director is entitled by his agreement to a commission of 3 per cent of the net profits for the year before providing for such commission, directors' fees, and all taxation, and before crediting interest on investments.

The directors' fees are fixed under the Articles at 5 per cent of the net profit for the year, after providing for the year's dividend (gross) on the preference shares, in addition to all expenses (including such fees), but before crediting interest in investments and before all taxation charges.

The estimated taxation liabilities on the profits of the year to 31st December, 19.4, are: Corporation Tax, £38,000.

The directors propose to pay the outstanding half-year's Preference Dividend and to recommend an Ordinary Dividend of 10 per cent. The Deferred Shares do not rank for dividend until the following year.

You ascertain the following—

(a) £50,000 Depreciation on Freehold Properties and Plant and Machinery has been charged in the Trading Account. The Audit Fee for the year of £850 and audit expenses of £55 have been agreed and are to be provided for.

(b) Extras Ltd. is an associated company.

(c) The investment in Imports Ltd. is of a temporary nature, and this company's shares are quoted on the Stock Exchange on 31st December, 19.4, at 75p–85p.

(d) A dividend of 10 per cent (less tax) was received during the year from Imports Ltd. Interest on investments also includes a year's Debenture Interest from the subsidiary company, the balance being from Extras Ltd.

(e) The company had entered into contracts for capital expenditure of £25,000 for which no provision has been made in the books.

(f) The turnover for the year ended 31st December, 19.4, was £628,550 derived from the sale of products for credit and for cash.

(g) The subsidiary company is Ayardorto Ltd., registered in England. Givortake's holding in Ayardorto Ltd. is 50,000 Ordinary Shares of £1 each and this represents 60 per cent of the nominal value of the Ordinary Share Capital of Ayardorto Ltd.

(h) The issued share capital of Extras Ltd. is 80,000 Ordinary Shares of £1 each. Extras Ltd. is registered in England.

The amount provided for Corporation Tax on the profits of the year ended 31st December, 19.4 was £32,000. The actual liability has been agreed with the Inland Revenue at £32,650. Assume the rate of Corporation Tax and of Income Tax to be 40 per cent.

There are three directors of the company. The managing director, N. Charge is full-time; the chairman O. Seer is part-time; A. Sleep, the third director, is also part-time. The directors' fees are payable: chairman 45 per cent, managing director 35 per cent, and director 20 per cent. *(Adapted from C.A. Final.)*

34. Write a short criticism of the following Balance Sheet.

BALANCE SHEET, 31ST DECEMBER

	£		£	£
Authorized Capital—		Investments at Cost—		
7% Cumulative Preference Shares of £1		Shares in Subsidiary and Associ-		
each fully paid	16,384	ated Companies	58,110	
Ordinary Shares of £1 each fully paid	32,238	Other Industrial Investments	700	
Deferred Shares of 50p each fully paid	9,548			58,810
		Preliminary Expenses		1,261
	58,170	Loans to Subsidiary Companies		8,345
General Reserve—		Sundry Debtors, including Income Tax		
Amount Transferred from Share £		suffered on Dividend Received		754
Premium Account 291		Office Furniture, etc.		40
Amount Transferred from Profit		Cash at Bankers and in Hand		661
and Loss Account 409				
	700			
Loans from Subsidiary and Associated				
Companies	7,651			
Creditors	846			
Profit and Loss Account before pro- £				
viding for Corporation Tax for the				
year ended 31st December. 4,567				
Less—				
Amount carried to Gen- £				
eral Reserve 409				
Corporation Tax 125				
Carried forward 83				
— 617				
		Note. Contingent liabilities existed at		
Profits recommended for Dividend 3,950		31st December in connection with offers		
Less—		open at that date, shares of certain com-		
Interim Preference Divi- £		panies for cash or by the issue of share		
dend 561		capital, and in connection with the guar-		
Interim Ordinary Divi-		antee of a bank overdraft of a subsidiary		
dend, 3% 968		company.		
— 1,529				
Balance available for further Distribution 2,421				
To be carried forward as above 83				
£69,871				£69,871

(C.A. Final.)

35. Gamma Delta Ltd. has a large number of shareholders. When a dividend is declared, the sum necessary to pay the same is transferred to a special "Dividend Account" at the bank, and after a lapse of six months any balance on this account is transferred to a "Deposit Account for Dividends Unpaid", in which are collected all unpaid dividends since the incorporation of the company.

Describe a method of record which will enable the various unpaid warrants from time to time to be identified and reconciled with the balance of this Deposit Account, and describe the procedure to be adopted when a warrant (say) two years old is presented by a shareholder for payment. *(L.C.C.)*

36. McArthurs Ltd. presented accounts to their shareholders for the year ended 31st December, 19.., showing a profit for the year of £19,784, and a balance brought forward from the previous year of £3,745.

It was proposed (*a*) to carry £5,000 to the Reserve Account (making that account £20,000); (*b*) to pay the half-year's dividend due on the 7 per cent preference capital (£50,000); and (*c*) to pay a dividend of 10 per cent on the ordinary capital (£100,000); and (*d*) to carry forward the balance to next year.

As on 1st February following, the warrants representing the above dividends had all been duly paid, with the exception of those in respect of holdings of 500 and 100 ordinary shares, which remained unpresented.

You are required to show the Appropriation Account presented to the shareholders and state the entries necessary to record the above particulars as on 1st February. Take tax at 40 per cent. *(L.C.C.)*

37. On 31st October, 19.., the directors of the G. H. Co. Ltd. declared and paid an interim dividend at the rate of 6 per cent per annum in respect of the half-year ended 30th September, 19.., on 100,000 ordinary shares of £1 each fully paid, held by a large number of shareholders. W. Jones holding fifty shares and J. Brown holding five shares had not "claimed" their dividends. State what entries should be made in the books of the company on 31st March next, the close of the financial year. Take tax at 40 per cent. *(C.A. Final.)*

38. The following particulars have been extracted from the Balance Sheet of Soleil d'Or Ltd., as on 31st December, 19...

	CAPITAL	£	£
Nominal:	10,000 5 per cent Preference Shares of £5 each .	50,000	
	100,000 Ordinary Shares of £1 each . . .	100,000	
		£150,000	
Issued:	5,000 5 per cent Preference Shares of £5 each .	25,000	
	50,000 Ordinary Shares of £1 each . . .	50,000	
			75,000
Reserve Fund			20,000
Profit and Loss Account (Balance)			12,000

During the year 19.. resolutions were duly passed as follows—

(1) A resolution converting the preference shares into preference shares of £1 each.

(2) A resolution declaring a bonus of 20 per cent on the ordinary shares to be provided as to £6,000, out of the reserve fund, and as to the remainder out of the balance of Profit and Loss Account.

The bonus to be satisfied by the issue of one fully paid ordinary share for five ordinary shares held.

Give the Journal entries which are necessary to carry out the above resolutions, and show how they would affect the Balance Sheet of the company as on 31st December, 19... Assume that the profit for the year 19.. amounted to £4,000. *(C.A. Final.)*

39. The directors of a limited company, believing that the undertaking is making substantial profits, desire to declare an interim dividend.

As auditor to the company, the directors ask you (*a*) whether they are entitled to do this, (*b*) whether in the circumstances it will be wise and, if so, (*c*) what rate of dividend should be paid. No accounts have been prepared since the publication of the annual accounts seven months previously.

What advice should you offer, and what special circumstances would need consideration in arriving at your decision? (*C.A. Final.*)

40. Gay & Perkins Ltd., a company which is neither a holding nor a subsidiary company, was registered with a nominal capital of £270,000 divided into 100,000 6 per cent preference shares of £1 each, 150,000 ordinary shares of £1 each, and 200,000 deferred shares of 10p each. After the ordinary shares had received a dividend of 10 per cent in respect of any year, any further sums distributed by way of dividend were to be divisible equally between the ordinary and deferred shareholders.

Accounts were made up annually to 31st March. The balance at credit of Profit and Loss Account at 31st March, 19.7, was £6,159.

On 31st March, 19.8, all the ordinary and deferred shares and 50,000 of the preference shares were issued and fully paid, and the dividend on the preference shares had been paid up to 30th September, 19.7; 25,000 of these preference shares had been offered for subscription to existing shareholders at 107½p per share on 1st October, 19.7. The issue was fully subscribed and paid up.

At the annual general meeting, held on 17th June, 19.8, the following recommendations of the directors were confirmed—

(*a*) To pay the final six months' dividend on the preference shares, and dividends for the year of 12 per cent on the ordinary shares and at the appropriate rate on the deferred shares.

(*b*) To write £5,000 off the Goodwill Account (previously standing at £20,000) and to transfer £3,500 to general reserve (previously standing at £2,172).

(*c*) To carry forward the balance.

In addition to the balances resulting from the above particulars the following were extracted from the company's books as on 31st March, 19.8—

BALANCES	£
Gross Trading Profit for the year	109,357
Freehold Land and Factory (at cost)	87,000
Machinery 31st March, 19.7 (cost £150,000)	105,480
Machinery and Plant sold, 1st April, 19.7	600
Stock, 31st March, 19.8	27,156
Work in Progress, 31st March, 19.8	34,237
Sundry Creditors	22,989
Sundry Debtors	33,175
Office Furniture, 31st March, 19.7 (cost £1,000)	720
Cash at Bank and in Hand	27,367
Office Salaries (including Managing Director, £3,000)	13,365
Travellers' Salaries and Commission	5,174
Bad Debts Provision	275
Office Expenses	1,731
Directors' Emoluments	4,500
Office Rent and Rates	2,507
Preference Dividend, paid 30th September, 19.7 (*less* Income Tax at 40 per cent)	450
Corporation Tax (*Dr.* balance)	565

You are required to prepare the company's Profit and Loss Account for the year ended 31st March, 19.8, and a Balance Sheet as on that date for publication purposes.

When preparing these accounts the following information and instructions are to be taken into consideration.

(*a*) The bad debts provision is to be made up to an amount equal to 4 per cent on the sundry debtors.

(*b*) Depreciation is to be provided as follows: machinery, 15 per cent; office furniture, 5 per cent, on written-down values.

(*c*) The machinery sold during the year stood in the books at £840 (original cost £1,000).

(*d*) The estimated Corporation Tax Liability arising out of these accounts is £25,600.

There are three directors, two are full-time and the chairman is part-time. Directors' Emoluments comprises the other full-time director's salary of £2,750, the chairman's fees of £1,000, and the managing director's fees of £750.

The turnover for the year derived from the sale of the company's product to customers was £343,720.   (*Adapted from C.A. Final.*)

41. The directors of a limited company possessing secret reserves, estimated to amount to £80,000, decide to adjust the Balance Sheet so as to disclose the true position. The £80,000 is made up as follows—

	£
Deduction of 10 per cent from the value of the Stock . . .	8,500
Profit on the Sale of Investments operating to reduce the Value of the remaining Investments below Cost and Market Value . .	10,000
Over-provision for Income Tax.	5,000
Under-valuation of Machinery, resulting from excessive Provision for Depreciation	55,000
Motor Vans written off	1,500

That portion of the £80,000 representing the extent to which revenue has been penalized in the past is to be placed to a reserve for the equalization of dividends. The remainder is to be placed to a pension fund, an equivalent amount to be specifically invested in a gilt-edged security so as to provide for the payment of the pensions.

Give Journal entries to record these operations, and state what effect the adjustments might have on the costing calculations of the company.   (*C.A. Final.*)

42. The annual accounts of Rayon d'Or Ltd. showed a balance to the credit of Profit and Loss Account of £5,950 as on 31st December, 19... The nominal capital of the company consisted of 10,000 shares of £1 each, all of which had been subscribed and fully paid up. At the annual meeting in February, 19.., it was decided (*a*) to increase the nominal capital of the company to £15,000 by the creation of 5,000 6 per cent preference shares of £1 each; (*b*) to pay a dividend for the year 19.. of 55 per cent, 50 per cent to be discharged by the issue of fully paid preference shares at par, and the balance, 5 per cent, to be paid in cash.

Give the entries necessary to record these transactions.   (*R.S.A.*)

43. A successful rubber plantation company found that its £5 shares rose to such a premium that the market became restricted. A special resolution was therefore duly passed dividing the company's 10,000 ordinary shares of £5 each into 200,000 shares of 25p each.

Show the entries which are necessary in order to give effect to the above resolution.
(*R.S.A.*)

44. The capital of Edward Herriott Ltd. consisted of 100,000 shares of £5 each, all fully paid. The reserve fund amounted to £200,000. Further capital was needed for the development of the business, and it was decided to divide each £5 share into three ordinary shares of £1 each and two 5 per cent preference shares of £1 each. Both classes of shares were to be deemed as paid up to the extent of 50p per share. It was also decided to make a call of 50p per share on both classes of shares, 25p per share of which was to be met by a transfer from the reserve and 25p per share was payable in cash. Give the entries necessary to record these transactions.   (*L.C.C.*)

45. Forsyth & Co. Ltd., finding themselves unable to make repayment to loan creditors amounting to £45,000, entered into negotiations for the sale to Bain, Pearson & Co. Ltd. of their Birmingham Branch, the book value of which was £50,000. (Assets £60,000, liabilities £10,000.)

Ultimately the sale was carried through, the purchase price, £60,000, being discharged by the issue to Forsyth & Co. Ltd. of 60,000 £1 ordinary shares, fully paid in Bain, Pearson & Co. Ltd.

By arrangement, Forsyth & Co.'s loan creditors agreed to take in repayment of their loans, 30,000 £1 shares in Bain, Pearson & Co. Ltd., and these shares were duly transferred to them by Forsyth & Co. Ltd.

Frame the Journal entries necessary to give effect to the above transactions in the books of Forsyth & Co. Ltd.

46. The business of X Ltd. is to own and let a sports ground, pavilion and equipment, which stand in its books at £10,800 and are let to the N Sports Club for a rent of £700 a year; the rent has been paid to 31st March, 19.7.

The issued share capital of the company is 480 shares of £5 each, fully paid. There are also outstanding 200 6 per cent debentures of £25 each, on which interest has been paid to 30th November, 19.7, and there is a loan of £4,000 on mortgage at 5 per cent on which interest has been paid to 31st December, 19.7.

On 31st March, 19.8, the company owed £78 to sundry creditors and had a debit balance on Profit and Loss Account of £128.

On the same date the N Sports Club's only assets were stocks valued at £80, and it owed £48 for wages and £122 for supplies.

A reconstruction as on 1st April, 19.8, was arranged, with the consent of all parties, on the following basis—

(1) X Ltd. to go into liquidation and to sell its assets to a new company, N Sports Club Ltd.

(2) N Sports Club Ltd. to take over the liabilities of X Ltd., except that to the debenture holders.

(3) The shareholders to receive a deferred share of 25p fully paid in N Sports Club Ltd. for each share in X Ltd.

(4) The debenture holders to receive a 10 per cent preference share of £5 fully paid in N Sports Club Ltd. for each debenture in X Ltd.

(5) The mortgage debt (including accrued interest) to be reduced by immediate payment to £3,500.

(6) N Sports Club Ltd. to issue 150 5 per cent debentures of £10 for cash at par.

(7) The club to surrender its lease, and N Sports Club Ltd. to take over its assets and liabilities.

These arrangements were duly carried through on 1st April, 19.8.

Show in Journal form the entries, including cash entries, which should be made in the books of N Sports Club Ltd. on 1st April, 19.8.

Ignore costs. Take Income Tax at 40 per cent. (*C.A. Final.*)

47. The Staffordshire Car Co. Ltd., having obtained the sanction of the debenture stockholders and the Court, decided to reduce its capital, and reorganize as at 30th September, 19.., and the following Balance Sheet shows the position as at that date—

THE STAFFORDSHIRE CAR CO. LTD.
BALANCE SHEET, 30TH SEPTEMBER, 19..

	£			£
Share Capital: Authorized, Issued, and Fully-paid:		Fixed Assets—		
15% Preference Shares of £1		Land, Buildings, and Plant .		46,700
each	40,000	Current Assets—		
Deferred Shares of £1 each .	100,000	Stock . .	£81,250	
	————	Debtors . .	46,750	
	140,000	Cash at Bank .	2,450	
Reserves	45,350		————	130,450
	————			
	185,350			
Less Profit and Loss Account	55,650			
	————			
	129,700			
10% Mortgage Debenture Stock	20,000			
Creditors	27,450			
	————			————
	£177,150			£177,150

The following are the details of the scheme—

(1) Each £1 of debenture stock is to be exchanged for 50p of new 12 per cent debenture stock, one new 20 per cent preference share of 25p, and one new deferred share of 25p.

(2) Each existing preference share is to be reduced from £1 to 37½p, of which 20p will be represented by new 20 per cent preference shares, and 17½p by new deferred shares.

(3) Each existing deferred share is to be reduced from £1 to 25p, and then both preference and deferred shares are to be consolidated into shares of £1 each.

The reduction of capital and the reserves are to be applied in eliminating the debit balance of Profit and Loss Account, and the balance, if any, is to be utilized in writing down the land, buildings, and stock *pro rata*.

(*a*) Submit Journal entries giving effect to the above scheme; and

(*b*) Draft the abbreviated opening Balance Sheet after reconstruction.

48. The books of Blank Co. Ltd. contained the following balances at 30th November, 19..—

	£	£
Share Capital—12,000 Shares		12,000
Creditors		14,000
Patents	12,000	
Plant and Machinery	4,000	
Stock	3,000	
Debtors	5,000	
Cash	125	
Preliminary Expenses	725	
Profit and Loss Account	1,150	
	£26,000	£26,000

The company being unable to raise further capital, and the patents standing in the books at a figure largely in excess of their value, the following scheme was submitted to the shareholders and creditors—

(*a*) The company to go into voluntary liquidation and a new company, Blank Co. (19..) Ltd., to be formed with a nominal capital of £20,000 to take over the assets and liabilities.

(*b*) Liabilities to be discharged by the new company as follows: preferential creditors for £200 to be paid in full, and unsecured creditors to be paid 25p in the £ in cash and 50p in the £ in 6 per cent debentures in the new company.

(*c*) 12,000 shares of £1 each, 50p per share paid, to be issued to the shareholders of the old company, the balance of 50p per share being payable on allotment.

(*d*) The costs of liquidation to be paid by the new company as part of the purchase consideration. These amounted to £175.

Assuming that the scheme has been approved and sanctioned, you are asked—

(*a*) To prepare Realization Account of Blank Co. Ltd.

(*b*) To write up Cash Book and Journal entries for opening the books of Blank Co. (19..) Ltd.

(*c*) To prepare Balance Sheet on completion.

49. A company having a paid-up capital of £500,000 (300,000 8 per cent cumulative preference shares of £1 each and 200,000 ordinary shares of £1 each) decides on a scheme for reduction of capital which is duly authorized.

The scheme provides as follows—

(1) Preference shareholders, to receive:

(*a*) One 6 per cent cumulative preference share of £1
One 10 per cent preferred ordinary share of £1
One ordinary share of 25p

for every three 8 per cent cumulative preference shares held.

(*b*) The arrears of preference dividend amount to £48,000, which is to be settled by the issue of one ordinary share of 25p per £1 of arrears.

(2) Ordinary shareholders to receive one new ordinary share of 25p (fully paid up) for each old ordinary share held.

The Balance Sheet of the company is as follows—

	£			£
Capital—		Fixed Assets—		
300,000 8% Cumulative Preference Shares of £1 each	300,000	Buildings (less Depreciation)	£100,000	
200,000 Ordinary Shares of £1 each	200,000	Plant (less Depreciation)	80,000	
				180,000
	500,000	Current Assets—		
Less Profit and Loss Account	114,000	Stock	£65,000	
		Investments at Cost	170,000	
	386,000	Sundry Debtors	70,500	
Sundry Creditors	100,000	Bank and Cash	500	
				306,000
	£486,000			£486,000

The scheme further provides that the value of the reduction in capital will be utilized as follows—

(1) Write off balance at debit of Profit and Loss Account.
(2) Reduce by 10 per cent the value of (a) buildings and (b) plant.
(3) Reduce by 15 per cent the value of investments.
(4) Any balance remaining to reduce further the value of investments.

Frame Journal entries for recording the foregoing in the company's books and show Balance Sheet giving effect to same.

50. The following are the abridged Balance Sheets of A Ltd., and B Ltd.

	A £	B £		A £	B £
Share Capital—			Sundry Assets	11,300	5,000
All £1, fully paid	10,000	8,000	500 Shares in B Ltd.—Cost	700	
Profit and Reserves	2,000		1,000 Shares in A Ltd.—Cost		1,200
			Profit and Loss Account (Dr.)		1,800
	£12,000	£8,000		£12,000	£8,000

A new company, called A, B Ltd., is to be formed to amalgamate the above companies. Assuming no adjustment of asset values, show the share exchange. Ignore expenses and fractions.   (*Institute of Company Accountants' Final.*)

51. On 1st January, 19.., the Balance Sheet of H Ltd. was—

	£		£
Authorized and Issued Share Capital—		Goodwill	55,000
50,000 6% Cumulative Preference Shares of £1 each, fully paid	50,000	Sundry Assets	164,500
		Cash	500
150,000 Ordinary Shares of £1 each, fully paid	150,000	Profit and Loss Account	30,000
5% Debentures	30,000		
Creditors	20,000		
Preference Dividends are in arrears for four years.			
	£250,000		£250,000

A scheme of reconstruction was agreed upon as follows—

(1) A new company to be formed called J Ltd. with authorized capital of £325,000, all in Ordinary Shares of £1 each.

(2) One Ordinary Share, 50p paid, in the new company, to be issued for each Ordinary Share in the old company.

(3) Two Ordinary Shares, 50p paid, in the new company to be issued for each Preference Share in the old company.

(4) "Arrears" to be cancelled.

(5) Debenture holders to receive 30,000 Ordinary Shares in the new company credited as fully paid.

(6) Creditors to be taken over by the new company.

(7) The remaining unissued shares to be taken up and paid for in full by the directors.

(8) The new company to take over the old company's assets, subject to—

    (a) Writing down Sundry Assets by £35,000.

    (b) Adjusting Goodwill as required.

Show—

    (i) Realization Account of H Ltd.

    (ii) Opening entries of J Ltd.

    (iii) Balance Sheet of J Ltd.

Ignore costs.

52. A company, limited by shares, was incorporated on 1st April, 19.., with a nominal capital of £20,000 divided into 20,000 Ordinary Shares of £1 each, to acquire as a going concern as from 1st January, 19.., a company limited by guarantee, which had been formed some years previously.

The only items in the Balance Sheet of the latter company to which attention need be drawn are 4 per cent Debentures, £10,000; Preliminary Expenses, £405; and Revenue Account (accumulated deficiency), £2,595. The agreement, which was entered into by the old company, its liquidator, and the new company, provided that the members of the old company were released from their guarantee, and that the new company, which took over all assets and liabilities at book values, should also undertake to repay such of the Debentures in the old company as were not converted into either Shares or Debentures in the new company, the purchase consideration being fixed at the amount at which the intangible assets appeared in the books of the old company. The old debenture-holders had the option of being repaid in full or of taking Shares or 5 per cent Debentures of an equivalent amount in the new company, the latter carrying interest, payable half-yearly, from 1st April.

Debenture-holders were circularized and replies received as follows: holders to the value of £3,000 elected to be repaid; those to the value of £2,500 and £4,000 elected to take Shares and Debentures respectively in the new company.

In addition, applications were received for 3,600 Shares of £1 each, which were fully paid with the exception of 50p per Share on 400 Shares, and for £3,000 Debentures (all paid for at par).

Prepare the opening Balance Sheet of the new company after giving effect to the above arrangements, ignoring Expenses and Tax.   (*Adapted from C.A. Final.*)

53. The following is the Trial Balance of Y Ltd. on 31st March, 19.6—

	Dr. £	Cr. £
Authorized Share Capital—		
50,000 Shares of £1 each .		
Issued Share Capital—		
40,000 Shares of £1 each, 75p called .		30,000
Calls in arrear (in respect of 2,000 Shares)	500	
Stock .	2,720	
Purchases and Sales .	29,120	42,310
Wages and Salaries .	4,100	
Other Expenses .	3,820	
Investments—		
Quoted at cost .	8,000	
Unquoted at cost .	1,000	
General Reserve .		10,000
Plant, etc. .	8,000	
Debtors and Creditors .	14,200	2,030
Goods out on Consignment .	720	
Cash at Bank .	21,730	

Taxation Provision	. . . .		10,000
Investment Income (net)	. . . . .		620
Tax paid	. . . .	9,100	
Profit and Loss Account (Balance)	. . .		8,050
		£103,010	£103,010

You are required to prepare (not for publication purposes) Trading and Profit and Loss Account for the year ended 31st March, 19.6, and Balance Sheet as at that date, having regard to the following—

(1) Closing Stock, £4,090.

(2) Included in Sales are £3,200 Goods on Sale or Return, which are not to be regarded as sales (the cost price of such goods is £2,500).

(3) A Bad Debt Provision of 20 per cent on trade debtors is to be created.

(4) Taxation Provision on year's profit.

(5) A dividend of 10 per cent is proposed.

(6) Interest on calls in arrear to be charged at 5 per cent per annum. (Due date, 1st October, 19.5.)

(7) Table A provisions apply to dividends.

(8) The manager is entitled to 10 per cent of the net profit of the company *after* charging such percentage, *excluding* income from investments and *before* charging taxation.

(9) Provide depreciation on Plant, etc., at 10 per cent per annum.

(10) Transfer £5,000 to General Reserve.

(11) All the goods out on consignment have been sold for £900, subject to Agents' Commission of 5 per cent.

(12) Included in Creditors is £1,200 outstanding (excluding deposit) for Plant purchased on hire-purchase on 1st October, 19.5, purchase price being payable in four equal quarterly instalments commencing 1st January, 19.6 (cash value of such Plant, £1,040), against which a deposit of £200 was paid on 1st October, 19.5, included in the item of Debtors.

Essential working accounts are required. Calculations to nearest £. Assume Income Tax at 40 per cent.   (*Institute of Company Accountants' Final.*)

54. A company made an issue of 20,000 shares of £1 each at par, 25p payable on application, 50p on allotment, and 25p on call.

87,650 shares were applied for, including an application for 600 shares from a person who paid for the whole 600 applied for in full. Owing to the heavy oversubscription, allotments were drastically scaled down as follows—

Applicants for 23,650 (in respect of applications for 1,000 or less) received 11,500 shares (including the applicant for 600, who got 300 shares).

Applicants for 64,000 (in respect of applications for over 1,000) received 8,500 shares.

Any amounts received were first applied towards allotment and call moneys (after satisfying amount due on application), and any balance was returned. All moneys due on allotment and call were paid.

Write up Cash Account and Ledger relating to the issue.

55. The following is the Trial Balance extracted from the books of Penn & Mass Ltd., on 31st December, 19.5—

	Dr. £	Cr. £
Penn's Capital		10,000
Mass's Capital		8,000
Penn's Drawings Account	1,000	
Mass's Drawings Account	900	
Sundry Debtors (including partnership debtors of £1,730) .	11,210	
Sundry Creditors (partnership creditors paid off) .		8,364
Purchases	27,118	
Sales		29,161
Discounts allowed	674	

Discounts received		724
Cash in hand	50	
Bad Debts written off	624	
Bank Overdraft		1,210
Stock, 1st January, 19.5	7,979	
Furniture and Fixtures at cost . . .	1,100	
Provision for Bad Debts, 1st January, 19.5 . . .		500
Rent and Rates	384	
Salaries	1,132	
Wages	1,758	
Plant and Machinery, at cost	2,000	
General Expenses	631	
Advertising	999	
Formation Expenses	400	
	£57,959	£57,959

The Stock-in-trade on 31st December, 19.5, was valued at £19,653.
You are given the following information—

(1) Penn & Mass had been carrying on the business in partnership, sharing profits equally. On 1st May, 19.5, Penn & Mass Ltd. was incorporated with a nominal capital of £30,000 (£20,000 in 50p Ordinary Shares and £10,000 5 per cent Preference Shares) to take over the business hitherto carried on by the partnership, as from 1st January, 19.5.
The vending agreement provided—

(a) The company to take over all the assets, with the exception of the Sundry Debtors, which at 1st January, 19.5, amounted to £7,200. The liabilities to Sundry Creditors at 1st January, 19.5, £6,100, were not to be taken over but were to be paid by the company on behalf of the vendors out of the amounts collected from debtors, any balance to be accounted for in cash (without interest). The Bank overdraft was not taken over by the company. There was no cash in hand at 31st December, 19.4.
(b) The purchase consideration to consist of £10,000 in fully-paid 5 per cent Preference Shares of £1 each, and £10,000 in fully-paid Ordinary Shares of 50p each.
(c) Penn & Mass to be appointed directors at salaries of £1,000 per annum each.
(d) Each of the vendors to subscribe in cash for 10,000 Ordinary Shares at par.

(2) Penn & Mass have subscribed in cash for the shares required by the vending agreement to be taken up by them, the amounts having been credited to their Capital Accounts. The cash adjustment between the vendors and the company in respect of the debts collected and the liabilities paid has not been made.
(3) Penn & Mass agree to divide the Preference Shares received as part of the purchase consideration in proportion to their capitals as at 31st December, 19.4.
(4) The business being a seasonal one, carrying a uniform rate of gross profit, average monthly sales to 30th April, 19.5, are double those of the average monthly sales during the remainder of the period.
(5) The Discounts Allowed and Received respectively on amounts received from debtors and paid to creditors were £450 and £280, whilst of the Bad Debts written off during the year, £160 were in respect of the debts outstanding at 1st January, 19.5.
(6) No entries relating to the formation of the company have been made in the books, which have been carried on without a break.
(7) Plant and Machinery to be written off at 10 per cent per annum. Provision for Bad Debts to be 15 per cent of the debtors.
You are required to—

(i) Prepare Journal entries to put the books in order.
(ii) Show the Vendors' Account as it will appear in the company's books after all necessary adjustments have been made.
(iii) Show the share-holdings acquired by the partners respectively and the partnership position at 31st December, 19.5, ignoring shares separately subscribed as men-

tioned in (1) (*d*), reconciling it with the goodwill item shown in the purchasing company's books.

(iv) Prepare the company's Trading and Profit and Loss Account for the year ended 31st December, 19.5, and Balance Sheet as on that date.

Ignore taxation and Realization Expenses. Calculate to nearest £.

(*Institute of Company Accountants' Final.*)

56. X Ltd. has a nominal capital of £150,000 divided into 100,000 6 per cent Preference Shares of £1 each and 50,000 Ordinary Shares of £1 each, the former all being issued and fully paid. The Ordinary Shares, which were issued at a premium of 25p per share, were all allotted; 75p per share (including the premium) had been called and paid up with the exception of 25p per share on 600 shares, which was unpaid.

On 31st March, 19.8, 500 5 per cent Debentures of £100 each were issued at 97, and were fully subscribed and paid up. These debentures were repayable at par by 25 equal half-yearly drawings, the first of which had taken place on 30th September, 19.8.

No provision had been made in the company's books for interest due on these debentures on 30th September, 19.8.

In addition to the balances arising out of the above, the following balances appeared in the company's books at 30th September, 19.8—

	£
Freehold Premises at cost	96,200
Plant and Machinery (*less* depreciation at 10 per cent per annum for the year)	28,350
Rent and Rates (Office)	1,627
Office Salaries	5,340
Stock, 30th September, 19.8	62,835
Directors' Emoluments paid	8,250
Travellers' Salaries, Commission, and Expenses	4,863
Cash in hand	124
Balance at Bank	10,777
Insurance	426
Sundry Debtors	22,950
Goodwill at cost	10,000
General Reserve	15,000
Sundry Creditors	8,786
Motor Lorries, 30th September, 19.7	3,500
Motor Lorries, running expenses	2,372
Office Furniture at cost	800
Loose Tools as valued at 30th September, 19.8	1,246
Profit and Loss Account (*credit* balance) 30th September, 19.7	6,352
Provision for Bad Debts, 30th September, 19.7	600
Manufacturing Account (*credit* balance)	43,172
Preference Dividend, year to 30th September, 19.8	6,000
Income Tax	2,400
Corporation Tax year to 30th September, 19.7	5,500

You are asked to prepare a Trial Balance ruled into Profit and Loss and Balance Sheet columns, giving effect to the following—

(1) The Motor Lorries were valued at 30th September, 19.8, at £3,100.

(2) Surplus Plant and Machinery (the book value of which on 30th September, 19.7, was £1,600) was sold for £1,750 in September, 19.8, but the sale had not been recorded in the books.

(3) Sundry Debtors, known to be bad, amounting to £750 were to be written off, and the Provision for Bad Debts was to be increased to an amount equal to 5 per cent of the Sundry Debtors.

(4) Directors' Fees, £250, were owing.

(5) Provision for Corporation Tax on current year's profits, £4,700.

(6) Discount on Debentures is to be written off. (*C.A. Inter.*)

57. Barrett & Co. sold their business on 31st July, 19.3 to Barrett & Co. Ltd., the latter being incorporated on that date. The purchasing company took over the business as from 1st July, 19.3, at which date the following Assets and Liabilities appeared in the books of Barrett & Co.—

	£
Land and Buildings	5,000
Plant and Machinery	4,500
Fixtures and Fittings	700
Debtors	3,600
Stock-in-trade	1,800
Cash in hand and at Bank	1,000
Creditors	1,700

The purchase agreement, *inter alia*, provided that—

(*a*) The vendors should discharge all liabilities.

(*b*) The vendors should retain the Debtors and Cash, but the purchasing company should collect outstanding debts as agents of the vendors, deducting a collecting charge of 2½ per cent on cash collected.

(*c*) The purchase consideration was to be £12,500, made up as under—

(i) A cash payment of £5,000.

(ii) The allotment of 4,000 6 per cent Preference Shares of £1 each, fully paid.

(iii) The allotment of 7,000 Ordinary Shares of £1 each credited as 50p paid.

All amounts collected from Debtors (*less* discounts and commission) to be credited in reduction of the unpaid liability on these shares at 30th June, 19.4, any balance to be paid by the vendors at that date.

Barrett & Co. Ltd. issued to the general public 10,000 6 per cent Preference Shares at a premium of 12½p. At 30th June, 19.4, calls amounting to 75p, plus the 12½p premium, had been made; one shareholder of 1,000 shares had paid all his calls in advance, while another holder of 500 shares had failed to pay the last call of 12½p per share.

Miscellaneous Expenses included £500 for Underwriting Commission, which was discharged by the issue of 500 £1 Ordinary Shares credited as fully paid, with the option to purchase a further 500 Ordinary Shares at a premium of 12½p within the next five years.

Cash collected by the purchasing company from the vendors' debtors amounted to £2,850, after allowing discounts of £150.

The following balances appeared in the books of Barrett & Co. Ltd. at 30th June, 19.4, in addition to those arising from the foregoing transactions—

	£
Sales	56,000
Purchases	24,000
Wages	17,000
Discounts (on *all* Debtors)	600
Preliminary Expenses	250
Miscellaneous Expenses	4,500
Debtors (old and new)	4,000
Creditors	2,100

Prepare the Trial Balance of Barrett & Co. Ltd. as at 30th June, 19.4, and show the Cash Book entries.

58. Atomic Electric Co. Ltd. purchased the business of K. Watt as on 1st January, 19.7. The following accounts intended for presentation to the shareholders were prepared by the secretary of the company, and you are instructed to comment on them.

BALANCE SHEET 31ST DECEMBER, 19.7

	£		£
Capital	250,000	Land and Buildings . .	210,000
£65,000 10% Mortgage De-		Goodwill and Work in Progress	47,300
bentures issued at 10% dis-		Debtors.	29,039
count	58,500	Calls in arrear . . .	200
Bank Loan	20,000	Stock	52,100
Reserve	620	Suspense . . .	7,176
Taxes	500	Investments . . .	5,300
Profit for year and		Cash at Bank. . . .	10
Balance forward £9,945		Cash on hand . . .	2,190
Less proposed		Loans to Directors . . .	1,700
Dividend of 2% 5,000			
————	4,945		
Creditors—			
Goods . . 17,200			
Debenture Interest 3,250			
————	20,450		
	£355,015		£355,015

MANUFACTURING, TRADING, AND PROFIT AND LOSS ACCOUNT FOR THE YEAR ENDED 31ST DECEMBER, 19.7

	£		£
To Stock of Finished Goods .	6,600	By Sales	6,200
„ Wages and Salaries . .	10,700	„ Stock of Finished Goods .	62,100
„ Purchases . .	37,200	„ Appreciation of—	
„ Rent and Rates . .	2,140	Goodwill . .	10,000
„ Power, Light, and Heat .	3,760	Investments . .	3,400
„ Carriage Inwards . .	240	„ Forfeited Shares . .	375
„ Office Expenses . .	6,180		
„ Directors' Fees . .	4,500		
„ Travelling Expenses . .	1,200		
„ Bad and Doubtful Debts .	620		
„ Profit . . .	8,935		
	£82,075		£82,075

You ascertain the following facts—

(1) The amount at 1st January, 19.7, due by directors was *nil*, and the amount lent to them during the year ended 31st December, 19.7, was £2,900.

(2) The amount of Directors' Fees comprises—

	£
Managing Director's remuneration (from subsidiary company) .	500
Managing Director's Salary.	1,500
Paid to a Director as Secretary	200
Directors' Fees	1,500
Directors' Fees paid by subsidiary company . . .	800
	£4,500

59. The Balance Sheets of Gonne Ltd. and Drie Ltd. at 31st December, 19.., contain the following—

	Gonne £	Drie £
Authorized and Issued Capital—		
Shares £1 fully paid	50,000	30,000
Creditors	14,000	16,000
Debentures, 5 per cent	10,000	
Debenture Redemption Fund	5,000	
Profit and Loss Account . . . . .(Cr.)	9,000 (Dr.)	7,000
Fixed Assets	51,000	37,000
Current Assets	33,400	5,000
Leasehold Redemption Fund.		3,000
Investments in Drie Ltd.: 3,000 Shares at cost .	3,600	

Gonnedrie Ltd. is formed to amalgamate the two businesses. The net purchase consideration, payable in cash, is agreed at £100,000 for Gonne Ltd. (excluding the Shares of Drie Ltd.), and £45,000 for Drie Ltd. The new company agrees to discharge the creditors of the old vendor companies and to issue £10,000 4½ per cent Debentures in exchange for the Debentures in Gonne Ltd. The creditors of Gonne Ltd. and Drie Ltd. were paid off for £13,500 and £15,800 respectively. Close off the books of the vendor companies.   (*Institute of Company Accountants' Final.*)

60. A Deed of Trust securing an issue of 500,000 4½ per cent Debentures of £1 each contained, *inter alia*, the following terms—

(1) Interest shall be paid half-yearly on the 30th June and 31st December.

(2) 25 per cent of the company's profits of any year shall be applied in redeeming Debentures, such redeemed Debentures to be thereafter cancelled.

(3) The company is further authorized to purchase its Debentures in the open market without limit at or under par.

(4) Debentures redeemed, otherwise than by purchase, shall be drawn by lot and surrendered at £1·05.

(5) Any Debentures purchased in excess of the obligatory amount shall be kept alive for reissue or cancelled at the option of the company.

(6) On giving three months' notice, the company is authorized to redeem Debentures outstanding at £1·10.

The position on 1st January, 19.4, was as under—

1. £241,000 Debentures had been redeemed and cancelled.
2. The profits for the calendar year 19.3 were £210,000.
3. The company held £141,000 of its own Debentures (cost £126,900).

The Debentures to be redeemed and cancelled were appropriated out of the company's holding, and three months' notice was given to redeem the Debentures not in the hands of the company. The redemption was completed on 1st April, 19.4, the interest to that date being duly paid. On 30th June, 19.4, it was resolved that the remaining Debentures should be cancelled.

What entries are required to give effect to the transactions referred to above? Tax may be ignored.

61. Y Ltd. takes over the business of X, but it is agreed that the vendor's debtors should be collected by the purchaser, who should out of the proceeds pay the vendor's creditors. The same books are continued by Y Ltd.

From the following information write up the accounts relating to cash, debtors, creditors, and discounts (to the nearest £)—

	£
Debtors at take-over	4,000
Creditors at take-over	2,200
Y Ltd. Sales during the first year	30,000
Y Ltd. Purchases during the first year . . .	17,000
Y Ltd. Debtors at end of first year	8,421
X's Creditors at end of first year	1,789
Discounts received from Y Ltd. Creditors . .	200

Discounts allowed and received on all Debtors and Creditors are 5 per cent and 2½ per cent respectively. There are no bad debts or other allowances, and no closing provision is to be made for discounts.

62. A & B and C & D, whose businesses are similar in character, decide to amalgamate and form a limited company to carry on the combined business, and they consult you upon the matter.

The respective Balance Sheets at 31st December, 19.6, were—

	A & B	C & D
	£	£
Current Assets—		
Cash at Bank and in hand	5,250	2,175
Debtors, *less* Provision for Bad Debts . . .	8,326	5,982
Stock	8,218	7,146
Fixed Assets, at Cost *less* Depreciation—		
Motor Vehicles	2,000	1,640
Fixtures and Fittings	1,049	1,629
Plant and Machinery	4,629	5,761
Freehold Premises	8,500	6,450
	£37,972	£30,783

	A & B	C & D
	£	£
Current Liabilities—		
Creditors	6,442	5,110
Accrued Charges	280	323
Current Accounts—		
A	800	
B	450	
Capitals—		
A	16,000	
B	14,000	
C		15,500
D		9,850
	£37,972	£30,783

The profits for each of the three years to 31st December, 19.6, after charging Depreciation but before charging Interest on Capital and Taxation, were—

	A & B	C & D
	£	£
19.4	8,270	6,580
19.5	10,100	7,250
19.6	9,950	7,782

A & B share profits in the ratio of 8:7 and C & D in the ratio of 3:2.
State briefly your suggestion as to—

(1) the basis for amalgamation; and

(2) the capitalization of the company and the division of the capital amongst the four partners.

63. Black & White carried on business as partners, sharing profits and losses equally. Their business was divided into A and B Departments, and the following is a detailed copy of their Balance Sheet as on 31st March, 19. .—

	£	£		£	£
Creditors—A Dept. . .	15,400		Land and Buildings at Cost .		18,650
B Dept. . .	2,600		Fixtures, at Cost *less* Deprecia-		
		18,000	tion		500
Loans		1,200	Debtors—A Dept. . .	6,400	
Bank Overdraft . . .		8,950	B Dept. . .	10,800	
Capital Accounts—					17,200
Black . . .	26,300		Stock-in-trade—		
White . . .	16,200		A Dept. . . .	23,000	
		42,500	B Dept. . . .	11,250	
					34,250
			Cash in Hand . . .		50
		£70,650			£70,650

As from 31st March, 19.., it was arranged that the business should be taken over by two limited companies, one called Black & Co. Ltd., to take over A Department, and the other White & Co. Ltd., to take over B Department. The loan holders agreed to accept 7 per cent preference shares of £1 each fully paid for their loans, 720 of these being in Black & Co. Ltd., and 480 in White & Co. Ltd.

Black & Co. Ltd. took over the premises, fixtures, and cash, and the liability to the bank. The assets and liabilities were transferred at the Balance Sheet figures, and the partners were to be paid £5,000 for the goodwill of A Department and £4,000 for that of B Department.

The whole of the purchase price was satisfied by the allotment of fully-paid ordinary shares of £1 each in the respective companies as follows—

Black: 23,750 shares in Black & Co. Ltd.
The balance by shares in White & Co. Ltd.
White: 15,920 shares in White & Co. Ltd.
The balance by shares in Black & Co. Ltd.

The bank overdraft was paid off out of the proceeds of a mortgage of £10,000 which was raised on the land and buildings by Black & Co. Ltd. The costs of the mortgage were £350.

Ordinary shares, as follows, were issued to employees and paid for in full.

Black & Co. Ltd., 1,000. White & Co. Ltd., 1,500.

The formation expenses, which were payable by the respective companies, were Black & Co. Ltd., £650; White & Co. Ltd., £400.

Set out the Balance Sheets of the new companies after the foregoing transactions had taken place.   (*C.A. Final.*)

64. B Ltd. has the following abridged Balance Sheet at 31st December, 19.9.

	£		£
Authorized and Issued Capital—		Net Tangible Assets . .	76,000
50,000 6 per cent Cumulative		Goodwill	15,000
Preference Shares of £1 each,		Profit and Loss Account Debit	
fully paid . . .	50,000	Balance	34,000
75,000 Ordinary Shares of £1			
each, fully paid . . .	75,000		
	£125,000		£125,000

The Preference Shares are preferential as to Capital in a winding up, but without right of participating in any surplus.

Each share carries one vote. The last preference dividend was paid in respect of the year ended 31st December, 19.5.

The net tangible assets are estimated to be worth £68,000 and the goodwill worth nothing. It is estimated that the annual profits will be £5,000 (ignoring tax).

Outline a scheme of reconstruction, mentioning the main matters which would require consideration; redraft the Balance Sheet, and state the effect on the two classes of shareholders.   (*Institute of Company Accountants' Final.*)

65. A Ltd. has £20,000 6 per cent Debentures; interest payable on 30th June and 31st December. The company's financial year ends 31st December.

A Ltd. purchased in the open market £2,000 own Debentures at 102½ on 1st March and £8,000 own Debentures at 104 on 1st April.

On 1st December, A Ltd. purchased on the open market the remaining Debentures at 99½ x.d.

Ignore Tax and Sinking Fund.

Show the appropriate accounts in the books of A Ltd. for the year ended 31st December.

66. A Ltd. proposes to redeem its 4 per cent Debenture Stock of £500,000 at a premium of 2 per cent, and offers the holders the following alternatives to the normal repayment—

To leave the redemption money with the company to be applied as to—

(a) 7 per cent Cumulative Preference Shares of £1 each fully paid at £1·12½ per share—accepted by holders of £188,100 Debenture Stock; *or*

(b) 5 per cent Debenture Stock at 96 per cent redeemable in 15 years at par— accepted by holders of £200,000 Debenture Stock.

Show the Journal entries (including cash) to give effect to the above arrangements.

67. Soccerballs Ltd. was incorporated on 1st July, 19.8, with an authorized capital of £10,000, divided into shares of £1 each, for the object of acquiring, as from 1st April, 19.8, the sports business carried on by Ivor Pill in his freehold shop. The vending agreement provided that—

(1) the company should acquire, as from 1st April, 19.8, the shop fittings and furniture for £3,000, the stock of goods for £3,600, and the goodwill of the business for a sum equal to one-half of the gross profit earned in the half-year ended 31st December, 19.8;

(2) the consideration should be satisfied by the issue at par of 6,500 shares of £1 each fully paid on 1st July, 19.8, and the balance by a cash payment on 31st January, 19.9;

(3) the company should collect the debts on behalf of the vendor and use the proceeds, together with the balance at the Southland Bank (which was transferred to an account in the name of the company) for the discharge of the vendor's trade liabilities;

(4) the vendor should charge the company, as from 1st April, 19.8, with a rent at the rate of £840 per annum for the use of the freehold shop;

(5) the company's articles of association should make provision for the payment of director's remuneration to Ivor Pill at the rate of £100 a month and to his wife at the rate of £10 a month; and

(6) profit apportionments should be made on the assumption that the gross profit remained constant and that sales, purchases, wages and salaries, rates and sundry expenses were spread evenly over the year.

The cost of the agreement and preliminary expenses were paid and borne by Ivor Pill personally.

The company used, without interruption, Ivor Pill's books of account, which had last been closed as on 31st December, 19.7. No entries were made in the books in respect of the above agreement.

Before 31st December, 19.8, all the trade creditors existing on 31st March, 19.8, were paid, and all the trade debts collected with the exception of a debt for £60, which proved bad and which it was decided should be written off.

The Trial Balance extracted from the books as on 31st December, 19.8, showed—

	£	£
Trade creditors (£700 on 31st March, 19.8) . . .		960
Trade debtors (£500 on 31st March, 19.8) . . .	2,100	
Balance with Southland Bank Ltd. (£400 on 31st March, 19.8)	360	
Sales		18,600
Purchases	12,000	
Wages and salaries	1,500	
Rates	400	
Sundry expenses	1,800	
Shop fittings and furniture on 1st January, 19.8 . .	2,000	
Stock of goods on 1st January, 19.8 . . .	3,450	
Capital account on 1st January, 19.8 . . .		15,200
Freehold shop	9,550	
Drawings	1,600	
	£34,760	£34,760

The directors decided—

(i) to provide for depreciation of shop fittings and furniture as from 1st April, 19.8, at the rate of 10 per cent per annum,

(ii) to make provision for auditors' fees of £100, and

(iii) to value the stock of goods on 31st December, 19.8, at £4,050.

You are required—

(a) to draft journal entries in the books of Soccerballs Ltd. recording the purchase of the business and the satisfaction of the purchase consideration and making such other adjustments as you consider necessary, and

(b) to prepare Trading and Profit and Loss Accounts for the nine months ended 31st December, 19.8, and a Balance Sheet as on that date. Assume that the Accounts are not for publication. Ignore taxation.

68. Storm Ltd. was incorporated on 1st April, 19.8, with an authorized capital of £200,000, all in ordinary shares of £1 each, and immediately acquired the whole issued share capital of Cloud Ltd. for £40,000, satisfied by the issue of 40,000 fully paid shares in Storm Ltd.

Storm Ltd. issued the remainder of its authorized capital and £60,000 5 per cent debentures to the public at par, and the full proceeds were received by 30th April, 19.8. Debenture interest was payable half-yearly on 30th September and 31st March, and the first payment (for a full half-year) was made on 30th September, 19.8.

Storm Ltd. paid preliminary expenses £3,000, and, in May, 19.8, purchased fixed assets for £120,000.

On 31st December, 19.8, Storm Ltd. purchased for redemption £4,000 of its own debentures for £3,970, and also acquired for cash the whole of the issued share capital of Thunder Ltd., for £75,000.

The annual accounts of Cloud Ltd. were made up to 31st December, 19.8, and, in January, 19.9, Cloud Ltd. declared and paid a dividend of £2,400 (gross) for the year 19.8; this dividend absorbed the whole of its profit for that year.

On 28th February, 19.9, Storm Ltd. purchased the fixed assets and goodwill of Thunder Ltd. for £30,000 and £18,000 respectively. Thunder Ltd. was wound up and, on 31st March, 19.9, the liquidator made a first and final distribution, wholly in cash, of £80,000.

For the year ended 31st March, 19.9, Storm Ltd. incurred a loss on trading of £10,200 after charging depreciation £9,000, and directors' remuneration, £6,500 (of which £500 fees was unpaid on 31st March, 19.9), but before charging debenture interest. With the exception of £7,350 owing to trade creditors and £8,480 owing by customers on 31st March, 19.9, all purchases had been paid for and cash had been received in respect of all sales. On 31st March, 19.9, stock-in-trade amounted to £10,430, at cost, and all expenses charged in arriving at the loss on trading (except the outstanding directors' fees) had been paid and nothing had been paid in advance.

Income tax to be taken at 40 per cent and the taxation liability for the year ended 31st March, 19.9, had been agreed at £200, i.e. £500 at 40 per cent, but was unpaid on 31st March, 19.9. Preliminary expenses are to be written off.

You are required to prepare—

(a) a summary of the Cash Account of Storm Ltd. for the year ended 31st March, 19.9, and

(b) the company's Profit and Loss Account for the year ended 31st March, 19.9, and Balance Sheet as on that date, in a form suitable for presentation to the members, but without the notes which are required for submission with the Accounts.

Consolidated accounts and the directors' and auditors' reports are not required.

69. X and Y, sharing profits 11:9, sold their business to XY Ltd. as and from 1st January, 19.6, the new company being incorporated on 1st April, 19.6. The purchase consideration is £35,000 made up of—

Sundry Fixed Assets £25,000; Stock on hand £3,000; Goodwill £7,000.

The Authorized Capital of XY Ltd. is £50,000 in shares of £1 each; and 35,000 were allotted as fully paid to X and Y in satisfaction of the agreed purchase consideration.

The business books of X and Y contain all the entries, except those arising out of the sale of the assets in respect of the transactions to 30th April, 19.6, when the partnership books were closed and the opening entries in the books of XY Ltd. were made.

TRIAL BALANCE AT 30TH APRIL, 19.6

	£	£
General Expenses	4,000	
Sundry Fixed Assets	22,000	
Loss on Sale of Fixed Assets	1,000	
Debtors	7,500	
Creditors		8,000
Stock, 1st January, 19.6.	3,000	
Cash at Bank	2,000	
Purchases and Sales	19,500	37,000
XY Ltd.	8,000	
Capital—X		12,000
Capital—Y		10,000
	£67,000	£67,000

Closing Stock £2,100.

The item XY Ltd., £8,000, is in respect of cash paid for 8,000 shares of £1 each allotted to X and Y and paid by them into a temporary Banking Account in the name of XY Ltd. A cheque was paid out of this account for Preliminary Expenses £700 and Bank Charges are £20.

All purchases and sales are paid for by or to X and Y, except for transactions in April, which are to be dealt with by the new company. The outstandings for the latter period are Debtors £5,500 and Creditors £5,700.

The loss on sale £1,000 represents a sale of certain sundry assets on 7th April, 19.6, which were in the books at £1,200, but which were included in the sale price of Fixed Assets at £1,700.

The gross profit is to be apportioned in the ratio of 4:1 and the general expenses on a time basis.

In order to close off the partnership affairs X and Y agreed that when the debtors were realized the partners should take over personally the loan due to XY Ltd. in the partnership ratio and have their shares in XY Ltd. in like ratio; the balance of the Capital Accounts to be balanced by a cash payment to or by a partner.

The debts realized £1,800, the loss by agreement being borne by the firm.

Ignore depreciation, taxation, interest, etc.

You are required to—

(1) Write up the account of XY Ltd. in the books of X and Y;

(2) Show the Balance Sheet of X and Y at 30th April, 19.6, and the Capital Accounts of X and Y, giving effect to the final agreed adjustments between them.

(3) Prepare Journal entries recording the acquisition in the books of XY Ltd. together with the Trading and Profit and Loss Account for the four months ended 30th April, 19.6, and Balance Sheet as at that date.

70. A converts his business into a limited company as on 1st January, and issues for cash 10,000 shares of £1 each at par to his business friends and customers.

From the proceeds the vendor was paid £8,000 plus the amount for reimbursement of his outlay in forming the company, amounting to £400, and £20 for his expenditure of time thereon; the balance due being settled by the allotment of the remaining 2,000 shares at par. No new books are opened.

The Trial Balance at 31st December is—

	£	£
Capital (at 1st January) £6,400	2,700	
A Ltd., for Shares issued and Expenses re Flotation . .	320	8,000
Purchases and Sales	18,000	22,450
Stock (Closing Stock £2,550)	1,300	
General Expenses	1,600	
Bad Debts	145	
Debtors and Creditors	3,350	2,750
Fixtures and Fittings	700	
Cash at Bank	5,085	
	£33,200	£33,200

The Fixtures are revalued at £1,050 and Debtors at £3,200. Of the latter £110 proved to be bad.

A is to have a salary of £2,700 per annum commencing on the date of incorporation (1st March) and interest at 6 per cent per annum to that date on the cash (principal only) due to him.

Profit prior to incorporation is to be calculated strictly on time basis, excluding A's salary and interest charged against such profit.

Prepare Trading and Profit and Loss Account for the year ended 31st December, and Balance Sheet as at that date, giving effect to all necessary adjustments, none of which has been entered in the books, except that A's Capital has been debited with the cash proceeds of the share issue paid to him, promotion expenses, and £1,000 on account of salary. Tax to be ignored.

The salary and interest due to A have not been paid, except the foregoing £1,000.

71. On 1st January, 19.3, A Ltd. issued £62,500 5 per cent Debentures at £99 per cent. The debenture deed provided that commencing on 1st January, 19.4, the company should pay to trustees for the debenture holders the sum of £3,000 each year to be applied by them in redemption of the debentures by purchases below par in the open market. It was further provided that, commencing in 19.8, debentures should be redeemed each year by an amount equal to one-fifteenth of the nominal value of debentures outstanding on 1st January, 19.8, and as far as redemptions by purchase during any calendar year do not reach this figure, redemption of the balance is to be effected by drawings for redemption at par on the following 31st December. Moneys not applied by the trustees for redemption are to be invested by them.

On 31st December, 19.6, £55,000 5 per cent Debentures were outstanding, and the trustees held £1,800 3 per cent Funding Loan (cost £1,675: interest payable 1st February and 1st August) and a balance at the bank of £97.

The trustees—

(1) purchased 5 per cent Debentures for redemption as follows—
on 1st July, 19.7, £2,500, cost £2,450; on 31st March, 19.8, £1,500 cost £1,492;

(2) invested in 3 per cent Funding Loan (in units of £100) the sums available on 30th September, 19.7 (price £94 per cent) and on 30th April, 19.8 (price £95 per cent);

(3) repaid on 31st December, 19.8, the debentures drawn for redemption, any necessary additional funds being provided by the sale on 10th November, 19.8, at a price of £96 per cent of an appropriate amount of 3 per cent Funding Loan (in units of £100).

The company kept accounts recording the cash and investment transactions of the trustees.

You are required to show the following accounts for the years 19.7 and 19.8 as they would appear in the books of A Ltd.—

(a) 5 per cent Debentures account, and
(b) Trustees for 5 per cent Debenture holders—

        Cash Account;
        Investment Account.

Treat income tax as 40 per cent and any profit or loss on realization of Funding Loan, Debenture Interest, and expenses of purchases and sales of investments.

72. Archers Ltd. agreed to absorb Bowmen Ltd. as on 1st January, 19.4, by acquiring that company's undertaking and assets (other than its bank balance), the consideration being—

(i) The assumption of its liabilities;

(ii) The discharge of the £40,000 5 per cent Debentures held outside the company at a premium of 10 per cent by the issue of 4½ per cent Debentures in Archers Ltd., carrying a full six months' interest payable 1st July, 19.4;

(iii) A payment in cash of 50p per share in Bowmen Ltd.; and

(iv) The issue of shares of £1 each in Archers Ltd., credited as fully paid, to the members of Bowmen Ltd., on the basis of two Ordinary Shares (valued at £1·62½ each), and one 4½ per cent Cumulative Preference Share (valued at £1·12½) for every five shares held in Bowmen Ltd.

(v) The whole of the share capital of £120,000 consists of share holdings in exact multiples of five, except the following holdings—

$$
\begin{array}{r}
114 \\
92 \\
72 \\
22 \\
10 \text{ (10 members holding one share each)} \\
\hline
310 \\
\end{array}
$$

It was arranged to pay for fractional share equivalents at £1 a share, for fractions of shares after dividing by 5.

The summarized Balance Sheet of Bowmen Ltd., as on 31st December, 19.3, was as follows—

	£			£
Share Capital—		Fixed Assets at cost, *less* ac-		
160,000 shares of £1 each,		cumulated Depreciation—		
75p paid . . .	120,000	Land		5,100
General Reserve . . .	75,000	Buildings. . . .		22,850
Profit and Loss Account .	21,550	Plant		45,050
Insurance Fund[1] . .	10,000			
5 per cent Debentures . .	45,000			73,000
Creditors	17,800	Stocks		85,800
		Debtors. . . .		45,000
		Investments—		
		On account of In-		
		surance Fund .	£10,000	
[1] The company had been carrying its own insurance risk, crediting amounts equivalent to premiums to the fund and charging losses thereto.		General—		
		£5,000 5 per cent		
		Debentures in		
		Bowmen Ltd.	4,800	
				14,800
		Bank Balance. . .		50,750
		Goodwill . . .		20,000
	£289,350			£289,350

It was agreed that for absorption purposes 5 per cent should be written off stocks and a provision of 2½ per cent made for doubtful debts. The remaining assets, other than goodwill, were considered to be properly valued for the purpose of the absorption.

The absorption was completed on 1st March, 19.4, by the issue of the necessary shares and debentures in Archers Ltd. and payment of cash. Bowmen Ltd. was thereupon wound up and distribution of its assets made to its members. Expenses payable by Bowmen Ltd. amounted to £750.

You are required to draft the Journal entries (to include cash items necessary) to record—

(a) the closing entries in the books of Bowmen Ltd.;

(b) the entries in the books of Archers Ltd. in respect of the absorption and the public issue.

Ignore narratives.

73. Sandpits Ltd. (Authorized Capital, £12,500 in shares of 25p each) was formed with the object of working a gravel pit, estimated to contain 800,000 cubic yards of gravel, under a lease which provided for a royalty of 7½p per cubic yard of gravel produced with a minimum rent of £2,500 per annum and a right of recovery of short-workings. A premium of £10,000 was paid in Year 9 for the grant of the lease.

The balances in the company's books on 31st December, Year 19, were as follows—

	£
Bank overdraft	5,600*
Cash in hand	50
Creditors and accrued charges	2,100*
Debtors	5,723
General Expenses	78,035
Manager's Fixed Remuneration	1,800
Old Motor Lorries *less* Depreciation to 31st December, Year 18 (Cost £3,000)	500
Plant and Machinery *less* Depreciation to 31st December, Year 18 (Cost £19,000)	10,450
Premium on Lease, *less* Amortization to 31st December, Year 18	6,100
Profit and Loss, 31st December, Year 18 (*Cr.*)	2,547*
Royalty Payments (three quarters to September, Year 18)	1,875
Sales (61,600 cubic yards)	91,931*
Share Capital, fully paid	10,000*
Shortworkings to 31st December, Year 18	4,400
Stock at 31st December, Year 18 (110 cubic yards)	120
Vehicle Suppliers Ltd. (Lorries on Hire Purchase)	2,925*
New Lorries	5,400
Hire Purchase Interest Suspense	650

[Items marked * are credit balances.]   £230,206

Stocks of gravel as on 31st December, Year 19, amounted to 150 cubic yards valued at £160, and it was ascertained that 200 cubic yards of the gravel raised during the year were unaccounted for.

The debit balance "Vehicle Supplies Ltd., £1,200" represents the initial deposits (£600 each) paid on 1st January, Year 19, and the instalments paid on two motor lorries purchased that day on an instalment purchase system of 24 equal monthly instalments of £225 payable on the first of each month commencing 1st February, Year 19. The *cash* price of each lorry was £2,700.

Depreciation is to be provided on Plant and Machinery at 7½ per cent on cost and on the new lorries on the basis of a seven-year life with a residual value of £100 each. The old lorries had been written down to residual value by 31st December, Year 18.

The manager is entitled to a commission bearing the following relation to the net profits *after* charging interest, depreciation and all expenses, including such commission—

First £1,000 of such profit	*Nil*
Next £500 of such profit	10 per cent
Balance thereof	20 per cent

You are required to prepare (not for publication) the company's Trading and Profit and Loss Account for the year ended 31st December, Year 19, and the Balance Sheet as on that date. Ignore taxation.   (*C.A. Final.*)

74. B Ltd. agrees to acquire the undertaking of S Ltd. (which will then be liquidated) for the following consideration—

(1) Issue of its own shares of £1 each fully paid in the ratio of four shares in S Ltd. for every five shares in B Ltd., the market value of the shares of B Ltd. being £3 per share.

(2) Issue of its own debentures in exchange for those of S Ltd. at the rate of £110 B Debentures for every £100 S Debentures.

Ignoring expenses and fractions, show—

(1) Journal entries of S Ltd.; and
(2) Journal entries of B Ltd.,

to record the foregoing transactions.

Ignore narrations and make full use of composite journal entries, without sacrificing clarity.

It can be assumed that there are no goodwill items and Sundry Assets are to be brought into B Ltd.'s books without change.

The following is the abridged Balance Sheet of S Ltd. immediately prior to the above agreement—

	£		£
Share Capital (£1 fully paid) .	10,000	Sundry Assets . . .	21,040
Reserves	6,000	Own Debentures [£1,000 at cost]	960
Debentures	4,000		
Creditors	2,000		
	£22,000		£22,000

HOLDING COMPANIES

1. The Craigmount Trust Ltd. was formed on 1st January, 19.4, with a capital of 200,000 shares of £1 each, which were fully subscribed, and on the same day purchased shareholdings in the following companies—

(a) In R.R. Ltd. . . 20,000 shares, price paid, £25,000.
(b) In S.S. Ltd. . . 50,000 shares, price paid, £56,000.
(c) In T.T. Ltd. . . 80,000 shares, price paid, £69,000.

Abridged Balance Sheets of the Companies as at 31st December, 19.4, are—

Assets	R.R.	S.S.	T.T.
	£	£	£
Goodwill		10,000	25,000
Land and Buildings	9,000	20,000	11,000
Plant	10,000	40,000	65,000
Stock	7,000	12,000	23,000
Debtors	10,000	13,000	14,000
Cash	4,000	1,000	1,000
Profit and Loss Account . . .			6,000
	£40,000	£96,000	£145,000

Capital and Liabilities	R.R.	S.S.	T.T.
	£	£	£
Capital.	25,000	60,000	100,000
Reserve	4,000		17,000
Profit and Loss Account. . . .	5,000	10,000	
Debentures (6%)		10,000	
Creditors	6,000	16,000	28,000
	£40,000	£96,000	£145,000

R.R. Ltd. owes £2,000 to the Craigmount Trust Ltd., S.S. Ltd. owes R.R. Ltd. £1,000, and the Craigmount Trust Ltd. owes £3,000 to T.T. Ltd.

It has been decided to write off £10,000 from the plant of T.T. Ltd., since the above Balance Sheet was prepared. The Land and Buildings of S.S. Ltd. were revalued at £26,000 at the date of the acquisition, but effect has not been given to this in the accounts.

R.R. Ltd. and S.S. Ltd. had credit balances on Profit and Loss Account at 31st December, 19.3, of £2,000 and £5,000 respectively, all of which were distributed within one month in dividends. In T.T. Ltd. there was a debit balance on Profit and Loss Account of £4,000 at 31st December, 19.3. Reserves of R.R. Ltd. and T.T. Ltd., at 31st December, 19.3, were £4,000 and £17,000 respectively.

The Goodwill of the Craigmount Trust Ltd. at 31st December, 19.4, stands at £10,000. The dividends for 19.4 are: R.R. Ltd., 9 per cent; and S.S. Ltd., 15 per cent, which have been paid.

Prepare a consolidated Balance Sheet of the Craigmount Trust Ltd. and its subsidiaries at 31st December, 19.4. Ignore tax.

2. The following are the draft Balance Sheets of H Ltd. and S Ltd. at 31st December, 19..—

	H Ltd. £	S Ltd. £		H Ltd. £	S Ltd. £
Share Capital (£1 fully paid)	20,000	10,000	Sundry Assets	13,250	13,820
Revenue Reserves	1,800	2,000	Shares in S Ltd., at cost	14,000	
Profit and Loss Account	1,700	1,600	Goodwill		2,000
Profit for year, *less* Transfer to Reserve	750	700			
Creditors	3,000	1,520			
	£27,250	£15,820		£27,250	£15,820

In the case of H Ltd., there is no transfer to reserve. In the case of S Ltd., profit for the year is £1,200, and transfer to reserve is £500.

The holding of H Ltd. in S Ltd. is 90 per cent, acquired a year ago. Write off from Sundry Assets of H Ltd. £1,800, and S Ltd. £620 out of current year's profits. Draft a Consolidated Balance Sheet of H Ltd. and its subsidiary.

3. From the following Balance Sheets prepare a Consolidated Balance Sheet of Bishop & Co. Ltd., and Subsidiary Company.

BISHOP & CO. LTD.

BALANCE SHEET, 31ST DECEMBER, 19..

	£		£
Share Capital—		Freehold Property at cost, *less*	
Authorized: 100,000 Shares of £1 each	100,000	Depreciation	95,000
		Plant and Machinery at cost, *less* Depreciation	14,000
Issued: 100,000 Shares of £1 each fully paid	100,000	Shares in Webster & Co. Ltd. at cost, 9,000 Shares of £1	
General Reserve (Revenue)	50,000	each	18,000
Profit and Loss Account	10,000	Stock	30,000
Creditors	30,000	Debtors	20,000
		Bank Balance	13,000
	£190,000		£190,000

WEBSTER & CO. LTD.

BALANCE SHEET, 31ST DECEMBER, 19..

	£		£
Share Capital—		Investments at Cost	2,000
Authorized: 10,000 Shares of £1 each	10,000	Stock	5,000
		Debtors	7,000
		Bank Balance	13,000
Issued: 10,000 Shares of £1 each fully paid	10,000		
Profit and Loss Account	15,000		
Creditors	2,000		
	£27,000		£27,000

(*C.A. Inter.*)

4. The General Manufacturing Company Limited acquired the whole of the shares in the Component Company Limited, as at 1st July, 19.7, at total cost of £112,000.

The Balance Sheets at 30th June, 19.8, when accounts of both Companies were prepared, were as under—

GENERAL MANUFACTURING COMPANY LIMITED

BALANCE SHEET, 30TH JUNE, 19.8

	£		£
Share Capital—		Freehold Premises . . .	103,000
Authorized and Issued:		Machinery	30,000
15,000 Shares of £10 each		Stock (b)	34,000
fully paid . . .	150,000	Debtors.	28,000
General Reserve (Revenue) .	95,000	Investment . . .	112,000
Profit and Loss Account (a) .	80,000	Cash	33,000
Creditors (c) . . .	15,000		
	£340,000		£340,000

(a) Includes interim dividend at the rate of 10 per cent per annum, gross, from
the Component Company Ltd.

(b) Includes £3,000 Stock at cost purchased from the Component Company Ltd.,
part of £6,000 purchases (see Note (c)).

(c) Includes £6,000 for purchases from the Component Company Ltd., on which
the latter Company made a profit of £1,500.

COMPONENT COMPANY LIMITED

BALANCE SHEET, 30TH JUNE, 19.8

	£		£
Share Capital—		Freehold Premises . . .	30,000
Authorized and Issued:		Machinery	27,100
50,000 Shares of £1 each		Stock	20,200
fully paid . . .	50,000	Debtors	15,800
General Reserve as at 1st July,		Cash	11,000
19.1.	2,000		
Profit and Loss Account .	36,000		
Creditors . . .	16,100		
	£104,100		£104,100

Note. The balance on Profit and Loss Account at 1st July, 19.7, was £28,000, an
interim dividend of 10 per cent per annum, gross, having been paid during the year
in respect of the year ended 30th June, 19.8.

Make the necessary adjustments and show a consolidated Balance Sheet as at 30th
June, 19.8. No final dividends are proposed.

5. X & Co. Ltd. are interested in three companies, A Ltd., B Ltd., and C Ltd.,
as follows—

	A Ltd.	B Ltd.	C Ltd.
Total Issued Capital	100,000 Ordinary Shares of £1 each fully paid	650,000 Ordinary Shares of 25p each and 500,000 Cumulative Preference Shares of £1 each, all fully paid	30,000 Ordinary Shares of £1 each 62½p paid up
Holding of X & Co. Ltd.	50,000 Shares	All the Ordinary Shares	20,000 Shares
Cost to X & Co. Ltd. .	Par	£150,000	50p a Share
Financial year end .	31st October, 19.9	30th September, 19.9	31st August, 19.9
Result	Loss, £2,000	Profit, £50,000	Loss, £1,500
Ordinary Dividend paid .	*Nil*	5% on 1st November, 19.9	*Nil*

B Ltd. owed X & Co. Ltd. £3,000 on 31st December, 19.9.

In each company one share carries one vote, and X & Co. Ltd. have no powers as regards the appointment of directors beyond their ordinary rights as members.

The auditors' reports to the members are qualified as follows—

A Ltd.: "The investments are included at an amount in excess of the market value."

C Ltd.: "The provision for depreciation of leasehold properties is, in our opinion, inadequate."

The directors of X & Co. Ltd. have decided to make proper proportionate provision for the loss incurred by C Ltd.

X & Co. Ltd. closed their books on 31st December, 19.9.

In relation to the above facts—

(1) State what provisions of the Companies Acts 1948 and 1967 are relevant, and how they apply.

(2) Draft the items to be included in the Balance Sheet and Accounts of X & Co. Ltd. to be laid before the members at the annual general meeting, and state what further information, if any, should be given. *(C.A. Final.)*

6. From the following Balance Sheets of the Parent and Subsidiary Companies prepare Consolidated Balance Sheet as at 31st March, 19..—

PARENT COMPANY LTD.
BALANCE SHEET AS AT 31ST MARCH, 19..

	£	£		£	£
Capital, Authorized, Issued, and Fully Paid—			Sundry Assets . .		107,168
250,000 Shares of £1 each .		250,000	Investments in Subsidiary Companies at cost—		
General Reserve . . .		75,000	A, Subsidiary Ltd.:		
Profit and Loss Account . .		23,192	3,760 5% Preference Shares of £1 each .	2,820	
		348,192	10,000 Ordinary Shares .	10,000	
4½% 1st Mortgage Debenture Stock—			B, Subsidiary Ltd.:		
As issued . . . £50,000			5,000 7% Preference Shares of £10 each .	50,000	
Less Purchased and Cancelled to date . 44,600			18,800 Ordinary Shares of £10 each .	200,000	
		5,400	C, Subsidiary Ltd.:		
Loan from B, Subsidiary Ltd. .		19,600	50,000 Ordinary Shares of £1 each .	54,000	
Trade Creditors . . .		4,500	£1,900 4% Debenture Stock . .	1,500	
Current Taxation . . .		48,463			318,320
			Advances to Subsidiary Companies—		
			A, Subsidiary Ltd., Current Account .	620	
			B, Subsidiary Ltd., Current Account .	47	
					667
		£426,155			£426,155

A, SUBSIDIARY LTD.
BALANCE SHEET AS AT 31ST MARCH, 19..

	£	£		£
Capital, Authorized, Issued, and Fully Paid—			Sundry Assets . .	35,966
5,000 Preference Shares of £1 each . .	5,000		Profit and Loss Account . .	19,602
10,000 Ordinary Shares of £1 each . .	10,000			
		15,000		
Trade Creditors . .		6,403		
Advances by Group Companies		34,165		
		£55,568		£55,568

B, SUBSIDIARY LTD.

BALANCE SHEET AS AT 31ST MARCH, 19..

	£	£		£	£
Capital, Authorized, Issued, and Fully Paid—			Sundry Assets . .		180,309
5,000 7% Preference Shares of £10 each . .	50,000		Investments—		
20,000 Ordinary Shares of £10 each . .	200,000		47,000 Ordinary Shares in Parent Co. Ltd., at cost .	53,000	
		250,000	3½% War Stock at cost .	70,000	
Profit and Loss Account . .		37,429			123,000
Trade Creditors . . .		16,433	Parent Co. Ltd.—Advance Account		19,600
Current Taxation . .		19,000			
Parent Co. Ltd.—Current Account . . .		47			
		£322,909			£322,909

C, SUBSIDIARY LTD.

BALANCE SHEET AS AT 31ST MARCH, 19..

	£		£
Capital, Authorized, Issued, and Fully Paid—		Sundry Assets	72,730
50,000 Ordinary Shares of £1 each	50,000	Loan to Group Company . .	33,545
Profit and Loss Account . .	11,656		
4% Debenture Stock (Secured) . .	20,000		
Trade Creditors . . .	14,916		
Current Taxation . . .	9,703		
	£106,275		£106,275

7. The directors of Holding Ltd. ask you to draft a Consolidated Balance Sheet of the whole undertaking, by amalgamating the assets and liabilities of the subsidiary companies, A Ltd. and B Ltd. with those of Holding Ltd.

Your detailed workings should be shown.

The following is an abstract of the Balance Sheets of the three companies as on 31st December, 19.9.

	Holding Ltd.		A Ltd.		B Ltd.	
	£	£	£	£	£	£
Share Capital, Authorized and Issued—						
Ordinary Shares of £1 each, fully paid .		100,000		40,000		30,000
Share Premium Account (Premium on issue of 20,000 Shares issued in payment for 30,000 Shares in A Ltd.)		10,000				
Sundry Creditors		19,000		20,000		3,000
Bills Payable (all issued to Holding Ltd.) .				18,000		
Profit and Loss Account—						
Balance brought forward . . .	5,000				6,000	
Add Interim Dividend from B Ltd. . .	6,000					
Profit for year to date . . .	12,000				12,000	
		23,000			18,000	
Deduct Interim Dividend of 30% per annum					9,000	
						9,000
		£152,000		£78,000		£42,000

Note. Holding Ltd. had a contingent liability in respect of bills discounted, £10,000. Sundry creditors of A Ltd., £20,000, includes £15,000 owed to Holding Ltd.

	Holding Ltd.		A Ltd.		B Ltd.	
	£	£	£	£	£	£
Goodwill, at cost				6,000		
Land, Buildings, Plant and Machinery, at cost		25,000		30,000		20,000
Investments, at cost—						
30,000 Ordinary Shares in A Ltd. .	30,000					
20,000 Ordinary Shares in B Ltd. .	40,000					
		70,000				
10,000 Ordinary Shares in B Ltd. .				20,000		
Stocks		10,000		3,000		8,000
Sundry Debtors		10,000		2,000		7,000
Advance to A Ltd.	15,000					
		25,000				
Bill Receivable (accepted by A Ltd.) .		8,000				
Balances at Bankers . . .		14,000		10,000		7,000
Profit and Loss Account—						
Balance brought forward . .			4,000			
Deduct Interim Dividend from B Ltd. .			3,000			
				1,000		
Add Loss for year to date . . .			6,000			
				7,000		
		£152,000		£78,000		£42,000

On 1st January, 19.8, the date when Holding Ltd. purchased the 30,000 shares in A Ltd. the debit balance on the latter company's Profit and Loss Account was £1,000. Holding Ltd., and A Ltd., both purchased their shares in B Ltd., on 1st January, 19.9. *(C.A. Final.)*

8. The following information relates to the three constituent members of a group of companies. The issued capitals of A Ltd. and B Ltd. and the relative holdings therein have remained unaltered since their formation some years ago. There were no pre-acquisition profits.

	Holdings Ltd.	A Ltd.	B Ltd.
	£	£	£
Issued Capital—			
Ordinary Stock	1,000,000	400,000	250,000
Cumulative Preference Stock . .	600,000	200,000	100,000
Rate of Preference Dividend . .	5%	5%	6%
Inter-company Holdings—			
Held by Holdings Ltd.:			
Ordinary Stock . . .		400,000	150,000
Cumulative Preference Stock . .		100,000	50,000
Held by A Ltd:			
Ordinary Stock			50,000
Balances at 31st March, 19.7—			
Revenue Reserves . . .	300,000	100,000	41,000
Profit and Loss Account (credit) . .	51,430	21,820	18,480
Year ended 31st March, 19.8—			
Inter-company Dividends received (gross) .	78,000	10,000	—
Interest on British Government Securities (gross)	25,000	8,000	2,000
Trading Profit (subject to Depreciation and Directors' Fees, etc., shown below) . .	157,634	122,352	206,515
Depreciation	6,500	3,000	7,500
Directors' Fees and Remuneration . .	5,000	2,000	6,000
Income Tax (suffered by deduction) . .	10,000	3,200	800

	Holdings Ltd. £	A Ltd. £	B Ltd. £
Dividends paid (gross)—			
Preference Dividend for year. . . .	30,000	10,000	6,000
Interim Ordinary Dividend	80,000	40,000	50,000
Rate of Interim Ordinary Dividend (gross) .	8%	10%	20%
Provision is to be made for—			
Corporation Tax for year ended 31st March,			
19.8	64,000	45,000	69,100
Proposed Final Ordinary Dividend (gross) .	17%	12½%	27%

The directors of Holdings Ltd. (who constitute the entire directorate of A Ltd. and B Ltd.) decide to frame that company's Profit and Loss Account as a Consolidated Profit and Loss Account.

You are required to show this Consolidated Profit and Loss Account for the year to 31st March, 19.8, and also how the items stated above would appear in the Consolidated Balance Sheet at that date. Group election has been made to pay dividends without deduction of Income Tax.

Show any necessary working schedules.   (*Adapted from C.A. Final.*)

9. X Ltd. is the Parent Company of Y Ltd. and Z Ltd.

The share capitals of Y Ltd. and Z Ltd, are £100,000 and £40,000 respectively (all in £1 fully paid shares). Particulars of the holdings are as follows—

	Undistributed Profit at date of purchase of shares	
	Z Ltd. £	Y Ltd £
Y Ltd. acquired 5,000 Shares in Z Ltd. . .	5,000	
X Ltd. acquired 30,000 Shares in Z Ltd. . .	7,000	
X Ltd. acquired 80,000 Shares in Y Ltd. . .	8,000	30,000

At 31st December, 19.9, the undistributed profits are: Y Ltd., £40,000, and Z Ltd., £10,000. No dividends have been paid or declared and no losses incurred in any of the relevant years.

Show how the total profits of the subsidiary companies will be dealt with in preparing the Consolidated Balance Sheet.

10. Assuming the same facts as in the preceding question, except that the Revenue Reserves of Z Ltd., when X Ltd. acquired its shares in Y Ltd., were £3,400 (instead of £7,000), show how the "derived" profits of Y Ltd. would be dealt with, the Balance Sheets being as shown below—

BALANCE SHEETS

	X Ltd. £	Y Ltd. £	Z Ltd. £		X Ltd. £	Y Ltd. £	Z Ltd. £
Share Capital (£1 f.p.)	200,000	100,000	40,000	Sundry Net Assets .	4,000	135,500	50,000
				Shares in Y Ltd.			
				(80,000) at cost .	160,000		
				Shares in Z Ltd.			
Revenue Reserves .	—	40,000	10,000	(30,000) at cost	36,000		
				Shares in Z Ltd.			
				(5,000) at cost .		4,500	
	£200,000	£140,000	£50,000		£200,000	£140,000	£50,000

11. The following are the Balance Sheets of H Ltd. and its subsidiaries at 31st December—

	H Ltd. £	S Ltd. £	T Ltd. £		H Ltd. £	S Ltd. £	T Ltd. £
Share Capital (£1 fully				Fixed Assets . .	20,000	30,000	20,000
paid) . . .	50,000	40,000	20,000	Debtors—			
Revenue Reserves .	10,000	4,000		External . .	9,500	5,000	800
Profit and Loss .	+12,000	+6,000	−2,000	Internal—			
				H Ltd. . .		4,100	1,000
	72,000	50,000	18,000	T Ltd. . .	3,500	1,800	
Creditors—				Cash at Bank . .	5,000	1,900	1,400
External . .	11,000	5,000	5,500	Stock . . .	4,000	9,000	5,000
Internal				Shares in subsidiaries			
S Ltd. . .	4,000		1,800	at cost—			
T Ltd. . .	1,000			S Ltd., 36,000			
H Ltd. . .			2,900	shares .	38,000		
				T Ltd., 12,000			
				shares .	8,000		
				T Ltd., 3,000			
				shares .		3,200	
	£88,000	£55,000	£28,200		£88,000	£55,000	£28,200

At the date S Ltd. bought the shares in T Ltd., the latter's debit balance was £11,000; but when H Ltd. bought its shares in T Ltd. at a date later than S Ltd.'s purchase of T Ltd.'s shares, the latter's debit balance had been reduced to £4,000.

The credit balance of the Profit and Loss Account of S Ltd., at the date H Ltd. bought its shares, was £2,000, and the Revenue stood at *nil*.

At 31st December, there were Goods in Transit (at cost) from H Ltd. to S Ltd., £600; and Cash in Transit £100 from H Ltd. to S Ltd. These had been entered only in the books of the "sending" company.

Dividends paid by S Ltd., £2,000 (ex pre-acquisition) and £10,000, all of which so far as attributable thereto had been credited in the books of H Ltd. Ignore Taxation.

Prepare Consolidated Balance Sheet of H Ltd. and its subsidiaries in draft form at 31st December.

12. The Balance Sheets of A Ltd., B Ltd., and C Ltd., at 31st December, 19.7, contained the following items relating to the profits and losses of the companies—

	A Ltd. £		B Ltd. £		C Ltd. £
Net Profit (or Loss) for year . . .	800		1,800	*Dr.*	480
Add Balance forward . .	Profit 1,500	*Loss*	800	Profit	1,920
	£2,300		£1,000		£1,440

A Ltd. acquired 75 per cent of the Share Capital of B Ltd. on 1st August, 19.6.
A Ltd. acquired 10 per cent of the Share Capital of C Ltd. on 1st December, 19.7.
B Ltd. acquired 80 per cent of the Share Capital of C Ltd. on 1st September, 19.7.

Prepare draft Schedule of Consolidated Profit and Loss Account of the Group, showing the amounts to be transferred to other essential accounts to be included in the Consolidated Balance Sheet, i.e. the credit total of £4,740 (as above).

13. The following are the Balance Sheets of H Ltd. and S Ltd. at 31st December, 19.9. H Ltd. does not trade in any substantial way, the operating company being S Ltd.

The shares in S Ltd. were all acquired on 1st January, 19.9. All the shares are £1 fully paid.

BALANCE SHEETS (ABRIDGED) AS AT 31ST DECEMBER, 19.9

	H Ltd. £		S Ltd. £			H Ltd. £	S Ltd. £
Share Capitals	20,000			10,000	Sundry Assets . . .	10,520	20,600
Profit and Loss Brought forward	£10		£2,500		Shares (10,000) in S Ltd. at cost	11,000	
Current Profit .	1,510		9,600				
	1,520		12,100				
Less Dividend .	—	1,520	1,500 (c)	10,600			
		£21,520		£20,600		£21,520	£20,600

Show Consolidated Balance Sheets as at 31st December, 19.9, assuming that the dividend is declared out of the Profit and Loss Account—

(1) at 31st December, 19.8.

(2) for the year ended 31st December, 19.9.

14. Assuming the same figures as in the preceding question, except that H Ltd. purchased (for £11,000) 8,000 shares in S Ltd., show the Consolidated Balance Sheet as at 31st December, 19.9.

CHAPTER XXV

DOUBLE ACCOUNT SYSTEM

1. From the following particulars draw up (1) Balance Sheet of a company as on 30th June, 19.4, on the single account system; and (2) the Capital Account and General Balance Sheet as on the same date on the double account system: nominal capital, £300,000, subscribed capital, £260,000; debentures at 5 per cent, £40,000; trade creditors, £16,000; reserve, £15,000; trade debtors, £38,000; cash in hand and in bank, £35,000; investments (reserve), £15,000; stock, £24,000.

Expenditure to 30th June, 19.3: land, £12,000; shafting, etc., £135,000; machinery, £40,000; buildings, £13,000,

The expenditure during the year ended 30th June, 19.4, was £25,000, £25,000, and £10,000 on the last three items, and a Renewals Fund of £25,000 had been created. The balancing item of £16,000 may be taken, for the purposes of this question, as profit of the company.

What advantages and disadvantages does the double account system possess?
Illustrate your answer from the above problem.

2. From the following Balance Sheet, drawn according to ordinary commercial methods, construct Balance Sheets according to the requirements of the double account system.

THE X LAND RAILWAY COMPANY
BALANCE SHEET, 31ST DECEMBER

	£		£
Ordinary Stock issued .	3,000,000	Fixed Assets—	
Revenue Account. .	60,000	Cost of Permanent Assets	3,880,000
8% Debenture Stock issued	1,000,000	Current Assets—	
Sundry Creditors . .	100,000	Stores, Fuel, and Supplies	
		in hand . . .	110,000
		Sundry Debtors . .	90,000
		Cash at Bank . . .	80,000
	£4,160,000		£4,160,000

Cost of Permanent Assets comprises:

	£
Lines Open for Traffic	2,990,000
Rolling Stock	890,000

(C.A. Final.)

3. A water company decided to replace three-quarters of its mains and lay down an auxiliary for the remaining quarter. Ten years ago the mains were laid down at a cost of £30,000, costs of materials and labour having gone up by 25 per cent. Old materials realized £500 in cash; £150 worth were used in the renewal, and £100 worth in the construction of the auxiliary main.

Show how these matters will be dealt with in the books of the water company.

149

CHAPTER XXVI

INVESTMENT TRUSTS AND UNIT TRUSTS, AND VALUATION OF SHARES

1. The directors of an old established company, of which you are the auditor, inform you that they have been approached by another company with a tentative proposal to acquire the whole or part of the company's shares. The company has a large factory manufacturing ironmongery, and owns 20 freehold and 10 leasehold shops where its goods, many of a proprietary and patented brand, are sold, and at the same time it has a subsidiary company manufacturing and selling lawn-mowers. The Balance Sheets of the main and subsidiary companies as at 31st December, 19.9, are summarized as follows—

	Main Co. £	Sub-sidiary £		Main Co. £	Sub-sidiary £
Issued Capital—			Fixed Assets—		
100,000 6% Pref. Shares of £1 each, fully paid	100,000		Freeholds at Cost	276,076	24,337
300,000 Ordinary Shares of £1 each, fully paid	300,000		Leaseholds at Cost	97,245	
50,000 Ordinary Shares of £1 each, fully paid		50,000	Plant and Machinery, *less* Depreciation	29,262	9,314
Reserves	100,000		Fixtures and Fittings	5,467	2,104
Profit and Loss Account	69,997	7,559	Patterns, etc.	23,858	100
			Goodwill		1
	569,997	57,559	Investment in Subsidiary at Cost	50,000	
Trade Creditors	56,286	14,318	Current Assets—		
			Stock	105,462	8,389
			Trade Debtors	8,394	22,214
			Cash at Bank	30,519	5,418
	£626,283	£71,877		£626,283	£71,877

The profits have been as follows—

	Main £	Subsidiary £			Main £	Subsidiary £
19.4	36,000	6,300	19.7		47,000	6,000
19.5	47,000	6,400	19.8		35,000	5,700
19.6	68,000	7.000	19.9		42,000	7,100

The directors instruct you to write to the other company stating a basis on which the company's shares might be acquired, and stating the reasons for arriving at the basis. Any further figures which you consider necessary may be inserted, and it can be assumed that your recommendation and the price suggested by you have been accepted by the directors of your client company.

A similar company has recently paid 7 per cent on its ordinary shares, which are quoted at par. Ignore tax. *(C.A. Final.)*

2. The Balance Sheet shows the position of a private limited company as on 30th June, 19.., as follows—

BALANCE SHEET, 30TH JUNE, 19..

Capital—	£	£	Fixed Assets—	£	£
Authorized:			Goodwill at Cost on formation of Company	5,000	
35,000 5% Preference Shares of £1 each	35,000		Freehold Properties as per valuation of Surveyor & Co. on 30th June, 19..	27,500	
35,000 6% Preferred Ordinary Shares of £1 each	35,000		Plant and Machinery at Cost, *less* Depreciation	32,300	
5,000 Deferred Ordinary Shares of £1 each	5,000				
	£75,000		*Carried forward*		64,800

(Continued on next page)

BALANCE SHEET, 30TH JUNE, 19.. (*Contd.*)

Capital—	£	£	Fixed Assets—	£	£
Issued:			*Brought forward*		64,800
32,000 5% Preference			Current Assets—		
Shares of £1 each fully			Sundry Debtors . £16,200		
paid . . .	32,000		*Less* Provision for		
20,000 6% Preferred			Bad Debts . 1,000		
Ordinary Shares of £1				15,200	
each fully paid .	20,000		Bills Receivable .	1,100	
5,000 Deferred Ordinary			Stock and Work in Progress		
Shares of £1 each fully			as valued by the Directors	16,700	
paid . . .	5,000		Cash at Bank and in hand .	7,500	
		57,000			40,500
Capital Reserve		25,000			
Debenture Redemption Reserve .		5,000			
Profit and Loss Account (Balance) . .		6,800			
		93,800			
6% Debentures redeemable 31st December, 19.., being part of an issue of £20,000, the balance of which the Company has power to reissue before the date mentioned		5,000			
Sundry Creditors		6,500			
		£105,300			£105,300

The company has in recent years only made sufficient profits to pay the dividends on the preference and the preferred ordinary shares. No dividend has been paid on the deferred ordinary shares.

The directors recommend the following dividends for the year to 30th June, 19.., and there is no reason to suppose that the recommendation will not be adopted: Preference and preferred, the full dividend: Deferred ordinary, 50 per cent.

The company's Articles of Association provide that the price at which shares shall change hands in any year shall be the price as fixed by the company at its last preceding annual general meeting.

You are appointed auditor of the company, and at the completion of your audit for the year to 30th June, 19.., you are asked by the directors to advise them as to the value of each class of share for submission to the annual general meeting.

Submit your reply, giving your reasons for, and showing how you arrive at the values you suggest. (*C.A. Final.*)

3. In dealing with accounts of Trust Investments, where there have been Purchases and Sales at varying prices, do you consider that the profit or loss arising on each transaction should be based on the valuation of the earliest holding of the particular investment or on the average price of the total holding? Illustrate your answer by reference to the following example—

X LTD. 5 PER CENT PREFERENCE STOCK

(i) 1st January. Bought £50 Stock at 101.
(ii) 1st April. Bought £50 Stock at 95.
(iii) 1st July. Sold £25 Stock at 99.
(iv) 1st October. Bought £100 Stock at 102.
(v) 31st December. Sold £150 Stock at 105.

4. Notebridge Ltd. is a private company. A suggestion has been made to the largest shareholder to sell to P a number of his shares. Subject to the valuation being made by you, it is agreed to make the proposed sale as at 1st January, 19.7, on the basis that assets are to be taken at book values, except Goodwill, which is to be computed at two years' purchase of the profits available for dividend for the ordinary shareholders, based upon the average of the last three years. Profits, before providing for debenture interest and preference dividends, were—

						£
Year ended 31st December, 19.4	.	.	.	.	.	3,600
,, ,, ,, ,, 19.5	.	.	.	.	.	5,900
,, ,, ,, ,, 19.6	.	.	.	.	.	5,700

The Balance Sheet at 31st December, 19.6, is—

	£		£
Share Capital—		Fixed Assets at Cost—	
Authorized and Issued:		Goodwill	6,000
10,000 6% Cumulative Preference		Leasehold Land and Buildings .	14,000
Shares of £1 each, fully paid .	10,000	Plant, etc.	10,000
1,200 Ordinary Shares of £10 each,			
fully paid . . .	12,000		30,000
	22,000	Investments at Cost—	
Debenture Redemption Fund . .	2,000	Leasehold Amortization Fund .	4,000
Profit and Loss Account—		Debenture Redemption Fund .	2,000
Balance, 1st January, 19.6 £4,750		Current Assets—	
Profit for year . . 4,350		Stock . . . £6,000	
	9,100	Debtors, *less* Provision £500 7,000	
		Cash at Bank . . 7,600	
	33,100		20,600
5% Debenture Stock	10,000		
Leasehold Amortization Fund . .	4,000		
Depreciation Fund (Plant, etc.) . .	1,500		
Creditors	8,000		
	£56,600		£56,600

The preference shareholders are preferential as to capital in a winding-up without participating rights in any surplus.

Compute the fair value of the ordinary shares, having regard to the fact that after completion of the Balance Sheet an invoice for goods supplied to the company on 31st December, 19.6, amounting to £350, was found to have been omitted from the books, and that £250 is the yearly contribution to the Debenture Redemption Fund.

5. What is a Unit Trust and what are its main advantages?

CHAPTER XXVII

INSURANCE CLAIMS

1. On 31st December, 19.., a fire occurred on the premises of a limited company which carried on the business of general house furnishers. The most important books were not destroyed, from which it was possible to ascertain the following particulars—

Sales from 1st January to 31st December, 19.. . . . . . £128,0C0
Purchases from 1st January to 31st December, 19.. . . . 84,000
Stock on hand at 1st January, 19.. 23,600
The gross profit for the past five years had averaged 35 per cent on turnover.
The value of the salvaged stock was agreed at £3,000.

Assuming all to be in order, draft a statement showing amount of the claim upon the insurance company.

2. A fire occurred on the premises of a merchant on 15th June, 19.., and a considerable part of the stock was destroyed. The value of the stock salved was £450.
The books disclosed that on 1st April, 19.., the stock was valued at £3,675, the purchases to the date of the fire amounted to £10,494, and the sales to £15,650.
On investigation it is found that during the past five years the average gross profit on the sales was 36 per cent.
You are required to prepare a statement showing the amount the merchant should claim from the insurance company in respect of stock destroyed or damaged by the fire. (*R.S.A.*)

3. A fire occurred at the premises of M. Ewer, glass and china merchant, on 31st May, destroying a great part of his stock, which at 1st January appeared in the books at £4,000. The value of the stock saved from the fire was £900. The gross profit on sales was 30 per cent, and these amounted to £10,200 from 1st January to the date of the fire, while for the same period the purchases amounted to £6,900.
Prepare a Statement of Claim for M. Ewer to present to the insurance company, showing clearly the amount which you consider he would be entitled to recover.

4. Owing to a city improvement scheme a proprietor of a retail business has been forced to sell same. The property was held on a lease, with 4 years yet to run. You are instructed to prepare a claim for compensation, and having examined the books, etc., for the past three years, you find as follows—

	June, 19.4 £	June, 19.5 £	June, 19.6 £
Proprietor's Salary	1,400	1,400	1,400
Income Tax	600	500	600
Interest on Capital at 5 per cent	300	325	400
Depreciation of Fittings, etc., at 10 per cent	100	90	81
Profits (before charging above)	2,300	3,000	2,100

The business was purchased in 19.1, when £4,000 was paid for goodwill; in 19.3 £1,000 was expended on new fittings, counters, and electric light installation. When the stock and fittings were sold by auction losses of £300 and £500 were made respectively.
Prepare a Statement of Claim and a short report thereon.

5. A fire destroyed part of the factory of Dickson. The damage sustained was as follows—

	Cost £	Book value £	Amount claimed £	Claim admitted £
(1) Machinery destroyed	3,500	2,950	3,200	3,000
(2) Machinery damaged	1,200	1,100	360	350
(3) Stock destroyed	4,850	4,000	4,750	4,500
(4) Stock damaged	1,000	1,000	400	300
(5) Expenses incurred in extinguishing fire	35	—	35	35

How would you record this settlement in the books of Dickson? (*L.C.C.*)

6. A fire occurred on 31st December, 19.7, and the business was disorganized until 31st May, 19.8, the amount insured being £12,000 and the period of indemnity seven months.

The net profit of the business for the year ended 30th September, 19.7, was £6,000 on a turnover of £80,000, after debiting the standing charges (all duly covered) of £14,000.

The turnover for the year ended 31st December, 19.7 (i.e. the year immediately preceding the fire) was £60,000; during the period of dislocation it was £9,000, as compared with the corresponding period in the preceding year of £26,000.

To mitigate the effect of the loss £1,760 was expended and accepted without limitation, there being no saving of standing charges in consequence of the fire.

Show the draft claim against the insurance company.

7. A Ltd. insured for Consequential Loss for £18,000.

The net profit for the year ended 31st December was £6,000 and the Insurable Standing Charges £15,000, but only £14,000 was included in the definition of Insured Standing Charges.

The period of indemnity is six months and the fire occurred on 1st April and the interruption continued till 31st July.

Additional Cost of Working to mitigate the effect of the damage is £2,000 and the Saving in Insured Standing Charges is £200.

	Turnover last financial year	Turnover for financial year in which the damage occurred	Reduction in Period of Interruption
	£	£	£
Jan.–Mar. . . .	25,000	25,600	
Apr.–Jul. . . .	20,000	6,000	14,000
Aug.–Dec. . . .	35,000	37,400	
	£80,000	£69,000	

The damage caused was severe, and but for the expenditure of the above £2,000 the business would have shut down for the period after the fire till 31st July, but by that time full restoration of normal conditions would have been effected.

Show details of draft claim against the insurance company.

8. On 2nd August, 19.9, the premises of Messrs. Black & Sons were destroyed by fire. The business books and records were saved, and from these the following particulars were ascertained—

	£
Stock, at cost, on 31st March, 19.8	8,860
Stock, as per Balance Sheet, 31st March, 19.9	7,510
Purchases, year to 31st March, 19.9	20,770
Sales, year to 31st March, 19.9	30,500
Purchases, from 1st April, 19.9, to 2nd August, 19.9 . . .	7,470
Sales, from 1st April, 19.9, to 2nd August, 19.9	11,800

In valuing the Stock on 31st March, 19.9, £160 had been written off a particular line of goods which had originally cost £360 and which was sold in May, 19.9, for £350. Except as regards this transaction, the ratio of gross profit has remained unchanged throughout.

The value of Stock salvaged from the burnt-out premises was £1,021.

You are required to calculate the amount of claim to be presented to the Insurance Company in respect of loss of Stock.

9. X Ltd., which deals in sweets, stationery, and fancy goods, prepares accounts annually to 31st December. The ratio of gross profit to sales in each category respectively is constant throughout.

On 30th April, 19.8, the Stock was partly destroyed by fire. The books and records were saved, and from these the following information was obtained—

	Sweets £	Stationery £	Fancy Goods £
Stock, including old Stock, all at cost—			
31st December, 19.6	90	940	1,510
31st December, 19.7	220	1,230	1,530
Purchases, 19.7	2,251	3,710	1,960
Sales, 19.7	3,030	4,560	2,870
Purchases, January–April, 19.8. . .	835	1,110	650
Sales, January–April, 19.8 . . .	1,040	1,720	1,273

Included in the stock of fancy goods at 31st December, 19.6, was a certain amount of old shop-soiled stock, in respect of which a special provision of £120, representing half the original cost, was made in the financial accounts, but had not been brought into the stock-sheets; one-half of this old stock had been sold during 19.7, for £70, and a further quarter was sold during the period to April, 19.8, for £33. These amounts are included in the figures of total sales given above. The remaining quarter was destroyed in the fire.

The value of the stock salvaged, which was undamaged, was—

	£
Sweets	72
Stationery	*nil*
Fancy Goods	370

You are required—

(a) To ascertain the value of the stock destroyed, including the remainder of the shop-soiled goods at their depreciated value; and

(b) To set out the account recording the provision in respect of shop-soiled stock.

10. Z Ltd. is a manufacturing company. Included in its Balance Sheet as at 31st March, 19.5, were the following assets—

		£
Fixed Assets—		
Freehold Factory at cost		25,000
Plant at cost	£14,000	
Less Accumulated Depreciation	4,000	
		10,000
Current Assets—		
Stock		18,500

These assets were insured for the following sums—

	£
Factory Buildings	30,000
Plant	16,000
Stock	16,000

On 30th June, 19.5, the factory and its contents, which included all the items shown above, were totally destroyed by fire, apart from stock salvaged. The following losses were agreed with the fire assessors—

	£
Factory Buildings	28,000
Plant	15,000
Stock (subject to average)	24,000

The total stock at the date of the fire was valued at £30,000, of which £6,000 was salvaged. The claims were paid on 30th September, 19.5.

The freehold land was estimated by the directors to have cost £4,000 out of the total cost of land and buildings of £25,000.

Record the foregoing in the books of the company and show how these items would be disclosed in the accounts of the company for the year ended 31st March, 19.6.

CHAPTER XXVIII

BANKRUPTCY

1. A B, finding himself in difficulties, asks you to ascertain his business position, and you prepare the following Balance Sheet—

	£	£		£
Creditors—			Plant and Tools . . .	435
Trade		3,688	Furniture, Fittings and Fixtures	273
Rent (3 months) . .		125	Motor Vehicles . . .	326
Rates (6 months) . .		65	Stock	1,370
Income Tax . . .		87	Book Debts	2,146
For Cash lent . . .		300	Cash in hand	14
Bank Overdraft . . .		1,837	Capital Account as *per Contra* .	1,538
Capital, 31/12/19..	£2,430			
Less Drawings £2,185				
Loss . 1,783				
	3,968			
Deficiency .	£1,538			
		£6,102		£6,102

The bank holds as security the deeds of his private house, valued at £1,650. The household furniture is valued at £478. The cash creditor holds as security an endowment policy on the life of A B, the surrender value of which is £425.

Prepare Statement of Affairs for presentation to a meeting of creditors, assuming any further information you may consider necessary.

2. Wright & Johnson, who trade in partnership, find themselves unable to meet their obligations and instruct you to prepare a Statement of Affairs for submission to a meeting of creditors.

You are able to ascertain the following particulars from the books as at 1st November, 19.8—

	£
Unsecured Creditors	12,000
Loan from Williams	1,000
Creditors partly secured	2,300
Estimated value of security . . .	2,000
Preferential Claims	140
Stock-in-trade (at Cost)	1,000
Cash at Bank	145
Cash in hand	55
Fixtures	200
Debtors (Good)	450
Debtors (Bad)	34
Debtors (Doubtful)	23

There was an excess of assets over liabilities at 1st January, 19.6, of £2,160, but since that date there has been a loss on trading of £9,180. Partners' drawings from 1st January, 19.6, to 1st November, 19.8, amounted to £4,513.

Johnson is a limited partner who brought in capital of £1,000, Wright being a general partner, whose separate estate has been entirely absorbed in financing the business. The loan from Williams was made under an arrangement by which he was to receive interest at a rate varying with the profits.

For the purposes of the Statement of Affairs it was estimated that stock would realize £850 and fixtures £100, while bad and doubtful debts would produce nothing.

Add such explanatory notes to the Statement as are necessary to convey to creditors the true position of affairs.

3. On 31st March, 19.., the Balance Sheet of Messrs. A and B was—

	£		£
Trade Creditors	2,000	Machinery	2,000
Bills payable	2,500	Buildings	2,100
Bank	1,500	Book Debts	2,000
12 months' Rent	800	Cash	100
1 month's Salaries	500	Stock	3,100
Capital—			
A . . . £1,000			
B . . . 1,000			
	2,000		
	£9,300		£9,300

A owed £1,800 personally, and he had in addition to his interest in the firm a house which cost £5,000, furniture £800; and life policies on which he had paid premiums amounting to £100. B owed £2,300, and he had paid life premiums amounting to £300, and had furniture which cost £1,000. The bank held the deeds of A's property and his life policies.

It became necessary to call the creditors together.

The partnership assets were valued as follows: machinery, £1,090; buildings, £500; good book debts, £1,000, doubtful, £500 (estimated at £300), bad, £500; stock, £2,000.

A's property was considered to be worth £6,000, his life policies £50, and his furniture £350. B's life policies were worth £150, his furniture £500.

Prepare Statements of Affairs and Deficiency Accounts. *(C.A. Inter.)*

4. Victor Mont filed his Petition in Bankruptcy on 30th September, 19... The details of his assets and liabilities were as follows: cash in hand, £5; book debts: good, £4,800, doubtful, £2,100, estimated to produce £980, bad, £450; stock-in-trade, £8,000, estimated to produce £6,500; bills receivable, good, £1,450; office furniture, £350, estimated to produce £250; machinery and plant, £600, estimated to produce £450; private house, £1,600, subject to a mortgage of £800; private furniture, £300, estimated to produce £220; unsecured creditors, £24,000; creditors partly secured, £14,000, estimated value of security held, £8,500.

Outstanding liabilities at the date of the petition not otherwise included: rent, 6 months, £250; salaries of office staff (2 months), £150; loan from wife, £2,000, and interest thereon at 8 per cent per annum, £120; rates (3 months), £50.

Prepare the Statement of Affairs in official form.

5. A Receiving Order in bankruptcy has been made against A and B, trading as A, B & Co., dated 4th February, 19.4. Particulars of the firm's financial affairs are as follows—

	£
Unsecured Creditors.	36,800
Creditors holding Security—	
(a) Midland Bank Limited, secured by hypothecation of Stock valued at £18,000 .	15,000
(b) Mortgage on business premises .	10,000
Add Interest Accrued, less Tax	180
The premises are valued at £12,300 at which amount they stand in the books.	
(c) Trade Creditors for £7,000 (not included in the total of £36,800) holding policies on the life of A, valued at £4,300.	
Income Tax owing: Sch. D, 19.3–19.4, £600; 19.4–19.5, £400	
Rates accrued .	450
Wages owing (preferential).	60
Cash in hand .	130

			£
Stock (not hypothecated)			2,420
Motor Vehicles.			600
Book Value	£1,000		
Book Debts: Good			14,460
Doubtful and Bad	£27,800		
Estimated to produce			2,300
Office Furniture, Fixtures, etc.			150
Book Value	£300		
Bills Receivable, discounted but not matured			1,200

       Note. It is anticipated that the Bills will be paid in full by the acceptors on maturity

Surplus from Separate Estate of A, estimated at   200

At 30th June, 19.3, the deficiency of the firm was, according to the books, £1,500. Since that date, the loss on trading (excluding bad debts) has been £5,920; bad debts, £10,160; and drawings (including debits to partners for income tax), A, £1,100; B, £900.

Prepare Statement of Affairs of the firm at 4th February, 19.4, and Deficiency Account from 30th June, 19.3.   *(C.A. Final.)*

CHAPTER XXIX

LIQUIDATION

1. At the date of appointment of a liquidator of Horner and Mudd Ltd., the position was as follows—

		£
Freehold Premises		10,000
Machinery, Plant, etc.		3,000
Fixtures, Fittings, etc.		450
Stock-in-trade		2,000
Goods out on Consignment		50
Investments		400
Cash in hand		10
Sundry Debtors		900
Goodwill		500
Mortgage on Freehold Premises		5,000
Interest accrued due thereon		75
Preferential Creditors		320
Unsecured Creditors		25,000
Bank Overdraft (unsecured)		90
Share Capital authorized and issued—		
8,000 Ordinary Shares of £1 each		8,000
10,000 Deferred Shares of 5p each		500
The assets were estimated to realize—		
Freehold Premises		8,000
Machinery, Plant, etc.		900
Fixtures, Fittings, etc.		120
Stock-in-trade		1,680
Goods on Consignment		30
Investments		300
Sundry Debtors		650

Prepare approximate Statement of Affairs as at the date of appointment of liquidator.

2. All the liabilities having been discharged and all costs provided for, the liquidator of a company had cash remaining amounting to £40,521. There were 25,000 cumulative preference shares of £1 each, and 25,000 deferred shares of 5p each.

At the date of the liquidation there were no arrears of preference dividend, but these shares were entitled to interest at 5 per cent per annum from the commencement of the winding up (1st January, 19..) until date of payment (30th November, 19..).

The surplus assets are to be distributed *pro rata* between the preference and the deferred shareholders, according to the nominal amount of their shares.

Prepare Distribution Account, showing the amount payable to each class of shareholder and the dividend on each class of share.

3. The liquidator of the Western Land Co. Ltd. had for distribution between preference and ordinary shares an available surplus, which after payment of all costs, proved to be £215,809. The share capital consisted of 25,000 cumulative preference shares of £5 each and 25,000 ordinary shares of 5p each. No arrears of dividends were payable on the preference shares at the date of the liquidation, but they were entitled to interest at 5 per cent per annum from the commencement of the winding up until payment—a period of eleven months.

On applying to the Court the liquidator was directed that the surplus assets must be distributed rateably between the preference and the ordinary shareholders according to the nominal amount of their shares, each preference share being entitled to 100 times the amount payable on each ordinary share.

Prepare a Distribution Account and show the respective dividends per share payable on both classes of shares; calculation to nearest £. (*C.A. Final.*)

4. A limited company, having carried out its business objects, went into voluntary liquidation with the following liabilities: Trade creditors, £12,000; bank overdraft,

£20,000; capital (preference shares, 10,000 of £10, £7 called), £70,000; ordinary shares (10,000 of £10, £9 called), £90,000, less calls in arrears £2,000, £88,000. Cash received from shareholders in anticipation of calls: on preference shares, £24,000; on ordinary shares, £4,000. The assets realized £200,000.

Describe the liquidator's process of winding up, and prepare a general liquidation account, allowing £2,000 as the expenses of the liquidation.

Note. No interest need be brought into account. The preference shares have no prior capital rights. (*C.A. Final.*)

5. The Birmingham Theatre Co. Ltd. passed a resolution for a members' voluntary winding up on the 1st January, 19... The company's articles of association contained the following provisions—

(*a*) That in the event of winding up, any surplus after discharging the whole of the liabilities of the company should be applied—

(1) In redeeming the preference share capital of the company.

(2) In redeeming the ordinary share capital of the company.

(3) The balance remaining, if any, to be divided equally between preference, ordinary, and deferred shareholders.

The position of the company at the date of the resolution to wind up was as follows—

Issued share capital:

5,000 preference shares of £1 each (fully paid).
5,000 ordinary shares of £1 each (fully paid).
5,000 ordinary shares of £1 each (75p paid).
5,000 deferred shares of 25p each (12½p paid).

The assets realized £25,750, and the liabilities amounted to £7,500. The costs of the liquidation (including the liquidator's remuneration) were £250. The liquidator duly made calls of 25p on the ordinary shares, and 12½p on the deferred shares, and the whole of the cash was received with the exception of a call on 1,000 deferred shares.

Prepare the liquidator's final Statement of Account, showing the amounts returned to the shareholders.

6. The following particulars were extracted from the books of the Loamshire Farming Co. Ltd. on 1st January, 19.., on which day a winding-up order was made: ordinary share capital, 20,000 shares of £1 each, 50p paid up, £10,000; 6 per cent preference share capital, 20,000 shares of £1 each fully paid, £20,000, 5 per cent first mortgage debentures, secured by a floating charge upon the whole of the assets of the company, exclusive of uncalled capital, £15,000; fully-secured creditors (value of securities, £3,500), £3,000; partly-secured creditors (value of securities, £1,000), £2,000; preferential creditors for rates, taxes, wages, etc., £600; bills payable, £10,000; unsecured creditors, £7,000; Union Bank Ltd. overdraft, £1,000; Bills receivable: in hand £1,500, discounted (one bill for £1,000 known to be bad) £4,000; book debts: good £1,000, doubtful (estimated to produce 50p in the £1) £700, bad £600; land and buildings (estimated to produce £10,000), £15,000; stock-in-trade (estimated to produce £4,000), £5,000; machinery, tools, etc. (estimated to produce £200), £500; cash in hand, £10.

Prepare a Statement of Affairs. (*C.A. Final.*)

7. The books of Accessories Ltd. at 31st July, 19.., contained the following balances—

	£	£
Share Capital—		
20,000 Shares of £1 each, fully paid		20,000
Sundry Creditors		15,000
Plant and Machinery	6,000	
Stock	4,000	
Patent Rights and Trade Marks	16,000	
Sundry Debtors	6,000	
Preliminary Expenses	500	
Profit and Loss Account	2,475	
Cash	25	
	£35,000	£35,000

The following scheme of reconstruction was submitted to the shareholders and creditors—

The company to go into voluntary liquidation and a new company, with a nominal capital of £40,000, to be formed to take over all the assets from the liquidator on the following terms—

(a) Preferential creditors for £500 to be paid in full.

(b) Unsecured creditors to have the option of receiving cash for 50p in the £ in full settlement of their claims or par value in 7½ per cent debentures in the new company.

(c) 20,000 shares of £1 each, 50p per share paid, to be distributed *pro rata* to shareholders of the old company.

(d) The new company to pay the costs of the liquidation.

One-half of the unsecured creditors exercised their option to be paid in cash, and the funds for this and for payment of the liquidation expenses (which amounted to £300) were obtained by calling up the balance of 50p per share.

Three shareholders holding 1,500 shares dissented, and required their interest to be purchased. The price of 33½p was agreed upon, and was paid to the liquidator by one of the assenting shareholders in return for the transfer of such shares.

Prepare the Liquidator's Account for presentation to the final meeting of members.

8. Makers Ltd. got into financial difficulties, and on 30th October, 19.7, a Receiver was appointed by the debenture-holders (under powers in the instrument which gave a floating charge, but no fixed charge) and a liquidator was appointed on 30th November, 19.7.

On the date of the Receiver's appointment the position of the company was as follows—

	£				£
80,000 6% Cumulative Preference Shares of £1 each, fully paid	80,000	Freehold Property	.	.	202,500
100,000 Ordinary Shares of £1		Leasehold Property	.	.	25 000
each, fully called up £100,000		Fixed Plant and Machinery.	.	.	20,000
Less Calls in arrear—		Loose Plant and Tools	.	.	4,000
20p a Share on 5,000 Shares 1,000		Stocks—			
	99,000	Finished . . £20,000			
5% Debentures, including Interest to		Raw Materials 5,000			
date	70,000				25,000
Bank Loan, including Interest to date .	10,000	Debtors	.		6,000
Landlord for Rent to date . .	2,500	Profit and Loss Account	.	.	15,000
Commissioners of Inland Revenue .	5,728				
Sundry Creditors . . .	30,272				
	£297,500				£297,500

The only security held by the Bank was the personal guarantees of the directors for £7,000. The amount due to the Inland Revenue was for accounting year ended 19.6, £1,600; p.a.y.e. 19.7, £3,728; and p.a.y.e. 19.8, £400.

By agreement of all parties, the landlord took Fixed Plant of a book value of £5,500 in full satisfaction of the sum due to him. The directors implemented their guarantees. The Receiver sold the Freehold Property for £190,000 and made his obligatory payments; his remuneration was £3,500 and his expenses £400. The balance of cash in his hands was duly paid over to the liquidator.

Sundry Creditors include the following items—

(a) Three months' salary due to the managing director, £300.

(b) Managing director for payment of two months' salary due to the chief accountant, £600.

(c) Contributions due under the National Insurance Act, £180.

P Ltd. was under contract to deliver certain goods to the company in December, 19.7, which the company had contracted to supply to W Ltd. P Ltd. refused to make delivery, but admitted (and paid) a claim made by the liquidator for £170 damages. W Ltd. claimed for damages against the liquidator, who admitted the claim to the extent of £90.

The liquidator realized £15,000 from Stocks and £4,120 from Debtors, excluding W Ltd., which was allowed to set off the claim of £90 from its debt of £300, the net balance being duly paid. The remaining assets realized £21,000 *less* than book values. The costs of realization were £850 and the liquidator's remuneration £2,250.

The company's regulations provided that, in the event of liquidation, the assets, after payment of liabilities and costs, were to be applied in repaying to the preference shareholders £1·12½ a share, any surplus then remaining to belong to the ordinary shareholders.

Prepare Receipts and Payments Accounts, showing the order in which the payments should be made, of—

    (a) The receiver; and
    (b) The liquidator.

Ignore interest after 30th October, 19.7.

9. X Ltd. was ordered to be wound up on 28th February, 19.., on which date the Balance Sheet was—

	£	£		£
Issued Capital—			Goodwill	25,000
100,000 Shares of £1 each,			Leasehold Premises	11,000
50p called . .	£50,000		Plant	15,000
Less Calls in arrear .	500		Fixtures	500
			Stock	32,250
	49,500		Debtors £9,005	
Add Calls in advance .	500		*Less* Provision . . 205	
		50,000		8,800
5% Debentures . .	60,000		Cash	50
Interest accrued . .	1,000		Profit and Loss Account . . .	51,750
		61,000		
Bank Overdraft . . .		5,000		
Sundry Creditors—				
Trade	22,100			
Expense . . .	5,050			
Bills Payable . . .	1,200			
		28,350		
		£144,350		£144,350

The amounts estimated to be realized are: Goodwill, £500; Leasehold Premises, £10,000; Plant, £6,000; Fixtures, £100; Stock, £31,000. Debtors: £7,400 (Good) and £300 in respect of the remainder; and Calls in arrear, £350.

Expense Creditors include Wages of 5 men, £100; Rent for nine months, £450; Tax deducted from interest, previous tax year, £600, current tax year, £700; Telephone, £40; and Directors' Fees, £500,

The Bank is secured by a fixed charge on the Leasehold Premises and the Debentures have a floating charge on all the assets of the company.

Three years ago the debit balance on Profit and Loss Account was £35,089, and since that date the accounts of the company (made up each year to 28th February) have shown the following figures—

	Year 1	Year 2	Year 3
	£	£	£
Gross Profit	16,200	8,940	7,360
Transfer Fees	10	8	5
Discounts received	44	18	27
Wages and Salaries	6,290	5,440	5,069
Rent, Rates, and Taxes	1,200	1,200	1,180
Debenture Interest	3,000	3,000	3,000
Bad Debts	860	904	1,203
Depreciation	5,000	—	—
Directors' Fees.	1,000	1,000	1,000
Miscellaneous Expenses	3,190	2,960	2,777

It is estimated that contingent liabilities on contracts, £6,000, will involve proofs of at least £5,500.

Prepare Statement of Affairs and Deficiency Account.

10. The Liquidator of X Ltd. realized £2,436 of the company's assets and paid off the preferential creditors, amounting to £736, and also paid the bank £1,200 on account (which was a creditor for £4,270 secured by floating charge); the remaining assets produced £4,924. The bank was paid off and a first dividend of 66⅔p in the £ paid to the unsecured creditors, amounting to a payment of £1,796.

The Ordinary Share Capital consisted of 24,000 "A" of £1 each, 90p called and paid; and 6,000 "B" of £1 each, 70p called and paid, the shares being *pari passu*. The Costs of Liquidation were £485.

After these payments, the Liquidator made a call on the Ordinary Shareholders sufficient to pay the Unsecured Creditors a final dividend of 33½p in the £ and the Preference Shareholders the full amount due thereto, viz. 2,000 Shares of £1 each at £1·12½.

Write up the Liquidator's Cash Account, ignoring Taxation.

(Adapted from C.A. Final.)

CHAPTER XXX

MANUFACTURING ACCOUNTS

1. The following extract of costing information relates to Commodity A for the six months ended 30th June, 19..—

	£
Purchases—Raw Materials.	30,000
Direct Wages	25,000
Rent, Rates, Insurance, and Works Overhead	10,000
Carriage Inwards	360
Stock: 1st January, 19..—	
Raw Materials	5,000
Finished Product: 1,000 tons	4,000
Stock: 30th June, 19..—	
Raw Materials	5,560
Finished Product: 2,000 tons	8,000
Work in Progress—	
1st January, 19..	1,200
30th June, 19..	4,000
Cost of Factory Supervision	2,000
Sales—Finished Product	75,000

Advertising, discounts allowed, and selling costs 25p per ton sold. 16,000 tons of the commodity were produced during the period.

You are required to ascertain—

(a) The value of the raw materials used.
(b) The cost of the output for the period.
(c) The total cost applicable to the turnover for the period.
(d) The net profit for the period.
(e) The net profit per ton of the commodity.

2. From the following balances extracted at 31st March, 19.3, prepare accounts in such form as to disclose—

(a) Cost of raw materials consumed.
(b) Works cost.
(c) Gross profit on manufacture.
(d) Cost of own manufactured goods to Sales Department.
(e) Gross profit on sales.
(f) Percentage of net profit to sales.

Stocks on 1st March, 19.3—

	£
Manufactured Goods	974
Raw Materials	300
Depreciation of Plant and Machinery	1,300
Discounts allowed	374
Printing and Stationery.	93
Purchases—	
Manufactured Goods	1,274
Raw Materials	8,726
Debtors	2,174
Cash at Bank	171
Repairs to Machinery	250
Office Rent and Rates	650
Plant and Machinery	7,521
Coal	579
Carriage Inwards.	391
Office Salaries	940
Carriage Outwards	233
General Expenses.	317
Factory Rent and Rates	2,271

	£
Cash in hand	57
Manufacturing Salaries and Wages	11,029
Travelling Expenses	279
Sales	29,942
Capital	7,782
Creditors	2,179

Stocks on 31st March, 19..3, were: Manufactured goods, £2,794; raw materials, £200. Goods manufactured are to be debited to the Sales Department at net realizable value, viz. £27,150.

Note. A Balance Sheet is not required.

3. P Ltd. is a manufacturing company having an authorized capital of £160,000, divided into 50,000 7 per cent preference shares, 100,000 ordinary shares, and 10,000 deferred shares, all of £1 each.

The following was the Trial Balance extracted from the books as on 31st January, 19..—

TRIAL BALANCE	£	£
30,000 Preference Shares, fully paid		30,000
70,000 Ordinary Shares, 75p called		52,500
Calls in Arrear (on Ordinary Shares)	250	
10,000 Deferred Shares, fully paid		10,000
General Reserve		5,000
Purchases *less* Returns	39,207	
Bought Ledger Balances		3,595
Sales *less* Returns		121,770
Sales Ledger Adjustment Account	11,449	
Wages and Salaries—Factory	35,372	
Wages and Salaries—Office	12,146	
Travellers' Salaries and Commission	6,530	
Rent (Factory nine-tenths, Office one-tenth) . . .	4,220	
Carriage Inwards	1,332	
Carriage Outwards	1,519	
Factory Power, and Expenses	2,370	
Rates, Heating, Lighting, and Insurance—Factory . .	1,942	
Rates, Heating, Lighting, and Insurance—Office . .	1,227	
Machinery and Plant—1st February, 19.., (cost £97,000) .	58,200	
Machinery and Plant—Purchased during year . . .	3,000	
Manufactured Stock, 1st February, 19.. . . .	21,518	
Raw Materials, 1st February, 19...	5,163	
Postage, Stationery, and Office Expenses	510	
Office Machinery and Equipment (cost £10,000) . .	5,800	
Office Fixtures and Fittings (cost £1,000) . . .	620	
Legal Expenses and Audit Fee	1,325	
Directors' Remuneration	9,000	
Advertising	2,370	
Bank Interest		146
Discount		512
Dividends Unpaid		141
Interest on Calls in Arrear		25
Preliminary Expenses	2,100	
Profit and Loss Account—Balance, 1st February, 19.. .		19,202
Dividend Paid—		
On Preference Shares, year to 31st January, 19.. . .	2,100	
On Ordinary Shares—Interim on account of year to 31st January, 19	5,250	
Cash at Bank	8,146	
Cash in Hand	225	
	£242,891	£242,891

You are required to prepare in columnar form a Manufacturing Account and a Profit and Loss Account for the year ended 31st January, 19.., and a Balance Sheet as on that date, taking into consideration the following information and instructions—

(*a*) The Trial Balance of the Sales Ledger was as follows—

	£	£
Debit Balances	11,592	
Credit Balances		143
General Ledger Adjustment Account		11,449
	£11,592	£11,592

(*b*) Manufactured stock on hand on 31st January, 19.., was valued at £29,310; and raw materials were valued at £7,369.

(*c*) Depreciation on plant and machinery is to be written off at 15 per cent on the reducing balance and on Office Machinery and Equipment at 10 per cent on cost, and the office fixtures and fittings are to be depreciated 5 per cent on cost.

(*d*) Unused office stationery, stamps, etc., were valued on 31st January, 19.., at £19.

(*e*) £800 is to be reserved for rent due and unpaid, and £346 for travellers' commission.

(*f*) Half the balance of preliminary expenses is to be written off.

(*g*) Provision is to be made for Corporation Tax of £875 on the profits of the year.

(*h*) The following dividends are proposed—Ordinary, 6 per cent (payable on the called up capital), Deferred, 12 per cent. (*Adapted from R.S.A.*)

4. The Paper Products Co. Ltd. owns: a paper mill, all the output of which is sold to the factory at 10 per cent above mill cost price; the factory, which sells all its output to the selling department at 10 per cent above factory cost price; the selling department.

From the following figures calculate (*a*) the factory cost of output, showing the proportion "Paper" bears to "Other Goods, Wages, and Charges"; (*b*) the profit made by the company in the year, allowing for (*c*) the provision required to eliminate the unrealized profit on increase in stocks in the year, assuming that the selling department increase is in the same proportion as in (*a*).

Factory: opening stock on hand—paper, £18,700; other goods, £14,800; paper purchases from mill, £73,300; other goods, wages, charges, etc., £43,900; closing stock on hand—paper, £24,200; other goods, £13,500.

Selling Department: opening stock on hand, £27,400; sales, £148,000; wages, charges, etc., £16,400; closing stock on hand, £37,300. Workings to nearest £.

(*C.A. Final.*)

5. A concern manufacturing one type of goods has three factories in different parts of the country, and a warehouse at head office from which sales are also made.

For accounting purposes the branches are regarded as separate entities, and goods supplied to head office are treated as sales and charged up to head office by the branches at the same price as to outside customers.

The following are the Manufacturing and Trading Accounts of the branches for the year ended 31st December, 19..—

	Branch A	Branch B	Branch C		Branch A	Branch B	Branch C
	£	£	£		£	£	£
Stock of Raw Materials at 1st Jan., 19..	10,500	12,200	14,900	Sales— Head Office	12,200	10,800	14,500
Purchases	38,100	29,700	34,300	Customers	23,900	23,500	23,200
	£48,600	£41,900	£49,200		£36,100	£34,300	£37,700
Less Stock of Raw Materials at 31st Dec., 19...	32,400	26,500	31,800	Stock of Finished Goods at 31st Dec., 19..	25,000	22,500	27,500
	£16,200	£15,400	£17,400		£61,100	£56,800	£65,200
Wages	12,300	11,500	13,100	Less Stock of Finished Goods at 1st Jan., 19..			
Factory Expenses	2,700	2,600	3,100				
	£31,200	£29,500	£33,600				
Selling Expenses	1,500	1,400	1,600		20,000	18,000	21,000
	£32,700	£30,900	£35,200				
Trading Profit	8,400	7,900	9,000				
	£41,100	£38,800	£44,200		£41,100	£38,800	£44,200

At 1st January, 19.., head office had on hand goods from branches valued for Balance Sheet purposes as follows—

	£
Goods from Branch "A" . . .	2,450
,, ,, ,, "B" . . .	1,725
,, ,, ,, "C" . . .	2,100

On the footing that during the year ended 31st December, 19.., head office sold 75 per cent of the goods it had available for sale, prepare a Statement bringing out (to nearest £) the value at which the stock of goods on hand at head office should be included in the Balance Sheet at 31st December, 19...

6. Keep Fit Ltd. manufactures medicinal salts and sells them in tins of one standard size. The books of the company reveal balances and information as follows—

	£		£
Stock at Cost on 1st January, 19.. —		Distribution Charges . .	1,500
		Selling Expenses . . .	3,290
Tinned Salts . . .	1,800	Advertising	3,225
Ingredients . . .	500	Directors' Fees . . .	1,000
Tins, Labels, etc. . .	350	Sales	30,000
Purchases—		Freight and Carriage Inwards .	781
Ingredients . . .	6,190	Stocks at Cost on 31st December,	
Tins, Labels, etc. . .	3,200	19.. —	
Manufacturing Wages . .	4,688	Ingredients	370
Factory Expenses . . .	2,344	Tins, Labels, etc.. . .	425
Factory Rent . . .	1,562		

Certain ingredients purchased at £1·40 a cwt. during the previous year proved unsuitable, and 50 cwt. had been sold in the current year at £1 a cwt., the proceeds being included in sales; 50 cwt. were still in stock on 31st December, 19.., when the market value was £1·10 a cwt.

The stock of tinned salts on 31st December, 19.., was 50,000 tins (all produced during the year); in addition, 20,000 tins produced during the year were still held by consignees on 31st December. These had been invoiced at 5p a tin and treated as sales.

750,000 tins of salts were produced during the year.

The directors decided that the charge to Profit and Loss Account for the year in respect of advertising should be 10 per cent of the total manufacturing cost.

Prepare from the above information Manufacturing, Trading, and Profit and Loss Account for the year ended 31st December, 19... *(Adapted from C.A. Final.)*

7. The following is the Trial Balance of Manfac Ltd. as on 30th September, 19.6.

	£	£
Share Capital—Authorised and Issued		200,000
Freehold Land and Buildings at cost	96,550	
Leasehold Land and Buildings at cost	48,220	
Plant and Machinery at cost	385,000	
Depreciation on Plant and Machinery as at end of previous year		218,400
New Plant (purchased 30th June, 19.6). . . .	80,000	
Purchase of Raw Materials	196,640	
Sales.		533,660
Returns Inwards	3,400	
Returns Outwards		1,968
Trade Debtors	39,220	
Trade Creditors		15,520
Manufacturing Wages.	36,480	
Factory Expenses	31,364	
Selling Expenses, Commission, etc.	35,478	
Carried forward	952,352	969,548

	Brought forward	952,352	969,548
Office Salaries and Administration Expenses . . .		53,610	
Unquoted Investment.		100,000	
Loan from Frendnede Ltd.			20,000
Interest on Loan (net) [Paid 31st August, 19.6] . .		900	
Auditors' Remuneration and Expenses		1,550	
Investment Income (Received 31st January, 19.6) . .			12,000
Income Tax Schedule F		800	
Ordinary Dividend of 5% (Paid 1st March, 19.6) . .		10,000	
Advertising		4,800	
Balance at Bank.		59,534	
Corporation Tax Account			60,000
General Reserve.			80,000
Profit and Loss Account (balance)			95,250
Stocks at beginning of year:			
Raw Materials		37,412	
Finished Goods		15,840	
		£1,236,798	£1,236,798

The following further information is available:

(a) The Stocks at the date of the Trial Balance were—

Raw Materials	£40,572
Finished Goods	19,634

The company's stocks of Raw Materials and Finished Goods have been valued by the directors at the lower of cost and net realizable value and this has been the basis of valuation adopted by the directors for a number of years.

(b) The item "Office Salaries and Administration Expenses" includes £25,000 for Directors' Salaries and £3,000 for Directors' Fees. There are two directors of Manfac Ltd. These are the Chairman, whose salary is £15,000 and another director whose salary is £7,000. This latter director also receives the fees of £3,000.

(c) Depreciation at 12½ per cent per annum is to be provided for on the new plant, and on the written down value of the old Plant and Machinery.

(d) General Reserve is to be increased by £50,000.

(e) The balance at the credit of Corporation Tax Account represents the liability to Corporation Tax for the accounting year to 30th September, 19.5, estimated and provided at the date of the previous Balance Sheet. The liability has now been agreed at £58,150.

The estimated liability to Corporation Tax on the current profits is £67,600.

(f) The directors recommend a dividend of 20 per cent.

(g) The unquoted investment consists of 100,000 £1 Ordinary Shares in Intake Ltd. (not a subsidiary). The directors estimate the value of this investment to be £100,000.

The issued Ordinary Share Capital of Intake Ltd. is 1,500,000 Ordinary Shares of £1 each. Intake Ltd. was incorporated in Scotland.

(h) The loan from Frendnede Ltd. requires to be repaid by not later than 30th September, Year 17. The rate of interest is 7½ per cent per annum and the loan is unsecured.

(i) The company's Leasehold Land and Buildings comprise—Leases which expire on 30th September, Year 85, £38,220; Leases which expire on 30th December, Year 55, £10,000.

You are required to prepare in vertical form, from the foregoing information, Manufacturing, Trading, Profit and Loss and Appropriation Account for the year ended 30th September, Year 19.6, showing Cost of Materials Consumed, Cost of Finished Goods and Cost of Sales, together with a Balance Sheet as at that date. The Profit and Loss Account and Balance Sheet are to be in a form suitable for publication and circulation to shareholders and are to comply with the requirements of the Companies Acts 1948 and 1967. Assume Income Tax to be 40 per cent.

CHAPTER XXXI

MANAGEMENT ACCOUNTING, AIDS AND TECHNIQUES

1. The summarized revenue accounts of a business for two years show the following—

	31st December 19.4 £	31st December 19.5 £
Sales	90,000	120,960
Direct Labour and Direct Materials . . .	60,000	65,000
	30,000	55,960
Overheads	40,000	44,000
Profit (Loss)	(£10,000)	£11,960

New production methods were put into operation on 1st January, 19.5, and from that date sales prices were increased by 20 per cent.

Assuming that all goods produced each year are sold during each year prepare a statement for management showing concisely the composition of the increase in the gross profit.

2. The following are the trading results of four departments of Adept Ltd. for the past year—

	Dept A £	Dept B £	Dept C £	Dept D £
Direct Materials	4,000	6,000	5,000	8,000
Direct Labour	20,000	12,000	8,000	16,000
Overheads—Variable	8,000	4,000	6,000	8,000
Fixed	16,000	14,000	3,000	12,000
Total Cost	48,000	36,000	22,000	44,000
Profits (+) or Loss (—)	+12,000	—6,000	+2,000	+10,000
Sales	£60,000	£30,000	£24,000	£54,000

The directors are dissatisfied with the results of Department B and are considering closing it. They have received an offer from a prospective sub-tenant, who states that he is prepared to rent any one of the four departments at £7,000 per annum. Assume that the total fixed overheads are not likely to be reduced if one department is closed down.

Advise the directors whether or not to accept.

3. The variable cost per unit of a certain product is 60p, and its selling price per unit, £1·50.

Prepare a table showing the profit or loss on outputs of 30, 40 and 60 units assuming that the fixed expenses for the period amount to £1·30.

Represent this information on a break-even graph, and calculate the sales value at the break-even point.

4. X commences business on 1st January with £5,000 Capital, all in fixed assets. The following are the relevant details of his operations for the past four months of trading—

£4,000 purchases were made, payment therefor mid-February.

Sales: January £6,000; February £10,000; March £9,000; April £9,000. (Average credit period two calendar months.)

Purchases, exclusive of initial outlay, £19,960 (average credit period 6½ weeks).

Wages £6,630 (lag in payment 1½ weeks).

Rent £800 (£600 usual quarter days in arrear).

Depreciation of Fixed Assets £720.

Salaries £2,176 (lag in payment ½ week).

General Expenses £824, calculated at £206 per calendar month (average credit 1 calendar month).

Closing Stock £3,100. Net Profit £1,990.

Arrangements are made with bankers to provide the additional Working Capital. There are no drawings, and ignore Bank Interest.

Show—

(1) Statement of additional Working Capital to be provided.

(2) Trading and Profit and Loss Account for the four months ended 30th April, and Balance Sheet on that date.

5. Prior to the formation of a company to be known as Rockets Limited the promoters ask you to advise them as to the amount they should allow for working capital.

You are given the following information—

(1) Budget for 19.9, being the first year's trading.

	£	*Notes*
Sales (own manufactured products).	150,000	Credit allowed: 2 months.
Raw materials consumption .	36,000	Credit received: 2 months.
Wages	72,000	Lag in payment: 4 days (say ⅛ month).
Power	2,400	Payable quarterly in arrear on 1st January, April, July and October.
Insurance	480	Payable yearly in advance on 1st January.
Rent	1,500	Payable quarterly in advance on the usual quarterly days.
General administrative charges .	14,400	Lag in payment: 1½ months.
Travellers' commission (payable on all sales). . . .	7,500	Payable on 1st of month following that in which sales *effected*.
Depreciation	3,720	
	138,000	
Profit	12,000	
	£150,000	

(2) Manufacturing will proceed at *an even rate* throughout the year and *all* goods manufactured *will be sold* by the end of the year at which date there will be no finished stock and the value of the work in progress will be so negligible that it may be ignored.

(3) Raw material stocks will be maintained at approximately £15,000 and the initial stock will be acquired immediately.

(4) The heaviest sales will be effected towards the end of the year, with estimated peaks in October of £30,000, November £34,000, and December £50,000. Apart from these peak months the turnover will be equally spread over the other months of the year.

You are required to set out your computation of the working capital that will be required on 30th November, 19.9, and to illustrate your answer by a statement of current assets and current liabilities as on that date. All workings should be submitted.

(C.A. Final.)

6. The abridged Balance Sheets of Beta Ltd. as on 31st March, 19.6 and 31st March, 19.7, are set out below—

BALANCE SHEET, 31ST MARCH, 19.6

	£	£		£	£
Capital—			Fixed Assets—		
Ordinary Share Capital .	200,000		Freehold Property at		
Revenue Reserves—			cost . . .	145,000	
General Reserve . £30,000			Leaseholds at cost . .	5,000	
Profit and Loss Account . 12,000			Plant and Machinery—		
			Cost . . . £180,000		
		42,000	Less Depreciation 72,000		
		242,000			108,000
8 per cent Debentures . .		50,000	Investment—		258,000
Current Liabilities—			Shares in Associated Company		
Sundry Creditors . .	84,000		at cost	16,000	
Current Taxation . .	14,000		Current Assets—		
Proposed Dividend (net) .	10,000		Stock-in-trade .	44,000	
		108,000	Debtors. . . .	62,000	
			Balance at Bankers .	19,800	
					125,800
			Preliminary Expenses . . .		200
		£400,000			£400,000

BALANCE SHEET, 31ST MARCH, 19.7

	£	£		£	£
Capital—			Fixed Assets —		
Ordinary Share Capital .	250,000		Freehold Property at Cost	185,000	
Capital Reserves—			Plant and Machinery—		
Share Premium Account. . . £10,000			Cost . . . £210,000		
Profit on sale of Leaseholds . . 2,500			Less Depreciation 93,000		
Profit on redemption of Debentures . 400				117,000	
		12,900			302,000
Revenue Reserves—			Investment—		
General Reserve . £35,000			Shares in Associated Company, at		
Profit and Loss Account. . 12,500			cost	16,000	
		47,500	Loan to Associated Company . .	6,400	
		310,400	Current Assets—		
8 per cent Debentures . .		40,000	Stock-in-trade . .	51,000	
Current Liabilities—			Debtors. . . .	67,000	
Sundry Creditors . .	82,150		Balance at Bankers . .	18,400	
Current Taxation . .	15,750				136,400
Proposed Dividend (net) .	12,500				
		110,400			
		£460,800			£460,800

The following is a summary of the company's Profit and Loss Account for the year to 31st March, 19.7—

PROFIT AND LOSS ACCOUNT

	£		£
Depreciation. . . .	21,000	Profit on trading . . .	70,510
Debenture Interest (gross) .	4,000	Dividend received (gross). .	1,600
Preliminary Expenses . .	200	Corporation Tax over-provided	
Taxation on Profits of year .	16,710	for previous year. . .	300
Proposed Dividend (gross) .	25,000	Balance brought forward from	
Transfer to General Reserve .	5,000	previous year . . .	12,000
Balance carried forward .	12,500		
	£84,410		£84,410

You are required to prepare a statement showing a reconciliation of the company's working capital at 31st March, 19.7, with that at 31st March, 19.6. The reconciliation should show the sources of increases, and the application of decreases, in the company's working capital during the year under review.

Ignore taxation except when dealing with the items shown.

7. The following are the estimated figures for 19.4 in respect of a General Agency. The proportions of Gross Sales by departments to gross turnover of the agency are estimated to be—

Department A 20 per cent.
„ B 30 „ „
„ C 50 „ „

The average commissions to be earned, calculated on selling price, are—

Department A 10 per cent.
„ B 20 „ „
„ C 30 „ „

Fixed Expenses £4,000.
Variable expenses for the first £8,000 of commissions earned amount to half of the commissions, and thereafter they represent one-tenth of the further commissions earned.
From the foregoing information on—

(a) Prepare a Break-even Chart, with four pass points.
(b) Calculate the estimated profit or loss on a gross turnover, during 19.4, of £50,000.
(c) Show the workings to reconcile with the Break-even figure as disclosed in (a).
                                                        (*Adapted from C.A. Inter.*)

8. A haulage contractor operates a motor vehicle which he hires out for a fixed charge of £6 per week plus a mileage charge of 2p per mile run.
The weekly cost of operating the van, based on mileage of 300 weekly, is made up of—

Fixed Charges £8
Running Charges. . . . £3

You are required—

(a) To prepare a Break-even chart showing the mileage at which the revenue earned in a week equals the total operating costs for a week.
(b) To indicate on the chart, and to state, the profit or loss which would have arisen had the mileage run been (i) 400 per week; (ii) 600 per week.
(c) To ascertain from the chart, and to state, the amounts of the fixed charge and mileage charge for which the contractor would have to hire out the vehicle, in order to make a profit (whatever mileage is run) of (i) £3 for week; (ii) £4 per week.
                                                        (*Adapted from C.A. Final.*)

9. The following are the Trading Accounts of Y & Co.—

	19.8 £	19.9 £				19.8 £	19.9 £
Cost of Sales .	60,000	70,000	Sales	.	.	90,000	135,000
Gross Profit .	30,000	65,000					
	£90,000	£135,000				£90,000	£135,000

In 19.9 selling prices were 25 per cent higher than in 19.8.
Show the increase of gross profit as reflected by—

(a) Price increase;
(b) Volume increase;
(c) Efficiency increase.

For this purpose it can be assumed that there is no increase in the cost prices making up Cost of Sales.

10. A company intends to expand its turnover and profit by (*a*) extensive advertising; (*b*) price reduction; and (*c*) increase in the rate of commission to travellers, as follows—

(*a*) Extra expenditure on advertising, £3,000 in 19.6;

(*b*) Decrease prices by 5 per cent in 19.6;

(*c*) Increase travellers' commissions by ½ per cent to 3½ per cent in 19.6.

It is estimated that expenses unrelated to turnover will remain unchanged, except for an increase of £140 in Travellers' Expenses.

There is one selling "line" only, and the turnover in 19.5 consisted of Sales of 80,000 units at 50p each; resulting from the policy outlined above there was a considerable increase in sales in 19.6. Sales are not subject to seasonal fluctuations and earned a Gross Profit of 25 per cent and 22½ per cent in 19.5 and 19.6 respectively before charging *any* expenses (general or selling). Show—

(1) comparative figures and percentages on sales for 19.5 and 19.6;

(2) "break-even" sales required to absorb—

(*a*) the charges *not* variable with sales, and

(*b*) the *extra* charges variable with sales;

(3) the increase in gross and net profit credited to Profit and Loss attributable to (*a*) increase in volume, *less* (*b*) decrease in price.

It can be assumed that the proposed expenditure for 19.6 is exactly incurred.

The abridged Profit and Loss Account for 19.5 is—

	£	£
Sales		40,000
Gross Profit—25 per cent		£10,000
Expenses—		
Advertising	800	
Travellers' Commissions	1,200	
Travellers' Salaries and Expenses . . .	1,500	
Sales Department Expenses	1,700	
General Expenses	1,800	
		7,000
Net Profit		3,000
		£10,000

The Gross Profit for 19.6 amounted to £17,100.

11. Airton & Co. Ltd., whose share capital was £10,000 in shares of £1 each, commenced business on 1st April, 19.8, paying into the bank £10,000.

The trading profit is £2,685 *after* charging thereto depreciation at 10 per cent per annum on the Fixed Assets. Such gross profit takes account of Cash Sales £100 and Closing Stock £2,800.

General Expenses are £1,435 and Directors' Fees, £850, the former all paid in cash (no accruals) and the latter partly in cash taking into account a debit of £100 for goods taken out of stock (at selling price) by the Directors and not paid for, and an accrual of £150.

Closing Debtors and Creditors are £6,000 and £4,800 respectively. Fixed assets were purchased and paid for: (i) on 1st April, 19.8, £4,000; (ii) on 31st December, 19.8, £600.

Prepare in draft form—

(1) Trading and Profit and Loss Account for the year ended 31st March, 19.9, together with Balance Sheet on that date.

(2) Cash Account, together with an explanatory schedule or account.

Ignore Taxation, General Expenses detail and Preliminary Expenses. It can be assumed that the goods taken by the Directors were so taken equally between them.

12. From the following information you are required, for year ending 31st December, 19.4, to prepare—

(*a*) by quarters, a cash budget; and

(*b*) for the year, a budgeted source and disposal of funds statement.

It is expected that the working capital at 1st January, 19.4 will be as follows—

	£
Cash in hand and at bank	35,000
Stock	65,000
Debtors	50,000
Creditors	40,000

Budgeted profit statement—

	First quarter £	Second quarter £	Third quarter £	Fourth quarter £
Sales	150,000	135,000	165,000	150,000
Cost of sales	102,000	94,000	110,000	102,000
Gross profit	48,000	41,000	55,000	48,000
Administrative, selling and distribution expenses and interest	23,000	21,000	25,000	23,000
Net profit	£25,000	£20,000	£30,000	£25,000

Budgeted balances at the end of each quarter—

	31st March, 19.4 £	30th June, 19.4 £	30th Sept., 19.4 £	31st Dec., 19.4 £
Stock	65,000	75,000	60,000	65,000
Debtors	60,000	45,000	65,000	55,000
Creditors	50,000	40,000	55,000	48,000

Dividends amounting to £40,000 will be paid during the first quarter. Corporation tax amounting to £30,000 will be paid during the third quarter. Capital expenditure amounting to £88,000 is expected to be incurred during the fourth quarter and will be partly financed by a further issue of debentures amounting to £25,000 and the proceeds of the sale of old plant and equipment £5,000.

Depreciation amounting to £5,000 is included in the budgeted expenditure for each quarter. *(I.C.M.A.)*

13. Before introducing an electronic computer into a business a feasibility study should be undertaken. What steps would be involved and what matters should be considered in the feasibility study and how should the staff be prepared for the new arrangements necessary for the data processing work?

14. Will Power owns a merchanting business which is run by a manager, Mark Tyme. The accounts for the year to 31st March, 19.4 and the balance sheet as at the end of the year are as follows—

TRADING AND PROFIT AND LOSS ACCOUNT
FOR THE YEAR ENDED 31ST MARCH, 19.4

	£		£	£
Opening Stock . . .	13,000	Sales:		
Purchases . . .	42,000	Cash . . .	8,000	
Gross Profit c/d . . .	6,000	Credit . .	32,000	
				40,000
		Closing Stock. . .		21,000
	£61,000			£61,000
Depreciation	1,310	Gross Profit b/d . . .		6,000
Other Expenses . . .	2,090			
Manager's Salary . . .	1,600			
Net Profit	1,000			
	£6,000			£6,000

BALANCE SHEET AS AT 31ST MARCH, 19.4

	£		£	£
Capital Account		Fixed Assets:		
at 1st April, 19.3. . .	37,200	at Cost . .	35,740	
Add Profit for Year . .	1,000	*Less* Depreciation	5,240	30,500
	38,200			
Less Drawings . . .	2,000	Current Assets:		
		Stock. . . .		21,000
	36,200	Debtors . . .		16,000
Current Liabilities:				
Bank Overdraft . . .	17,300			
Trade Creditors . . .	14,000			
	£67,500			£67,500

Will Power is dissatisfied with these results, dismisses Mark Tyme and engages a new Manager, W. Izzard. In his first year, W. Izzard—

(*a*) doubles the rate of stock turnover, calculated on the average of the opening and closing stocks;
(*b*) increases the rate of gross profit to sales by one-third;
(*c*) by careful buying reduces the stock by £6,000 by the end of the year;
(*d*) doubles the ratio of cash to credit sales;
(*e*) takes as remuneration 25 per cent of the net profit remaining after charging all expenses, including his own remuneration. Other expenses, including depreciation, are unchanged from the previous year.

The ratios of trade creditors to stock and of debtors to credit sales are the same at the end of the year as at the beginning, and Will Power's drawings are the same as in the previous year.

Draft the accounts of the business for the new manager's first year and the balance sheet at the end of the year, and comment briefly on any striking changes disclosed by a comparison of the two balance sheets.

15. Shrapnell (Engineering) Ltd. sell metal offcuts from their product to a local scrap dealer. Recently production has been increased to meet a considerable growth in demand and in consequence the volume of offcuts has risen. Proposals have been made to utilize the offcuts for the manufacture by Shrapnell of an additional product. To do this Shrapnell will require to lease additional premises, and will need to purchase and install plant and machinery. Additional working capital will also be required. The details are as follows—

	£
Cost of Plant and Machinery	120,000
Installation costs	22,500
Additional working capital—19.1	22,500
19.2 and thereafter	30,000
Lease of premises per annum	7,500
Fixed costs per annum—19.1	18,000
19.2	21,000
Thereafter	22,500
Variable costs (per unit)	22½p
Sales value (per unit)	50p
Sales volume (number of units)—19.1	192,000
19.2	264,000
19.3	300,000
Thereafter	300,000

The revenue which the company will receive if it continues to sell the offcuts is—19.1 4,800
19.2 6,600
Thereafter per annum 7,500

The project attracts a Government grant of 25 per cent which will be receivable in 19.1.

Writing Down Allowances—20 per cent on the reducing balance.

Corporation Tax—40 per cent payable in the year following that in which the liability is incurred.

All cash flows may be assumed to take place on the last day in each year, apart from the initial outflows for the capital cost of the equipment, installation cost, and the initial working capital, which take place at the beginning of the first year. Assume the realization value of the plant and machinery at the end of 19.5 to be equal to its written down value for taxation purposes.

Calculate a rate of return for the project.

Table of Present Values of £1

Year	Present Values of £1		
	10%	12%	14%
19.1	·91	·89	·88
19.2	·83	·80	·77
19.3	·75	·71	·68
19.4	·68	·64	·59
19.5	·62	·57	·52
19.6	·56	·51	·46

CHAPTER XXXII

MISCELLANEOUS

1. Six producers, A, B, C, D, E, and F, are members of the Central Producers' Association. The Association takes, at a uniform price fixed year by year, and markets the whole of the output produced by the members.

Each member has a standard percentage and, in any year in which a member produces in excess of his standard percentage, he incurs a penalty, for each unit of the excess, calculated at twice the profit per unit of output earned by the Association in that year; the proceeds of the penalties are divided among members who produce less than their standard percentages, *pro rata* to their deficiencies.

The Association's profits of each year are distributed in proportion to the actual output of the year.

The relevant balances in the books of the Association on 31st December, 19.., were as follows—

	£
Stock on 1st January, 19..	2,000
Purchases from Members	750,000
Sales	860,000
General Expenses of the Association	6,000
Bad Debts	2,500
Due for Purchases: B, £4,000; D, £500	4,500

The Stock on 31st December, 19.., was valued at £500.
The respective standard percentages and the actual output for 19.. were—

	Standard Percentage	Actual Output (in thousands of units)
A	25	600
B	10	180
C	15	300
D	17½	300
E	27½	500
F	5	120

Prepare the Association's Revenue Account, Revenue Distribution Account, and Penalty Account for the year ended 31st December, 19.., and a statement showing the amount due to or by each member. (*C.A. Final.*)

2. The European agents of a London firm are instructed to pay to an American firm $6,000 out of the balance of 60,000 francs owing to their principals and remit the balance to London.

The rates of exchange may, for this purpose, be assumed to be—

(1) 12 francs to £ (conversion rate in the books of London principals).
(2) 4 francs to $ (cost of remittance to U.S.A.). (Or $3 to £.)
(3) 11·8 francs to £ (remittance to London).

The London firm had entered into a forward exchange transaction at 119 to £ in respect of 25,000 francs.
Write up the books of the London firm.

3. The following balances (*inter alia*) appear in the books of X Ltd. on 30th June, 19.8—

	£
Process 1—Raw Materials purchased	20,000
Process 2—Raw Materials purchased (other than goods from Process 1)	6,000
General expenses paid	3,600
Vendor	10,000

	£
Debtors	4,550
Creditors (Trade)	10,700
Cash at Bank	2,000
Share Capital	20,300
Preliminary Expenses (£600 paid).	700

X Ltd. had acquired the business from Vendor on 1st July, 19.7, for a purchase consideration of £15,000, payable as to £10,000 in cash and settlement in shares of £1 each fully paid at par. The book-keeper had not dealt with the opening entries fully, having opened up accounts for debtors and creditors and debited vendor with the cash paid to him, viz. £10,000.

The Share Capital balance of £20,300 represents the issue of 20,000 shares of £1 each to outsiders which are fully paid, except for a shareholder with 2,000 shares who failed to pay the last call of 25p per share. His shares were forfeited and 1,000 were reissued as fully paid for 80p a share. The book-keeper had credited moneys received to Share Capital, but had made no other entries in the Share Capital Account *re* the forfeiture and reissue.

The assets taken over from Vendor were—

	£	
Fixed Assets	6,000	
Stock	5,000	(all sold for £5,550)
Debtors.	3,000	

Creditors taken over were £2,000.

Process 1 transfers the whole of its output to Process 2 at a profit of 10 per cent on cost; the latter transferring its production to a Selling Department at a profit of 15 per cent on cost. The general expenses are to be apportioned as to one-half to Selling Department and the other half as between the two processes in proportion to their respective goods *consumed*. The Selling Department makes a gross profit of 20 per cent on its sales (apart from the goods which had been taken over and sold at a profit of £550). It has sold exactly 50 per cent of the goods it has received from Process 2.

The Stocks on hand at 30th June, 19.8, are—

Process 1—Raw Materials	£5,000
Process 2—Raw Materials ex Process 1 . . .	£9,600
Other Raw Materials	£2,000

There are no finished goods nor work in progress in either process and no stock deficiencies or surpluses.

Show Process Accounts, Selling Department Trading and Profit and Loss Account for the year ended 30th June, 19.8, together with Balance Sheet as at that date, making suitable provision for unrealized profit on goods unsold. Draft accounts only need be shown, not necessarily as they would be published. Tax and depreciation to be ignored. Workings must be shown.

(Institute of Company Accountants' Final.)

ANSWERS

CHAPTER I

1. DOUBLE Entry book-keeping is the system of keeping accounts which takes advantage of the twofold aspect of every transaction, whereby one account—that relating to the receiving of a benefit—is debited, and another account—that relating to the yielding of a benefit—is credited. By means of books of prime entry, postings of certain accounts may be performed in total.

Double Entry book-keeping is so-called so as to distinguish it from Single Entry—the system that takes into account only the personal aspect of each transaction.

The term "Single Entry" may be extended to cover any system which falls short of full Double Entry.

2. (i) Personal: credit side.   (iv) Personal: credit side.

 (ii) Nominal: debit side.   (v) Real: debit side.

 (lii) Nominal: debit side.   (vi) Real: debit side.

3.

PURCHASES DAY BOOK

			£	£
19..				
Jan. 1	B. Pitt—			
	(Details)		600	
	Less 33⅓% Trade Discount		200	
				400

[Posted to the debit of Purchases Account.]

RETURNS OUTWARD BOOK

			£	£
19..				
Jan. 1	B. Pitt—			
	(Details)		300	
	Less 33⅓% Trade Discount		100	
				200

[Posted to the credit of Returns Outward (or Purchases) Account.]

CASH BOOK, CREDIT SIDE

		Discount	Cash	Bank
		£	£	£
19..				
Jan. 1	By B. Pitt	10	—	190

Dr.				B. PITT				*Cr.*
19..			£	19..				£
Jan. 1	To Returns . . .	200		Jan. 1	By Goods . . .			400
	,, Cash and Discount . .	200						
		£400						£400

4. *Dr.*   B. WISE   *Cr.*

19..							£	19..				£
Jan. 1	To Goods	.	.	.	.	.	240	Jan. 4	By Cheque on account .	.	.	150
6	,, ,,	.	.	.	.	.	150	10	,, Returns .	.	.	75
15	,, ,,	.	.	.	.	.	20	12	,, Cheque and Discount	.	.	90
20	,, ,,	.	.	.	.	.	80	15	,, Cash[1] .	.	.	20
								25	,, Cheque and Discount	.	.	90
								31	,, Balance .	.	c/d	65
							£490					£490

Feb. 1	To Balance	.	.	.	b/d	65

[1] Alternatively, the Cash Sale may be debited to cash and posted direct to Cash Sales, the above items not appearing in the Ledger Account.

5.   JOURNAL

									£	£
[Date]	Cash .	.	.	.	.	.	.	. *Dr.*	4	
	Bank.	.	.	.	.	.	.	. *Dr.*	150	
	Stock.	.	.	.	.	.	.	. *Dr.*	400	
	Buildings	.	.	.	.	.	.	. *Dr.*	1,000	
	Fixtures	.	.	.	.	.	.	. *Dr.*	90	
	Debtors	.	.	.	.	.	.	. *Dr.*	10	
	Machinery .	.	.	.	.	.	. *Dr.*		300	
	To Bills Payable	.	.	.	.	.				350
	,, Creditors	.	.	.	.	.				75
	,, A. Mann—Loan	.	.	.	.					150
	,, Capital .	.	.	.	.	.				1,379
	Being assets and liabilities introduced into the business on this date.								£1,954	£1,954

6.   JOURNAL

								£	£
(1) Purchases .	.	.	.	.	.	.	. *Dr.*	200	
To A. Text .	.	.	.	.	.	.	.		200
(2) Returns Inward .	.	.	.	.	.	.	. *Dr.*	25	
To B. Jones	.	.	.	.	.	.	.		25
(3) Carriage Inwards .	.	.	.	.	.	.	. *Dr.*	5	
To Cash	.	.	.	.	.	.	.		5
(4) A. Wood .	.	.	.	.	.	.	. *Dr.*	75	
To Bank .	.	.	.	.	.	.	.		70
,, Discounts Allowed .	.	.	.	.	.	.			5
(5) Insurance .	.	.	.	.	.	.	. *Dr.*	10	
To Cash	.	.	.	.	.	.	.		10
(6) Cash .	.	.	.	.	.	.	. *Dr.*	5	
To Office Furniture	.	.	.	.	.	.			5
(7) Bad Debts .	.	.	.	.	.	.	. *Dr.*	15	
To M. Stone	.	.	.	.	.	.	.		15

JOURNAL—(contd.)

		£	£
(8) No entry till acceptance.			
If accepted—			
Bills Receivable . . . . Dr.		100	
To A. Rose			100
(9) N. Town . . . . Dr.		40	
To Sales			40

Narratives ignored.

7.

	Debit	£		Credit	£
(a)	Machinery	500·00	Cash		500·00
(b)	Bank	170·00			
	Discounts Allowed . .	2·63	J. Robinson		172·63
(c)	Bank	600·00	Insurance Company . .		600·00
	Insurance Company . .	600·00	Insurance Claim . .		600·00
(d)	Bank	75·00	Motor Van[1] . . .		75·00
(e)	J. Fitter	260·75	Bank		250·00
			Interest		10·75

[1] Depreciation to date of sale and loss (if any) will be written off by crediting Motor Vans Account and debiting Profit and Loss Account.

8.

PURCHASES DAY BOOK

19.. May 16	G. Long— 10 doz. Pairs of Blankets at £5·25 a pair . . . . *Less* 10% Trade Discount	£ 630 63	£ £567

PURCHASES RETURNS BOOK

19.. May 18	G. Long— 20 Pairs of Blankets at £5·25 a pair . . . . *Less* 10% Trade Discount	£ 105·00 10·50	£ £94·50

CASH BOOK—CREDIT SIDE

		Discount	Cash	Bank
		£	£	£
19.. May 27	By G. Long	23·63		448·87

Dr. G. LONG **Cr.**

19..		£	19..		£
May 18	To Returns . . .	94·50	May 16	By Goods . . .	567·00
27	„ Cheque and Discount .	472·50			
		£567·00			£567·00

9. A Trial Balance is a schedule of the Ledger balances (including cash and bank) drawn up at a given date after all the postings and additions have been made, the debits appearing in a debit column, the credits in a credit column. The totals of the two columns if in agreement will be prima facie evidence of total arithmetical accuracy of the book-keeping.

The Trial Balance may be out of balance (*inter alia*) for the following reasons—

(1) Error in posting, e.g. transposition of figures.
(2) Balance unextracted.
(3) Balance extracted, but placed on wrong side of Trial Balance.
(4) Incomplete double entry of item or items.
(5) Errors in the balancing of the opening figures.
(6) Errors in addition.

10. (*a*) Errors not disclosed by the Trial Balance may be—

(i) Errors of omission: both aspects of the Double Entry unposted; omission of an original entry.

(ii) Errors of commission: a posting made to the wrong account, but correct in amount, through similarity of name, for example.

(iii) Errors of principle: a fundamental rule of book-keeping violated, such as Returns Inward debited to Purchases Account; Repairs posted to Asset Account.

(iv) Compensating errors: a debit and a credit balance both overcast or undercast to the same extent; an incorrect posting compensated for by one or more incorrect postings (of the same total amount) on the opposite side of the Ledger, e.g. an overcast of the Sales Day Book of £10 compensated by an overcast of the Sales Returns Book of £6 and an undercast of Discount Received Account of £4.

(*b*) In a Trial Balance the following would ordinarily be found—

(1) Capital Account: on the credit side (Personal Accounts: credit supplier).
(2) Purchases: on the debit side (Real Accounts: debit what comes in).
(3) Returns Inward: debit side (Real Accounts: debit what comes in).
(4) Bills Payable: credit side. The equivalent of a creditor.
(5) Bank overdraft: credit side. A balance in favour of the banker makes him a creditor. (Personal Accounts: credit supplier.)
(6) Drawings: a deduction from Capital, and hence a debit balance. (Personal Accounts: debit receiver.)

11.   Trial Balance, 31st December, 19..

	Dr. £	Cr. £
Capital		3,000
Premises	1,500	
Fixtures	500	
Plant and Machinery	400	
Purchases	7,640	
Sales		10,500
Returns Inwards	150	
Returns Outwards		70
Carriage Inwards	40	
Carriage Outwards	75	
Discounts Received		175
Discounts Allowed	240	
Wages	730	
Insurance, Rates, etc.	135	
Rent Receivable		110
General Expenses	325	
Creditors		1,224
Debtors	3,420	
Drawings	300	
Bills Payable		100
Cash in Hand	12	
Bank Overdraft		288
	£15,467	£15,467

12.   Trial Balance, 31st December, 19..

	Dr. £	Cr. £
B. Blank: Capital		1,556
B. Blank: Drawings	564	
Leasehold Premises	741	
Sales		2,756
Debtors	530	
Purchases	1,268	
Purchases Returns		264
Creditors		528
Loan from Bank		250
Trade and Office Expenses	784	
Bank	142	
Bills Payable		100
Salaries and Wages	598	
Stock (as at 1st January, 19..)	264	
Rent, Rates, etc.	465	
Sales Returns	98	
	£5,454	£5,454

13. *Dr.*   CAPITAL   *Cr.*

			19..	£
			Apr. 1 By Balance . . b/d	3,000

Dr.   DRAWINGS   *Cr.*

19..				£	
Mar. 19	To Balance .	.	. b/d	330	
30	,, Cash	.	. .	30	

Dr.   FREEHOLD PROPERTY   *Cr.*

19..				£
Apr. 1	To Balance .	.	. b/d	1,200

Dr.   FURNITURE AND FITTINGS   *Cr.*

19..				£
Apr. 1	To Balance .	.	. b/d	150

Dr.   STOCK   *Cr.*

19..				£
Apr. 1	To Balance .	.	. b/d	1,436

Dr.   SALES   *Cr.*

			19..		£
			Mar. 19	By Sundries . . .	8,041
			31	,, ,, . . .	248

Dr.   RETURNS INWARDS   *Cr.*

19..			£	
Mar. 19	To Sundries	. . .	159	
31	,, ,,	. . .	25	

Dr.   PURCHASES   *Cr.*

19..			£	
Mar. 19	To Sundries .	. . .	6,735	

Dr.   RETURNS OUTWARDS   *Cr.*

			19..		£
			Mar. 19	By Sundries . . .	252

Dr.   CASH PURCHASES   *Cr.*

19..			£	
Mar. 23	To Cheque	. . .	82	

Dr.   OFFICE EXPENSES   *Cr.*

19..				£	
Mar. 19	To Balance .	.	. b/d	510	
30	,, Cash	.	. .	16	

Dr.   SALARIES AND COMMISSION   *Cr.*

19..				£	
Mar. 19	To Balance .	.	. b/d	455	
24	,, Cash	.	. .	23	

Dr.   CARRIAGE OUTWARDS   *Cr.*

19..				£	
Mar. 19	To Balance .	.	. b/d	159	
24	,, Cash	.	. .	5	

Dr.   CARRIAGE INWARDS   *Cr.*

19..				£	
Mar. 19	To Balance .	.	. b/d	145	

Dr. **BAD DEBTS** *Cr.*

19..				£	
Mar. 19	To Balance .	.	b/d	131	
23	,, W. Wright	.	.	11	

Dr. **DISCOUNT** *Cr.*

		19..				£
		Mar. 19	By Balance	.	b/d	15

Dr. **CASH SALES** *Cr.*

		19..				£
		Mar. 31	By Cash	. .	.	36

Dr. **F. DRAKE** *Cr.*

19..				£	19..				£
Mar. 19	To Balance .	.	b/d	74	Mar. 21	By Cheque .	.	.	74
24	,, Goods .	.	.	154	30	,, Returns	.	.	25

Dr. **W. WRIGHT** *Cr.*

19..				£	19..				£
Mar. 19	To Balance .	.	b/d	33	Mar. 22	By Cheque	.	.	22
						,, Bad Debts	.	.	11
				£33					£33

Dr. **H. NELSON** *Cr.*

19..		£	19..				£
Mar. 29	To Cheque on account .	100	Mar. 19	By Balance	.	b/d	318

Dr. **C. BLAKE** *Cr.*

		19..				£
		Mar. 19	By Balance	.	b/d	152

Dr. **G. COOK** *Cr.*

19..				£	
Mar. 22	To Goods .	.	.	94	

JOURNAL

19..			£	£
Mar. 23	Bad Debts . . . . . . *Dr.*		11	
	To W. Wright			11
	Being balance of account written off.			

SALES DAY BOOK

19..		£
Mar. 22	G. Cook.	94
24	F. Drake	154
		£248

SALES RETURNS BOOK

19..		£
Mar. 30	F. Drake	25

Dr.   CASH BOOK   **Cr.**

19..		Dis-count £	Cash £	Bank £
Mar. 19	To Balances b/d		37	224
21	,, F. Drake			74
23	,, W. Wright			22
30	,, Bank—*contra*		50	
31	,, Cash Sales		36	
			£123	£320
Apr. 1	To Balances b/d		49	88

19..		Dis-count £	Cash £	Bank £
Mar. 23	By Cash Purchases			82
24	,, Carriage Outwards		5	
	,, Salaries and Commission			100
	,, H. Nelson, on account		23	
29	,, Cash—*contra*			50
30	,, Office Expenses		16	
	,, Drawings		30	
31	,, Balances c/d		49	88
			£123	£320

TRIAL BALANCE, 31ST MARCH, 19..	Dr. £	Cr. £
Capital		3,000
Drawings	360	
Freehold Property	1,200	
Furniture and Fittings	150	
Stock	1,436	
Sales		8,289
Returns Inwards	184	
Purchases	6,735	
Returns Outwards		252
Cash Purchases	82	
Office Expenses	526	
Salaries and Commission	478	
Carriage Outwards	164	
Carriage Inwards	145	
Bad Debts	142	
Discount		15
Cash Sales		36
F. Drake	129	
H. Nelson		218
C. Blake		152
G. Cook	94	
Cash	49	
Bank	88	
	£11,962	£11,962

14. The agreement of the opening figures should be proved in ROUGH form, and items which require no further attention put straight into the Trial Balance; thus—

TRIAL BALANCE AS AT 1ST JANUARY, 19..		Dr. £		Cr. £
Capital			T.	4,750
Debtors	S.	800		
Creditors			P.	800
Stock	T.	2,000		
Motor Vans	T.	2,000		
Insurance (prepaid)	T.	50		
Rent (owing)			N.	200
Post-dated Cheques	N.	150		
Bank	C.	750		
		£5,750		£5,750

Items marked T. may be inserted direct into the final Trial Balance; accounts being opened for the remainder marked S. for Sales Ledger; P. for Purchases Ledger; C. for Cash Book; N. for Nominal Ledger.

The Accounts will be duly posted after writing up the Cash Book, Petty Cash Book, and the Day Books, the totals from the Discount columns of the Cash Book, and from Petty Cash Book and Day Books being "posted" direct to the Trial Balance.[1]

The following abbreviations are used—

D.B. = Day Books.	C.B. = Cash Book.
P.C.B. = Petty Cash Book.	O. = Opening Balances.
S. = Sales Ledger.	P. = Purchases Ledger.
N. = Nominal Ledger.	T.B. = Trial Balance.

[1] In examinations set by the professional bodies, this system should always be employed unless otherwise stated. Non-professional examining bodies, e.g. Royal Society of Arts, however, often prefer detailed accounts to be opened.

Dr.   CASH BOOK   Cr.

19..		Folio	Discount Allowed £	Bank £	19..		Folio	Discount Received £	Bank £
Jan. 1	To Balance b/d	O.		750	Jan. 1	By Petty Cash	P.C.B.		5
4	,, A. Black & Co.	S.		50	2	,, Rent	N.		200
	,, W. Cox	S.		250		,, F. Flint	P.	13	337
5	,, A. Black &	S.				,, Petty Cash	P.C.B.		15
6	Co.	S.	5	195	5	,, Motor Expenses	T.B.		23
7	,, T. Green: First and Final Dividend	S.		25	7	,, J. Smith	P.	3	142
						,, Balance	c/d		548
			£5	£1,270				£16	£1,270
			T.B.					T.B.	
Jan. 8	To Balance	b/d		548					

Dr.   PETTY CASH BOOK   Cr.

Receipts £	C.B. Folio	Date	Details	Voucher No.	Total £	Wages £	Postages £	Telephone £
5	C.B.	19.. Jan. 1	Cash					
15	C.B.	2	Cash					
			Postages . . .		4		4	
			Wages . . .		12	12		
			Telephone . . .		3			3
					19	£12	£4	£3
						T.B.	T.B.	T.B.
		7	Balance . . .	c/d	1			
£20					£20			
1		Jan. 8	Balance . . .	b/d				

SALES DAY BOOK

19.. Jan. 1	W. Cox, 240 yds. of Lino at 60p a yard . . .	£144	
	Less Trade Discount at 8½%	12	
			£132
			T.B.

PURCHASES DAY BOOK

19.. Jan. 4	F. Flint, 360 yds. of Cloth at 20p a yard	£72
		T.B.

PURCHASES RETURNS AND ALLOWANCES BOOK

19.. Jan. 7	J. Smith, Goods Damaged	£5
		T.B.

NOMINAL LEDGER

				£						£
Dr.			POST-DATED CHEQUES						*Cr.*	

19..				£	19..					£
Jan. 1	To Balance . . b/d	O.	150		Jan. 7	By Cooper, Cheque Dis-				
7	,, Post-dated Cheques .	S.	300			honoured[1] . .	S.	150		
						,, Balance . . .	c/d	300		
			£450						£450	
Jan. 8	To Balance . . . b/d		300							

[1] To the debit of Cooper's Account.

Dr.			RENT						*Cr.*	
19..				£	19..					£
Jan. 1	To Cash . . . C.B.		200		Jan. 1	By Rent Owing . b/d O.				200

SALES LEDGER

Dr.			T. GREEN						*Cr.*	
19..				£	19..					£
Jan. 1	To Balance . . b/d	O.	100		Jan. 7	By Cash for First and				
						Final Dividend of				
						25p in £ . .	C.B.	25		
						,, Bad Debts . .	T.B.	75		
			£100						£100	

Dr.			W. COX						*Cr.*	
19..				£	19..					£
Jan. 1	To Balance . . b/d	O.	300		Jan. 5	By Cash . . . C.B.				250
	,, Sales . . . D.B.		132		7	,, Balance . . . c/d				182
			£432						£432	
Jan. 8	To Balance . . . b/d		182							

Dr.			J. COOPER & CO.						*Cr.*	
19..				£	19..					£
Jan. 1	To Balance . . b/d	O.	150		Jan. 7	By Post-dated Cheques .	N.	300		
7	,, Post-dated Cheque									
	Dishonoured . .	N.	150							
			£300						£300	

Dr.			A. BLACK & CO.						*Cr.*	
19..				£	19..					£
Jan. 1	To Balance . . b/d	O.	250		Jan. 4	By Cash . . . C.B.				50
					6	,, Cash and Discount . C.B.				200
			£250						£250	

PURCHASES LEDGER

Dr.			F. FLINT & CO.						*Cr.*	
19..				£	19..					£
Jan. 2	To Cash and Discount . C.B.		350		Jan. 1	By Balance . . b/d	O.	650		
7	,, Balance . . . c/d		372		4	,, Purchases . . D.B.		72		
			£722						£722	
					Jan. 8	By Balance . . . b/d		372		

Dr.			J. Smith & Co.		Cr.	
19..			£	19..		£
Jan. 7	To Allowance . . . D.B.		5	Jan. 1 By Balance . . b/d O.		150
	„ Cash and Discount . C.B.		145			
			£150			£150

Trial Balance as at 7th January, 19..

		Dr.	Cr.
		£	£
Capital	O.		4,750
Stock, 1st January, 19..	O.	2,000	
Motor Vans	O.	2,000	
Insurance.	O.	50	
Bad Debts	S.[1]	75	
Motor Expenses	C.B.	23	
Discount Allowed	C.B.	5	
Discount Received	C.B.		16
Petty Cash	P.C.B.	1	
Wages	P.C.B.	12	
Postages	P.C.B.	4	
Telephone	P.C.B.	3	
Sales	D.B.		132
Purchases	D.B.	72	
Purchases (Allowances)	D.B.		5
Cox	S.	182	
Flint	P.		372
Cash at Bank	C.B.	548	
Post-dated Cheques	N.	300	
		£5,275	£5,275

[1] Direct from Green's Ledger Account.

CHAPTER II

1.   CASH BOOK ADJUSTMENT

		£
Balance as per Cash Book	*Dr.*	327·95
Less Bank Interest charged		12·33
	Dr.	£315·62

BANK RECONCILIATION STATEMENT AS AT 31ST DECEMBER, 19..

		£
Balance as per Bank Statement.	*Cr.*	267·89
Add Unpresented Cheque		32·94
	Cr.	300·83
Less Uncleared Cheque.		616·45
Balance as per Cash Book (adjusted)	*Dr.*	£315 62

2.   CASH BOOK ADJUSTMENT

		£
Balance as per Cash Book	*Dr.*	557·50
Less Bank Interest and Charges		8·11
	Dr.	£549·39

BANK RECONCILIATION STATEMENT AS AT 30TH JUNE, 19..

		£
Balance as per Bank Statement.	*Dr.*	1,401·63
Less Unpresented Cheques—	£	
P.	29·20	
Q	801·17	
R	5·74	
S.	132·32	
		968·43
	Dr.	433·20
Add Uncleared Cheques		116·19
Balance as per Cash Book (adjusted).	*Dr.*	£549·39

3.   CASH BOOK ADJUSTMENTS

		£
Balance as per Cash Book	*Dr.*	1,257·47
Less Bank Commission.		2·53
		1,254·94
Add Bank Interest		18·63
Adjusted Balance as per Cash Book	*Dr.*	£1,273·57

BANK RECONCILIATION STATEMENT AS AT 31ST JANUARY, 19..

		£
Balance as per Bank Statement (overdrawn) . . . . *Cr.*		539·83
Less Uncleared Cheque.		2,500·00
	Dr.	1,960·17
	£	
Less Unpresented Cheques—		
[Details]	100·11	
	89·63	
	247·75	
	92·42	
	113·58	
	43·11	
		686·60
Balance as per Cash Book (adjusted). . . . . *Dr.*		£1,273·57

4. CASH BOOK ADJUSTMENTS

	£	£
Balance as per Cash Book (overdrawn) . . . . *Cr.*		812·94
Add Commissions	5·50	
,, Interest	13·57	
,, Transfer to Customs Duties Account . . .	2,500·00	
,, Transfer to Deposit Account	2,000·00	
		4,519·07
	Cr.	5,332·01
Less Transfer from Deposit Account	5,450·00	
,, Transfer from Customs Duties Account . . .	1,088·68	
		6,538·68
Adjusted Balance as per Cash Book . . . . . . *Dr.*		£1,206·67

BANK RECONCILIATION STATEMENT AS AT . . . .

	£	£
Balance as per Bank Statement. . . . . *Dr.*		1·34
Add Uncleared Cheques		1,507·61
	Dr.	1,508·95
Less Unpresented Cheques—		
[Details]	102·28	
	50·00	
	150·00	
		302·28
Balance as per Cash Book (adjusted). . . . . *Dr.*		£1,206·67

5. Dr.   PETTY CASH BOOK   *Cr.*

Date		Fol.	£		Date		Total	Postages and Stationery	Travelling Expenses	Carriage	Sundries[2]
			£				£	£	£	£	£
19.. Jan. 4	To Balance	b/d	2·50		19.. Jan. 4	By Postages	1·50	1·50			
	,, Cash	C.B.	17·50		Jan. 5	,, Travelling Expenses	0·45		0·45		
						,, Telegrams	0·46	0·46			
						,, Shorthand Notebooks	0·55	0·55			
					6	,, Carriage	0·27			0·27	
						,, Fares	0·37		0·37		
						,, Envelopes	1·15	1·15			
					8	,, Repairs to Typewriter	4·22				4·22
					9	,, Carrier[1]	1·84			1·84	
						,, Cleaner	5·00				5·00
							15·81	£3·66	£0·82	£2·11	£9·22
						,, Balance c/d	4·19				
			£20·00				£20·00				
Jan.10	To Balance	b/d	4·19								

[1] This item would be inserted in the analysis column for "Ledger Accounts," but this is not provided for in the question.
[2] Sundries column would be analysed at the foot and postings made to relevant nominal ledger accounts.

195

6.   CASH BOOK ADJUSTMENTS

		£	£
Balance as per Cash Book (overdrawn).	Cr.		80
Add Commission		8	
„ Error Adjusted.		20	
			28
	Cr.		108
Less Error Adjusted.			50
Adjusted Balance as per Cash Book (overdrawn)	Cr.		£58

BANK RECONCILIATION STATEMENT AS AT........................

		£
Balance per Bank Statement	Dr.	60
Add Uncleared Cheques		26
		86
Less Unpresented Cheques		144
Balance overdrawn as per Cash Book (adjusted)	Cr.	£58

7.   BANK RECONCILIATION STATEMENT, 31ST DECEMBER, 19.4

		£	£
Balance overdrawn per Bank Statement . . .	Cr.		1,026·64
Add Cheques drawn not yet cleared		12·00	
		1,021·14	
		98·12	
		112·80	1,244·06
	Cr.		2,270·70
Less Cash received not banked		2,100·00	
Bill paid not credited		250·00	2,350·00
	Dr.		79·30
Add Cash Book corrections—			
Bank Interest unentered		151·06	
Cheque Book unentered		1·00	
Subscription unentered		4·20	156·26
	Cr.		76·96
Less Cheque Book entered twice			0·25
Apparent Bank Balance per Cash Book	Cr.		£76·71

8. A's books.

Dr. CASH BOOK Cr.

		Bank No. 1	Bank No. 2			Bank No. 1	Bank No. 2	
		£	£			£	£	
	To Balances . . b/d	85	3,094	By Cheque dishonoured .			20	(2)
(3)	,, Remittance D. & Co. .	22		,, Adjustment *re* £20 Australia to Sterling .			4	(4)
(6)	,, Cheque No. 2 charged to No. 1 in error (*contra*)	32		,, Cheque No. 2 charged to No. 1 in error (*contra*) . .			32	(6)
				,, Payment S.O. . .			10	(8)
(11)	,, Transfer (*contra*) . .		200	,, Cheque £21 entered as £12 . . .			9	(9)
(12)	,, Cheque paid in £18 entered as £17 . .			,, Bank Charges . .		3	4	(10)
	,, Balance . . c/d	64	1	,, Transfer (*contra*) . .		200		
				,, Balance . . c/d			3,216	
		£203	£3,295			£203	£3,295	
	,, Balance . . b/d		3,216	,, Balance . . b/d		64		

BANK RECONCILIATION STATEMENT, 31ST DECEMBER, 19.9

			No. 1.		No. 2.
	Balances in credit for Bank Sheets	£	£ 809	£	£ 2,009
(2)	Add cheques not yet credited .		200		140 (2)
			1,009		2,149
(5) (7)	Transfers	—73[1]		+73	
	Transfers	—1,000[1]	1,073	+1,000	1,073
			64		3,222
(13)	Less unpresented cheque .				6
	Per Cash Book . . .		£64 *Dr.*)		£3,216

[1] To be notified to the Bank.

9. (*a*)

Dr. CASH BOOK Cr.

		Income	Capital			Income	Capital
		£	£		By Funeral Expenses, to	£	£
To Balances . . b/d		1,600	4,941	correct entry of £100 to £110 . . .			10
,, Deposit Interest . .		9		,, Balances . . c/f		1,609	4,931
		£1,609	£4,941			£1,609	£4,941

(*b*) BANK RECONCILIATION—

	Current	Deposit
	£	£
Balance per Bank Statement	1,869	4,930
Amounts paid in not cleared	141	
Interest on deposit	9	
	2,019	
Cheque drawn on wrong account 10		10
		4,940
Less Interest on deposit (credited to wrong account) . .		9
Cheques not cleared 400		
	410	
Balance per Cash Book	£1,609	£4,931

The bank should be instructed to transfer £1 from Current Account to Deposit Account to correct the error *re* professional charges, *less* deposit interest due to income.

CHAPTER III

1. Cost price is $\frac{5}{6} \times$ £180 = £150. (The profit is 20 per cent, i.e. $\frac{1}{5}$, of cost, which is $16\frac{2}{3}$ per cent or $\frac{1}{6}$ of selling price.)

2. Selling price is $1\frac{1}{4} \times$ £180 = £225. (The profit is 20 per cent, i.e. $\frac{1}{5}$, of selling price, which is 25 per cent or $\frac{1}{4}$ of cost.)

		£	£
3. Opening stock at Balance Sheet value (i.e. cost less 25 per cent)	.		180
Add $33\frac{1}{3}$ per cent to bring up to cost			60
			240
Packages invoiced during the year (at cost plus 50 per cent) .	.	2,200	
Less returns at invoice price	.	1,600	
		600	
Less $33\frac{1}{3}$ per cent to reduce to cost	.	200	
			400
Closing stock "out" at cost			640
Less 25 per cent reduction			160
Closing Stock at Balance Sheet value.			**£480**

4. A   B   C   D

$5 + 2 + 2 + 1 = 10$

		£
A receives $\frac{5}{10} \times$ £1,500 =		750
B ,, $\frac{2}{10} \times$ £1,500 =		300
C ,, $\frac{2}{10} \times$ £1,500 =		300
D ,, $\frac{1}{10} \times$ £1,500 =		150
		£1,500

If A drops out, then B   C   D

$2 + 2 + 1 = 5$

		£
B receives $\frac{2}{5} \times$ £1,500 =		600
C ,, $\frac{2}{5} \times$ £1,500 =		600
D ,, $\frac{1}{5} \times$ £1,500 =		300
		£1,500

5. If the average sales of the first three months are taken as 1, the average for the next four months will be 2 and that for the last five months 4.

3 months in the ratio of 1:1 =   3   i.e. (3 × 1)
4   ,,   ,,   ,,   ,,   of 2:1 =   8   i.e. (4 × 2)
5   ,,   ,,   ,,   ,,   of 4:1 = 20   i.e. (5 × 4)

31 units

The sales in the four months, April to July, will therefore be

$$\frac{8}{31} \times £15,500 = £4,000.$$

Taking the four months in question, it may be assumed that the average sales of April, May, and July are 1, so that June sales will be 5.

3 months in the ratio of 1:1 = 3
June   ,,   ,,   ,,   ,, 5:1 = 5
                                        ――
                                        8 units
                                        ＝

June sales will therefore be $\frac{5}{8}$ × £4,000 = £2,500.

6. The final amount realized will be—

$$\frac{5,000}{80} \times \frac{85}{1} \times \frac{1}{95} \times \frac{102}{1} = £5,704 \text{ (to the nearest £).}$$

The flat rate on the 5 per cent Stock is $\frac{5}{95}$ × 100 = 5·26 per cent p.a.
The profit on redemption is $\frac{7}{95}$ × 100, which is
$\frac{7}{95} \times \frac{100}{10}$ yearly = $\frac{70}{95}$ = 0·74 per cent p.a.

The redemption yield is therefore   6·00 per cent p.a.

	£
7. Costs actually to be incurred	1,900
Add for contingencies 5 per cent of the total cost, i.e. $\frac{1}{19}$th of the actual costs.	100
Total costs including contingencies.	2,000
Add for profit 20 per cent of the contract price, i.e. 25 per cent of the total costs	500
Contract price.	£2,500

8. The book debts are—

$$\frac{100}{96\frac{1}{4}} \times \frac{100}{95} \times \frac{100}{98} \times £89,608·75$$

$$= \frac{100}{96\frac{1}{4}} \times \frac{20}{19} \times \frac{50}{49} \times £89,608·75$$

$$= \frac{400,000}{358,435} \times £89,608·75$$

$$= \frac{400,000}{358,435} \times \frac{358,435·00}{4} = £100,000$$

The debts are therefore dealt with as follows—

	£
Book debts	100,000·00
Less Bad Debts: 2 per cent on £100,000 . .	2,000·00
	98,000·00
Less Cash Discount: 5 per cent on £98,000. .	4,900·00
	93,100·00
Less Commission: 3¾ per cent on £93,100 . .	3,491·25
Net amount due to X Ltd.	£89,608·75

[Alternatively, the book debts may be calculated by—

adding to £89,608·75, $\frac{3\frac{3}{4}}{96\frac{1}{4}}$ thereof, i.e. £3,491·25., giving £93,100;

adding to £93,100, $\frac{5}{95}$ thereof, i.e. £4,900, giving £98,000; and by
adding to £98,000, $\frac{2}{98}$ thereof, i.e. £2,000, giving £100,000.]

9. STATEMENT OF COMMISSION DUE TO MANAGER

	Total	Retained by Company	Due to Manager	
	£	£	£	
Profit (1)	2,000	2,000	—	
Profit (2)	2,200	2,000	200	10% of £2,000 or $\frac{10}{100}$ of £2,200
Profit (3)	2,300	2,000	300	15% of £2,000 or $\frac{15}{115}$ of £2,300
Profit (4)	1,200	1,000	200	20% of £1,000 or $\frac{20}{120}$ of £1,200
	£7,700	£7,000	£700	

10. COMPUTATION OF ESTIMATED CONTRACT PRICE

As the estimate of profit is $\frac{1}{6}$ of "selling" price (i.e. contract price) this is $\frac{1}{5}$ of *total* cost (i.e. materials, labour, depreciation, overheads, contingency provision and manager's commission).

The manager is entitled to 10 per cent of the net profit, that is, the excess of contract price over the *total* cost, which includes his commission; as the latter must be $\frac{1}{10}$ of profit, and such profit $\frac{1}{5}$ of cost, the commission is therefore $\frac{1}{50}$ of total cost.

The provision for contingencies is $\frac{1}{10}$ of total cost (including this provision). The calculation is—

Let R = Reserve,
C = Total Cost,
R = $\frac{1}{10}$ × C,
C = 3,000 + R + Commission.

As, however, commission is $\frac{1}{50}$ Cost,

$$C = 3,000 + R + \tfrac{1}{50} \times C.$$
$$\therefore \qquad 50C = 150,000 + 50R + C.$$
$$49C = 150,000 + 50R$$

but as R = $\frac{1}{10}$C

$$49C = 150,000 + 50 \left(\frac{C}{10}\right)$$
$$49C = 150,000 + 5C$$
Hence
$$44C = 150,000$$
$$C = £3,409$$

The statement is—

	£
Cost of Materials, Labour, Depreciation and Overheads . . .	3,000
Contingency Reserve $\frac{1}{10}$ × £3,409	341
Manager's Commission $\frac{1}{50}$ × £3,409 or 10% of £682 . .	68
Total Cost.	3,409
Profit (estimate) $\frac{1}{5}$ × £3,409; or $\frac{1}{6}$ × £4,091. . . .	682
Estimated Contract Price	£4,091

[*Note.* If the Commission had already been known, then the cost *before* charging up Contingency Reserve would be £3,068 (£3,000 + £68) and the Contingency Reserve would be ascertainable therefrom, i.e.—

$$\tfrac{1}{9} \times £3,068 = £341 \text{]}$$

The problem may be worked out arithmetically, as follows—

Assume that the total cost is £100 and the Contingency Reserve accordingly is £10. As the profit would be £20 (i.e. $\frac{1}{5}$ of Cost) the Manager's Commission is £2, that is 10 per cent of profit of £20 (or, as shown in the algebraic workings, $\frac{1}{50}$ of Cost). Hence the materials and cost figure is £88, thus—

	£	Result £
Materials and cost	88	3,000
Contingency Reserve	10	341
Manager's Commission	2	68
Total Cost	£100	£3,409

Therefore the total cost, where materials and cost are £3,000, is $\frac{100}{88} \times 3,000 =$ £3,409. The resultant figures are obtained quite simply by taking the fractions of $\frac{1}{50}$ and $\frac{1}{10}$ of £3,409 for Contingency Reserve and Commission respectively.

It will be observed that the question can be solved by ascertaining any *one* of the unknown factors (Reserve, Commission, Cost).

11.   "BREAK-EVEN" SALES

	%
Profit on Sales [= 33⅓% on Cost] . . .	25
Selling Costs	10
Gross Profit	15

Sales, therefore, required to "break even" are $\frac{100}{15} \times$ £1,500 = £10,000.

Thus—

	£
Profit on Cost (33⅓% of £7,500 = 25% of £10,000) .	2,500
Selling Costs 10% of £10,000	1,000
Profit available, equalling Standing Charges . .	£1,500

CALCULATION OF A'S COMMISSION

12. The question may be dealt with arithmetically by taking the two parts of the commission separately—

	£
(a) Commission 5 per cent of £4,800	240
(b) Commission $\frac{10}{100}$ of [£4,800 − (£3,000 + £240) − $\frac{1}{11}$ of £1,560] .	142
	£382

Alternatively, it may be calculated by simple algebra—

Let C = Total Commission
then $C = 240 + \frac{1}{10}(4,800 - 3,000 - C)$
$= 240 + \frac{1}{10}(1,800 - C)$
$10C = 2,400 + 1,800 - C$
∴ $11C = 4,200$
$= £382$

Proof—

	£	£	£
(1) Commission on Sales 5 per cent of £4,800 . .			240
(2) Commission on "excess" Sales		4,800	
Less Cost (¾ of £4,000)	3,000		
Less Total Commission	382		
		3,382	
		£1,418	
10 per cent thereof			142
			£382

CHAPTER IV

1.

Date	Amount	Days from 18th July	Products
19..	£		
July 18	500	0	0
Aug. 12	600	25	15,000
Nov. 16	800	121	96,800
	£1,900		111,800

Calculations—

(1) Average due date:

$$\frac{111,800}{1,900} = 59 \text{ (to the nearest whole number)} = \text{15th September.}$$

(2) Therefore the drawings are deemed to have been made at this date, so that interest is chargeable for 107 days, i.e. 15th September to 31st December.

(3) Interest:

£1,900 at 5 per cent per annum—

$$1,900 \times \frac{5}{100} \times \frac{107}{365}$$

$$= 1,900 \times \frac{5}{100} \times \frac{107}{365}_{73}$$

$$= £27 \cdot 85$$

2.

Due Date	Amount	Days from 18th April	Products
19..	£		
April. 18	220	0	—
May 24	125	36	4,500
June 30	200	73	14,600
July 18	350	91	31,850
	£895		50,950

Calculation—

$$\text{Average due date} = \frac{50,950}{895} = 57 \text{ days after 18th April}$$
(to the nearest whole number)

$$= \text{14th June}$$

3.

Date	Amount	Days from 4th July	Products
19.. July 4	£ 364	0	
30	523	26	13,598
Sept. 10	462	68	31,416
	£1,349		45,014

Calculation—

Average date $= \dfrac{45,014}{1,349} = 33$ days from 4th July (to the nearest whole number)

$= $ 6th August

4. Dr. — L. M. GIBSON IN ACCOUNT CURRENT WITH F. K. JOHNSON — Cr.

Dr.

Date	Particulars	Days	Products	Principal
19..				£
July 1	To Balance . . . b/d	184	94,550	513·86
Aug. 17	,, Goods	167	6,680	40·00
,, 19	,, ,,	134	96,570	720·67
,, 30	,, ,,	123	1,845	15·00
Nov. 12	,, ,,	49	681	13·90
Dec. 31	,, Interest on Products of £65,576 for one day at 5% p.a. (from contra)			8·98
			200,326	£1,312·41
19..				
Jan. 1	To Balance . . . b/d			42·41

Cr.

Date	Particulars	Days	Products	Principal
19..				£
Aug. 1	By Cash	152	76,000	500·00
Sept. 1	,, ,,	121	48,400	400·00
,, 1	,, 3 months' Draft due 4th Dec.	27	8,100	300·00
Oct. 22	,, Goods	70	1,400	20·00
Dec. 14	,, Cash	17	850	50·00
,, 31	,, Balance of Products (to contra) . c/d		65,576	
,, 31	,, Balance			42·41
			200,326	£1,312·41

5. Dr. — V. PARK IN ACCOUNT CURRENT WITH M. SIDE — Cr.

Dr.

Date	Particulars	Days	Products	Principal
19..				£
July 2	To Goods	182	72,800	400·00
Aug. 1	,, ,,	152	212,800	1,400·00
Oct. 1	,, ,,	91	91,000	1,000·00
Dec. 1	,, 2 months' Bill due 4th Feb.,			1,000·00
,, 15	,, Cash	16	4,800	300·00
,, 31	,, Balance of Products (to contra) . c/d		5,100	0·70
			386,500	£4,100·70

Cr.

Date	Particulars	Days	Products	Principal
19..				£
July 10	By Sight Draft	174	34,800	200·00
Sept. 15	,, Goods	121	181,500	1,500·00
Oct. 15	,, Cash	77	61,600	800·00
Nov. 15	,, Goods	46	73,600	1,600·00
Dec. 31	,, Products on Bill (contra)	35	35,000	
,, 31	,, Interest on Products of £5,100 for one day at 5% p.a. (from contra)			0·70
			386,500	£4,100·70
19..				
Jan. 1	By Balance . . . b/d			0·70

6.

R. U. DINN IN ACCOUNT WITH WESTERN BANK

Date	Particulars	Debits £	Credits £	Balances Dr. £	Balances Cr. £	No. of Days	Products Dr.	Products Cr.
19..								
July 1	Balance	200·00		200		15	3,000	
15			340		140·00	16		2,240
31		40·00			100·00	15		1,500
Aug. 15			120		220·00	16		3,520
31		70·00	50		200·00	15		3,000
Sept. 15			60		260·00	15		3,900
30		180·00	20		100·00	31		3,100
Oct. 31		240·00		140		30	4,200	
Nov. 30		110·00	170	80		15	1,200	
Dec. 15			290		210·00	16		3,360
31		80·00	110		240·00			
31	Interest[1]	0·59						
	Commission[2]	1·16						
	Balance c/d	238·25				184	¹ (a) 8,400	¹ (b) 20,620
		£1,160·00	£1,160·00	238·25	238·25			
19..								
Jan. 1	Balance b/d		238·25					

£
1·15
0·56
___
59

¹ (a) £8,400 at 5% per annum for one day
  (b) £20,620 at 1% per annum for one day
² 10p per cent on £1,160.

CHAPTER V

1. (*a*) THE Profit and Loss Account is an account showing on the debit side the current expenses of administration, selling, and distribution, and on the credit side the gross profit from the Trading Account (or debit in the case of gross loss on trading), and other gains not attributable directly to trading, e.g. discounts received, rents receivable.

The account will include full provision for depreciation, bad and doubtful debts, and accrued expenses. The balance of Profit and Loss Account is the net profit or net loss, and is carried to the Capital Account of a sole trader, to individual partners' Capital or Current Accounts in partnerships, and to Profit and Loss Appropriation Account in limited companies.

Where manufacturing takes place (as distinct from pure merchanting, i.e. where goods are purchased and sold in the same condition), it is usual to subdivide the Trading Section into (*a*) Manufacturing, and (*b*) Trading. The former will include all the appropriate expenses and costs of manufacturing or producing goods in a suitable condition for sale, and hence raw materials, manufacturing wages, and depreciation of plant will be therein included in order to arrive at the costs of the output; the Trading Account will then be debited with the cost of the manufactured goods and credited with the sales (the opening and closing stocks of manufactured goods will be dealt with in the usual way). If, *in addition*, merchanted goods are dealt with, the transactions in them will also appear in the same Trading Account (under separate headings) or be shown in separate columns or under a separate account, e.g. Merchanting Trading Account to distinguish from the transactions in connection with the Manufactured Goods.

(*b*) The purpose of the Trading Account is to arrive at gross profit or gross loss on sales, whilst that of the Profit and Loss Account is to arrive at the net profit or net loss of the business for the same period, after charging all the costs, charges, and expenses and crediting all revenue gains, not included in the Trading Account. The disposal of the balance on each account is (i) in the case of the Trading Account to the Profit and Loss Account, (ii) in the case of the latter account to proprietor's or partner's Capital or Current Accounts, or if a limited company to Profit and Loss Appropriation Account.

Both accounts deal with a specific period (the same in each case), and only gains or losses actually *attributable* to the period under review must be included, so that adjustments in both accounts may be necessary.

Thus, briefly distinguished, the Trading Account will be charged with the cost entailed in getting goods into saleable condition, and the Profit and Loss Account with all other relevant expenses, costs and charges of a revenue nature, including necessary provisions and accruals, other than those appertaining to Trading.

2.   JOURNAL

19..			£	£
Dec. 18	Office Furniture . . . . . . *Dr.*		20	
	To Acme Manufacturing Co.			20
	Being purchase on credit of filing cabinet . .			
31	Rent (above the "line") . . . . *Dr.*		50	
	To Rent (below the "line").			50
	Being accrual for rent for quarter to date.			

3. *Dr.*   RENT   *Cr.*

19.9			£	19.9		£
Apr. 3	To Cash: Rent for quarter to March 31, Year 9 .		60	Dec. 31	By Profit and Loss Account	240
July 2	,, Cash: Rent for quarter to June 30, Year 9 . .		60			
Oct. 1	,, Cash: Rent for quarter to September 30, Year 9 .		60			
Dec. 31	,, Rent accrued . . c/d		60			
			£240			£240
19.0				19.0		
Jan. 5	To Cash: Rent for quarter to December 31, 19.9 .		60	Jan. 1	By Balance accrued . b/d	60

PROFIT AND LOSS ACCOUNT FOR THE YEAR ENDED 31ST DECEMBER, 19.9
(*includes*)
                                                           £ |
Rent   .   .   .   .   240 |

BALANCE SHEET AS AT 31ST DECEMBER, 19.9 (*includes*)
        Liabilities   £ |
Creditors for Expenses—Rent   .   .   60 |

Note. Should rent be due on the usual quarter days, then six days will be deducted from the first payment, and six days' extra accrual will be included at the end of the year.

4. (*a*)

Dr.   WAGES   *Cr.*

19..			£	19..		£
Dec. 31	To (Details) . . .		?	Dec. 31	By Trading Account . .	?
	,, Wages accrued . c/d		98			
				19..		
				Jan. 1	By Balance accrued . b/d	98

(*b*)

Dr.   GEORGE DICKSON   *Cr.*

19..		£	19..		£
Dec. 28	To Returns	17	?	By (Details) . . .	?

Dr.   PURCHASES   *Cr.*

19..		£	·19..		£
Dec. 31	To Sundries	?	Dec. 28	By Returns— (George Dickson) .	17
			31	,, Trading Account . .	?

Alternatively, the adjustment may be made by crediting above the "line" and debiting below the "line" £17, and passing the item through Purchases Returns Book on 1st January, 19... [Unless sold, such returned stock will be included in Stock on hand at 31st December, 19...]

(*c*)

Dr.   INSURANCE   *Cr.*

19..		£	19..		£
Dec. 31	To (Details) . . .	?	Dec. 31	By Profit and Loss Account	?
					,, Insurance prepaid . c/d	21
19..						
Jan. 1	To Balance prepaid . b/d	21				

5. *Dr.* TELEPHONE *Cr.*

19.6		£	19.6		£
Jan. 15	To Cash: Rent to 31st March, 19.6	5·00	Jan. 1	By Calls accrued . .	12·00
	,, ,, : Calls to 31st December, 19.5	12·00	Dec. 31	,, Profit and Loss Account	79·93
Apr. 16	,, ,, : Rent to 30th June, 19.6 .	5·00			
	,, ,, : Calls to 31st March, 19.6.	16·27			
July 12	,, ,, : Rent to 30th September, 19.6 .	5·00			
	,, ,, : Calls to 30th June, 19.6 .	15·33			
Oct. 15	,, ,, : Rent to 31st December, 19.6 .	5·00			
	,, ,, : Calls to 30th September, 19.6 .	14·16			
Dec. 31	,, Calls accrued . c/d	14·17			
		£91·93			£91·93
19.7			19.7		
Jan. 17	To Cash: Calls to 31st December, 19.6 .	14·17	Jan. 1	By Calls accrued . b/d	14·17
	,, ,, : Rent to 31st March, 19.7 .	5·00			

6. B. HINDER

TRADING AND PROFIT AND LOSS ACCOUNT FOR THE SIX MONTHS ENDED 30TH SEPTEMBER, 19..

	£		£
To Stock at 31/3/19.. .	8,345	By Sales	41,567
,, Purchases	25,467	,, Stock at 30/9/19.. . .	8,840
,, Wages	2,454		
,, Gross Profit . . . c/d	14,141		
	£50,407		£50,407
To Rates	500	By Gross Profit . . b/d	14,141
,, Discounts allowed . .	1,647	,, Discounts received . .	1,476
,, General Expenses[1] . .	2,550		
,, Carriage[2] . . .	945		
,, Bad Debts . . .	994		
,, Depreciation— Plant and Machinery . .	133		
,, Net Profit transferred to Capital Account . . .	8,848		
	£15,617		£15,617

BALANCE SHEET AS AT 30TH SEPTEMBER, 19..

		£			£
Capital—			Fixed Assets—		
Balance at 31st March, 19... . .	£19,972		Freehold Land and Buildings . .		5,500
Less Drawings . .	3,715		Plant and Machinery .	£2,676	
	16,257		*Less* Depreciation .	133	
Add Net Profit per Profit and Loss Account . .	8,848		Furniture		2,543 384
		25,105			8,427
Sundry Creditors—			Current Assets—		
Trade	4,908		Bank		3,749
Rates . . .	125		Sundry Debtors . .	£10,891	
		5,033	*Less* Bad Debts Provision	1,894	
					8,997
			Insurance Premium prepaid[1] . .		125
			Stock		8,840
		£30,138			£30,138

[1] Assumed Insurance Premiums are included in General Expenses.
[2] Assumed Carriage Outwards.

7.   JOURNAL

19.9 Dec. 31		£	£
	Stock . . . . Dr.	9,327	
	To Trading and Profit and Loss Account (Trading section)		9,327
	Being closing Stock brought into books.		
	Depreciation . . . . Dr.	1,105	
	To Plant and Machinery		1,105
	Being Depreciation at 6¼% per annum for half-year on £164 (£5) and for year on £17,600 (£1,100).		
	Loss on Sale of Plant and Machinery . . Dr.	103	
	To Plant and Machinery		103
	Being loss on Sale [£164—(£5 + £56)].		
	Bad Debts Provision (above the "line") . . Dr.	617	
	To Bad Debts Provision (below the "line") . .		617
	Being new Bad Debts Provision at this date, viz. 5% of £12,345		
	Dad Debts , ... Dr.	42	
	To Bad Debts Provision		42
	Being balance of Bad Debts Provision (£617—£575) transferred.		
	Suspense (19.9) . . . . . . Dr.	4	
	To Difference in Balance		4
	Being difference in books of short debit kept in suspense.		
	Customer . . . . Dr.	9	
	To Suspense (19.8)		9
	Being error in 19.8 of Sale £110 posted as £101 adjusted.		
	Trading and Profit and Loss Account (Profit and Loss section) . . . . Dr.	1,435	
	To Depreciation		1,105
	,, Loss on Sales of Plant and Machinery . .		103
	,, Bad Debts[1]		227
	Being balances transferred.		

[1] Bad Debts (per question) plus transfer, i.e. £185 + £42.

[Plant and Machinery Account will appear—

Dr.			PLANT AND MACHINERY		Cr.	
19.9		£	19.9			£
Jan. 1	To Balance . .	b/d 17,764	June 30	By Sale		56
			Dec. 31	,, Depreciation on Plant sold (3¼%) .		5
				,, Loss on Sale . .		103
				,, Depreciation on £17,600 (6¼%) .		1,100
				Balance .	c/d	16,500
		£17,764				£17,764
19.0						
Jan. 1	To Balance . .	b/d 16,500				

Alternatively, the adjustments in respect of Bad Debts may be made by first transferring debts written off as bad to the Bad Debts Provision, making the new provision
and balancing off the account to Profit and Loss Account. (See next question, Bad
Debts Provision.)]

8.

PROFIT AND LOSS ACCOUNT FOR THE YEAR ENDED 28TH NOVEMBER, 19.6

	£	£		£
Gross Losses¹—			Gross Profits¹—	
Wheat	27		Cattle	595
Manures	185		Horses	117
Feeding Stuffs	141	353	Hens	217
Wages		484	Straw and Hay	13
Rent and Taxes		91	Oats	102
Carriage		27	Vegetables	532
Heating and Lighting		101	Grazing	10
Postages		11	Sundries	156
Depreciation—Implements		33		
Repairs to Property		45		
Horse Expenses		25		
Insurance		129		
Implements Upkeep		113		
Bad Debts		8		
Sundries		12		
Net Profit for Year		310		
		£1,742		£1,742

¹ Gross Losses may be deducted inset from Gross Profits and the final figure carried out.

210

BALANCE SHEET AS AT 28TH NOVEMBER, 19.6

	£				£
Capital—			Fixed Assets—		
Balance at 29th November,	£		Implements—		
19.5 . . .	1,560		Balance at 29th	£	
Less Drawings . .	1,071		November, 19.5 . .	259	
	———		*Plus* Additions . .	70	
	489			———	
Add Net Profit				329	
for year . .	310		*Less* Depreciation .	33	
	———	799		———	296
Sundry Creditors. . . .		252			
			Current Assets—		
			Cash at Bank . .	274	
			„ in Hand . .	13	
				———	287
			Sundry Debtors . .	75	
			Less Bad Debts Pro-		
			vision . .	8	
				———	67
			Stocks		401
		£1,051			£1,051

Creditors (£42) may be deleted and credited to Drawings Account. [See Rent and Taxes Account in rough Adjustment Sheet.]

ROUGH ADJUSTMENT SHEET

		£			£
Bad Debts Provision . . .		8	Profit and Loss		8

		£			£
Rent and Taxes (per T.B.) . .		258	*Drawings*		42
			Drawings		125
			Profit and Loss . . .		91

	£			£
Drawings—		Capital		1,071
Wages	650			
Rent and Taxes . . .	42			
Vegetables . . .	80			
Rent and Taxes . . .	125			
Repairs to Property . .	63			
Heating and Lighting . .	101			
Insurance . . .	10			

		£			£
Wages (per T.B.)		1,084	*Drawings*		650
Vegetables		50	Profit and Loss . . .		484

		£			£
Repairs to Property (per T.B.) .		108	*Drawings*		63
			Profit and Loss . . .		45

		£			£
Heating and Lighting (per T.B.) .		202	*Drawings*		101
			Profit and Loss . . .		101

		£			£
Insurance (per T.B.) . . .		139	*Drawings*		10
			Profit and Loss . . .		129

		£			£
Profit and Loss		532	Vegetables (per T.B.) . . .		402
			Drawings		80
			Wages		50

Heavy type items appear in the Profit and Loss Account; items in italics are transfers.

9.

WELL

TRADING AND PROFIT AND LOSS ACCOUNT FOR THE YEAR ENDED 30TH SEPTEMBER, 19.8

	£		£
Stock at 1/10/19.7 . . .	394	Sales	47,102
		Stock at 30/9/19.8 . . .	932
Purchases . . . £26,805			
Less Returns . 5			
	26,800		
Carriage and Cartage Inwards . .	8,531		
Sack Hire	131		
Gross Profit . . . c/d	12,178		
	£48,034		£48,034
Carriage and Cartage Outwards .	4,254	Gross Profit . . . b/d	12,178
Wagon Hire	198	Cartage Earnings . . .	219
Commission on Sales . .	210	Wagon Hire Earnings . .	84
Rents, Rates, Taxes and Insurance .	356		
Telephone Rent and Calls . .	66		
Legal and Professional Charges .	169		
Salaries and Wages . . .	3,589		
Motor Expenses . . .	152		
Trade Expenses . . .	868		
Bank Charges and Interest . .	45		
Discounts allowed . . .	53		
Travelling Expenses . . .	924		
Bad Debts (*less* recoveries)[1] .	86		
Wagon Repairs . . .	476		
Depreciation—			
Wagons . . . £44			
Motor-car . . 95			
Furniture, Fixtures and			
Fittings . . 4			
	143		
Net Profit transferred to Capital			
Account . . .	992		
	£12,481		£12,481

[1] Alternatively— (i) Bad Debts, debit to Profit and Loss Account, £103.
(ii) Bad Debts recovered, credit to Profit and Loss Account, £17.

BALANCE SHEET AS AT 30TH SEPTEMBER, 19.8

	£			£
Well—Capital:		Fixed Assets—		
Balance at 1st	£	Furniture, Fixtures	£	
October, 19.. . .	2,405	and Fittings . .	160	
Less Drawings .	1,907	*Less* Depreciation .	4	
				156
	498	Wagons . . .	886	
		Less Depreciation .	44	
Add Net Profit for				842
year . .	992	Motor-car . . .	475	
	1,490	*Less* Depreciation .	95	
				380
				1,378
		Current Assets—		
Sundry Creditors—		Cash in hand . . .		47
Trade . . .	5,102	Sundry Debtors .	6,717	
Expenses—		*Less* Bad Debts		
Rent . £65		Provision . .	189	
Audit . . 42				6,528
	107	Insurance Premium prepaid . .		12
	5,209	Stock-in-trade . . .		932
Bank Overdraft . . .	2,198			
	£8,897			£8,897

10.

M. DORE

TRADING AND PROFIT AND LOSS ACCOUNT FOR THE YEAR ENDED
31ST DECEMBER, 19..

		£	£
Sales.			150,380
Less Cost of Goods Sold—			
Purchases		49,300	
Opening Stock		26,600	
		75,900	
Deduct Closing Stock . .		14,300	
		61,600	
Carriage Inwards . . .		2,300	
			63,900
Trading Profit for Year			86,480
Salaries and Wages		52,200	
Heating, Lighting and Cleaning .		2,520	
Rents, Taxes, etc.		2,200	
Advertising		3,300	
Bad Debts		1,880	
Discounts		1,579	
Loan Interest (Gross) . . .		6,400	
Bank Charges		1,640	
Depreciation—			
Buildings and Plant . . £8,000			
Delivery Vans. . . . 1,500			
		9,500	
			81,219
Net Profit for Year			£5,261

BALANCE SHEET
AS AT 31ST DECEMBER, 19..

		£	£
Fixed Assets—			
Goodwill			6,700
		£	
Buildings and Plant at 1/1/19..		80,000	
Less Depreciation for Year		8,000	
			72,000
Delivery Vans at 1/1/19..		6,000	
Less Depreciation for Year		1,500	
			4,500
			83,200
Current Assets—			
Cash.		720	
Debtors £16,020			
Less Bad Debts Provision . . . 860			
	15,160		
Less Discounts Provision . . 379			
		14,781	
Stock		14,300	
(A) £29,801			
Current Liabilities—			
Creditors		£9,620	
Bank Overdraft		15,280	
Loan Interest Accrued		3,200	
(B) £28,100			
Working Capital (A)–(B)			1,701
Total Net Capital Employed			£84,901
Represented by—			
M. Dore—Capital:			
at 1/1/19..		1,640	
Add Net Profit for Year		5,261	
		6,901	
Less Drawings for Year		2,000	
			4,901
Loan			80,000
			£84,901

11.

(a)

Dr.				OLD CAR				Cr.	
19.9				£	19.9				£
Jan. 1	To Balance . . . b/d			110	May 31	By Cash . . .			60
					Dec. 31	,, Depreciation—			
						5 months at 20%			
						per annum . .			9
						,, Profit and Loss Account .			41
				£110					£110

Dr.				NEW CAR				Cr.	
19.9				£	19.9				£
May 1	To Cash			300	Dec. 31	By Depreciation—			
						8 months at 20%			
						per annum . .			40
						,, Balance . . c/d			260
				£300					£300
19.0									
Jan. 1	To Balance . . b/d			260					

(b)

Dr.				OLD LEASE				Cr.	
19.9					19.9				£
Jan. 1	To Balance . . b/d			1,050	Dec. 31	By Depreciation—1 year .			150
						,, Balance . . c/d			900
				£1,050					£1,050
19.0									
Jan. 1	To Balance . . b/d			900					

Dr.				NEW LEASE				Cr.	
19.9				£	19.9				£
June 30	To Cash			975	Dec. 31	By Depreciation—			
	,, Materials . . .			125		$\frac{1}{13}$ of £1,248[1] .			96
	,, Wages . . .			148		,, Balance . . c/d			1,152
				£1,248					£1,248
19.0									
Jan. 1	To Balance . . b/d			1,152					

[1] *Note.* The lease has 6½ years to run. Half a year's depreciation (one-thirteenth) must be written off.

12.   A. STREET

TRADING AND PROFIT AND LOSS ACCOUNT FOR THE YEAR ENDED 31ST DECEMBER, 19..

19..		£	19..		£
Stock at 1/1/19..		3,080	Sales, *less* Returns	. . .	17,040
Purchases, *less* Returns	. . .	7,575	Stock at 31/12/19..	. . .	4,380
Carriage .	. . .	377			
Wages .	. . .	4,231			
Gross Profit	. . . c/d	6,157			
		£21,420			£21,420
Rates and Taxes	. . .	194	Gross Profit	. . . b/d	6,157
Salaries .	. . .	806			
Lighting and Heating	. . .	82			
Electric Power	. . .	192			
Travellers' Commission	. . .	207			
Insurance	. . .	93			
Advertising	. . .	57			
Bad Debts	. . .	335			
Discounts	. . .	20			
General Expenses	. . .	302			
Postages, Telephone, etc.	. . .	111			
Loss on Machinery	. . .	310			
Depreciation—					
Plant and Machinery	. £194				
Furniture & Fittings	. 12				
		206			
Net Profit transferred to Capital Account	. . .	3,242			
		£6,157			£6,157

	£	£			£	£	£
Capital—				**Fixed Assets—**			
Balance at 1st Jan. 19..	16,000			Land and Buildings			7,920
Less Drawings	2,120			Plant and Machinery—			
	13,880			Balance at 1st Jan 19...		2,017	
Add Profit for year	3,242			*Less* Sale	£190		
		17,122		Loss on Sale	310		
Creditors—						500	
Trade	2,211					1,517	
Wages	250			*Plus* Addition		420	
		2,461				1,937	
				Less Depreciation		194	
							1,743
				Furniture and Fittings—			
				Balance at 1st Jan., 19..		189	
				Plus Additions		50	
						239	
				Less Depreciation		12	
							227
							9,890
				Current Assets—			
				Stock		4,380	
				Debtors	£3,085		
				Less Bad Debts Provision[1]	299		
					2,786		
				Less Discounts Provision	68		
						2,718	
				Insurance prepaid		10	
				Cash at Bank		2,585	
							9,693
		£19,583					£19,583

Notes—

(1) Assumed that the goods omitted (see (*h*) in question) are included in the stock or accounted for in sales.

(2) The item of Electric *Power* appears heavy and seems inappropriate to a stationery retailer.

(3) Assumed that the £30 item (see (*l*) in question) is to be re-debited to the Debtor and not to be written off.

It is assumed that the cheques dishonoured had been paid into bank and included in the bank balance before the adjustments were made.

[1] 10% of £2,986 [£3,086—£100 (*contra*).]

217

Rough Adjustment Sheet

	£		£
Drawings (per T.B.)	2,000	Capital	2,120
Purchases	120		

	£		£
Purchases (per T.B.)	7,805	Drawings	120
Creditors	120	Plant (new)	230
		Profit and Loss	7,575

	£		£
Insurance (per T.B.)	103	Prepayment	10
		Profit and Loss	93

	£		£
Advertising (per T.B.)	107	Furniture	50
		Profit and Loss	57

	£		£
Bad Debts (per T.B.)	31	Profit and Loss	335
Debtors	5		
Bad Debts Reserve . . .	299		

	£		£
Balance (Reserve)	68	Discounts (per T.B.)	48
		Profit and Loss	20

	£		£
Wages (per T.B.)	3,981	Profit and Loss	4,231
Balance (Reserve)	250		

	£		£
Debtors (per T.B.)	3,040	Bad Debts	5
Cash at Bank	30	Balance	3,085
Cash at Bank	20		

	£		£
Balance	2,211	Creditors (per T.B.)	2,091
		Purchases	120

	£		£
Furniture (per T.B.)	189	Profit and Loss	12
Advertising	50	Balance	227

	£		£
Plant (old) (per T.B.)	2,017	Plant (new)	190
		Profit and Loss (Loss) . . .	310
		Profit and Loss (Depreciation)[1] . .	152
		Balance	1,365

	£		£
Plant (new)		Profit and Loss (Depreciation)[1] . .	42
Purchases	230	Balance	378
Plant (old)	190		

	£		£
Cash at Bank (per T.B.)	2,635	Debtors	30
		Debtors	20
		Balance	2,585

	£		£
Balance (Reserve)	299	Bad Debts	299

[1] £194 per Profit and Loss.

13.

X

TRADING AND PROFIT AND LOSS ACCOUNT FOR THE YEAR ENDED
31ST DECEMBER, 19..

	£		£
Stock at 1/1/19..	350	Sales	9,235
Purchases	8,120	Stock at 31/12/19..	495
Wages	720		
Gross Profit c/d	540		
	£9,730		£9,730
General Expenses	517	Gross Profit b/d	540
Net Profit transferred to Capital Account	23		
	£540		£540

BALANCE SHEET AS AT 31ST DECEMBER, 19..

	£	£		£
Capital—			Debtors.	1,920
Introduced at 1st January, 19..	3,000		Stock	495
Add Net Profit for year	23		Fixtures.	400
			Goodwill	300
	3,023			
Less Drawings[1].	468			
		2,555		
Creditors		390		
Bank Overdraft		170		
		£3,115		£3,115

[1] Alternatively, drawings may first be deducted.

[The opening entries (in Journal form) are—

JOURNAL

		£	£
Goodwill .	Dr.	300	
Fixtures .	Dr.	400	
Debtors .	Dr.	1,200	
Stock .	Dr.	350	
To Creditors			250
„ Y .			2,000
Cash .	Dr.	3,000	
To X—Capital			3,000
Y .	Dr.	2,000	
To Cash			2,000]

14.   CALCULATION OF VALUE OF STOCK AS ON 31ST OCTOBER, 19..

	£	£
Value of Stock on 3rd November, 19...		15,918
Add Sales during period 1st/3rd November.	195	
Less Gross Profit (28%)	55	
		140
		16,058
Less Purchases during period 1st/3rd November .	151	
Less Goods received after 3rd November	53	
		98
		15,960
Add Goods invoiced in October, received after 3rd November		29
Value of Stock on 31st October, 19..		£15,989

15.   JOURNAL

19.9		£	£

Apr. 1	Employers' Liability Insurance . . . . *Dr.*
	    To Insurers Ltd. . . . .
	    Premium, 1 per cent on Wages for year ended 31st
	March, 19.9, £100,000.
		1,000	1,000

June 30	Profit and Loss Account . . . . . *Dr.*
	    To Employers' Liability Insurance . . .
	    Premium, 1 per cent on Wages for three months ended
	30th June, 19.9, £20,000.
		200	200

19.0
Apr. 1
	Employers' Liability Insurance . . . . *Dr.*
	    To Insurers, Ltd. . . . .
	    Premium, 1½ per cent on Wages for year ended 31st
	March, 19.0, £90,000.
		1,350	1,350

7	Insurers, Ltd. . . . . *Dr.*
	    To Employers' Liability Insurance . . .
	    Adjustment of premium to actual Wages for the year
	ended 31st March, 19.0.—1 per cent on £90,000, £900,
	against payment of premium of £1,000.
		100	100

June 30	Profit and Loss Account . . . . . *Dr.*
	    To Employers' Liability Insurance. . . .
	    Premium on Wages for year ended 30th June, 19.0—
	Nine months ended 31st March, 19.0: 1 per cent
	    on £70,000 . . . . . . £700
	Three months ended 30th June, 19.0: 1½ per cent
	    on £30,000 450
	
	                          £1,150
		1,150	1,150

CHAPTER VI

BILLS PAYABLE BOOK

1.

No. of Bill	Date Given	To whom Sent	Drawer	Payee	Acceptor	Where Payable	Date of Bill	Teror	Due Date	Folio	Amount	Remarks
?	19.. July 1	Tyre	Tyre	Tyre	Self	?	19.. July 1	2 months	19.. Sept. 1		£ ?	
?	Aug. 1	Carr	Spoule	Carr	Self	?	Aug. 1	4 months	Dec. 1		400	

2.   *G's books*

Dr.   H   Cr.

		£			£
To Balance . . . . b/d		500·00	By Bills Receivable		500·00
,, Bank—Bill dishonoured . .		500·00	,, Bills Receivable		511·52
,, Bank—Discounting Charges .		5·00			
,, Interest		6·52			
		£511·52			£511·52

Dr.   BILLS RECEIVABLE   Cr.

	£			£
To H	500·00	By Bank		500·00
,, H	511·52			

Dr.   BANK   Cr.

	£		£
To Bills Receivable	500·00	By Discounting Charges . . .	5·00
		,, H—Bill dishonoured . . .	500·00

Dr.   DISCOUNTING CHARGES   Cr.

	£			£
To Bank	5·00	By H		5·00

Dr.   INTEREST   Cr.

		£
	By H—	
	Interest on £500 at 7% per annum	
	for two months and seven days .	6·52

              H's books

Dr.   G   Cr.

	£			£
To Bills Payable	500·00	By Balance . . . . b/d		500·00
,, Bills Payable	511·52	,, Bills Payable—		
		Bill dishonoured . .		500·00
		,, Discounting Charges . .		5·00
		,, Interest		6·52
	£511·52			£511·52

Dr.   BILLS PAYABLE   Cr.

	£			£
To G—Bill dishonoured . . .	500·00	By G		500·00
		,, G		511·52

Dr.	DISCOUNTING CHARGES	Cr.

To G . . . . . . £ 5·00 |

Dr.	INTEREST	Cr.

To G . . . . . . £ 6·52 |

Note. It is assumed that interest is to be calculated for the period of two months, plus seven days (period elapsing from the dishonour of the first bill).

3. (*a–b*) An Inland Bill is one which is, or purports to be, drawn and payable in the British Isles *or* drawn in the British Isles upon a person resident therein.

All other bills are foreign bills.

From the viewpoint of the Stamp Act, 1891, a foreign bill is a bill which is both drawn and payable outside the United Kingdom, but paid, endorsed, or negotiated in the United Kingdom.

All other bills are inland bills.

(*c*) An Accommodation Bill is a bill of exchange which has been accepted, drawn, or endorsed by a person without valuable consideration, enabling the person accommodated to discount the bill on the strength of the first person's name.

(*d*) The retiring of a bill means its withdrawal before maturity, either because the acceptor wishes to avoid its dishonour or because he is desirous of paying the amount without awaiting its due date.

4.   *Smith's books*

Dr.		JONES		Cr.	
19..		£	19..		£
July 1	To Bills Payable . .	600·00	July 1	By Bills Receivable . .	600·00
Nov. 1	,, Bank—		Nov. 1	,, Bills Receivable .	607·85
	Bill dishonoured .	600·00			
	Expenses . .	0·35			
	,, Interest . .	7·50			
		£607·85			£607·85

Dr.		BILLS PAYABLE		Cr.	
19..		£	19..		£
Nov. 1	To Bank . . .	600·00	July 1	By Jones . . .	600·00

Dr.		BILLS RECEIVABLE		Cr.	
19..		£	19..		£
July 1	To Jones . . .	600·00	July 1	By Bank . . .	600·00
Nov. 1	,, Jones . . .	£607·85	19.. Feb. 1	,, Bank . . .	£607·85

Dr.		BANK		Cr.	
19..		£	19..		£
July 1	To Bills Receivable . .	600·00	July 1	By Discounting Charges .	10·00
19..			Nov. 1	,, Bills Payable .	600·00
Feb. 1	,, Bills Receivable . .	607·85		,, Jones—	
				Bill dishonoured .	600·00
				Expenses . .	0·35

Dr.   DISCOUNTING CHARGES   Cr.

			£	
19..				
July 1	To Bank	. . .	10·00	

Dr.   INTEREST   Cr.

			£
19..			
Nov. 1	By Jones	. . .	7·50

Note. It is assumed that 5 per cent means 5 per cent *per annum.*

5.

	19..	£
Due Date of Bill	May 15	500
,, ,, ,, ,,	June 5	300
,, ,, ,, ,,	July 8	500
,, ,, ,, ,,	Sept. 19	600
		£1,900

CALCULATION OF INTEREST

Original Due Dates	Dates of Payment			Days	Products
19..	19..	£	£		
May 15	Sept. 1	500		109	54,500
June 5		300		88	26,400
July 8		200		55	11,000
		—	1,000		
	Nov. 1	300		116	34,800
Sept. 19		600		43	25,800
		—	900		
					152,500

Interest on £152,500 for 1 day at 4 per cent per annum = £20·89.
Balance due on 1st November, 19.. = £900 + £20·89 = £920·89

Alternative solution—

1. Average due date of original Bills:

Due		Days from 15th May	Products
19..	£		
May 15	500	0	0
June 5	300	21	6,300
July 8	500	54	27,000
Sept. 19	600	127	76,200
	£1,900		1,900)109,500
			58

Average due date = 58 days from 15th May, 19.. = 12th July, 19..

2. Calculation of Interest—

Interest at 5 per cent per annum on—

		£
£1,900 from 12th July, 19.., to 1st September, 19.. . . .		13·27
£ 900 from 1st September, 19.., to 1st November, 19.. . .		7·52
		£20·79

or—

1,900 × 51 (12th July, 19.., to 1st September, 19..) . . .		96,900
900 × 61 (1st September, 19.., to 1st November, 19..) . .		54,900
		151,800

Interest on £151,800 for one day at 5 per cent per annum . . £20·79

Note. The alternative solution does not give a perfectly accurate result, because the average due date calculation involves a fraction of a day—in the foregoing example $57\frac{12}{19}$.

6.   *B's books*
JOURNAL

19..		£	£
Jan. 1	Bills Receivable . . . . *Dr.*	850	
	To A		850
	Being three months' bill drawn on A.		
?	Bank . . . . *Dr.*	840	
	Discounting Charges . . . . . . *Dr.*	10	
	To Bills Receivable		850
	Being amount received and discounting charges on discounting A's bill.		

Note. The last entry would, in practice, be made through the Cash Book, the bill £850 being debited to Bank, **and** the discounting charges £10 credited to Bank.

7.   *Walkden's ledger*

Dr.   SCHOFIELD   *Cr.*

19..			£	19..			£
June 1	To Balance . . b/d		2,000	June 1	By Bills Receivable . .		1,000
					,, ,, .		1,000

Dr.   BILLS RECEIVABLE   *Cr.*

19..		£	19..			£
June 1	To Schofield—2 months' Bill	1,000	June 1	By Bank . . .		1,000
,, ,, —4 months' Bill		1,000	Aug. 1	,, ,, .		1,000

Dr.   BANK   *Cr.*

19..			£	19..		£
June 1	To Bills Receivable . .		1,000	June 1	By Discounting Charges .	4
Aug. 1	,, ,, ,, . .		1,000			

Dr.   DISCOUNTING CHARGES   *Cr.*

19..			£	
June 1	To Bank		4	

8.   *X's books*

| Dr. | | | | | | | Y | | | | | Cr. |

						£						£
To Bills Payable	.	.	.	.		800	By Bills Receivable	.	.	.	.	800

| Dr. | | | | | | | BILLS RECEIVABLE | | | | | Cr. |

						£	
To Y	.	.	.	.	.	800	

| Dr. | | | | | | | BILLS PAYABLE | | | | | Cr. |

										£
						By Y	.	.	.	.	.	800

Y's books

| Dr. | | | | | | | X | | | | | Cr. |

						£						£
To Bills Payable	.	.	.	.		800	By Bills Receivable	.	.	.	.	800

| Dr. | | | | | | | BILLS RECEIVABLE | | | | | Cr. |

						£						£
To X	.	.	.	.		800	By Bank	.	.	.	.	800

| Dr. | | | | | | | BILLS PAYABLE | | | | | Cr. |

										£
						By X	.	.	.	.	.	800

| Dr | | | | | | | BANK | | | | | Cr. |

						£						£
To Bills Receivable	.	.	.	.	800	By Discounting Charges	.	.	.	.	?

9. *(a)*

£1,000

Address......................................
Date ....*Jan. 1st,* 19............

     TWO MONTHS after date pay to me or my order the
sum of One Thousand Pounds, value received.

                               Moss & Co.

To Saul Bros. (Addressed)

Accepted payable L. C. & M.
Bank: Saul B.

Note. As a result of the Finance Act 1970, *ad valorem* stamp duties on bills of
exchange, cheques and promissory notes have been abolished as from February 1971.

(b) and (c).

(1) *Moss & Co's books*

Dr.   SAUL BROS.   Cr.

19..			£	19..			£
Jan. 1	To Balance	. . b/d	1,000	Jan. 1	By Bills Receivable	. .	1,000
Mar. 3	,, Bank—Bill dishonoured .		1,000				
	Noting Charges, etc,		*?*				

Dr.   BILLS RECEIVABLE   Cr.

19..		£	19..			£
Jan. 1	To Saul Bros.—2 months' Bill	1,000	?	By Bank	. . .	1,000

Dr.   BANK   Cr.

19..			£	19..		£
?	To Bills Receivable	. .	1,000	?	By Discounting Charges .	?
				Mar. 3	,, Saul Bros.—	
					Bill dishonoured .	*1,000*
					Noting Charges, etc. .	*?*

Dr.   DISCOUNTING CHARGES   Cr.

19..		£	
?	To Bank	?	

Note. If the amount due by Saul Bros. proves bad it will be written off to Bad Debts Account.

(2) *Saul Bros.' books*

Dr.   MOSS & CO.   Cr.

19..			£	19..			£
Jan. 1	To Bills Payable .	. .	1,000	Jan. 1	By Balance	. . b/d	1,000
				Mar. 3	,, *Bills Payable*	. .	*1,000*
					,, *Expenses*	. . .	*?*

Dr.   BILLS PAYABLE   Cr.

19..		£	19..			£
Mar. 3	To Moss & Co.—		Jan. 1	By Moss & Co.—		
	Bill dishonoured .	*1,000*		2 montns' Bill	.	1,000

Dr.   EXPENSES   Cr.

19..		£	
Mar. 4	*To Noting Charges, etc.* .	*?*	

Notes. (1) There will be the usual entries in the Bill Books. Items in italics comprise the entries relative to the dishonour of the bill.

(2) Banks are now closed on Saturdays and consequently Saturday is now deemed to be a non-business day. Bills which notionally fall due on a Saturday will be payable on the next business day. Accordingly the three days of grace formerly added to the times of payment no longer apply.

10.

BILLS DISCOUNTED REGISTER

No.	Date	Name	Drawer	Payee	Acceptor	Date of Bill	Tenor	When Due	Amount	Total	Days to Run	Discount		Remarks
												Rate	Amount	
	19..					19..		19..	£				£	
Feb. 1				John Cubley	A Debtor	Feb. 1	3 months	May 1	600		93	6%	8·78	Dis-honoured
May 6				John Cubley	A Debtor	May 5	3 months	Aug. 5	400		94	6%	6·05	

DISCOUNT LEDGER

	Date			Acceptor	Date Due	Dr.	Cr.	Balance
19..					19..	£	£	£
Feb. 1.	.	.	.	A Debtor	May 1	600		Dr. 600
May 1	.	.	.	A Debtor	Dishonoured		600	
6.	.	.	.	A Debtor	Aug. 5	400		Dr. 400

CURRENT ACCOUNTS LEDGER
JOHN CUBLEY

				Dr.	Cr.	
19..				£	£	Balance
Feb. 1	Bills Discounted	.	.		600·00	
	Discount on Bills			8·78		
May 1	Bills Discounted	.	.	600·00		
	Noting Charges, etc..		.	?		
	Cash	.	.		200·00	
6	Bills Discounted	.	.		400·00	
	Discount on Bills	.	.	6·05		

There will, in addition, be entries in the Bill Diary, Cash Book, and Bills Discounted Account.

11.

Dr.	A. BAKER [*In Sales Ledger*]		Cr.
	£		£
To Balance . . . . b/d 1,000	By *Contra Account* . . .	.	585
	,, Discount (2½% on £1,000)	.	25
	,, Bills Receivable Account	.	390
£1,000			£1,000

Dr.	A. BAKER [*In Purchases Ledger*]		Cr.
	£		£
To Allowance: Defective Goods . 15	By Balance . . . b/d		600
,, *Contra Account* . . . 585			

Dr.	BILLS RECEIVABLE		Cr.
	£		£
To A. Baker 390	By Bank		390

Dr.	BANK		Cr.
	£		£
To Bills Receivable . . . 390·00	By Discounting Charges		
	(5% on £390 for one month)	.	1·62

Dr.	DISCOUNTING CHARGES	Cr.
	£	
To Bank . . . . . 1·62	

12. *V. R. & Co.'s books*

Dr.	H. V. & Co.		Cr.
19..	£	19..	£
Oct. 1 To Bank . . . 4,937·50		Oct. 1 By Bills Receivable	5,000·00
,, Discounting Charges 62·50			
£5,000·00			£5,000·00
19..			
Jan. 1 To Bank . . . 5,000·00			

Dr.   BILLS RECEIVABLE   Cr.

19..		£	19..		£
Oct. 1	To H. V. & Co. . .	5,000·00	Oct. 1	By Bank . . .	5,000·00

Dr.   BANK   Cr.

19..		£	19..		£
Oct. 1	To Bills Receivable .	5,000·00	Oct. 1	By H. V. & Co. . .	4,937·50
				,, H. V. & Co.—	
				, Discounting Charges .	62·50
		£5,000·00			£5,000.00

H. V. & Co.'s books

Dr.   V. R. & Co.   Cr.

19..		£	19..		£
Oct. 1	To Bills Payable . .	5,000·00	Oct. 1	By Bank . . .	4,937·50
				,, Discounting Charges .	62·50
		£5,000·00			£5,000·00
			19..		
			Jan. 1	By Bank . . .	5,000·00

Dr.   BILLS PAYABLE   Cr.

19..		£	19..		£
Jan. 1	To Bank . . .	5,000·00	Oct. 1	By V. R. & Co. . .	5,000·00

Dr.   BANK   Cr.

19..		£	19..		£
Oct. 1	To V. R. & Co. . .	4,937·50	Jan. 1	By Bills Payable . .	5,000·00
19..					
Jan. 1	,, V. R. & Co. . .	5,000·00			

Dr.   DISCOUNTING CHARGES   Cr.

19..		£
Oct. 1	To V. R. & Co. . .	62·50

13.   EXPORT BANK LTD.

Dr.   BALANCES OF ADVANCES ON BILLS   Cr.

19..			£	19..			£
May 31	To Advances on Bills .		832·00	Mar. 31	By Balance . .	b/d	6,535·00
	,, Balance . .	c/d	5,780·00	May 31	,, Advances on Bills .		77·00
			£6,612·00				£6,612·00
				June 1	By Balance . .,	b/d	5,780·00

Dr.   EXPORT BANK LTD.—SPECIAL MARGINS   Cr.

19..			£	19..			£
Mar. 31	To Balance .	b/d	816·00	May 31	By Balance . .	c/d	879·75
Apr. 30	,, Advances on Bills .		63·75				
			£879·75				£879·75
June 1	To Balance .	b/d	879·75				

Export Bank Ltd.: Advances on Bills

	Fol.	Bill No. 308	Fol.	Bill No. 316	Fol.	Bill No. 317	Fol.	Bill No. 320	Fol.	Bill No. 324
		£		£		£		£		£
Debits—										
Bills		150·00		104·10		55·00		200·00		350·00
Cash								4·75		
Suspense for partial delivery .						77·00				
Transfer to Balances of Advances on Bills . .										
		£150·00		£104·10		£132·00		£204·75		£350·00
Credits—										
Balances of Advances on Bills .		120·00		100·00		132·00		200·00		280·00
Interest		3·50		4·10				4·75		6·25
Cash		26·50								63·75
Special Margins . . .										
		£150·00		£104·10		£132·00		£204·75		£350·00

231

Dr.			X Y			Cr.
19..			£	19..		£
Apr. 20	To Bill No. 316—			May 20	By Cash—	
	Not accepted	.	125·00		Sale of Goods	
May 20	„ Warehousing Ex-				covered by Bill	
	penses .	.	10·00		No. 316. . .	70·00
				31	Balance . . c/d	65·00
			£135·00			£135·00
June 1	To Balance .	b/d	65·00			

Dr.		INTEREST			Cr.
19..		£	19..		£
Apr. 3	To Export Bank Ltd. .	3·50	May 31	By Balance . . .	18·60
12	„ „ „ „ .	4·75			
20	„ „ „ „ .	4·10			
30	„ „ „ „ .	6·25			
		£18·60			£18·60
June 1	To Balance . . b/d	18·60			

Dr.			BILLS RECEIVABLE			Cr.
19..			£	19..		£
Mar. 31	To Balance .	b/d	8,620·00	Apr. 3	By Export Bank Ltd.—	
					Bill No. 308 . .	150·00
				12	„ „ 320 . .	200·00
				15	„ Cash—Bill No. 312 .	185·00
				20	„ XY— „ „ 316 .	125·00
				30	„ Export Bank, Ltd.—	
					Bill No. 324 . .	350·00
				May 31	Balance . . c/d	7,610·00
			£8,620·00			£8,620·00
June 1	To Balance .	b/d	7,610·00			

Dr.			SUSPENSE			Cr.
19..			£	19..		£
May 31	To Balance .	c/d	55·00	May 23	By Export Bank Ltd.—	
					Receipt on account	
					of Bill No. 317 .	55·00
				June 1	By Balance . . b/d	55·00

14. *Ledger entries in the books of Johnson & Co.—*

Dr.			BILLS RECEIVABLE			Cr.
19.0			£	19.0		£
Oct. 20	To Trade Bank	.	3,500·00	Oct. 20	By Trade Bank Bill	
					discounted . .	3,500·00
19.1				19.1		
Jan. 23	To Trade Bank	.	4,000·00	Jan. 23	By Trade Bank Bill	
					discounted . .	4,000·00

Dr. TRADE BANK **Cr.**

19.0		£	19.0		£
Oct. 20	To Bill discounted	3,500·00	Oct. 20	By Bill Receivable..	3,500·00
19.1				„ Discounting	
Jan. 23	„ „ retired	3,500·00		Charges[1]	50·50
				„ Commission[1]	17·50
				„ Cash, Net Proceeds of Bill discounted	3,432·00
		£7,000·00			£7,000·00

19.1			19.1		
Jan. 23	To Bill discounted	4,000·00	Jan. 23	By Bill Receivable	4,000·00
24	„ Balance c/d	4,000·00		„ Discounting Charges[1]	50·00
				„ Commission[1]	20·00
				„ Cash, Net Proceeds of Bill discounted	3,930·00
		£8,000·00			£8,000·00
			19.1		
			Jan. 24	By Balance b/d	4,000·00

Dr. BANK (IN CASH BOOK) **Cr.**

19.0		£	19.0		£
Oct. 20	To Trade Bank— Bill discounted	3,432·00	Oct. 21	By Bills Payable	3,500·00
19.1			19.1		
Jan. 23	„ Trade Bank— Bill discounted	3,930·00	Jan. 23	„ Trade Bank (to meet Bill retired)	3,500·00
				„ Balance c/d	362·00
		£7,362·00			£7,362·00
19.1					
Jan. 24	To Balance b/d	362·00			

Dr. ROSENKRANZ **Cr.**

19.0		£	19.0		£
July 18	To Bills Payable	3,500·00	July 18	By Goods	4,375·00

Dr. BILLS PAYABLE **Cr.**

19.0		£	19.0		£
Oct. 21	To Bank	3,500·00	July 18	By Rosenkranz	3,500·00

The position on 24th January, 19.1, is that Johnson & Co. still owe £875 to Rosenkranz and £4,000 to the Trade Bank. This is reflected in the Bank Account which shows a balance of £362. The balance thereof, but for Trade Bank charges, would have been increased by £138, that is £500. Against this, the liability is £4,000 to Trade Bank and £875 to Rosenkranz. Thus the liability is £4,875 as against the original debt of £4,375.

[1] These items—discounting charges and commission—will be posted to the debit of accounts in the ordinary way (totals, £138).

15. *Dr.*   BANK   *Cr.*

19.9		£	19.9		£
To Credit Bank Advance			By Interest—		
Bill No. 300 . . .		120	Credit Bank Advance		
302 . . .		100	Bill No. 303 . .		5
303 . . .		200	302 . .		104
304 . . .		280	Balance . . . c/d		992
305 . . .		130			
306 . . .		60			
,. Credit Bank Collection Bill					
No. 301 . . .		185			
„ Credit Bank Advance Bill					
No. 300 Balance . .		26			
		£1,101			£1,101
19.0			19.0		
To Balance . . . b/d		992	By Balance . . . c/d		1,032
„ Credit Bank—					
Bill No. 305 . . .		18			
306 . . .		22			
		£1,032			£1,032
19.1					
To Balance . . . b/d		1,032			

Dr.   INTEREST   *Cr.*

19.9		£	19.9		£
To Credit Bank Advance			By Balance . . . c/d		13
Bill No. 300 . . .		4			
303 . . .		5			
302 . . .		4			
		£13			£13

Dr.   BILLS RECEIVABLE   *Cr.*

19.9			£	19.9		£
No. of						
Bill				By Credit Bank Advance		
300	To Balance . b/d		150	Account . .		150
301	„ „ . „		185	,, Bills for Collection Account .		185
302	., „ . „		125	,. Credit Bank Advance		
303	., „ . „		200	Account . . .		125
304	„ „ . „		350	,, „ „ „ .		200
305	„ „ . „		165	,, „ „ „ .		350
306	„ „ . „		100	,, „ „ „ .		165
				,, „ „. ., .		100
			£1,275			£1,275

Dr.   CREDIT BANK BILLS FOR COLLECTION   *Cr.*

19.9	No. of	£	19.9		£
	Bill				
301	To Bills Receivable Account . .	185	By Bank		185

CREDIT BANK ADVANCE

	Fol.	Bill No. 300	Fol.	Bill No. 302	Fol.	Bill No. 303	Fol.	Bill No. 304	Fol.	Bill No. 305	Fol.	Bill No. 306
		£		£		£		£		£		£
DEBITS—												
Bills		150		125		200		350		165		100
Cash		—		104		5		—		—		—
Transfer		—		—		—		—		—		30
		£150		£229		£205		£350		£165		£130
CREDITS—												
Advance		120		100		200		280		130		60
Interest		4		4		5		6		3		1
Expenses		—	2	—		—	1	—		2		—
Transfer		—		125		—	1	64		12		47
Cash		26		—		—		—		18		22
		£150		£229		£205		£350		£165		£130

Dr.	INTEREST				Cr.
19.0			£	19.0	£
	To Balance . . .	b/d	13	By Balance . . c/d	23
	„ Credit Bank				
	Bill No. 304		6		
	305		3		
	306		1		
			£23		£23
19.1					
	To Balance . . .	b/d	23		

Dr.	SPECIAL LOAN		Cr.
19.0	£	19.0	£
To Bill No. 304	64	By Balance . . . b/d	?

Dr.	SUSPENSE (*Bill No. 306*)		Cr.
19.0	£	19.1	£
To Balance of Bill No. 306 . .	47	By Transfer from Advance Account	30

Notes. (1) BILL No. 306 must be divided into two parts, as follows—

		No. 1 £				No. 2 £
Advance	. . .	30	Advance	. . .		30
Bank Remittance	. .	22	Balance	. . .		17
Interest .	. . .	1				
Total.	. .	£53				£47

£100

(2)   [TOTAL ACCOUNTS] CUSTOMERS' ACCOUNTS

To Bill No. 302 . . . . . [2]125 £   By [Bills 300–306] . . . . 1,275 £

[1] Shown in Trial Balance on page 236.
[2] The item of £125 will be debited to the customer in the ordinary way, in addition to other expenses, e.g. warehousing charges.

(3) "Trial Balance" at 31st December, 19.9.

	£	£	£
Advance—			
Bill No. 304	70		
„ „ 305	35		
„ „ 306	40		
	—	145	
Bank		992	
[1]Interest		13	
[2]Customers' Accounts			1,150
		£1,150	£1,150

(4) Transactions subsequent to 31st December, 19.9, are shown in italics.
(5) "Trial Balance" at 31st December, 19.0.

	£	£
Advance	*nil*	
Bank	*1,032*	
[1]*Interest*	*23*	
Special Loan	*64*	
Suspense (Bill No. 306)	*17*	
[1]*Expenses*	*2*	
[1]*Exchange*	*12*	
[2]*Customers' Accounts*		*1,150*
	£1,150	*£1,150*

[1] Actually these items would be transferred to Profit and Loss Account.
[2] Customers' Accounts would have been debited with the sale price of goods and Sales Account credited.

CHAPTER VII

1. By Depreciation is meant the permanent and continuing diminution in the quality, quantity, or value of an asset from any cause whatsoever.

In consequence of natural laws it follows that any asset must suffer, in some way and to some extent, from the effects of time, in spite of effective repairs, Depreciation is quite separate from cost of maintenance.

Examples of the application of Depreciation are—(1) Wear and tear on Machinery; (2) Obsolescence of Plant, owing to the invention of better and more economic methods. (3) Shrinkage in the value of securities owing to a fall in market values.

(The latter, if the cause of decline is transitory, is merely a fluctuation.)

2. (1) *Goodwill.* Capacity to maintain the super profits of the business on the same amount of capital, as measured by the trend of profits. Any state of affairs likely to cause diminution of the earning capacity of the business must be considered, e.g. general economic conditions, general conditions of trade, conditions in the particular class of trade, conditions in the particular business; continuity of management, ruling rates of interest, growth of competitive class of business (Radio and Stereograms); effluxion of time (approaching expiry of lease where situational advantage constitutes a prime factor).

(2) *Leasehold Land and Works erected thereon.* Length of lease—terms of lease—appropriate covenants as to repairs, fixtures, and dilapidations. Where the lease is a long one, the current market conditions as to property.

(3) *Fixed Machinery and Plant, including Engine Power.* Estimated effective life—residual value—obsolescence—dependence upon outside factors (e.g. frigidaire, where ice-cream may be manufactured only if permission granted by local authority); danger of loss if licence withdrawn—effectiveness and regularity of repairs and maintenance—effects of a physical nature, e.g. vibration, careless handling and use, damp atmosphere, etc.

(4) *Loose Tools.* Estimated life of tools; as life short, frequent revaluations required.

(5) *Book Debts.* Investigations as to whether the amounts are debts, or in reality "debit" balances like drawings, loans (long term), goods on sale or return, hire-purchase items. Validity of the transaction—sale of goods to infant, enforceability, e.g. statute barred, set off—contra account, deductions for trade discount and other customary deductions. Inquiry as to term of credit allowed, age of debt, regularity of settlement, payments in instalments, or by bills, payments on account; dishonoured cheques, evidence of insolvency, bankruptcy, death, deed of arrangement, etc., of customer, debtors in hands of solicitor, "Guardian" Societies or other debt-collecting agency. Knowledge that customer has suffered severely in the default of *his* customers.

In case of foreign debtors, especially as to whether the debt is a sterling debt or a currency debt. Blocked or "frozen" accounts. Exchange Regulations.

In case of a limited company being a debtor, the fact of limited liability is important (although some businesses require the personal guarantee of the directors of the limited company to whom goods or services are supplied).

(6) *Investments in Gilt-edged or other Securities.* Where the investments are revalued the governing considerations are as shown hereunder, although it is customary to leave the investments in the Balance Sheet at book value and insert a note against the item showing the current valuation.

Where securities are officially quoted on a recognized Stock Exchange the "middle" price (i.e. half the difference between the two quotations) is usually taken.

Where securities are dealt in, but not officially quoted on a recognized Stock Exchange, the last bargain recorded, or the mean (if several bargains), is taken.

Where securities are not dealt in on a recognized Stock Exchange an estimate is made based upon the price of the last known transaction—if reasonably recent—consideration being given to the lack of marketability of the security. If a recent Balance Sheet is available, an estimate may be made on the "net asset" value, or if accounts are available the earning capacity of the concern.

Where an investment is made in a Subsidiary Company by a Holding Company a valuation may be made based upon the earning capacity of the Subsidiary Company in relation to the capital involved.

The prices in question relate to those as at the date of the Balance Sheet of the concern holding the securities.

(7) *Amount expended on partly completed Contracts.* The estimated worth of Materials and Plant on hand; an estimate of work in progress taking into account a proportion of profit earned to date, subject to possible default on the part of contractee and claim for damages under the contract.

Where there is a profit to date an ample reserve is made, often one-third of the profit; occasionally only such proportion of the remaining two-thirds is taken as is represented by the ratio that the cash received bears to the work certified.

Where the work on the contract is almost complete, the profit (subject to suitable reserve) is ascertained by estimating the further cost entailed to complete, thus finding the total cost of the contract. Therefrom may be computed the profit by measuring the total cost against the total contract price. The proportion of the work certified to date to the contract price is taken as profit to date, subject to suitable reserve.

3. (1) The additions, if of such a nature as to become attached to the property itself, must be left undisturbed by the lessee at the end of the lease; otherwise they become assets in the ownership of the lessee.

In both instances the amount should be transferred out of Leasehold Works and debited to a separate account. In the former case the amount should either be charged to current revenue or written off in yearly instalments based upon the fourteen years remaining. If the latter, the writing off will be based upon the life of the asset irrespective of the length of the lease.

(2) Repairs are a current revenue charge, the lessee being liable for dilapidations.

(3) The provision for depreciation is inadequate. It should be provided upon the cost of the lease—without any other additions—either by equal instalments, Annuity Method, or the Sinking Fund Method, the latter being particularly appropriate if it is intended to renew this lease or acquire on its expiry an entirely new one.

The account may be shown in amended form as follows—

Dr.			LEASEHOLD WORKS			Cr.
19..		£	19..			£
Jan. 1	To Cost of Lease . .	10,000	Dec. 31	By Depreciation—		
				$\frac{1}{15}$ of £10,000 (say) .		667
				„ Balance . . c/d		9,333
		£10,000				£10,000
19..						
Jan. 1	To Balance . . b/d	9,333				

Alternatively, the £10,000 may be left undisturbed and entries made thus—

(1) Debit Profit and Loss Account.[1]
    Credit Leasehold Amortization Account.

(2) Debit Leasehold Amortization Investment Account.
    Credit Bank.

4. FREEHOLD LAND AND BUILDINGS AT COST

It is evident from the description in the Balance Sheet that no provision at all has been made for the depreciation of this item. With regard to the land no exception can be taken to such treatment, unless the value of the land has permanently fallen, when provision may be made to reduce the value standing in the books to the lower realizable figure. Such a provision is, however, rather different from a normal depreciation charge and should therefore be shown separately in the Profit and Loss Account. The Buildings and the additions thereto are, however, quite a different matter, for buildings are not of the same permanent quality as land. Quite apart from any temporary fall in market value there is thus need to provide for depreciation since the Buildings are gradually wearing out. A rate of 1 per cent to 2 per cent per annum on the original cost in advisable, provision being made for replacement if this is desired. Information

---

[1] The figure will be ascertained from Sinking Fund tables.

as to the present value and state of these assets would be helpful in determining the amount of the provision now required.

PATENT ACCOUNT

It is evident that the original patent is absolutely valueless (both legally and commercially) in itself, and that £3,000 at least in respect of its cost still stands in the books of the Company. However, the original patented process together with the later experimenting may have built up the foundation of a new line of business, and in such a case it is submitted that it is perfectly correct to continue to carry a proportion of such Capital expenditure in the books.

Thus, before any advice can be given as to the adequacy or inadequacy of the depreciation provided, it is essential that knowledge be had as to the successful or unsuccessful outcome of the later experiments, and as to whether, if successful, the original patented process contributed to such success.

At all events, in view of the present facts disclosed, to maintain a conservative attitude, it is suggested that the cost of the original patent should be eliminated from the books.

LOOSE TOOLS

It is assumed that the tools are used in the course of the Company's business. In these circumstances it is considered that revaluation at the date of each annual Balance Sheet, and the writing off of any difference arising, is a more satisfactory method to adopt than the writing off of an arbitrary percentage. If, however, this percentage is the percentage of depreciation which has been disclosed by the revaluation method in past years, this treatment will pass criticism.

PATTERNS

The same remarks apply to Patterns as have been applied to Loose Tools. In this case, however, it is made clear that the Patterns are used in the course of the Company's business, some to a greater extent than others. It thus becomes evident that an arbitrary rate of 10 per cent per annum depreciation on the diminishing balance system is unlikely to be the best method of depreciation available—unless such percentage has been disclosed by actual revaluation, or by scientific investigation in the past. Where it has been established that half the patterns are in constant use, depreciated by 15 per cent per annum and the remainder by only 5 per cent per annum, the adoption of a flat 10 per cent rate over all may be justified.

In both the case of Loose Tools and Patterns, there arises the question whether additions during the year should suffer a full year's depreciation.

In view of the lack of information as to actual rates of depreciation of these assets, and as to their scrap value when no longer of use to the business, it is submitted that no definite judgment can be passed as to the adequacy of the depreciation provided in these cases. As, however, the rate employed, 10 per cent (even on original cost as distinct from diminishing balance method), indicates at least a ten-year life, it would appear, particularly so in the case of Loose Tools, that the estimated effective life is greatly over-calculated, indicating a need for substantially more depreciation.

The following general comments may also be made—

(1) As far as possible depreciation should be provided on a consistent basis.

(2) The charge against Profit and Loss Account which must be made before a true profit for the year can be obtained must be distinguished from any temporary rise or fall in value of the assets concerned.

5. Depreciation being a charge against, and not an appropriation of, profits it follows that provision therefor is a necessary element in arriving at the true results of carrying on a business. Hence it should appear as a debit to Manufacturing, Trading, or Profit and Loss Account regardless of the effect of its inclusion. The amount of profit earned has no direct bearing on the question of the need for providing an adequate sum by way of depreciation. In exceptional cases the largeness of the profit might serve as an index to the amount of depreciation to be provided, e.g. in an abnormally busy year exceptional profits may have arisen, necessitating heavy use of machinery and other assets; on the other hand, a falling off in business may indicate the need for abnormal depreciation, e.g. where it can be attributed to inefficient, worn-out, or obsolete plant, loss of goodwill, or monopoly use of patents.

As all attachable and incidental revenue expenses must be provided for before the true profits can be computed, whether the particular expense is wages, repairs or depreciation, it follows that a proportion (exact or as approximately so as the circumstances permit) for the use or consumption of an asset must be included in the charge of running the business.

Occasionally, a lapse in writing off depreciation may in exceptional circumstances be justified, but only where it can reasonably be shown that in the immediate past excessive depreciation has been written off. A better method is to charge the normal depreciation to Profit and Loss Account and to write back the previous excess by crediting Profit and Loss Appropriation Account. The mere fact that an asset has been used on a much less scale is not sufficient justification for the *omission* to write off depreciation, yet if, in the meantime, the asset has been properly maintained a somewhat smaller amount than normal may be written off, but against this the point has to be borne in mind that an asset may become *obsolete* before its normal functioning life is over.

6. A Reserve is an amount set aside out of profits or other surpluses which is **not** designed to meet any liability, contingency, commitment, or diminution in value of assets known to exist at the Balance Sheet date. Reserves are divided into Revenue and Capital, according to whether they are, or are not, free for distribution through the Profit and Loss Account. (This is a matter of importance in limited companies.)

A Reserve Fund is an alternative term to Reserve, frequently taken to signify that the amount of the Fund is represented by a corresponding Investment made outside the business. Actually, a Reserve Fund may be represented by the ordinary assets of the business.

A Sinking Fund may either be a charge against profits for the writing off of an asset, or an appropriation of profits for the redemption of a liability. It is nearly always represented by an investment outside the business, the interest on the investment being generally re-invested immediately on receipt, the Sinking Fund increasing proportionally at Compound Interest rates.

A Reserve Account is a synonymous term to Reserve or Reserve Fund, often being employed to signify that an outside investment is made to represent it.

A Depreciation Fund is a **charge against** profits to cover the estimated diminution in quality, quantity, or value of an asset. It is built up during the life of the asset so that a just proportion of the asset in question may be written off in ratio to the shrinkage in value.

A Provision is an amount set aside out of profits or other surpluses (or charged to Profit and Loss Account) to **provide** for depreciation, renewals, or diminution in value of assets or to meet a liability, contingency, or commitment known to exist at the Balance Sheet date but the amount whereof cannot be determined with substantial accuracy.

7. *Dr.* SINKING FUND *Cr.*

			£			£
Year 1	To Balance	c/d	90·4875	Year 1 By Profit and Loss Account		90·4875
Year 2	To Balance	c/d	185·4994	Year 2 By Balance b/d		90·4875
				„ Interest		4·5244
				„ Profit and Loss Account		90·4875
			£185·4994			£185·4994
Year 3	To Balance	c/d	285·2619	Year 3 By Balance b/d		185·4994
				„ Interest		9·2750
				„ Profit and Loss Account		90·4875
			£285·2619			£285·2619
Year 4	To Balance	c/d	390·0125	Year 4 By Balance b/d		285·2619
				„ Interest		14·2631
				„ Profit and Loss Account		90·4875
			£390·0125			£390·0125
Year 5	To Lease Account		500·0000	Year 5 By Balance b/d		390·0125
				„ Interest		19·5000
				„ Profit and Loss Account		90·4875
			£500·0000			£500·0000

8. *Dr.*   POLICY   *Cr.*

			£					£
Year 1 (com-mence-ment) (end)	To Cash—Premium	. .	70·00	Year 1 (end)	By Balance	. . c/d		72·10
„	„ Interest on £70 at 3% per annum .	. .	2·10					
			£72·10					£72·10
Year 2 (com-mence-ment)	To Balance	. . b/d	72·10	Year 2 (end)	By Balance	. . c/d		146·36
„ (end)	„ Cash—Premium . „ Interest on £142·10 at 3% per annum .	. . . .	70·00 4·26					
			£146·36					£146·36
Year 3 (com-mence-ment)	To Balance	. . b/d	146·36					

Dr.   ASSET AMORTIZATION   *Cr.*

			£					£
Year 1 (end)	To Balance	. . c/d	72·10	Year 1 (end) „	By Profit and Loss Account . „ Policy Account	. .		70·00 2·10
			£72·10					£72·10
Year 2 (end)	To Balance	. . c/d	146·36	Year 2 (com-mence-ment) (end) ,	By Balance . By Profit and Loss Account . „ Policy Account	. . b/d . .		72·10 70·00 4·26
			£146·36					£146·36
				Year 3 (com-mence-ment)	By Balance	. . b/d		146·36

In the final year the policy will be liquidated, the Policy Account being closed by a transfer to Cash (*Dr.* Cash, *Cr.* Policy Account). When the policy matures there will almost invariably be a difference between the book value of the policy (e.g. by erroneous loading for interest) and the amount due upon the policy at maturity. This difference will be transferred from the Policy Account to the Asset Amortization Account. For example, the book value of a £1,000 policy may be £978 at the maturity date. Obviously, the Asset Amortization Account will stand at £978, so that the Policy Account will be debited with £22 and the Asset Amortization Account credited with the like amount. The Asset Amortization Account balance will be transferred to the corresponding asset account (*Dr.* Asset Amortization Account, *Cr.* Asset).

Frequently only the surrender value of the policy is taken into account in valuing the policy at the end of each year. In that case, the surrender value will be the amount brought down annually as a debit balance on the Policy Account, and as a credit balance on the Asset Amortization Account, the difference between the premium paid and the increase in surrender value of the policy being transferred from Policy Account to Asset Amortization Account.

9. *Dr.*   POLICY   *Cr.*

			£			£
Year 1	To Cash—Premium	. .	100	Year 1	By Asset Amortization Account	100
Year 2	To Cash—Premium	. .	100	Year 2	By Asset Amortization Account	15
					„ Balance (surrender value)	
					c/d	85
			£100			£100
Year 3	To Balance	. . b/d	85	Year 3	By Asset Amortization Account	5
	„ Cash—Premium	. .	100		„ Balance (surrender value)	
					c/d	180
			£185			£185
Year 4	To Balance	. . b/d	180			

10. It is not essential for the amount put aside by Directors, out of profits, to be invested in interest-bearing securities. There are distinct advantages to the practice, as the Reserve Fund will not depend on the prosperity of the company, and will earn compound interest regardless of the trading results of the financial years. However, the Directors may be of opinion that the funds can be better employed in the business itself, so that no outside investing is undertaken. It is as well to notice, however, that in the mind of the public at large the term "Reserve Fund" is generally taken as indicating an investment made outside the business.

The interest, on being received, will be credited to Reserve Fund and cash debited; on being re-invested, the Reserve Fund Fund Investment Account will be debited and cash credited.

The purpose of the Reserve Fund is an important consideration. Where the object is to provide liquid funds at some future date, the Directors would be defeating the very object of the Reserve Fund by failing to invest in first-class outside investments (or in an Endownment Insurance Policy). Further, the Directors in certain cases may be bound to invest the Reserve Fund "outside," e.g. where Debentures have been issued and a Reserve Fund (usually designated Debenture Redemption Fund) is according to the Debenture Trust Deed definitely to be invested in, say, "gilt-edged" or other approved securities.

11. A Secret Reserve is a reserve which actually exists but is not disclosed in the Balance Sheet. It may take the form of a Hidden, Inner, or purely Secret Reserve, but in all cases the existing reserve is not discernible from an inspection of the published Balance Sheet.

Bankers create secret reserves by—

(1) Inclusion of free reserves amongst current liabilities.

(2) Crediting profits on realization of investments to a reserve (included in liabilities) and writing off losses on realization of investment out of current revenue.

The practice is criticized on the following grounds—

(1) Profits are actually higher than those disclosed, and, as a result, customers ought to have a proportion of benefit by being able to borrow at cheaper rates of interest.

(2) By the use of secret reserves a bank may hide from its customers for a lengthy period a severe decline in stability, earning capacity, and liquidity.

(3) The accounts cannot be said to represent a true and fair view.

12. *Dr.*   PLANT AND MACHINERY   *Cr.*

Year 89		£	Year 89		£
Jan. 1	To Balance . . . b/d	19,515		By Cash: Sale of Plant. .	35
Jan. 1	,, Purchases . . .	2,950		[Purchased Year 77,	
to				written down value	
Dec.31	,, Profit and Loss Account:			*nil*]	
	Profit on Sale . .	35		,, Profit and Loss Account:	
				Depreciation—	
				Year 80 Purchases £1,700	
				Year 81–Year 88	
				Purchases 25,200	
				Year 89 Purchases 2,950	
					£29,850
				10% thereon . .	2,985
				,, Balance . . c/d	19,480
		£22,500			£22,500

Year 90		£	Year 90		£
Jan. 1	To Balance . . . b/d	19,480	?	By Cash: Sale of Plant .	350
Jan. 1				[Purchased Year 86 for	
to				£700, written down value	
Dec.31	,, Purchases . . .	1,800		1st Jan., Year 90	
				£700 − £280 = £420]	
			Dec. 31	,, Profit and Loss Account:	
				Loss on Sale	
				[£420 − £350] . .	70
				,, Depreciation—	
				Year 81–Year 88	
				Purchases . £25,200	
				Less Cost of	
				Plant sold 700	
					24,500
				Year 89 Purchases 2,950	
				Year 90 Purchases 1,800	
					£29,250
				10% thereon . .	2,925
				,, Balance . . c/d	17,935
		£21,280			£21,280

Year 90			
Jan. 1	To Balance . . . b/d	17,935	

13.

(a) Dr.   LORRIES   *Cr.*

19.9		£	19.9		£
Jan. 1	To No. 1	1,000	Dec. 31	By Balance . . c/d	2,400
July 1	,, No. 2	1,400			
		£2,400			£2,400

19.0		£	19.1		£
Jan. 1	To Balance . . . b/d	2,400	Dec. 31	By Sale of Lorries Account	
19.1				at cost—	
Apr. 30	,, No. 3 . . .	1,600		No. 1 . . .	1,000
Oct. 1	,, No. 4 . . .	1,100		No. 2 . . .	1,400
				,, Balance (Nos. 3 and 4)	
				c/d	2,700
		£5,100			£5,100

19.2			
Jan. 1	To Balance . . . b/d	2,700	

Dr.   PROVISION FOR DEPRECIATION OF LORRIES   *Cr.*

19.9			£	19.9			£	
Dec. 31	To Balance	c/d	340	Dec. 31	By Profit and Loss Account—Depreciation at 20 per cent per annum on cost			
					No. 1. 1 year		200	(a)
					No. 2. 6 months		140	(d)
			£340				£340	
19.0				19.0				
Dec. 31	To Balance	c/d	820	Jan. 1	By Balance	b/d	340	
				Dec. 31	„ Profit and Loss Account—Depreciation at 20 per cent per annum on cost			
					No. 1. 1 year		200	(b)
					No. 2. 1 year		280	(e)
			£820				£820	
19.1				19.1				
Dec. 31	To Sale of Lorries Account—			Jan. 1	By Balance	b/d	820	
	No. 1. (a + b + c)		450	Dec. 31	Profit and Loss Account—Depreciation at 20 per cent per annum on cost			
	No. 2. (d + e + f)		630		No. 1. 3 months		50	(c)
					No. 2. 9 months		210	(f)
	To Balance (g and h)	c/d	295		No. 3. 9 months		240	(g)
					No. 4. 3 months		55	(h)
			£1,375				£1,375	
				19.2				
				Jan. 1	By Balance	b/d	295	

Dr.   SALE OF LORRIES ACCOUNT   *Cr.*

19.1		£	19.1			£
Apr. 1	To Lorries Account No. 1 (a)	1,000	Apr. 1	By Sale Price No. 1 . (a)		800
Oct. 1	„ „ „ No. 2 (b)	1,400		Provision for Depreciation Account No. 1		
Dec.31	„ Profit and Loss Account (separately shown)—			(a)		450
	Profit on Sale of No. 1	250[1]	Oct. 1	Sale Price—No. 2. (b)		500
	(£800 + £450 − £1,000) (a)			„ Provision for Depreciation Account No. 2		
				(b)		630
			Dec. 31	„ Profit and Loss Account (separately shown)—		
				Loss on Sale of No. 2 .		
				(£1,400 − £500 − £630) (b)		270[1]
		£2,650				£2,650

Dr.   MOTOR DEALER   *Cr.*

19.1		£	£	19.1		£	£
Apr. 1	To Cash, No. 3	800		Dec. 31	By Lorries Account—		
	„ Lorries Account—Transfer exchange value No. 1	800			No. 3 .	1,600	
			1,600		No. 4 .	1,100	
Oct. 1	Cash No. 4	600					2,700
	Lorries Account—Transfer exchange value No. 2	500					
			1,100				
			£2,700				£2,700

[1] The two items may be brought into Profit and Loss Account at £20 (loss) by contra of £250 against £270 within the above account.

Although somewhat more complicated, the last two accounts may be dispensed with and the entries all worked in within the Motor Lorries Account, thus—

Dr.				LORRIES				Cr.	
19.9			£	19.9					£
Jan. 1	To No. 1	. . . .	1,000	Dec. 31	By Balance	. c/d			2,400
July 1	„ *No. 2*	. . .	1,400						
			£2,400						£2,400
19.0				19.1					
Jan. 1	To Balance	. . b/d	2,400	Dec. 31	By No. 1—				
19.1					Provision for Deprecia-				
Apr. 1	„ No. 3 (£800 + £800) .	.	1,600		tion Account	£450			
Oct. 1	„ No. 4 (£600 + £500) .	.	1,100		Sale Price .	. 800			
Dec. 31	„ Profit on No. 1 (£1,250 −					——		1,250	
	£1,000) .	. .	250		„ *No. 2—*				
					Provision for Deprecia-				
					tion Account	£630			
					Sale Price .	. 500			
						——		*1,130*	
					„ *Loss on No. 2*				
					(£1,400 − £1,130)	.		270	
					„ Balance	. c/d		2,700	
			£5,350						£5,350
19.2									
Jan. 1	To Balance	. . b/d	2,700						

(b)   JOURNAL

19.1				£	£
Dec. 31	Profit and Loss Account—				
	Loss on Sale of No. 2	(1)	Dr.	270	
	Depreciation	(2)	Dr.	383	
	Profit and Loss Account—				
	Profit on Sale of No. 1	(1)			250
	Provision for Depreciation Account . . .	(3)			295
	Lorries Account	(4)			108

Being entries for the amended Lorries Account, profit and loss on Sale of Lorries, correction of Depreciation Charge and Provision for Depreciation as per Schedules hereunder—

(1) Profit and Loss on Sale of Motors £250 and £270 respectively and as per Memorandum Accounts.

(2) Correction of Depreciation charge—

Correct Charges		Memo Account £	Actual Lorry Account £	Extra Charge £
Per Memorandum Accounts	19.9	340	200	140
Per Actual Account (Lorry Ac-				
count)	19.0	480	440	40
	19.1	555	352	203
		£1,375	£992	£383
			(See below)	(Debit to Profit and Loss Account)

(3) Provision for Depreciation Account per Memorandum Account.

(4) Lorries Account—

	£
Per actual (Lorries) account	2,808
Per Memorandum Account	2,700
Credit to Lorries Account	£108

There will be no time available in the examination to break down the depreciation adjustments, but the details are given below—

Actual write-off made in books—

	No. 1 £		No. 2 £		No. 3 £	No. 4 £	Total £
19.9 Dec. 31	20 per cent of £1,000	200					200
19.0 Dec. 31	20 per cent of £800	160	20 per cent of £1,400	280			440
19.1 Dec. 31	20 per cent of £640	128	20 per cent of £1,120	224	nil	nil	352
A. (See below)		£488		£504	(as there was no balance on these at commencement of the year (see p. 245) 19.1)		£992

Write off (by credit to Provision for Depreciation as amended).

	No. 1 £		No. 2 £		No. 3 £		No. 4 £		Total £
19.9 Dec. 31	20 per cent of £1,000	200	20 per cent of £1,400 (½ year)	140					340
19.0 Dec. 31	20 per cent of £1,000	200	20 per cent of £1,600	280					480
19.1 Dec. 31	20 per cent of £1,000 3 months	50	20 per cent of £1,400 6 months	210	20 per cent of £1,600 9 months	240	20 per cent of £1,100 3 months	55	555
B.		450		630		240	55 (see p. 245)		1,375
A. (Deducted as above)		488		504		—	— (see p. 245)		992
	Over-depreciation charge	£38	Under-depreciation charge	£126	Under-depreciation charge	£240	Under-depreciation charge	£55	£383

CHAPTER VIII

1. BRIEFLY, capital expenditure is that incurred in the acquisition or increase of an asset or in the increase of the earning capacity of a business; revenue expenditure is that incurred in the maintenance of the assets and earning capacity of the business and in the sound running of the business.

The following considerations are necessary to determine whether an item is capital or revenue.

Debit items—

(1) Where the amount has been incurred or expended in the acquisition of a fixed asset or assets, the name of the item will be no more than prima facie evidence as to the fundamental object of the outlay, e.g. a Repair expense may be in reality part of the cost of a newly acquired asset.

It is immaterial whether the item represents a strictly permanent asset like Land, or a semi-permanent asset like Machinery, so long as it indicates the acquiring of part of the equipment of the business.

The same principle applies to the purchase of a business as a going concern. Not only will the bare cost directly incurred on the acquisition of a fixed asset or business be considered capital, but the incidental costs connected therewith like conveyance and mortgage charges in connection with a purchase of Land and Buildings, brokerage on the purchase of investments, experimental work on patents, and preliminary expenses of a limited company.

Where expenditure is incurred as a *necessary* element in construction or acquisition of an asset or required to enable a business to be started, even if the visible and tangible results of such pioneer and preliminary work are obliterated or obscured, such expenditure is nevertheless considered as a proper capital charge. An instance of this may be seen in the construction of a reservoir involving expenditure in building (and later demolishing) workmen's cottages, temporary railway lines, etc.

Where such preliminary expenditure is **not** necessary, or where by reason of the introduction of more modern equipment, particularly after a lengthy period of time during which the first capital expenditure was sufficient to enable the business to function, there is conflict of opinion, although the law permits the prior expenditure to be considered capital (*Cox* v. *Edinburgh District Tramways Co.*).

(2) Where the item represents expenditure made in enhancing earning capacity as distinct from merely maintaining or holding it, such expenditure is considered capital. Such expenditure may involve the destruction of a tangible asset, e.g. where part of the structure or fixtures are destroyed to give more space. Advertising expenses may accordingly be either Capital or Revenue.

(3) Where the item represents expenditure on the acquisition of a fixed asset (though not enhancing earning capacity) which is saleable, e.g. non-income producing investment, it is nevertheless capital.

(4) An item may, on the other hand, be a capital loss, e.g. destruction of property uninsured, development work cost in connection with an abandoned mine.

(5) Conventionally, many items are considered "capital" when the expenditure is somewhat abnormal in nature and amount, and the management is averse to writing it off against the current year.

(6) Expenditure of a revenue nature which is in the nature of Deferred Revenue, i.e. carried forward to be written off in future years, is considered as capital for the particular Balance Sheet it concerns.

(7) Expenditure (subject to (6)) incurred in the acquisition of stock for sale or manufacture and all current operating costs and expenses, including depreciation and necessary provisions, in running the business are considered Revenue charges.

(8) Dispositions of profits constitute a debit against disposable profits.

Credit items—

Conversely treated, similar principles will apply to credit items.

Briefly, if the item represents a reduction in the earning capacity or saleable value of a fixed asset; or the increase of a fixed liability; or a rebate in respect of capital expenditure or loss; or a return of the purchase price (wholly or in part) of a fixed

247

asset or of a business (e.g. dividend received on a recently acquired investment) it is capital.

If the item represents a normal receipt or gain of an ordinarily recurring nature, being the outcome of the ordinary function and object of the business, it is revenue, and is none the less such merely because the debit which represents it is not in the form of cash.

Should the item represent the excess of realization of a fixed asset, it is considered capital, but accountancy practice declines to recognize a mere estimate of an appreciation in the value of a fixed asset as profit. If the asset be written up, the book profit should be transferred to Capital Reserve.

Note. (i) In capital expenditure involving a protracted period, it is usual to charge with it all expenditure thereon until completion, e.g. wages on construction, rates, and not infrequently interest on capital.

(ii) Where the renewals system of providing for depreciation is employed, cost of the renewal is charged to revenue, although a portion of the cost may virtually be capital.

2. (See Chapter VIII, Q. 1, page 247.)

Printing Machine. The total cost of the asset, including the necessary expenses entailed in making it ready for use, is a capital charge. In addition to the cost of the asset itself will be Carriage, Freight and Duty (if imported), possible Loss on Exchange (if imported), Insurance, Wages, and Materials in fixing; the cost of essential subsidiary assets, e.g. type, etc., repairs if essential to rendering it fit for use (particularly likely if second-hand), compensation claims for accidents involved in above, less rebates and discounts arising out of the above.

Renewals of parts, cost of upkeep, e.g. power, lubrication, depreciation, current repairs, cost of inspection, are chargeable to Revenue.

Motor Vans—Purchase price, delivery charges, signwriting, are chargeable to Capital. Repairs, if necessary to put them in condition, will be charged to Capital.

Expenses chargeable to Revenue are—

Upkeep of Motor Vans—Current repairs, painting, etc., wages and materials used in cleaning.

3. Expenditure on sinking shafts and driving levels incurred by a mining concern is in the nature of capital expenditure. It was stated in the case of *Lee* v. *Neuchatel Asphalte Co.* that there is no obligation on the part of a limited company to make good such capital sunk (i.e. charge to Revenue) before distributing profits, although the directors may consider it advisable to write off the expenditure over a period of years. It is, however, recognized in investment circles that every payment of a mining dividend partly represents a return of the capital sunk in, and expended on, the mine.

		£	£
4. Book value of Old Building (cost)			10,500
Less Depreciation		8,600	
Less Old Materials realized		50	
Less Old Materials used on New Building		200	
			8,850
Amount chargeable to Profit and Loss Account			£1,650

The debit to new building is, therefore, £23,900, i.e. £22,250 + £1,650.

5. It is assumed that the benefit of the first seven years' advertising cost is received within that period, although an assumption of continuance of benefit beyond the first seven years may be reasonable. The expenditure involved is—

£14,000 + £12,000 + £10,000 + £8,000 + £6,000 + £4,000 + £2,000 = £56,000.

Average = £8,000 to be charged annually for the first seven years.

An Advertising Suspense (or Equalization) Account will be opened and a balance of £8,000 will be transferred to Profit and Loss Account in the first year, and £6,000 carried forward to the second. At the end of the sixth year the balance on the account will be £6,000. At the end of the seventh year this sum, together with the expenditure of £2,000, will be debited to Profit and Loss Account.

The Balance Sheet at the end of the seventh year would show the account thus—

Assets	£	£
Advertising Suspense Account (Balance) . . .	6,000	
Add Expenditure during year	2,000	
	8,000	
Less Written off during year	8,000	....

Note. The answer assumes that from the outset the advertising expenditure in the future is a known quantity, otherwise the annual allocation must be estimated on probabilities.

6. Wages, Salary of Engineer, and Law Costs in connection with the construction of Works and Plant are normally legitimate charges of a capital nature, whilst interest on bank loan, directors' fees, and salary of secretary are revenue charges, but the item of interest may be capitalized if solely incurred during the period and for the purpose of construction. As to the directors' fees and salary of secretary, these should be charged to revenue, unless part of the time has been spent on construction, in which case a due proportion of fees and salary may be capitalized.

In any case, the capital expenditure should be separately featured under distinct heads: (*a*) Works, and (*b*) Plant.

7. (*a*) Chargeable to Capital.:
   (*b*)   ,,   ,,   ,,   } Cost of, or applicable to, acquisition of assets or
   (*c*)   ,,   ,,   ,,   } raising capital.
   (*d*)   ,,   ,,   ,,
   (*e*) Chargeable to Revenue. The first dividend received will be credited wholly to Revenue, the excess of the latter over the amount debited to Revenue upon purchase being the amount attributable to the period since the date of purchase.

8. (1) The cost of the patent rights, leasehold buildings, plant, etc., and machinery will be debited to the respective asset accounts.

The cost of advertising will be debited to Advertising Account.

The cost of defence is virtually one incurred in the acquisition of the asset itself, and may be debited to Patent Rights Account.

The foreign rights of the patent disposed of is a capital receipt, and will be credited to the Patent Rights Account.

(2) The patent after the adjustment for profit or loss on the sale of the foreign rights should be written off at the latest by the expiry of the legal life of sixteen years, but although legally protected the patent right may rapidly become obsolete; hence the nature of the patent right and its commercial utility will be very important factors in determining what proportion should be written off yearly.

The leasehold buildings will be written off on the basis of their life of 99 years, either by an equal sum yearly or a proportion representing the return on a terminable annuity. The Sinking Fund Method may be used, but as the period is extremely long this is not advisable.

The plant and machinery may be written off by any of the usual methods of depreciation, due regard being had to estimated life and residual values after calculating cost of dismantling. The same principle, however, that arises in the patent must be considered, viz. possible early obsolescence.

The cost of advertising to the extent that it *creates* rather than *maintains* the goodwill may be capitalized either by opening an Advertising Account (as mentioned), or by a transfer to Goodwill Account. The proportion, if any, attributable to current necessities should be charged to Revenue. Notwithstanding its capitalization, a steady writing off of any intangible asset such as this is generally considered advisable. (See Chapter VIII, Q. 5, page 248.)

The item of defence being considered as part of the cost of the patent will be dealt with in the Patent Rights Account.

If the foreign right is sold at a profit, the total sale price having been credited to the Patent Rights Account, such profit will be transferred to Reserve or used to write down fictitious and intangible assets. (Debit Patent Rights Account, Credit Reserve or Asset.) If, however, a loss has been incurred, a transfer should be made to Loss on Sale of Foreign Rights Account. (Debit Loss on Foreign Rights Accounts, Credit Patent Rights Account.) As the former account is fictitious it should be written off at the earliest possible date.

The question of the sale above-mentioned may affect the future sales of the company, so that a portion of the advertising cost may become ineffective; hence, if ascertainable, the abortive expenditure thereon should be written off at the earliest possible date, and if there is a profit on the sale of the foreign right it should be used to offset the foregoing non-productive advertising expense.

9. The contributions to the Sinking Fund are equivalent to depreciation provided that (1) the cost thereof is charged regularly to the undertaking; (2) the period of the loan is conterminous with that of the life of the assets acquired; (3) the contributions are regularly made; and (4) the Sinking Fund actually utilized to write off the assets upon their full amortization. As the item of goodwill cannot suffer the visible and regular depreciation identified with the other assets, there will be a surplus (or deficiency) of the fund measurable by the excess (or deficiency) of the value attachable to the goodwill over its book value.

Assuming, for example, the assets enumerated at £3,000, £10,000 and £27,000 respectively, the items will appear (assuming that "life" of the loan equals that of the fixed assets)—

	£		£
Sinking Fund	40,000	Sinking Fund Investment. .	40,000
Loan	40,000	Goodwill	3,000
		Land and Buildings . .	10,000
		Buses	27,000

The Sinking Fund and the assets will be written off; the investments realized and used to pay off the loan, but if the asset goodwill is estimated to be worth, say, £1,800, the Sinking Fund transfer to the credit of the assets will be £38,200, leaving £1,800 in the Sinking Fund, available for other uses. The same principle will apply if the period of the loan is less than the life of the assets, e.g. assuming that at the date of repayment the three assets were worth £7,000, the transfer from the Sinking Fund would be £33,000 only.

If the loan extends over a period longer than the estimated life of the assets (a very unlikely contingency), the contributions to the Sinking Fund to the extent that the rate of amortization is greater than the provision for the repayment of the loan, e.g. assuming the loan is for 25 years and the assets have an estimated life of 20 years, there will be an annual undercharge for depreciation to the extent of the difference between a Sinking Fund contribution built up on a 20-year and 25-year table.

10.   JOURNAL

19.0		£	£
June 30	Leasehold Redemption Policy . . . *Dr.*	37,250	
	To Leasehold Redemption Fund . . .		37,250
	Being entries for converting the secret reserve of the above amount, being the accumulation of annual premiums of £6,005 charged under the terms of the Debenture Trust Deed to Profit and Loss Account, into an open reserve in respect of Leasehold Redemption.		

BALANCE SHEET AS AT 30TH JUNE, 19.0 (*includes*)

	£		£
		Lease at Cost	237,000
Leasehold Redemption Fund . .	37,250	Leasehold Redemption Policy at Surrender Value . . .	37,250

It is assumed that it is intended to bring back the surrender value, otherwise the appropriate figure based on premiums without allowing for interest will be £36,030 (on the assumption the first premium was paid on 30th June, 19.5, and the 30th June, 19.0, premium paid before the above adjustment has been made). If the question intends that the adjustment is to be made on the footing that the premium for 19.0 has been properly made (disclosing the truly secret reserve, i.e. as at 30th June, 19.9) the Journal entries, ignoring narratives, are—

JOURNAL

19.0				£	£
June 30	Leasehold Redemption Policy	Dr.		6,005	
	To Bank.				6,005
	Profit and Loss Account	Dr.		6,005	
	To Leasehold Redemption Fund . .				6,005
	Leasehold Redemption Policy . . .	Dr.		30,134	
	To Leasehold Redemption Fund . .				30,134
	Leasehold Redemption Policy . . .	Dr.		1,111	
	To Leasehold Redemption Fund . .				1,111

BALANCE SHEET AS AT 30TH JUNE, 19.0 (*includes*)

	£	£		£	£
Leasehold Redemption Fund—			Lease at Cost . . .		237,000
Balance at 1st July, 19.9	30,134[1]		Leasehold Redemption		
Add Contribution £6,005			Policy—		
Increase of Sur-			Balance at 1st July, 19.9	30,134	
render Value 1,111			*Add* Premium £6,005		
	7,116[1]		Increase of Sur-		
		37,250	render Value 1,111		
				7,116	
					37,250

If interest is brought into account (by debiting the policy—no cash being received—and crediting the fund) the above figures will be proportionally greater.

11.   BRICKS LIMITED

BRICKYARD ACCOUNT FOR THE YEAR ENDED 31ST DECEMBER, 19.5

	Bricks	£		Bricks	£
Wages		3,255	Bricks spoiled . . .	50,000	
Employers' Liability Insur-			Cost of Usable Bricks pro-		
ance		16	duced . . . c/d	3,050,000	5,485
Stores, Fuel, etc. . . .		1,300			
Salaries		350			
Head Office and Sundry Ex-					
penses		564			
Bricks produced . . .	3,100,000				
	3,100,000	£5,485		3,100,000	£5,485
Cost of Usable Bricks pro-			Bricks used for new Kiln at		
duced . . . b/d	3,050,000	5,485	Cost . . .	950,000	1,708
			Cost of Bricks for Sale c/d	2,100,000	3,777
	3,050,000	£5,485		3,050,000	£5,485
Opening Stock . . .	100,000	175	Sales	2,050,000	4,305
Cost of Bricks for Sale b/d	2,100,000	3,777	Closing Stock . . .	150,000	270
Profit		623			
	2,200,000	£4,575		2,200,000	£4,575

---

[1] If based purely on contributions, i.e. ignoring interest and surrender value, the amounts will be respectively £30,025 and £6,005.

Abridged account, ignoring quantities, is—

	Rev- enue	Cap- ital	Total		Rev- enue	Cap- ital	Total
	£	£	£		£	£	£
Stock . . .	175		175	Sales . . .	4,305		4,305
Wages . . .	3,255	1,000	4,255	Transfer . .	1,708		
Employers' Liability				Stock . . .	270		270
Insurance .	16	5[1]	21	Cost of Kiln. .		5,508	4,885[3]
Stores, Fuel, etc. .	1,300	2,500	3,800				
Salaries . .	350	150	500				
Head Office and Sun-							
dries . .	564	145	709				
Transfer of Bricks .		1,708					
Profit . . .	623						
	£6,283	£5,508	£9,460[2]		£6,283	£5,508	£9,460[2]

Alternative answer—

BRICKS LIMITED
BRICKYARD ACCOUNT FOR THE YEAR ENDED 31ST DECEMBER 19.5

	Bricks	£		Bricks	£
Wages. . . .		4,255	Transfer to Kiln . . .	950,000	5,508
Employers' Liability Insur-			Bricks spoiled . . .	50,000	
ance . . .		21	Transfer to Trading . .	2,100,000	3,777
Stores, Fuel, etc. . .		3,800			
Salaries . . .		500			
Sundries . . .		709			
	3,100,000	£9,285		3,100,000	£9,285
Opening Stock . .	100,000	175	Sales	2,050,000	4,305
Cost of Bricks produced .	2,100,000	3,777			
	2,200,000	3,952			
Less Closing Stock .	150,000	270			
		3,682			
Profit . . .		623			
	2,050,000	£4,305		2,050,000	£4,305

(1) Wages cost of making bricks—

(*a*) Cost per 1,000 bricks in 19.5 is 5 per cent on 19.4 cost per 1,000 bricks.

$$\text{Cost in } 19.4 = \frac{\text{wages paid}}{\text{bricks produced}} \times 1,000$$

$$= £\frac{2,500}{2,700,000-200,000} \times 1,000$$

$$= £1.$$

∴ 19.5 cost per 1,000 bricks = £1 plus 5 per cent thereof
= £1·05

(*b*) Bricks produced in 19.5 are 3,100,000
(*c*) Bricks produced are 3,100,000
   Less used in new kiln 950,000

Bricks produced for sale (including spoiled) . . . 2,150,000

---

[1] It is assumed that the transfer of £150 Head Office Expenses includes the charge for Employers' Liability Insurance. [2] Per question. [3] £5,508 − £623 = £4,885.

(*d*) Wages chargeable to production—   £
    (i) For sale 2,150,000 at £1·05 per 1,000 . . . . 2,257½
    (ii) For kiln 950,000 at £1·05 per 1,000 . . . . 997½

                                              3,255
(*e*) Wages on construction of kiln (£4,255–£3,255) 1,000

      Accounting for wages item of £4,255

(2) Cost of making bricks—

	Bricks	£
Wages (as above)		3,255
Salaries (£500 – £150)		350
Stores, Fuel, etc. (£3,800 – £2,500) . . .		1,300
Head Office and Sundries (£730 – £21 – £145) . . .		564
Employers' Liability Insurance (£21 – £5)		16
Bricks Manufactured	3,100,000	
Less Spoilage	50,000	
Total	3,050,000	£5,485

(3) Transfer cost of bricks to kiln—

$$\frac{950,000}{3,050,000} \times £5,485 = £1,708 \text{ (to nearest £)}$$

(4) Cost of kiln—

	£
Wages	1,000
Bricks	1,708
Salaries	150
Stores, Fuel, etc.	2,500
Head Office and Sundries	145
Employers' Liability Insurance . . .	5
	£5,508

CHAPTER IX

CASES STOCK

Dr.

		Price D	Quantity	£
19.. Jan. 1	To Stock—			
	In hand	15	4,000	600
	With Customers	15	8,000	1,200
Dec. 31	" Purchases	25	5,000	1,250
			17,000	£3,050
19.. Jan. 1	To Stock—			
	In hand: Old	15	2,040	306
	New	25	5,000	1,250
	With Customers	15	3,800	570

Cr.

		Price D	Quantity	£
19.. Dec.31	By Cases Trading Account—			
	Cases retained by Customers	15	6,000[1]	900
	Loss on Cases Scrapped			19
	Cash: Sales for Scrap	15	160	5
	" Stock—			
	In hand: Old	15	2,040	306
	New	25	5,000[2]	1,250
	With Customers	15	3,800	570
			17,000	£3,050

[1] Opening Stock "out" 8,000 plus dispatched during year 6,400, less returned, 4,600 and closing stock "out" 3,800.

[2] Assumed all new cases still in stock.

CASES TRADING ACCOUNT

Dr.

		Price D	Quantity	£
19.. Dec.31	To Customers—			
	Cases returned	25	4,600	1,150
	" Cases Stock—			
	Cases retained by Customers	15	6,000	900
	Loss on Cases Scrapped			19
	" Provision for Liability on Returnable Cases in Customers' hands c/d	25	3,800	950
	" Profit and Loss Account—			
	Profit on Hire			
	Profit on Sales			} 1,400[3]
			14,400	£4,419

Cr.

		Price D	Quantity	£
19.. Jan. 1	By Provision for Liability on Returnable Cases in Customers' hands b/d	25	8,000	2,000
Dec.31	" Customers—			
	Cases Charged out	37½	6,400	2,400
	" Profit and Loss Account—			
	Loss on Cases Scrapped			19
			14,400	£4,419
19.. Jan. 1	By Provision	25	3,800	950

[3] This figure may be checked as follows, assuming that all cases "out" at 1st January are returned—

Charged out during the year	6,400
Less retained by customers (i.e. sold)	6,000
Hired out during the year	400

Profit at 22½ (37½ less 15) on 6,000	£1,350	= Sale
Profit at 12½ (37½ less 25) on 400	50	= Hire
	£1,400	

2. *Dr.*   CASES STOCK   *Cr.*

19.8			£	19.8			£
Jan. 1	To Balances—	b/d		Dec. 31	By Cases Reserve—		
	Stock on hand .	.	596		Sales . . .	.	140
	Stock in hands of				„ Balances—	c/d	
	Customers .	.	336		Stock on hand .	.	280
Dec. 31	„ Materials used	.	38		Stock in hands of		
	„ Wages (Repairs)	.	156		Customers .	.	232
					„ Profit and Loss Account .		474
			£1,126				£1,126
19.9							
Jan. 1	To Balances—	b/d					
	Stock on hand .	.	280				
	Stock in hands of						
	Customers .	.	232				

Dr.   CASES RESERVE   *Cr.*

19.8			£	19.8			£
Dec. 31	To Cases Stock: Sales .	.	140	Jan. 1	By Balance .	b/d	840
	„ Debtors—Returns .	.	3,260	Dec. 31	„ Debtors—		
	„ Balance .	c/d	580		Cases charged out	.	3,140
			£3,980				£3,980
				19.9			
				Jan. 1	By Balance .	b/d	580

The stock of cases (on hand and with customers) will appear in the Balance Sheets at 31st December, 19.7 and 19.8, as £932 and £512 respectively under heading of cases on hand and with customers at cost less depreciation. The credit balance on Cases Reserve, being the invoiced price of cases in hands of customers (and so being included in the list of debtors), will be deducted from the total debtors, thus reducing the latter to the amount due for goods supplied.

Note. The opening item of cases "out" (£336) is 50 per cent of £840 = £420, less 20 per cent £84 = £336. The closing item of cases "out" (£232) is 50 per cent of £580 = £290, less 20 per cent £58 = £232.

3. *Dr.*   CASES CONTROL ACCOUNT   *Cr.*

	Quantity	£		Quantity	£
To Cases charged out per Cases Columns in Sales Day Book . . .	1,800	2,700	By Cases returned per Cases Columns in Sales Returned Book .	1,200	1,800
			„ Balance Cases in hands of customers . . c/d	600	900
	1,800	£2,700		1,800	£2,700
To Balance (b) . . b/d	600	900			

Dr.   CASES STOCK   *Cr.*

	Quantity	£		Quantity	£
To Purchases . .	1,000	1,000	By Cases charged . .	1,800	1,800
„ Cases returned (cost) .	1,200	1,200	(Cost) . . .		
			„ Balance, Cases on hand . c/d	400	400
	2,200	£2,200		2,200	£2,200
To Balance (a) . . b/d	400	400			

Dr.   CASES PROFIT SUSPENSE ACCOUNT   *Cr.*

	Quantity	£		Quantity	£
To Surcharge on Cases returned	1,200	600	By Surcharge on Cases dispatched . . .	1,800	900
„ Balance—unrealized Profit on Cases still in customers' hands . c/d	600	300			
	1,800	£900		1,800	£900
			By Balance (c) . . b/d	600	300

The Balance Sheet for Stock of Cases will be—

	Quantity	£	£
(a) Cases in hand	400		400
(b) Cases in hands of customers (at loaded price)} .	900		
(c) *Less* Cases Profit Suspense Account } .	600	300	
		—	600
	1,000		£1,000

Obviously there is no profit as all the cases have been, or will be, returned.

There may be required (apart from dealing with the situation arising from non-returns) explanations of the adjustments, as can be seen from the next question.

4. *Dr.*   CASES CONTROL ACCOUNT   *Cr.*

		Quantity	£		Quantity	£
To Balance . . b/d		*600*	*900*	By Cases returned . .	2,000	3,000
,, Cases charged out . .		1,600	2,400	. Cases retained by customers (= Sale) . .	40	60
				,, Balance Cases in hands of customers . . c/d	160	240
		2,200	£3,300		2,200	£3,300
To Balance (b) . . b/d		160	240			

Dr.   CASES STOCK   *Cr.*

		Quantity	£		Quantity	£
To Balance . . b/d		*400*	*400*	By Cases charged (cost)	1,600	1,600
,, Cases returned (cost) .		2,000	2,000	,, Sale of Scrap Cases .	30	5
,, Repairs . . .			35	,, Profit Suspense for Profit on Cases retained by customers . .		20
				,, Profit and Loss Account. (d)		40
				,, Balance, cases on hand c/d	770	770
		2,400	£2,435		2,400	£2,435
To Balance (a) . . b/d		770	770			

Dr.   CASES PROFIT SUSPENSE ACCOUNT   *Cr.*

	Quantity	£		Quantity	£
To Surcharge on Cases returned . . .	2,000	1,000	*By Balance* . . b/d	*600*	*300*
,, Profit on Cases retained (= Sale) . .	40	20	,, Surcharge on Cases dispatched . .	1,600	800
,, Balance— Profit on cases still in customers' hands. c/d	160	80			
	2,200	£1,100		2,200	£1,100
			By Balance (c) . . b/d	160	80

The Balance Sheet for Cases will be—

	Quantity	£	£
(a) Cases on hand	770		770
(b) Cases in the hands of customers (at loaded price)} .	160	240	
(c) *Less* Cases Profit Suspense account } .		80	
		—	160
	930		£930

(*d*) The charge of Profit and Loss Account is analysed as follows—

	£	£
Loss on Cases scrapped and sold: 30 at £1 each . . .	30	
Less Sale price	5	
		25
Repairs		35
		60
Less profit realized on 40 Cases retained by customers at 50p each		20
		£40

An alternative method relating to stock (on balance preferable, but under the severe time conditions obtaining in examinations, the method illustrated already would suffice) is to exclude profit and loss elements and to transfer cases scrapped to a separate account at cost; and to bring down all the stock whether on hand or with customers, bringing down the stock so held by customers as a *credit*.

Dr.   CASES STOCK   *Cr.*

	Quantity	£		Quantity	£
To Balance . . b/d	400	400	By Cases charged Cost . .	1,600	1,600
,, Cases Returned Cost .	2,000	2,000	,, Transfer Scrapped Cases .	30	30
,, Balance, Cases in customers' hands . . c/d	160	160	,, Balance, Cases on hand c/d	770	770
			,, Balance, Cases in customers' hands . . c/d	160	160
	2,560	£2,560		2,560	£2,560
To Balance on hand . b/d	770	770	By Balance with customers b/d	160	160
,, Balance with customers b/d	160	160			

Dr.   CASES PROFIT AND LOSS ACCOUNT   *Cr.*

	Quantity	£		Quantity	£
To Transfer Cases scrapped (cost)	30	30	By Cases Profit Suspense— Profit on Cases retained by customers . .		20
,, Repairs		35	,, Cash Sale of Scrapped Cases . .	30	5
			,, Profit and Loss Account: Loss . . .		40
	30	£65		30	£65

The Cases Control and Cases Profit Suspense Accounts are not affected.

It will be seen that the total Cases Stock is ascertainable from the Cases Stock Account (Debit Balance), the Credit Balance being used as part cancellation of the Debit Balance in the Cases Control Account and the Credit Balance in the Cases Suspense Account, thus—

	£	£
Debit balance of Cases Control	240	
Credit balance of Cases Profit Suspense . . .		80
Credit balance of Cases Stock Account . .		160
(The quantity column thereof 160 cases.)		
	£240	£240

The Cases Profit and Loss Account shows clearly the composition of the loss of £40.

5. The Department of Trade and Industry in Account with the Owners of m.v. "Mary Rose." Voyage No. 5

Swansea–Montreal–Liverpool: 15th June to 30th September, 19..

	£	£	£
Freights received—			
Outward—8,000 tons Anthracite at £4 per ton			32,000
Homeward—7,000 tons Grain at £3 per ton			21,000
			53,000
Expenses—			
Bunkers—30,000 gallons at 40p per gallon		12,000	
Managers' Fittage thereon—50p per 100 gallons		150	
Loading at Swansea—			
Dock Dues, Pilotage, Towage, etc.	806		
Trimming Cargo	408		
Trimming Bunkers	175		
		1,389	
Discharging and Landing at Montreal—			
Dock Dues, Pilotage, Towage, etc.	910		
Cleaning Holds	240		
Loading Grain	734		
		1,884	
Discharging at Liverpool—			
Dock Dues, Pilotage, Towage, etc.	718		
Discharging Grain	450		
		1,168	
Crew's Overtime re Cargo Work		856	
Address Commission—2% on £32,000		640	
Brokerage—½ of 5% on £32,000		533	
Managers' Commission—1% on £32,000			
less £1,173		308	
			18,928
Balance due to Department			£34,072

Note. There is no indication in the question of commission or brokerage on homeward freight.

6. Goods Sent on S. or R. Journal

19..		£
Jan. 1	B	50
9	C	25
16	D	70
23	C	25
30	B	40
31	E	50
		£260

Goods on S. or R. Sold and Returned Journal

19..		Returned £	Sold £
Jan. 4	B		50
10	C	15	10
19	D		70
25	C	25	
		£40	£130

Dr. Goods on S. or R. Total Account *Cr.*

19..			£	19..			£
Jan. 31	To Returns		40	Jan. 31	By Goods sent out on		
	„ Sales		130		S. or R.		260
	„ Balance	c/d	90				
			£260				£260
				Feb. 1	By Balance	b/d	90

Dr.						B						Cr.	
19..					£	19..							£
Jan. 1	To Goods	.	.	.	50	Jan. 4	By Sales	.	.	.			50
30	„ Goods	.	.	.	40	31	„ Balance	.	.	c/d			40
					£90								£90
Feb. 1	To Balance	.	.	b/d	40								

The balance on Goods on Sale or Return Total Account of £90 at 31st January represents outstanding goods, i.e. B £40 plus E £50.

7.   C.O.D. JOURNAL

Date	Name, etc.	Invoice Price	Post, etc.	Total per T.C.F	Cash Received	Goods Returned	Post, etc., on Returns
		£	p	£		£	p
19..							
Dec. 1	B	10	28	10·28	Dec. 6		
3	C	3	10	3·10	7		
7	D	5	12	5·12		5	12
15	E	7	14	7·14	22		
30	F	10	24	10·24			c/d
		£35	88	£35·88		£5	12
19..							
Jan. 1	F b/d	10	24	10·24			

CASH RECEIVED BOOK

	19..									£
	Dec. 6	B	.	.	.	.	.	.	.	10·28
	7	C	.	.	.	.	.	.	.	3·10
	22	E	.	.	.	.	.	.	.	7·14
										£20·52

Dr.				C.O.D. TOTAL ACCOUNT				Cr.	
19..				£	19..				£
Dec. 31	To Sales	.	.	35·00	Dec. 31	By Cash	. . .		20·52
	„ Cash: Postages, etc.	.		0·88		„ Returns	. . .		5·00
						„ Postage, etc., on Returns	.		0·12
						„ Balance	.	c/d	10·24
				£35·88					£35·88
19..									
Jan. 1	To Balance	.	b/d	10·24					

CHAPTER X

1. THE system of Self-balancing Ledgers or Sectional Balancing is utilized to prove the total arithmetical accuracy of a particular ledger, in the same way as a Trial Balance is used to prove the total arithmetical accuracy of the book-keeping entries in all the books.

The principle involves the preparation of a Total Account for each ledger concerned, such account giving, in summarized form, all the entries in the appropriate ledger. A Sales Ledger Total Account, for example, will represent all the entries posted to the Sales Ledger as if only one debtor existed.

In order to carry out the system it is essential that columns be provided in the subsidiary books appropriate to each ledger; or that such books be analysed according to the ledger to which the postings are made; or entirely separate subsidiary books employed.

Where transfers are made from one ledger to another or there are transactions other than those appearing in the usual subsidiary books, it will be necessary to employ a Transfer Journal with analysis columns relating to each ledger. Where transfers are made from one account to another *within* the same ledger there is theoretically no need to employ a transfer journal, as the total of the particular ledger is not affected, but as the transfer must be put through a journal in any case, it is convenient to make the entry through the Transfer Journal.

The Total Accounts (separate for each ledger) will be constructed at convenient dates; such accounts may be "dual", i.e. in the particular ledger on reverse side, and in the Nominal Ledger on the same side as the details appear in the relative ledger. The component items (taking a Sales Ledger Total Account as an example) will be: Debit side (*a*) opening balance, (*b*) sales, (*c*) interest charged, (*d*) other debits, e.g. transfers; and on the Credit side (*a*) opening balance (if credit balances appear in the Sales Ledger), (*b*) cash received, (*c*) discounts allowed, (*d*) returns, (*e*) allowances, (*f*) bad debts written off, (*g*) bills receivable accepted by customers, and (*h*) other credits, e.g. transfers.

The account will be balanced off either as a net "carry down" or separately for debit balances and for credit balances.

The above items being on "same" side would appear in the Nominal Ledger, and if the accounts are "dual," on the reverse side in the Sales Ledger.

The items on the debit side will be posted from the subsidiary books as follows: (*a*) brought down from previous period, (*b*) sales day book, (*c*) interest charged book, (*d*) appropriate subsidiary book, e.g. transfer journal.

The items on the credit side will be posted from the subsidiary books as follows: (*a*) brought down from previous period, (*b*) cash book for cash received, (*c*) cash book for discount allowed, (*d*) returns inwards book, (*e*) allowances journal, (*f*) transfer journal, (*g*) bills receivable journal or transfer journal, (*h*) appropriate subsidiary book, e.g. transfer journal.

The balance (or balances) of a Total Account will, in the absence of errors, represent in total the balances of the accounts in the ledger with which it is concerned.[1]

The principle of construction is identical in other ledgers.

---

[1] In the Balance Sheet the debit balances will be shown as Debtors; the credit balances as Creditors.

EXAMPLE

Dr.   SALES LEDGER TOTAL ACCOUNT   Cr.

19..			£	19..			£
Jan. 1	To Balances . . b/d		3,000	Dec. 31	By Returns . . .		120
Dec. 31	,, Sales		10,500		,, Cash and Discount .		8,810
	,, Bills Dishonoured . .		200		,, Bills Receivable . .		1,000
	,, Interest Charged on Over-				,, Bad Debts . . .		95
	due Accounts . .		75		,, Allowances . .		121
	,, Transfers of *Contra* Ac-				,, Balances . . c/d		3,724
	counts to Purchases						
	Ledger . . .		95				
			£13,870				£13,870
19..							
Jan. 1	To Balances . . b/d		3,724				

It should be noted that—

(i) The Total Account may be a memorandum account only.

(ii) The Sales Ledger itself may be regarded as memorandum, the Total Account, with entries on the same sides as the Sales Ledger, being part of the Double Entry.

(iii) The Sales Ledger may still be part of the Double Entry, the Sales Ledger Total Account being opened in the Nominal Ledger with entries on the same sides as the Sales Ledger. A further account will then be opened in the Sales Ledger itself, headed Nominal Ledger Adjustment (or Total) Account, with sides reversed to the Sales Ledger. The effect on the Trial Balance would be (taking the figures in the illustration given)—

	£	£
Sales Ledger (*Dr.* Balance)	3,724	
Nominal Ledger Total Account (*Cr.* Balance) . . .		3,724
Sales Ledger Total Account (*Dr.* Balance) . . .	3,724	

Advantages of the system are—

(1) If affords a check upon the total arithmetical accuracy of the book-keeping.

(2) In conjunction with other precautions, it provides a check upon the honesty of the ledger clerks, so long as the total accounts are not under their control.

(3) Location of errors is simplified.

(4) It enables draft accounts to be prepared without the delay entailed by extraction of separate ledger balances relating to Debtors and Creditors.

2.   SALES LEDGER CONTROL ACCOUNT
Dr.   [IN NOMINAL LEDGER]   Cr.

19..			£	19..			£
Jan. 1	To Balances . . b/d		37,262	June 30	By Sales Returns . .		741
June 30	,, Sales . . .		73,127		,, Cash . . .		70,813
	,, Cheques dishonoured.		289		,, Discount . . .		1,782
	,, Bills dishonoured .		360		,, Bills Receivable .		2,690
	, Interest . .		68		,, Bad Debts . .		632
	,, Carriage Outwards .		120		,, Balances . . c/d		34,568
			£111,226				£111,226
July 1	To Balances . . b/d		34,568				

Notes. (i) The Provision for Doubtful Debts does not appear in the Sales Ledger, and consequently not in its Total Account.

(ii) The Bad Debts recoveries will be posted direct from the Cash Book to the credit of Bad Debts Account (hence not appearing in the Sales Ledger and its Total Account) as assumed above; or credited from the Cash Book to the customers' accounts, like amounts being debited to the customers' accounts and credited to Bad Debts Account, in which event the total will appear (as in the ledger) on both sides of the Total Account.

3. The totals do not agree with the details given, as shown by the subjoined Total Accounts—

Dr.			TOTAL DEBTORS						Cr.
19.7			£	19.8					£
Oct. 1	To Balances	b/d	1,926	Mar. 31	By Cash				12,993
19.8					,, Bad Debts				55
Mar. 31	,, Interest		5		,, Returns				93
	,, Cheques dishonoured		76		,, Discounts				356
	,, Sales		13,308		,, Balances		c/d		1,818
			£15,315						£15,315
19.8									
Apr. 1	To Balances	b/d	1,818						

Dr.			TOTAL CREDITORS						Cr.
19.8			£	19.7					£
Mar. 31	To Cash		7,613	Oct. 1	By Balances		b/d		1,215
	,, Discount		285	19.8					
	,, Returns		182	Mar. 31	,, Purchases				8,848
	,, Bills Payable		890		,, Bills Payable withdrawn				200
	,, Balances	c/d	1,295		,, Interest				2
			£10,265						£10,265
				19.8					
				Apr. 1	By Balances		b/d		1,295

	Sales Ledger £	Bought Ledger £
Balances per Schedules	1,807	1,290
Balances per Total Accounts	1,818	1,295
Discrepancies	£11	£5

4.   TRIAL BALANCE, 30TH JUNE, 19.5

	Dr. £	Cr. £
Loan Creditor		1,000
Capital		1,586
Buildings	900	
Furniture and Fittings	140	
Stock-in-trade	1,582	
Bills Receivable	50	
Sundry Debtors	1,816	
Bad Debts Reserve		100
Sundry Creditors		1,100
Purchases	3,166	
Discounts	182	153
Returns	113	59
Sales		4,750
Drawings	433	
Loan Interest	38	
General Expenses	397	
Bank Overdraft		312
Cash in hand	243	
	£9,060	£9,060

TRIAL BALANCE, 1ST JULY, 19.5 [*after preparing final accounts*]

	Dr.	Cr.
	£	£
Loan Creditor		1,000
Capital.		2,410
Buildings	900	
Furniture and Fittings	140	
Stock-in-trade	1,773	
Bills Receivable	50	
Sundry Debtors	1,816	
Bad Debts Provision		100
Sundry Creditors		1,100
Bank Overdraft		312
Cash in Hand	243	
	£4,922	£4,922

Dr.   PURCHASES LEDGER CONTROL ACCOUNT   **Cr.**

19.5			£	19.4			£
June 30	To Cash		4,213	July 1	By Balances	b/d	2,359
	,, Discount received		153	19.5			
	,, Returns Outward		59	June 30	,, Purchases		3,166
	,, Balances	c/d	1,100				
			£5,525				£5,525
				19.5			
				July 1	By Balances	b/d	1,100

Dr.   SALES LEDGER CONTROL ACCOUNT   **Cr.**

19.4			£	19.5			£
July 1	To Balances	b/d	1,670	June 30	By Cash		4,199
19.5					,, Discount allowed		182
June 30	,, Sales		4,750		,, Returns Inward		113
					,, Bills Receivable		110
					,, Balances	c/d	1,816
			£6,420				£6,420
19.5							
July 1	To Balances	b/d	1,816				

Dr.   BILLS RECEIVABLE   **Cr.**

19.4			£	19.5			£
July 1	To Balance	b/d	295	June 30	By Cash		355
19.5					,, Balance	c/d	50
June 30	,, Debtors		110				
			£405				£405
19.5							
July 1	To Balance	b/d	50				

Dr.   CAPITAL   **Cr.**

19.5			£	19.4			£
June 30	To Drawings		433	July 1	By Balance	b/d	1,586
	,, Balance	c/d	2,410	19.5			
				June 30	,, Profit and Loss Account		1,257
			£2,843				£2,843
				19.5			
				July 1	By Balance	b/d	2,410

The following accounts are essential to the proper working of the question—

CASH BOOK

Dr.		Cash	Bank			Cash	Bank	Cr.
		£	£			£	£	
19.4				19.5				
July 1	To Balances . . . b/d	39	419	June 30	By Creditors . . .	4,213		
19.5					,, General Expenses .	397		
June 30	,, Debtors . . .	4,199			,, Loan Interest . .	38		
	,, Bills Receivable . .	355			,, Drawings . . .	433		
	,, Cash (contra) . .		4,545		,, Bank (contra) . .	4,545		
	,, Bank (contra) . .	5,276			,, Cash (contra) . .		5,276	
	,, Balance . . c/d		312		,, Balance . . c/d	243		
		£9,869	£5,276			£9,869	£5,276	
19.5				19.5				
July 1	To Balance . . . b/d	243		July 1	By Balance . . . b/d		312	

TRADING AND PROFIT AND LOSS ACCOUNT FOR THE YEAR ENDED 30TH JUNE, 19.5

		£	£			£	£
Stock (Opening) . . .			1,582	Sales		£4,750	
Purchases . . .		£3,166		Less Returns . .		113	4,637
Less Returns . .		59					
			3,107	Stock (Closing) . .			1,773
Gross Profit . . .			1,721				
			£6,410				£6,410
General Expenses . .			397	Gross Profit . . . b/d			1,721
Loan Interest . . .			38	Discount received . .			153
Discount allowed . .			182				
Net Profit to Capital Account			1,257				
			£1,874				£1,874

CHAPTER XI

1.

SAMUEL WOOD

TRADING AND PROFIT AND LOSS ACCOUNT FOR THE YEAR ENDED
31ST DECEMBER, 19.5

		£			£
Stock (Opening)		876	Sales		6,037
Purchases		4,011	Stock (Closing)		854
Gross Profit . . .	c/d	2,004			
		£6,891			£6,891
Wages		743	Gross Profit	b/d	2,004
General Expenses . . .		627			
Depreciation—					
Machinery and Plant . . .		58			
Bad Debts		150			
Net Profit transferred to Capital					
Account		426			
		£2,004			£2,004

BALANCE SHEET AS AT 31ST DECEMBER, 19.5

		£				£
Capital—			Machinery and Plant—			
Balance 1st January, 19.5	£3,150		Balance 1st January, 19.5 .	£420		
Cash introduced . .	200		*Plus* Additions . . .	160		
Add Net Profit for year .	426			580		
	3,776		*Less* Depreciation . .	58		
Less Drawings . . .	574				522	
		3,202	Freehold Premises . . .		1,560	
						2,082
Creditors		816	Current Assets—			
			Stock		854	
			Debtors . . .	£880		
			Less Bad Debts Provision	150		
					730	
			Cash		352	
						1,936
		£4,018				£4,018

It is assumed that there are no discounts and no bad debts actually written off.

Working accounts in outline—

DEBTORS

	£		£
Balance (opening) . . .	982	Cash	4,276
Sales	4,212	Balance	918
	£5,194		£5,194
Balance	918	Drawings	38
		Balance (closing) . . .	880
	£918		£918

CREDITORS

	£		£
Cash	3,954	Balance (opening) . . .	721
Balance (end)	816	Purchases	4,049
	£4,770		£4,770

CASH

	£		£
Balance	33	Creditors	3,954
Debtors	4,276	*Wages*	*743*
Cash Sales . . .	1,863	*Expenses*	*627*
Capital	200	Machinery . . .	160
		Drawings	536
		Balance	352
	£6,372		£6,372

SALES

	£		£
Transfer to Purchases . .	38	Debtors. . . .	4,212
Trading	*6,037*	Cash	1,863
	£6,075		£6,075

PURCHASES

	£		£
Creditors	4,049	Transfer from Sales . .	38
		Trading	*4,011*
	£4,049		£4,049

DRAWINGS

	£		£
Cash	536	*Capital*	*574*
Debtors	38		
	£574		£574

Items in italics "transferred" direct to final accounts.

2.   STATEMENT OF ESTIMATED BUSINESS PROFITS FOR THE SIX YEARS
ENDED 31ST DECEMBER, 19.9

	1st January, 19.4		31st December, 19.9	
	£	£	£	£
Total Capitals—				
Business: Cash	947		1,945	
Debtors.	145		592	
Stock	542		674	
	1,634		3,211	
Less Creditors . . .	732		840	
		902		2,371
Personal: House	2,000		2,000	
Car			750	
Investment . . .			750	
Loan			300	
				3,800
	2,000			
Less Loan	400	1,600		6,171
		£2,502		
Less Capital at 1st January, 19.4				2,502
Increase of Capital				3,669
Add Living Expenses			£3,400	
Money stolen			300	
				3,700
Estimated Business Profits				7,369
Profits per Accounts				5,777
Estimated under-statement of Business Profits				£1,592

Note. It is assumed that income from investment and loan, and charges upon loan, payments for income tax Schedule D are included in item of living expenses. If they are included in the business figures, the above income will be deducted from, and the above charges and payments added to, the foregoing figures.

[In practice a statement will be required for *each* of the relevant years, and schedules for non-business sources of income.]

3. (i) An opening Statement of Affairs must *first* be prepared, the figures therein, excluding Debtors and Creditors, being posted to the various accounts, which will be opened. Capital will be the balancing item of the Statement of Affairs. Debtors and Creditors will be dealt with as shown in paragraph (iii).

(ii) The Cash Book will be completely analysed, all cognate items being summarized together, so that a Receipts and Payments Account can be prepared. The opening and closing balances of the Receipts and Payments Account should agree with the balances in the Cash Book.

(iii) The ledgers will then be completely analysed into Total Accounts. Each side of each Ledger Account will be extracted on to schedules as shown below, the totals of the various columns being built into the Total Accounts. The ledger schedules will appear as below—

BOUGHT LEDGER ANALYSIS SCHEDULE

Fo.	Name of Personal Account	Closing Balances	Cash and Discount	Returns	Total	Purchases	Opening Balances
	£	£	£	£	£	£	£

Other columns may be used if necessary.

The Sales Ledger will similarly be analysed into—

Opening Balances—Sales—Total—Cash and Discount—Bills Accepted—Returns—Allowances—Bad Debts—Closing Balances. Other columns may be used if necessary.

(iv) The Total Accounts will then be compared to see that Cash paid to Creditors and Cash received from Debtors agree with the figures shown by the Receipts and Payments Account. Similarly, discounts will be checked up in total from Receipts and Payments Account and posted to the Discounts Accounts.

(v) Accounts will then be opened for Allowances, Bad Debts, Returns Inward and Outward, which will be posted up from the Total Accounts.

(vi) Nominal Accounts such as Carriage and Freight, Telephone, Electricity, Rent, and others, will be posted from the Receipts and Payments Account to the relevant accounts.

(vii) The Journals will be cast and the totals compared with the corresponding amounts in the Total Accounts. The Purchases Journal total will be posted to Purchases Account, and the Sales Journal total to the Sales Account; with reverse entries for Returns.

(viii) The Trial Balance may now be extracted by listing all the balances of the nominal items, capital, cash, bank, and the totals of debtors and creditors.

Note. Care must be exercised to see that every item in a ledger is analysed appropriately, e.g. if many debtors' accounts have been struck out it will be necessary to utilize a Bad Debts column in the Sales Ledger analysis; on the other hand, exceptional items (e.g. where only a small number of bad debts have arisen, or where a customer accepts a bill of exchange) will be inserted in a "Sundries" analysis column, the nature of the item being shown against each amount and finally sub-analysed on completion of the analysis.

If there are **credit** items in the Sales Ledger and **debit** items in the Bought Ledger, suitable columns must be inserted in the Analysis Sheets.

4.   STATEMENT OF AFFAIRS AS AT 1ST JANUARY, 19..

	£		£
Creditors	341	Cash in Hand . . .	3
Capital	812	Cash at Bank . . .	100
		Debtors. . . .	175
		War Loan . . .	625
		Stock	250
	£1,153		£1,153

I. Rally

Trading and Profit and Loss Account for the Year Ended 31st December, 19..

		£				£
Stock		250	Sales			3,200
Purchases		2,019	Stock			187
Gross Profit	c/d	1,118				
		£3,387				£3,387

		£				£
Salaries		150	Gross Profit		b/d	1,118
General Expenses		350				
Stationery and Wrapping Paper		87				
Rent and Rates		70				
Lighting, etc.		25				
Net Profit transferred to Capital Account		436				
		£1,118				£1,118

Balance Sheet as at 31st December, 19..

		£	£			£	£
Capital—				Stock			187
Balance at 1st January, 19..		812		Sundry Debtors			250
Less Drawings		405		War Loan			625
		407		Cash in Hand		5	
Add Net Profit for year		436		„ at Bank		150	155
			843				
Sundry Creditors			374				
			£1,217				£1,217

Rough Working Accounts—

Cash Book

	Cash	Bank		Cash	Bank
	£	£		£	£
To Balances	3	100	By *Salaries*	150	
„ Debtors	3,125		„ *General Trade Charges*	350	
„ Cash (*contra*)		1,875	„ *Stationery, etc.*	87	
„ Drawings		25	„ *Rent and Rates*	70	
			„ *Lighting, etc.*	25	
			„ Creditors	475	1,525
			„ Drawings		325
			„ Drawings	91	
			„ Bank (*contra*)	1,875	
			„ Balances	5	150
	£3,128	£2,000		£3,128	£2,000

Debtors

	£		£
To Balances	175	By Receipts	3,125
„ *Sales*	3,200	„ Balances	250

CREDITORS

	£		£
To Payments	2,000	By Balances	341
,, Balances	374	,, Purchases	2,033

PURCHASES

	£		£
To Creditors	2,033	By Drawings	14
		,, *Purchases (Net)*	*2.019*

DRAWINGS

	£		£
To Cheques	325	By Bank	25
,, Cash	91	,, *Capital*	*405*
,, Purchases	14		

Notes. (i) Difficulty is likely to arise in connection with the two items: "Payments through Bank and by Cash for Goods, £2,000"; and "Payments out of Bank—Business, £1,525." The matter is simplified if the cash columns are first built up, inserting the closing balance of cash £5. This will disclose a shortage of cash payments of £475, which item will be written into the credit column of cash, leaving £1,525 (£2,000–£475) representing the payments out of Bank. Assuming that the expenses are paid out of cash, it will be obvious that if £2,000 is made up of Bank and Cash payments and £1,525 thereof is the bank payments proportion, £475 remain for cash payments.

(ii) Opening entries in heavy type; final account transfers in italics.

(iii) As the War Loan appears as an asset of the business the interest thereon should appear as a credit to Profit and Loss Account. No amount is given as to the nominal amount held, so that the receipt of War Loan interest cannot be ascertained. The item of £25 described as "personal" in the question may be applicable to this source of income.

If, therefore, the £25 represent War Loan interest it should be—to be logical—credited to Profit and Loss Account; if the item has not come into the books at all Drawings Account should be debited and Profit and Loss Account credited with the correct figure.

(iv) It is assumed that there are no bad debts.

(v) No fixed assets appear in the accounts.

5. Under pure Single Entry the twofold aspect of each transaction is completely ignored, the only accounts kept being Personal Accounts of Debtors and Creditors.

Actually, however, the term Single Entry is stretched to embrace all systems of book-keeping where the principle of complete double entry is not adhered to. Pure Single Entry is very rarely met with, as usually a Cash Book is kept.

The obvious disadvantages of Single Entry are that only a very haphazard figure for Profit or Loss can be ascertained, namely, by finding the difference between the opening and closing capitals of the period under review, adjustments being made for Drawings and introductions of Capital. In point of fact the system is only accurate in so far as a composite result is obtainable by comparisons of opening and closing capitals compiled from unsystematic records, as no statistical facts can be extracted from the books with any accuracy.

One of the chief advantages of Double Entry book-keeping is the facility with which the arithmetical accuracy of the entries can be checked in the Trial Balance, and the further check in the Profit and Loss Account afforded by the agreement of the Balance Sheet. These advantages are completely lacking under Single Entry. Moreover, under Double Entry, the system of book-keeping can easily be amended in the case of expansion of the business.

Accounts prepared from books kept on the Double Entry system will be more readily accepted by outside parties, such as revenue authorities, bankers, and executors.

6. Conversion to Single Entry for a period is dealt with in Question 3. Conversion at a given date is given in Question 7. It should be noted that, should no Cash Book be kept, conversion to Double Entry over a period would be difficult, as Rent, Carriage, and other expenses paid in cash could not be computed and posted to their respective accounts, unless from records covering all expenses, drawings, introductions of capital, cash sales, etc., a notional Cash Account could be compiled.

7. As requested, I have pleasure in setting out in concise form instructions for keeping your accounts on a complete double-entry system—

(1) List of books of account required: (*a*) Sales Journal, (*b*) Sales Returns Journal, (*c*) Purchases Journal, (*d*) Purchases Returns Journal, (*e*) Cash Book, (*f*) Journal, (*g*) Sales Ledger, (*h*) Purchases Ledger, (*i*) Private Ledger.

(2) Rules for writing up books of account.

A statement must first be prepared as at the date on which you desire the new system to commence. On one side will be tabulated the whole of your business assets, including expenses prepaid; and on the other will be tabulated all your business liabilities, including expenses accrued and accruing. The difference between the total of the two sides will represent either your capital or deficiency of capital, according to whether your assets exceed your liabilities, or *vice versa*. Such difference will be inserted in the Schedule of Assets and Liabilities on the side showing the smaller total.

The foregoing figures will doubtless be available from the books you have already kept on the single entry system, but I strongly recommend you to permit me to go carefully into the position before any entries are made in the new set of books, and also to make the initial entries for you, so that at the outset the books will be in balance.

The entries necessary to commence the new system will be first shown in the Journal, and will take the following form—

JOURNAL

					£	£
Assets [detailed]	.	.	.	. *Dr.*	1,200	
To Liabilities [detailed]	.	.	.			630
„ Capital	.	.	.	.		570

The figures inserted in the above Journal are imaginary and given merely to make the instruction more concrete.

From the above entries will be made what are termed postings to the Ledger, all the items in the first column of the Journal being entered on the debit (or left-hand) side of the Ledgers, viz. the debtors in the Sales Ledger, the cash and bank balances in the Cash Book, and other assets, e.g. Fixtures, in the Private Ledger.

From the second column of the Journal postings will be made to the credit (or right-hand) side of the Ledgers, viz. creditors in the Purchases Ledger and Capital in the Private Ledger.

The books mentioned in paragraph (1) may be briefly outlined.

(*a*) *Sales Journal.*

All credit sales will be entered in the Sales Journal with such detail as you desire for reference, and posted to the debit of the customers making the purchases in the Sales Ledger. At periodic intervals the Sales Journal will be added and the total posted to the credit of Sales Account in the Private Ledger.

(*b*) *Sales Returns Journal.*

All returns from customers will be entered in the Sales Returns Journal and the entries treated in the opposite way to (*a*).

(*c*) *Purchases Journal.*

All purchases (assumed to be all on credit) will be entered in the Purchases Journal together with such detail as you require, and postings made to the credit of the suppliers in the Purchases Ledger, and at suitable intervals the Purchases Journal will be added and the total posted to the debit of Purchases Account in the Private Ledger.

(d) Purchases Returns Journal.

All returns to your suppliers will be entered in the Purchases Returns Book and treated in the opposite way to (c).

(e) The Cash Book.

You will require a Cash Book with, say, four columns on each side, the columns on the left hand being for (i) Cash Sales, (ii) Discounts allowed, (iii) Cash received, and (iv) Receipts into Bank. The right-hand columns will be shown after dealing with the debit (or left-hand) side.

After dealing with the entries from the Journal in respect of opening balances, the rules of procedure are—

(1) Receipts from Cash Sales. The amounts will be entered in columns (i) and (iii).

(2) Receipts from customers will be entered in columns (ii) and (iii) respectively for discounts allowed and cash received. The total of columns (ii) and (iii) will be posted to the credit side of the customer's account in the Sales Ledger.

The right-hand side of the Cash Book will contain columns for (i) Drawings, (ii) Discounts received, (iii) Cash, and (iv) Bank.

The procedure is—

(1) Private withdrawals will be entered into columns (i) and (iii) or (iv) according to whether you withdraw out of cash or by cheque.

(2) Payments to creditors will be entered in columns (ii) and (iii) or (iv) respectively for discounts received and cash (or cheque) payments. The total of the two columns will be posted to the debit of the supplier in the Purchases Ledger.

(3) Payments for expenses will be entered in columns (iii) or (iv) and posted to the debit of the expense account in the Private Ledger.

All transfers from Cash to Bank will be entered in column (iii) on the credit side of the Cash Book, and on the debit side in column (iv), and conversely for transfers from Bank into Cash, i.e. credit of column (iv) and debit of column (iii).

The Cash and Bank columns will be balanced off periodically, and the totals of columns (i) and (ii) of the debit side of the Cash Book will be posted to the credit of Sales and debit of Discount allowed (in the Private Ledger) respectively.

The totals of columns (i) and (ii) of the credit side of the Cash Book will be posted to the debit of Drawings (in the Private Ledger) and credit of Discount received (in the Private Ledger) respectively.

(f) Journal.

This book, apart from the use already indicated, will be used only occasionally when entries are required which cannot be properly entered in other books or journals.

(g) Sales Ledger.

This ledger will contain the accounts of customers written up from the relative foregoing journals and the Cash Book, and at the end of your accounting period the balances therein will require extraction and listing.

(h) Purchases Ledger.

This ledger will contain the accounts of suppliers written up from the relative foregoing journals and the Cash Book, and at the end of your accounting period the balances therein will require extraction and listing.

(i) Private Ledger.

This ledger will contain the remaining accounts, and after being written up balances will be extracted and listed as in (g) and (h).

In addition, it will be necessary to keep a Petty Cash Book on the Imprest System, that is, each month (or other suitable interval) the amount expended will be recouped by a payment from your ordinary Cash Account. The expenses will be analysed by means of columns used in the Petty Cash Book, and posted to the debit of the appropriate expense accounts in the Private Ledger.

It is also advisable to have your Purchases and Sales Ledgers built up on the Sectional Balancing principle.

When all the balances are extracted, the debits being listed in one column and credits in another, a Trial Balance may be prepared from which a Profit and Loss Account and Balance Sheet may be drawn up. For this latter purpose outstandings, accruals, prepayments, and stock on hand will be required to be incorporated.

I suggest that until such time as you are thoroughly conversant with the practical working of the Double Entry system, I call upon you daily to supervise and assist; and thereafter once at the commencment of each month to check through the preceding month's entries. This arrangement will not only keep the audit work up to date, but enable any modification of the system, necessary in the light of experience, to be made quickly and effectively.

[The question is such that a practical answer cannot very well be given, involving as it does, an explanation of double entry book-keeping, which in the examination hall must be as concise as possible, whilst in practice a much more elaborate explanation must be given to the client. Indeed little short of a detailed instruction in book-keeping would be necessary before the client could be expected to carry out the book-keeping on the proper lines.]

8.   TRADING AND PROFIT AND LOSS ACCOUNT FOR THE YEAR ENDED
                        31ST DECEMBER, 19..

				£						£
Stock (opening)	.	.	.	1,000	Sales .	.	.	.	.	12,800
Purchases	.	.	.	8,135	Stock (closing) ,	.	.	.	750
Gross Profit	.	.	c/d	4,415					
				£13,550						£13,550
Wages	.	.	.	2,000	Gross Profit	.	.	.	b/d	4,415
Rent and Rates	.	.	.	100					
Lighting and Heating	.	.	50					
Delivery Expenses	.	.	350					
General Expenses	.	.	230					
Net Profit transferred to Capital								
Account	.	.	.	1,685					
				£4,415						£4,415

BALANCE SHEET AS AT 31ST DECEMBER, 19..

			£	£					£	£
Capital—					Stock	.	.	.	.	750
Balance at 1st Janaury, 19..	.	3,250		Sundry Debtors	.	.	.	.	1,000
Less Drawings	.	.	1,665		Investments	.	.	.	.	2,500
					Cash in Hand	.	.	.	20	
			1,585		„ at Bank	.	.	.	600	
Add Net Profit for year	.	1,685							620
Private dividends	.	100						
				3,370					
Sundry Creditors	.	.	.	1,500					
				£4,870						£4,870

Notes. (i) As the business premises are occupied also domestically, a proportion of expenses, particularly Rent, Rates, Lighting, and Heating, may be (and must be in Income Tax Accounts) considered private. The estimated amount—say, one-third of such expenses—will be debited to Drawings and credited to the appropriate expense accounts.

(ii) The same point as was considered in Chapter XI, Q. 4 (see Note (i) thercon, page 270), arises in reference to items £8,000 and £6,100, i.e. £1,900 is the *Cash* payment for purchases.

(iii) The working accounts will be built up as previously outlined, viz. Opening Statement of Affairs, Cash, Bank, Debtors, and Creditors Accounts. Opening Capital is £3,250, i.e. £1,000 + £400 + £15 + £700 + £2,500 − £1,365.

9.
MISS MARY JONES
BALANCE SHEET AS AT 31ST MARCH, 19.5

	£		£
Sundry Creditors	181	Cash	13
		Sundry Debtors	35
		Stock	297
Capital—			
Balance at 1st April, 19.4 . £164			
Add Net Profit for the year . 1,108			
————			
1,272			
Less Drawings . . . 1,108			
————			
164			
	£345		£345

[1] Drawings and profit must be increased by £624 "own" remuneration.

CHAPTER XII

1.

INCOME AND EXPENDITURE ACCOUNT FOR THE YEAR ENDED 31ST DECEMBER, 19..

	£		£
To Law Costs and Damages . . .	444	By Interest on Investments (net) . .	225
,, Depreciation . . .	100	,, Mortgage Interest (net) . .	210
,, Provision for Income Tax on Bank Interest .	24	,, Bank Interest (gross) . .	60
,, Personal Expenditure . . .	951	,, Directors' Fees (after deduction of tax) .	390
		,, Balance, excess of Expenditure over Income	634
	£1,519		£1,519

BALANCE SHEET AS AT 31ST DECEMBER, 19..

	£	£		£	£
Capital—			Cash at Bank—		
Balance as at 1st January, 19..	12,285		Current Account . .	150	
Less Excess of Expenditure over Income for year.	634		Deposit Account . .	1,125	
		11,651			1,275
Provision for Income Tax . . .		24	Investments—		
			Balance as at 1st January, 19...	4,625	
			Add Purchases . .	625	
				5,250	
			Less Sales . .	750	
					4,500
			Mortgages . .		5,000
			Household Furniture—		
			Balance as at 1st January, 19...	1,000	
			Less Depreciation . .	100	
					900
		£11,675			£11,675

275

Notes. (1) Mortgage Interest is £350, less tax at 40 per cent, £140 = £210.

(2) No mention is made of liability for tax on Bank Interest, so that provision has been made on the current year's interest, although assessment would normally be on a preceding year basis. It is assumed that all income tax allowances are made against the officer's pension of which there is no mention; such allowances are normally taken into account automatically in the P.A.Y.E. system. No mention is made of payment during the year of the preceding year's income tax, so that it is possible that there are sufficient allowances to cover Bank Interest, in which case there might be a question of a repayment claim. An alternative treatment would be to show all income gross with a corresponding tax debit.

(3) Accruals ignored.

(4) In accordance with the requirements of the question Interest on Investments has been taken on the investments standing at 31st December, 19.., although actually this would be unlikely, unless the changes in the investments took place at the commencement of the year.

(5) Commencing Capital is—

	£
Investments [£4,500 + £750 − £625]	4,625
Mortgages	5,000
Furniture.	1,000
Cash at Bank: Deposit Account	1,500
Current Account	160
	12,285
Less Income Tax accruing	?
	£12,285

(6) In the absence of information it is impossible to make any adjustment for profit or loss on sale of investments, or any possible liability (Capital Gains Tax).

(7) Bank Accounts are shown on page 277.

BANK ACCOUNTS

Dr.		Current	Deposit
19..		£	£
Jan. 1	To Balances . . . b/d.	160	1,500
Dec.31	„ Investment Income . .	225	
	„ Mortgage Interest . .	210	
	„ Directors' Fees . .	390	
	„ Bank Interest . .		60
	„ Deposit Account . .	435	
	„ Investments Sold . .	750	
		£2,170	£1,560

Cr.		Current	Deposit
19..		£	£
Dec. 31	By Current Account		435
	„ Law Costs, etc. . .	444	
	„ Investments purchased	625	
	„ Personal Expenditure .	951	
	„ Balances . . . c/d.	150	1,125
		£2,170	£1,560

277

2. The differences between a Receipts and Payments Account and an Income and Expenditure Account may be tabulated as follows—

RECEIPTS AND PAYMENTS ACCOUNT	INCOME AND EXPENDITURE ACCOUNT
(1) Cash Account (Real Account)	Nominal Account.
(2) Is made up of Capital and Revenue items; introductions and withdrawals of Capital.	Records Revenue items.
(3) No record of accruals, prepayments or stock.	Records accruals, prepayments, and stock.
(4) No record of depreciation or appreciation.	Gives effect to depreciation or appreciation.
(5) Debit items herein appear in Income and Expenditure Account as credits (if not Capital items) and vice versa.	Credit items herein appear in the Receipts and Payments Account on the debit side, and vice versa.
(6) The opening and closing balances represent cash in hand, at Bank (or overdraft).	The opening or closing balances (if any) represent respectively the accumulated Revenue at the commencement, and that balance plus current year's income (or less current year's loss).
	[The yearly balance is usually transferred to Capital or its equivalent account.]
(7) Usually (though not necessarily) presented where accounts are not on the double entry system.	Usually (though not necessarily) presented where accounts are kept on the double entry system. If this system has been employed there will be, in addition, a Balance Sheet.

3.

BACHELORS' CLUB

REVENUE ACCOUNT FOR THE YEAR ENDED 30TH APRIL, 19..

	£		£
Mortgage Interest . . .	820	Subscription and Entry Moneys	11,311
Debenture Interest . . .	755	[1]Profit—	
Rates, Taxes, and Insurance .	1,925	Wines and Spirits . .	1,852
Wages	5,721	Mineral Waters . . .	403
Heat, Light, and Power . .	1,303	Cigars	135
Laundry	1,008	Provisions . . .	1,237
Newspapers	280	Billards	282
Telephone	35	Bedrooms	991
Printing and Stationery . .	381	Deposit Receipt Interest . .	165
Books and Binding . . .	131	Balance, being excess of Expenditure over Income for the year	475
Management Expenses . .	1,003		
Postages and Miscellaneous Expenses . . .	601		
Repairs and Renewals . .	1,738		
Alterations to Buildings . .	1,150		
	£16,851		£16,851

Separate Trading Accounts should be opened for Wines and Spirits, etc., as shown on page 279.

Dr.				WINES AND SPIRITS		Cr.	
				£			£
Stock	.	.	.	.	887	Sales	9,751
Purchases	.	.	.	.	7,985	Stock	973
Profit	.	.	.	.	1,852		
					£10,724		£10,724

Dr.				MINERAL WATERS		Cr.	
				£			£
Stock	.	.	.	.	125	Sales	1,511
Purchases	.	.	.	.	1,125	Stock	142
Profit	.	.	.	.	403		
					£1,653		£1,653

Dr.				CIGARS		Cr.	
				£			£
Stock	.	.	.	.	73	Sales	784
Purchases	.	.	.	.	657	Stock	81
Profit	.	.	.	.	135		
					£865		£865

Dr.				PROVISIONS		Cr.	
				£			£
Stock	.	.	.	.	310	Sales	7,235
Purchases	.	.	.	.	5,892	Stock	204
Profit	.	.	.	.	1,237		
					£7,439		£7,439

4.

SERF CLUB

TRADING ACCOUNTS FOR THE YEAR ENDED 31ST MARCH, 19.8

	Restaurant £	Bar £		Restaurant £	Bar £
Opening Stock	4	36	Takings	1,616	1,305
Purchases	1,078	822	Maintenance of Staff	250	25
Gross Profit c/d	787	501	Closing Stock	3	29
	£1,869	£1,359		£1,869	£1,359

INCOME AND EXPENDITURE ACCOUNT FOR THE YEAR ENDED 31ST MARCH, 19.8

	£	£		£	£
Rent and Rates		349	Gross Profit—		
Wages		623	Restaurant	787	
Maintenance of Staff		275	Bar	501	1,288
Repairs and Renewals of China, Glass, Cutlery, and Linen		179	Subscriptions		315
Fuel and Light		175	Billiards and Sundry Receipts		256
Sundry Expenses		134	Interest on Deposit		8
Depreciation—					
Furniture	14				
Fixtures and Fittings	1				
Billiard Table and Accessories	13	28			
		104			
Balance, being the excess of income over expenditure for the year c/d		104			
		£1,867			£1,867
Balance	c/f	566	Balance	b/f	462
			"	b/d	104
		£566			£566

Alternatively, the Trading Accounts may be shown as follows—

TRADING ACCOUNTS FOR THE YEAR ENDED 31ST MARCH, 19.8

	Restaurant £	Bar £		Restaurant £	Bar £
Goods Consumed	829	804	Takings	1,616	1,305
Gross Profit c/d	787	501			
	£1,616	£1,305		£1,616	£1,305

BALANCE SHEET AS AT 31ST MARCH, 19.8

	£			£	£
Creditors	175	Cash in Hand . . .		13	
Income and Expenditure Account—		Bank Balance . . .		91	
Credit Balance	566				104
		Bank Deposit . . .		.	283
		Debtors			74
		Stocks—			
		Restaurant . .		3	
		Bar . . .		29	
					32
					493
		Current Assets—			
		China, Glass, Cutlery and Linen as at 31st March, 19.7 . . .		.	20
		Billiard Table and Accessories as at 31st March, 19.7 . . .		89	
		Less Depreciation .		13	
					76
		Fixtures and Fittings as at 31st March, 19.7 .		29	
		Less Depreciation .		1	
					28
		Furniture as at 31st March, 19.7 . . .		84	
		Plus Additions . .		54	
				138	
		Less Depreciation[1] .		14	
					124
	£741				£741

5. GENERAL INCOME AND EXPENDITURE ACCOUNT FOR THE YEAR ENDED 31ST DECEMBER, 19..

	£			£	£
Payments to Pensioners . .	1,265	Donations	(?)		
Rent	100	Subscriptions . . .	(?)		1,272
Office Expenses and Salaries .	275	Legacies			200
Collectors' Commission . .	37	Interest on Investments . .			135
Printing Year Book . . .	26	Interest on Deposit . . .			24
Postages	18	Advertisements . . .			15
		Net Income from Special Fund .			27
		Balance—Excess of Expenditure over Income			48
	£1,721				£1,721

SPECIAL FUND INCOME AND EXPENDITURE ACCOUNT FOR THE YEAR ENDED 31ST DECEMBER, 19..

	£		£
Gratuities	143	Donations	170
Net Income transferred to General Account	27		
	£170		£170

Note. No information is given as to what expenses (if any) included in the General Account are properly chargeable to Special Fund Account.

[1] In the absence of information as to dates, a full year's depreciation has been provided on additions to Furniture.

6.   BLANKSHIRE BENEVOLENT CHARITY

INCOME AND EXPENDITURE ACCOUNT FOR THE YEAR ENDED
30TH JUNE, 19..

	£		£
Annuities	805	Interest on Investments . . .	418
Salary—		Donations	383
Secretary £75		Special Appeal	182
Treasurer 75		Rent Received	84
————	150	Bank Interest	18
Incidentals	4	Deficiency transferred to Accumulated	
Printing	18	Fund	22
Chief Rent	105		
Law Charges	9		
Bank Commission	8		
Sundries	8		
	£1,107		£1,107

BALANCE SHEET AS AT 30TH JUNE, 19..

	£	£		£
Accumulated Fund—			Property	?
Balance as at 1st July, 19. . .	10,620		Investments (at cost ?) . . .	10,162
Less Deficiency for the			(Market value ?)	
year . . .	22		Cash at Bank	499
	————	10,598		
Suspense Account . . .		63		
		£10,661		£10,661

The Statement of Accounts is merely a Receipts and Payments Account.

There is an error on the Receipts side of £63 in addition. Assuming that opening and closing balances are correct and agreed, subject to an error of £1 in the opening balance, it follows that a Suspense Account must be opened and inserted on the Liabilities side of the Balance Sheet. If there were anything to show that this was a revenue item, it would be inserted in the Income and Expenditure Account.

It can be seen from the Receipts and Payments Account that no sales or purchases of Investments have taken place during the year.

No accruals, depreciation (if any), or stock is mentioned.

The amount in the accounts under Interest on Investments should be shown gross, less income tax. The item presumably includes Mortgage Interest. The basis of the investment figures, e.g. cost, nominal, might be stated and the current market value.

No amount is disclosed relating to reclaim for Income Tax.

A separate account should be shown relating to gross income and expenditure of the Special Appeal.

Although no assets, apart from Investments and Bank balance, are shown it is clear that the Charity owns property and pays chief rent thereon. In the absence of data it is assumed that the property is leasehold, in respect of which suitable provision for depreciation is necessary.

Criticism may be made on the fact that the *auditor* has not certified as to existence of the securities; in any case the certificate should definitely stipulate that the whole of the securities have been examined at one "sitting" and that they conform to the list given.

It is assumed that the actual transactions conform to the rules of the Charity and the statutory regulations concerning Charity Accounts, although the errors appearing in the audited accounts do not inspire confidence.

Accumulated Fund—Opening Balance—

	£
Investments	10,162
Bank	457
Error[1]	1
	£10,620

[1] Alternatively, this may be carried forward and added to Suspense Account.

7.   TRIAL BALANCE AS AT 30TH JUNE, 19.6   *Dr.*   *Cr.*

	£	£
Sundry Investments	155,000	
Profits on Realization of Investments		15,500
Losses on Realization of Investments	23,000	
Reserve for Depreciation of Investments.		24,000
Dividends and Interest received		7,600
Capital as at 1st July, 19.5		159,760
Drawings	8,500	
Provision for Tax Liability		1,500
Properties	14,000	
Rents Received		1,600
Outgoings *re* Properties	230	
Sundry Debtors for Rents	450	
Sundry Creditors		500
Deposit Interest Received		220
Cash at Bank (Current Account)	4,500	
Cash at Bank (Deposit Account)	5,000	
	£210,680	£210,680

INCOME AND EXPENDITURE ACCOUNT FOR THE YEAR ENDED
30TH JUNE, 19.6

	£		£
Outgoings *re* Properties	230	Dividends (net)	7,600
Net Income for year c/d	9,190	Rents	1,600
		Deposit Interest	220
	£9,420		£9,420
Reserve for Depreciation Investments	7,000	Balance b/d	9,190
Taxation on Current Year's Profit	950	Tax Over-provided for Previous Year	300
Balance to Capital Account	1,540		
	£9,490		£9,490

BALANCE SHEET AS AT 30TH JUNE, 19.6

		£			£
Sundry Creditors		500	Cash at Bank—		
Provision for Current Taxation		1,200	Current Account	£4,500	
Provision for Future Taxation		950	Deposit Account	5,000	
Capital Account—					9,500
Balance at 1st July, 19.5	£159,760		Sundry Debtors		450
Less Drawings	8,500		Sundry Investments	£155,000	
	151,260		*Less* Provision for Depreciation	31,000	
Add Balance of Income and Expenditure Account	1,540		Properties		124,000
					14,000
	152,900				
Deduct Loss on Sale of Investments £23,000					
Less Profit on Sale of Investments 15,500					
	7,500				
		145,300			
		£147,950			£147,950

Note: The income may be "grossed" and the tax liability shown as a debit.

8.   LOAMSHIRE ENTOMOLOGICAL SOCIETY

INCOME AND EXPENDITURE ACCOUNT FOR THE YEAR ENDED
31ST DECEMBER, 19..

	£		£
Salaries and Wages	1,675	Entrance Fees (60 at £30) . . .	1,800
Secretary's Salary	850	Fees for Life Membership (10 at	
Rent, Rates, etc.	1,264	£52)	520
Printing and Postages. . . .	136	Annual Subscriptions . . .	1,685
Repairs to Premises	324	Interest on Treasury Stock . .	120
Interest on Bank Loan . . .	57	Sundry Receipts	62
Expenses	42	Balance, being excess of Expenditure over Income, transferred to Accumulated Fund	161
	£4,348		£4,348

BALANCE SHEET AT 31ST DECEMBER, 19..

	£		£		£
Accumulated Fund—				Leasehold Premises at Cost. . .	2,124
At 1st Jan., 19.. . .	£4,330[1]			Treasury Stock at Cost (market value?)	1,970
Less Balance on Income and Expenditure A/c		161		Debtors	121
			4,169	Cash on hand and at Bank . .	1,911
Bank Loan (secured on leasehold premises)			1,000		
Creditors			957		
			£6,126		£6,126

[1] The Accumulated Fund at 1st January, 19.., is—

	£
Cash on hand and at Bank	1,236
Treasury Stock	1,970
Leasehold Premises	2,124
	5,330
Less Bank Loan	1,000
	£4,330

(1) The account, as presented by the society, is not an Income and Expenditure Account, but a Receipts and Payments Account, except that the secretary's salary of £850 has been included as a payment whereas the treasurer's note says that the amount is outstanding. £850 should therefore be deleted, increasing the closing cash to £1,911.

(2) Expenditure should appear as a debit and Income as a credit.

(3) An Income and Expenditure Account covers a period, not the position at a specific date.

(4) Being a cash account the statement submitted does not distinguish between capital and revenue items, nor does it take cognizance of the period to which the receipt or expense relates; but in preparing an Income and Expenditure Account accruals and prepayments both as to income and expenditure (commencing and ending) will be dealt with along the usual lines.

(5) As regards the Entrance Fees and Life Membership Fees consideration must be given to the question as to whether they should be apportioned over a period of years or otherwise transferred direct to the Accumulated Fund, and not shown in the Income and Expenditure Account at all. Before coming to a decision the former accounts and the rules of the society should be studied.

(6) As such an account as submitted cannot disclose depreciation—unless an asset has been purchased and sold within the same period—this omission alone is a serious flaw, and will require attention (if necessary) in the Income and Expenditure Account.

(7) In absence of the amount of holding of Treasury Stock its composition cannot be ascertained.

(8) If the Balance on hand is solely cash held by the treasurer, the amount appears to be excessive.

(9) The accounts should be put on a double entry basis, so that the Income and Expenditure Account and Balance Sheet can be properly prepared.

CHAPTER XIII

1. BY tabular book-keeping is meant the employment of columns to reduce the number of ledger accounts, where certain entries are numerous and regular. By the use of this system postings can be made with greater speed, particularly as the scattered arrangement of ledger accounts is avoided.

The extent to which the method is capable of fullest use must depend upon the nature of the business, but nearly all accounting systems incorporate the underlying principle, as is seen in the use of columnar cash books, day books, and analysed petty cash books. The method might be used in the accounts of—

(1) Estate companies for tenants' accounts.
(2) Gas, water, electricity and similar undertakings for customers' accounts.
(3) Hotels for visitors' accounts.
(4) Insurance companies in respect of premiums.
(5) Merchants, for goods out on sale or return.
(6) Businesses with branches and departments.
(7) All businesses employing the sectional balancing system.

Advantages are—

(1) Economy of time in posting.
(2) Quick reference to both the posted item and original is possible.
(3) Frequently (as in hotels) the entry into the Ledger may be made direct from slips without first entering the amount into a book of prime entry.
(4) Facilitates mechanization.

Disadvantages are—

(1) Congestion owing to multiplicity of columns may arise.
(2) Risk of error of posting to wrong column.
(3) Frequently sub-analyses and adjustments of details entered into columns are required.
(4) If a reverse entry is required where a column normally contains items of a similar nature (e.g. credit items), it may be necessary to use red or coloured ink therefor, thus tending to complicate obtaining totals.

2. [In designing the system consideration must be given to the size of the hotel, whether the custom is regular or seasonal, whether supplies are wholly or mainly from outside sources, or through own organization (e.g. own farm).]

The chief books will be—

(1) *Visitors' Ledger.*

The Visitors' Ledger will be ruled with a column for each room, and the pages will be printed with suitable headings for the various items of charges and payments, e.g. apartments, meals, refreshments, laundry, cash paid, and allowances. The debits and credits will appear rather differently from the usual Ledger, the charges occupying the upper portion of the page, and the cash, allowances, etc., the lower portion. A separate page is used for each day, balances being carried forward. In addition to the daily balancing of the accounts the various items will be extended into a total column, and the charges will be posted either direct to the Nominal Ledger or to an Abstract Book ruled with columns for apartments, meals, etc.; the cash will have been posted from the Cash Book and the allowances will be debited to Allowances Account.

(2) *Analysed Cash Book.*

The debit side of the Cash Book will be ruled with columns for cash received from Visitors (per Visitors' Ledger), Restaurant, Bar, Billiards, etc., and Sundries, together with total columns for Cash and Bank. The gross daily takings should preferably be paid direct into the bank and in this case the bank will be the only total column, and it will be advisable to have a Petty Cash Book on the imprest system for small cash payments.

The credit side of the Cash Book will be ruled with columns for payments made for (*a*) provisions, (*b*) beer, wine, and minerals, (*c*) utensils, (*d*) rent, rates, heating, and lighting, (*e*) telephone and telegrams, (*f*) sundries, (*g*) drawings, and any other columns which the circumstances may require. The totals of the various expense columns will be posted periodically to the Nominal Ledger, and Bought Ledger items will be posted to the debit of the individual creditors' accounts.

(3) *Bought Ledger.*

The Bought Ledger will be kept on the usual lines, postings being made from the Bought Journal, Returns Journal, and Cash Book.

(4) *Bought Journal and Returns Journals.*

These books will be ruled with columns for provisions, beer, wines, minerals, etc., the totals being posted to the Nominal Ledger.

(5) *Nominal Ledger.*

Apart from the usual asset accounts and capital accounts the Nominal Ledger will contain accounts for Apartments, Meals, Refreshments, Laundry, and the usual expense items.

Frequently separate accounting is in operation for the Bar, Restaurant, Laundry, etc., and it will be necessary to allocate the various items of expense over the separate sections.

Provision will have to be made for the meals and lodging of the staff, and transfers accordingly may have to be made, e.g. from Provisions to Wages.

A correct record must be kept of the stocks and stores in the Kitchen, Restaurant, Bar, etc.

3. *Dr.* RENTAL LEDGER Half-year to Christmas 19.7 (25th December) *Cr.*
Half-year to Midsummer 19.8 (24th June)

No. of Street, etc.	Name of Tenant	Arrears Brought Forward	Rent	Sundries	Total Debits	Date of Receipt	Receipt No.	C.B. Folio	Cash Received	Allowances	Empties	Sundries	Arrears Carried Forward	Total Credits	Observations
3 Spring Road.	A. Butcher	£ 15	£ 20	£	£ 35	19.7/19.8			£ 30		£		£ 5	£ 35	£
		5	*20*		*25*	*Dec. 25*							*25*	*25*	
5 Spring Road.	H. Sadler		17·50		17·50	Dec. 25			17·50					17·50	
			17·50		*17·50*	*June 24*			*17·50*					*17·50*	
7 Spring Road.	P. Baker		21		21	Dec. 25			21					21	
			21		*21*	*June 24*			*21*					*21*	
9 Spring Road.	R. Merchant		25		25	Dec. 25			25					25	
			25		*25*	*June 24*			*25*					*25*	
Garage	A. Driver		10		10				10					10	
			10		*10*	*June 24*			*10*		*10*			*10*	
Flower Farm	J. Handcock		95	2·50	97·50	Dec. 25			97·50					97·50	
			95	*2·50*	*97·50*	*June 24*			*80*				*17·50*	*97·50*	
Croft	C. Toiler		5		5	Dec. 25			5					5	
			5		*5*	*June 24*			*5*					*5*	
Stable and Garage	M. Dealer		15		15	Dec. 25			15					15	
		6	*9*		*9*	*June 24*			*9*					*9*	
Fenhead Farm	G. Digger		105		105	Dec. 25			105					105	
			105		*105*	*June 24*			*105*					*105*	

Assumed rents are received on due dates (apart from arrears).

The figures in italics will be shown on the page following the Christmas half-year, if, as is probable, the Rental Ledger is ruled with the "repeat" pages, the first two columns being in the form of a short leaf so as to avoid repetition in each half-year of the tenants' names and addresses.

4.   Visitors' Ledger, 17th January, 19..

	(a)	Room 1	Room 3	Room 5	Total
Dr.		£	£	£	£
Brought forward . . .		3·25	4·72		7·97
Apartments		1·50		1·25	2·75
Breakfast		0·50	0·50	0·50	1·50
Lunch		0·75			0·75
Tea				0·20	0·20
Dinner or Supper . . .		1·00		0·25	1·25
Wines, Spirits, Cigars, etc. .		1·52		0·43	1·95
Baths				0·15	0·15
Sundries	(b)	0·48	0·32	0·12	0·92
		£9·00	£5·54	£2·90	£17·44
Cr.					
Cash			5·54		5·54
Allowances					
Transfers					
Carried forward . . .		9·00		2·90	11·90
		£9·00	£5·54	£2·90	£17·44

Notes. (a) The columns will be ruled for each room, 1, 2, 3, 4, etc.
     (b) This item may be further analysed as required.

5.

RENTAL LEDGER

Situation of Premises	Room No.	Name of Tenant	Arrears Brought Forward £	Rent for Quarter £	Gas for Quarter £	Cleaning for Quarter £	Total £	Receipt No.	DEDUCTIONS Income Tax Sch 'A' £	DEDUCTIONS Commission £	DEDUCTIONS Repairs £	DEDUCTIONS Sundries £	CASH Date	CASH Cash Book Folio	CASH Amount £	Total Cash and Deductions £	Arrears Carried Forward £	Observations
57 Princess Street	4/1	W. Pickles		50	5·75	9·50	65·25	G.F. 172	23·26	2·90	4·20				30·36	34·89		
				(a)	(b)¹	(c)			(d)	(e)	S				(g)		(h)	

Additional columns for water and electricity if charged up.

290

The tabular system is embodied in the rulings shown on p. 290, the first three columns being "short leaf" so as to avoid constant rewriting of the details contained therein.

The details, upon receipt of the agents' statements, will be entered direct in the Rental Ledger, and the totals posted to the appropriate accounts. The Ledger is really an Agents' Account, any balance due being either included in the Arrears column and carried forward or transferred to a separate Ledger Account.

The items (in total) referenced by letter will be posted as follows—

(a) Credit Rent Account, (b) Credit Gas Account, (c) Credit Cleaning Account, (d) Debit Income Tax Account, (e) Commission Account, (f) Repairs Account.

As regards (g) the individual items will appear on the debit side of the Cash Book, whilst the individual items in (h) will be carried forward or debited to Agents' Account.

It is assumed that the company reimburses separately the outlay of the agents for Cleaning and Gas charges, so that these will be charged up to the appropriate account, off-setting items marked (b) and (c) above.

CHAPTER XIV

1. *Dr.* SUSPENSE *Cr.*

			£					£
To Difference in Balance	.	.	97·41	By Sales	.	.	(a)	100·00
,, Returns Outwards	(b)	.	30·58	,, Barton Bros.	.	(c)	.	2·88
, Bad Debts	.	(d)	1·37	, J. Smithson	.	.	(e)	26·48
			£129·36					£129·36

2. (a) JOURNAL

	£	£
Office Furniture . . . . . *Dr.* To Office Expenses . . . . . Being adjustment for a capital expense posted to a Revenue Account.	152·50	152·50

(b) Insert an amount of £78·36 to the debit of Discount Account. This will have the effect of cancelling the error and completing the original double entry.

If a Suspense Account were raised for £78·36, the necessary adjustment would then be—

JOURNAL

	£	£
Discount Allowed . . . . . *Dr.* To Suspense . . . . . Being correction of posting of discount allowed to the credit instead of the debit side of Discount Account.	78·36	78·36

(c) JOURNAL

	£	£
Returns Outwards . . . . . *Dr.* To X & Co. . . . . . Being correction of posting of Returns Outwards as £10 instead of £7.	3·00	3·00

3. (a) Loose Tools Account (an asset in the Balance Sheet) must be debited with £476, and Purchases Account credited with £318 and wages with £158.

(b) Insurance Claims Account must be debited and Wages credited with £56.

(c) J. B. Robinson, provided the title to the goods has *not* yet passed, must be debited and Purchases credited with £21.

Otherwise, Stock in Transit must be debited and Trading Account credited.

(d) It is presumed that Goods on Consignment Account has already been credited with £1,287 and Consignment Account debited. The former account will then be debited and Purchases or Trading Account credited, whilst the balance on Consignment Account will appear as an asset on the Balance Sheet at the lower of cost or net realizable value.

Notes—

(i) With regard to (b), on the claim being agreed, the insurance company will be debited and Insurance Claims Account credited, and any balance thereon closed off as a probable loss or a possible gain.

(ii) With regard to (d), the entries might have been put through erroneously as Debit Consignee and credit Sales Account, either with the cost or estimated selling price of the goods. In that case an adjustment would be necessary to ensure that Goods on Consignment was credited and Consignment Account debited at cost.

All expenses paid in connection with the consignment should also be debited to the Consignment Account, *not* the normal Expense Accounts.

4. The effect of each set of errors is—

(1) Sales are excessive by £75, i.e. £100 recorded in respect of a sale of £25, and debtors are excessive by £75. Provided this error is adjusted, the inclusion of the value of the stock at £50 (or at market value if lower) in the Trading Account is correct. It is assumed that it is known that £25 goods have been actually sold.

(2) Gross (and Net) Profit and Drawings are too small by £250. Trading Account should be credited with £250 (assuming that this covers the loss) and Fire Loss Account (or Insurance Company) debited. The £250 received should have been credited to the latter account.

(3) Gross (and Net) Profit are excessive by £200 because of the inclusion of the stock without the appropriate entry in the Purchases Day Book. If the Purchases Day Book has been closed it will be necessary to debit Purchases Account above the "line" and credit it below the "line." It is assumed that the £200 represents the actual purchase price and that it is lower than market value.

(4) Net Profit is excessive by £10 as is the debtors' balance.

The adjustments are, in summary form—

JOURNAL

				£	£
Sales	. (1)	Dr.	75	
Drawings	. (2)	Dr.	250	
Purchases	. (3)	Dr.	200	
Legal Expenses	. (4)	Dr.	15	
To Debtor	. (1)			75
„ Fire Loss	. (2)			250
„ Creditor	. (3)			200
„ Discount Received . . .	. (4)			5
„ [1]Debtor	. (4)			10
Being adjustment of sundry errors.				

[1] This item will not be posted, inasmuch as the error will be corrected by amending the schedule of debtors.

5. *Dr.*   SUSPENSE   *Cr.*

		£				£
To Difference in Trial Balance .	.	151·00	By Goods purchased for Resale .	(a)	15·00
„ Customer	(d)	21·00	„ Supplier . . .	(b)	49·75
			„ Sundry Debtors . .	(f)	60·00
			„ Discount Allowed .	(g)	2·25
			„ Rates . . .	(h)	45·00
		£172·00			£172·00

(c) To rectify this entry, debit customer and credit Bills Receivable. The situation arising from the customer's default may require provision for Bad Debt.

(e) To rectify this entry, debit Sales and credit Plant. Depreciation and Profit or Loss on Sale will be written off the book value of the Plant sold to reduce it to *nil*;

The above corrections reduce the profit by £362·25, made up as follows—

	£
(a)	15·00
(e)	300·00
(g)	2·25
(h)	45·00
	£362·25

Total accounts will be affected as follows—

(a) Since the total column in the Purchase Journal was correct, no alteration will be required in the total account.

(b) Total accounts not affected.

(c) Sales Ledger Adjustment Account   .   .   .   *Dr.* £200
        To Nominal Ledger Adjustment Account   .   .   . £200

(d) No correction needed.

(e) No correction required if the purchaser has been treated as a Sales Ledger customer throughout; otherwise the sale must be eliminated from the Total Accounts.

(f) No correction needed.

(g) Nominal Ledger Adjustment Account.   .   .   *Dr.* £2·25
        To Sales Ledger Adjustment Account   .   .   .   . £2·25

(h) Not applicable.

6. *Dr.*   SUSPENSE   *Cr.*

	£		£
To Difference in Trial Balance . .	38·57	By Bank	9·00
,, J. Jones	9·00	,, Salaries	10·00
,, R. Foley	1·44	,, S. Minett	30·01
	£49·01		£49·01

Note. Only items (c) and (e) affect the actual books of account, the remainder being errors of extraction in the Trial Balance.

7. (a) The steps necessary to correct the records are—

(1) Credit Sales Ledger Control Account £20 bad debt.

(2) Debit Discounts Allowed £36; Credit Sales Ledger Control Account £36.

(3) No posting required—merely addition to Schedule of Debtors £14.

(4) Debit C £10 for sale posting omitted; credit C £1 for discount omitted *and* credit Sales Ledger Control Account £1 discount.

(5) Debit Bought Ledger Control Account £25; credit Sales Ledger Control Account £25.

(6) Debit E £42 for omitted Sale; credit Credit Sales £42 *and* debit Sales Ledger Control Account £42.

(b)

     Dr.   SALES LEDGER CONTROL ACCOUNT   *Cr.*

	£			£
To Balance (original extraction		By Bad Debt . . .	(1)	20
per question) . . .	1,569	,, Discount Allowed .	(2)	36
,, Sales (6)	42	,, ,, ,, .	(4)	1
		,, Bought Ledger Control		
		Account . .	(5)	25
		,, Balance (as below) .	c/d	1,529
	£1,611			£1,611
To Balance . . . c/d	1,529			

The Sales Ledger debit balances arising from the corrections will be—

		£
Total per question (before corrections)		1,464
B	(3)	14
C [£10 − £1]	(4)	9
E	(6)	42
		£1,529

Assuming that no other errors exist, the closing balance of the Sales Ledger Control Account must equal the aggregate net debtors [i.e. debit balances *less* credit balances] in the Sales Ledger, which taking into account the entries in the Control Account will give an "opening" figure of £1,569.

CHAPTER XV

1. (*a*) A Mineral Rent is the Royalty payable by the lessee of a mine to the lessor as the consideration wholly or in part for the right to extract minerals included in the property leased, calculated upon minerals extracted at an agreed figure.

(*b*) Surface Rent is the sum payable by the lessee of a mine (in addition to mineral royalties) for the use of the land itself and includes the estimated damage resultant upon such use, e.g. subsidence of the land.

(*c*) Minimum Rent is the annual or periodic minimum sum payable by the lessee of a mine to the lessor, arising if the Mineral Royalty is less than such sum. Usually the lease provides for recoupment of the excess of the Minimum Rent over the Mineral Royalty, either (*a*) for a restricted period from the commencement of the lease or from the end of the year of deficiency; or (*b*) throughout the whole period of the lease.

(*d*) Rack Rent is the annual rent based upon a fair commercial letting value. It is, as it were, the annual value stretched to full capacity, without the intrusion of any consideration other than that of letting the property on the basis of proper payment for beneficial occupation, that is on a normal competitive basis.

2. "Power to recoup Short Workings over a term of years" is the right enjoyed by virtue only of a clause in a lease whereby the lessee is empowered to deduct from the Royalty payable to the lessor (not beyond the defined period, if any) in those years when the Royalty payable *exceeds* the Minimum Rent, the amount by which in previous years the Minimum Rent exceeded the Royalty payable computed on the agreed basis. Such deduction is limited so that in any year the lessor receives no less than the Minimum Rent. If, for example, the Minimum Rent payable is £50, and in previous years the Royalties payable have fallen short of the required minimum by £20 and the current year's Royalty payable is £65, the lessee will be able to recoup £15 of the £20, leaving a balance of £5 to be recouped (unless the time limit for recoupment has expired) in future years. In the above-mentioned year no greater recoupment than £15 is permissible, because the lessor is entitled to the **minimum** sum of £50.

3. Dr.   MINIMUM RENT   Cr.

		£			£
Year 1	To Owner	300	Year 1	By Royalty . . .	140
				,, Short Workings . .	160
2	,, ,, ...	300	2	,, Royalty . . .	275
				,, Short Workings . .	25
3	,, ,, . . .	300	3	,, Royalty . . .	375
	,, Short Workings . .	75			
4	,, Owner . . .	315	4	,, ,, . . .	425
	,, Short Workings . .	110			
5	, Owner	475	5	,, . . .	475

Dr.   OWNER   Cr.

		£			£
Year 1	To Cash	300	Year 1	By Minimum Rent . .	300
2	,, ,, ...	300	2	, ,, ,, . .	300
3	,, ,, ...	300	3	,, ,, ,, . .	300
4	,, ,, . . .	315	4	,, ,, ,, .	315
5	,, ,, . . .	475	5	,, ,, ,, .	475

Dr.   SHORT WORKINGS   Cr.

		£			£
Year 1	To Minimum Rent . .	160	Year 3	By Minimum Rent . .	75
2	,, ,, . .	25	4	,, ,, ,, . .	110

Dr.		ROYALTY			Cr.
		£			£
Year 1	To Minimum Rent .	140	Year 1	By Production Account .	140
2 ,, ,, ,, .		275	2 ,, ,, ,, .		275
3 ,, ,, ,, .		375	3 ,, ,, ,, .		375
4 ,, ,, ,, .		425	4 ,, ,, ,, .		425
5 ,, ,, ,, .		475	5 ,, ,, ,, .		475

Income tax ignored.

4. (*a*) Being Royalties at 2½p a ton on 40,000 tons raised, and sum charged to Short Workings for future recoupment, and total Minimum Rent of £1,500, as per terms of lease dated............

(*b*) Being Royalties at 2½p a ton on 48,000 tons raised, as per terms of lease dated............

(*c*) Being Short Workings recouped, as per terms of lease dated............

(*d*) Being Short Workings irrecoverable, by reason of time bar, as per terms of lease dated............, and Royalties Account transferred to Profit and Loss Account.

[*Note to Student.* These entries have no relation to each other.]

5. Dr.		ROYALTIES PAYABLE			Cr.
19.4		£	19.4		£
June 30	To R. S. . . .	125	June 30	By Production Account .	125
			19.5		
Dec. 31	,, ,, ,, . .	125	June 30	,, ,, ,, .	625
19.5					
June 30	,, ,, ,, . . .	500			
		£625			£625
			19.6		
Dec. 31	,, ,, ,, . .	750	June 30	,, ,, ,, .	1,375
19.6					
June 30	,, ,, ,, . .	625			
		£1,375			£1,375

Dr.		¹SHORT WORKINGS			Cr.
19.4		£	19.5		£
June 30	To R. S. . . .	375	Dec. 31	By R. S. . . .	250
Dec. 31	,, ,, ,, . .	375	19.6		
			June 30	,, ,, ,, . .	125
				,, Balance . . c/d	375
		£750			£750
19.6					
July 1	,, Balance . . b/d	375			

Dr.		ROYALTIES RECEIVABLE			Cr.
19.5		£	19.4		£
June 30	To Production Account .	412·50	Dec. 31	By X Y Co., Ltd. .	187·50
	[See Note (a) p. 297]		19.5		
			June 30	,, ,, ,, ,, ,, .	225·00
		£412·50			£412·50
19.6			19.5		
June 30	,, Production Account .	675·00	Dec.31	,, ,, ,, ,, ,, .	225·00
	[See Note (b) p. 297]		19.6		
			June 30	,, ,, ,, ,, ,, .	450·00
		£675·00			£675·00

¹ This account will be balanced yearly and shown in the Balance Sheet as an asset.

Dr. ¹PROVISION FOR SHORT WORKINGS ALLOWABLE Cr.

	£			£
19.6		19.4		
June 30 To X Y Co. Ltd.[2] . .	75·00	Dec. 31 By X Y Co. Ltd. . .		187·50
,, Profit and Loss		19.5		
Account[2] .	112·50	June 30 ,, ,, ,, ,, ,, . .		150·00
,, Balance . c/d	300·00	Dec. 31 ,, ,, ,, ,, . .		150·00
	£487·50			£487·50
		19.6		
		July 1 ,, Balance . . b/d		300·00

Note. The Royalties Receivable may be transferred to Royalties Payable Account, the net balance being written off to Production Account.

Alternatively, transfers may be made from Royalties Receivable Account to Royalties Payable Account on the basis of 2½p a ton on the sub-lessee's output, and to Profit and Loss Account of 1½p a ton on such output.

[1] This account will be balanced yearly and shown in the Balance Sheet as a liability.
[2] As the short workings of X Y Co. Ltd., for the half-year to 31st December, 19.4, can only be recouped at the latest by 30th June, 19.6, the balance of £112·50 is a gain to A B Co. Ltd.; the sum of £75 being the maximum recoupable, so as to leave A B Co. Ltd., with its minimum [£450 Royalties *less* Minimum Rent £375].
Note. According to the question A B Co. Ltd.'s output in the six months to 31st December, 19.4, is *nil*, since that of X Y Co. Ltd. is the same as the combined total.

The result will be as follows—

	Royalties Payable at 2½p a Ton	Royalties Receivable at 2½p a Ton	Net Royalties Payable	Royalties Receivable at 1½p a Ton
	£	£	£	£
Half-year ended—				
30th June, 19.4 . .	125		125	
31st December, 19.4 .	125	(a) 125		(a) 62·50
30th June, 19.5 . .	500	(a) 150	350	(a) 75·00
31st December, 19.5 .	750	(b) 150	600	(b) 75·00
30th June, 19.6 . .	625	(b) 300	325	(b) 150·00
	[1] £2,125	[2] £725	[3] £1,400	[4] £362·50

[1] *Total* output—85,000 tons at 2½p a ton.
[2] *Sub-lessee's* output—29,000 tons at 2½p a ton.
[3] *Net* output—56,000 tons at 2½p a ton.
[4] *Sub-lessee's* output—29,000 tons at 1½p a ton.

Notes (a) and (b).
The transfers from Royalties Receivable Account will be—

		£
Year ended 30th June, 19.5—(a) Production Account . .		275·00
(a) Profit and Loss Account .		137·50
,, ,, ,, ,, 19.6—(b) Production Account . .		450·00
(b) Profit and Loss Account .		225·00

6. Dr. MINIMUM RENT Cr.

	£		£
19.5		19.5	
Dec. 31 To Lessor	2,000	Dec. 31 By Short Workings . .	2,000
19.6		19.6	
Dec. 31 ,, ,, . . .	2,000	Dec. 31 ,, Royalties . . .	650
		,, Short Workings . .	1,350
19.7		19.7	
Dec. 31 ,, ,, . . .	2,000	Dec. 31 ,, Royalties . . .	1,850
		,, Short Workings . .	150

Dr.				ROYALTIES				Cr.
19.6			£	19.6				£
Dec. 31	To Minimum Rent . .		650	Dec. 31	By Production Account .			650
19.7				19.7				
Dec. 31	,, ,, ,, . .		1,850	Dec. 31	,, ,, ,, .			1,850
19.8				19.8				
Dec. 31	,, Royalties . .		2,250	Dec. 31	,, ,, ,, .			2,250
19.9				19.9				
Dec. 31	,, . . .		2,800	Dec. 31	,, ,, ,, .			2,800
19.0				19.0				
Dec. 31	,, ,, . .		3,500	Dec. 31	,, ,, ,, .			3,500
19.1				19.1				
Dec. 31	,, ,, . .		1,900	Dec. 31	,, ,, ,, .			1,900
19.2				19.2				
Dec. 31	,, ,, . .		3,000	Dec. 31	,, ,, ,, .			3,000

Dr.				[1]SHORT WORKINGS				Cr.
19.5			£	19.8				£
Dec. 31	To Minimum Rent . .		2,000	Dec. 31	By Lessor . .			250
19.6				19.9				
Dec. 31	,, ,, ,, . .		1,350	Dec. 31	,, ,, . .			800
19.7				19.0				
Dec. 31	,, ,, ,, . .		150	Dec. 31	,, ,, . .			1,500
				19.1				
				Dec. 31	,, Short Workings Irrecoverable[2] . .			800
				19.2				
				Dec. 31	,, Lessor . .			150
			£3,500					£3,500

Notes. (i) Total Royalties, £15,950; Cash paid to Lessor, £16,750; Irrecoverable Short Workings, £800.

(ii) The Short Workings of 19.5 are recoverable by the end of 19.0; this has been effected, together with £550 of Short Workings of 19.6. This leaves £800 Short Workings to be recovered by the end of 19.1. As there was no excess of Royalty over Minimum Rent in the latter year there was no opportunity to recover this balance, so that it must be written off. The fact of the strike, whilst it enables the lessee to avoid payment of the Minimum Rent, does not extend the period of recoupment of the Short Workings.

[Alternatively, so long as the lessor is receiving his minimum, even where there are excess royalties but not sufficient to eliminate short workings, the Minimum Rent Account may be employed; thus in 19.8 the accounts would be written up as follows—

Dr.				LESSOR				Cr.
19.8			£	19.8				£
Dec. 31	To Cash . . .		2,000	Dec. 31	By Minimum Rent .			2,000

Dr.				MINIMUM RENT				Cr.
19.8			£	19.8				£
Dec. 31	To Lessor . . .		2,000	Dec. 31	By Royalties . .			2,250
	,, Short Workings .		250					

Dr.				SHORT WORKINGS				Cr.
19.8			£	19.8				£
Jan. 1	To Balance (as above) .		3,500	Dec. 31	By Minimum Rent .			250

Income tax ignored. [See also Chapter XV, Question 3, p. 295.]

---

[1] This account will be balanced yearly and shown in the Balance Sheet as an asset. The account is not actually asked for in the question, but is shown for completeness.
[2] Debited to Profit and Loss Account.

CHAPTER XVI

JOINT VENTURE WITH ANDREW STEWART

Williams's books.

1. Dr.   **Cr.**

		Mths.	Interest £	£			Mths.	Interest £	£
19.. Nov. 1	To Bills Payable (Bill due 4th April, 19..)	1	6·25	1,250·00	19.. May 1	By Interest to *contra*		7·15	
	,, Expenses	6	0·90	30·00		,, Cheque			1,407·86
19.. May 1	,, Interest from *contra*		7·15	7·15					
	,, Share of Profit			120·71					
			£7·15	£1,407·86				£7·15	£1,407·86

JOINT VENTURE WITH WILLIAMS

Stewart's books.

Dr.   **Cr.**

		Mths.	Interest £	£			Mths.	Interest £	£
19.. Apr. 1	To Expenses	1	0·18	35·00	19.. Feb. 1	By Cash—Sales	3	9·00	600·00
May 1	,, Interest to *contra*		13·57	120·71	Apr. 1	,, ,, ,,	1	4·75	950·00
	,, Share of Profit			1,407·86	May 1	,, Interest from *contra*			13·57
	,, Cheque								
			£13·75	£1,563·57				£13·75	£1,563·57

Memorandum Joint Venture Account

		Mths.	Interest £	£
19..				
Nov. 1	To Goods (as at 4th April, 19..) . .	1	6·25	1,250·00
,,	,, Expenses . .	6	0·90	30·00
19..				
Apr. 1	,, Expenses . .	1	0·18	35·00
,,	,, Balance of Interest to *contra* . .		6·42	
May 1	,, Share of Profit— Stewart, ½ £120·71, Williams, ½ 120·71			241·42
			£13·75	£1,556·42

		Mths.	Interest £	£
19..				
Feb. 1	By Sales	3	9·00	600·00
Apr. 1	,, ,, . . .	1	4·75	950·00
May 1	,, Interest from *contra*			6·42
			£13·75	£1,556·42

2. *Adams's books*

Dr.   JOINT VENTURE WITH BELL   Cr.

19..		£	19..			£
June 25	To Cost of Pictures .	1,600·00	July 17	By Sale of Picture . .		630·00
	,, Expenses . .	25·00	Aug. 5	,, Cheque—		
July 17	,, Commission . .	31·50		[£756 — £37.80] .		718·20
25	,, Carriage and Insur-		Sept. 30	,, Picture taken over .		400·00
	ance . . .	7·80		,, Balance . . c/d		91·01
Sept. 30	,, Share of Profit .	174·91				
		£1,839·21				£1,839·21
Oct. 1	To Balance . . b/d	£91·01	Oct. 5	By Cheque . . .		£91·01

Dr.   *Memorandum* JOINT VENTURE ACCOUNT   Cr.

19..			£	19..				£
June 25	To Cost of Pictures .		1,600·00	July 10	By Sale of Picture .	(1)		892·50
	,, ,, ,, ,,		1,350·00	17	,, ,, ,, ,, .	(2)		630·00
	,, Expenses—			29	,, ,, ,, ,, .	(3)		819·00
	[£25 + £10] . .		35·00	Aug. 5	,, ,, ,, ,, .	(4)		756·00
July 10	,, Commission .	(1)	44·63	Sept. 30	,, Picture taken over .			400·00
17	,, ,, .	(2)	31·50					
	,, Carriage and Insur-							
	ance . .		7·80					
29	,, Commission .	(3)	40·95					
Aug. 5	,, ,, .	(4)	37·80					
Sept. 30	,, Profit—	£						
	Adams, ½ . 174·91							
	Bell, ½ . 174·91							
			349·82					
			£3,497·50					£3,497·50

3. *Green's books.*

Dr.   BROWN, BOMBAY   Cr.

19..		£	19..		£
Apr. 15	To Cash for Goods—		Apr. 15	By Bills Receivable—	
	(1,000 Transistors)	8,750·00		Bill drawn on	
	,, Freight and Insurance	565·60		Brown payable 1	
	,, Discounting Charge .	118·47		month after sight,	
?	,, Sundry Expenses .	17·25		140,000 Rupees at	
June 29	,, Profit on Joint Ven-			£5·35 per 100 rupees	7,490·00
	ture—½ share .	1,226·49	?	,, Sight Draft—	
				59,585 Rs, at £5·35	
				per 100 rupees .	3,187·81
		£10,677·81			£10,677·81

Dr.   BILLS RECEIVABLE   Cr.

19..		£	19..		£
Apr. 15	To Brown (140,000 Rs.) .	7,490	Apr. 15	By Bank	7,490

Dr.   BANK   Cr.

19..		£	19..		£
Apr. 15	To Bills Receivable .	7,490·00	Apr. 15	By Discounting Charge .	118·47

Brown's books.

Dr.   GREEN, LONDON   Cr.

19..		Rupees	19..		Rupees
June 24	To Landing, etc., Charges.	1,475	June 29	By Sales (1,000 Transistors)	224,000
29	„ Bill Payable . .	140,000		„ Discount . . .	325
?	„ Sundry Expenses. .	340			
	„ Profit on Joint Venture:				
	½ share [£1,226·48] .	22,925			
July 4	„ Sight Draft. . .	59,585			
		Rs. 224,325			Rs. 224,325

Dr.   *Memorandum* JOINT VENTURE ACCOUNT   Cr.

19..		£	19..		£
Apr. 15	To Goods—		June 29	By Sales (1,000 Transis-	
	(1,000 Transistors)	8,750·00		tors) 224,000 Rs. .	11,984·00
	„ Freight & Insurance.	565·60		„ Discount (325 Rs.) .	17·39
	„ Discounting Charge .	118·47			
?	„ Sundry Expenses .	17·25			
June 24	„ Landing and Ware-				
	house Charges—				
	(1,475 Rs.) .	78·91			
?	„ Sundry Expenses—				
	(340 Rs.) . .	18·19			
?	„ Net Profit—				
	Green, ½ £1,226·48				
	Brown, ½ 1,226·49				
		2,452·97			
		£12,001·39			£12,001·39

Note. There is no necessity to enter in the Joint Venture Account a rupee equivalent. If, however, this is done the total profit in rupees will be Rs. 45,850.

Dr.   JOINT VENTURE   **Cr.**

Date	Particulars	£	£
19..	To Kahla Capital—		
Feb. 1	Printing and Dispatch of Prospectus	350·00	
	Advertising Prospectus	3,000·00	
26	Professional Charges *re* Expert Reports and Valuations	750·00	
Mar. 1	Printing Allotment Letters and Share Certificates	45·00	
5	Solicitors' Charges *re* Prospectus and Public Issue of Capital	525·00	
	Brokerage—1¼p per share on 75,000 Shares	937·50	
	3,000 Preference Shares taken up under Underwriting Agreement	3,000·00	8,607·50
	" Bateman Capital—		
Jan. 1	Capital Duty	1,400·00	
	Solicitors' Charges *re* Formation of Company	105·00	
	Printing Memorandum and Articles	35·00	
20	Printing Books of Account and Statutory Books	95·00	
Mar. 31	Office Rent and Rates	50·00	
	Salaries of Office Staff	250·00	
	Sundry Petty Cash	35·00	
	2,000 Preference Shares, taken up under Underwriting Agreement	2,000·00	3,970·00
	" Net Profit—Kahla, ⅗	4,978·50	
	Bateman, ⅖	3,319·00	8,297·50
			£20,875·00

Date	Particulars	£	£
19..	By Cash—		
Mar. 15	Underwriting Commission 2½p per share on 125,000 Preference Shares		3,125·00
31	" Cash—Proceeds of 5,000 Preference Shares at 90p (a)	4,500·00	
	" Cash—Proceeds of 15,000 Ordinary Shares at 95p (b)	14,250·00	
			18,750·00
	Less Expenses of Sale (20,000 Shares at 5p)		1,000·00
			17,750·00
			£20,875·00

If sold on the Stock Exchange the expenses would be—

		£	£
(a)	On £4,500—		
	Brokers' Commission 1·25%	56·25	
	Contract Stamp	0·60	56·85
(b)	On £14,250—		
	Brokers' Commission:		
	1·25% on £5,000	62·50	
	0·625% on £9,250	57·81	
	£14,250		
	Contract Stamp	0·60	120·91
			£177·76

Dr.   CAPITAL   **Cr.**

		Kahla	Bateman			Kahla	Bateman
		£	£			£	£
19.. Mar. 31	To Cash	13,586·00	7,289·00	19.. Feb.– Mar. 31	By Joint Venture [per details therein]	8,607·50	3,970·00
					" Share of Profit	4,978·50	3,319·00
		£13,586·00	£7,289·00			£13,586·00	£7,289·00

303

5. A's books.

JOINT VENTURE

Dr.

Date	Particulars	Nominal	Principal £
19.. Sept. 30	To Broker— Purchase of Shares:		
	A.B. Plantations Ltd., Ordinary	200	384·00
	X.Y. Tobacco Co. Ltd., Ordinary	200	757·00
	Z. Insurance Co. Ltd., Ordinary	40	733·00
Nov. 15	,, Bonus Dividend—		
	A.B. Plantations Ltd., Ordinary Shares	100	
19.. Jan. 31	,, Broker—Interest		16·63
Mar. 31	,, ,, ,,		8·48
		540	£1,899·11
19.. Apr. 1	To Balance b/d		1,490·50

Cr.

Date	Particulars	Nominal	Principal £
19.. Oct. 12	By Cash—		
	Dividend 5% *less* tax on 200 X.Y. Tobacco Co. Ltd., Ordinary Shares		6·00
Nov.10	,, Broker—		
	Dividend of 55p per share, *less* tax, on 40 Z. Insurance Co. Ltd., Ordinary Shares		13·20
15	,, Cash—		
	Dividend 25%, *less* tax, on 200 A.B. Plantations Ltd., Ordinary Shares		30·00
	,, Bonus—		
	Dividend of one share for two on 200 A.B. Plantations, Ltd., Ordinary Shares *per contra*		
19.. Jan. 12	,, Broker—		
	Dividend 9% *less* tax on 200 X.Y. Tobacco Co. Ltd., Ordinary Shares		10·80
20	,, Broker—Sale of Shares:		
	X.Y. Tobacco Co. Ltd., Ordinary (ex div.)	100	348·25
Mar.31	,, Balance—Shares:		
	A.B. Plantations Ltd. c/d	300	384·00
	X.Y. Tobacco Co. Ltd. (a) c/d	100	373·50
	Z. Insurance Co. Ltd. c/d	40	733·00
	,, Net Loss—		
	B		0·18
	Profit and Loss Account		0·18
		540	£1,899·11

(a) In the absence of essential details as to the proportion of dividend accruing in the price and current market price, shares are brought down at cost; except for X.Y. Tobacco Co. Ltd., where the 12th October gross dividend has been deducted from the price, i.e. $\dfrac{£757 - £10}{2}$

Notes. (i) Income Tax on Broker's Loan ignored, as usually tax not deducted.

(ii) The due dates of settlement of account to or by broker will not be the date of purchase or sale, but the following settlement day—Tuesday week following the close of the "account" in which the transaction took place.

(iii) Notes will be made in the Ledger as to the custody of the Investments.

(iv) The question is somewhat ambiguous in its requirements, as the examiner may require separate accounts to be shown, together with such entries as are necessary in A's books.

The above transactions appearing in A's books will form part of the Double Entry. A "Trial Balance" may be obtained by taking the cash items and writing up a Cash Account. This will result in a credit balance of cash of £373·19. The balances are, therefore—

	£	£
Joint Venture Account	1,490·50	
Broker—Loan Account		708·48
B		409·01
Profit and Loss Account (from Joint Venture Account) . .	0·18	
Cash Account		373·19
	£1,490·68	£1,490·68

If separate books for the Joint Venture are in use the Trial Balance will be—

	£	£
Joint Venture Account	1,490·50	
Broker—Loan Account		708·48
A		373·01
B		409·01
	£1,490·50	£1,490·50

Dr.			*Rough* CAPITAL ACCOUNTS			Cr.
	A £	B £		A £	B £	
To Cash . .	177·81	177·81	By Cash . .	587·00	587·00	
,, Dividends—						
X.Y. . .	6·00					
A.B. . .	30·00					
,, Loss . .	0·18	0·18				
,, Balances .	373·01	409·01				
	£587·00	£587·00		£587·00	£587·00	

Dr.		CASH		Cr.
	£			£
To A	587·00	By Broker . . .	.	1,174·00
,, B	587·00	,, A . . .	.	177·81
,, Broker	355·62	,, B . . .	.	177·81
	£1,529·62			£1,529·62

BROKER

Dr.		£			Cr.		£
19.. Sept. 30	To Broker—Loan	700·00					£ 1,874·00
	" Cash	587·00			19.. Sept. 30	By Joint Venture	
	" B	587·00					
		£1,874·00					£1,874·00
19.. Jan. 20	To Joint Venture	£348·25			19.. Jan. 20	By Broker—Loan	£348·25

BROKER—LOAN [7½% per annum on securities (detailed)]

Dr.		Days	Interest	Principal			Cr.		Days	Interest	Principal
			£	£						£	£
19.. Nov. 10	To Joint Venture	82	0·22	13·20			19.. Sept. 30	By Broker	123	17·68	700·00
19.. Jan. 12	" Joint Venture	19	0·04	10·80			19.. Jan. 31	By B			177·81
Jan. 20	" Broker	11	0·79	348·25				" Cash			177·81
Jan. 31	" Interest to contra		16·63	700·00				" Interest from contra			16·63
	" Balance c/d										
			£17·68	£1,072·25						£17·68	£1,072·25
19.. Mar. 31	To Balance			708·48			19.. Feb. 1	By Balance	b/d		700·00
				£708·48			Mar. 31	" Interest on £700 at 7½% per annum			8·48
											£708·48
							19.. April 1	By Balance	b/d		708·48

B

Dr.		£			Cr.		£
19.. Jan. 31	To Broker	177·81					£ 587·00
Mar. 31	" Joint Venture—Half Share of Loss	0·18			19.. Sept. 30	By Broker	
	" Balance c/d	409·01					
		£587·00					£587·00
					19.. Apr. 1	By Balance	b/d 409·01

306

As a result, the only entries in A's books will be those involved in writing up (and posting) B's account; that is, *debiting* B with moneys put into the Joint Venture and A's share of Profits, and *crediting* B with the amount received from the Joint Venture, thus—

Dr.					B						Cr.
					£						£
To Cash	.	.	.	.	587·00	By Cash	.	.	.	.	177·81
						„ Dividends—					
						X.Y.	.	.	.	.	6·00
						A.B.	.	.	.	.	30·00
						„ Loss	.	.	.	.	0·18
						„ Balance	.	.	.	c/d	373·01
					£587·00						£587·00
To Balance	.	.	.	b/d	373·01						

B thus owes A £373·01 as shown in the latters' books and agreeing with the credit balance due to A in the Joint Venture books.

B's books would be as follows—

Dr.					A						Cr.
					£						£
To Cash	.	.	.	.	587·00	By Cash	.	.	.	.	177·81
						„ Loss	.	.	.	.	0·18
						„ Balance	.	.	.	c/d	409·01
					£587·00						£587·00
To Balance	.	.	.	b/d	409·01						

Assuming that the shares on hand were sold at book values out of £1,490·50 the broker would be paid £708·48, leaving £782·02 payable to A (£373·01) and to B (£409·01). Each venturer would debit his own cash or bank and credit his co-venturer, e.g. in A's books the entries are debit Cash £373·01 and credit B £373·01.

[If the same circumstances are assumed to arise in the main solution, A would be left with £373·01 after paying both the broker and B, thus almost restoring the overdrawn sum of £373·19, leaving a balance of £0·18 representing loss.]

6. Books of C D Ltd.

Dr.			JOINT VENTURE WITH A B			Cr.
19..		£	19..			£
Jan. 6	To Goods, 56,600 kr. at 14.15 . .	4,000·00	Jan. 20	By Sales to X Y— 484,000 esc.		
13	„ Freight and Other Charges— 10,800 kr. at 14.40 .	750·00		*Less* Allowance for Damage 26,400		
Feb. 3	„ Balance . . c/d	750·00				
				[at 88] 457,600		5,200·00
			Feb. 3	„ Carriers *re* Damage— 4,377 kr. at 14.59 .		300·00
		£5,500·00				£5,500·00
19..			19..			
Feb. 4	To Cash—A B . .	424·13	Feb. 3	By Balance . b/d		750·00
	„ Office Expenses .	25·00				
	„ Profit and Loss Account . .	300·87				
		£750·00				£750·00

The whole of the profit of the venture subject to the proportion due to A B is arrived at as follows—

			£
Proceeds of Sale: 457,600 escudos at 86.	.	.	5,320·93

	Kronor		
Purchases	56,600		
Freight and other Charges .	10,800		
	67,400		
Less Damage . . .	4,377		
	63,023 at 14.25 .	4,422·67

Profit .	.	.	.	.	.	£898·26

One-half thereof	.	.	.	.	449·13
Less Office Expenses[1]	.	.	.	.	25·00
					£424·13

[1] It is assumed that the charge for £25 is against A B solely and not against the venture.

7. *Tower's books.*

(a) Dr.   CASTLE   Cr.

19.4			£	19.4		£
Jan. 2	To Goods purchased—			Jan. 3	By Cash from Castle . .	3,500
	Cash . £4,800			9	,, Sales—	
	Bill Payable 800				Bill Receivable	
	,, ,, 1,200				(Brown) . £420	
			6,800		Bill Receivable	
9	,, Bills Receivable transferred				(Green) . 250	
	to Castle (£420 + £250)		670			670
Apr. 30	,, Profit and Loss Account—			Feb. 2	,, Sales (£1,800) *less* Re-	
	Joint Venture—				turns (£90) .	1,710
	Commission on Sales		176	Mar. 5	,, Bill payable paid by Castle	800
	Joint Venture—			31	,, Sales (balance of goods in	
	Share of Profit .		1,162		Tower's hands) . .	2,910
	Cash to Castle—settlement		1,044	Apr. 30	,, Bad Debts—	
					Bill dishonoured—	
					Green . . £250	
					Castle's Debtors 12	
						262
			£9,852			£9,852

Dr.   DEBTORS   Cr.

19.4			£	19.4		£
Jan. 9	To Sales—Brown .	.	420	Jan. 9	By Bill Receivable—Brown .	420
	,, ,, Green .	.	250		,, ,, ,, Green .	250
			£670			£670
Feb. 3	,, Sales . .	.	1,800	Feb. 3	,, Returns . .	90
Mar. 31	,, ,, . .	.	2,910	Mar. 31	,, Cash . .	4,590
					,, Bad Debts .	30
			£4,710			£4,710

Dr.   BILLS RECEIVABLE   Cr.

19.4			£	19.4		£
Jan. 9	To Brown .	.	420	Jan. 9	By Castle—transfer of Bills .	670
	,, Green .	.	250			
			£670			£670

Dr.   BAD DEBTS   Cr.

19.4		£	19.4		£
Mar. 31	To Joint Venture Debtors per Tower . . .	30	Mar. 31	By Profit and Loss Account .	292
Apr. 30	„ Joint Venture Debtors per Castle . .	12			
	„ Joint Venture Debtors per Green's Bill . .	250			
		£292			£292

Dr.   BILLS PAYABLE   Cr.

19.4		£	19.4		£
Mar. 5	To Castle—cash paid by him to meet the bill . .	800	Jan. 2	By Castle . . .	800
	„ Cash	1,200		„ „ . . .	1,200
		£2,000			£2,000

Castle's books.

Dr.   TOWER   Cr.

19.4		£	19.4		£
Jan. 2	To Cash to Tower .	3,500	Jan. 9	By Bills Receivable—	
Feb. 11	„ Cash Payment of dishonoured Bill (Green) .	250		Brown . . £420	
Mar. 5	„ Cash Payment of Bill accepted by Tower	800		Green . 250	670
31	„ Bad Debt . . .	12	Feb. 3	„ Sales . . .	110
Apr. 30	„ Profit and Loss Account— Share of Profit on Joint Venture . .	1,162	Mar. 31	„ „ . . .	3,400
			Apr. 30	„ Goods taken over .	500
				„ Cash from Tower—settlement . . .	1,044
		£5,724			£5,724

Dr.   DEBTORS   Cr.

19.4		£	19.4		£
Feb. 3	To Sales . . .	110	Mar. 31	By Cash . . .	3,498
Mar. 31	„ „ . . .	3,400		„ Tower—Bad Debt .	12
		£3,510			£3,510

Dr.   BILLS RECEIVABLE   Cr.

19.4		£	19.4		£
Jan. 9	To Tower—Brown .	420	Jan. 9	By Cash (Bank) . .	670
	„ „ Green .	250		(Proceeds of Bills discounted) . .	
		£670			£670

(b) Dr.   *Memorandum* JOINT VENTURE ACCOUNT   Cr.

	£			£
To Goods purchased . . .	6,800	By Sales less Returns		
„ Tower — 2 per cent Commission on Sales of £8,800 .	176	„ Proceeds £8,598 — £90 . . £8,508		
Net Profit: Towers ½ £1,162		Bad Debts charged		
Castle ½ 1,162	2,324	to Tower .	292	8,800
		„ Goods taken over by Castle .		500
	£9,300			£9,300

		£
Sales £420 + £250 + £1,800 + £110 + £2,910 + £3,400		8,890
Less Returns		90
		£8,800

		£
Cash collected		8,508
Bad Debts borne by Tower and **not** by the Joint Venture £250 + £30 + £12		292
		£8,800

8. *A's books.*

Dr.	B		Cr.

	£			£
To Goods to Joint Venture .	1,000	By Goods returned (10 articles)		100
„ Carriage	20	„ Carriage thereon . .		2
„ Profit and Loss Account:		„ Sales (5 Articles at £18		
Share of Net Profit as		each) . . .		90
Joint Venture . .	156	„ Balance . . .	c/d	984
	£1,176			£1,176
To Balance . . .	b/d	984		

B's books.

Dr.	A		Cr.

	£			£
To Carriage	4	By Sales (82 articles at £14 each)		1,148
„ Commission, 10 per cent on		„ Goods taken over (3 articles		
£1,148 (see note (i) on next		at £11 each) . . .		33
page)	115			
„ Profit and Loss Account;				
Share of Net Profit on				
Joint Venture . .	78			
„ Balance . . .	c/d 984			
	£1,181			£1,181
		By Balance . . .	b/d	984

MEMORANDUM JOINT VENTURE
(A AND B)

Dr.	Articles	£	Cr.	Articles	£
To Goods (See note (a)) . .	100	1,000	By Goods (returned) (See note		
„ Carriage (See note (b)) .		24	(a))	10	100
„ Commission . . .		115	„ Carriage thereon (See note		
„ Net Profit—			(b)) . . .		2
A, ⅔ . . . £156			„ Sales by—		
B, ⅓ . . . 78			A	5	90
		234	B	82	1,148
			„ Goods taken over by B .	3	33
	100	£1,373		100	£1,373

(a) This item could be shown "net" on debit side, i.e. 90 Articles—£900.
(b)   „   „   „   „   „   „   „   „   .   „   , Carriage—£22.

Notes. (i) The amount of commission due to B, in the absence of clarity in the agreement, is tentative only, as the view taken by A may differ from that of B. (The agreement, written or verbal, might have provided for dealing with the situation.)

The agreement, however, so far as is revealed by the question, indicates that B is to have his commission on Sales—not stated as sales *by B.* A might take the view that the inference is that the commission due to B should be confined to sales by B and that A should be entitled to commission on his sales of Joint Venture goods (i.e. 5 articles). Against this, the agreement as revealed makes no mention of *any* commission due to A.

Theoretically, in the absence of agreement, either legal proceedings or arbitration would be taken, but in view of the triviality of the sum involved, it is extremely unlikely that such course of events would follow and some compromise be made.

In the answer, a reasonable compromise solution (not necessarily the only one) is given, viz. that B takes his commission on his Sales, i.e. £148, and A none.

(Some comment on these lines is an essential part of the answer.)

(ii) The student may find a minor difficulty in differentiating between (*a*) the goods returned (to be struck out of the Joint Venture Account) and (*b*) those returned for A to sell on behalf of the Joint Venture.

As regards (*a*) the entry relating to those goods represents a *pro tanto* reversal of the goods originally sent (i.e. 100 articles at £10 each) so that A must make a cancelling entry.

B makes no entry against A. He had made none when he received them from A as he had not *bought* them, so that when he returns them to A, he will make no entry.

As regards (*b*), again B will make no entry in A's account, but (differing from (*a*) A makes no entry in favour of B) the transfer of these goods (5 articles) is merely one of location and of no more consequence than removing them from one room to the other, and of course they are still Joint Venture goods.

(iii) Each party will make the appropriate entries in his Stock Register.

9. (Where a bank account is opened for the Joint Venture, it is maintained as a separate entity and forms part of the double entry and no cash or bank entries therefrom appear in the partners' own books, except for any moneys paid from the account to the partners, or vice versa.)

Jasper Rhode's books.

Dr.   JOINT VENTURE ACCOUNT WITH MORTIMER RHODE   Cr.

	£		£
To Transfer from Purchases (*a*) .	6,600	By Transfer to Purchases (*c*) .	380
,, Cash—		,, Transfer to Debtors (*d*) .	5,200
Wages	48	,, Cash—Received from J. V.	
Advertising . . .	30	Bank Account . .	1,987
Transport . . .	10		
,, Net Profit on Joint Venture .	879		
	£7,567		£7,567

Mortimer Rhode's books.

Dr.   JOINT VENTURE ACCOUNT WITH JASPER RHODE   Cr.

	£		£
To Cash—		By Cash—Received from J. V.	
Hire of Hall . . .	60	Bank Account . .	663
Insurance . . .	12		
Transport . . .	5		
,, Net Profit on Joint Venture .	586		
	£663		£663

Dr.   JOINT VENTURE BANK ACCOUNT   Cr.

	£		£
To Sales—Caravans. . .	1,250	By Cash, Nu Homes Ltd. (b)—	
„ Sales—Accessories .	450	Accessories Sold . .	300
„ Deposits—Credit Sales .	1,300	Accessories for Prizes .	50
		„ Cash— . . . . _ .	
		Jasper	1,987
		Mortimer . . .	663
	£3,000		£3,000

Dr. JOINT VENTURE—MEMORANDUM PROFIT AND LOSS ACCOUNT   Cr.

	£		£
To Purchases—		By Sales—	
Caravans (f) . . .	6,220	Caravans (e) . . .	7,750
Accessories . .	300	Accessories . . .	450
„ Wages	48		
„ Advertising. . .	30		
„ Hire of Hall . .	60		
„ Insurance . . .	12		
„ Transport . . .	15		
„ Prizes	50		
„ Net Profit—			
Jasper Rhode ($\frac{3}{5}$) . .	879		
Mortimer Rhode ($\frac{2}{5}$). .	586		
	£8,200		£8,200

(a) Since Jasper supplies the caravans at cost he will debit the Joint Venture Account with the cost thereof, and credit his Purchases Account.

(b) As accessories are bought by Mortimer on sale or return, no entries need to be made until goods are paid for. The *pro forma* cost was £470, of which £120 is returned, and of the difference of £350, £50 is used for prizes, and the balance sold.

(c) The caravan taken back by Jasper is a Rhode "Rider", and the cost thereof is redebited to Jasper's purchases (£400 less 5 per cent).

(d) Total Credit Sales £6,500, Cash Deposits £1,300; balance represents Debtors taken over by Jasper.

(e) Sale of Caravans made up as to—

	£
Cash Banked	2,550
Debtors—Jasper	5,200
	£7,750

(f) Cost of Caravans taken over from Jasper £6,600, *less* rebate on one returned £380.

CHAPTER XVII

1. Account Sales of 10 cases of hardware, ex S.S.................sold for and on account of G. McArthur & Co., London, by—

R. UPRICHARD, CAPE TOWN

Marks						£	£
and	8 Cases at £42 per case	.	.	.	.	336·00	
Numbers	*Less* 5% Cash Discount .	.	.	.	.	16·80	
							319·20
	2 Cases at £43·53 net per case	.	.	.	.		87·06
	Less—				£		406·26
	Dock and Landing Charges	.	.	.	3·98		
	Warehouse Charges	.	.	.	2·20		
	Insurance	.	.	.	.	3·38	
	Cartage	.	.	.	.	1·99	
						11·55	
	Commission—						
	2½% of £406·26	.	.	.	.	10·16	
	Del credere—						
	1% of £406·26	.	.	.	.	4·06	
						14·22	
							25·77
	Balance due to G. McArthur & Co. per sight Draft						£380·49

E. & O.E.
Cape Town
(Date) 21st February, 19..   (Signed) R. UPRICHARD.

It should be noted that the consignee being in Cape Town, his Account Sales will be rendered in South African rands and cents.

Note. It is assumed that the consignee sent Sight Draft with Account Sales on 21st February, 19..

[1 Rand = 56p.]

2. *Dr.*   CONSIGNMENT TO A B, JAMAICA   *Cr.*

19..		£	19..		£
Jan. 10	To Goods on Consignment .	625	Jan. 28	By A B—Sales . . .	150
	„ Carriage and Freight .	40	Feb. 20	„ „ „ . . .	590
	„ Insurance . .	25	Mar. 2	„ Profit and Loss Account—	
Mar. 2	„ A B—Expenses . .	15		Loss on Consignment .	2
	„ A B—Commission .	37			
		£742			£742

Dr.   GOODS ON CONSIGNMENT   Cr.

19..		£	19..		£
Mar. 2	To Purchases or Trading Account . . .	625	Jan. 10	By Consignment to A B .	625

Dr.   A B, JAMAICA   Cr.

19..		£	19..		£
Jan. 28	To Consignment—		Jan. 10	By Bill Receivable . .	400
	Sales . . .	150	Mar. 2	,, Consignment—	
Feb. 20	,, Consignment—			Expenses . . .	15
	Sales . . .	590		Commission . .	37
	,, Interest . . .	5		,, Bill Receivable . .	293
		£745			£745

Note. The Consignment Account automatically reflects the loss due to faulty packing.

CONSIGNMENT

19..		Cases	£			19..		Cases	£
Apr. 15	To Goods	100	2,126·00			May 31	By Insurance Claim— Goods lost in transit	2	44·00
May 31	" Insurance		35·50			June 16	" Sales— 42,400 Rupees at £5·35 per 100	80	2,268·40
	" Freight, etc.		86·75			July 31	" Stock . . c/d	18	(a)410·68
	" Landing Charges— 415 Rupees at £5·35 per 100		22·20						
	" Storage and Insurance— 80 Cases for one month = 80 Rupees at £5·35 per 100		(d) 4·28						
June 16	" Commission— 2¼% on 42,400 Rupees = 850 Rupees at £5·35 per 100		56·71						
July 31	" Reserve— Storage and Insurance: 18 Cases for two months = 36 Rupees at £5·35 per 100 . . c/d		(c) 1·93						
	" Net Profit to Profit and Loss Account		389·71						
		100	£2,723·08					100	£2,723·08
Aug. 1	To Stock . . . . b/d	18	410·68			Aug. 1	By Accrual Sales—		1·93 [1 b/d]
	" Storage and Insurance— 18 Cases for three months = 54 Rupees at £5·35 per 100 [1]		(d) 2·89			15	" Sales— 9,300 Rupees at £5·35 per 100	18	481·50
15	" Commission— 2¼% on 9,000 Rupees = 225 Rupees at £5·35 per 100		(c) 12·04						
	" Net Profit to Profit and Loss Account		57·82						
			£483·43					18	£483·43

[1] Net charge 18 at £5·35 per 100 = £1·20, i.e. £3·60 — £2·40.

315

JONES AND WARE

19..		Rupees	£		19..		Rupees	£
June 16	To Consignment—				May 31	By Landing Charges	415	22·20
	Sales	42,400	2,268·40		June 16	„ Storage and Insurance . .	80	4·28
July 18	„ Difference on Exchange . .		(b) 5·63		July 18	„ Commission	1,060	56·71
					31	„ Draft	37,500	2,011·88
						„ Balance . . . . c/d	3,345	178·96
		42,400	£2,274·03				42,400	£2,274·03
Aug. 1	To Balance . . . . b/d	3,345	178·96		Aug. 1	By Storage and Insurance . .	54	2·89
15	„ Consignment—				15	„ Commission	225	12·04
	Sales	9,000	481·50		16	„ Draft	12,066	645·53
		12,345	£660·46				12,345	£660·46

INSURANCE COMPANY

19..		£
May 31	To Claim for Goods lost in transit .	(c) 44·00

316

Notes. (*a*) Stock valuation is—

		£
$\frac{18}{100} \times$ £2,248·25		404·69
$\frac{18}{98} \times$ 415 rupees, *plus* 36 rupees = 76 + 36 = 112 @ £5·35 per 100 .		5·99

£410·68

(*b*) The profit on exchange is—

Sales by Agent: .	Cases	Rupees
16th June, 19.. . . .	80 @ 530	42,400
15th August, 19.. . .	18 @ 500	9,000

		51,400
Less 2½% Commission on Sales .	1,285	
„ Landing Charges . .	415	
„ Storage and Insurance. .	134	
	—	1,834

	Rs. 49,566 @ £5·35	
	per 100 Rs.	2,651·78
Sterling amount of Drafts . .		2,657·41

	Profit on Exchange	£5·63

[As all the transactions are recorded at the rate of £5·35 per 100 rupees, except the remittance from the agent of Rs. 37,500, which produces £5·365 per 100 rupees, the profit on exchanges is 375 × £0·015 = £5·63.]

(*c*) The total profit is made up of—

		£
(1) Remittances from Agent		2,657·41
Less Consignor's Expenses, including Cost of Goods		
[see 15th April, 19.., transactions]. . .		2,248·25
		409·16
(2) Amount due from Insurance Company *re* Claim . .		44·00
		£453·16

This sum is reflected in the following items—

		£
(1) Profit on Consignment, 31st July, 19... . .		389·71
(2) „ „ „ 15th Aug., 19.. . .		57·82
(3) Profit on Exchange, 31st July, 19.. . .		5·63
		£453·16

(*d*) It is assumed that the payments for storage and insurance relate to complete months, so that no rebate will be granted if the goods are removed during the month, e.g. the storage and insurance item on 80 cases relates to one month, i.e. June, notwithstanding withdrawal on 15th June. The charge of 54 rupees relates to 18 cases from 1st June to 31st August.

(*e*) Alternatively, the storage charge of £7·17 [80 + 54 rupees] may be calculated thus—

	Rupees	£
98 for one month (June)	98	
18 for two months (July and August) . .	36	
	Rs. 134 @ £5·35 per	
	100 Rs. =	7·17

4.   JOURNAL

19..		£	£
Dec. 2	Sales . . . . *Dr.*	35·50	
	To A B		35·50
	Being adjustment of excess of credit to Sales over net proceeds of consignment.		
23	X Y . . . . *Dr.*	6·75	
	To Sales		6·75
	Being adjustment of excess of net proceeds of consignment over credit to Sales.		

The open shipment already credited to Sales £2,225 will be adjusted by debiting Sales, and either bringing the amount down below the "line" or by crediting an Open Shipments Account, the latter off-setting the debits of £2,225 against the Consignees. The Stock at cost (including consignment non-recurring expenses debited to the expense accounts) or net realizable value, if lower, will be introduced into the Trading Account and (Consignment) Stock Account in the usual manner.

The adjusting entries are made in accordance with the system of book-keeping adopted by the consignors, but included in each adjusting entry should be a debit for the appropriate expenses, and a credit to Sales in order that the gross proceeds and all expenses relevant to each consignment may be clearly disclosed. Further, no attempt in the system shown in the question is made to show the consignee's expenses and commission.

Taking the first consignment as an illustration, assuming the consignor's expenses are £40, and the consignee's £180, the adjusting entries (ignoring narratives) are—

JOURNAL

		£	£
Consignment Expenses (Consignee) . .[1] *Dr.*		180·00	
,, ,, (Consignor) . .[1] *Dr.*		40·00	
To Sales			144·50
,, General Expenses			40·00
,, A B			35·50

This will give the Sales as £1,150 (already credited) plus £144·50 = £1,294·50 and a charge of £180 incurred by the consignee, leaving a net amount due from the consignee of £1,114·50. The item of £40 does not affect the figure of gross Sales.

In the above adjustment it is assumed that the phrase "net proceeds" means the gross proceeds of Sales less the expenses and commission of the consignee.

The firm should deal with each consignment by means of Consignment Accounts, as needless labour and complications will otherwise arise.

[1] Or in one item £220.

The following entries will be entailed, using the same facts as in the foregoing—

JOURNAL

		£	£
Sales . . . . *Dr.*		1,150·00	
To A B			1,150·00
[Cancellation of original entry.]			
Consignment . . . . . *Dr.*		925·00	
To Goods on Consignment Account . .			925·00
[Goods sent at cost.]			
Consignment . . . . . *Dr.*		220·00	
To General Expenses			40·00
„ A B			180·00
[For all consignment expenses.]			
A B . . . . . . *Dr.*		1,294·50	
To Consignment			1,294·50
[A B's sales.]			
Cash . . . . . . *Dr.*		1,114·50	
To A B			1,114·50
[Settlement of balance.]			
Consignment . . . . . *Dr.*		149·50	
To Profit and Loss on Consignment Account.			149·50
[Profit.]			

The profit on the first consignment, as shown above, may be reconciled with the figures given in the question and the Journal entry on page 318 thus—

	£	£
Sales originally credited with net proceeds . .		1,150·00
Less Sales debited in Journal entry on page 318 . .	35·50	
„ Cost of Goods included in purchases . . .	925·00	
„ Consignment expenses	40·00	
		1,000·50
Profit		£149·50

Reconciliation with the Journal entry on page 318 is as follows—

	£	£
Sales originally credited with expected net proceeds . .		1,150·00
Add Sales credited in Journal entry on page 318 . .		144·50
		1,294·50
Less Consignment Expenses debited in Journal entry on page 318.	220·00	
„ Cost of Goods included in purchases . . .	925·00	
		1,145·00
Profit		£149·50

No difficulty arises with the balance due by A B, because after credit of £35·50 as shown in the Journal entry, he is a debtor for £1,114·50, i.e. £1,150 as originally debited less £35·50. This amount is the same as shown in the last set of Journal entries where the original debit to A B was cancelled, the usual entries being made in reference to A B's sales and expenses, leaving finally the entry of £1,114·50 for the remittance of the net proceeds.

5.

ACCOUNT SALES

of two cars, *ex* S.S. *Silver Bullet*, sold for and on account of Midland Motors Ltd.
by Agents of Bombay

Marks			Rupees
and	Proceeds of One Car		6,500
Numbers	„ „ „ „		7,150
			13,650

		Rupees	
Less—			
	Landing Charges	650	
	Commission, 8%	1,092	
	Del Credere Commission, 2% . . .	273	
			2,015
			11,635
	Less Draft remitted on Account		5,200
		Rs.	6,435

E. & O. E.

Agent's Signature
(*Date*).

Consignor's books.

Dr.   CONSIGNMENT TO BOMBAY   **Cr.**

	£		£
To Cars on Consignment: 2 Cars . .	600	By Agent—Sales per Account Sales	
„ Cartage, Freight, and Insurance .	175	(13,650 Rupees at 13 to £) . .	1,050
„ Landing Charges (650 Rupees at 13 to £)	50		
„ Commission (1,365 Rupees at 13 to £)	105		
„ Profit and Loss on Consignment Account	120		
	£1,050		£1,050

Note. The consignee, being a *del credere* agent, must bear the loss arising from the bad debt.

Dr.   AGENT   **Cr.**

	Rupees	£		Rupees	£
To Consignment to Bombay—Sales . .	13,650	1,050	By Draft	5,200	400
			„ Landing Charges . .	650	50
			„ Commission . .	1,365	105
			„ Draft	6,435	495
Rs.	13,650	£1,050	Rs.	13,650	£1,050

Dr.   CARS ON CONSIGNMENT   **Cr.**

	£		£
To Purchases or Trading Account . .	600	By Consignment to Bombay—2 Cars .	600

Consignee's books.

Dr.   MIDLAND MOTORS LTD.   Cr.

	Rupees		Rupees
To Landing Charges	650	By Sundry Debtors	6,500
„ Draft	5,200	„ „	7,150
„ Commission	1,365		
„ Draft	6,435		
	13,650		13,650

Dr.   COMMISSION   Cr.

	Rupees		Rupees
To Bad Debt	1,300	By Midland Motors Ltd.	1,365
„ Profit and Loss Account	65		
	1,365		1,365

Note. If the agent bears the cost of landing charges the consignor's profit would be increased by £50 to £170, and the consignee would incur a loss of 650 − 65 = 585 rupees.

6. (1) All consignments sent out must be passed through a special Consignments Day Book. This will contain columns for the name of the consignee, the cost price of the goods dispatched, the invoice price (where the cost price for any reason is not to be disclosed), and an additional foreign currency column.

(2) The cost price of the goods will be debited, not to the personal account of the consignee, but to a "Consignment to ⸺ Account," each consignment having its own separate account. This account is a subsidiary Profit and Loss Account and not a Personal Account.

(3) The cost price column of the Consignment Day Book will be cast and posted to the credit of Goods on Consignment Account.

(4) All expenses incurred by the consignors in connection with dispatch of the goods will be debited to the Consignment Account. This account will be furnished with memorandum columns to record the invoice price of the goods and, where necessary, the foreign currency.

(5) On receipt of details regarding the results of the transaction the Consignment Account will be debited with all expenses incurred by the consignee in connection therewith, including commission on the realization. These will be credited to the consignee's Personal Account. The gross proceeds will be debited to the consignee and credited to the Consignment Account.

(6) Should all the goods have been disposed of the balance on the Consignment Account, which will represent a profit in the case of a credit balance and a loss in the case of a debit balance, will be transferred to a Profit and Loss on Consignment Account.

(7) On receipt of the proceeds from the consignee, his account will be credited in the usual way and Cash or Bills Receivable debited.

(8) At the end of the financial period, in the case of any consignment not completely disposed of, stock must be brought down on the Consignment Account before Profit or Loss can be computed. The amount of stock unsold must be brought down plus any charges directly attributable thereto, such as cost of dispatch, landing charges, duties, etc. No proportion of the selling expenses, however, must be included, such as commission and carriage outwards. After the balance of stock has been brought down the Profit or Loss on Consignment will be the balancing figure.

(9) Where the net realisable value of the goods unsold has fallen below the figure of cost plus charges attributable, the stock should be brought down at this lower figure. This will have the effect of decreasing the profit or increasing the loss on the consignment.

(10) At the end of the financial year the Profit or Loss on Consignment Account balance will be transferred to the general Profit and Loss Account, the stocks brought down on the Consignment Accounts will appear as assets in the Balance Sheet, and the balance of Goods on Consignment Account will be credited to Trading Account.

(11) Profits (or losses) on exchange, if any, will be transferred to the credit (or debit) of Profit and Loss on Exchange Account, or Reserve.

7.   DICKENS'S JOURNAL

		£	£
Consignment Account . . . . . *Dr.*		2,200	
To Goods sent on Consignment Account . . .			2,000
„ Cash Account			200
Being goods consigned to Jones in Gibraltar and Freight and Insurance thereon.			
Bills Receivable . . . . *Dr.*		2,000	
To Jones			2,000
Bill for 60 days drawn on Jones this day.			
Jones . . . . *Dr.*		2,950	
Consignment Account—Jones's expenses . . *Dr.*		200	
Jones's commission . . *Dr.*		350	
To Consignment Account—Sales . . .			3,500
Being sale by Jones of nine-tenths of consignment and his expenses and commission of 10 per cent on sales in respect thereof.			
Stock on Consignment Account . . . . *Dr.*		220	
To Consignment Account			220
Being stock at this date in Jones's hands at cost (£200) plus freight and insurance applicable thereto (£20).			
Consignment Account . . . . . *Dr.*		970	
To Profit and Loss Account			970
Being transfer of Profit made on Consignment to Jones to date.			
Bills Receivable . . . . *Dr.*		950	
To Jones			950
Being sight draft from Jones for balance of account.			
Goods sent on Consignment Account . . . *Dr.*		2,000	
To Purchases Account			2,000
Being transfer of balance.			

JONES'S JOURNAL

		£	£
Dickens . . . . *Dr.*		2,000	
To Bills Payable			2,000
Being bill for 60 days drawn by Dickens and accepted this date.			
Dickens . . . . *Dr.*		550	
To Cash—Expenses			200
„ Commission Account			350
Being expenses (£200) incurred in connection with Consignment from Dickens and Commission of £350 in respect thereof.			
Cash . . . . *Dr.*		3,500	
To Dickens			3,500
Being sales in respect of Consignment from Dickens.			
Dickens . . . . *Dr.*		950	
To Bills Payable			950
Being sight draft for balance of account sent this day.			

CHAPTER XVIII

Elizabeth Garage Co.

1. DEPARTMENTAL TRADING ACCOUNTS FOR THE YEAR ENDED
31ST DECEMBER, 19..

Car Trading Department

		£			£
Purchases	. . . .	25,000	Sales	. . . . .	29,500
Carriage	. . . .	230			
Gross Profit	. . . c/d	4,270			
		£29,500			£29,500

Hire Department

		£			£
Expenses—Hire Cars	. . .	450	Customers	. . .	810
Depreciation—Hire Cars	. .	260			
Gross Profit	. . . c/d	100			
		£810			£810

Repairs Department

		£			£
Cost of Repairs			Customers	. . .	1,900
(Material, Wages, etc.)	. .	1,750			
Repairs to Plant	. . .	54			
Depreciation—					
Loose Plant and Tools	.	90			
Gross Profit	. . . c/d	6			
		£1,900			£1,900

Petrol, Oil, etc., Department

		£			£
Petrol, Oil, etc., used	. .	1,250	Sales	. . .	1,950
Yard Wages	. . .	310			
Gross Profit	. . . c/d	390			
		£1,950			£1,950

Accessories Department

		£			£
Accessories used			Sales	. . .	5,470
(Tubes, Tyres, etc.)	. . c/d	4,700			
Gross Profit	. . .	770			
		£5,470			£5,470

PROFIT AND LOSS ACCOUNT FOR THE YEAR ENDED
31ST DECEMBER, 19..

		£				£
Salaries	. . . . .	1,020	Gross Profit—		b/d	
Bad Debts	. . . .	150	Car Trading	. . .	£4,270	
Loan Interest	. . . .	250	Hire	. . .	100	
Depreciation—			Repairs	. . .	6	
Fixtures and Fittings	. . .	8	Petrol, Oil, etc.	. .	390	
			Accessories	. .	770	
		1,428				5,536
Manager's Commission—			Sundry Receipts	. .		330
5% of £4,398[1]	. . . .	220	Garage Rents	. . .		180
Net Profit	. . . c/d	4,398				
		£6,046				£6,046
Balance	. . . . c/f	5,698	Balance	. . . .	b/f	1,300
			,,	. . . .	b/d	4,398
		£5,698				£5,698
			,,	. . . .	b/f	5,698

Notes. (i) It has been assumed that Loan Interest is a debit item.

(ii) Depreciation of loose plant and tools and Repairs to plant are assumed to be charged to Repairs Department.

(iii) No indication of internal transfers is given, e.g. petrol and accessories used in repair and other departments, cost of repairs to Hire Cars.

If the firm owns its premises (as would appear) an allocation should be made to each department for Rent, the total being credited to Profit and Loss Account.

(iv) As the question indicates Petrol, etc., and Accessories used and the closing Stocks have already been credited, hence the item £750 Stock of Accessories is not again credited, but will appear in the Balance Sheet as an asset.

(v) No closing stock of Petrol is given in question. This information would be essential if a Balance Sheet was required.

[1] $\frac{1}{21}$ of £4,618 (i.e. £6,046 — £1,428).

2. DEPARTMENTAL TRADING ACCOUNTS FOR THE THREE MONTHS ENDED 30TH SEPTEMBER, 19 ..

	Mail	Town	Country	Foreign		Mail	Town	Country	Foreign
	£	£	£	£		£	£	£	£
Stocks (opening)	2,500	3,500	1,000	500	Sales	6,000	3,500	3,000	500
Purchases	3,000	2,500	2,000	1,000	Stocks (closing) (est.)	1,900	3,550	750	1,100
Gross Profit c/d	2,400	1,050	750	100					
	£7,900	£7,050	£3,750	£1,600		£7,900	£7,050	£3,750	£1,600
Direct Expenses c/d	1,000	750	350	300	Gross Profit b/d	2,400	1,050	750	100
Profit c/d	1,400	300	400		Loss c/d				200
	£2,400	£1,050	£750	£300		£2,400	£1,050	£750	£300
Loss b/d				200	Profit b/d	1,400	300	400	

GENERAL TRIAL BALANCE AT 30TH SEPTEMBER, 19..

	£	£
Cash at Bank	9,100	
Sundry Debtors	8,500	
Stock-in-trade (closing).	7,300	
Fixtures and Fittings	2,437	
Machinery and Plant	9,500	
Indirect Expenses.	1,000	
Interest on Loan	6	
„ „ Capital	313	
Depreciation—	£	
Machinery and Plant. 500		
Fixtures and Fittings. 63		
	563	
Departmental Profits (Net)		1,900
Sundry Creditors.		7,506
Partners' Current Accounts		4,313
Partners' Capital Accounts		25,000
	£38,719	£38,719

3.　　　　　　　　　　STORES CONSUMED

	Wines	Spirits	Beers	Min-erals	Cigars and Cigar-ettes	Sundry Pro-visions and Stores	Fish and Poultry	Meat
	£	£	£	£	£	£	£	£
Stocks, 1st January 19.. . .	413	126	55	49	38	61		
Add Purchases .	627	730	384	350	80	1,740	1,320	1,209
	1,040	856	439	399	118	1,801	1,320	1,209
Less Stocks, 31st December, 19..	399	111	58	119	23	47		
Stores Consumed .	£641	£745	£381	£280	£95	£1,754	£1,320	£1,209

TRADING AND PROFIT AND LOSS ACCOUNT
FOR THE YEAR ENDED 31ST DECEMBER, 19..

	£	£		£	£
Stores Consumed—			Sales—		
Wines	641		Wines	1,290	
Spirits	745		Spirits	1,445	
Beers	381		Beers	621	
Minerals	280		Minerals . . .	720	
Cigars and Cigarettes . .	95		Cigars and Cigarettes .	130	
Sundry Provisions and Stores .	1,754				4,206
Fish and Poultry . . .	1,320		Meals	£7,943	
Meat	1,209		Rooms	3,125	
		6,425	Fires	194	
Wages		1,435	Laundering . . .	73	
Heating		737			11,335
Electric Light		376			
Rates, Taxes, and Insurance . .		571			
Laundry		317			
Gross Profit	c/d	5,680			
		£15,541			£15,541
Salaries		800	Gross Profit	b/d	5,680
General Expenses . . .		570			
Repairs Renewals, and Depreciation—					
Premises . . .	£116				
Furniture and Fittings . .	220				
Glass and China . .	203				
Linen	130				
Cutlery and Plate . .	69				
		738			
Net Profit to Capital Account . .		3,572			
		£5,680			£5,680

BALANCE SHEET AS AT 31ST DECEMBER, 19..

	£	£			£
Capital Account—			Fixed Assets—		
Balance 1st January, 19..	18,895		Freehold Premises. . . .		15,600
Less Drawings . .	2,500		Furniture and Fittings . . .		2,978
	16,395		Glass and China		367
Add Net Profit per Profit and Loss Account .	3,572		Linen		280
			Cutlery and Plate		130
		19,967			19,355
Sundry Creditors		1,130	Current Assets—		
			Stocks on hand (*a*) . .	£790	
			Debtors . . .	163	
			Cash at Bank . .	716	
			„ in hand . .	73	
					1,742
		£21,097			£21,097

Note (*a*) Stocks per Departmental Section £710, plus Provisions £47, plus Solid Fuel £33 = £790.

Alternatively, the Trading and Profit and Loss Account may be shown as follows—

TRADING AND PROFIT AND LOSS ACCOUNT FOR THE YEAR ENDED 31ST DECEMBER, 19..

	Wines	Spirits	Beers	Minerals	Cigars and Cigarettes	Total
	£	£	£	£	£	£
Stocks	413	126	55	49	38	681
Purchases	627	730	384	350	80	2,171
Balances c/d	649	700	240	440	35	2,064
	£1,689	£1,556	£679	£839	£153	£4,916

	Wines	Spirits	Beers	Minerals	Cigars and Cigarettes	Total
	£	£	£	£	£	£
Sales	1,290	1,445	621	720	130	4,206
Stocks (a)	399	111	58	119	23	710
	£1,689	£1,556	£679	£839	£153	£4,916

Debit	£	£	Credit	£	£
Meat		1,209	Balances	b/d.	
Fish and Poultry		1,320	Wines	649	
Provisions and Stores [£61 + £1,740 − £471] (a)		1,754	Spirits	700	
Glass and China		203	Beers	240	
Linen		130	Minerals	440	
Cutlery and Plate		69	Cigars and Cigarettes	55	2,064
Laundry		317	Meals		7,943
Heating [£50 + £720 − £33] (a)		737	Rooms		3,125
Electric Light		376	Fires Charged		194
Salaries		800	Laundering Charged.		73
Wages		1,435			
Rates, Taxes, and Insurance		571			
General Expenses		570			
Repairs, Renewals, and Depreciation—					
Premises	£116				
Furniture and Fittings	220	336			
Net Profit to Capital Account		3,572			
		£13,399			£13,399

(a) See note (a) on page 327.

328

DEPARTMENTAL TRADING AND PROFIT AND LOSS ACCOUNTS FOR THE YEAR ENDED 30TH JUNE, 19..

4.

	Dept. A	Dept. B	Total		Dept. A	Dept. B	Total
	£	£	£		£	£	£
Stock	1,140	980	2,120	Sales, *less* Returns	7,050	6,350	13,400
Purchases	3,960	3,740	7,700	Transfers	250		250
Carriage Inwards[1]	160	80	240	Stock	2,960	1,700	4,660
Transfers		250	250				
Gross Profit c/d	5,000	3,000	8,000				
	£10,260	£8,050	£18,060		£10,260	£8,050	£18,060
Wages and Salaries	1,100	550	1,650	Gross Profit b/d	5,000	3,000	8,000
Advertising and Catalogues	540	270	810				
Rent, Rates, Taxes, and Lighting	1,220	610	1,830				
Sundry Expenses	520	260	780				
Bad Debts[2]	190	95	285				
Depreciation	100	50	150				
Balances c/d	1,330	1,165	2,495				
	£5,000	£3,000	£8,000		£5,000	£3,000	£8,000
Net Profit to Current Account			2,600	Balances—			
				Dept. A	b/d 1,330		
				Dept. B	b/d 1,165		2,495
				Dividends received			105
			£2,600				£2,600

[1] *All* expenses are to be allocated, in the ratio 2:1 but Carriage Inwards may more properly be allocated according to purchases.
[2] Bad Debts written off, £120, plus increased provision, £165.

BLACK

BALANCE SHEET AS AT 30TH JUNE, 19..

	£	£		£	£
Capital Account		10,000	*Fixed Assets*		
Current Account—			Shares in X Y & Co. Ltd. (at cost?) .		2,300
Net Profit per Profit and			Furniture and Fixtures . . 1,500		
Loss Account . . 2,600			*Less* Depreciation . . . 150		
Less Drawings . . 2,000					1,350
		600			3,650
Sundry Creditors. . . 2,974					
Expenses Outstanding . . 40			*Current Assets*		
		3,014	Stock-in-trade—		
			Department A . . 2,960		
			„ B . . 1,700		
					4,660
			Catalogues in hand		60
			Sundry Debtors . . . 4,800		
			Less Provision for Bad and		
			Doubtful Debts . . 240		
					4,560
			Bank Balance		684
		£13,614			£13,614

5. TRADING AND PROFIT AND LOSS ACCOUNT FOR THE YEAR ENDED 30TH JUNE, 19.. .

Debit side

	Pictures £	Pottery £	Total £
Stock	94,427	33,155	127,582
Purchases	97,028	52,318	149,346
Renovation and Framing Expenses—			
Wages and Salaries	525		525
Workshop Expenses	293		293
Packing Materials and Carriage	633	211	844
Balance c/d	25,193	7,191	32,384
	£218,099	£92,875	£310,974
Commissions Paid	1,074	238	1,312
Balance c/d	27,350	7,550	34,900
	£28,424	£7,788	£36,212
Salaries and Wages	3,354	1,118	4,472
Rent and Rates	5,241	1,747	6,988
Heating, Lighting, and Insurance	693	231	924
Advertising	2,325	775	3,100
Catalogues [£63 + £9]	54	18	72
Office and Trade Expenses	1,005	335	1,340
Repairs to Buildings	123	41	164
Travelling Expenses	231	77	308
Directors' Fees	450	150	600
Bad Debts	561	187	748
Depreciation of Lease	1,800	600	2,400
„ „ Fixtures and Fittings	189	63	252
Debenture Interest	1,969	656	2,625
Net Profit c/d	9,355	1,552	10,907
	£27,350	£7,550	£34,900
Debenture Discount			1,000
Redemption Fund			5,000
Interim Dividend on Preference Shares			750
Balance c/f			6,494
			£13,244

Credit side

	Pictures £	Pottery £	Total £
Sales	118,416	38,557	156,973
Stock	99,683	54,318	154,001
	£218,099	£92,875	£310,974
Balance b/d	25,193	7,191	32,384
Commissions Received	3,231	597	3,828
	£28,424	£7,788	£36,212
Balance b/d	27,350	7,550	34,900
	£27,350	£7,550	£34,900
Balance b/f			2,337
Net Profit—			
Pictures b/d		£9,355	
Pottery b/d		1,552	10,907
			£13,244

331

ART SALES LTD.

BALANCE SHEET AS AT 30TH JUNE, 19..

	£			£
Capital and Surplus—		**Fixed Assets—**		
Share Capital—Authorized, Issued and fully-paid:		Goodwill		15,000
		Lease:		
25,000 6% Preference Shares of £1 each	25,000	Balance at 1st July, 19.. £19,200		
125,000 Ordinary Shares of £1 each	125,000	*Less* written off during the year (⅛) .	2,400	
	150,000			16,800
Debenture Redemption Fund:		Fixtures and Fittings:		
Balance at 1st July, 19.. £25,000		Balance at 1st July, 19.. £3,100		
Add Appropriation made during the year . 5,000		*Add* Purchases during the year . .	260	
	30,000		3,360	
Profit and Loss Account . .	6,494	*Less* Depreciation (7½%)	252	
	186,494			3,108
				34,908
5% Debentures—		**Current Assets—**		
Balance at 1st July, 19... £55,000		Stock:		
Less repaid during the year 5,000		Pictures . . . £99,683		
	50,000	Pottery . . 54,318		
Current Liabilities—			154,001	
Trade Creditors . . £15,191		Packing Material . £37		
Expenses accruing:		Catalogues . . 45		
Heating and Lighting £107			82	
Office Expenses . . 22			154,083	
Advertising. . .146		Sundry Debtors . £53,600		
	275	*Less* Provision (1%) 536		
	15,466		53,064	
		Rates prepaid . .	312	
		Cash at Bank . .	7,374	
		Cash in hand . .	219	
				215,052
		Debenture Discount—		
		Balance at 1st July, 19.. £3,000		
		Less written off during the year . . .	1,000	
				2,000
	£251,960			**£251,960**

Notes.

<table>
<tr><th colspan="2">TRIAL BALANCE</th><th>Dr.</th><th>Cr.</th></tr>
<tr><td></td><td>£</td><td>£</td><td>£</td></tr>
<tr><td>Total per List of Balances . . . .</td><td>604,033</td><td></td><td></td></tr>
<tr><td>*Less* Credits—   £</td><td></td><td></td><td></td></tr>
<tr><td>Debenture Redemption Fund . . . . 25,000</td><td></td><td></td><td></td></tr>
<tr><td>Sales . . . . . . 156,973</td><td></td><td></td><td></td></tr>
<tr><td>Commissions Received . . . . 3,828</td><td></td><td></td><td></td></tr>
<tr><td>Creditors . . . . . . 15,191</td><td></td><td></td><td></td></tr>
<tr><td>Profit and Loss Account . . . . 2,337</td><td></td><td></td><td></td></tr>
<tr><td></td><td>203,329</td><td></td><td></td></tr>
<tr><td></td><td></td><td>400,704</td><td>203,329</td></tr>
<tr><td>*Add* Ledger items not in List—</td><td></td><td></td><td></td></tr>
<tr><td>Share Capital . . . .</td><td></td><td></td><td>150,000</td></tr>
<tr><td>5% Debentures . . . .</td><td></td><td></td><td>50,000</td></tr>
<tr><td>Debenture Interest . . . .</td><td></td><td>2,625</td><td></td></tr>
<tr><td></td><td></td><td>**£403,329**</td><td>**£403,329**</td></tr>
</table>

Debenture Interest—		£
Half-year's Interest on £55,000 at 5% per annum		1,375
,, ,, £50,000 ,, ...		1,250
		£2,625

Catalogues—					£	
Opening Stock	.	.	.	.	390 at 30p =	117
Less Distributed	.	.	.	.	210 at 30p =	63 (Dr. P. and L.)
Balance	.	.	.	.	180 at 30p =	54
Less Loss 180 at 5p	.	.	.		=	9 (Dr. P. and L.)
Closing Stock	.	.	.	.	180 at 25p =	£45 (Asset)

Adjustments—

	Heating, Etc.	Office Expenses	Adver- tising	Rates, Etc.
	£	£	£	£
Per Trial Balance	817	1,318	2,954	7,300
Accruals (Liabilities)	+ 107	+ 22	+ 146	
Prepayment (Asset)				− 312
Profit and Loss Account	£924	£1,340	£3,100	£6,988

6. As there are "cross" charges each dependent upon the other, it is essential to make the computation by algebra, thus—

Let cost of water be represented by W; and cost of electricity by E, then

$$E = 500 + \tfrac{2}{5}W, \text{ and } W = 200 + \tfrac{1}{4}E$$

∴

$E = 500 + \tfrac{2}{5}(200 + \tfrac{1}{4}E)$ OR	$W = 200 + \tfrac{1}{4}(500 + \tfrac{2}{5}W)$
$= 500 + 80 + \tfrac{1}{10}E$	$= 200 + 125 + \tfrac{1}{10}W$
$= 580 + \tfrac{1}{10}E$	$= 325 + \tfrac{1}{10}W$
$10E = 5800 + E$	$10W = 3250 + W$
$9E = 5800$	$9W = 3250$
$E = £644 \text{ (to nearest £)}$	$W = £361 \text{ (to nearest £)}$

As **total** cost of E is £644, the charge for water is £144 (£644 − £500).

As **total** cost of W is £361 the charge for electricity is £161 (£361 − £200).

Electricity					£
General cost	.	.	.	.	500
Cost of own electricity used = $\tfrac{1}{4}$					
× **£644**	.	.	.	.	**161**
Charge for water	.	.	.	.	144
					£805

Water				£
General cost.	.	.	.	200
Charge for electricity	.	.	.	161
				£361

	£
Transfer (300,000 units) to Factory	
($\tfrac{3}{5}$ × £805)	483
Transfer (100,000 units) to Electricity	
($\tfrac{1}{5}$ × £805)	161
Supplied to Splash Ltd. ($\tfrac{1}{5}$ × £805) .	161
	£805

	£
Transfer to Factory ($\tfrac{3}{5}$)	. 217
Supplied to Flash Ltd. ($\tfrac{2}{5}$)	. 144
	£361

Note. As the 100,000 units of electricity used by generating department is merely a contra, it need not be brought into the foregoing calculations. It can be seen that such cost is $\tfrac{1}{5}$ × £805 = £161, and this itself is part of the cost, so that the remainder of the units is $\tfrac{4}{5}$ × £805 = £644 allocated as $\tfrac{3}{8}$ (£483) to Factory; $\tfrac{1}{8}$ (£161) to Splash Ltd. This is the same result as $\tfrac{3}{4}$ × £644 (£483) and $\tfrac{1}{4}$ × £644 (£161).

7.

STATEMENT OF COST ALLOCATIONS
FOR THE YEAR ENDED 31ST DECEMBER, 19..

	Total	Allocation Basis	A	B	Boiler Room	Office
	£		£	£	£	£
Indirect Wages . .	20,000	Actual . . .	12,000	5,200	1,700	1,100
Rent and Rates . .	1,000	Floor space . .	500	300	100	100
Depreciation—						
Machinery . .	2,000	Per question . .	900	600	400	100
Buildings . . .	400	Floor space . .	200	120	40	40
Repairs—						
Machinery . .	2,940	Depreciation basis except office which is actual . . .	1,350	900	600	90
Buildings . . .	1,500	Floor space . . .	750	450	150	150
Insurance—						
Machinery . .	290	Depreciation except office which is actual .	135	90	60	5
Buildings . . .	200	Floor space . .	100	60	20	20
Coal and Water . .	2,311	Actual . . .			2,311	
Cleaning Materials—						
Machinery . .	190	Depreciation . .	90	60	40	
Buildings . . .	240	Floor space . .	120	72	24	24
Printing, Postage, etc. .	201	Actual . . .				201
Space Light and Heat .		Floor space . .	100	60[1]	−180	20
					5,265	1,850
Power . . .		Transfer A ⅔; B ⅓ .	3,510	1,755	−5,265	
Cost Office . . .		Equally to A and B .	925	925		−1,850
	£31,272		£20,680	£10,592		

[1] Space, heat and light.

	A £	B £	Boiler £	Office £
Per question (£200)	¹⁄₁₀ 100	⁶⁄₁₀ 60	¹⁄₁₀ 20	¹⁄₁₀ 20
Charged out			200	
	+£100	+£60	−180	+£20

This is an interdepartmental adjustment and does enter into the total.

	Total £	A £	B £
Materials used (outside purchases) . . .	59,623	38,258	21,365
Direct Wages	39,105	21,062	18,043
Overhead Charges	31,272	20,680	10,592
	£130,000	£80,000	£50,000

Computation of transfer of Finished Goods to be used in other Factory Departments—

Let $\quad$ A = TOTAL Cost (i.e. including the cost of Goods from B)

and $\quad$ B = ,, ,, $\frac{1}{10}$,, ,, ,, ,, ,, ,, A)

$$A = 80,000 + \tfrac{1}{10}(B)$$
$$B = 50,000 + \tfrac{1}{5}(A)$$
$$10A = 800,000 + B$$

substituting—

$$10A = 800,000 + 50,000 + \frac{A}{5}$$
$$= 850,000 + \frac{A}{5}$$
$$50A = 4,250,000 + A$$
$$49A = 4,250,000$$
$$A = £86,735$$

		£
	As the **total** cost is	86,735
and	Cost (*before* transfer) . . .	80,000
	Transfer Cost of B goods to A . .	£6,735

There is no need to compute separately the total cost to B as it can be computed from the information now available thus—

	Total £	A £	B £
Cost (before transfer)	130,000	80,000	50,000
Transfer from B		6,735	
Transfer from A			17,347
Total Cost.		86,735	67,347
of which $\frac{1}{5}$ transferred to B		17,347	
of which $\frac{1}{10}$ transferred to A			6,735
	£130,000	£69,388	£60,612

DEPARTMENTAL SUMMARY OF COST AND PROFIT
FOR THE YEAR ENDED 31ST DECEMBER, 19..

	A £	B £	Total £
Cost of materials *before* transfer . . .	38,258	21,365	59,623
Transfers (as below)	6,735	17,347	24,082
Cost of materials including transfers . . .	44,993	38,712	83,705
Direct Wages	21,062	18,043	39,105
Overhead charges	20,680	10,592	31,272
Total Cost, subject to deduction for transfers . .	86,735	67,347	154,082
Transfers (as above)	17,347	6,735	24,082
Total Cost	69,388	60,612	130,000
Add 20 per cent	13,877	12,123	26,000
Transfer price to Selling Departments . .	£83,265	£72,735	£156,000

(If the reader wishes to work from B instead of A, the total cost of B will be calculated—

$$B = 50,000 + \tfrac{1}{5}A$$
$$5B = 250,000 + A$$
but $$A = 80,000 + \tfrac{1}{10}B$$

substituting—

$$5B = 250,000 + 80,000 + \tfrac{1}{10}B$$
$$= 330,000 + \tfrac{1}{10}B$$
$$50B = 3,300,000 + B$$
$$49B = 3,300,000 \qquad = 67,347$$

As the cost of B goods excluding transfer from A is . 50,000

Transfer from A £17,347

8.   Let A = Total Cost to A
          and B = Total Cost to B
          $A = 3,000 + \tfrac{1}{8}B + \tfrac{2}{125}A$ (See note page 336)

proceed either—

(1)	*or*	(2)
$6A = 18,000 + B + \tfrac{12}{125}A$		$125A = 375,000 + \tfrac{125}{8}B + 2A$
$750A = 2,250,000 + 125B + 12A$		$123A = 375,000 + \tfrac{125}{8}B$
$738A = 2,250,000 + 125B$		$738A = 2,250,000 + 125B$
		(from here the working is the same)
but $B = \dfrac{30,000 + 6A}{29}$ (see page 336)	but	$B = \dfrac{30,000 + 6A}{29}$ as in (1)

substituting—

$$738A = 2,250,000 + 125 \left(\frac{30,000 + 6A}{29} \right)$$
$$21,402A = 65,250,000 + 3,750,000 + 750A$$
$$20,652A = 69,000,000$$
$$= £3,341^1$$

B as shown above is computed—

$$B = 1,000 + \tfrac{1}{6}A + \tfrac{4}{120}B$$
$$= 1,000 + \tfrac{1}{6}A + \tfrac{1}{30}B$$
$$30B = 30,000 + 6A + B$$
$$29B = 30,000 + 6A$$
$$B = \frac{30,000 + 6A}{29}$$

[See page 335.]

(This note forms no part of answer, but from the answer the above total for B is verified.)

$$B = \frac{30,000 + 6 \times 3,341^1}{29}$$

$$\frac{30,000 + 20,046}{29} = \frac{50,046}{29}$$

$$= £1,725$$

STATEMENT OF DEPARTMENTAL COST AND PROFIT OF FACTORY

	A £		B £	Total £
Cost (before Commission and Transfer) . .	3,000		1,000	4,000
Add Transfer B Goods to A	287			
„ „ *A* „ „ *B* . . .			668	
Manager's Commission (10% of £534) . .	54	20% of £287	57	111
	3,341		1,725	
Less Transfers.	668		287	
Cost of Factory Goods delivered to Selling Departments	2,673		1,438	4,111
Add 20% of Cost (¼ of "Selling" i.e. Invoice Price to Selling Departments)	534		287¹	821
Invoice price of Factory Goods to Selling Departments	£3,207		£1,725	£4,932

The total invoice price to the Selling Departments is £4,932 of which 16⅔ per cent (or ⅙) thereof is "loading," i.e. ⅙ × £4,932 = £822, the odd £1 difference being attributable to taking the departmental profits to nearest £.

In computing the unknown components, viz. Transfers and Commissions, the aim is to arrive at total cost to either department, i.e. Cost "before" *plus* Transfers and Commissions. Therefrom flows the requisite remaining figures (there is no need to calculate both). It is immaterial whether the department chosen for the "key" figure is A or B.

Note. In the workings A has been taken for the basic calculation.

---

¹ A = £3,341 as above.
² Apart from commission which has not been charged in arriving at the cost of Departments A and B, the other adjustments are internal, so that the only addition to the cost of £4,000 is the commission of £111, hence a final total cost of £4,111.

9.   ORCHARD

(a)   TRADING AND PROFIT AND LOSS ACCOUNT
                 FOR YEAR ENDED 31ST DECEMBER, 19.8

	Farm £	Cannery £		Farm £	Cannery £
Opening Stocks . . .	400	1,650	Sales	530	9,950
Purchases . . .	250	1,190	Fruit transferred to Can-		
Fruit from Farm . .		2,200	nery	2,200	
Wages	1,600	2,400	Closing Stocks . . .	300	1,720
Depreciation of Plant and					
Machinery . . .	210	360			
Gross Profit . . c/d	570	3,870			
	£3,030	£11,670		£3,030	£11,670
Salaries	350	1,050	Gross Profit . . b/d	570	3,870
Pippin, Commission—5%			Loss for year . . c/d	260	
on £1,200 . . .		60			
Repairs	80	360			
Trade Expenses . .	250	750			
Administration and Motor					
Expenses . . .	30	90			
Interest on Loan . .	120	360			
Net Trading Profit for year					
c/d		1,200			
	£830	£3,870		£830	£3,870

		£			£
Loss on Farm . . . b/d		260	Net Profit of Cannery . . b/d		1,200
Net Profit for year transferred to Capital			Profit on sale of Tractor . . .		200
Account		1,590	,, ,, ,, ,, Freehold Land . .		450
		£1,850			£1,850

                                  ORCHARD

(b)   BALANCE SHEET AS AT 31ST DECEMBER, 19.8

		£			£
Orchard, Capital Account—			*Fixed Assets—*		
Balance at 1st January, 19.8 . .		13,500	Freehold Land and Premises at cost .		14,550
Add Net Profit for year . .		1,590	Plant and Machinery—		
		15,090	Farm at cost . .	£2,100	
			Less Provision for Depreci-		
Less Drawings . .	£1,200		ation . . .	810	
Charge for private use					1,290
of car . .	104		Cannery at cost . .	£4,800	
		1,304	*Less* Provision for Depreci-		
		13,786	ation . . .	2,000	
Loan at 6 per cent . . .		8,000			2,800
Current Liabilities—			Fruit Trees and Bushes, at cost . .		800
Trade Creditors—					19,440
Farm . . .	£200				
Cannery . . .	720		*Current Assets—*		
	920		Balance at Bank . .	£864	
Accruals . . .	260		Sundry Debtors . .	642	
		1,180	Stocks on hand . .	2,020	
					3,526
		£22,966			£22,966

WORKING SCHEDULES

	£			£
(1) Plant and Machinery—Farm	1,900	(4) Bought Ledger Balances—		
Less Plant sold, at cost .	600	Cannery . . .	.	740
	———	Add Outstandings .	.	140
	1,300			———
New Plant at cost . .	800			880
		Less Allowance on sub-		
		standard cans . .	.	160
	———			———
	£2,100			£720

	£			£
(2) Provision for Depreciation—		(5) Administration and Motor		
Farm	1,100	Expenses . . .	.	584
Less Depreciation on Plant		Less Loan interest (9 months).		360
sold	500			———
	———			224
	600			
Depreciation for year — 10%		Less charged to Orchard for		
on £2,100 . . .	210	private use of car .	.	104
	———			———
	£810			£120

	£			£
(3) Purchases—Cannery . .	1,210	(6) Loan Interest . . .	.	480
Add Outstandings . .	140			
	———			£
	1,350	(7) Accruals—		
Less Allowance on substan-		Trade Expenses . .	.	80
dard cans . . .	160	Loan Interest . .	.	120
	———	Commission . .	.	60
	£1,190			———
				£260

CHAPTER XIX

1. THE method adopted of converting all the items in the French and Brazilian Trial Balances to sterling at the exchange rates ruling on 31st December cannot be considered to be an accurate treatment. The rates ruling at the end of the year may be quite abnormal, due to temporary causes, and results obtained by adopting such rates may be quite at variance with results that would have been obtained by adopting a more accurate and scientific basis of conversion giving a true reflection of the trading of the branches in the light of rates of exchange obtaining throughout the period.

It is submitted that, according to whether the exchange in question is of a stable or fluctuating nature, the following methods would be preferable to that employed.

(1) Where the exchange is stable: To convert all the items at a fixed rate, any difference arising from remittances at a different rate to be transferred to Profit and Loss on Exchange Account.

(2) Where the exchange is widely fluctuating: To adopt Method (1) and make periodic adjustments if a permanent move takes place in either direction.

(3) Where the exchange is fluctuating within narrow limits: To convert all the items at different rates according to their nature—

Fixed Assets. At the rate ruling at date of contract, delivery, payment(s) or of remittance therefor.

Long-term Liabilities. At rate ruling at date of contract, or date incurred. If the long-term liabilities are payable in the foreign currency and are not in sterling, it is considered preferable to convert them at the rate ruling at each year-end, particularly if a change in the rate has increased the ultimate liability; in this way the liabilities are, so to speak, kept up to date and each Balance Sheet shows as true a state of affairs as possible; moreover, the "final" period in which the liabilities are repaid does not stand a large loss on exchange.

Current Assets and Liabilities. At rate ruling at the end of the accounting period.

Remittances. At actual rates.

Transfer of Goods. At rate ruling at date of dispatch.

Profit and Loss Items. At average or weighted average rate ruling over the whole period, save for depreciation of fixed assets which will be taken at rate ruling at the date of acquiring the asset; and opening and closing stocks which will be taken at the opening and closing rates.

Any difference arising in the Trial Balance under this method will be transferred to Profit and Loss on Exchange Account.

Note. An important point to consider is that in many countries there is a rigid control of foreign exchange, and as a result transferences of funds abroad can only be effected through official channels. In some cases two rates are in use, an official rate and a "free" market rate, a proportion of remittances being allowed to be converted at the latter rate.

2. In the case of a plantation of this kind it is customary to transfer capital expenditure at the end of each annual period to the books of the head office, leaving only the current assets in the books of the branch.

It would seem that the best method to adopt in this case is to convert the various items in the Trial Balance at different rates according to their nature, although this method may be quite inadequate to meet the situation where the currency moves permanently to a relatively higher or lower than normal figure.

However, assuming that this is not the case, the procedure will be as follows: to convert—

(*a*) Capital expenditure — at rate ruling when incurred.

(*b*) Revenue items — at average or weighted average rate for the period.

(*c*) Current assets and liabilities — at rate ruling at the close of the period.

(*d*) Remittances — at actual rate obtained.

This method will smooth out the effect of temporary fluctuations in the trading results, giving a true picture of the trading activities of the period. In the event of permanent depreciation a Provision will have to be created against the book value of

339

fixed assets. Any difference arising on the Trial Balance after conversion will be transferred to Profit and Loss on Exchange Account.

If the exchanges fluctuate so much as to render it impracticable to adopt the foregoing method (much depending upon the meaning in the question of "considerable" fluctuations) it would be preferable to have the whole of the assets kept in the Head Office books, and the receipts and payments of the Branch incorporated into the Head Office books at a fixed rate (see pages 1983–5 of *Accountancy*).

3. The necessary entries in Journal form are—

	£	£
India Branch Current Account . . . . . Dr.[1]	7,500	
To Bank		7,500
India Branch Current Account . . . . Dr.[1]	2,500	
To Bills Payable		2,500
Profit and Loss Account . . . . . Dr.	1,800	
To India Branch Current Account. . . .		1,800

4. (*a*) Unless there is a system in force whereby all transactions in lire are to be converted to sterling at a fixed rate—when such system will be followed—the invoices should be recorded in the books of L & Co. in both lire and sterling, being converted at the rate ruling at the date of the invoices.

(*b*) Remittances to the creditors will again be recorded in both lire and sterling. Any difference between the sterling cost of the goods recorded and the sterling cost of payment will represent a profit or loss on exchange, and will be transferred to a Profit and Loss on Exchange Account. The currency columns will be Memorandum only.

Payment can be made by—

(1) Sterling Bill.
(2) Lire Bill.
(3) By set-off against an amount owing to L & Co. by the creditor in question.

5. *Head Office books.*

Dr.　　　　　　　BIRMINGHAM BRANCH STOCK　　　　　　　Cr.

19..		£	19..			£
Jan. 1	To Stock . . . b/d	2,200	Dec. 31	By Debtors . . .		20,020
Dec. 31	,, Goods . . .	15,400		,, Stock . . . c/d		1,980
	,, Profit and Loss Account—					
	Gross Profit . .	4,400				
		£22,000				£22,000
19..						
Jan. 1	To Stock . . . b/d	1,980				

Dr.　　　　　BIRMINGHAM BRANCH ADJUSTMENT ACCOUNT　　　　　Cr.

19..		£	19..			£
Dec. 31	To Balance . . c/d	180	Jan. 1	By Balance . . b/d		200
	,, Profit and Loss Account—		Dec. 31	,, Goods Sent to Branches		
	Handling Charge . [2]1,420			Account . . .		1,400
		£1,600				£1,600
			19..			
			Jan. 1	By Balance . . b/d		180

[1] Or India Branch Remittance Account.
[2] Profit is $\frac{1}{11} \times$ (£20,020 − £4,400) = $\frac{1}{11} \times$ £15,620 = £1,420.

Dr.   BIRMINGHAM BRANCH DEBTORS   Cr.

19..				£	19..				£
Jan. 1	To Balances	.	b/d	80	Dec. 31	By Cash .	.	.	20,000
Dec. 31	,, Stock Account	.	.	20,020		,, Balances	.	c/d	100
				£20,100					£20,100
19..									
Jan. 1	To Balances	.	b/d	100					

Dr.   GOODS SENT TO BRANCHES   Cr.

19..			£	19..			£
Dec. 31	To Branch Adjustment Account	. .	1,400	Dec. 31	By Branch Stock	. .	15,400
	,, Trading Account	.	14,000				
			£15,400				£15,400

Dr.   CASH (includes)   Cr.

19..			£
Dec. 31	To Branch Debtors	. .	20,000

6. Dr.   BRANCH GOODS   Cr.

				£					£	£
To Balance (Opening)	.	.	b/d	1,500	By Sales—Credit	.	.	.	6,000	
,, Goods from H. O.	.	.	.	5,080	Cash	.	.	.	3,350	
,, Returns from Customers	.	.	.	58						9,350
,, Gross Profit to Branch Profit and Loss Account	.	.	c/f	4,172	,, Returns to H. O.	.	.	.		70
					,, Stock (Closing)	.	.	c/d		1,390
				£10,810						£10,810
To Stock (Opening)	.	.	b/d	1,390						

Dr.   BRANCH DEBTORS   Cr.

				£						£
To Balances (Opening)	.	.	b/d	2,620	By Returns	.	.	.	.	58
,, Sales	.	.	.	6,000	,, Allowances	.	.	.	.	32
					,, Cash	.	.	.	.	4,920
					,, Discounts	.	.	.	.	240
					,, Bad Debts	.	.	.	.	60
					,, Balances (Closing)	.	.	.	.	3,310
				£8,620						£8,620
To Balances (Opening)	.	.	b/d	3,310						

Dr.   BRANCH EXPENSES   Cr.

			£		£
To Rent, Rates, etc.	.	.	180	By Branch Profit and Loss Account	910
,, Wages and Salaries	.	.	600		
,, General Trade Charges	.	.	130		
			£910		£910

Dr.   BRANCH PROFIT AND LOSS ACCOUNT   Cr.

			£			£
To Branch Expenses	.	.	910	By Gross Profit from Branch Goods Account	b/f	4,172
,, Allowances	.	.	[1]32			
,, Discounts	.	.	240			
,, Bad Debts	.	.	60			
,, Net Profit	.	.	2,930			
			£4,172			£4,172

[1] This may alternatively be debited to Trading Account (Branch Goods Account).

7.

		Henley	Kingston	Sutton			Henley	Kingston	Sutton
19.. Jan. 1	To Balances . . b/d [Book Debts and Stock]	£ 3,500	£ 2,940	£ 1,930	19.. June 30	By Cash . . . ,, Balances . . c/d [Book Debts and Stock] ,, Net Loss . . .	£ 9,251 3,814	£ 11,319 2,773	£ 6,436 1,879 555
June 30	,, Goods . . . ,, Salaries and Expenses . ,, Rent and Rates . . ,, Net Profit . . .	5,998 1,604 304 1,659	7,602 2,659 581 310	5,438 1,240 262					
		£13,065	£14,092	£8,870			£13,065	£14,092	£8,870

Memorandum BRANCH TRADING AND PROFIT AND LOSS ACCOUNT FOR THE SIX MONTHS ENDED 30TH, JUNE 19..

		Henley	Kingston	Sutton			Henley	Kingston	Sutton
19.. Jan. 1 June 30	To Stock . . . ,, Purchases . . . ,, Gross Profit . c/d	£ 1,400 5,998 3,646	£ 1,280 7,602 3,612	£ 1,290 5,438 947	19.. June 30	By Credit Sales, *less* Returns . ,, Cash Sales . . . ,, Stock . . .	£ 6,358 3,011 1,675	£ 6,761 4,718 1,015	£ 4,637 1,633 1,405
		£11,044	£12,494	£7,675			£11,044	£12,494	£7,675
	To Salaries and Expenses . ,, Rent and Rates . . ,, Bad Debts . . . ,, Net Profit . . .	1,604 304 79 1,659	2,659 581 62 310	1,240 262		By Gross Profit . . b/d ,, Net Loss . . .	3,646	3,612	947 555
		£3,646	£3,612	£1,502			£3,646	£3,612	£1,502

Memorandum BRANCH DEBTORS ACCOUNT

		Henley	Kingston	Sutton			Henley	Kingston	Sutton
19.. Jan. 1 June 30	To Balances . . b/d ,, Sales . . .	£ 2,100 6,409	£ 1,660 6,815	£ 540 4,701	19.. June 30	By Cash . . . ,, Returns, etc. . . ,, Bad Debts . . . ,, Balances . . c/d	£ 6,240 51 79 2,139	£ 6,601 54 62 1,758	£ 4,803 64 474
		£8,509	£8,475	£5,341			£8,509	£8,475	£5,341

Accounts in full will be as follows—

BRANCH STOCK

		Henley	Kingston	Sutton			Henley	Kingston	Sutton
		£	£	£			£	£	£
19.. Jan. 1	To Stock . . . b/d	1,400	1,280	1,290	19.. June 30	By Sales— Credit	6,409	6,815	4,701
June 30	,, Goods . . .	5,998	7,602	5,438		Cash	3,011	4,718	1,633
	,, Returns and Allowances	51	54	64		,, Stock . . c/d	1,675	1,015	1,405
	,, Gross Profit transferred to Branch Profit and Loss Account	*3,646*	*3,612*	*947*					
		£11,095	£12,548	£7,739			£11,095	£12,548	£7,739
19.. July 1	To Stock . . . b/d	*1,675*	*1,015*	*1,405*					

BRANCH DEBTORS

		Henley	Kingston	Sutton			Henley	Kingston	Sutton
		£	£	£			£	£	£
19.. Jan. 1	To Balances . . b/d	2,100	1,660	640	19.. June 30	By Cash	6,240	6,601	4,803
June 30	,, Sales . . .	6,409	6,815	4,701		,, Returns and Allowances	51	54	64
						,, Bad Debts	79	62	
						,, Balances . . c/d	2,139	1,758	474
		£8,509	£8,475	£5,341			£8,509	£8,475	£5,341
19.. July 1	To Balances . . b/d	2,139	1,758	474					

BRANCH CASH

		Henley	Kingston	Sutton			Henley	Kingston	Sutton
		£	£	£			£	£	£
19.. June 30	To Debtors . .	6,240	6,601	4,803	19..				
	,, Sales . . .	3,011	4,718	1,633					

The items in italics will be posted to Branch Profit and Loss Account, giving the same result as shown in the Memorandum Account on page 342 above and on page 344.

Dr. BRANCH EXPENSES Cr.

		Henley £	Kingston £	Sutton £			Henley £	Kingston £	Sutton £
19.. June 30	To Salaries and Expenses	1,604	2,659	1,240	19.. June 30	By *Branch Profit and Loss Account*	*1,987*	*3,302*	*1,502*
	" Rent and Rates	304	581	262					
	" Bad Debts	79	62	—					
		£1,987	£3,302	£1,502			£1,987	£3,302	£1,502

Dr. GOODS SENT TO BRANCHES Cr.

		£
19.. June 30	By Stock Accounts—	
	Henley	5,998
	Kingston	7,602
	Sutton	5,438

The items in italics will be posted to Branch Profit and Loss Account in detail, giving the same result as shown in the Memorandum Account on page 342 above and on page 343.

8.

TRADING AND PROFIT AND LOSS ACCOUNTS FOR THE YEAR ENDED 31ST MARCH, 19..

	London £	Ipswich £	Ipswich (Invoice Price) £		London £	Ipswich £	Ipswich (Invoice Price) £
Stock	11,482	1,431	1,792 [1]	Sales	25,331	9,575	9,575
Purchases	28,724	6,305	7,715	Transfers to Branch	6,305	1,542	1,847
Gross Profit c/d	6,857	3,381	1,915	Stock	15,427		
	£47,063	£11,117	£11,422		£47,063	£11,117	£11,422
Salaries and Wages	2,280	846	846	Gross Profit b/d	6,857	3,381	1,915
Rent and Rates	743	212	212				
Sundry Expenses	656	157	157				
Depreciation— Furniture and Fittings	37	12	12				
Manager's Commission— ½—£688		344	344				
Net Profit	3,141	1,810	344				
	£6,857	£3,381	£1,915		£6,857	£3,381	£1,915

[1] £1,847 — £1,792 + [2](£9,575).   [2] 20 per cent of £9,575.

BALANCE SHEET AS AT 31ST MARCH, 19..

	£	£			£	£
Sundry Creditors—			*Current Assets*			
London. . .	931		Stock—			
Ipswich. . .	27		London . .	15,427		
Manager (Ipswich).	344		Ipswich . .	1,542		
		1,302				16,969
			Sundry Debtors—			
			London .	3,973		
			Ipswich .	1,438		
Capital	20,000					5,411
Add Profit—			Cash—			
London £3,141			London . .	1,793		
Ipswich . 1,810			Ipswich . .	49		
	4,951		In Transit .	100		
		24,951				1,942
			Fixed Assets			
			Furniture and Fittings			
			(*less* Depreciation)—			
			London . .	703		
			Ipswich . .	228		
						931
			Goodwill. . . .			1,000
		£26,253				£26,253

9. *Dr.*   LIVERPOOL BRANCH CURRENT ACCOUNT   *Cr.*

19..			£	19..				£
Apr. 1	To Balance . . b/d		18,750	Mar. 31	By Cash			29,800
19..					,, Returns . . .			423
Mar. 31	,, Goods . . .		22,025		,, Balance . . c/d			19,860
	,, Expenses . . .		5,832					
	,, Profit carried to Profit							
	and Loss Account .		3,476					
			£50,083					£50,083
Apr. 1	To Balance . . b/d		19,860					

The above account would appear in the Head Office books on the completion of the accounts for the year. The balance £19,860 represents the value of the Head Office's investment in the Liverpool Branch. This amount can be proved by ascertaining the assets and liabilities of the Liverpool Branch at 31st March, 19.., and finding the difference, which should be a surplus of assets over liabilities to the extent of £19,860.

If detailed proof of the composition of the account is required a Memorandum Trading and Profit and Loss Account will be drawn up with the aid of Branch Stock, Branch Debtors, and Branch Expenses Accounts.

10. *Dr.*   BRANCHES CURRENT ACCOUNT   *Cr.*

19..			£	19..			£
Dec. 31	To Balance . . b/d		60	Dec. 31	By Balance—	c/d	£
	,, Balance— c/d				Cash .	£1,500	
	Rent and Rates £6,320				Debts .	2,410	
	Salaries . 1,000				Stock .	20,400	
			7,320		Fittings .	9,900	
							34,210
	,, Profit carried to Profit						
	and Loss Account .		26,830				
			£34,210				£34,210
19..				19..			
Jan. 1	To Balance . . b/d		34,210	Jan. 1	By Balance . . b/d		7,320

Memorandum BRANCHES TRADING AND PROFIT AND LOSS ACCOUNT
FOR THE YEAR ENDED 31ST DECEMBER, 19..

	£	£		£	£
Stock		16,380	Sales—		
Purchases—			Cash	413,680	
Cash	4,360		Credit	14,350	
Credit	226,500			428,030	
		230,860	*Less* Allowances	480	
Wages		112,500			427,550
Gross Profit c/d		88,210	Stock		20,400
		£447,950			£447,950
Rent and Rates[1]		22,180	Gross Profit b/d		88,210
Salaries		33,300			
Sundry Expenses[2]		4,800			
Depreciation of Fittings		1,100			
Net Profit to Profit and Loss Account		26,830			
		£88,210			£88,210

Memorandum BRANCHES BALANCE SHEET AS AT 31ST DECEMBER, 19..

		£			£
Head Office Account—			*Fixed Assets*		
Balance £60			Fittings as at 1st		
Add Net Profit per			January, 19..	£10,000	
Profit and Loss			*Plus* Additions	1,000	
Account 26,830				11,000	
		26,890	*Less* Depreciation[3]	1,100	
Rent and Rates £6,320					9,900
Salaries 1,000			*Current Assets*		
		7,320	Stock		20,400
			Debtors		2,410
			Cash		1,500
		£34,210			£34,210

[1] Cash paid £20,200, *plus* closing outstanding £6,320, *less* opening outstanding £4,340.
[2] Expenses paid by Branches £2,320, *plus* expenses paid by Head Office £2,480.
[3] Depreciation on additions taken for whole year.

11. *Bombay books.*

JOURNAL

19..Dec. 31		Rupees	Rupees
	Sales . . . . *Dr.*	225,676	
	Stock . . . . *Dr.*	148,500	
	To Trading Account		374,176
	Being Sales transferred to Trading Account and closing stock introduced.		
	Trading Account. . . . . *Dr.*	261,604	
	To Purchases		261,604
	Being Balance transferred to Trading Account.		
	Trading Account. . . . . *Dr.*	112,572	
	To Profit and Loss Account . . .		112,572
	Being Gross Profit transferred to Profit and Loss Account.		
	Profit and Loss Account . . . . *Dr.*	101,724	
	To Wages and Salaries		43,868
	,, Freight and Insurance . . .		26,608
	,, General Expenses		31,248
	Being Expenses transferred to Profit and Loss Account.		
	Profit and Loss Account . . . . *Dr.*	10,848	
	To Head Office		10,848
	Being Net Profit transferred to Head Office Account.		

Head Office books.

BOMBAY CURRENT ACCOUNT

Dr.   Cr.

19..		Rupees	£	19..			Rupees	£
Jan. 8	To Cash	64,000	4,200·00	Dec. 31	By Loss on Exchange			145·20
Apr. 6	" "	96,000	5,800·00		" Balance . c/d.		218,848	13,678·00
Aug. 17	" "	48,000	3,100·00					
Dec. 31	" Profit and Loss Account	10,848	723·20					
	Rs.	218,848	£13,823·20		Rs.		218,848	£13,823·20
19..								
Jan. 1	To Balance[1] . b/d.	218,848	13,678·00					

[1] Balance of 208,000 + 10,848 (profit).   See also page 349.

348

The closing balance on the account on page 348 is made up of—

		£
Cash at Bank	. . . .	790·06
„ in Hand	. . . .	97·69
Debtors	. . . .	6,653·88
Stock	. . . .	9,281·25
		16,822·88
Less Creditors	. . . . .	3,144·88
		£13,678·00

These, being current assets and liabilities, are all converted at the closing rate of £6·25 per 100. The converted Trial Balance, if required, will appear—

TRIAL BALANCE, 31ST DECEMBER, 19..

	Dr.	Cr.		Dr.	Cr.
	Rupees	Rupees	Rate per 100 £	£	£
London Account		208,000			13,100·00
Profit and Loss Account		10,848			723·20
Cash at Bank	12,641		6·66⅔	790·06	
„ in Hand	1,563		6·25	97·69	
Sundry Debtors	106,462		6·25	6,653·88	
Stock	148,500		6·25	9,281·25	
Sundry Creditors		50,318	6·25		3,144·88
Loss on Exchange			6·25	145·20	
Rs.	269,166	Rs. 269,166		£16,968·08	£16,968·08

COPENHAGEN AGENTS

19..		Kroner	£	19.. Oct. 31			Kroner	£
Aug. 31	To Agents' Remittance Account . . . c/d	1,206,000	70,000		By May Shipment . . .		252,000	14,000
Oct. 31	,, Balance . . . . c/d	51,840	2,880		,, Carriage . . .		90,000	5,000
					,, June Shipment . .		180,000	10,000
					,, ,, Shipping Charges .		72,000	4,000
					,, July Shipment . .		216,000	12,000
					,, August Shipment .		324,000	18,000
					,, Commission—			
					May . . .		5,040	280
					June . . .		3,600	200
					July . . .		4,320	240
					August . .		6,480	360
					,, Net Profit—			
					July . . .		14,400	800
					August . .		18,000	1,000
					,, Profit and Loss on Exchange Account			3,000
					,, Balance . . . c/d		72,000	4,000
		1,257,840	£72,880				1,257,840	£72,880
	To Balance . . . . b/d	72,000	4,000		By Balance . . . b/d		51,840	2,880
		72,000	£4,000		,, ,, . . . c/d		20,160	1,120
Nov. 1	To Balance . . . . b/d	20,160	1,120				72,000	£4,000

350

TIMBER PROFIT AND LOSS ACCOUNTS

Dr.

	May £	June £	July £	August £
To Agents—				
Purchases	14,000	10,000	12,000	18,000
Carriage and Freight	5,000	4,000	6,000	9,000
Freight and Insurance	7,000	1,000		
„ Agents—				
Commission 2%	280	200	240	360
$\frac{1}{10}$ Net Profit			800	1,000
„ Profit and Loss Account—				
Net Profit			7,200	9,000
	£26,280	£15,200	£26,240	£37,360

Cr.

	May £	June £	July £	August £
By Cash—				
Sales	24,280	12,200	26,240	37,360
„ Profit and Loss Account—				
Net Loss	2,000	3,000		
	£26,280	£15,200	£26,240	£37,360

Dr.				FREIGHT AND INSURANCE				Cr.

19..			£	19..				£
May	To Cash		7,000	May	By Timber Profit & Loss Account			7,000
June	,, ,,		1,000	June	,, ,, ,, ,, ,,		,,	1,000
July	,, ,,		6,000	July	,, ,, ,, ,, ,,		,,	6,000
Aug.	,, ,,		9,000	Aug.	,, ,, ,, ,, ,,		,,	9,000

Dr.			PROFIT AND LOSS ACCOUNT			Cr.

19..			£	19..		£
Oct. 31	To May Shipment—Loss		2,000	Oct. 31	By July Shipment—Profit	7,200
	,, June Shipment—Loss		3,000		,, August Shipment—	
	,, Loss on Exchange[1]		3,000		Profit	9,000
	,, Net Profit		8,200			
			£16,200			£16,200

[1] This is accounted for by the fact that £70,000 remitted to agents produces 1,206,000 Kroner as against 1,260,000 on the basis of 18 Kroner to £, thus entailing a loss of 54,000 Kroner. The latter at 18 to £ is £3,000.

13. CONVERTED TRIAL BALANCE, 30TH JUNE, 19..

		Francs	Rate	Profit and Loss Account		Balance Sheet	
				Dr.	Cr.		
				£	£	£	£
Head Office	(x)	451,373					5,218
Remittances		236,062				2,641	
Fixtures and Fittings		26,040	124			210	
Sundry Debtors		171,288	91½			1,872	
Stock, 1st January		87,365	86½	1,010			
Sundry Creditors	(x)	57,828	91½				632
Purchases		186,989	89[2]	2,101			
Sales	(x)	270,738	89		3,042		
Discount Allowed		4,183	89	(a) 47			
,, Received	(x)	5,429	89		(a) 61		
Salaries		46,369	89	(a) 521			
Rent and Rates		20,826	89	(a) 234			
Bad Debts		2,403	89	(a) 27			
Cash in Hand		3,843	91½			42	
Stock, 30th June, 19..		91,863	91½		(b) 1,004[3]	1,004	
		(c)		3,940	4,107	5,769	5,850
Difference in Exchange				248			
Net Loss (after allowing for Difference in Exchange)					81	81	
				£4,188	£4,188	£5,850	£5,850

2 $\frac{86½ + 91½}{2}$.   [3] Calculated to the nearest £.

(a) The net profit is arrived at as follows— £

Gross Profit [*per Trading Account*] (see page 353)					935
Less Expenses [*marked (a)*]				£829	
,, Discount Received [*marked (a)*]			61		
					768
Net Profit [*per Journal entry*] (see page 353)					£167

(b) The closing stock is introduced into the books in the ordinary way.

(c) The total of the Francs column (eliminating closing stock, which in fact is not a balance but merely a note) is—

					Francs
Total					1,570,736
Less Credits (4 items (x))					785,368 = Cr.
Balance, i.e. same as credits					785,368 = Dr.

Dr.		BRANCH TRADING ACCOUNT				Cr.
19..		£	19..			£
Jan. 1	To Stock . . .	1,010	June 30	By Sales . . .		3,042
June 30	,, Purchases . .	2,101		,, Stock . . .		1,004
	,, Gross Profit[1] . .	935				
		£4,046				£4,046

Gross Profit = 30·74 per cent on Sales.

After conversion of items as above Journal entries will be made as follows—

JOURNAL

19..		£	£
June 30	Branch[1] . . . . Dr.	167	
	To Profit and Loss Account		167
	Being profit for six months to date.		
	Difference on Exchange Account . . . Dr.	248	
	To Branch		248
	Being difference on exchange.		

The Branch will then show a debit balance of £2,496, made up as follows—

			£
Opening Balance . . . . . . Dr.			5,218
Less Remittances			2,641
			2,577
Less Journal transfers [*as above*]			81
Closing Balance . . . . . . Dr.			£2,496

[1] See Note (a) on page 352.

14. London books.

(a) Dr.

BRANCH

Dr.	Francs	Rate	£		Cr.	Francs	Rate	£
To Goods	25,250	25·25	1,000·00		By Remittance	25,250	25·25	1,000·00
„ Exchange Reserve	125	25·25	4·95		„ Balance	125		4·95
	F.25,375		£1,004·95			F.25,375		£1,004·95
To Balance b/d	125	25·25	4·95					

EXCHANGE RESERVE

Dr.					Cr.	Francs	Rate	£
					By Branch	125	25·25	4·95

Branch books.

HEAD OFFICE

Dr.	£	Rate	Francs		Cr.	Francs	Rate	£
To Remittance	1,000·00	25·25	25,250		By Goods	25,125	25·25	995·05
„ Balance c/d	4·95		125			125	25·25	4·95
	£1,000·00		F.25,250			F.25,250		£1,000·00
					By Balance b/d	125	25·25	

London books.
(b) *Dr.* **BRANCH ACCOUNT** *Cr.*

	Francs	Rate	£		Francs	Rate	£
To Goods . . . c/d	25,000	25	1,000·00	By Remittance .	25,000	25	1,000·00
,, Balance .	125	25	5·00	,, Exchange Reserve .	125	25	5·00
	F.25,125		£1,005·00		F.25,125		£1,005·00
				By Balance . . b/d	125	25	5·00

Dr. **EXCHANGE RESERVE** *Cr.*

	Francs	Rate	£
To Branch .	125	25	5·00

Branch books.
Dr. **HEAD OFFICE ACCOUNT** *Cr.*

	Francs	Rate	£		Francs	Rate	£
To Remittance . .	25,125	25	1,005·00	By Goods . .	25,000	25	1,000·00
	F.25,125		£1,005·00	,, Balance . . c/d	125	25	5·00
To Balance . . b/d	125	25	5·00		F.25,125		£1,005·00

355

15.   Trading and Profit and Loss Account for the Year Ended 31st December, 19..

	H.O.	Branch		H.O.	Branch
	£	£		£	£
Stock	9,846	5,844	Sales	74,562	24,042
Purchases	49,218		Transfer to Branch		
Transfer from H.O.		18,819	(Wholesale Price)	18,819	
Gross Profit c/d	43,777	6,279	Stock	9,460	6,900
	£102,841	£30,942		£102,841	£30,942
Sundry Expenses	26,584	3,499	Gross Profit b/d	43,777	6,279
Balance c/d	17,193	2,780			
	£43,777	£6,279		£43,777	£6,279
Increase in Branch Adjustment Account	352		Balance b/d	17,193	2,780
Net Profit c/d	16,841	2,780			
	£17,193	£2,780		£17,193	£2,780
Balance c/f	45,021		Balance b/f	25,400	
			Profit—		
			H.O. b/d	16,841	
			Branch b/d	2,780	
	£45,021			£45,021	

Balance Sheet as at 31st December, 19..

	£			£
Share Capital—		Branch Fixtures		600
Authorized, Issued and fully paid:		H.O. Fixed Assets		49,266
50,000 Shares of £1 each	50,000	Stock-in-trade—		
Profit and Loss Account	45,021	H.O.	£9,460	
	95,021	Branch[1]	4,600	
Trade Creditors	6,080			14,060
		Trade Debtors—		
		H.O.	£17,280	
		Branch	1,425	
				18,705
		Cash at Bank—		
		H.O.	£18,210	
		Branch	200	
				18,410
		Cash on hand		60
	£101,101			£101,101

Branch Adjustment

	£		£
To Closing—		By Opening—	
33⅓% of £6,900[1]	2,300	33⅓% of £5,844	1,948
		„ Trading Account	352
	£2,300		£2,300

[1] The item of £4,600 is the closing stock as per Trading Account, £6,900, *less* Branch Adjustment Account, £2,300. £4,600 is £9,200 *less* 50 per cent.

It will be observed that if the cost price is represented by 100, the wholesale price is 150 and the retail selling price is 200: therefore the reduction from retail selling price to wholesale price is 50, i.e. 25 per cent thereof. The reduction from wholesale price to *cost* is also 50, i.e. 33⅓ per cent of the wholesale price.

16. (a)   BRANCH TRADING AND PROFIT AND LOSS ACCOUNT FOR
 Dr.   THE YEAR ENDED 31ST DECEMBER, 19.9   *Cr.*

	£		£
Opening Stock . . .	24,500	Sales	642,240
Goods from Head Office . . .	340,000	Closing Stock . . .	31,000
Branch Purchases . . .	5,000		
Gross Profit . . . c/d	303,740		
	£673,240		£673,240
Rent, Rates, and Insurance . .	30,030	Gross Profit . . . . b/d	303,740
Wages	169,000		
Salaries	47,000		
Sundry Expenses . . .	5,180		
Petty Cash	3,500		
Bad Debts . . .	120		
Allowances . . .	715		
Depreciation of Fixtures . .	2,440		
Net Profit . . . c/f	45,755		
	£303,740		£303,740

(b) *Dr.*   GOODS SENT TO BRANCHES   *Cr.*

19 9		£	19.9		£
Dec. 31	To Purchases (or Trading Account). . .	£340,000	Dec. 31	By Branches Trading Account . .	£340,000

 Dr.   BRANCH DEBTORS   *Cr.*

19.9			£	19.9			£
Jan. 1	To Balances . . b/d		1,300	Dec. 31	By Branch Cash . .		18,600
Dec. 31	,, Branch Sales—				,, Branch Trading Account:		
	Credit Sales . .		21,500		Bad Debts . .		120
					Allowances . .		715
					,, Balances . c/d		3,365
			£22,800				£22,800
19.0							
Jan. 1	To Balance . . b/d		3,365				

 Dr.   BRANCH CASH   *Cr.*

19.9			£	19.9			£
Jan. 1	To Balance . . b/d		700	Dec. 31	By Remittances to H.O. . .		460,150
Dec. 31	,, Branch Sales—				., Branch Expenses—		
	Cash Sales . .		620,740		Wages . .		169,000
	,, Branch Debtors . .		18,600		Purchases . .		5,000
					Petty Cash . .		3,500
					,, Balance . c/d		2,390
			£640,040				£640,040
19.0							
Jan. 1	To Balance . . b/d		2,390				

 Dr.   BRANCH SALES   *Cr.*

19.9		£	19.9			£
Dec. 31	To Branch Trading Account	642,240	Dec. 31	By Branch Debtors—		
				Credit Sales .		21,500
				,, Branch Cash—		
				Cash Sales .		620,740
		£642,240				£642,240

Dr.   BRANCH EXPENSES   **Cr.**

		£			£
19.9			19.9		
Jan. 1	To Rates and Insurance paid in advance . b/d	900	Dec. 31	By Branch Trading Account—	
Dec. 31	„ Branch Cash—			Purchases . .	5,000
	Wages . . .	169,000		Rent, Rates, and Insurance . .	30,030
	Purchases . .	5,000		Salaries . .	47,000
	Petty Cash . .	3,500		Sundry Expenses .	5,180
	„ Head Office—			Wages . . .	169,000
	Rent, Rates, and Insurance . .	30,180		Petty Cash . .	3,500
	Salaries . .	47,000		„ Rates and Insurance paid in advance c/d	1,050
	Sundry Expenses .	5,180			
		£260,760			£260,760
19.0					
Jan. 1	To Rates and Insurance paid in advance . b/d	1,050			

Dr.   BRANCH FIXTURES   **Cr.**

		£			£
19.9			19.9		
Jan. 1	To Balance . . b/d	12,000	Dec. 31	By Branch Trading Account: Depreciation	2,440
Oct. 1	„ Head Office—Additions . .	800		„ Balance . . c/d	10,360
		£12,800			£12,800
19.0					
Jan. 1	To Balance . . b/d	10,360			

17.   TRADING ACCOUNT

	H.O.	Branch		H.O.	Branch
	£	£		£	£
Purchases . . .	20,000		Sales . . .	17,000	5,000
Transfer H.O. Goods . .		8,000	Transfer to Branch . .	8,000	
Gross Profit—			Stock—		
Outside Sales (See Note[1] page 360) . .	8,500	1,000	Cost Price . .	6,500	
Branch . . .	3,000		Invoice Price . .		4,000
	£31,500	£9,000		£31,500	£9,000

H.O. PROFIT AND LOSS ACCOUNT

	£			£
Provision for unrealized Profit on H.O. Goods at Branch—		Gross Profit . . . b/d		11,500
37½% × £4,000. . .	1,500	Gross Profit: Branch . . .		1,000
"Net" Profit[1] (See Note[1] page 360) .	11,000			
	£12,500			£12,500

[1] There would be expenses to be charged before true net profit was arrived at, but their introduction into the problem would merely lengthen the question, and the examiner clearly intended that the candidate should be left to deal with the real problem without the intrusion of extraneous detail.

The question does not indicate the closing stocks, but these can be computed quite easily.

The closing stock of goods in Head Office is arrived at as follows—

			£
Goods purchased.			20,000
Deduct—			
Cost price of goods sold to customers . .	£17,000		
Less 50% profit	8,500		
		£8,500	
Deduct—			
Cost price of goods "sold" to Branch . .	8,000		
Less 37½% profit	3,000		
		5,000	
			13,500
Closing Stock			£6,500

The gross profit is—

		£
(a) 100% of £8,500		8,500
(b) 60% of £5,000		3,000
		£11,500

The closing stock of goods at Branch at invoice price is arrived at as follows—

			£
Goods received			8,000
Deduct—			
Invoice price of goods sold to customers . . .	£5,000		
Less 20% profit	1,000		
		4,000	
Closing Stock at invoice price			£4,000

The gross profit is 20% of £5,000 = £1,000

A rough proof can be made of the final profit of the company by ignoring the transfer price from H.O. to Branch and compiling a total Trading Account, thus—

TRADING ACCOUNT

	£			£
Purchases	20,000	Sales		22,000
Net Profit (50% × £22,000) . .	11,000	Stock		9,000
	£31,000			£31,000

The Stock is £9,000 at cost, corresponding with the closing Stock figures of H.O. £6,500 and Branch £4,000 less Reserve £1,500.

This provision effectually brings down the goods at branch to £2,500. This can be seen at a glance from the question, as the selling price of the goods transferred to Branch is £10,000 (being invoiced to Branch at £8,000, i.e. £10,000, less 20 per cent) and the *cost* price thereof is **£5,000** (as the selling price carries a profit of 100 per cent on cost) and, as obviously half the quantity has been sold, **one-half** of the stock transferred to Branch remains on hand, i.e. £2,500 at cost.

This type of problem causes much confusion to examination candidates, but it is really a matter of applying the elementary principles of percentages. Thus, if it is assumed that the—

					£	£
	Cost price is .	.	.	.		100
then	Selling price is .	.	.	.		200
so that the	Price to Branch is	.	.	.	200	
	Less 20%	.	.	.	40	
						160

Hence the invoice price to Branch is the cost (£100) plus profit (£60), i.e. true cost plus 60 per cent. Conversely, the cost price of the goods, calculated from the invoice price of £160 is £100, i.e. £160 — £60, i.e. £160 — 37½ per cent of £160.

Note to students. If the Head Office keeps the accounts of Branch transactions it will have the following—

BRANCH STOCK

		£								£
Goods	. . . . .	8,000	Sales	.	.	.	.	.	.	5,000
Branch Adjustment Account	. .	1,000	Stock	.	.	.	.	c/d		4,000
Stock	. . . . b/d	4,000								

GOODS SENT TO BRANCH

		£						£
Purchases or Trading Account	. .	5,000	Branch Stock	.	.	.	.	8,000
Branch Adjustment Account	. .	3,000						

BRANCH ADJUSTMENT ACCOUNT

			£				£
Provision	. . . . c/d		1,500	Goods sent to Branch	. . .		3,000
Profit[1]	. . . . .		2,500	Branch Stock	. . . .		1,000
				Provision	. . . . b/d		1,500

[1] As shown in Trading Accounts (page 358) in H.O. columns: £3,000 — Provision £1,500 + Profit in Branch column £1,000 = £2,500; this, together with H.O. Gross Profit on Sales £8,500, totals £11,000.

18.   COMPUTATION OF MANAGERS' COMMISSION

	Branch P			Branch Q		
	£	£	£	£	£	£
Sales			45,160			29,280
Opening Stock at Cost		9,342			6,242	
Goods sent to Branches		36,210			21,740	
		45,552			27,982	
Less Closing Stock at Selling Price . .	15,416			7,976		
„ 25% to reduce to Cost . . .	3,854			1,994		
		11,562			5,982	
			33,990			22,000
Gross Profit			11,170			7,280
Less Chargeable Expenses			6,140			4,510
Net Profit subject to Managers' Commission . .			£5,030			£2,770
Commission at 10%			503			277
Less 25% of Stock deficiency—						
Standard Gross Profit: 25% on Sales . .		11,290			7,320	
Actual Gross Profit		11,170			7,280	
			£120			£40
25% thereof			30			10
Commission for the year			473			267
Less paid on account			300			200
Balance due			£173			£67

Note. It is assumed that the opening stocks are correct.

19.
(a)

EASTERN BRANCH TRIAL BALANCE
31ST MARCH, 19.5

	Dr. Ficals	Cr. Ficals	Conversion Rate	Dr. £	Cr. £
Balance at Bank	183,400		100	1,834	
Creditors		117,900	100		1,179
Debtors	388,800		100	3,888	
Local Expenses	377,100		90	4,190	
Head Office—					
Goods Account		1,762,400	80		22,030
Remittance Account:					
Received	1,048,000		—	14,500	
In Transit	297,000		—	3,000	
Purchases and Import Duties—					
Head Office Goods	1,762,400		80	22,030	
Local and Import Duties . . .	889,000		90	9,878	
Sales		3,065,400	90		34,060
	F.4,945,700	F.4,945,700		59,320	57,269
Adjustments for Stocks at 31st March, 19.5					
Goods ex Head Office (at cost to Branch):					
Trading Account		522,800	80		6,535
Balance Sheet	522,800		100	5,228	
Local Purchases and Import Duties—					
Trading Account		166,500	90		1,850
Balance Sheet	166,500		100	1,665	
				66,213	65,654
Profit on Exchange					559
	F.5,635,000	F.5,635,000		£66,213	£66,213
Adjustment for Head Office Profit included in					
Branch Stock—					
20% of F.522,800 = 104,560:					
Trading Account			80	1,307	
Balance Sheet			100		1,046
Profit on Exchange					261
				£1,307	£1,307

(b) Dr.   EASTERN BRANCH ACCOUNT   Cr.

	Ficals	£			Ficals	£
To Goods . . .	1,762,400	22,030	By Remittances . .		1,048,000	14,500
,, Branch Profit . .	726,200	6,347	,, Remittances (in transit)			
,, Profit on Exchange .		559		c/d	297,000	3,000
			,, Balances . .	c/d	1,143,600	11,436
	F.2,488,600	£28,936			F.2,488,600	£28,936
To Balances . . b/d	1,143,600	11,436				
,, Remittance in transit b/d	297,000	3,000				

This account in Head Office books contains (memo.) Fical figures reverse to those appearing in the books of the Branch; the balances brought down represent the net assets of the Branch, viz.—

		Ficals	£
Bank		183,400	1,834
Debtors		388,800	3,888
Stocks.		689,300	6,893
		1,261,500	12,615
Less Creditors		117,900	1,179
		F.1,143,600	£11,436

The Branch profit is found from the Branch Trading Account as follows—

BRANCH TRADING ACCOUNT

	Ficals	£		Ficals	£
Purchases—			Sales . . .	3.065,400	34,060
Head Office . .	1,762,400	22,030	Stock—		
Local & Import Duties	889,000	9,878	Ex Head Office .	522,800	6,535
Expenses . . .	377,100	4,190	Local . . .	166,500	1,850
Profit . . .	726,200	6,347			
	F.3,754,700	£42,445		F.3,754,700	£42,445

(c) PROFIT AND LOSS ACCOUNT FOR THE YEAR ENDED
31ST MARCH, 19.5

	£		£
Sundry Expenses . . .	10,881	Trading Profit—	
Net Profit to Capital . .	61,268	Head Office	67,109
		Branch	6,347
			73,456
		Less unrealized Profit in Branch Stock	1,307
	£72,149		£72,149

BALANCE SHEET AS AT 31ST MARCH, 19.5

		£		£
Capital—			Sundry Assets	184,328
At 1st April, 19.4 .	£228,947		Stock (d)	106,347
Add Profit . .	61,268		Debtors (c)	86,394
		290,215	Cash in Transit	3,000
Less Drawings .	20,000		Cash at Bank (e)	27,051
		270,215		
Exchange Reserve (b) . . .		820		
Creditors and Accruals (a) .		136,085		
		£407,120		£407,120

(a) H.O. £134,906 + Branch £1,179.
(b) Per Eastern Branch Trial Balance: £559 + £261.
(c) H.O. £82,506 + Branch £3,888.
(d) H.O. £100,500 + Branch £6,893 — Stock Adjustment £1,046.
(e) H.O. £25,217 + Branch £1,834.

20.   Lyria Trial Balance, 31st December   *Cr.*

	Dr.	*Cr.*	Rate	*Dr.*	*Cr.*
	Lyras	Lyras		£	£
Creditors . . .		27,750	185		150
Head Office . . .		1,911,250	—		(a) 10,000
Sales		900,000	180		5,000
Buildings . . .	2,000,000		200	10,000	
Debtors . . .	18,500		185	100	
Bank	55,500		185	300	
Purchases . . .	180,000		180	1,000	
Goods from H.O. . .	400,000		(Invoice)	(b) 2,000	
Rent	18,500		[1]185	100	
Trade Salaries, etc.. .	166,500		180	925	
Loss on Damaged Goods . . .				(b) 500	
Loss on Exchange . .				225	
	2,839,000	2,839,000		£15,150	£15,150

Head Office Trial Balance, 31st December

	Dr.	*Cr.*
	£	£
Capital		125,000
Sales		120,000
Creditors		25,000
Transfer to Lyria		(b) 2,500
Buildings	80,000	
Debtors	40,250	
Bank	26,000	
Lyria Branch	(a) 10,000	
Cash in Transit (see below)	1,250	
Purchases	80,000	
Trade Salaries and Expenses	25,000	
Stock	10,000	
	£272,500	£272,500

As there are two separate Trial Balances, the combined Balance Sheet will be prepared, the items (*a*) and (*b*), as shown above, cancelling out, the latter being inserted in the appropriate column, but not carried out in the total column (see *x* on page 364).

The two accounts will be fully reflective when the remittance and Loss on Damaged Goods have been inserted (as on page 364), but in the Head Office Trial Balance the cash in transit has been segregated. In the Branch Trial Balance the loss of £500 has also been segregated and the sterling figure of £10,000 shown separately. The item of £10,000 in the branch books has already incorporated the above loss of £500.

[1] Average for year.

TRADING AND PROFIT AND LOSS ACCOUNT
FOR THE YEAR ENDED 31ST DECEMBER

	H.O.	Lyria	Total		H.O.	Lyria	Total
	£	£	£		£	£	£
Stock . .	10,000		10,000	Sales . . .	120,000	5,000	125,000
Purchases . .	80,000	1,000	81,000	Transfer (net) (x)	2,500		
Transfer (net) (x)		2,500		Stock . .	22,500	200	22,700
Gross Profit c/d	55,000	2,200	57,200	Loss on Damaged			
				Goods . .		500	500
	£145,000	£5,700	£148,200		£145,000	£5,700	£148,200
Rent . .		100	100	Gross Profit b/d	55,000	2,200	57,200
Trade Salaries							
and Expenses .	25,000	925	25,925				
Loss on Damaged							
Goods . .		500	500				
Net Profit . .	30,000	675	30,675				
	£55,000	£2,200	£57,200		£55,000	£2,200	£57,200

THE LONDON-LYRIA TRADING CO. LTD.

COMBINED BALANCE SHEET AS AT 31ST DECEMBER

	£	£		£	£
Capital . . .		125,000	Buildings—		
Profit and Loss			London . .	80,000	
Account .	30,675		Lyria . . .	10,000	
Less Loss on					90,000
Exchange .	225		Stock—		
		30,450	London . .	22,500	
			Lyria . .	200	
Sundry Creditors—					22,700
London .	25,000		Sundry Debtors—		
Lyria . .	150		London . .	40,250	
		25,150	Lyria . . .	100	
					40,350
			Cash in Transit .		1,250
			Bank—		
			London . .	26,000	
			Lyria . .	300	
					26,300
		£180,600			£180,600

The actual entries will be made on the principle of adjusting the Branch Current Account in the head office books. These will be—

Head Office books.

Dr.   LYRIA BRANCH   Cr.

	Lyras	Rate	£			Lyras	£
To Cash . .	2,000,000	200	10,000	By Remittances . .		248,750	1,250
,, Goods— . .							
400,000 (*a*)		(*a*) 200	2,000	,, Returns . . .		298,500	1,500
298,500 (*b*)		(*b*) 199	1,500	,, Balance . . c/d		2,250,750	11,250
	698,500						
,, Damages . .	99,500	199	500				
	2,798,000		£14,000			2,798,000	£14,000
To Balance . b/d	2,250,750		11,250	By Cash in Transit .		240,000	1,250
				,, Balance . . c/d		2,010,750	10,000
	2,250,750		£11,250			2,250,750	£11,250
To Balance . b/d	2,010,750		10,000	By Balance . . c/d		2,083,250	10,450
,, Profit and Loss Account—				,, Loss on Exchange .			225
Lyria Profit[1]	72,500		675				
	2,083,250		£10,675			2,083,250	£10,675
To Balance[2] . b/d	2,083,250	[3]	10,450				

[1] See below.
[2] See page 366.
[3] See page 366.

Branch books—

TRADING AND PROFIT AND LOSS ACCOUNT

	Lyras		Lyras
Stock	*nil*	Sales	900,000
Purchases . . .	180,000	Stock	37,000
Transfers . . .	400,000		
Gross Profit . . c/d	357,000		
	937,000		937,000
Rent	18,500	Gross Profit . . b/d	357,000
Trade Salaries, etc. .	166,500		
Loss *re* Damaged Goods .	99,500		
Net Profit to Head Office .	72,500		
	357,000		357,000

Dr.   HEAD OFFICE   Cr.

			Lyras				Lyras
To Remittances	.		248,750	By Cash (Buildings)	.	(a)	2,000,000
„ Returns	.	(a)	298,500	„ Goods (Trading			
„ Cash in Transit	.		240,000	Account)	.	(a)	698,500
„ Balance	.	c/d	1,911,250				
			2,698,500				£2,698,500
To Balance	.	c/d	2.083,250	By Balance	.	b/d[1]	1,911,250
				„ Damages (Profit and Loss Account)	.		99,500
				„ Profit for Year	.		72,500
			2,083,250				2,083,250
				By Balance	.	b/d[2]	2,083,250

(a) These items appear net (inset) in the Trial Balance.

The above account is reverse to the currency columns of Lyria Branch Account in the head office books, and as will be now clear to the student is the equivalent of a Capital Account. The profit of 72,500 Lyras is transferred to the credit of Head Office Account by means of a Journal entry, thus—

JOURNAL

	Lyras	Lyras
Trading and Profit and Loss Account Dr.	72,500	
To Head Office		72,500
Being profit for year transferred		

BALANCE SHEET, 31ST DECEMBER

			Lyras				Lyras
Creditors	.	T.B.	27,750	Bank	. .	T.B.	55,500
Head Office[3]	.	L.	2,083,250	Debtors	. .	T.B.	18,500
				Stock	. .	T.	37,000
				Buildings	. .	L.	2,000,000
			2,111,000				2,111,000

[1] Per Trial Balance (see page 363).
[2] See page 365.
[3] The valuation for insertion in Branch Account in head office books is made up—

					£	£	Lyras	Lyras
Bank	.	.	.	.	300		55,500	
Debtors	.	.	.	.	100		18,500	
Stock	.	.	.	.	200		37,000	
Buildings	.	.	.	.	10,000		2,000,000	
						10,600		2,111,000
Less Creditors	.	.	.		150		27,750	
						£10,450		£2,083,250

The Balance Sheet (combined) will therefore be—

THE LONDON-LYRIA TRADING CO. LTD.

COMBINED BALANCE SHEET AS AT 31ST DECEMBER

	H.O.	Lyria	Total		H.O.	Lyria	Total
	£	£	£		£	£	£
Capital	125,000		125,000	Cash in Transit	1,250		1,250
Sundry Creditors	25,000	150	25,150	Bank	26,000	300	26,300
Profit and Loss				Sundry Debtors	40,250	100	40,350
Account—				Stock	22,500	200	22,700
Head Office £30,000				Buildings	80,000	10,000	90,000
Lyria (675—225) 450				Branch Current Account	10,450		
	30,450		30,450				
Head Office Current Account		10,450					
	£180,450	£10,600	£180,600		£180,450	£10,600	£180,600

The Balance Sheet of the Head Office is merely a Balance Sheet prepared in the usual way, together with the Profit less Loss on Exchange obtained by the incorporation of the branch results.

The dates in the question are vital.

For instance, all the purchases of the branch are in the second half-year; therefore the conversion of 180,000 is at 180 to £; but rent of 18,500 is in respect of the whole year, hence the rate for the year must be taken, i.e. 185 to £.

The remittance in transit is converted at actual. The question shows that 488,750 lyras have been remitted, the sum of 248,750 being absorbed in the first remittance of £1,250, leaving a balance of 240,000. In point of fact the latter figure is given in the question, but it is deducible from other data supplied.

21.   LEEDS BOOKS

JOURNAL

		£	£
Stock in Transit Account (£636 + £159) . . . Dr.		795	
Cash in Transit Account . . . . Dr.		200	
To Liverpool Current Account			995
Being adjustment for £795 stock in transit and £200 cash in transit.			
Leeds Profit and Loss Account . . . Dr.		618	
To Branch Stock Suspense Account . . .			618
	£		
Being Stock in hand Liverpool . .	3,525		
„ Stock in transit to Liverpool .	795		
	£4,320		
⅕ thereof	864		
Less Balance brought forward . .	246		
	£618		

£

Balance Sheet includes—
Stock-in-trade—
    Leeds   8,273
    Liverpool: In hand £3,525
           Stock in Transit . . .   795

                                    4,320
        Less Branch Stock Suspense Account . .   864   3,456

                                          £11,729

With the adjustment of £995 the two current accounts are equal, the figures being £18,629.

22. [Most examination candidates experience difficulty in knowing where to begin "sorting out." Generally, when a start is made the question although lengthy, becomes less formidable.

The start should be made by taking the foreign branch Trial Balance, ignoring all questions of foreign exchange, adjusting by means of rough working ledger accounts the various matters arising (including the introduction with its double entry of the closing stock). After this is done, the conversions should be made, giving in effect the basis of the final sterling figures of the Branch, except that the sterling equivalent cannot be inserted until the Branch Account in Head Office is adjusted. Lastly the adjustments required in the Head Office books should be made.]

UTOPIA BRANCH TRIAL BALANCE
30TH SEPTEMBER, 19.9

	Dr.	*Cr.*	Rate of Conversion	*Dr.*	*Cr.*
	Topas	Topas		£	£
Bank and Cash . . .	7,000		850	5,950	
Sales		311,800	825		257,235
Purchases—					
Local Para (1)	40,000		825	33,000	
At London	176,800		825	145,860	
Stock, 1st October, 19.8 . .	41,250		800	33,000	
Wages	48,400		825	39,930	
Carriage, etc. . . .	2,800		825	2,310	
Debtors and Creditors . .	48,500	28,800	850	41,225	24,480
Head Office		28,750	Actual		21,540
(The above require no adjustment and represent all the items in the Trial Balance, except Plant and Depreciation)					
Plant Para (5)	14,200		750	10,650	
Provision for Depreciation ,, .		10,700	750		8,025
Profit on Sale of Plant ,, .		320	750		240
Depreciation for year ,, .	1,420		750	1,065	
Stock, 30th September, 19.9—					
Local	11,000	11,000[1]	825	9,075[1]	9,075
Ex London	22,000	22,000[1]	825	18,150[1]	18,150
Manager's Commission and Provision .	1,600	1,600[2]	825	1,320	1,320
Profit on Exchange . . .					1,470
	414,970	414,970		£341,535	£341,535

[1] See note on page 369.
[2] See page 371.

Trading Accounts
FOR THE YEAR ENDED 30TH SEPTEMBER, 19.9

	London	Utopia	Total		London	Utopia	Total
	£	£	£		£	£	£
Stocks in hand and transit at 1st October, 19.8 .	64,983	33,000	97,983	Sales . . .	642,270	257,235	899,505
				Transfer . .	145,860		
Purchases . .	620,000	33,000	653,000	Stocks in hand and awaiting shipment at 30th			
Transfer . .		145,860		September, 19.9[1]	53,700	27,225	80,925
Gross Profit . c/d	156,847	72,600	229,447				
	£841,830	£284,460	£980,430		£841,830	£284,460	£980,430
Wages, etc. .	145,000	39,930	184,930	Gross Profit b/d	156,847	72,600	229,447
Carriage, etc. .	8,025	2,310	10,335				
Depreciation .	3,480	1,065	4,545				
Manager's Commission .		1,320	1,320				
Net Trading Profit . c/d	342	27,975	28,317				
	£156,847	£72,600	£229,447		£156,847	£72,600	£229,447

[1] Included therein is £1,700, the cost price of goods invoiced to Branch at £1,870 awaiting shipment; i.e. $\frac{10}{11} \times £1,870 = £1,700$.

PROFIT AND LOSS ACCOUNT

	£		£
Directors' Remuneration .	10,500	Net Trading Profit for year	
Net Profit carried to Appropriation Account . .	18,327	London	342
		Utopia	27,975
		Profit on Sales of Plant .	240
		Transfer of Excess Reserve on unrealized profit on Branch Stock	270
	£28,827		£28,827

APPROPRIATION ACCOUNT

	£		£
Stock Reserve: Amount to make up Stock Reserve to 12 per cent on Stock as brought into Trading Accounts . .	676	Balance forward . . .	34,500
		Net Profit for year . .	18,327
Proposed Dividend 10 per cent on £85,000 . .	8,500		
Balance forward . .	43,651		
	£52,827		£52,827

The usual procedure will follow in preparing the Combined Balance Sheet.

The debit of £51,225 (see Branch Account in Head Office books, *infra*) against the Branch is reflected in the converted figures of Branch Assets and Liabilities as follows—

	£	£
Cash and Bank	5,950	
Plant	10,650	
Provision for Depreciation		8,025
Debtors and Creditors	41,225	24,480
Manager, *re* Commission		1,320
Stock	27,225	
	85,050	33,825
Balance Head Office		51,225
	£85,050	£85,050

Rough working accounts at Head Office—

Dr.	BRANCH ACCOUNT			*Cr.*
	£			£
Per T.B.	23,410	Sales—reversal of entry *re* Goods		
		awaiting shipment (*a*)		1,870
		Balance . . . c/d		21,540
	21,540 (*underlined*)			21,540 (*underlined*)
Balance		Balance forward . . .		51,225
(Sterling equivalent of balance in Branch books) b/d	21,540			
Incorporation of Branch profits, Profit and Loss Account—				
Net Trading Profit .	27,975			
Profit on Sale of Plant	240			
Exchange Suspense—				
Profit on Exchange .	1,470			
	£51,225			£51,225

Dr.	SALES AND INTERNAL TRANSFERS		*Cr.*
	£		£
Branch Account (*a*) . .	**1,870**	Per T.B.	790,000
Trading Account . .			
Branch Transfers			
(See Purchases, Branch T.B.)	145,860		
Sales	642,270		
	£790,000		£790,000

Dr.		STOCK RESERVE	Cr.
	£		£
Profit and Loss Account— Excess Reserve for un-realized Profit—amount written back		Per T.B.	9,305
		„ Appropriation Account .	676
	£		
Branch Open-ing Stock	33,000		
Branch Clos-ing Stock	18,150		
	£14,850		
$\frac{1}{5} \times \frac{10}{110} \times$ £14,850 . .	270		
Balance—12% of £80,925 .	9,711		
	£9,981		£9,981

Rough Working Accounts (Branch Books)—

Dr.		PLANT	Cr.
	Topas		Topas
Per T.B. . . .	14,000	Plant Disposal Account (b) .	600
Plant Disposal Account (Sale) (a) . . .	800	Balance . . . T.B.	14,200

Dr.		PROVISION FOR DEPRECIATION	Cr.
	Topas		Topas
Disposal Account—2 years Depreciation (£60 per an-num) (c) . . .	120	Per T.B.	9.400
Balance . . . T.B.	10,700	P. & L. Dep. 14,200 at 10% . . T.B.	1,420

Dr.		PLANT DISPOSAL ACCOUNT	Cr.
	Topas		Topas
Plant Cost (b) . . .	600	Plant (Sale) (a) . . .	800
Profit . . . T.B.	320	Depreciation (c) . . .	120

Computation of Branch Manager's Commission—

	Topas
Opening Debtors	56,700
Sales (assumed all Credit Sales) . . .	311,800
	368,500
Less Closing Debtors	48,500
Amount collected	320,000
$\frac{1}{2}$ per cent thereon [as per T.B., page 368] Topas	1,600

23. Before the accounts can be compiled it is necessary to complete the English Branches Control Account and the Goods sent to English Branches Account. The opening Branch Stock at selling price on opposite sides will form part of these accounts, and as this is shown in the Trial Balance at £10,200, i.e. 66⅔ per cent of selling price, the latter is £15,300. These accounts built up in detail are—

Dr. ENGLISH BRANCHES CONTROL ACCOUNT *Cr.*

	£			£
To Balance (opening Stock at selling price) b/d . . . (a)	15,300	By Expenses and Remittance . .		86,746
,, Goods from H.O. . . (b)	90,330	,, Balance . . . . c/d		18,884
	£105,630			£105,630
To Balance (per T.B.) . . b/d	18,884	By Bad Debts . . . (c)		40
		,, Stock Shortage . . (d)		180
		,, Balance c/d—		
		Cash . . £150		
		Debtors [£3,284 − £40] 3,244		
		Closing Stock at sell-		
		ing price . . 15,270		
				18,664
	£18,884			£18,884
To Balance b/d—				
Cash . . £150				
Debtors. . . 3,244				
Stock (See note *infra*) 15,270				
	18,664			

Dr. GOODS SENT TO ENGLISH BRANCHES ACCOUNT *Cr.*

	£			£
To Balance . . . c/d	105,630	By Balance b/d . . (a)		15,300
		,, Goods to English Branches. (b)		90,330
	£105,630			£105,630
To Stock Shortage . . (d)	180	By Balance (per T.B.) . b/d		105,630
,, Sales . . . (e)	90,180			
,, Closing Stock at selling price c/d	15,270			
	£105,630			£105,630
		By Balance b/d (See note *infra*) .		15,270

Note. It will be seen that the closing stock at selling price is included in the debit balance of the Control Account and in the credit balance of the Goods sent to Branches Account, cancelling themselves out in the Balance Sheet, so that the stock at cost will be introduced into the final accounts in the ordinary way.

Items (c) £40 and (e) £90,180 will be transferred direct to Profit and Loss Account.

Balance

— £40 (Bad Debts)

English Branches Control[1] *Dr.* £18,884 — £180 (Goods sent to Branches) £18,664

— £180 (English Branches Control)

Goods sent to Branches[1] *Cr.* £105,630— £90,180 (Sales) . . . £15,270

[1] As proof it can be seen that the net credit of the two accounts above is £86,746 and this will be "disposed of" as follows—

			£	£
Credits	Sales	.	90,180	
	Balance of Goods sent to Branches .	.	15,270	105,450
Debits	Bad debts	.	40	
	Balance of Branches Control .	.	18,664	18,704
				£86,746

The Dublin Head Office Control Accounts will require reconciliation by entries in the Head office (being reverse to those in Dublin).

Dr.			DUBLIN CURRENT ACCOUNT		Cr.
		£			£
Opening Balance . .	b/d	287	Claim (Balance Sheet) . .		200
Closing Balance . .	c/d	363	Cash in Transit (Balance Sheet)		450
		£650			£650
			Balance . . .	b/d	363

(a)   DISTRIBUTORS LTD.
TRADING AND PROFIT AND LOSS ACCOUNT
FOR THE YEAR ENDED 31ST MARCH, 19.6

	H.O.	Dublin	Total		H.O.	Dublin	Total
	£	£	£	Sales—	£	£	£
Opening Stock .	29,700	1,970	31,670	H.O. .	59,980		
Purchases[1] . .	127,520	10,038	137,558	Branches .	90,180		
Transfers . .		11,800[1]			150,160	33,012	183,172
Gross Profit . c/d	39,920	12,004	51,924	Transfers[1] .	11,800		
				Closing Stock .	35,180	2,800	37,980
	£197,140	£35,812	£221,152		£197,140	£35,812	£221,152
General Expenses .	25,535	5,000	30,535	Gross Profit b/d	39,920	12,004	51,924
Bad Debts . .	40		40				
Net Profit . .	14,345	7,004	21,349				
	£39,920	£12,004	£51,924		£39,920	£12,004	£51,924

[1] Dublin Branch has debited Head Office in respect of goods lost (£200) and credited Transfers £200.

Head Office will have credited Dublin with this loss and debited claim: but in addition must debit transfer with £200 to bring it into line with the Dublin reduced figure (£12,000 − £200 = £11,800) and credit purchases: alternatively, instead of making the latter credit it could be separated and credited to Trading Account.

(b)   FINAL TRIAL BALANCE
AT 31ST MARCH, 19.6

	H.O.		Dublin	
	Dr.	Cr.	Dr.	Cr.
	£	£	£	£
Sundry Assets and Liabilities . . .	35,874	16,137	4,985	1,144
Dublin Current Account		363		
Head Office Current Account . .			363	
English Branches Control . . .	18,664			
Goods sent to Branches Control . .		15,270		
Share Capital		40,000		
Stocks H.O. £25,000 + Branches £10,180 .	35,180		2,800	
Stock Claim	200			
Profit and Loss—				
Forward		4,253		
Profit for year		14,345		7,004
Cash in Transit	450			
	£90,368	£90,368	£8,148	£8,148

24.

TRADING AND PROFIT AND LOSS ACCOUNT
FOR THE YEAR ENDED 31ST DECEMBER

	Head Office	Branch		Head Office	Branch
	£	£		£	£
Goods purchased and transferred . £11,000		3,800	Sales . . .	8,500	3,000
Less Closing Stock . . 1,000		950	Transfers to Branch at Invoice price . .	3,800	
	10,000	2,850			
Less Goods transferred as below . 3,200					
	6,800				
Add Gross Profit 25% (*a*) . . 1,700					
	8,500				
Goods transferred as above . £3,200					
Add Gross Profit $\frac{3}{16} = 18\frac{3}{4}$% (*b*) . 600					
	3,800	150			
	£12,300	£3,000		£12,300	£3,000
Provision for unrealized Profit on Unsold Branch Stock . .	150		Gross Profit [(*a*) and (*b*)] b/d	2,300	150
Net Profit . . .	2,150	150	Sales . . £1,700		
			Transfers . 600		
			£2,300		
	£2,300	£150		£2,300	£150

SUMMARY OF HEAD OFFICE TRADING ACCOUNT
FOR THE YEAR ENDED 31ST DECEMBER

	£		£
Purchases . . .	11,000	Sales (£8,500 + £3,000) . .	11,500
Less Closing Stock (£1,000 + £800) .	1,800		
	9,200		
Gross Profit 25% . .	2,300		
	£11,500		£11,500

The cost of goods sold is 80 per cent of Sales.

	£
The Head Office Sales are (Receipts from Debtors £6,100 + Closing Debtors £400 + Cash Sales £2,000)	8,500
Less 20 per cent thereon	1,700
Cost of Sales at Head Office (Profit 25 per cent thereof) . . .	6,800
But Goods were transferred to Branch (Cost)	3,200
Total Cost of Goods sold at Head Office and Branch . . .	£10,000

As the transfers to Branch are at selling price, the invoice price to Branch is—

	£
Cost of Goods	3,200
Add 25 per cent	800
	4,000
Less 5 per cent of £4,000	200
	£3,800
Profit thereon accruing to Head Office £3,800 − £3,200	£600

There is no provision for unrealized profit on unsold goods required at Branch as the Stock thereat is taken to it at "cost," i.e. invoice price from Head Office.

The provision for such unrealized profit is—

$\dfrac{20 - 5}{100 - 5} = \tfrac{15}{95} \times £950$ . . . . . (see below) £150

Cost price of Goods £950 − 150 . . . . (see below) £800

i.e. $\tfrac{100}{95} \times \tfrac{80}{100} \times £950$ . . . . . . (see below) £800

	£
Alternatively the various percentages may be shown thus—	
Assumed Cost	16
Profit 25 per cent	4
Selling price	20
Less 5 per cent deduction from selling price ($\tfrac{1}{20} \times 20$)	1
Price to Branch	£19

Therefore for every £19 of Branch Goods at "invoice" price to Branch (£19)
£3 is loading (£4 − £1) therefore $\tfrac{-3}{6} \times £950$ is Reserve = £150, leaving
true cost $\tfrac{16}{19} \times £950$ £800

25. *Method 1—*

Dr.   BRANCH STOCK   Cr.

	£			£
To Goods from Head Office	10,000	By Returns to Head Office	.	500
		,, Sales (See Note 4)	.	8,400
		,, Closing Stock .	c/d	1,100
	£10,000			£10,000
To Stock . . . b/d	1,100			

Dr.   GOODS SENT TO BRANCH   Cr.

	£			£
To Returns from Branch .	500	By Goods to Branch .	.	10,000
,, Returns from Customers	50			
,, Purchases Account	7,560			
,, Branch Adjustment Account . .	1,890			
	£10,000			£10,000

Dr.		BRANCH ADJUSTMENT ACCOUNT		Cr.
	£			£
To Provision for unrealized profit on Goods at Branch – 20% of £1,100 c/d	220	By Goods sent to Branch .		1,890
„ Branch Profit and Loss— 20% of £8,350 . .	1,670			
	£1,890			£1,890
		By Provision . . b/d		220

Dr.		BRANCH DEBTORS[1]		Cr.
	£			£
To Branch Stock— Sales . . .	8,400	By Goods sent to Branch— Returns to Head Office .		50
		„ Cash		6,010
		„ Balance . . . c/d		2,340
	£8,400			£8,400
To Balance . . b/d	2,340			

BRANCH CASH[1]

	£			£
To Branch Debtors . .	6,010	By Bank Remittances from Branch . . .		5,000
		„ Balance . . . c/d		1,010
	£6,010			£6,010
To Balance . . b/d	1,010			

[See *Accountancy*, 4th ed., page 1918 *et seq.*]

Method 2—

Instead of the first three accounts in (1) there will appear one account only—

Dr.			BRANCH STOCK		Cr.	
	Memorandum (selling price)			Memorandum (selling price)		
	£	£		£	£	
To Goods from Head Office	10,000	8,000	By Sales (see Note 4) . .	8,400	8,400	
„ Returns from customers .	50[1]	50[1]	„ Goods to Head Office .	500	400	
„ Gross Profit . .		1,670	„ Goods to Head Office .	50[1]	40[1]	
			„ Closing Stock . c/d	1,100	880	
	£10,050	£9,720		£10,050	£9,720	
To Stock . . . b/d	1,100	880				

[1] Branch Debtors and Branch Cash as in (1), i.e. as above.

The Returns from customers direct to Head Office will be passed through the Branch Stock Account "in" (credit to customers at *Selling* price) and "out" (debit to Purchases at *cost* price).

[See *Accountancy*, 4th ed., page 1927 *et seq.*]

Method 3—

Dr.　　　　　　　　　　　　BRANCH　　　　　　　　　　　Cr.

	£		£
To Goods . . .	8,000	By Cash remitted . . .	5,000
„ Balance, Gross Profit .	1,670	„ Goods returned . .	400
		„ Goods returned ex custo-	
		mers	40
		„ Closing Balances c/d—	
		Cash . . £1,010	
		Debtors . 2,340	
		Stock . . 880	
			4,230
	£9,670		£9,670
To Balances . . b/d	4,230		

[See *Accountancy*, 4th ed., page 1904 *et seq.*]

Method 4—

Dr.　　　　　　　　　　　BRANCH STOCK　　　　　　　　　Cr.

	£		£
To Goods from Head Office	10,000	By Returns to Head Office .	500
		„ Sales (See Note 4) . .	8,400
		„ Closing Stock . . c/d	1,100
	£10,000		£10,000
To Stock (See Note 3) .	1,100		

Dr.　　　　　　　　GOODS SENT TO BRANCH　　　　　　　Cr.

	£		£
To Returns from Branch .	500	By Goods to Branch . .	10,000
„ Returns from customers	50		
„ *Branch Trading Account—*			
Sales, less Returns .	8,350		
„ Closing Stock . c/d	1,100		
	£10,000		£10,000
		By Stock (See Note 3) . b/d	1,100

BRANCH TRADING ACCOUNT

	£		£
To Purchases, *less* Returns	7,560	*By Sales, less Returns* . .	8,350
„ Gross Profit . .	1,670	„ Closing Stock (See Note 3)	880
	£9,230		£9,230

Notes—

(1) The item of purchases (Branch) will be transferred from Head Office Purchases direct to Branch Trading Account (£8,000 — £400 — £40).

(2) The item of Sales will be transferred from Goods sent to Branch Account.

(3) The item of Closing Stock will be **introduced** in to the Branch Trading Account in the usual way—

Debit Branch Stock: Credit Branch Trading Account.

This procedure is necessary as the debit brought down on Branch Stock (£1,100) has a reciprocal credit brought down on Goods sent to Branch (£1,100), one eliminating the other.

(4) A difficulty may arise in Methods (1) (2) and (3) because the sales by Branch are not given in the question. As, however, the Branch Cash received must be (*a*) £5,000 remitted to Head Office, *plus* (*b*) Branch Cash in hand (£1,010) it follows that the receipts from Debtors are £6,010. As the Closing Debtors are £2,340 the receipts from Debtors £6,010 and returns from Debtors £50, the gross sales made by Branch are £8,400. (The net sales are £8,350, as there are £50 Returns from customers direct to Head Office).

[See *Accountancy*, 4th ed., page 1928 *et seq.*]

Six per cent per annum with half-yearly rests is equivalent to 3 per cent per annum. The present value of an annuity of £1 for six years is £5·4172.

By simple proportion, therefore, £600 is the present value of six equal instalments of—

$$£\frac{600}{5\cdot4172} = £110\cdot7583 = £110\cdot76$$

This calculation may be proved as follows:

Half-Year No.	Balance at Commencement (i)	Interest at 3% (ii)	Instalment Paid (iii)	Amount of Capital Repaid (iv) [(iii) — (ii)]
	£	£	£	£
1	600·00	18·00	110·76	92·76
2	507·24	15·22	110·76	95·54
3	411·70	12·35	110·76	98·41
4	313·29	9·40	110·76	101·36
5	211·93	6·36	110·76	104·40
6	107·53	3·23	110·76	107·53
		£64·56	£664·56	£600·00

The hire-purchase price is £600 + £200 initial deposit + £64·56 interest = £864·56.

2. *Hire Purchaser's books.*

Dr.   MACHINE   Cr.

	£			£
Year 1 To Hire Vendor . .	2,578·51	Year 1 By Depreciation . .		128·92
		,, Balance . . c/d		2,449·59
	2,578·51			2,578·51
Year 2 To Balance . . b/d	2,449·59	Year 2 By Depreciation . .		122·48
		,. Balance . . c/d		2,327·11
	2,449·59			£2,449·59
Year 3 To Balance . . b/d	2,327·11	Year 3 By Depreciation . .		116·35
		,, Balance . c/d		2,210·76
	£2,327·11			£2,327·11
Year 4 To Balance . . b/d	2,210·76			

Note. Depreciation provided on the diminishing balance method.

Dr.   HIRE VENDOR   Cr.

		£		£
Year 1 To Cash (Deposit) . .		600·00	Year 1 By Machine . . .	2,578·51
,, Cash . . .		640·00	,, Interest	
,, Balance . . c/d		1,536·36	[10% on £1,978·521 . .	197·85
		£2,776·36		£2,776·36
Year 2 To Cash		890·00	Year 2 By Balance . . b/d	1,536·36
,, Balance . . c/d		800·00	,, Interest . . .	153·64
		£1,690·00		£1,690·00
Year 3 To Cash . . .		880·00	Year 3 By Balance . . b/d	800·00
			,, Interest . . .	80·00
		£880·00		£880·00

(*See notes at end of answer.*)

Hire Vendor's books.

Dr.				SALES				Cr.
								£
				Year 1	By Hire Purchaser	.	.	2,578·51

Dr.				HIRE PURCHASER				Cr.
				£				£
Year 1	To Sales .	.	.	2,578·51	Year 1	By Cash .	. .	600·00
	,, Interest	.	.	197·85		,, Cash .	. .	640·00
						,, Balance	. . c/d	1,536·36
				£2,776·36				£2,776·36
Year 2	To Balance	.	b/d	1,536·36	Year 2	By Cash .	. .	890·00
	,, Interest	.	.	153·64		,, Balance	. . c/d	800·00
				£1,690·00				£1,690·00
Year 3	To Balance	.	b/d	800·00	Year 3	By Cash .	. .	880·00
	,, Interest	.	.	80·00				
				£880·00				£880·00

Dr.			INTEREST				Cr.
			£				£
Year 1	To Profit and Loss Acct.	.	197·85	Year 1	By Hire Purchaser	. .	197·85
Year 2	To Profit and Loss Acct.	.	153·64	Year 2	By Hire Purchaser	. .	153·64
Year 3	To Profit and Loss Acct.	.	80·00	Year 3	By Hire Purchaser	. .	80·00

Notes. (i) The answer must be worked backwards to find the original purchase price. The beginning balances are—

		£
Third year	$\frac{10}{11}$ × £880	800·00
Second year	$\frac{10}{11}$ × £1,690	1,536·36
First year	£600 plus $\frac{10}{11}$ × £2,176·36	2,578·51

The figure can be found by algebra, e.g. in the third year, letting x be the beginning figure, then the answer is: $x + \frac{10x}{100} = $ £880, i.e. £800.

(ii) The answer assumes that the transaction took place at the commencement of the year. (See page 401.)

3. *Hire Vendor's books.*

Dr.				A				Cr.
				£				£
Year 1	To Hire Sales	.	.	3,000·00	Year 1	By Cash	. .	1,200·00
	,, Interest	.	.	300·00		,, Balance	. . c/d	2,100·00
				£3,300·00				£3,300·00
Year 2	To Balance	.	b/d	2,100·00	Year 2	By Cash .	. .	1,110·00
	,, Interest	.	.	210·00		,, Balance	. . c/d	1,200·00
				£2,310·00				£2,310·00
Year 3	To Balance	.	b/d	1,200·00	Year 3	By Hire Sales Returns		
	,, Interest					Account[1]	.	668·31
	($\frac{1}{2}$ year on £1,200)	.		60·00		,, Cash .	. .	60·00
	,, Interest					,, Cash .	. .	558·27
	($\frac{1}{2}$ year on £531·69)	.		26·58				
				£1,286·58				£1,286·58

[1] The Machinery will be taken into Stock at revaluation and the account be credited with re-sale price (and debited with appropriate expenses).

Hire Purchaser's books.

| Dr. | | | | MACHINES | | | Cr. |

			£				£
Year 1	To Vendor	. .	3,000·00	Year 1	By Depreciation . .		300·00
					,, Balance . . c/d		2,700·00
			£3,000·00				£3,000·00
Year 2	To Balance . b/d		2,700·00	Year 2	By Depreciation . .		270·00
					,, Balance . . c/d		2,430·00
			£2,700·00				£2,700·00
Year 3	To Balance . .		2,430·00	Year 3	By Vendor—Returns .		668·31
					,, Depreciation [½ year on £810 at 10% per annum] .		40·50
					,, Loss on Sale . .		101·19
					,, Depreciation [year on £1,620 at 10% per annum] .		162·00
					,, Balance . . c/d		1,458·00
			£2,430·00				£2,430·00
Year 4	To Balance . b/d		1,458·00				

| Dr. | | | | HIRE VENDOR | | | Cr. |

			£				£
Year 1	To Cash . .		1,200·00	Year 1	By Machines . .		3,000·00
	,, Balance . c/d		2,100·00		,, Interest . .		300·00
			£3,300·00				£3,300·00
Year 2	To Cash . .		1,110·00	Year 2	By Balance . b/d		2,100·00
	,, Balance . c/d		1,200·00		,, Interest . .		210·00
			£2,310·00				£2,310·00
Year 3	To Machines . .		668·31	Year 3	By Balance . b/d		1,200·00
	,, Cash . .		60·00		,, Interest . .		60·00
	,, Cash . .		558·27		,, Interest . .		26·58
			£1,286·58				£1,286·58

The position may be summarized as follows—

	Machines Retained	Machines Returned	Total
	£	£	£
Cost	2,000·00	1,000·00	3,000·00
Depreciation—Year 1 . . .	200·00	100·00	300·00
	1,800·00	900·00	2,700·00
Depreciation—Year 2 . . .	180·00	90·00	270·00
	1,620·00	810·00	2,430·00
Depreciation—Year 3 . . .	162·00	[1]40·50	202·50
	1,458·00	769·50	2,227·50
Less Allowance by Hire Vendor .		668·31	668·31
		101·19	1,559·19
Less Loss on Sale		101·19	101·19
Balance per Accounts . . .	£1,458·00		£1,458·00

The amount paid by the purchase, £2,928, is accounted for as follows—

	£
Interest	596·58
Depreciation	772·50
Loss on Sale	101·19
Balance	1,458·00
	£2,928·27

	£
Allowance price is calculated thus—	
Cost of Machine	1,000·00
Less Depreciation, 15%	150·00
	850·00
Less Depreciation, 15%	127·50
	722·50
Less Depreciation, 15% (½ year) . .	54·19
	£668·31

The question is capable of several answers, because—

(1) Depreciation may be taken on the fixed or equal instalment method, although the words "with yearly rests" would appear to mean the diminishing balance method.

(2) The amount payable annually, £900, may include principal and interest.

(3) (a) The interest payable by the purchaser may be (in the third year) on the proportion of the debt (at the end of the second year) reduced by the allowance price, or (b), interest may be fully discharged on the whole balance due (at the end of the second year) for the first half-year, i.e. to the date the machine is returned, and for the second half-year on the balance.

---

[1] ½ year only.

Assuming (1), (2), and (3*b*), the accounts are—

Hire Vendor's books.

Dr.			A				Cr.	
			£					£
Year 1	To Sales		3,000	Year 1	By Cash . . .			900
	,, Interest . . .		300		,, Balance . . .	c/d		2,400
			£3.300					£3,300
Year 2	To Balance . . .	b/d	2,400	Year 2	By Cash . . .			900
	,, Interest . . .		240		,, Balance . . .	c/d		1,740
			£2,640					£2,640
Year 3	To Balance . . .	b/d	1,740	Year 3	By Returns[1] . .			700
	,, Interest—				,, Cash . . .			900
	½ year on £700 . £35				,, Balance . . .	c/d		279
	Year on £1,040 . 104							
			139					
			£1,879					£1,879
Year 4	To Balance . . .	b/d	279					

Hire Purchaser's books.

Dr.			MACHINES				Cr.	
			£					
Year 1	To Vendor . . .		3,000	Year 1	By Depreciation . . .			300
					,, Balance . . .	c/d		2,700
			£3,000					£3,000
Year 2	To Balance . . .	b/d	2,700	Year 2	By Depreciation . . .			300
					,, Balance . . .	c/d		2,400
			£2,700					£2,700
Year 3	To Balance . . .	b/d	2,400	Year 3	By Vendor—Returns[1] . .			700
					,, Depreciation			
					[½ year on £1,000 at			
					10% per annum] .			50
					,, Loss on Sale . . .			50
					,, Depreciation			
					[Year on £2,000 at			
					10% per annum] .			200
					Balance . . .	c/d		1,400
			£2,400					£2,400
Year 4	To Balance . . .	b/d	1,400					

[1] I.e. £1,000 *less* £300 which is £150 per year for two years on the straight line method. If depreciation at 15 per cent per annum is to be taken up to the middle of the third year, the allowance will be £1,000 *less* £300 *less* £75. i.e. £625.

Dr.			HIRE VENDOR				Cr.
			£				£
Year 1	To Cash		900	Year 1	By Machines . . .		3,000
	,, Balance . . . c/d		2,400		,, Interest . . .		300
			£3,300				£3,300
Year 2	To Cash		900	Year 2	By Balance . . . b/d		2,400
	,, Balance . . . c/d		1,740		,, Interest . . .		240
			£2,640				£2,640
Year 3	To Machines—			Year 3	By Balance . . . b/d		1,740
	Returns . . .		700		,, Interest—		
	,, Cash . . .		900		½ year on £700 . £35		
	,, Balance . . . c/d		279		Year on £1,040 . 104		
						—	139
			£1,879				£1,879
				Year 4	By Balance . . . b/d		279

4. Dr.   TALLBOY & CO. LTD.   Cr.

19.4				£	19.4				£
Jan. 1	To Hire Sales . . .			1,500	Jan. 1	By Cash			200
Dec. 31	,, Interest . . .			65	Dec. 31	,, Cash . . .			300
						,, Balance . . c/d			1,065
				£1,565					£1,565
19.5					19.5				
Jan. 1	To Balance . . b/d			1,065	Dec. 31	By Cash			300
Dec. 31	,, Interest . . .			53		,, Balance . . c/d			818
				£1,118					£1,118
19.6					19.6				
Jan. 1	To Balance . . b/d			818	Dec. 31	By Cash . . .			300
Dec. 31	,, Interest . . .			41		,, Balance . . c/d			559
				£859					£859
19.7					19.7				
Jan. 1	To Balance . . b/d			559	Dec. 31	By Cash . . .			300
Dec. 31	,, Interest . . .			28		,, Balance . . c/d			287
				£587					£587
19.8					19.8				
Jan. 1	To Balance . . b/d			287	Dec. 31	By Cash			300
Dec. 31	,, Interest . . .			13					
				£300					£300

Notes. (i) £1,500 will be included in the entries in the Sales Journal and form part of the total Hire Sales for the year.

(ii) Interest, £65 etc., will be posted to the credit of Interest Account, or (if necessary) included in the entries in the Interest Journal, the total of which will be posted to the credit of Interest Account.

(iii) The transactions, being high in value, have been entered on the sales plan and interest separately recorded. Consequently the profit on the delivery has been credited to the 19.4 Trading Account, and a provision may be necessary to cover possible loss. Alternatively, the Interest Suspense Method may be adopted.

(iv) The balance standing to the debit of Tallboy & Co. Ltd. will be shown in the Vendor's Balance Sheet as Stock out on Hire Purchase (*less* provision, if any).

An alternative plan is as follows—

1st year.	Debit Hire Sales.	*With the debit balance against the Hire Purchaser at the end of the first year.*
	Credit Hire Purchaser's Suspense.	

The above entries leave Hire Sales with a credit corresponding with the amounts actually paid by Hire Purchaser on account of principal, and at the same time eliminate the debit balance against the Hire Purchaser. In the above instance, the transfer is £1,065—sales thus being £435, i.e. £1,500 — £1,065, as the total of the payments is £500, which discharges £435 Principal and £65 Interest.

As the portion of Sale is eliminated it must be taken into Stock at cost price, that is, credited to Trading Account and shown in Balance Sheet.

Subsequent years. Each year a transfer will be made so as to eliminate the balance due by the Hire Purchaser, and the amount reduced to cost and incorporated into the Trading Account, e.g. in the second year (in reference to the foregoing example) Hire Sales Account will be credited with £247 (£1,065 — £818).

Thus, the net credits to Trading Account as Sales are—

						£
19.4	.	.	.	.	.	435
19.5	.	.	.	.	.	247
19.6	.	.	.	.	.	259
19.7	.	.	.	.	.	272
19.8	.	.	.	.	.	287
	Total	.	.	.	.	£1,500

Assuming that the cost price of the goods is £1,000, the Trading Account will contain closing and opening Stock (to nearest £)—

					Dr.	Cr.
					£	£
19.4	.	.	.	.	Nil	710 (⅔ of £1,065)
19.5	.	.	.	.	710	545 (⅔ of £818)
19.6	.	.	.	.	545	373 (⅔ of £559)
19.7	.	.	.	.	373	191 (⅔ of £287)
19.8	.	.	.	.	191	Nil

The Hire Purchaser's Suspense Account will be—

Dr.					HIRE PURCHASER'S SUSPENSE				Cr.	
				£						£
19.5	To Hire Sales	.	.	.	247	19.4	By Hire Sales	.	.	.	1,065
	,, Balance	.	.	c/d	818					
19.6	To Hire Sales	.	.	.	259	19.5	By Balance	.	.	b/d	818
	,, Balance	.	.	c/d	559					
19.7	To Hire Sales	.	.	.	272	19.6	By Balance	.	.	b/d	559
	,, Balance	.	.	c/d	287					
19.8	To Hire Sales	.	.	.	287	19.7	By Balance	.	.	b/d	287

5. *Dr.*   WAGONS   *Cr.*

19.. Jan.	1	To Cash	.	.	.	.	£ 600	19.. Dec. 31	By Depreciation—10% on 4,600 „ Balance . . c/d	£ 460 140
19.. Jan.	1	To Balance . „ Cash	. .	. .	b/d .	140 800		19.. Dec. 31	By Depreciation—10% on £4,600 „ Balance . . c/d	460 480
19.. Jan.	1	To Balance . „ Cash	. .	. .	b/d .	480 800		19.. Dec. 31	By Depreciation—10% on £4,600 „ Balance . . c/d	460 820
19.. Jan.	1	To Balance . „ Cash	. .	. .	b/d .	820 800		19.. Dec. 31	By Depreciation—10% on £4,600 „ Balance . . c/d	460 1,160
19.. Jan.	1	To Balance . „ Cash	. .	. .	b/d .	1,160 800		19.. Dec. 31	By Depreciation—10% on £4,600 „ Balance . . c/d	460 1,500
19.. Jan.	1	To Balance . „ Cash	. .	. .	b/d .	1,500 800		19.. Dec. 31	By Depreciation—10% on £4,600 „ Balance . . c/d	460 1,840
19.. Jan.	1	To Balance[1]	.	.	b/d	1,840				

Interest Account will be debited in the ordinary way, thus—

Year						£
1	5% on £4,000	.	.	.	.	200
2	5% on £3,200	.	.	.	.	160
3	5% on £2,400	.	.	.	.	120
4	5% on £1,600	.	.	.	.	80
5	5% on £800	.	.	.	.	40

[1] Cost £4,600 *less* 60% aggregate depreciation, £2,760 = £1,840.

The above solution has been worked on the assumption that the annual payments are made on the anniversary of the initial payment of £600. If the first payment of £600 *does* occur within the same period as the initial payment, say 31st December, the Wagons Account will appear—

Dr.		WAGONS		Cr.

19..			£	19..			£
Jan. 1	To Cash	. . . .	600	Dec. 31	By Depreciation—10% on £4,600		460
Dec. 31	,, Cash	. . . .	800		,, Balance . . . c/d		940
			£1,400				£1,400
19..				19..			
Jan. 1	To Balance	. . b/d	940	Dec. 31	By Depreciation—10% on £4,600		460
Dec. 31	,, Cash	. . . .	800		,, Balance . . .		1,280
			£1,740				£1,740
19..				19..			
Jan. 1	To Balance	. . b/d	1,280	Dec. 31	By Depreciation—10% on £4,600		460
Dec. 31	,, Cash	. . . .	800		,, Balance . . . c/d		1,620
			£2,080				£2,080
19..				19..			
Jan. 1	To Balance	. . b/d	1,620	Dec. 31	By Depreciation—10% on £4,600		460
Dec. 31	,, Cash	. . . .	800		,, Balance . . . c/d		1,960
			£2,420				£2,420
19..				19..			
Jan. 1	To Balance	. . b/d	1,960	Dec. 31	By Depreciation—10% on £4,600		460
Dec. 31	,, Cash	. . . .	800		,, Balance . . . c/d		2,300
			£2,760				£2,760
19..							
Jan. 1	To Balance[1]	. . b/d	2,300				

[1] Cost £4,600 *less* 50% aggregate depreciation, £2,300 = £2,300.

6. Dr.   HIRE PURCHASE STOCK   Cr.

19..			£	19..			£
Jan. 1	To Stock . . b/d		1,620	Dec. 31	By Sales . . .		2,480
Dec. 31	,, Goods on Hire Purchase .		6,534		, Stock . . c/d		5,674
			£8,154				£8,154
19..							
Jan. 1	To Stock . . b/d		5,674				

Dr.   GOODS ON HIRE PURCHASE   Cr.

19..		£	19..		£
Dec. 31	To Stock . . .	4,083·75	Dec. 31	By Hire Purchase Stock	6,534·00
	,, Hire Purchase Adjustment Account .	2,450·25			
		£6,534·00			£6,534·00

Dr.   HIRE PURCHASE ADJUSTMENT ACCOUNT   Cr.

19..			£	19..			£
Dec. 31	To Gross Profit to Profit and Loss Account .		930·00[1]	Jan. 1	By Balance . . b/d		607·50
	,, Reserve . c/d.		2,127·75	Dec. 31	,, Goods on Hire Purchase . .		2,450·25
			£3,057·75				£3,057·75
				19..			
				Jan. 1	By Balance . . b/d		2,127·75

[1] Profit of ⅜ of £2,480.

Dr.					SUNDRY DEBTORS			*Cr.*
19..				£	19..			£
Dec. 31	To Hire Purchase Stock—				Dec. 31	By Cash . . .		2,100
	Sales .	.	.	2,480		„ Balances .	. c/d	380
				£2,480				£2,480
19..								
Jan. 1	To Balances	.	. b/d	380				

Notes. Entries will be made in the Memorandum Ledger containing the details of each customer's account.

The reduction from sale price to cost price is $\frac{100}{160}$, i.e. $\frac{5}{8}$ of selling price; e.g. £6,534 selling price = £4,083·75 (i.e. $\frac{5}{8}$ × £6,534) loading being £2,450·25 (i.e. 60% of cost, £4,083·75).

7. *Dr.*   Z LOAN   *Cr.*

				£					£
Period 1	To Cash	.	. .	100·00	Period 1	By Cash	.	. .	866·00
	„ Balance	.	c/d	783·32		„ Interest	.	. .	17·32
				£883·32					£883·32
Period 2	To Cash	.	. .	100·00	Period 2	By Balance	.	. b/d	783·32
	„ Balance	.	c/d	698·99		„ Interest	.	. .	15·67
				£798·99					£798·99
Period 3	To Cash	.	. .	100·00	Period 3	By Balance	.	. b/d	698·99
	„ Balance	.	c/d	612·97		„ Interest	.	. .	13·98
				£712·97					£712·97
Period 4	To Cash	.	. .	100·00	Period 4	By Balance	.	. b/d	612·97
	„ Balance	.	c/d	525·23		„ Interest	.	. .	12·26
				£625·23					£625·23
Period 5	To Cash	.	. .	100·00	Period 5	By Balance	.	. b/d	525·23
	„ Balance	.	c/d	435·73		„ Interest	.	. .	10·50
				£535·73					£535·73
Period 6	To Cash	.	. .	100·00	Period 6	By Balance	.	. b/d	435·73
	„ Balance	.	c/d	344·44		„ Interest	.	. .	8·71
				£444·44					£444·44
Period 7	To Cash	.	. .	100·00	Period 7	By Balance	.	. b/d	344·44
	„ Balance	.	c/d	251·33		„ Interest	.	. .	6·89
				£351·33					£351·33
Period 8	To Cash	.	. .	100·00	Period 8	By Balance	.	. b/d	251·33
	„ Balance	.	c/d	156·36		„ Interest	.	. .	5·03
				£256·36					£256·36
Period 9	To Cash	.	. .	100·00	Period 9	By Balance	.	. b/d	156·36
	„ Balance	.	c/d	59·49		„ Interest	.	. .	3·13
				£159·49					£159·49
Period 10	To Cash	.	. .	60·68	Period 10	By Balance	.	. b/d	59·49
						„ Interest	.	. .	1·19
				£60·68					£60·68

If the firm purchases the machine on the hire purchase system from R Co. Ltd., it will have to pay £1,000 in five yearly instalments of £200 each. On the other hand, if the firm accepts a loan from Z on the terms proposed, the total amount payable will be £960·68 spread over five years in half-yearly instalments of £100 until the final instalment of £60·68.

In the circumstances it is considered that the latter method is preferable.

As an additional factor, the title in the machines will, if Z's offer be accepted, have passed to the firm, a consideration which may be of importance.

The account of the Hire Vendor, if the hire purchase terms are accepted, would be—

Dr.					HIRE VENDOR				Cr.
				£					£
Year 1	To Cash	.	.	. 200·00	Year 1	By Machine	.	.	. 866·00
	,, Balance	.	.	. 709·30		,, Interest	.	.	. 43·30
				£909·30					£909·30
Year 2	To Cash	.	.	. 200·00	Year 2	By Balance	.	.	. 709·30
	,, Balance	.	.	. 544·77		,, Interest	.	.	. 35·47
				£744·77					£744·77
Year 3	To Cash	.	.	. 200·00	Year 3	By Balance	.	.	. 544·77
	,, Balance	.	.	. 372·01		,, Interest	.	.	. 27·24
				£572·01					£572·01
Year 4	To Cash	.	.	. 200·00	Year 4	By Balance	.	.	. 372·01
	,, Balance	.	.	. 190·61		,, Interest	.	.	. 18·60
				£390·61					£390·61
Year 5	To Cash	.	.	. 200·00	Year 5	By Balance	.	.	. 190·61
						,, Interest[1]	.	.	. 9·39
				£200·00					£200·00

[1] Interest in the last year is not exact, as five yearly instalments of £200 do not discharge a debt of £866 at 5% per annum. The precise instalment is £200·03.

8. JOURNAL

			£	£
1st Quarter	Wagons . . . . . . *Dr.*		200·00	
	Interest[1] . . . . . . *Dr.*		70·00	
	Repairs . . . . . . *Dr.*		50·00	
	To Hire Vendor			320·00
	Being instalment of Principal and Interest on Wagons and Repairs.			
2nd Quarter	Wagons . . . . . . *Dr.*		200·00	
	Interest[1] . . . . . . *Dr.*		67·50	
	Repairs . . . . . . *Dr.*		50·00	
	To Hire Vendor			317·50
	Being instalment of Principal and Interest on Wagons and Repairs.			
3rd Quarter	Wagons . . . . . . *Dr.*		200·00	
	Interest[1] . . . . . . *Dr.*		65·00	
	Repairs . . . . . . *Dr.*		50·00	
	To Hire Vendor			315·00
	Being instalment of Principal and Interest on Wagons and Repairs.			
4th Quarter	Wagons . . . . . . *Dr.*		200·00	
	Interest[1] . . . . . . *Dr.*		62·50	
	Repairs . . . . . . *Dr.*		50·00	
	To Hire Vendor			312·50
	Being instalment of Principal and Interest on Wagons and Repairs.			

[1] Interest at $1\frac{1}{4}$% on £5,600, £5,400, £5,200, and £5,000 respectively.

Notes. (i) Assumed that the first payment is made at the end of the first quarter.

(ii) Assumed that interest is calculated in quarterly rests.
(iii) Assumed that the charge for repairs is made quarterly.
(iv) Assumed that the instalments of £200 are payable *in addition to* interest.
(v) Cash price is £200 × 28, viz. twenty-eight quarterly payments of £200.

9. *Dr.* FURNITURE *Cr.*

19.6		£	19.7			£
Apr. 1	To Universal Stores—Cash Value of Furniture on Hire Purchase . . .	2,500·00	Mar. 31	By Depreciation—5% on £2,500 . .		125·00
				„ Balance . .	c/d	2,375·00
		£2,500·00				£2,500·00
19.7			19.8			
Apr. 1	To Balance . . b/d	2,375·00	Mar. 31	By Depreciation—5% on £2,375 .		118·75
				„ Balance . .	c/d	2,256·25
		£2,375·00				£2,375·00
19.8						
Apr. 1	To Balance . . b/d	2,256·25				

Dr.				UNIVERSAL STORES				*Cr.*
19.6				£	19.6			£
June 30	To Cash	.	.	330·00	Apr. 1	By Furniture . .		2,500·00
	,, Balance	.	c/d	2,201·25	June 30	,. Interest at 5% per annum . .		31·25
				£2,531·25				£2,531·25
Sept. 30	To Cash .	.	.	330·00	July 1	By Balance .	b/d	2,201·25
	,, Balance	.	c/d	1,898·77	Sept. 30	,, Interest at 5% per annum .		27·52
				£2,228·77				£2,228·77
Dec. 31	To Cash .	.	.	330·00	Oct. 1	By Balance .	b/d	1,898·77
	,, Balance	.	c/d	1,592·50	Dec. 31	,, Interest at 5% per annum .		23·73
				£1,922·50				£1,922·50
19.7					19.7			
Mar. 31	To Cash .	.	.	330·00	Jan. 1	By Balance .	b/d	1,592·50
	,, Balance	.	c/d	1,282·41	Mar. 31	,, Interest at 5% per annum .		19·91
				£1,612·41				£1,612·41
June 20	To Cash .	.	.	330·00	Apr. 1	By Balance .	b/d	1,282·41
	,, Balance	.	c/d	968·44	June 30	,, Interest at 5% per annum .		16·03
				£1,298·44				£1,298·44
Sept. 30	To Cash .	.	.	330·00	July 1	By Balance .	b/d	968·44
	,, Balance	.	c/d	650·55	Sept. 30	,, Interest at 5% per annum .		12·11
				£980·55				£980·55
Dec. 31	To Cash .	.	.	330·00	Oct. 1	By Balance .	b/d	650·55
	,, Balance	.	c/d	328·68	Dec. 31	,, Interest at 5% per annum .		8·13
				£658·68				£658·68
19.8					19.8			
Mar. 31	To Cash .	.	.	330·00	Jan. 1	By Balance .	b/d	328·68
	,. Interest	.	.	2·79	Mar. 31	,, Interest at 5% per annum .		4·11
				£332·79				£332·79

Alternative Solution—

Dr.			FURNITURE			Cr.
		£	19.7			**£**
19.6			Mar. 31	By Balance . . c/d	1,217·59
June 30	To Cash in part discharge[1]					
	of Principal . .	298·75				
	,, Cash in part discharge					
	of Principal . .	302·48				
Dec. 31	,, Cash in part discharge					
	of Principal . .	306·27				
19.7						
Mar. 31	,, Cash in part discharge					
	of Principal . .	310·09				
		£1,217·59			£1,217·59
19.7			19.8			
Apr. 1	To Balance . . b/d	1,217·59	Mar. 31	By Balance . . c/d	2,500·00
June 30	,, Cash	313·97				
Sept. 30	,, Cash	317·89				
Dec. 31	,, Cash	321·87				
19.8						
Mar. 31	,, Cash . . .	328·68				
		£2,500·00			£2,500·00
Mar. 31	To Balance . . b/d	2,500·00	Mar. 31	By Depreciation . .	243·75
				,, Balance . . c/d	2,256·25
		£2,500·00			£2,500·00
19.8						
Apr. 1	To Balance . . b/d	2,256·25				

[1] See page 391. £330 − £31·25 = £298·75, and so on.

Dr.			INTEREST		Cr.
		£	19.7		**£**
19.6			Mar. 31	By Profit and Loss Account	102·41
June 30	To Cash	31·25			
Sept. 30	,, Cash	27·52			
Dec. 31	,, Cash	23·73			
19.7					
Mar. 31	,, Cash . . .	19·91			
		£102·41			£102·41
			19.8		
June 30	To Cash	16·03	Mar. 31	By Excess Interest . .	2·79
Sept. 30	,, Cash	12·11		,, Profit and Loss Account	37·59
Dec. 31	,, Cash	8·13			
19.8					
Mar. 31	,, Cash . . .	4·11			
		£40·38			£40·38

Dr.		DEPRECIATION		Cr.
19.8			19.7	
Mar. 31	To Furniture . .	243·75	Mar. 31	By Profit and Loss Account. 125·00
			19.8	
			Mar. 31	,, Profit and Loss Account 118·75
		£243·75		£243·75

10. *Dr.*   MACHINE   *Cr.*

19.4		£	19.4			£
Jan. 1	To X Discount Society— Cash Price . .	644·65	Dec. 31	By Depreciation . .		64·47
				,, Balance . . c/d		580·18
		£644·65				£644·65
19.5			19.5			
Jan. 1	To Balance . . b/d	580·18	Dec. 31	By Depreciation . .		58·02
				,, Balance . .		522·16
		£580·18				£580·18
19.6			19.6			
Jan. 1	To Balance . . b/d	522·16	Jan. 1	By Cash . . .		500·00
			Dec. 31	,, Loss to Profit and Loss Account . .		22·16
		£522·16				£522·16

Dr.   X DISCOUNT SOCIETY   *Cr.*

19.4		£	19.4			£
Jan. 1	To Cash	100·00	Jan. 1	By Machine . . .		644·65
Dec. 31	,, Cash	200·00	Dec. 31	,, Interest		
	,, Balance . . c/d	371·88		(5% on £544·65) .		27·23
		£671·88				£671·88
19.5			19.5			
Dec. 31	To Cash . . .	200·00	Jan. 1	By Balance . . b/d		371·88
	,, Balance . . c/d	190·47	Dec. 31	,, Interest		
				(5% on £371·88) .		18·59
		£390·47				£390·47
19.6			19.6			
Jan. 1	To Cash	£190·47	Jan. 1	By Balance . . b/d		£190·47

11.   TRADING AND PROFIT AND LOSS ACCOUNT
FOR THE YEAR ENDED 31ST DECEMBER, 19.8

	£			£
Opening Stock	6,900	Sales		
Purchases	34,400	Cash		10,400
Gross Profit . . . c/d	10,800	Hire Purchase . £48,400		
		Less provision for un- realized profit . 17,300		
				31,100
		Closing Stock		10,600
	£52,100			£52,100
General Expenses . . .	12,100	Gross Profit . . . b/d		10,800
Loss on Sale of Goods repossessed .	900	Net Loss for year . . . c/d		2,200
	£13,000			£13,000
Net Loss for year . . b/d	2,200	Net Loss transferred to Capital		
Adjustment for unrealized profit of previous years . . .	1,200	Account		3,400
	£3,400			£3,400

BALANCE SHEET AS AT 31ST DECEMBER, 19.8

		£			£
			Stock—		
X Capital—			On hand . . . £12,100		
Opening Balance . . £20,000			With customers on H.P.		
Less Loss . . 3,400			(£37,600 − £18,500) . 19,100		
		16,000			31,200
Creditors		16,600	Cash at Bank		2,000
		£33,200			£33,200

Working Accounts—

INSTALMENTS RECEIVABLE

	£		£
Per T.B. .	41,200	Goods repossessed .	3,600
		Balance . c/d	37,600
	£41,200		£41,200
Balance . b/d	37,600		

CASH SALES

	£		£
		Goods repossessed .	1,200
		Trading .	10,400
Per T.B. .	11,600		£11,600
	£11,600		

GOODS REPOSSESSED

	£		£
Instalments Receivable .	3,600	Sales .	1,200
		Balance at valuation . c/d	1,500
		Loss to P. & L. .	900
	£3,600		£3,600
Balance . b/d	1,500		

UNREALIZED PROFIT PROVISION

	£
P. & L. adj. for unrealized Profit—	
Previous years:	
40% of £3,000 .	1,200
Current year:	
50% of £34,600	17,300
	£18,500

SCHEDULES

	£
Stock	12,900
Less H.P. repossessed Stock at Cost .	2,300
	10,600
Add Stock repossessed at Valuation .	1,500
	£12,100

CALCULATION OF UNREALIZED PROFIT ON CURRENT YEAR'S TRANSACTIONS

By converting cash sales into notional Hire Purchase Sales the resulting notional Gross Profit and percentage can be ascertained thus—

		£
Hire purchases . . . . (actual)		48,400
Cash Sales as Hire Purchase Sales $\frac{100}{80}$ of £10,400 (£10,400 + £2,600)		
		13,000
	(notional)	£61,400

	£
Cost of Goods sold: Opening Stock £6,900 + Purchases £34,400 − Closing Stock £10,600	£30,700
Gross Profit, if all sales were on hire purchase = 50 per cent of sale price	£30,700

Alternative calculation—

	£
Sales £48,400 + £10,400	58,800
Add extra Sales if all H.P. ($\frac{1}{4} \times$ £10,400)	2,600
	61,400
Less Cost, as above	30,700
Gross Profit	£30,700

	£
Actual Gross Profit per accounts	10,800
Add Provision	17,300
	£28,100

The difference is £2,600, i.e. the amount by which the gross profit would have been increased had all sales been on hire purchase. (See (*a*) above.)

12.   TRADING ACCOUNT
FOR THE YEAR ENDED 31ST DECEMBER

			£					£
Cost of Sales—				Sales—				
Purchases . . .	£11,000			Cash . . .	(*y*)	£2,400		
Less Closing Stock .	3,800			Hire Purchase .	(*x*)	6,300		
			7,200					8,700
Provision for unearned profit on Hire								
Purchase Transactions . .		360						
Gross Profit on—								
Hire Purchase								
(£1,260 − £360) .	(*x*)	£900						
Cash Sales . .	(*y*)	240						
			1,140					
			£8,700					£8,700

(*x*) = 20 per cent (before provision).
(*y*) = 10 per cent.

£

Rate of Gross Profit on Hire Purchase transactions—
Hire Purchase Sales 6,300
Cash Sales converted to hire purchase basis—

$$2,400 \times \frac{112\frac{1}{2}}{100} \left(\frac{9}{8}\right) \quad . \quad . \quad . \quad . \quad . \quad . \quad . \quad 2,700$$

Sales if all made on hire purchase terms 9,000
Less Cost of Sales 7,200

Notional Gross Profit = 20 per cent of Sales £1,800

Provision on outstanding Debtors, 20 per cent of £1,800 (6,300 —
£4,500). £360

The Gross Profit for Cash Sales is £240, which, if the transactions had been on hire purchase would have been greater by 125 per cent, as the Cash Sales (if made on hire purchase) would have been greater by 12½ per cent, lifting the Gross Profit by £300 (i.e. £240 + 125 per cent thereof, £300) = £540, this being 25 per cent of the Cost of Sales attributable thereto, viz. £2,160 = £540 (20 per cent of Sales of £2,700).

If the Trading Account is split, the figures, which appear somewhat complicated, become self-explanatory.

TRADING ACCOUNT

	H.P. £		Cash £		H.P. £	Cash £
Cost of Sales . .	5,040		2,160	Sales . . .	6,300	2,400
Gross Profit (£1,500) (a)	1,260	(b)	240			
	£6,300		£2,400		£6,300	£2,400

(a) = 20 per cent.
(b) = 10 ,, ,,

Note. As the Gross Profit on Hire Purchase is 20 per cent and therefore £1,260, the Cost of Sales appropriate thereto is £5,040 (i.e. £1,260 × 4); this leaves the balance of Cost of Sales as £2,160 (£7,200 — £5,040) and the Gross Profit £240 (£1,500 — £1,260).

If the Cash Sales became Hire Purchase Sales they would be £2,400 + £300 (12½ per cent addition to Cash Sales) = £2,700, and the Gross Profit £540 (£240 + £300), which is 20 per cent on £2,700, or 25 per cent on Cost of Sales of £2,160.

13. HIRE PURCHASE TRADING ACCOUNT
FOR THE YEAR ENDED 30TH JUNE, 19.9

	£		£
Purchases Account . .	210	Cash instalments received .	102
Gross Profit . . .	33	Purchases Account—	
		Stock repossessed . . .	49
		Stock in hands of customers at	
		cost . . . . c/d	92
	£243		£243
Stock . . . b/d[1]	92		

[1] See page 397.

GENERAL TRADING ACCOUNT
FOR THE YEAR ENDED 30TH JUNE, 19.9

	£		£
Purchases . . .	5,400	Sales	6,200
Less Transfer to Hire		Stock (£700 + £49) . .	749
Purchase Trading Ac-			
count . . £210			
Less Repossession . 49			
———			
161			
5,239			
Gross Profit . . .	1,710		
£6,949			£6,949

MEMORANDUM

Hire Purchase Debtors

Dr.			(Total Account)			Cr.
		£				£
To Sale Price of Goods delivered			*By Cash—instalments received* .			*102*
on Hire Purchase . .	*310*		„ *Goods repossessed*			
			Balance of Account £100			
			— £30 . . .			*70*
			„ *Balances* . . . c/d			*138*
	£310					£310
To Balances . . b/d	138					

The goods repossessed are valued on the same basis as the goods in possession of the hire purchasers, i.e.—

$$\frac{\text{Instalments outstanding}}{\text{Sale Price}} \times \text{Cost Price}$$

These are—

						£
Television set $\frac{48}{60} \times$ £60 .	.	.	.	.	.	32
Washing machine $\frac{90}{120} \times$ £80	.	.	.	.	.	60
Refrigerator $\frac{70}{100} \times$ £70 .	.	.	.	.	.	49
						——
						141

Less Refrigerators eliminated from Hire Purchase Trading Account and (instead of being brought down as a
balance) transferred back to General Trading Account   49

As per page 396 . . £92

If the scale of hire purchase transactions was substantial and the repossessions frequent, there should be a separate recording for such repossessions. In that case the hire purchase transactions would be as follows—

Dr.	HIRE PURCHASE TRADING ACCOUNT		Cr.	
	£			£
To Purchases . . .	210	By Cash retentions . . .		72
„ Goods Repossessed Account	30	„ Cash repossessions . .		30
„ Gross Profit . . .	24	„ Goods Repossessed Account .		70
		„ Stock in hands of customers		
		at cost equivalent . c/d		92
	£264			£264
To Stock . . . b/d	92			

Dr.	GOODS REPOSSESSED ACCOUNT		Cr.	
To Hire Purchase Trading Ac-count—		By Hire Purchase Trading Ac-count		
Cost price of goods sent out (included in (£210)	70	Cash instalments received .		30
„ Gross Profit . . .	9	„ Stock at cost equivalent c/d .		49
	£79			£79
To Stock . . . b/d	49			

This account completely eliminates the accounting of repossessed goods from the Hire Purchase Trading Account.

The refrigerator is taken into account at the cost equivalent, i.e. the unrealized proportion of cost, but it would probably be necessary to create a provision to cover the reduced value where, as is frequent, the article has been subject to rough treatment in the hands of the customers.

The following table may assist in checking up the figures in the accounts—

	Cost	H.P. Sale price	Dep-osit	Instalments paid		Instalments outstanding		Cost equivalent
	£	£	£		£		£	£
Television Set . .	60	90	10	8 × £4 =	32	12 × £4 = 48 $\frac{48}{90}$ × £60 =		32
Washing Machine .	80	120	12	2 × £9 =	18	10 × £9 = 90 $\frac{90}{120}$ × £80 =		60
Refrigerator . .	70	100	10	4 × £5 =	20	14 × £5 = 70 $\frac{70}{100}$ × £70 =		49
	£210	£310	£32		£70			£141
					£102			

14.   CONTRIVANCES LTD.

(*a*) (i)   TELEVISION TRADING ACCOUNT
FOR THE YEAR ENDED 31ST DECEMBER, 19.2

	Sets	£		Sets	£
Purchases	515	30,900	Sales—		
Gross Profit, exclusive of interest on Hire Purchase transactions		10,261	Hire Purchase at Cash selling price . . .	450	36,930
			Cash	15	1,231
			Closing Stock . . .	50	3,000
	515	£41,161		515	£41,161

(ii)

BICYCLES TRADING ACCOUNT
FOR THE YEAR ENDED 31ST DECEMBER, 19.2

	Bicycles	£		Bicycles	£
Transfer from Purchases.	12,100	108,900	Hire Purchase instalments received—		
Less Returns (See below) . . .	100	900	Sales	12,100	60,300
			Less Returns . .	100	300
	12,000	108,000		12,000	60,000
			Transfer—Repossessed Bicycles Account—received on goods repossessed . .		
Transfer Deposits received and retained on repossessed goods . .		300	possessed . . .		300
Gross Profit, inclusive of interest . . .		24,000	Hire Purchase instalments outstanding at cost price, i.e. hire purchase goods in possession of customers proportionate to cost price . . .		
					72,000
	12,000	£132,300	[See page 400]	12,000	£132,300

Dr.   BICYCLES PURCHASES   Cr.

	Bicycles	£		Bicycles	£
To Sundries . . .	13,100	117,900	By Transfer to Hire Purchase Trading Account .	12,100	108,900
			,, Stock	1,000	9,000
	13,100	£117,900		13,100	£117,900

Dr.   REPOSSESSED BICYCLES ACCOUNT   Cr.

	Bicycles	£		Bicycles	£
To Transfer to Bicycles Trading Account (See above)	100	900	By Transfer from Bicycles Trading Account . .		300
Profit and Loss . .		100	,, Stock	100	700
	100	£1,000		100	£1,000

(iii)

PROFIT AND LOSS ACCOUNT
FOR THE YEAR ENDED 31ST DECEMBER, 19.2

	£			£
Salaries and General Expenses . .	20,000	Trading Profit—		
Net Profit	15,532	Television:		
		Gross Profit on Sales exclusive of interest .	£10,261	
		Interest Allocation .	1,171	
				11,432
		Bicycles:		
		Gross Profit based on instalments received inclusive of interest .	£24,000	
		Gross Profit on repossessed bicycles .	100	
				24,100
	£35,532			£35,532

(b)   **BALANCE SHEET**
                    AS AT 31ST DECEMBER, 19.2

	£		£	£
Issued Share Capital. . . .	100,000	Stocks on hand—		
Profit and Loss Account . . .	15,532	Television Sets at cost .	£3,000	
Sundry Creditors	17,969	New Bicycles at cost . .	9,000	
		Repossessed Bicycles at valuation . . .	700	
				12,700
		Stocks on hire purchase with customers—		
		Television Sets at selling price including total interest *less* provision for interest not yet accrued thereon.		
		Hire Purchase Debtors . .	£27,000	
		Less Interest Suspense .	2,399	
				24,601
		Bicycles at cost . . .	72,000	
				96,601
		Bank		24,200
	£133,501			£133,501

Notes and workings—

Dr.   HIRE PURCHASE DEBTORS (Televisic Sets)   *Cr.*

	£		£
To Sales: 450 at £90 . .	40,500	By Cash Deposits, 450 at £30 .	13,500
		,, Balance . . . c/d	27,000
	£40,500		£40,500
To Balance . . b/d	27,000		

The cost price of the bicycles out on hire purchase based upon the cost equivalent of unpaid instalments is—

(i) Cost price of bicycles delivered 12,000 at £9 . . . . . £108,000

(ii) As the total instalments arising amount to £180,000 (12,000 at £15) and instalments paid amount to £60,000 (the item of £300 paid on repossessed bicycles being struck out of the account), two-thirds is the fraction representing the cost price equivalent, i.e.—

$$\left(\frac{£120,000}{£180,000}\right) \times £108,000 \quad . \quad . \quad . \quad . \quad £72,000$$

		£
(iii) Bicycles "out," i.e. unpaid for . . .		120,000
Less Profit on Sales ($\frac{6}{15}$), i.e. 40% . .		48,000
		£72,000

An alternative method of arriving at the stock in hands of hire purchasers, where the Gross Profit rate is constant, is to reduce the amount of unpaid instalments by the percentage of profit thereon, i.e. £120,000 − £48,000 = £72,000. The item of £48,000 is 40 per cent of hire sale price seeing that the latter (per unit) is £15 and cost £9, i.e. profit $\frac{6}{15}$, or 40 per cent. The full details are as follows—

	One Set £	450 Sets £		One Set £	450 Sets £
To Cash Price	*82·06⅔* (*a*)	36,930	*By Deposit ("down" at purchase)*	*30·00* (*b*)	13,500
,, *Interest at 10 per cent per annum on £52·06⅔*	*5·20⅔*		,, *Balance (end of first year)* c/d	*57·27⅓*	25,773
,, £23.430 (*a − b*)		2,343			
	£87·27⅓	£39,273		*£87·27⅓*	£39,273
To Balance b/d	*57·27⅓* (*a*)	25,773	*By Cash (2nd instalment at* ***commencement*** *of this second year leaving £27·27⅓ per set (= £12,273) to carry interest*	*30·00* (*b*)	13,500
,, *Interest at 10 per cent per annum on £27·27⅓*	*2·72⅔*		,, *Balance (end of second year)*	*30·00*	13,500
,, £12,273 (*a − b*)		1,227			
	£60·00	£27,000		*£60·00*	£27,000
To Balance b/d	*30·00*	13,500	*By Cash (3rd instalment at* ***commencement*** *of this third year, leaving no balance and therefore no interest*	*30·00*	13,500
	£30·00	£13,500		*£30·00*	£13,500

As the transactions are evenly spread the interest will be apportioned—

		£	£
1st year	½ × 5·20⅔		2·60⅓
2nd year	½ × 5·20⅔	2·60⅓	
	½ × 2·72⅔	1·36⅓	3·96⅔
3rd year	½ × 2·72⅔		1·36⅓
Excess of H.P. over Cash Sale Price (£90 − £82·06⅔)			£7·93⅓

The interest is taken into profit in three accounting periods—

(1) $\frac{£2·60⅓}{£7·93⅓} = \frac{781}{2,380} \times £3,570 = £1,171$

(2) $\frac{£3·96⅔}{£7·93⅓} = \frac{1,190}{2,380}\ (= \tfrac{1}{2}) \times £3,570 = £1,785$

(3) $\frac{£1·36⅓}{£7·93⅓} = \frac{409}{2,380} \times £3,570 = £614$

Total £3,570

In the illustration given, as the interest in the first period on the cash price *less* deposit is 10 per cent per annum thereof, this is evened out to a half, i.e. 5 per cent, just as where the interest shown for one set at 10 per cent per annum is £5·20⅔, this is halved to £2·60⅓.

The interest carried to Profit and Loss Account is—

		£	£
1st year (as worked in the accounts)—			
10% p.a. on £36,930 − £13,500 (£23,430)	£2,343 (½)		£1,171
2nd year—			
10% p.a. on £36,930 − £13,500 (£23,430)	£2,343 (½)	1,172	
10% p.a. on £23,430 + 1st yr. interest			
£2,343 − £13,500 (£12,273)	£1,227 (½)	613	1,785
3rd year—			
10% p.a. on £23,430 + 1st yr. interest			
£2,343 − £13,500 (£12,273)	£1,227 (½)		614
			£3,570

Alternatively, all the transactions relating to the bicycles could be combined in one account, but it is suggested that it is preferable to keep the repossessed transactions separate from the normal transactions, particularly if the repossessions are numerous.

The combined account is—

BICYCLE TRADING ACCOUNT

	Bicycles	£		Bicycles	£
Purchases . . .	13,100	117,900	Hire Purchase instal-		
Bicycles repossessed .	100		ments received on		
Gross Profit, including			Sales . . .	12,100	60,300
Interest Hire Purchase			Hire purchase instal-		
Sales . . .		24,000	ments outstanding at		
Repossessed Bicycles .		100	cost price . . .		72,000
			Stocks on hand—		
			New Bicycles, at cost .	1,000	9,000
			Repossessed Bicycles		
			at valuation . .	100	700
	13,200	£142,000		13,200	£142,000

The individual customers' accounts in respect of the bicycle transactions will be outside the double entry accounting, i.e. "memorandum," but it is usual to build up Total Accounts, the balance of which should reconcile with the schedule of balances due by the customers.

Dr.		TOTAL DEBTORS		Cr.
	£			£
To Sales	181,500	By Cash		60,300
		„ Amount written off de-		
		faulting customers, i.e.		
		100 at £12 . . .		1,200
		„ Balance . . c/d		120,000
	£181,500			£181,500
To Balance . . b/d	120,000			

Dr.		TOTAL DEBTORS SUSPENSE		Cr.
	£			£
To Cash	60,300	By Sales		181,500
„ Amount written off .	1,200			
„ Balance . . c/d	120,000			
	£181,500			£181,500
		By Balance . . b/d		120,000

CHAPTER XXI

1. *Dr.*   Cᴀsʜ Bᴏᴏᴋ   *Cr.*

		£				£
19.3			19.4			
June 1	To Interest and Dividend A/c: Half-year's War Loan Interest (gross) .	7	Jan. 1	By Income Tax— Sch. A tax, 19.3–19.4 .		61
Sept. 29	„ Rent for half-year to date	126	3	„ Income Tax— Sch. D, Case I, 19.3– 19.4 (1st instalment)		350
Dec. 1	„ Ditto	7				
19.4			Mar. 1	„ Loan Interest (net) .		48
Mar. 25	„ Rent for half-year to date	126	Apr. 5	„ Balance . . c/d		357
31	„ Interest and Dividend A/c: Dividend (net) . .	550				
		£816				£816
19.4						
Apr. 6	To Balance . . b/d	357				

Dr.   Rᴇɴᴛ   *Cr.*

		£				£
19.4			19.3			
Apr. 5	To Profit and Loss Account .	252	Sept. 29	By Cash		126
			19.4			
			Mar. 25	„ Cash		126
		£252				£252

Dr.   Iɴᴛᴇʀᴇsᴛ ᴀɴᴅ Dɪᴠɪᴅᴇɴᴅs   *Cr.*

		£				£
19.4			19.3			
Mar. 1	To Cash— Loan Interest (net) .	48	June 1	By Cash— War Loan Int. (gross) .		7
	„ Income Tax Account— Tax thereon at 40% .	32	Dec. 1	War Loan Int. (gross) .		7
			19.4			
Apr. 5	„ Profit and Loss Account .	851	Mar. 31	Dividend (net) .		550
				„ Income Tax Account— Tax thereon at 40% .		367
		£931				£931

Dr.   Iɴᴄᴏᴍᴇ Tᴀx   *Cr.*

		£				£
19.4			19.4			
Jan. 1	To Cash— Sch. A Tax 19.3–19.4 .	61	Mar. 1	By Interest and Dividends Account . .		32
3	To Cash— Sch D, Case I, 19.3– 19.4 . .	350	Apr. 5	„ A,—Current Account .		1,102
Mar. 31	„ Interest and Dividends Account . .	367				
Apr. 5	„ Provisions c/d— Sch. D, Case I, 19.3– 19.4 (Balance) .	350				
	Sch. D, Case III, 19.31 19.4 (on War Loan Interest) .	[1]6				
		£1,134				£1,134
			19.4			
			Apr. 6	By Provisions . . b/d		356

[1] £14 at 40% to nearest £.

403

CORPORATION TAX ACCOUNT

19.6		£	19.6		£
Dec. 31	To Balance c/d:		Jan. 1	By Balance—	
	Current Liability—			Provided, Accounting	
	Corp'n Tax for			Year ended 31/12/19.5	10,200
	Accounting Year		Dec. 31	P & L A/c—	
	ended 31/12/19.5	10,400		Overprovided, Accounting	
	Future Liability—			year ended 31/12/19.5	200
	Corp'n Tax for			Provided, Accounting	
	Accounting Year			year ended 31/12/19.6	12,500
	ended 31/12/19.6	12,500			
		£22,900			£22,900
			19.7		
			Jan. 1	By Balance . . b/d	£22,900

ORDINARY DIVIDENDS ACCOUNTS

19.6		£	19.6		£
Aug. 15	To Bank—		Aug. 15	By P & L A/c . . .	2,000
	Interim dividend of		Dec. 31	„ P & L A/c . . .	1,000
	10% (net) . .	1,200			
15	„ Income Tax A/c				
	Schedule F—				
	Liability on Interim				
	dividend . .	800			
Dec. 31	„ Balance c/d—				
	Final dividend of 5%				
	proposed (gross) .	1,000			
		£3,000			£3,000
			19.7		
			Jan. 1	By Balance . . b/d	£1,000

DEBENTURE INTEREST ACCOUNT

19.6		£	19.6		£
June 15	To Bank—		Dec. 31	By P & L A/c . . .	1,200
	Half-year's interest to date.	360			
15	„ Income Tax Account—				
	Section 53 Income Tax re-				
	tained on payment .	240			
Dec. 15	„ Bank—				
	Half-year's interest to date.	360			
15	„ Income Tax Account—				
	Section 53 Income Tax				
	retained on payment .	240			
		£1,200			£1,200

DIVIDEND RECEIVED ACCOUNT
(FRANKED INVESTMENT INCOME)

19.6		£	19.6		£
Dec. 31	To P & L A/c . . .	350	Sept. 21	By Bank—	
				Dividend from Transfusions	
				Ltd. (net) . . .	210
			21	„ Income Tax Account—	
				Schedule F Income Tax	
				suffered on dividend rec'd	
				from Transfusions Ltd. .	140
		£350			£350

LOAN INTEREST RECEIVED ACCOUNT

19.6		£	19.6		£
Dec. 31	To P & L A/c . . .	255	July 18	By Bank— Interest on Loan (net) .	153
			18	,, Income Tax Account— Section 53 Income Tax suffered on Loan Interest received . .	102
		£255			£255

INCOME TAX ACCOUNT

19.6		Sch. F £	Sect. 53 £	19.6		Sch. F £	Sect. 53 £
July 5	To Loan Interest Received— Income Tax deducted .		102	June 15	By Debenture Interest— Income Tax deducted	240	
19	,, Bank— net Sect. 53 Income Tax remitted to Collector of Taxes		138				
Sept. 19	,, Bank— Sch. F Income Tax remitted to Collector of Taxes	800		Aug. 15	,, Ordinary Dividend— Income Tax on Interim Dividend paid .	800	
21	,, Dividend Received— Income Tax on dividend received from Transfusions Ltd. . .	140		Dec. 15	,, Debenture Interest— Income Tax deducted . .	240	
				31	,, Profit and Loss A/c— Income Tax on Franked Investment Income written off .	140	
Dec. 31	,, Balance c/d .		240				
		£940	£480			£940	£480
				19.7			
				Jan. 1	By Balance b/d .		240

Year ended 31st December 19.6

PROFIT AND LOSS ACCOUNT (Extract)

		£
Investment Income		
Trade (gross)		· 350
Loan Interest (gross) . . .		255
Deduction		
Debenture Interest (gross) . .		1,200

PROFIT AND LOSS APPROPRIATION ACCOUNT (Extract)

		£
Balance of Profit brought forward from previous year		x
Add Corporation Tax overprovided previous year		200
		x

Deductions:	£
Income Tax on Franked Investment Income	
now written-off	140
Corporation Tax on Current Profits . .	12,500

Dividends:			
Paid—			
Ordinary Interim of 10% (gross) .		£2,000	
Income Tax Schedule F .	800		
Net Dividend Paid .	1,200		
	£2,000		
Proposed—			
Ordinary Final of 5% (gross) . .	1,000		
		3,000	

BALANCE SHEET (Extract)
AS AT 31ST DECEMBER 19.6

	£
(Liabilities side)	
Future Liability—Corporation Tax—Accounting Year ended 31/12/19.6 .	12,500
Current Liabilities:	
Sundry Creditors (including Sect. 53 liability of £240)	
Corporation Tax—Accounting Year ended 31/12/19.5 . . .	10,400
Dividend proposed (gross)	1,000

Notes. (i) The debit balance of £140 in respect of Income Tax suffered on the dividend received from Transfusions Ltd. on 21/9/19.6 is available for set-off against Income Tax retained from subsequent dividend payments. However, it is common practice to write off such balances in order to reflect the true position at the year end. When in the next year the £140 is set-off against Income Tax retained on dividends paid the fact that relief was so obtained should be stated by way of note in the relevant published accounts.

(ii) There is no legal obligation to disclose in respect of dividends paid, the Income Tax Schedule F and the net dividend payable. This is sometimes done in practice, but the reason for so doing in this instance is to differentiate the taxation aspect regarding dividends paid and dividends proposed. Notice that the gross amount only of the dividend proposed is shown. Income Tax Schedule F liability arises only when a dividend is paid or declared, it does not arise when a dividend is merely proposed.

3. (*a*) The following items of expenditure are deductible in computing liability to long-term Capital Gains Tax:

(i) any amount expended on acquiring the asset, including incidental costs;
(ii) any amount expended on enhancing the value of the asset;
(iii) the incidental costs of disposing of the asset.

In (i) and (iii) above, incidental costs include cost of or remuneration paid for the professional services of any surveyor, valuer, auctioneer, accountant, agent or legal adviser but not in connection with the actual calculation of the resultant gain or loss.

(b) The assessments on individuals are made for a year of assessment beginning on 6th April (as for Income Tax), on the total amount of gains accruing in the year of assessment after deducting losses accruing in that year and any unallowed losses of earlier years. The assessments are normally made after the end of the year of assessment in which the gain arose.

4. Value Added Tax, commonly abbreviated to VAT, is theoretically, a tax paid by a trader in respect of the value which he adds to goods or services during his stage of the production or the distribution of those goods or services. However, in effect, VAT is a tax on the amount expended by the final consumer of goods or services. VAT is collected whenever goods or services are transferred for value during the production—wholesale—retail process. When a trader purchases goods or services liable to VAT he must pay the supplier a price which includes the standard rate of VAT on the taxable purchase price. In turn, the trader when selling goods or services to his customers must charge them a price which includes the standard rate of VAT on the taxable sales price. The trader must submit a quarterly return to the Commissioners of Customs and Excise at which time he must settle any net amount of VAT due. The net amount due is calculated by deducting from the VAT collected on goods or services sold (output tax) the VAT paid on goods or services purchased (input tax). If, however, the amount of VAT paid exceeds that collected a refund for the excess may be claimed.

VAT is chargeable at a single standard rate on the supply of all goods and services in the UK in the course of a business and on all imports of goods, except where specifically excluded. [1]Exceptions to tax at the standard rate take the form of either exemption or zero rating. In respect of goods or services which are exempt the trader does not charge his customer with any "output tax." Exemption, however, does not mean that VAT will not fall on exempt goods or services. What it means is that the purchaser does not pay tax directly on the goods or services purchased. The consequences of this are twofold viz. (i) the supplier is not able to set off any "output tax," in respect of the exempted goods or services, against his "input tax," (ii) the supplier in these circumstances, is a final consumer and the tax ends there; however to recover the tax he has paid he will doubtless increase the selling price of his goods or services. When goods or services are zero-rated it means that such goods or services are taxable but that the tax charged is nil. The zero-rated trader can sell his goods or services VAT free because he can reclaim any "input tax" which he paid to his suppliers. All persons trading in the UK, including non-residents, must register with the Commissioners of Customs and Excise unless specifically excluded by statute. In particular traders whose turnover does not exceed £5,000 are excepted. No special format of accounting for VAT is required and existing accounting systems may be adapted for the proper recording of VAT. Where goods or services are supplied to taxable customers an invoice should be issued showing the following particulars—(a) the supplier's name and address and VAT registration number; (b) the customer's name and address; (c) the description of the goods or services supplied; (d) the price excluding VAT; (e) the rate and amount of VAT; (f) the price including VAT.

VAT is payable quarterly in arrear with a month's grace for payment.

---

[1] VAT commenced on 1 April 1973 with one positive rate only—the standard rate which was 10 per cent. On 19 July 1974 the standard rate was reduced to 8 per cent and on 18 November 1974 the rate applied to petrol and related products was 25 per cent. From 1 May 1975 the 25 per cent rate, known as the higher rate, was extended to cover the following classes of goods and certain related services: domestic electric appliances; radio and television sets; boats and aircraft; caravans; photographic equipment, binoculars, etc.; furs; jewellery, goldsmiths' and silversmiths' wares, etc.

CHAPTER XXII

1.   PROFIT AND LOSS APPROPRIATION ACCOUNT

			£				£
To X—				By Balance . . . . b/d			28,700
¾ of £27,637 . . . £20,728				,, Z—Salary added back . . .			2,500
Less Excess per							
Memorandum Statement 894							
			19,834				
,, Y—¼ of £27,637			6,909				
,, Z—⅐ of £31,200			4,457				
			£31,200				£31,200

Memorandum Statement

		£
Share due to Z on—		
One-seventh basis		4,457
Alternative basis:		
Salary	£2,500	
Commission, $\frac{5}{105}$ of £28,700 . .	1,063	
		3,563
Excess chargeable to X . .		£894

Alternative Solution—

	Total	X	Y
	£	£	£
Balance of Profits after crediting Z . .	26,743		
Add amount back to firm's profit to be borne personally by X	894		
Balance of profit divisible between X and Y .	27,637	20,728	6,909
Less amount borne by X *personally* . .	894	894	
Final sharing of X and Y	£26,743	£19,834	£6,909

2.   JOURNAL

19..		£	£
Dec. 31	Profit and Loss Appropriation Account. *Dr.*	650·00	
	To Current Accounts—		
	X		300·00
	Y		200·00
	Z		150·00
	Being 5% Interest on Capital—X, £6,000; Y, £4,000; and Z, £3,000.		
	X Current Account . . . . *Dr.*	67·50	
	To Purchases		67·50
	Being transfer of goods taken by X for own use.[1]		
	Repairs . . . . . *Dr.*	137·65	
	To Wages		137·65
	Being transfer of Wages incurred on repairs to machinery.		

[1] See note on page 409.

TESTOUT—CURRENT ACCOUNT

		Months	Interest	Principal
			£	£
19..				
June 1	To Cash—Drawings .	7	16·04	550·00
Aug. 1	„ „ „ .	5	11·04	570·00
Oct. 1	„ „ „ .	3	7·19	575·00
Dec. 1	„ „ „ .	1	2·29	550·00
			£36·56	
31	To Goods—Drawings .			¹71·00
	„ Interest on Drawings			36·56
	„ Balance . c/d.			1,075·44
				£3,428·00

Cr.

			Principal
			£
19..			
Jan. 1	By Balance . b/d		3,128·00
Dec. 31	„ Interest on Capital .		300·00
			£3,428·00
19..			
Jan. 1	By Balance . b/d		1,075·44

¹ For the purpose of Income Tax, goods withdrawn for private use will be considered as so withdrawn at *selling* price (*Sharkey v. Wernher*). See *Accountancy*, 4th ed., page 2211.

See also notes on next page.

Notes. (i) The details of drawings may be shown separately in "Drawings Account" and the total thereof, including interest, transferred to Current Account, in one item.

(ii) The current account will include Testout's share of profit or loss, but the necessary figure is not disclosed in the question.

[Alternatively, the average due date may be computed. If this is done in months, it will be—

£						Product
550 × 7 months	.	.	.	.		3,850
570 × 5 ,,	.	.	.	.		2,850
575 × 3 ,,	.	.	.	.		1,725
550 × 1 ,,	.	.	.	.		550

£2,245   2,245 | 8,975 = approx. four months

Interest on £2,245 at 5% per annum for four months = £37·42. (If reckoned in days per page 409, £36·56.)]

4.   PROFIT AND LOSS APPROPRIATION ACCOUNT

To Capital (or Current) Accounts—	£	£	By Balance . . . . b/d	£ 2,821
A—	£			
⁴⁄₇ of £2,821 1,612				
Less				
⅔ of £347 231				
		1,381		
B—				
²⁄₇ of £2,821 806				
Less				
⅓ of £347 116				
		690		
C—				
¹⁄₇ of £2,821 403				
Add Transfer from A . 231				
Add Transfer from B . 116				
		750		
		£2,821		£2,821

Note. No mention is made of the right of recoupment of Guarantee [see *Accountancy*, 4th ed., 2261 *et seq.*]. Alternative solutions may be prepared on lines shown in *Accountancy*, 4th ed., page 2254 *et seq.*

The foregoing may be shown in statement form, as follows—

APPROPRIATION OF PROFITS

	Total		A	B	C
		£	£	£	£
Profits		£2,821			
A, ⁴⁄₇ . . .	£1,612		1,612		
B, ²⁄₇ . . .	806			806	
C, ¹⁄₇ . . .	403				403
		2,821			
			1,612	806	403
Add C		347			347
Less A, ⁴⁄₆ .	£231		231		
,, B, ²⁄₆ . .	116			116	
		347			
			£1,381	£690	£750

5. The reason for the practice of crediting each partner with interest on his capital is that before formal division of profits a proportionate share should be allocated as the reward due for the use of each partner's capital. Such a procedure is called for when the capitals of the partners differ from the profit-sharing ratio, because if they *are* in profit ratio the total amount due to each partner is the same whether interest on capital is charged or not, e.g. if A and B are partners sharing profits equally, their capitals being £2,000 each and the trading profits are £1,600, they receive £800 each as share of profits if no interest on capital is charged, whilst they each receive £100 and £700 if interest be charged, assuming a rate of 5 per cent per annum.

The procedure thus affords to a partner who has contributed more capital than another a compensation for his increased outlay. If, for instance, A contributes £10,000 and B £1,000 (being equal partners), by agreeing upon 5 per cent interest on capital A receives (out of profits) £450 more than B to compensate him for the extra capital he has provided, A being credited with £500 and B with £50. If, however, the ratio of profit sharing is 10:1 no provision is required for interest on capital, whilst if the ratio is, say 12:1 it would be definitely detrimental to A inasmuch as the first £500 of the profits are divided as interest on capital in the ratio of 10:1 only.

However unfair it may be to the "high contribution" partner to ignore interest on capital, it cannot be claimed unless the partnership agreement as originally framed or subsequently altered (e.g. by a course of dealing) so provides [see s. 24 (4), Partnership Act, 1890]. Furthermore, interest on capital is not interest in the usual sense, but **a proportion of profits** allocated as a reward for the use of capital contributed by the partners.

6.   BLACK & CO.

STATEMENT OF PROFITS FOR THE HALF-YEAR ENDED 30TH JUNE, 19..

	£	£			£	£
Commencing Capitals—				Closing Capitals		[1]6,976
White	3,000			Drawings—	£	
Green	2,520			White	603	
Brown	1,500			Green	410	
		7,020		Brown	300	
Balance	c/d	1,269				1,313
		£8,289				£8,289
Interest on Capitals—				Balance	b/d	1,269
White	75					
Green	63					
Brown	38					
		176				
Net Profit—						
White, $\frac{5}{10}$ . . .	547					
Green, $\frac{3}{10}$ . . .	328					
Brown, $\frac{2}{10}$ . . .	218					
		1,093				
		£1,269				£1,269

[1] See page 413.

Dr. CAPITALS **Cr.**

		White	Green	Brown			White	Green	Brown
19..		£	£	£	19..		£	£	£
June 30	To Drawings	603	410	300	Jan. 1	By Balances b/d	3,000	2,520	1,500
	„ Balances c/d	3,019	2,501	1,456	June 30	„ Interest on Capitals	75	63	38
						„ Net Profit	547	328	218
		£3,622	£2,911	£1,756			£3,622	£2,911	£1,756
					July 1	By Balances b/d	3,019	2,501	1,456

[Although not required by the question the resultant Statement of Affairs is appended.

BLACK & CO.

STATEMENT OF AFFAIRS AS AT 30TH JUNE, 19..

	£	£		£
Liabilities (per question)[1]		16,649	Assets (per question)[1]	23,625
Capitals—	£			
White	3,019			
Green	2,501			
Brown	1,456			
		6,976		
		£23,625		£23,625

[1] Net Assets = £6,976 per page 411.

It is assumed that Capitals are to include Interest on Capitals, etc.]

7. JOURNAL

		£	£
19.. Jan. 1	A—Current Account . . . . *Dr.*	253	
	To B—Current Account		100
	„ C—Current Account		153
	Being adjustment for interest on capital allowed for the years, 19.7, 19.8, and 19.9, as per Memorandum Adjustment Statement.		

Memorandum ADJUSTMENT STATEMENT

	19.7			19.8			19.9			
		"Profit"	Adjustment	Interest on Capital	"Profit"	Adjustment	Interest on Capital	"Profit"	Adjustment	Combined "Result"
	£	£	£	£	£	£	£	£	£	£
A	325	½ 313	− 12	350	⅖ 264	− 86	360	3/10 205	− 155	− 253
B	210	3/10 187	− 23	200	⅖ 264	+ 64	215	⅖ 274	+ 59	+ 100
C	90	⅕ 125	+ 35	110	⅕ 132	+ 22	110	3/10 205	+ 96	+ 153
	£625	£625		£660	£660		£685	£684		

8. STATEMENT OF DIVISION OF PROFITS FOR EIGHT MONTHS ENDED 31ST AUGUST, 19..

	A	B	C
	£	£	£
[1]First £4,000 [⅔ of £6,000]	⅓ 1,334	⅓ 1,333	⅓ 1,333
[1]Next £5,334 [⅔ of £8,000]	½ 2,667	⅜ 2,000	⅛ 667
Remainder £4,466	4/9 1,985	⅓ 1,489	2/9 992
[Total £13,800]	£5,986	£4,822	£2,992

[1] As the stages are £6,000 and £8,000 *per annum* they are £4,000 and £5,334 *per eight months.*

9. Assumed partners' capitals are fixed. [In order to show a variation in layout (*cf.* Ques. 7 above) the adjustments are as shown on page 414.]

Memorandum Adjustment Statement

Year	A		B		C	
	£	£	£	£	£	£
19.2 . . .	+60	−60 ($\frac{1}{2}$)	+30	−30 ($\frac{1}{4}$)	+30	−30 ($\frac{1}{4}$)
19.3 . . .	+60	−80 ($\frac{2}{3}$)	+30	−20 ($\frac{1}{6}$)	+30	−20 ($\frac{1}{6}$)
19.4 . . .	+60	−90 ($\frac{3}{4}$)	+30	−15 ($\frac{1}{8}$)	+30	−15 ($\frac{1}{8}$)
	+£180	−£230	+£90	−£65	+£90	−£65
		= Dr. £50		= Cr. £25		= Cr. £25

Journal

19.5		£	£
Jan. 1	A—Current Account . . . . . . *Dr.*	50	
	To B—Current Account		25
	,, C—Current Account		25
	Being interest on Capital for the last three years, as per Memorandum Adjustment Statement.		

As there was a loss in 19.3, there would be no profits to divide between the partners either as interest on capital or in profit-sharing ratio. As, however, the question states that interest is to be allowed for the *three* years, this has been done, thus increasing the 19.3 loss to be debited to the partners in their profit-sharing ratio.

As it is clear that there can be no alteration as between B and C, because their respective capitals and profit-sharing ratio are equal throughout, the calculation may be made as to A only, and the result divided equally in favour of B and C, thus—

Memorandum Statement *re* A

		£
Interest on Capital— £1,000 at 6% per annum for three years		+180
	£	
Less 19.2 $\frac{1}{2}$ of £120 =	60	
19.3 $\frac{2}{3}$,, =	80	
19.4 $\frac{3}{4}$,, =	90	
		230
Balance, equally between B and C		−£50

10.

Profit and Loss Appropriation Account
year ended 31st December, 19.9

	£	£				£
Interest on Capital—			Balance . . . . b/d			2,286
	£		Interest on Current Account—			
Southern	275		Weston			27
Weston	138					
		413				
Interest on Current Account—						
Southern . . .		10				
Net Profit—						
Southern	1,260					
Weston	630					
		1,890				
		£2,313				£2,313

Dr.		Capitals		*Cr.*
		19.9		Southern Weston
				£ £
		Jan. 1 By Balance b/d		5,500 1,650
		,, Cash .		1,100

Dr.   SOUTHERN CURRENT ACCOUNT   *Cr.*

		Interest	Principal			Interest	Principal
		£	£			£	£
19.9				19.9			
Mar. 31	To Cash . .	11·25	300	Jan. 1	By Balance b/d	22·50	450
June 30	,, ,, . .	7·50	300		,, Weston Current Account		
Sept. 30	,, ,, . .	3·75	300				
Dec. 31	,, ,, . .		300		Goodwill .	10·00	200
	,, Interest to *contra* .	10·00		Dec. 31	,, Profit and Loss Acct.		
	,, Balance c/d		995		Interest on Capital .		275
					Net Profit		1,260
					,, Interest from *contra* .		10
		£32·50	£2,195			£32·50	£2,195
				19.0			
				Jan. 1	By Balance b/d		995

Dr.   WESTON CURRENT ACCOUNT   *Cr.*

		Interest	Principal			Interest	Principal
		£	£			£	£
19.9				19.9			
Jan. 1	To Balance b/d	6·25	125	Dec. 31	By Profit and Loss Account—		
	,, Southern Current Account Goodwill .	10·00	200		Interest on Capital		138
Mar. 31	,, Cash . .	5·63	150		Net Profit		630
June 30	,, ,, . .	3·75	150		,, Interest to *contra* .	27·50	
Sept. 30	,, ,, . .	1·87	150		,, Balance c/d		184
Dec. 31	,, ,, . .		150				
	,, Interest from *contra* .		27				
		£27·50	£952			£27·50	£952
19.0							
Jan. 1	To Balance b/d		184				

Goodwill Adjustment—

Total profits for five years ended 31st December, 19.8 = £9,750

Three years' purchase of average profits $= \dfrac{9,750}{5} \times 3$

Weston's increased share—

$$\tfrac{1}{3} - \frac{1,650}{7,150} = \frac{715 - 495}{2,145} = \frac{220}{2,145}$$

The total charge to Weston is, therefore—

$$\frac{220}{2,145} \times \frac{9,750}{5} \times 3 = \text{£600}$$

Charged in three instalments commencing 1st January, 19.9 of £200

Alternatively, interest may be calculated as follows—

			Southern				Weston
			£				£
£650 for one year .	.	. Cr.	32·50	£325 for one year .	.	. Dr.	16·25
[1]£900 for six months	.	. Dr.	22·50	[1]£450 for six months	.	. Dr.	11·25
		Cr.	£10·00			Dr.	£27·50

[1] As there are three withdrawals (at equal intervals) of £300 each, the last being on 31st December, thus bearing no interest, the average due date is 30th June; in regard to Weston, as the withdrawals (at the same intervals) are £150 each, the interest is one-half of that charged to Southern.

The alternative method dispenses with the necessity for interest columns, enabling the current accounts to be written up in the familiar columnar way.

For P & L Appn. A/c purposes amounts have been rounded off to nearest £.

The question does not indicate *how* the adjustment of capitals is to be made, so that an equally correct procedure would be to make a transfer of £1,100 to the debit of Weston's Current Account (crediting his Capital Account); or transfers of £733 to the debit of Weston's Current Account and credit of Southern's Current Account respectively.

If the total capital is to remain the same as before the position will be as follows—

	Southern	Weston	Total
	£	£	£
Original Capitals	5,500	1,650	7,150
Cash paid out or credit Current Account .	733		
Cash paid in or debit Current Account . .		733	
	£4,767	£2,383	£7,150
Interest on Capital will be	£238	£119	£357

11. PROFIT AND LOSS ACCOUNT FOR THE YEAR ENDED
30TH SEPTEMBER, 19.8

	£			£
Office Salaries [£2,189 + £69] . .	2,258	Gross Profit . . . . b/d		34,628
Office Expenses . . .	622			
Insurance [£364 − £62] . .	302			
Delivery Expenses . . .	2,203			
Advertising [£4,339 − £878] . .	3,461			
Bad Debts [£801 − £600] . .	201			
Depreciation— £				
Patents . . . 400				
Machinery and Plant . 1,718				
Motor Lorries . . 100				
Office Furniture . . 30				
———	2,248			
Mortgage Interest [£450 + £150] .	600			
Net Profit . . . . c/d	22,733			
	£34,628			£34,628
Salary—White	1,000	Balance . . . . b/d		22,733
Interest on Capital— £		Interest on Drawings— £		
Black 1,000		Black 330		
White 250		White 80		
———	1,250	———		410
Interest on Current Accounts—				
Black 53				
White 140				
———	193			
Commission—White (10% of £20,700)	2,070			
Balance—				
Black, ⅘ . . . 14,904				
White, ⅕ . . . 3,726				
———	18,630			
	£23,143			£23,143

Footnote to Balance Sheet on page 417—

[1] £13,280 at 10% per annum . . .	£1,328
£1,560 at 25%	390
	£1,718

BLACK AND WHITE—BALANCE SHEET AS AT 30TH SEPTEMBER, 19.8

	Black	Black	White	White		£	£
	£	£	£	£			
Capitals		20,000		5,000			25,000
Current Accounts—							
As at 1st Oct., 19.7		1,060		2,800			
Add Interest on Capital		1,000		250			
Interest on Current Account		53		140			
Salary				1,000			
Commission				2,070			
Profit		14,904		3,726			
		17,017		9,986			
Less Drawings	£10,000		£3,000				
Interest thereon	330		80				
		10,330		3,080			
		£6,687		£6,906			13,593
							38,593
Mortgage on Freehold Premises				10,000			
Add Interest accrued				150			10,150
Sundry Creditors				24,150			
Salaries accrued				69			24,219
							£72,962

	£	£	£
Fixed Assets—			
Freehold Premises at Cost			15,000
Patents as at 1st Oct., 19.7		4,000	
Less Depreciation		400	3,600
Machinery and Plant as at 1st Oct., 19.7	13,280		
Add Additions during year	1,560		
		14,840	
Less Depreciation[1]		1,718	13,122
Motor Lorries as at 1st Oct., 19.7		900	
Less Depreciation		100	800
Office Furniture as at 1st Oct., 19.7		300	
Less Depreciation		30	270
			32,792
Current Assets—			
Stock			21,069
Sundry Debtors	£16,020		
Less Bad Debts Provision	801		15,219
Payments in Advance—			
Factory Expenses	70		
Insurance	62		
Advertising	878		1,010
Cash in Hand	31		
Cash at Bank	2,841		2,872
			40,170
			£72,962

[1] See footnote on page 416.

12.   PROFIT AND LOSS ACCOUNT FOR THE YEAR ENDED
31ST DECEMBER, 19..

		£			£
Salaries		12,500	Brokerage		44,000
Rent		3,500	Bank Interest		1,300
Stationery and Printing			Investment Interest		3,000
[1,250 + £35] . . .		1,285			
Accountancy and Audit Fee . .		815			
Subscriptions to Lloyds . .		2,530			
Travelling Expenses . . .		350			
Sundry Office Expenses . . .		520			
[£400 + £120]					
Bad Debts Provision . .		793			
Net Profit . . . . c/d		26,007			
		£48,300			£48,300
C—Salary		3,000	Balance . . . . . b/d		26,007
Interest on Capital . . .		120			
Mrs. X—$\frac{1}{20}$ of £22,887 . .		1,144			
General Reserve—					
7½% of £21,743					
[£26,007 − £3,000 − £120 − £1,144]		1,631			
Balance—	£				
A, ½	10,056				
B, ⅓	6,704				
C, ⅙	3,352				
		20,112			
		£26,007			£26,007

A, B, and C
Balance Sheet as at 31st December, 19..

Capitals—

	£	£
A	1,200	
B	800	
C	400	
		2,400

Current Accounts—

	A £	B £	C £
Salary			3000
Interest on Capital	60	40	20
Profit	10,056	6,704	3,352
	10,116	6,744	6,372
Less Debit Balances at 1st January 19..	600	400	200
	£9,516	£6,344	£6,172

	£
Current Accounts	22,032
General Reserve	1,631
Creditors	75,000
Outstanding Expenses [£35 + £120]	155
Mrs. X	1,144
	76,299
	£102,362

	£	£	£
Investments at cost (Market value £)			20,100
Debtors	63,500		
Less Bad Debts Provision	793		62,707
Debt owing by A[1]			1,500
Cash at Bank		18,000	
Cash in hand		55	18,055
			£102,362

[1] Alternatively, this balance may be transferred to the debit of A's Current Account.

419

13.   JOURNAL

19.5		£	£
Jan. 1	A Current Account—$\frac{3}{5}$ . . . . *Dr.*	495	
	B Current Account—$\frac{2}{5}$ . . . . *Dr.*	330	
	To C Current Account. . . .		825

ADJUSTMENT SCHEDULE

	19.2 £	19.3 £	19.4 £
C's share—old arrangement—			
Salary	1,600	1,600	1,600
Interest on Deposit—6% . . .	300	300	300
Bonus 5% on:			
£6,750 (£8,000 − £1,250) . . .	338		
£8,750 (£10,000 − £1,250) . .		437	
£12,750 (£14,000 − £1,250) . .			638
	£2,238	£2,337	£2,538

	£	£	£
C's share—new arrangement—			
Interest on Deposit—5% . . .	250	250	250
Share of Profit—$\frac{1}{4}$ of:			
£6,400	1,600		
£8,400		2,100	
£12,400			3,100
	1,850	2,350	3,350
Less C's share (old arrangement)			
as above	2,238	2,337	2,538
Additional sum to C	*Nil*[1]	£13	£812

[1] As the share under the old is more than that under the new, no adjustment is required.

14.   STATEMENT OF PROFIT FOR THE YEAR ENDED 31ST MARCH, 19..

19..		£	19..			£
Apr. 1	To Opening Capital	10,000	Mar. 31	By Drawings		2,800
Mar. 31	,, Depreciation— £			,, Balance[1]		11,671
	Motor Vans . 118					
	Fixtures and					
	Fittings . . 23					
	———	141				
	,, Bad Debts Provision .	300				
	,, Net Profit . . c/d	4,030				
		£14,471				£14,471
	To Interest on Capital— £			By Balance . . b/d		4,030
	Field . . 300					
	Paddock . . 200					
	———	500				
	,, Profit—					
	Field, ⁶⁄₁₀ . . 2,118					
	Paddock, ⁴⁄₁₀ . 1,412					
	———	3,530				
		£4,030				£4,030

STATEMENT OF AFFAIRS AS AT 31ST MARCH, 19..

	£	£		£	£
Capitals—			Current Assets—		
Field . . . 6,000			Stock-in-trade . . .		5,100
Paddock . . . 4,000			Sundry Debtors . . 7,600		
		10,000	Less Bad Debts Provision . 300		
Current Accounts—					7,300
Field . . . 618			Cash at Bank . . .		900
Paddock . . . 612			Fixed Assets		
		1,230	Fixtures and Fittings . . 230		
Sundry Creditors . . .		2,749	Less Depreciation . 23		
					207
			Motor Vans . . 590		
			Less Depreciation . 118		
					472
					679
		£13,979			£13,979

		Field	Paddock
		£	£
Current Accounts—			
Interest on Capital		300	200
Profit		2,118	1,412
		2,418	1,612
Less Drawings		1,800	1,000
		£618	£612

---

[1] Assets £14,420, *less* Creditors £2,749.

15. *Dr.*   DRAWINGS   *Cr.*

		A	B	C			A	B	C
		£	£	£			£	£	£
19.. Dec. 31	To Cash . ,, Balances c/d	2,500 2,150	2,000 1,320	1,500 1,180	19.. Jan. 1 Dec. 31	By Balances b/d ,, Interest on Capital . ,, Profit .	750 300 3,600	500 180 2,640	400 120 2,160
		£4,650	£3,320	£2,680			£4,650	£3,320	£2,680
					19.. Jan. 1	By Balances b/d	2,150	1,320	1,180

Statement of Division of Profit

		£
Balance		9,000
Less Interest on Capital . . .		600
		8,400

Proportion of £6,000—

	£	
A: $\frac{5}{10}$.	3,000	
B: $\frac{3}{10}$.	1,800	
C: $\frac{2}{10}$.	1,200	
		6,000
		2,400

Residue—

A: 25%	600	
B: 35%	840	
C: 40%	960	
		2,400

16.   COSTS, PROFIT AND LOSS AND APPROPRIATION ACCOUNT FOR
THE YEAR ENDED 30TH JUNE, 19..

		A B & Co. and D	A B & Co.		A B & Co. and D	A B & Co.
		£	£		£	£
Estimate of Costs not made up (Opening) . . . (i)		?	2,000	Bills of Costs rendered . .	1,500	6,000
Clients' Disbursements . (ii)		600	1,040	Estimate of Costs not made up (Closing) . . . (i)	1,050	2,200
Profit Costs— A B & Co. . c/d ($\frac{2}{3}$) D's Widow . . ($\frac{1}{3}$)		1,300 650	5,160			
		£2,550	£8,200		£2,550	£8,200
Salaries			1,430	Balances . . . b/d		6,460
Office Expenses . . .			870	Commission on Debts Collected for D		45
Depreciation—Furniture . .			60			
Net Profit . . . c/d			4,145			
			£6,505			£6,505
Interest on Capital— A . . . . B	£ 124 96		 220	Balance . . . . b/d		4,145
Balance— A, $\frac{2}{5}$ B, $\frac{3}{5}$	1,570 2,355		 3,925			
			£4,145			£4,145

A B & Co.

BALANCE SHEET AS AT 30TH JUNE, 19..

	£	£		£	£
Capitals—			Library	?	
A	2,480		Furniture	?	
B	1,920				
		4,400	Balance as at 1st July, 19..	500	
Current Accounts—			*Add* Purchases . . .	100	
A— Interest on Capital .	124				
Profit . .	1,570			600	
			Less Depreciation . .	60	
	1,694				540
Less Drawings . .	1,125		Estimate of Costs not made up	(i)	3,250
		569	Uncompleted Work . . .		?
B—Interest on Capital .	96		Debtors—		
Profit . .	2,355		Bills of Costs . . .	900	
			Sundry . . .	1,300	
	2,451				2,200
Less Drawings . .	1,250		Bank—Clients . . (iii)	1,210	
		1,201	Own . .	1,780	
D's Widow—					2,990
One-third Profit Costs attributable					
to D's Practice . .	650				
Furniture . . .	100				
Debts Collected . £900					
Less Commission . 45					
	855				
	1,605				
Deduct amount paid on account .	650				
		955			
Creditors—Sundry . .	670				
Clients . (iii)	1,185				
		1,855			
		£8,980			£8,980

Notes. (i) The opening and closing disbursements included in estimate of costs may be transferred to Disbursements Accounts.

(ii) It is assumed that the disbursements have actually been expended and charged and allocated properly as between the two sections.

(iii) There is an unexplained difference of £25 between Clients' Bank and credit balance of Clients.

17.   STATEMENT OF DIVISION OF PROFIT FOR THE YEAR ENDED
                                    31ST MARCH, 19..

	£	£
Balance		14,390
Less Black's Salary	2,000	
Black's Commission [5% of £11,800] . .	590	
		2,590
		11,800
Add Salary and Commission		2,590
	£	
Costello: ¾ of £11,800	8,850	14,390
Less Excess due to Black	288	
	8,562	
Bryant: ¼ of £11,800	2,950	
Black: ⅕ of £14,390	2,878	
		14,390

£2,878 — £2,590.

Alternatively, the statement may be presented thus—

	Total £	Costello £	Bryant £
Balance	14,390		
Less Black ⅕	2,878		
	11,512		
Add Excess not borne by Partnership but by Costello . . .	288		
	11,800	(¾) 8,850	(¼) 2,950
Less Excess charged to Costello .	288	288	
Final Sharing between Costello and Bryant	£11,512	£8,562	£2,950

Note. It is assumed that no salary has been credited to Black in arriving at the profit of £14,390.

18. On the admission of Perkins it will be necessary to estimate the value of the goodwill. If no Goodwill Account appears in the books one should be opened and debited with the total goodwill, the Capital Accounts of Collins and Dickson being credited in equal shares.

If a Goodwill Account is already in the books, the revised value will be brought into account by debiting the increase (or crediting the decrease) to Goodwill Account, and crediting (or debiting) the old partners equally.

Alternatively, Perkins may agree to purchase his share by instalments, in which case he will be debited with the *share* and the old partners credited equally, an adjustment as between the old partners themselves being necessary should they decide to alter their own relative proportions.

Assuming Perkins agrees on £500 as being the premium due from him for a fifth share, the old partners' ratios to be two-fifths each, the Journal entries, ignoring narratives, are—

JOURNAL

			£	£
Method 1—				
Goodwill	*Dr.*	2,500		
To Collins Capital			1,250	
„ Dickson Capital			1,250	
Method 2—				
Perkins—Loan	*Dr.*	500		
To Collins Capital				250
„ Dickson Capital				250

19.   APPROPRIATION ACCOUNT

YEAR ENDED 31ST DECEMBER, 19..

	£	£		£
Interest on Capital—			Balance	4,500
Alver . . .	400			
Clifton . . .	100			
		500		
Balance—				
Alver, ¾ . . .	3,000			
Clifton, ¼ . . .	1,000			
		4,000		
		£4,500		£4,500

Dr.   CAPITALS   *Cr.*

				Alver	Clifton
			19..	£	£
			Jan. 1 By Balance . b/d	8,000	
			,, Transfer to Pre-		
			mises[1] . .		2,000
			Dec. 31 ,, Current Account .		580
				8,000	2,580

Dr.   CURRENT ACCOUNTS   *Cr.*

			Alver	Clifton				Alver	Clifton
			£	£				£	£
19..					19..				
Dec. 31	To Drawings . .		1,900	490	Dec. 31	By Interest on Capital		400	100
	,, Capital . .			580		,, Profit . . .		3,000	1,000
	,, Balances . c/d		1,500	30					
			£3,400	£1,100				£3,400	£1,100
					19..				
					Jan. 1	By Balances . b/d		1,500	30

[1] It is assumed that the amount credited by Clifton is by way of gift.

20. It is assumed that (1) no Goodwill Account exists at the date of the introduction of Dumas as partner, (2) Byron and Scott are to continue to share the remaining four-fifths of the profits in the ratio of 2:1, (3) the capitals are to remain "fixed," (4) interest to be charged on capitals at 5 per cent per annum, and (5) no interest on Current Accounts.

The alternatives may be considered as follows—

(1) By the creation of the Goodwill Account the old partners gain £600 by way of interest on capital, losing four-fifths thereof by reason of diminished divisible profits of £600, that is, a gain of £600 *less* a loss of £480, viz. £120.

(2) By the creation of a Loan Account of £3,000 the old partners gain £150 by way of interest on capital, losing four-fifths thereof by reason of diminished divisible profits of £150, that is, a gain of £150 *less* a loss of £120, viz. £30.

If interest on the loan of £3,000 is charged at 5 per cent per annum there is a clear gain of £150 to the old partners, as there is a charge of £150 and a credit of the same sum for the old partners' and the new partner's interest on £3,000 respectively, that is, the debit and the credit to Profit and Loss Account cancel each other, the new partner and the old partners being respectively debited and credited with £150.

As compared with alternative (1) there is thus a loss to the old partners of £90 if no interest is charged on Dumas's loan, and a gain of £30 if interest at 5 per cent per annum is charged.

(3) The proposal to take out a joint policy will decrease the divisible profits by the amount of the annual premium, in addition to which the old partners receive none of the advantages enumerated above; but the annual payments of the premiums are virtually creating a benefit for all partners in the profit-sharing proportions, the ultimate effect being that the partners are sharing profits without any of the foregoing interest provisions, thus operating adversely to the old partners.

Furthermore, the annual payments may constitute a serious drain on the liquid resources of the firm, but in case of the death of a partner will provide cash towards the payment of the amount due to the estate of the deceased partner.

In a winding up of the partnership no difference arises in respect of the three alternatives.

The second method is the most equitable, provided interest is charged to Dumas, because it enables the old partners to obtain interest as if Dumas had paid in his premium, whilst the provision as to repayment affords a method of the gradual withdrawal—dependent upon the relative prosperity of the firm—of the premium payable by Dumas.

The third method is the least satisfactory solution of the difficulty.

21.

(1) BALANCE SHEETS AS AT 31ST MARCH, 19..

	£	£	£		£	£	£
Capitals—				Goodwill . . .	800	—	300
Robinson . .	1,760	¹1,360	960	Motor Van . . .	150	150	150
Bell . . .	880	¹680	480	Stock	880	880	880
Bank Overdraft .	320	¹120	1,020	Trade Debtors . .	1,600	1,600	1,600
Trade Creditors .	480	480	480	Cash	10	10	10
	£3,440	£2,640	£2,940		£3,440	£2,640	£2,940
Alternative . .	(a)	(b)	(c)		(a)	(b)	(c)

(2) No definite statement is given as to the value of goodwill, and consequently the amount indicated in (a) is assumed to represent the agreed value of the goodwill of the business.

In regard to sharing of profits the amount of capital is immaterial if no interest on capital is to be charged, otherwise the alternatives would require consideration, but in this instance no difference in total participation of profits arises, as in all three cases the respective capitals are in the ratio of 2:1, corresponding with the ratio of the formal division of profits.

In regard to goodwill, the treatment is correct in (a) but not in (b) and (c). In (b) the premium chargeable to Bell should be £267—one-third of £800—thus involving an overcharge of £133; whilst in (c) goodwill should appear at £800. This shows a gain of £167 to Bell. Alternative (c) is therefore the best from Bell's point of view.

If goodwill in (b) is to be taken as correct, goodwill in (a) and (c) should be £1,200.

Proof of the above may be afforded by assuming the firm is wound up, the general assets realizing the book values and goodwill £800.

	(a)	£		(b)	£		(c)	£
Balance . . .		880	Balance . .		680	Balance . .		480
			Add profit on sale of goodwill (⅓) . .		267	Add profit on sale of goodwill (⅓)² .		167
Bell receives . .		880			947			647
Bell originally paid into firm . . .		880			1,080			480
Profit (+) or Loss (−) .		—			−£133			+£167

¹ It is assumed that in (b) the premium is retained in the business, otherwise Bank will be £720, Robinson £960 and Bell £480.
² ⅓ of (£800 − £300).

22. *Axe and Coe*

(a) BALANCE SHEET AS AT 1ST JANUARY, 19.7

		£				£
Capitals—			Furniture, etc. . . .			380
Axe . . .	£3,900		Uncompleted Work . . .			410
Coe . . .	900		Sundry Debtors . . .			1,420
		4,800	Cash at Bank [£590 + £2,100] .			2,690
Sundry Creditors . . .		100				
		£4,900				£4,900

(b)   PROFIT AND LOSS APPROPRIATION ACCOUNT
                          YEAR ENDED 31ST. DECEMBER 19.7

		£	£			£
Interest on Capital—				Balance . . . . b/d		5,230
Axe	£345					
Coe	45					
			390			
Balance—						
Axe, ¾ . . .	£3,630					
Less amount to cover						
guarantee . . .	190					
		3,440				
Coe, ¼ . . .	£1,210					
Add amount due to Axe						
to cover guarantee .	190					
		1,400				
			4,840			
			£5,230			£5,230

[If the premium of £4,200 is not to be retained in the business Axe's Capital Account will remain at £2,700 and the Cash at the Bank £590 + £900 = £1,490. As a result (ignoring guarantee) interest on Capital will be: Axe, £135; and Coe, £45, the divisible profit £5,050, allocated as to Axe £3,788 and Coe £1,262. In this event Axe receives in all £3,923 and Coe £1,307, as against £3,975, and £1,255 shown in the above account. This is a loss of £52 to Axe and a gain to Coe of the like amount, being 5 per cent on £4,200 (£210) less three-quarters of £210 (£158).]

Calculation of premium—

$$\tfrac{1}{4} \times \frac{5,800 + 5,400 + 5,600}{3} \times 3 = £4,200.$$

23.   RED, WHITE AND BLUE
(a)   JOURNAL

19.8			£	£
(1) Dec. 31	White . . . . . Dr.		8,750	
	Blue . . . . . Dr.		8 750	
	To Red			17,500
	Being acquisition by White and Blue from Red of a one-ninth share each of the goodwill of the firm. (Value £78,750.)			
19.9				
(2) Jan. 1	Pink . . . . . Dr.		4,375	
	To White			2,500
	,, Blue			1,875
	Being acquisition by Pink of a further one-eighteenth share of the goodwill of the firm (value £78,750) and sale thereof to Pink by White as to four-sevenths and Blue three-sevenths.			
19.9				
(3) Dec. 31	Blue . . . . . Dr.		1,875	
	Pink . . . . . Dr.		15,000	
	To Red			10,625
	,, White			6,250
	Being sale of Red's share of goodwill of the firm and its acquisition by White, Blue and Pink in proportions to equalize the share of goodwill of firm as between the continuing partners.			

Calculation of Goodwill—   £

Profits for the four years ended 31st December, 19.8—

£25,000 + £30,000 + £28,000 + £43,000 .   . $\underline{126,000}$ = £31,500 annually

                                                                           £

Goodwill = 2½ years' purchase of average of four
years = $\frac{5}{8}$ × £126,000 .   .   .   .   . $\underline{78,750}$

Calculation of Goodwill adjustment at 31st December, 19.8—

	Red	White	Blue
Old Profit ratio .	(4) $\frac{4}{9}$	(3) $\frac{3}{9}$	(2) $\frac{2}{9}$
New ,, ,, .	(2) $\frac{2}{9}$	(4) $\frac{4}{9}$	(3) $\frac{3}{9}$
Seller . .	$\frac{2}{9}$	Buyer $\frac{1}{9}$	Buyer $\frac{1}{9}$
$\frac{2}{9}$ × £78,750 .	Cr. £17,500	Dr. £8,750	Dr. £8,750 Basis for first Journal entry.

[Each $\frac{1}{9}$ of £78,750 = £8,750]

The new partner Pink acquires his share of goodwill by (i) gift from Red and (ii) sale by White and Blue.

As to (i)—

The release by Red is a portion of the average profits, as shown above:

$$\frac{2,750}{31,500} = \frac{11}{126}$$

As to (ii)—

Pink is to acquire in total $\frac{1}{7}$ (or $\frac{18}{126}$) of the goodwill, so that he buys from White and Blue a further $\frac{7}{126}$ (i.e. $\frac{1}{18}$) in the ratio of 4:3, that is $\frac{4}{126}$ and $\frac{3}{126}$ respectively, as this ratio is that which obtained immediately before Pink was admitted a partner, as shown below.

(b) Calculation of revised profit sharing ratios for the purpose of goodwill adjustment on Pink's admission at 1st January, 19.8—

	Red	White	Blue	Pink
Ratio (as amended 31st Dec. 19.8) . =	$\frac{28}{126}$	= $\frac{56}{126}$	= $\frac{42}{126}$	
Release by Red to Pink	$\frac{11}{126}$			$\frac{11}{126}$
Purchase by Pink from White and Blue .	(Cr.)	$\frac{4}{126}$ (Cr.)	$\frac{3}{126}$ (Dr.)	$\frac{7}{126}$ Basis for second Journal entry
New Ratio . .	$\frac{17}{126}$	$\frac{52}{126}$	$\frac{39}{126}$	$\frac{18}{126}$ (= $\frac{1}{7}$)
The transfers for goodwill adjustment are:		$\frac{4}{126}$ × £78,750	$\frac{3}{126}$ × £78,750	$\frac{7}{126}$ × £78,750
		£2,500	£1,875	£4,375

The above is shown in full, but it is much quicker to take Pink's purchase as follows—

$\frac{7}{126} = \frac{1}{18}$ of £78,750 . . . . . . (Dr.) £4,375

sold to   White and Blue in the ratio of 4:3

which is   White $\frac{4}{7}$ × £4,375 . . . . . (Cr.) £2,500

         Blue $\frac{3}{7}$ × £4,375 . . . . . . (Cr.) £1,875

Calculation of Goodwill adjustment at 31st December, 19.8—

	Red	White	Blue	Pink
As fixed 1st January, 19.9	$\frac{17}{126}$	$\frac{52}{126}$	$\frac{39}{126}$	$\frac{18}{126}$
As now amended . .	Nil	($\frac{1}{3}$) $\frac{42}{126}$	($\frac{1}{3}$) $\frac{42}{126}$	($\frac{1}{3}$) $\frac{42}{126}$
Adjustment . .	Cr. $\frac{17}{126}$	Cr. $\frac{10}{126}$	Dr. $\frac{3}{126}$	Dr. $\frac{24}{126}$
[$\frac{1}{126}$ × £78,750 = £625].	£10,625	£6,250	£1,875	£15,000
	£625 × 17	£625 × 10	£625 × 3	£625 × 24
		£16,875		£16,875

24.   JOURNAL

19..		£	£
July 1	Cash at Bank . . . . . *Dr.*	630	
	Stock-in-trade . . . . . *Dr.*	4,687	
	Sundry Debtors . . . . . *Dr.*	3,120	
	Machinery and Plant . . . . *Dr.*	1,875	
	Freehold Premises . . . . . *Dr.*	4,375	
	To Sundry Creditors . . .		5,000
	„ Bad Debts Provision . . .		312
	„ Culme—Capital	1	5,625
	„ Burr—Capital		3,750
	Being Assets and Liabilities taken over by new firm on this date as per agreement . . .		
	Cash . . . . . . *Dr.*	3,750	
	To Land—Capital		3,750
	Being Cash introduced by Land . . .		
	Culme—Capital . . . . . *Dr.*	625	
	To Culme—Loan		625
	Being transfer to Culme's Loan Account to bring his Capital to £5,000.		

[1] Capital £6,250 after adjustments for profits and losses on revaluations.

BALANCE SHEET AS AT 1ST JULY, 19..

		£				£
Capitals—			Freehold Premises . . .			4,375
Burr . . .	£3,750		Machinery and Plant . . .			1,875
Land . . .	3,750		Stock . . .			4,687
Culme . . .	5,000		Sundry Debtors . .	£3,120		
		12,500	*Less* Bad Debts			
Culme—Loan . . .		625	Provision . .	312		
Sundry Creditors . . .		5,000				2,808
			Bank			4,380
		£18,125				£18,125

Notes. (i) It is assumed that the balance due to Culme has not been paid; otherwise the Loan Account would disappear and Cash in Bank be £3,750.

(ii) No adjustment has been made for goodwill in absence of data as to its agreed value. If the figure of goodwill is available Culme is a seller of 10/24; Burr is a buyer of 1/24; and Land is a buyer of 9/24.

(iii) The Capital Accounts may be shown under two headings—General Partners and Limited Partner.

25.   JOURNAL

19.. Jan. 1		£	£
	Revaluation Account . . . *Dr.*	1,800	
	To Investment Reserve . . .		1,200
	,, Plant		600
	Being adjustments in value of Investments and Plant on the admission of D into the partnership.		
	Capitals— *Dr.*		
	A	900	
	B	600	
	C	300	
	To Revaluation Account . . .		1,800
	Being apportionment of the loss arising from revaluation between the old partners.		
	Cash . . . . . *Dr.*	3,500	
	To A—Capital		1,000
	,, D—Capital		2,500

	Being introduction of Capital by D and pay-
	  ment to A in respect of purchase of Goodwill
	  retained in the firm by A.		

BALANCE SHEET AS AT 1ST JANUARY, 19..

		£			£
Capitals—			Plant . . .	£3,500	
A [£6,000 + £1,000 − £900]	£6,100		*Less* Depreciation .	600	
B [£4,000 − £600] .	3,400				2,900
C [£2,000 − £300] .	1,700		Furniture and Fittings . .		1,000
D . . .	2,500		Investments . .	£3,000	
		13,700	*Less* Reserve . .	1,200	
					1,800
Creditors		10,500	Stock		5,000
			Debtors		6,000
			Cash at Bank		7,500
		£24,200			£24,200

Dr.						CAPITALS					Cr.
		A	B	C	D			A	B	C	D
		£	£	£	£			£	£	£	£
19.. Jan 1	To Revaluation Acct.	900	600	300		19.. Jan. 1	By Balances b/d	6,000	4,000	2,000	
Dec 31	,, Drawings	3,000	3,000	1,500	1,500		,, Cash .	1,000			2,500
	,, Balances c/d	7,100	4,400	2,200	3,000	Dec. 31	,, Profit .	4,000	4,000	2,000	2,000
	£	11,000	8,000	4,000	4,500		£	11,000	£8,000	£4,000	£4,500
						19.. Jan. 1	By Balances b/d	7,100	4,400	2,200	3,000

A now obtains one-third of the profits, i.e. one-half — one-sixth sold to D.
Goodwill if brought into the books would be £24,000, as one-sixth share is £4,000.

The capitals, before the introduction of the new partner, were proportional to profit-sharing ratios, and if they are to be revised after D's admittance, cash adjustments will be as follows—

	A £	B £	C £	D £	Total £
Capitals	5,100	3,400	1,700	2,500	12,700
Cash paid in (+) or out (−) . .	−867	+833	+417	−383	
Revised Capitals [to nearest £1] .	($\frac{1}{3}$)£4,233	($\frac{1}{3}$)£4,233	($\frac{1}{6}$)£2,117	($\frac{1}{6}$)£2,117	£12,700

26. *Dr.*   PROFIT AND LOSS APPROPRIATION ACCOUNT   *Cr.*

		£			£
Q—Salary . . .		1,800	Balance . . . b/d		13,200
Interest on Capital—					
P . . .	£200				
Q . . .	100				
		300			
R—Salary		1,400			
R—Proportion of Profits [$\frac{1}{20}$ of £9,700] . .		485			
Balance . . . c/d		9,215			
		£13,200			£13,200
R—Extra Salary		350	Balance . . . b/d		9,215
P—$\frac{3}{5}$ of £9,215 .	£5,529				
Less Extra Salary due to R .	350				
		5,179			
Q—$\frac{2}{5}$ of £9,215 . .		3,686			
		£9,215			£9,215

[*Alternative Solution*—

PROFIT AND LOSS APPROPRIATION ACCOUNT

		£			£
R—Salary		1,750	Balance (after charging Q's salary and		
Balance	c/d	9,350	interest on Capital) . .	b/d	11,100
		£11,100			£11,100
R—Proportion of Profit—			Balance	b/d	9,350
$\frac{2}{40}$ of £9,700		485	R—Extra Salary . . .	c/d	350
Balance	c/d	9,215			
		£9,700			£9,700
R—Extra Salary . . .	b/d	350	Balance	b/d	9,215
P (as above)		5,179			
Q (as above)		3,686			
		£9,215			£9,215

		£
P thus obtains £5,179 + £200 . . =		5,379
Q „ £3,686 + £100 + £1,800 =		5,586
R „ £1,750 + £485 . . =		2,235
		£13,200

It is assumed that R's proportion of profit ($\frac{2}{40}$) is based upon the *firm's* profit, i.e. after charging £1,400, and not the extra £350, otherwise the amount would be 5 per cent of £9,350, in which case the final division between P and Q would be—

Profit £13,200 — (Q's salary £1,800, R's salary £1,750, R's profit £468) — Interest on Capital £300 = £8,882, adjusted thus—

	Total £	P £	Q £
Balance	8,882		
Add R's extra salary	350		
	9,232	5,539	3,693
Less R's extra salary borne by P . . .	350	350	
Final sharing	£8,882	£5,189	£3,693

		£
P thus obtains £5,189 + £200	=	5,389
Q „ £3,693 + £100 + £1,800	=	5,593
R „ £1,750 + £468	=	2,218
		£13,200

27.   JOURNAL

19..		£	£
Nov. 30	Stock . . . . *Dr.*	900	
	To Buildings		300
	„ Machinery and Plant		300
	„ Bad Debts Provision		200
	„ Revaluation Account		100
	Being revaluation of assets on the admission of C. Dun to the partnership.		
	Revaluation Account . . . . *Dr.*	100	
	To A. Dun—Capital		67
	„ B. Dun—Capital		33
	Being apportionment of profit on revaluation between the old partners.		
	Bank . . . . *Dr.*	5,500	
	To A. Dun—Capital		1,333
	„ B. Dun—Capital		667
	„ C. Dun—Capital		3,500
	Being introduction of Capital by C. Dun and payment for Goodwill to the old partners.		

BALANCE SHEET AS AT 1ST DECEMBER, 19..

Capitals—		£		Fixed Assets—			£
A. Dun . . .		9,800		Buildings			5,700
B. Dun . . .		4,950		Machinery and Plant . .			2,700
C. Dun . . .		3,500		Furniture and Fittings . .			400
			18,250	Current Assets—			
General Reserve . . .			1,300	Debtors . . .	£6,200		
Creditors . . .			6,700	Less Bad Debts Provision	200		
							6,000
				Stocks . . .			5,000
				Cash on Hand . .			50
				Cash in Bank . .			6,400
			£26,250				£26,250

Notes. (i) It is assumed that A. Dun and B. Dun share (as between themselves) as before, otherwise an adjustment between them is necessary in respect of the balance of goodwill retained by them. In the absence of the value of the share acquired by C. Dun the *whole* goodwill is not known, but only that part of the whole acquired by C. Dun.

(ii) If the general reserve represents undrawn profits, it is advisable that it be credited to A. Dun and B. Dun, or the reversal process used, that is, A. Dun and B. Dun credited in old ratios and the three new partners debited in new ratios, so that when dealt with at a later stage it will be divided between A. Dun, B. Dun, and C. Dun in the new partnership ratios.

28. *Dr.*   **CAPITALS**   *Cr.*

	C	P	T		C	P	T
	£	£	£		£	£	£
To Balance . .			1,500	By Balances . .	30,000	23,000	
,, Balances . c/d	31,720	23,860	20,000	,, Cash . . .			21,500
				,, T, re Goodwill .	1,000	500	
				,, Capital Adjustment Account .	720	360	
	£31,720	£23,860	£21,500		£31,720	£23,860	£21,500
To Drawings . .	2,000	2,000	2,000	By Balances . b/d	31,720	23,860	20,000
,, Balances . c/d	32,506	23,653	19,600	,, Interest on Capitals . .	1,586	1,193	1,000
				,, Profit and Loss Account . .	1,200	600	600
	£34,506	£25,653	£21,600		£34,506	£25,653	£21,600
To Balances . c/d [as amended]	37,880	18,940	18,940	By Balances b/d (b)	32,506	23,653	19,600
,, Cash . . .		¹4,713	¹660	,, Cash . .	¹5,374		
	£37,880	£23,653	£19,600		£37,880	£23,653	£19,600
				By Balances b/d (a)	37,880	18,940	18,940

¹ The difference of £1 arises because the resultant Capitals have been rounded off for each individual partner to the nearest £10, i.e.—

		£
(*a*) resultant Capitals (after equating)	.	75,760
(*b*) Capitals (before equating) . .	.	75,759
		£1

Dr.   **AGENT**   *Cr.*

	£		£
To Rents (*November, 19.2*) . . .	1,000	By Balance (per T.B.) . . .	4,815
,, *Rents 12 months ended 30th November, 19.3*	12,000	,, *Rates (to 31st March, 19.3—½ year)* . . .	1,540
		,, *Commission (November, 19.2, Rents)* . . .	75
		,, *Repairs (all 19.3)* . . .	1,480
		,, *Commission* . . .	900
		,, *Rates (to 31st March, 19.4—1 year)* . . .	3,120
		,, *Balance* . . . c/d	1,070
	£13,000		£13,000
To Balance . . . . b/d	1,070		

¹ The figures in italics introduced from the Agent's Statement.

The adjustment of Capitals could not in practice take place on 31st December, 19.3, because the profit for the year would not have normally been ascertained, so that the entries would be postponed until the accounts for the year ended 31st December, 19.3, had been prepared and the resulting balances of capitals ascertained.

Dr.		RATES		Cr.
	£			£
To Agent—½ year to 31st March, 19.3	1,540	By Transfer to Capital Adjustment Account—3 months ended 31st December, 19.2—$\frac{3}{6}$ × £1,540 .		770
		„ Prepayment, 3 months ended 31st		
To Agent—1 year to 31st March, 19.4	3,120	December, 19.3—$\frac{3}{12}$ × £3,120		
			c/d	780
		„ Profit and Loss Account . .		3,110[1]
	£4,660			£4,660
To Prepayment . . . b/d	780			

[1] 3 months ended 31st March, 19.3 ($\frac{3}{6}$ × £1,540) . . 770
   9 „   „   31st December, 19.3 ($\frac{9}{12}$ × £3,120) . 2,340
                                  £3,110

Dr.		RENTS RECEIVABLE		Cr.
	£			£
To Capital Adjustment Account—		By Agent—30th November, 19.2 .		1,000
Rent—2 months ended 31st		„ Agent, year ended 30th November,		
December, 19.2 . .	2,000	19.3		12,000
„ Profit and Loss Account . .	12,000	„ Rent accrued 1 month ended 31st		
		December, 19.3 . . c/d		1,000
	£14,000			£14,000
To Rent accrued . . . b/d	1,000			

Dr.		COMMISSION PAYABLE		Cr.
	£			£
To Agent—30th November, 19.2		By Capital Adjustment Account—		
[7½% on £1,000] . .	75	Commission—2 months ended		
„ Agent—year ended 30th November,		31st December, 19.2 [7½% on		
19.3 [7½% on £12,000] . .	900	£2,000]		150
„ Commission Accrued—31st Dec-		„ Profit and Loss Account		
ember, 19.3—1 month [7½% on		[7½% on £12,000] . .		900
£1,000] . . . . c/d	75			
	£1,050			£1,050
		By Commission Accrued . . b/d		75

Dr.		CAPITAL ADJUSTMENT ACCOUNT		Cr.
		£		£
To Commission . . .		150	By Rent	2,000
„ Rates . . .		770		
„ Balance C $\frac{2}{3}$ . . £720				
P $\frac{1}{3}$ . . 360				
		1,080		
		£2,000		£2,000

Dr.	BANK ADJUSTMENT re EQUATION OF CAPITAL			Cr.
		£		£
To Balance (per T.B.) . . .		2,984	By P	4,713
„ C		5,374	„ T	660
			„ Closing Balance . . c/d	2,985
		£8,358		£8,358
To Balance . . . b/d		2,985		

PROFIT AND LOSS ACCOUNT
FOR THE YEAR ENDED 31ST DECEMBER, 19.3

		£				£
Agent's Commission.		900	Rents Receivable	. . .		12,000
Rates . . .		3,110				
Repairs . .		1,480				
General Expenses .		200				
Insurance . .		131				
Net Profit for year .	c/d	6,179				
		£12,000				£12,000
Interest on Capitals—			Net Profit	. . .	b/d	6,179
C . . .	£1,586					
P . . .	1,193					
T . . .	1,000					
		3,779				
Balance divisible—						
C ½ . .	£1,200					
P ¼ . .	600					
T ¼ . .	600					
		2,400				
		£6,179				£6,179

BALANCE SHEET AS AT 31ST DECEMBER, 19.3

		£			£
Capitals—			*Fixed Assets—*		
C . . .	£37,880		Property at cost . . .		70,000
P . . .	18,940		*Current Assets—*		
T . . .	18,940		Debtors and Prepayments:		
		75,760	Agent . . .	£1,070	
			Rents Receivable *less* Agent's Commission thereon		
			(£1,000 — £75) .	925	
				1,995	
			Rates prepaid . .	780	
					2,775
			Cash at Bank		2,985
		£75,760			£75,760

29.   A, B AND C

PROFIT AND LOSS APPROPRIATION ACCOUNT
FOR THE YEAR ENDED 31ST DECEMBER, 19.9

		£			£
Net Trading Profit . .	c/d	17,400	Balance	b/d	12,000
			Partners' Salaries written out to Profit and Loss Appropriation . .		5,400
		£17,400			£17,400
Partner's Salaries—			Balance . . .	b/d	17,400
A . . .	2,600		Interest on Drawings deficiency—		
B . . .	2,800		C 5% (£1,800 — £1,200) . .		30
		5,400			
Interest on Drawings excess—					
A 5% (£7,200 — £5,800)	£70				
B 5% (£3,600 — £3,400)	10				
		80			
Net Divisible Profit—					
A $\frac{6}{10}$ × £12,050 . .	£7,230				
B $\frac{3}{10}$ + £12,050 . £3,615					
Less Benefits . 100					
	3,515				
C $\frac{1}{10}$ × £12,050 . .	1,205				
		11,950			
		£17,430			£17,430

		£
Profit = £12,000 + £30 − £80		11,950
Add Benefit in kind B.		100

i.e.   £7,230 + £3,615 + £1,205   £12,050

The basis figure of profit for the Interest adjustment is—

	A		B		C
	£	£	£	£	£
£12,000, i.e.	7,200		3,600		1,200
Drawings	5,800	6,000		4,600	
Less Salary since credited . . .		2,600		2,800	
			3,400		1,800
Excess or *Deficiency*	£1,400		£200		£600

If the benefits in kind adjustment had to be brought into account in calculating Interest all partners would benefit as regards Interest as to—

	£
A 5 per cent of £60 =	3·00
B 5 per cent of £30 =	1·50
C 5 per cent of £10 =	0·50
	£5·00

B would be debited with £5, leaving him with net diminution of £3·50 (i.e. £5 − £1·50) = the gain to A £3 plus C £0·50.

As the benefits in kind would be spread over the year it would theoretically not be correct to make the adjustment at 5 per cent for the full year but on average due date of the benefits, and obviously the difference in the amount of interest resulting therefrom is too insignificant to be brought into adjustment.

Dr.   MOTOR VEHICLE   *Cr.*

	£		£
To Balance	1,200	By Cost of Vehicle sold . . .	1,200
,, Transfer from Purchases, new vehicle	1,600	,, Balance . . . . c/d	1,600
	£2,800		£2,800
To Balance . . . . b/d	1,600		

Dr.   PROVISION FOR DEPRECIATION OF MOTOR VEHICLE   *Cr.*

	£		£
To Transfer to Motor Vehicle Sale Adjustment Account .	600	By Balance . . . . b/d	600
,, Balance . . . . c/d	160	,, Profit and Loss Adjustment Account—Depreciation 10% of £1,600	160
	£760		£760
		By Balance . . . . b/d	160

Dr.   MOTOR VEHICLE SALE ADJUSTMENT   *Cr.*

	£		£
To Cost Transferred . .	1,200	By Provision for Depreciation . .	600
,, Profit to Profit and Loss Adjustment Account . . .	200	,, Transfer from Sales *re* old vehicle sold	800
	£1,400		£1,400

PROFIT AND LOSS ADJUSTMENT ACCOUNT

	£		£
Sales correction	800	Balance from Profit and Loss Account[1]	16,560
Depreciation omitted . . .	160	Profit on Sale of Motor Vehicle .	200
Amended Profit to Appropriation Account	17,400	Purchases correction . . .	1,600
	£18,360		£18,360

[1] The profit (after charging Partners' Salaries £5,400) is £11,160, so that the amount for *Appropriation* is £11,160 + £5,400 = £16,560, the item of £5,400 being chargeable in the Appropriation Account.

30. JOURNAL

19..		£	£
Dec. 31	Freehold Premises. . . . . *Dr.*	1,000	
	To J. Lock—Capital . . .		500
	„ F. Lock—Capital . . .		500
	Being increase in value of Freehold Premises on revaluation.		
	Goodwill . . . . . . *Dr.*	500	
	Furniture . . . . . . *Dr.*	100	
	Stock . . . . . . *Dr.*	1,500	
	Debtors . . . . . *Dr.*	400	
	To A. Key—Capital . . .		2,500
	Being agreed value of assets brought into the firm.		
	Cash . . . . . . *Dr.*	2,000	
	To J. Lock—Capital		1,000
	„ F. Lock—Capital		1,000
	Being agreed payment by A. Key for his share of Goodwill.		
	J. Lock—Capital . . . . . *Dr.*	2,000	
	F. Lock—Capital . . . . . *Dr.*	1,000	
	To Cash		3,000
	Being Cash withdrawn to equalize partners' Capitals as agreed.		

BALANCE SHEET AS AT 1ST JANUARY, 19..

Capitals—		£			£
J. Lock . . .	£2,500		Goodwill		500
F. Lock . . .	2,500		Freehold Premises		3,000
A. Key . . .	2,500		Fixtures and Furniture . . .		600
		7,500	Stock		5,000
Creditors		5,000	Debtors		3,100
			Bank and Cash		300
		£12,500			£12,500

Note. Goodwill should be either written off equally against the partners, or increased by £6,000 (the value of goodwill of Lock & Co.) and credited equally to J. and F. Lock; in the latter case the cash balance will be insufficient to permit the payment to J. and F. Lock of the necessary amounts to equalize the capitals.

31.   PROFIT AND LOSS APPROPRIATION ACCOUNT FOR THE YEAR
ENDED........

	£			£
W—$\frac{4}{12}$ £3,200		Net Profit . . . b/d		9,600
Less Transfer to Z—				
$\frac{2}{10}$ × £400 . . . 160				
	3,040			
X—$\frac{3}{12}$ £2,400				
Less Transfer to Z—				
$\frac{3}{10}$ × £400 . . . 120				
	2,280			
Y—$\frac{3}{12}$ £2,400				
Less Transfer to Z—				
$\frac{3}{10}$ × £400 . . . 120				
	2,280			
Z—$\frac{2}{12}$ £1,600				
Add Transfers from W, X,				
and Y . . . 400				
	2,000			
	£9,600			£9,600

32. *Dr.*   REALIZATION ACCOUNT   *Cr.*

19..		£	19..		£
Feb. 1	To Freehold Property, Plant,		Feb. 1	By Cash . . .	45,000
	and Machinery . . 18,000			,, Creditors . . .	4,500
	,, Debtors . . . 11,000				
	,, Stock-in-trade . . 7,000				
	,, Realization Expenses 600				
	,, Profit on Realization— £				
	Brown, $\frac{1}{3}$ £6,000 (a) 2,000				
	$\frac{1}{2}$ £6,900 (b) 3,450				
	5,450				
	Green, $\frac{1}{3}$ £6,000 (a) 2,000				
	$\frac{1}{2}$ £6,900 (b) 3,450				
	5,450				
	White, £6,000 (a) . 2,000				
	£49,500				£49,500

Dr.   CASH   *Cr.*

19..		£	19..		£
Feb. 1	To Balance . . . b/d	600	Feb. 1	By Realization Account. .	600
	,, Realization Account. .	45,000		,, Brown—Capital . .	20,850
				,, Green—Capital . .	21,250
				,, White—Capital . .	2,900
		£45,600			£45,600

Dr.   CAPITALS   *Cr.*

		Brown	Green	White			Brown	Green	White
19..		£	£	£	19..		£	£	£
Feb. 1	To Cash	20,850	21,250	2,900	Feb. 1	By Balance b/d	15,000	15,000	
						Transfer-Current Accounts	400	800	900
						Realization Account—			
						Profit	5,450	5,450	2,000
		£20,850	£21,250	£2,900			£20,850	£21,250	£2,900

		£
Computation of Profit on Sale—		
Purchase Consideration		45,000
Less Net Assets taken over . . .		32,100
		£12,900

	£	£
Profit—		
(a) Profit on Sale of Machinery, etc.		
Sale Price . . .	24,000	
Less Book Value . . .	18,000	
		6,000 divisible between
		B, G, and W
(b) Profit on Sale of remainder (Debtors,		
less Creditors, Stock, and Cash):		
Sale Price [£45,000 − £24,000].	21,000	
Less Book Values . .	14,100[1]	
		6,900 divisible between
		B and G only
		£12,900

[1] It is assumed that the remaining net assets are sold at book values, leaving a profit of £6,900 in respect of Goodwill.

33.

STATEMENT OF PROFIT FOR THE YEAR ENDED
31ST DECEMBER, 19.. (a)

		£			£	£
Opening Capital—A		2,600	Drawings—A . . .	£3,600		
B—Cash introduced		500	B . . .	2,250		
Net Profit . . .	c/d	7,000				5,850
			Closing Capitals . . .			4,250
		£10,100				£10,100
Interest on Capital—	£		Net Profit	b/d		7,000
A	130					
B	25					
		155				
Balance—	£					
A, ⅔ . . .	4,563					
B, ⅓ . . .	2,282					
		6,845				
		£7,000				£7,000

STATEMENT OF PROFIT FOR THE YEAR ENDED
31ST DECEMBER, 19.. (b)

		£			£	£
Opening Capitals		4,250	Drawings—A . . .	£3,540		
Net Profit . . .	c/d	7,390	B . . .	2,250		
						5,790
			Closing Capitals . . .			5,850
		£11,640				£11,640
Interest on Capital—			Net Profit	b/d		7,390
		£				
A		188				
B		25				
		213				
Balance—						
A, ⅔		4,785				
B, ⅓		2,392				
		7,177				
		£7,390				£7,390

STATEMENT OF PROFIT FOR THE YEAR ENDED
31ST DECEMBER, 19.. (c)

		£				£
Opening Capital . . .		5,850	Drawings—A . . .	3,580		
Net Profit	c/d	6,780	B . . .	2,250		
					5,830	
			Closing Capitals . . .		6,800	
		£12,630			£12,630	

		£				£
Interest on Capital—			Net Profit . . .	b/d	6,780	
A	267					
B	25					
		292				
Balance—						
A, ⅔	4,325					
B, ⅓	2,163					
		6,488				
		£6,780			£6,780	

The position as regards the premium payable by B to A is as follows—

	£	£
Amount of Premium due		400
Less Amount paid year 1	57	
Amount paid year 2	167	
Amount paid year 3	Nil	
		224
Balance transferable out of future profits		£176

CAPITALS

Date	Particulars	A £	B £		Date	Particulars	A £	B £
19.. Dec. 31	To Drawings .	3,600	2,250		19.. Jan. 1	By Balance . b/d	2,600	500
	,, A—Transfer .		57 [1]		Dec. 31	,, Cash .		
	,, Balances . c/d	3,750	500			,, Interest on Capital .	130	25
						,, Net Profit .	4,563	2,282
						,, B—Transfer .	57	
		£7,350	£2,807				£7,350	£2,807
19.. Dec. 31	To Drawings .	3,540	2,250		19.. Jan. 1	By Balances . b/d	3,750	500
	,, A—Transfer .		167		Dec. 31	,, Interest on Capital .	188	25
	,, Balances . c/d	5,350	500			,, Net Profit .	4,785	2,392
						,, B—Transfer .	167	
		£8,890	£2,917				£8,890	£2,917
19.. Dec. 31	To Drawings .	3,580	2,250		19.. Jan. 1	By Balances . b/d	5,350	500
	,, Balances . c/d	6,362	438 [2]		Dec. 31	,, Interest on Capital .	267	25
						,, Net Profit .	4,325	2,163
		£9,942	£2,688				£9,942	£2,688
					19.. Jan. 1	By Balances . b/d	6,362	438

[1] B's share of profits is £2,307, i.e. Interest on Capital £25 + Share of Net Profit £2,282. It has been assumed that share of profits means share of divisible profits *and* Interest on Capital. If Interest on Capital is to be excluded the transfer (in the first year) is £32 only. i.e. £2,282 − £2,250.

For Premiums payable by B to A, see page 441.

[2] B's share of profits is £2,188. i.e. Interest on Capital £25 + £2,163. However, B has drawn £2,250, i.e. he has overdrawn (£2,250 − £2,188) £62 which, in effect, is a withdrawal of capital.

34. *Dr.* REALIZATION ACCOUNT *Cr.*

		£				£
19.. Dec. 31	To Sundry Assets	12,600	19.. Dec. 31	By Cash		8,700
	„ Expenses	270		„ Loss—A	£1,390	
				B	1,390	
				C	1,390	4,170
		£12,870				£12,870

Dr. CAPITALS *Cr.*

		A	B	C			A	B	C
		£	£	£			£	£	£
19.. Dec. 31	To Balance. b/d			900	19.. Dec.31	By Balances . b/d	6,000	3,000	
	„ Profit and Loss Account[1]	950	950	950		„ *Transfers*			
	„ Loss on Realization	1,390	1,390	1,390		$A \frac{6000}{9000} \times £3,240$			
	„ *Transfer C-Loss per Garner* v . *Murray*	2,160	1,080			$B \frac{3000}{9000} \times £3,240$			3,240
	„ Cash	1,500				„ Cash		420	
		£6,000	£3,420	£3,240			£6,000	£3,420	£3,240

Dr. CASH *Cr.*

		£			£
19.. Dec. 31	To Realization Account—		19.. Dec. 31	By Realization Account—	
	Assets	8,700		Expenses	270
	„ B—Capital	420		„ Creditors	6,300
				„ A—Loan and Interest	1,050
				„ A—Capital	1,500
		£9,120			£9,120

[1] £2,800 plus A interest on loan at 5 per cent per annum, £50, equals £2,850 [5 per cent per annum taken per s. 24, Partnership Act, 1890]. Income Tax has been ignored.

35. The capital and goodwill of A at the date of his retirement, £3,600, should be transferred to the remaining partners' Capital Accounts in profit-sharing ratio if there is a Goodwill Account open in the books. If there is not a Goodwill Account in the books, and it is not desired to open one, it will only be necessary to transfer the balance of A's Capital Account to the Capital Accounts of B and C. In the first instance the entries required will be—

							£	£
A Capital	.	.	.	.	.	*Dr.*	3,600	
To B Capital ($\frac{3}{5}$)	.	.	.	.				2,160
„ C Capital ($\frac{2}{5}$)	.	.	.	.				1,440

A's annuity for the following year will be £400, and this will be debited either to Profit and Loss Account, or to the partners' Capital or Current Accounts in the ratio 3:2 (if the partners B and C still maintain the same profit-sharing ratio between themselves).

Alternatively, the estimated liability in respect of the capital value of the annuity may be debited to B and C in the ratio of 3:2 and an Annuity Fund Account credited, and the amount of £400 charged to the latter instead of as in the preceding paragraph.

The partners will deduct income tax at the standard rate on the annuity and account or it to the Inland Revenue.

On any change in the constitution of the partnership or in profit ratios, the revised amount of goodwill and the estimated actuarial liability in respect of the annuity will have to be brought into account either permanently or temporarily.

36. Dr. REALIZATION ACCOUNT **Cr.**

19..		£	19..				£
June 30	To Sundry Assets . .	5,150	Aug. 16	By Cash—Sundry Assets .			3,920
Aug. 16	„ Expenses of Realization.	270		„ Loss on Realization—			
					X . . .	£750	
					Y . . .	750	
							1,500
		£5,420					£5,420

Dr. CASH **Cr.**

19..			£	19..			£
June 30	To Balance . . b/d		850	Aug. 16	By Realization Account—		
Aug. 16	„ Realization Account—				Expenses of Realiza-		
	Sundry Assets . .		3,920		tion . . .		270
	„ Y—Capital . . .		50		„ Sundry Creditors . .		2,300
					„ X—Capital . . .		2,250
			£4,820				£4,820

Dr. CAPITALS **Cr.**

		X	Y			X	Y
19..		£	£	19..		£	£
Aug. 16	To Realization Ac-			June 30	By Balances . b/d	3,000	700
	count: Loss .	750	750		„ Cash[1] . . .		50
	„ Cash . .	2,250					
		£3,000	£750			£3,000	£750

[1] It is assumed that Y is able to pay in £50; if not, the actual cash received from Y will be debited to cash and the balance to X.

37. Dr. APPROPRIATION ACCOUNT **Cr.**

			£			£
To A: Interest on Loan . . .			206	By Balance . . . . b/d		7,000
„ A: Loan Account—						
⅓ of £3,000 . . .			1,000			
„ Capitals—	£					
B	500					
C	500					
			1,000			
„ Current Accounts—						
B	. 2,397					
C	. 2,397					
			4,794			
			£7,000			£7,000

Dr.		A—Loan		Cr.	
	£				£
To Cash (1st Quarter)—		By Transfer from Capital . . .			1,000
Principal	250	,, Goodwill			3,500
Interest	56	,, Interest on £4,500 at 5% per annum			
,, Cash (2nd Quarter)—		(1st Quarter)			56
Principal	250	,, Interest on £4,250 at 5% per annum			
Interest	53	(2nd Quarter)			53
,, Cash (3rd Quarter)—		,, Interest on £4,000 at 5% per annum			
Principal	250	(3rd Quarter)			50
Interest	50	,, Interest on £3,750 at 5% per annum			
,, Cash (4th Quarter)—		(4th Quarter)			47
Principal , ...	250	,, Appropriation Account—			
Interest	47	One-third of profit . . .			1,000
,, Balance . . . c/d	4,500				
	£5,706				£5,706
		By Balance . . . . b/d			4,500

Notes. (i) Goodwill should be deducted equally from the partners, or increased by £7,000, £3,500 being credited to each partner.

(ii) No mention is made of an allocation of expenses, e.g. of collection in respect of £3,000 fees.

(iii) No interest in the above year is payable to A in respect of his £1,000 share of profits.

(iv) It is assumed that the figure £7,000 represents profit *before* the charge for interest.

(v) The phrase "payment of A's capital out of profits" is capable of many alternative interpretations.

BALANCE SHEET AS AT........

	£			£
Capitals—		Goodwill . .		3,500
B . .	1,500	Sundry Assets—		
C . .	1,500	Per Opening Capitals .	£3,000	
	3,000	*Add* Profit .	7,000	
A—Loan . .	4,500		10,000	
Current Accounts—		*Less* Cash paid to A—		
B . .	2,397	Principal .	£1,000	
C . .	2,397	Interest .	206	
	4,794		1,206	
				8,794
	£12,294			£12,294

38. *Dr.*

CAPITALS

	Devon	Dorset	Poole
	£	£	£
To Balance . . . b/d			900
„ Realization Account— Loss . . .	600	600	600
„ Poole [6:1] . . .	1,286	214	
„ Cash . . .	7,114	686	
	£9,000	£1,500	£1,500

Cr.	Devon	Dorset	Poole
	£	£	£
By Balances . . . b/d	9,000	1,500	1,500
„ Devon and Dorset .			
	£9,000	£1,500	£1,500

¹ Per *Garner v. Murray*.

447

39. *Dr.*   REALIZATION ACCOUNT   *Cr.*

	£		£
To Sundry Debtors . . .	7,000	By Cash—	
,, Fixtures and Furniture . .	450	Sundry Debtors . . .	6,230
,, Stock	4,300	Fixtures and Furniture . .	315
,, Expenses of Realization . .	580	Stock	3,548
		,, Loss—H	1,305
		,, Loss—M	932
	£12,330		£12,330

Dr.   CASH (OR BANK)   *Cr.*

		£		£
To Balance	b/d	1,850	By Expenses of Realization . .	580
,, Realization Account—			,, Sundry Creditors . . .	2,700
Sundry Debtors . .		6,230	,, H	4,745
Fixtures and Furniture . .		315	,, M	3,918
Stock		3,548		
		£11,943		£11,943

Dr.   PARTNERS' ACCOUNTS   *Cr.*

	H	M		H	M
	£	£		£	£
To Current Account .	250		By Balance (Capitals)		
			b/d	5,600	4,000
,, Sundry Creditors—			,, Current Account .		350
(additional liability as at 30th June, 19..) .	175	125	,, Reserve transferred	875	625
,, Realization Account:					
Loss . . .	1,305	932			
,, Cash . . .	4,745	3,918			
	£6,475	£4,975		£6,475	£4,975

40. *Dr.*   REALIZATION ACCOUNT   *Cr.*

19..		£	19..		£
Jan. 1	To *Sundry Assets* . .	1,900	Jan. 1	By Cash	350
	,, Realization Expenses .	100		,, Loss on Realization—	
				Z, ⅓ . . . £550	
				Y, ⅓ . . . 550	
				Z, ⅓ . . . 550	1,650
		£2,000			£2,000

Dr.   CASH   *Cr.*

19..			£	19..		£
Jan. 1	To *Balance* . .	b/d	100	Jan. 1	By Realization Account—	
	,, Realization Account .		350		Realization Expenses .	100
					,, X—Capital . . .	320
					,, Y—Capital . . .	30
			£450			£450

Dr.   CAPITALS   *Cr.*

		X	Y	Z			X	Y	Z
19..		£	£	£	19..		£	£	£
Jan. 1	To Realization Account—Loss	550	550	550	Jan. 1	By *Balances*[1] b/d	900	600	500
	,, Transfer: Z—					Transfers—			
	Per *Garner* v.					X, $\frac{900}{1500} \times £50$			30
	Murray	30	20			Y, $\frac{600}{1500} \times £50$			20
	,, Cash	320	30						
		£900	£600	£550			£900	£600	£550

[1] It is assumed that these are the last agreed Capitals.

41. *Dr.*   CAPITALS   *Cr.*

			Fay	Fry				Fay	Fry
19..			£	£	19..			£	£
June 30	To Loan	.	16,000		June 30	By Balances	b/d	16,000	14,000
	,, Balance	c/d		17,420		,, Revaluation Account	.		3,420
			£16,000	£17,420				£16,000	£17,420
					July 1	By Balance	b/d		17,420

Dr.   CURRENT ACCOUNTS   *Cr.*

			Fay	Fry				Fay	Fry
19..			£	£	19..			£	£
June 30	To Loan	.	1,924		June 30	By Balances	b/d	1,924	1,704

Dr.   REVALUATION ACCOUNT   *Cr.*

				£	19..			£
19..	To Plant and Machinery	.		1,000	June 30	By Stock . . .	.	700
June 30	,, Patents written off	.		600		,, Bad Debts Provision	.	400
	,, Profit on Revaluation—					,, Freehold Property .	.	1,340
	Fay—Loan.	£3,420				Goodwill . .	.	6,000
	Fry—Capital	3,420						
				6,840				
				£8,440				£8,440

Dr.   EXECUTOR OF FAY—LOAN   *Cr.*

			£	19..			£
19..				June 30	By Capital . . .	.	16,000
June 30	To Balance	c/d	21,344		,, Current Account	.	1,924
					,, Revaluation Account	.	3,420
			£21,344				£21,344
				July 1	By Balance	. .	b/d 21,344

Notes. (i) No information is given as to further adjustments, e.g. profits and interest to date of death.

(ii) Until payment, the executor of Fay is entitled to interest at the rate of 5 per cent (less tax), or profit, as the Court decides (s. 24, Partnership Act, 1890).

(iii) The Ledger accounts will be suitably amended, or if it is not intended to disturb them, the items in the Revaluation Account will be brought down and written off against Fry by the reversal process.

CAPITALS

Debit side

Date	Particulars	Alton (£)	Bowers (£)	Crann (£)
19.6 Dec. 31	To Drawings	750	750	750
	" Balances c/d	11,712	5,712	650
		£12,462	£6,462	£1,400
19.7 Dec. 31	To Drawings	750	750	750
	" Loss	573	573	573
	" Balances c/d	10,389	4,389	
		£11,712	£5,712	£1,323
	To Balance b/d	3,464	3,464	298
	" Loss on Realization		925	3,464
	" Cash	6,925		
		£10,389	£4,389	£3,762

Credit side

Date	Particulars	Alton (£)	Bowers (£)	Crann (£)
19.6 Jan. 1 / Dec. 31	By Sundries	11,250	5,250	188
	" Interest			
	" Profit	1,212	1,212	1,212
		£12,462	£6,462	£1,400
19.7 Jan. 1 / Dec. 31	By Balances b/d	11,712	5,712	650
	" Interest			375
	" Balance			298
		£11,712	£5,712	£1,323
	By Balances b/d	10,389	4,389	
	" Loan			3,762
		£10,389	£4,389	£3,762

Dr.   CRANN—LOAN   *Cr.*

19.7			£	19.6			£
Dec. 31	To Capital	. . .	3,762	June 30	By Cash .	. . .	7,500
	,, Cash .	. . .	3,738				
			£7,500				£7,500

Dr.   PROFIT AND LOSS ACCOUNTS   *Cr.*

19.6				£	19.6				£
Dec. 31	To Interest on Loan[1]	.		188	Dec. 31	By Trading Profit	.	b/d	3,824
	,, Profit—		£						
	Alton	.	1,212						
	Bowers	.	1,212						
	Crann	.	1,212						
				3,636					
				£3,824					£3,824
19.7					19.7			£	
Dec. 31	To Trading Loss	b/d		1,344	Dec. 31	By Loss—			
	,, Interest on Loan[2]	.		375		Alton	.	573	
						Bowers	.	573	
						Crann	.	573	
									1,719
				£1,719					£1,719

Profits and losses divided equally in the absence of agreement to the contrary (s. 24, Partnership Act, 1890).

Dr.   CASH   *Cr.*

19.7			£	19.7			£
Dec. 31	To Realization Account:			Dec. 31	By Creditors .	.	2,512
	Sundry Assets .		14,100		,, Crann—Loan	.	3,738
					,, Alton—Capital	.	6,925
					,, Bowers—Capital	.	925
			£14,100				£14,100

Dr.   REALIZATION ACCOUNT   *Cr.*

19.7			£	19.7			£
Dec. 31	To Sundry Assets	.	24,492	Dec. 31	By Cash .	. . .	14,100
					,, Loss—	£	
					Alton	. 3,464	
					Bowers	. 3,464	
					Crann	. 3,464	
							10,392
			£24,492				£24,492

[1] £7,500 at 5 per cent per annum for half-year.
[2] £7,500 at 5 per cent per annum for one year.

43. *Memorandum* OF DISTRIBUTIONS

| | Total | Creditors | Loans | | Capitals | | |
			X	Z	X	Y	Z
	£	£	£	£	£	£	£
1st . .	5,000	5,000					
2nd . .	10,000	5,000	3,000	2,000			
3rd . .	5,000		3,000	2,000			
4th . .	1,000				(a)1,000		
5th . .	4,400				(a)4,400		
	⌠100				(a) 100		
6th . .	⌡500				(b) [1]214	[1]286	
	£26,000	£10,000	£6,000	£4,000	£5,714	£286	

[1] Calculated to the nearest £.

The distributions to the partners are determined as follows—

			X	Y	Z
			£	£	£
Capitals			10,000	6,000	2,000
1st £5,500 (X) . .	(a)		−5,500		
			4,500	6,000	2,000
2nd £7,700 (3:4) . .	(b)		−3,300	−4,400	
			1,200	1,600	2,000
3rd £4,800 (3:4:5) . .			−1,200	−1,600	−2,000
£18,000					

(a) £5,500 all to X. (b) Cash not exceeding £7,700 the ratio is 3:4, hence the receipt of £500 is distributed in the ratio of 3:4.

44. Dr.   REVALUATION ACCOUNT   Cr.

19.7			£	19.7			£
Dec. 31	To Bad Debts Provision .		460	Dec. 31	By Capital Expenditure		
	,, Pension Fund . c/d		1,560		written back . .		292
	,, Balance—	£			,, Plant and Fixtures .		250
	A, 4/7 . . 2,246				,, Goodwill . . c/d	[1]5,408	
	B, 2/7 . . 1,123						
	C, 1/7 . . 561						
			3,930				
			£5,950				£5,950
19.8				19.8			
Jan. 1	To Goodwill . . b/d		5,408	Jan. 1	By Pension Fund . b/d		1,560
					,, Balance	£	
					A, 2/3 . . 2,565		
					E, 1/3 . . 1,283		
							3,848
			£5,408				£5,408

[1] See Note (ii) on page 453.

| Dr. | | | C—LOAN ACCOUNT (*includes*) | | Cr. |

19.7		£	19.7		£
Dec. 31	To Income Tax	42	Dec. 31	By Revaluation Account	561

Notes. (i) Capital Expenditure written back—

		£
19.5		400
Less Depreciation		40
19.6		360
Less Depreciation		36
19.7		324
Less Depreciation		32
		£292

(ii) Goodwill = $\frac{2}{4}$ × £10,816.

(iii) Strictly, the profits require amending in the light of the foregoing adjustments for the purpose of ascertaining goodwill, that is, to the profits will be added £292 and Bad Debts Provision arising out of the last four years' trading will be deducted.

45. Dr.   REALIZATION ACCOUNT   Cr.

	£				£
To Sundry Debtors	13,500	By Cash			17,450
,, Stock	5,050	,, Loss—		£	
,, Machinery and Plant	7,000		Jones, ⅓	2,700	
			Smith, ⅓	2,700	
			Brown, ⅓	2,700	
					8,100
	£25,550				£25,550

Dr.   CASH   Cr.

		£			£
To Balance	b/d	150	By Sundry Creditors		17,000
,, Realization Account		17,450	,, Jones		2,600
,, Smith		2,000			
		£19,600			£19,600

Dr.   PARTNERS' ACCOUNTS   Cr.

		Jones	Smith	Brown			Jones	Smith	Brown
19..		£	£	£	19..		£	£	£
July 1	To Current Accounts		500	1,500	July 1	By Balances b/d	6,000	2,000	1,000
	,, Realization Account—Loss	2,700	2,700	2,700		,, Current Account	1,700		
	,, Transfer from Brown per *Garner v. Murray* [3:1]	2,400	800			,, Transfer to Jones			2,400
	,, Cash	2,600				,, Transfer to Smith			800
						,, Cash		2,000	
		£7,700	£4,000	£4,200			£7,700	£4,000	£4,200

No figure given for realization costs.

46. *Dr.*   EXECUTORS OF N   *Cr.*

19.6				£	19.6				£
June 30	To Current Account	.		450	June 30	By Capital	.	. ¹	3,600
	,, Balance	. . c/d		9,770		,, Goodwill	.	. ¹	6,620
				£10,220					£10,220
July 1	To Capital Accounts—				July 1	By Balance	.	. b/d	9,770
	O, 4/7	. .		5,583					
	P, 3/7	. .		4,187					
				£9,770					£9,770

The purchase taking place on 1st July, 19.6, the whole of the capital and goodwill of N must be transferred to O and P, notwithstanding that the *payments* are to be made in instalments. If the partners pay out of the firm's moneys their accounts will be debited accordingly.

$$^1 \tfrac{9}{15} \times \tfrac{2}{4} \, £(8,800 + 7,040 + 5.520 + 2,176) = \underline{£6,620}.$$

EXECUTORS OF N

Dr.				Cr.		

Dr.

Date		£	£
19.6			
Dec. 31	To Cash—Principal:		
	O, $\frac{4}{7}$	1,396	
	P, $\frac{3}{7}$	1,047	2,443
	,, Cash—Interest:		
	O, $\frac{4}{7}$	139	
	P, $\frac{3}{7}$	105	244
	,, Balance . . . c/d		7,327
			£10,014
19.7			
June 30	To Cash—Principal:		
	O, $\frac{4}{7}$	1,396	
	P, $\frac{3}{7}$	1,047	2,443
	,, Cash—Interest:		
	O, $\frac{4}{7}$	105	
	P, $\frac{3}{7}$	78	183
	,, Balance . . . c/d		4,884
			£7,510
Dec. 31	To Cash—Principal:		
	O, $\frac{4}{7}$	1,396	
	P, $\frac{3}{7}$	1,047	2,443
	,, Cash Interest:		
	O, $\frac{4}{7}$	70	
	P, $\frac{3}{7}$	52	122
	,, Balance . . . c/d		2,441
			£5,006
19.8			
June 30	To Cash—Principal:		
	O, $\frac{4}{7}$	1,396	
	P, $\frac{3}{7}$	1,047	2,442
	,, Cash—Interest:		
	O, $\frac{4}{7}$	35	
	P, $\frac{3}{7}$	26	61
			£2,502

Cr.

Date		£	£
19.6			
July 1	By Balance . . . b/d		9,770
Dec. 31	,, Interest for six months at 5% per annum on £9,770		
	O, $\frac{4}{7}$	139	
	P, $\frac{3}{7}$	105	244
			£10,014
19.7			
Jan. 1	By Balance . . . b/d		7,327
June 30	,, Interest for six months at 5% per annum on £7,327		
	O, $\frac{4}{7}$	105	
	P, $\frac{3}{7}$	78	183
			£7,510
July 1	By Balance . . . b/d		4,884
Dec. 31	,, Interest for six months at 5% per annum on £4,884		
	O, $\frac{4}{7}$	70	
	P, $\frac{3}{7}$	52	122
			£5,006
19.8			
Jan. 1	By Balance . . . b/d		2,441
June 30	,, Interest for six months at 5% per annum on £2,441		
	O, $\frac{4}{7}$	35	
	P, $\frac{3}{7}$	26	61
			£2,502

Note. It will be observed that the interest diminishes each six months by £61, being interest for six months on £2,443 at 5 per cent per annum.

47. *Dr.* CAPITALS *Cr.*

	X	Y	Z			X	Y	Z
	£	£	£			£	£	£
To Balance . b/d			2,000	By Balances . . b/d		6,000	4,000	
,, Loss on Realization .	1,000	1,000	1,000	,, Transfer —				
,, Transfer from Z per				X . . .				1,800
Garner v. *Murray*				Y . . .				1,200
[3:2] . . .	1,800	1,200						
,, Bank . . .	3,200	1,800						
	£6,000	£4,000	£3,000			£6,000	£4,000	£3,000

Dr. BANK *Cr.*

		£			£
To Balance . . . . b/d		5,000	By X—Capital		3,200
			,, Y—Capital		1,800

48. P AND Q

TRADING AND PROFIT AND LOSS ACCOUNT FOR THE HALF-YEAR
ENDED 31ST MARCH, 19..

		£			£
Stock (opening)		2,749	Sales (*less* Returns) . . .		44,335
Purchases		21,470	Stock (closing)		2,874
Wages		6,636			
Gross Profit . . . . c/d		3,354			
		£47,209			£47,209
Salaries		8,755	Gross Profit . . . . b/d		16,354
Rent and Rates		1,263	Discounts (Balance) . . .		35
Travellers' Commission and Expenses		580			
General Expenses . . .		375			
Net Profit . . . . c/d		1,416			
		£16,389			£16,389
Interest on Capital—	£		Net Profit . . . . b/d		5,416
P 100					
Q 50					
		150			
Balance—					
P 2,633					
Q 2,633					
		5,266			
		£5,416			£5,416

Amount due to P's Estate

		£	£
1. Capital			4,000
2. Current Account: Interest on Capital .	.	100	
Share of Profit	.	2,633	
		2,733	
Less Drawings	.	2,450	
			283
3. Share of Goodwill:			
½ (£3,100 + £2,640 + £2,460) . .			4,100
			£8,383

BALANCE SHEET AS AT 31ST MARCH, 19..

[*Before* Goodwill Adjustment]

	£		£
Sundry Creditors	1,800	Plant and Machinery	2,150
Capitals—		Fixtures and Fittings	200
P (£4,000 + £100 + £2,633 − £2,450)	4,283	Stock	2.874
Q (£2,000 + £50 + £2,633 − £2,350)	2,333	Sundry Debtors	2,640
		Cash at Bank	552
	£8,416		£8,416

49. (1) C will be liable jointly with the other partners in respect of the debts contracted *prior* to his retirement as no contract of novation has been entered into.

A partner who retires from a firm does not thereby cease to be liable for partnership debts or obligations incurred before his retirement (s. 17 (2), Partnership Act, 1890).

(2) C will also be jointly liable in respect of the debts incurred *subsequent* to his retirement unless proper notice, as indicated by s. 36, Partnership Act, 1890, has been given. Under this section (*a*) persons dealing with the firm before the retirement must be notified of the change in constitution, and (*b*) an advertisement must be inserted in the London or Edinburgh (according to the situation of the place of business) *Gazette* for the notification of persons who had no dealings with the firm prior to the retirement.

(3) For the loan of £5,000 C will rank as a deferred creditor, i.e. he can receive no return on it until the ordinary unsecured creditors have been paid in full (s. 3, Partnership Act, 1890).

50. (1) The first method is to pay half-yearly sums of £1,800 to the widow of the deceased partner and to charge the amounts to Profit and Loss Account yearly.

In this case the necessary entries will be—

		£	£
Year 1. Annuity	*Dr.* 3,600		
To Cash			2,160
,, Income Tax (40%)			1,440
Profit and Loss Account[1] . .	*Dr.* 3,600		
To Annuity			3,600

(2) An alternative method is to purchase an annuity from an insurance company or similar concern. In this case a large sum of money will have to be found on the death of a partner, and the necessary entries will be—

		£	£
Year 1. Annuity	*Dr.* (say) 30,000		
To Cash			30,000
Capital Account of Surviving Partner	*Dr.* 30,000		
To Annuity			30,000

It is apparent that the first method will be advantageous if the widow dies earlier than normal expectation, and the latter method if she lives longer than normal expectation.

[1] Or Drawings, Current, or Capital Account in profit ratios.

51. *Dr.*   M. LANE—CAPITAL   *Cr.*

19.. Apr. 30		£	19.. Jan. 1 Apr. 30			£
To Drawings	. . .	570	By Balance	. . b/d	3.600
„ Representatives of M. Lane		5,907	„ Interest on Capital	. .	60
			„ Share of Profits[1]	. .	339
			„ Share of Goodwill	. .	2,478
		£6,477			£6,477

[1] If the share is to be calculated on true profits, i.e. after adjusting premium payable, this sum will be increased by $\frac{3}{8} \times \frac{1}{12} \times £400 = £50$.

		£
(1) The Share of Profits, £339, is arrived at as follows— Net Profits for the year preceding death		2,712
Profits for 4 months, $\frac{4}{12} \times £2,712$		904
M. Lane's share thereof, $\frac{3}{8} \times £904$		339

(2) The Share of Goodwill, £2,478, is arrived at as follows— Net Profits for the three years preceding death:			£
	Year 1	. .	2,800
	2	. .	3,200
	3	. .	2,712
			8,712
Add insurance premiums for three years		. . .	1,200
			£9,912
Two years' purchase of average profits $£\frac{9912}{3} \times 2$		. . .	£6,608
M. Lane's share thereof, $\frac{3}{8} \times £6,608$		. . . . .	£2,478

Note. The answer set out above follows the instructions given in the question, i.e. that a deceased partner should be credited with his capital as shown by the last balance sheet, etc. It might, however, be considered equitable for credit to be given in addition for a due proportion of the proceeds of the joint life policy. On this basis the representatives of M. Lane would be credited with £9,657, i.e. £5,907 as above, plus three-eighths of £10,000.

52.   PROFIT AND LOSS ACCOUNT FOR THE NINE MONTHS ENDED
30TH SEPTEMBER, 19..

		£	£				£
Life Assurance Premiums—				Net Profit	b/d	2,850
W. Edgar	. . .	318				
R. Ward	. . .	159				
Joint	. . .	742				
			1,219				
Interest on Capital—						
W. Edgar	. . .	398				
R. Ward	. . .	298				
			696				
Divisible Profit—						
W. Edgar $\frac{4}{7}$	. . .	534				
R. Ward $\frac{3}{7}$	. . .	401				
			935				
			£2,850				£2,850

DRAWINGS

Dr.

Date	Particulars	W. Edgar £	R. Ward £
19.. Sept. 15	To Drawings (9 months)	675	675
30	,, Premiums	159	318
	,, Capital	98	
		£932	£993
Oct. 1	To Balance . b/d		294

Cr.

Date	Particulars	W. Edgar £	R. Ward £
19.. Sept. 30	By Interest on Capital	398	298
	,, Profit	534	401
	,, Balance . c/d		294
		£932	£993

CAPITALS

Dr.

Date	Particulars	W. Edgar £	R. Ward £
19.. Sept. 30	To Cash .		
	,, Balance . c/d	10,698	7,950
		£10,698	£7,950

Cr.

Date	Particulars	W. Edgar £	R. Ward £
19.. Jan. 1	By Balance . b/d	10,600	7,950
Sept. 30	,, Sundries . Drawings	98	
		£10,698	£7,950
Oct. 1	By Balance . b/d	6,057	7,950
	,, Joint Policies—		
	W. Edgar[1]		4,543
	R. Ward	?	?

[1] Amount covered by this policy is £10,600.
See notes on page 460.

Notes. (i) The premiums debited to Drawings Account are—

> W. Edgar: 2% on *Ward's* Capital, £7,950 = £159.
> R. Ward: 3% on *Edgar's* Capital, £10,600 = £318.

(ii) The policies on which premiums are charged to Profit and Loss Account, being firm property, are divided between the partners at 1st October, 19.., in the ratio in which they share profits, which in this case is the same ratio as their capitals. Ward's policy will have to be evaluated for the purpose of dissolution.

(iii) The policies in respect of which premiums are charged to Drawings are assumed to be the personal property of the partners named, and are therefore not brought into account on Edgar's death.

53.

A AND B

JOURNAL

19..		£	£
Apr. 1	Realization Account. . . . . *Dr.*	8,000	
	To Premises		1,800
	„ Stock		3,000
	„ Debtors		1,200
	„ Investment		2,000
	Being transfer of assets to be taken over by the new firm as per agreement dated......		
	Creditors . . . . . *Dr.*	1,000	
	To Realization Account . . .		1,000
	Being transfer of creditors to be taken over by the new firm as per agreement dated......		
	Cash Trading Co. . . . . *Dr.*	7,500	
	To Realization Account . . .		7,500
	Being purchase price of assets to be paid by the new firm as per agreement dated......		
	Realization Account. . . . *Dr.*	500	
	To A—Capital		300
	„ B— „		200
	Being profit on realization.		
	Reserve . . . . . . *Dr.*	2,000	
	To A—Capital		1,200
	„ B— „		800
	Being transfer of Reserve to partners in profit-sharing ratio.		
	A—Capital . . . . . *Dr.*	4,500	
	B— „ . . . . . *Dr.*	3,000	
	To Cash Trading Co.—		
	A—Capital		4,500
	B— „		3,000
	Being purchase consideration satisfied by the creation of Capital Accounts in the new firm.		

X AND Y

JOURNAL

19..		£	£
Apr. 1	Realization Account. . . . . *Dr.*	5,000	
	To Stock		2,600
	,, Debtors		2,400
	Being transfer of assets to be taken over by the new firm as per agreement dated........		
	Creditors . . . . . *Dr.*	2,200	
	Bank Loan . . . . . . *Dr.*	800	
	To Realization Account . . .		3,000
	Being transfer of creditors to be taken over by the new firm as per agreement dated........		
	Cash Trading Co. . . . . *Dr.*	2,000	
	To Realization Account . . .		2,000
	Being purchase price of assets to be paid by the new firm as per agreement dated........		
	X—Capital . . . . . *Dr.*[1]	500	
	Y— ,, ... *Dr.*	500	
	To Goodwill		1,000
	Being transfer of Goodwill to partners in profit ratio.		
	X—Capital . . . . . *Dr.*	1,000	
	Y— ,, ... *Dr.*	1,000	
	To Cash Trading Co.— . . .		
	X—Capital		1,000
	Y— ,, ...		1,000
	Being purchase consideration satisfied by the creation of Capital Accounts in the new firm.		

[1] Alternatively, the item Goodwill may be debited to Realization Account and the loss of £1,000 transferred from the latter account to Capitals.

CASH TRADING CO.

JOURNAL

19.. Apr. 1		£	£
Premises . . . . . . *Dr.*		2,300	
Stock . . . . . . *Dr.*		3,000	
Debtors . . . . . . *Dr.*		1,200	
Investment . . . . . *Dr.*		2,000	
To Creditors			1,000
,, A and B			7,500
Being assets and liabilities taken over from A and B as per agreement dated.........			
A and B . . . . *Dr.*		7,500	
To A— Capital			4,500
,, B— ,, ...			3,000
Being satisfaction of purchase consideration by the creation of Capital Accounts as per agreement dated.........			
Stock . . . . . . *Dr.*		2,600	
Debtors . . . . . . *Dr.*		2,400	
To Creditors			2,200
,, Bank Loan			800
,, X and Y			2,000
Being assets and liabilities taken over from X and Y as per agreement dated........			
X and Y . . . . . . *Dr.*		2,000	
To X—Capital			1,000
,, Y— ,, ...			1,000
Being satisfaction of purchase consideration by the creation of Capital Accounts as per agreement dated.........			
Cash . . . . . . *Dr.*[1]		1,000	
To X—Capital Account . . .			500
,, Y— ,, ,, . . .			500
Being introduction of new capital by X and Y.			

[1] Journalized for completeness.

Alternatively, the foregoing entries may be curtailed as follows—

CASH TRADING CO.

JOURNAL

19..		£	£
Apr. 1	Premises . . . . *Dr.*	2,300	
	Stock . . . . *Dr.*	5,600	
	Debtors . . . . *Dr.*	3,600	
	Investment . . . . . . *Dr.*	2,000	
	To Creditors		3,200
	,, Bank—Loan		800
	,, A—Capital		4,500
	,, B— ,, ...		3,000
	,, X— ,, ...		1,000
	,, Y— ,, ...		1,000
	Being assets and liabilities taken over from A and B and X and Y as per agreement.		

54.

JOURNAL

19..		£	£
Apr. 30	Fixtures and Fittings . . . . *Dr.*	190	
	Motor Van . . . . . . *Dr.*	90	
	Stock . . . . . . *Dr.*	464	
	Sundry Debtors . . . . . *Dr.*	478	
	Cash at Bank . . . . . *Dr.*	50	
	To Bad Debts Provision		22
	,, Creditors		340
	,, E. Jackson—Capital		910
	Being assets and liabilities introduced by E. Jackson into the partnership on this date as per agreement dated........		
	Bank . . . . *Dr.*	90	
	To E. Jackson—Capital		90
	Being Cash introduced by E. Jackson to raise Capital Account to £1,000 as per agreement dated........		

DIVISION OF PROFIT

	Total	T. Parker	R. Parker	E. Jackson
	£	£	£	£
Profit for Year	2,200			
Less ⅕—E. Jackson	440			440
	1,760			
Less T. Parker, ⅝ . . . £1,100				
R. Parker, ⅜ . . . 660				
	1,760	1,100	660	
		£1,100	£660	£440

55.

SMITH AND JACKSON

JOURNAL

19..		£	£
Feb. 2	Bank . . . . *Dr.*	465	
	Sundry Debtors . . . . . *Dr.*	15,650	
	Stock-in-trade . . . . . *Dr.*	5,250	
	Motor Vehicles . . . . . *Dr.*	2,000	
	Fixtures and Fittings . . . . *Dr.*	500	
	Leasehold Premises . . . . *Dr.*	4,600	
	To Bad Debts Provision . . .		1,500
	,, Capital Reserve . . .		465
	,, Creditors of Wm. Brookshaw . .		26,500
	[£532 + ¾ × £34,624]		
	Being the purchase of assets and liabilities of William Brookshaw as per agreement dated........		
	Legal Expenses . . . . . *Dr.*	100	
	To Bank		100
	Being expenses in connection with the assignment of the business.		
	Bank . . . . *Dr.*	12,000	
	To Smith—Capital . . .		6,000
	,, Johnson—Capital . . .		6,000
	Being introduction of Capital by the partners.		
	Creditors of Wm. Brookshaw . . *Dr.*	10,000	
	To Bank		10,000
	Being payment of first instalment of the purchase consideration.		

The dissenting creditors amount to only £43, and thus are insufficient to present a petition in bankruptcy. The Deed of Arrangement entered into, if it has been properly registered and if the assent of a majority in number and value of creditors has been obtained within 21 days of registration, cannot be upset by these dissenters. Their only remedy, if they will not become parties to the Deed of Arrangement, is to sue their debtor, William Brookshaw, for the amount of their debts, which may be met out of any other property he owns.

56.   JOURNAL

19..		£	£
June 2	Leasehold Premises . . . . . . Dr.	3,250	
	Furniture, Fixtures, and Fittings . . Dr.	300	
	Stock . . . . Dr.	4,000	
	Debtors . . . . Dr.	2,160	
	Bank . . . . Dr.	35	
	Cash . . . . Dr.	10	
	To Bad Debts Provision		250
	,, Creditors—Trade		8,586
	,, Creditors—Expenses		133
	,, W. Blake—Capital Account . . . ¹		786
	Being assets and liabilities assigned to syndicate as per scheme of arrangement.		
	Bank . . . . Dr.	9,000	
	To Syndicate Advance Account . . .		9,000
	Being Cash introduced by syndicate.		
	Creditors—Trade	8,586	
	Creditors—Expenses.	133	
	To Bank		8,719
	Being payment of creditors as per scheme of arrangement.		

BALANCE SHEET AS AT 2ND JUNE, 19..

	£			£
Syndicate—Advance Account . .	9,000	*Fixed Assets*—		
W. Blake—Capital . . .	786	Leasehold Premises . . .		3,250
		Furniture, etc. . . .		300
		Current Assets—		
		Stock		4,000
		Debtors . . .	£2,160	
		Less Bad Debts Provision	250	1,910
		Bank [£35 + £9,000 − £8,719]		316
		Cash		10
	£9,786			£9,786

Notes. (i) Assumed that the creditors were paid on 2nd June, 19...

(ii) Costs in connection with the assignment will be charged to Blake's Capital Account.

(iii) When the position is clear, the balance due to Blake will be paid to him.

	£
¹ Profit on release of liability to Trade Creditors—62½p in £ on £22,896 =	14,310

	£	
Less Loss on revaluation—Furniture	265	
Stock	325	
Debtors	250	
		840
		13,470
Deduct Capital Account overdrawn		12,684
Balance—Capital Account (*Cr.*)		£786

PROFIT AND LOSS ACCOUNT FOR THE YEAR ENDED ...., 19..

	Repairs	Shops A	Shops B	Shops C	Total
Interest on Loan (b)	225	300	150	75	750
Balance c/d	600	6,100	5,455	4,125	16,280
	£825	£6,400	£5,605	£4,200	£17,030
C—Payment (c)	400				400
Shops Account to contra		750	525	375	1,650
Interest on Capitals (a)	200	546	499	378	1,423
Pool (contra)					1,423
Balance— Shops		4,914	4,491	3,402	12,807½
Pool		712	474	237	1,423½
	£600	£6,922	£5,989	£4,392	£17,703

	Repairs	Shops A	Shops B	Shops C	Total
Balance b/d	825				750
					16,280
	£825				£17,030
Balance b/d	600	6,100	5,455	4,125	16,280
Repairs from Contra		(55%)110	(30%)60	(15%)30	1,423
Shops		(½) 712	(½) 474	(½) 237	
	£600	£6,922	£5,989	£4,392	£17,703

Notes.

	Repairs	A	B	C
(a)		10% of (£6,210 − £750)	10% of (£5,515 − £525)	10% of (£4,155 − £375)
(b)	7½% of £3,000	7½% of £4,000	7½% of £1,000	Total Loans £10,000
(c)		7½% of £2,000	7½% of £10,000	7½% of £7,000 ... 7½% of £5,000 ... Total Capital £22,000

It is assumed that 7½ per cent per annum is actually paid on loans.

¹ Proof of divisible profits—

```
Profits
  Repairs                                      £825
  Shops—A              £6,400
         B               5,605
         C               4,200
                                             16,205
                                             17,030
Less Loan Interest and Interest on Capitals—
  7½% of £32,000       £2,400
  C—Payment               400
                                              2,800
                                           ────────
Divisible profits (as above)                £14,230
```

Alternatively, the answer may be presented as follows—

APPROPRIATION ACCOUNTS

	A Shop	B Shop	C Shop		A Shop	B Shop	C Shop
	£	£	£		£	£	£
Interest on Loan, etc.	1,050	675	450	Net Profit	6,400	5,605	4,200
Capitals—				*Repair Department*	*110*	*60*	*30*
A	4,914						
B		4,491					
C			3,402				
Pool	546	499	378				
	£6,510	£5,665	£4,230		£6,510	£5,665	£4,230

REPAIR SHOP

	£		£
Interest on Loan, etc.	225	Net Profit	825
C, Payment	400		
A Shop	*110*		
B ,,	*60*		
C ,,	*30*		
	£825		£825

GENERAL POOL

	£		£
A Capital—one-half	712	A Shop	546
B ,, —one-third	474	B ,,	499
C ,, —one-sixth	237	C ,,	378
	£1,423		£1,423

INTEREST ON LOAN AND CAPITALS

	£		£
Interest on Loan	750	A Shop	1,050
,, ,, Capital—A	750	B ,,	675
,, ,, ,, —B	525	C ,,	450
,, ,, ,, —C	375	Repair Shop	225
	£2,400		£2,400

58.   TRIAL BALANCE AS AT 31ST DECEMBER, 19..

	Folio	Dr. £	Cr. £
Johnson Capital			14,000
Williamson Capital			5,000
Premises at Cost		9,440	
Goodwill		6,000	
Partner's Salary—Johnson		2,300	
Johnson Drawings	7	2,900	
Williamson Drawings	7	2,040	
Agents' Deposits			260
Fixtures		1,000	
Stock, 1st January		3,100	
Purchases	4	35,200	
Sales	3		67,180
Sales Returns		2,460	
Wages and Salaries		8,120	
Rent and Rates	6	1,720	
General Expenses	5	937	
Debtors	8	15,160	
Creditors	10		8,130
Advertising	9	1,080	
Cash in Bank		1,450	
Bills Receivable		500	
Bad Debts	1	572	
Bank Interest			40
Discounts Net	2	631	
		£94,610	£94,610

The numbers in the folio column are references to rough accounts in the Adjustment Sheet on page 471.

TRADING AND PROFIT AND LOSS ACCOUNT FOR THE YEAR ENDED 31ST DECEMBER, 19..

		£	£			£	£
Stock (Opening)			3,100	Sales		£66,820(3a)	
Purchases	(4a)		35,356	*Less* Returns		2,460	64,360
Gross Profit	c/d		30,856	Stock (Closing)			4,952
			£69,312				£69,312
Wages and Salaries	(6a)		8,120	Gross Profit	b/d		30,856
Rates and Insurance	(5a)		1,810	Bank Interest			40
General Expenses			1,017	Sublet Rents and Rates			81
Bad Debts	(1a)		1,312				
Discounts	(2a)		982				
Advertising	(9b)		744				
Depreciation of Fixtures			100				
Balance	c/d		16,892				
			£30,977				£30,977
Partner's Salary, Johnson			2,300	Balance	b/d		16,892
Interest on Capitals—				Interest on Excess Drawings—Johnson			5
Johnson		£700					
Williamson		250	950				
Staff Thrift Fund, one-seventh of £11,941			1,706				
Balance, being Net Divisible Profits to							
Current Accounts—							
Johnson: ³⁄₇		£7,165					
Williamson: ⁴⁄₇		4,776	11,941				
			£16,897				£16,897

469

BALANCE SHEET AS AT 31ST DECEMBER, 19..

	£	£	£
Creditors—			
Trade (10a)	8,646		
Agents' Deposits	260		
		8,906	
Amounts Accrued and Accruing: Rent (6b)		300	
			9,206
Staff Thrift Fund			1,706
Capital Accounts—			
Johnson		14,000	
Williamson		5,000	
			19,000
Current Accounts—			
Johnson:			
Interest on Capital		700	
Share of Profits		7,165	
		7,865	
Less Drawings (7a) £3,040			
Interest on Excess Drawings 5		3,045	
			4,820
Williamson:			
Interest on Capital		250	
Share of Profits		4,776	
		5,026	
Less Drawings (7a)		2,180	
			2,846
			£37,578

	£	£	£
Fixed Assets—			
Goodwill			6,000
Premises at Cost			9,440
Fixtures		1,000	
Less Depreciation at 10%		100	
			900
			16,340
Current Assets—			
Stock:			
Goods	£4,952		
Advertising Material (9a)	150		
		5,102	
Debtors and Prepayment:			
Trade (8a)		£14,800	
Less Provisions:			
Bad Debts (1b) £740			
Discounts (2b) 351		1,091	
		13,709	
Rent and Rates		81	
Rates Prepaid (6c)		210	
Bills Receivable		1,450	
Cash at Bank		500	
			21,052
Deferred Revenue Expenditure—			
Advertising (9c)			186
			£37,578

The numbers in the folio columns refer to the rough accounts in the Adjustment Sheet on page 471.

ROUGH ADJUSTMENT SHEET

			£		£
1. Bad Debts	. .	Per Trial Balance .	572	Per Profit and Loss Ac-	
		Provision 5% on £14,800 (b)	740	count (a) . .	1,312
2. Discounts	. .	Per Trial Balance .	631	Per Profit and Loss Ac-	
		Provision 2½% on £14,060 (b)	351	count (a) . .	982
3. Sales	. . .	Per Trading Account (a)	66,820	Per Trial Balance .	67,180
		To Purchases (4)	360		
4. Purchases	. .	Per Trial Balance .	35,200	By Sales (3) . .	360
		To Creditors (10) .	516	,, Trading Account (a)	35,356
5. General Expenses	.	Per Trial Balance .	937	Per Profit and Loss Ac-	
		To Drawings (7) .	80	count (a) . .	1,017
6. Rates and Insurance	.	Per Trial Balance .	1,720	By Prepayment of Rates	
		To Insurance accruing (b)	300	(c . . .	
				Per Profit and Loss Ac-	210
				count (a) . .	1,810

			J.	W.		
7. Drawings Accounts	.	Per Trial Balance	£2,900	£2,040	By G. Expenses (5) .	80
		To Debtors (8) .	140	220	Per Balance Sheet (J.) £3,040	
					(a) (W.) . .	2,180

8. Debtors	. .	Per Trial Balance .	15,160	By Drawings (7) .	360
				Per Balance Sheet (a) .	14,800
9. Advertising	. .	Per Trial Balance .	1,080	By Stock (a) .	150
				Per Profit and Loss Ac-	
				count (b) . .	744
				Per Balance Sheet (c)	186
10. Creditors .	. .	Per Balance Sheet (a)	8,646	Per Trial Balance .	8,130
				By Purchases (4) .	516

Note 1. The items—Closing Stock (Goods), Subject Rents, and Depreciation—have been dealt with direct.

Note 2. The Interest against Johnson is 10 per cent on £200 for 3 months, as his excess drawing takes place on 1st October, having exhausted his limit of £2,700 by £200. No Interest is required on goods taken out, as the question limits it to *Cash* withdrawals.

Note 3. The calculation of Sublets is—

		£
Rent for 3 months at £240 per annum	60
Rates for 3 months at $\frac{1}{10}$ of £840 per annum . . .	21
	£81

Note 4. The Staff Thrift Fund appropriation is one-seventh of final divisible profits, i.e.—

$$\tfrac{1}{7} \times £11,941 \quad \text{or} \quad \tfrac{1}{8} \times £13,647$$

Note 5. The Salary is PAID to Johnson. If it had been credited to Johnson, his Salary Account would have been in credit therefor, unless the entry had not been made at the time of the Trial Balance, in which event an adjustment would be required, viz.—*Debit* Profit and Loss Account; *Credit* Partner's Salary or Current Account.

59.   JOURNAL

19.8		£	£
Dec. 31	Goodwill . . . . *Dr.*	1,200	
	Freehold Premises . . . . . . *Dr.*	330	
	To X Capital		765
	„ Y Capital		765
	Increase in valuation of assets for dissolution and Z's admission.		
19.9			
Jan. 1	Y Capital ⅔ . . . . *Dr.*	1,020	
	Z Capital ⅓ . . . . *Dr.*	510	
	To Goodwill		1,200
	„ Freehold Premises		330
	Reversal of revaluation at 31st December, 19.8		
	Cash . . . . *Dr.*	2,790	
	To Y Capital		1,515
	„ Z Capital		1,275
	Cash brought in by Y and Z to make their capitals proportionate to their profit ratios.		

Y's Capital to be ⅔ . . £5,100[1]
Less credit balance . . 3,585
————— £1,515

Z's Capital to be ⅓ . . £2,550[1]
Less contributed by X . . 1,275
————— £1,275

	X Capital . . . . *Dr.*	4,165	
	To Cash		2,890
	„ Z Capital		1,275
	Balance of X's Capital discharged by cash and transfer to Z's capital.		

Rough accounts are given below. They are not an essential part of the answer.

Dr.   CAPITALS   *Cr.*

	X	Y	Z		X	Y	Z
	£	£	£		£	£	£
Cash	2,890			Balance . . .	3,400	2,820	
Transfer to Z . .	1,275			Profit on Revaluation .	765	765	
Reversal of Revaluation .		1,020	510	Cash		1,515	1,275
Balance . . .		4,080	2,040	Transfer from X . .			1,275
	£4,165	£5,100	£2,550		£4,165	£5,100	£2,550

Dr.   CASH   *Cr.*

	£		£
Balance	1,100	X	2,890
Y	1,515	Balance	1,000
Z	1,275		
	£3,890		£3,890

[1] The total capital of the firm must be (before reversal or revaluation): Sundry assets £6,100, plus working cash £1,000, plus increase in valuation of assets £1,530; less creditors £980 = £7,650.

BALANCE SHEET

		£			£
Creditors		980	Assets per question (first 4 items) .		6,100
Capitals—			Cash		1,000
Y	£4,080				
Z	2,040				
		6,120			
		£7,100			£7,100

60. *Dr.* CAPITAL ADJUSTMENT ACCOUNTS *Cr.*

		A	B	C			A	B	C
		£	£	£			£	£	£
By Revaluation Account—					By Revaluation Account				
A and B . .		2,000	1,000	1,000	A and B . .		2,400	1,600	
C . .		480	320	800	C . .				1,600
,, Balance . . c/d				280	,, Balances . c/d		80		200
		£2,480	£1,600	£1,800			£2,480	£1,600	£1,800
To Balances . . b/d		80		200	By Balance . . b/d			280	

If all the above entries were made "memo," a Journal entry would be made thus—

JOURNAL

	£	£
A . . . . *Dr.*	80[1]	
C . . . . *Dr.*	200[1]	
To B		280
Adjustments for Goodwill on admission of C and taking over his business.		

[1] See page 474.

If the Premium Method is used whereby merely the *portions* of Goodwill sold and bought are entered, there would be a resultant amending entry required to adjust the altered ratios as between A and B, thus—

JOURNAL

	£	£
C . . . . *Dr.*	1,000	
To A		600
,, B		400
Premium charged to C for $\frac{1}{4}$ share of Goodwill of A and B ($\frac{1}{4}$ of £4,000).		
A $\frac{3}{10}$ . . . . *Dr.*	480	
B $\frac{1}{5}$ . . . . *Dr.*	320	
To C		800
Premium charged to A and B for $\frac{1}{2}$ share of C's Goodwill ($\frac{1}{2}$ of £1,600).		
A . . . . *Dr.*	200	
To B		200
Adjustment of Goodwill of £3,000 consequent on rearrangement of profit-sharing ratio as between A and B, viz. $\frac{1}{15}$ of £3,000.		

	A	B
Old ratio	$\frac{3}{5}$	$\frac{2}{5}$
New ratio	$\frac{2}{3}$	$\frac{1}{3}$
Purchase of $\frac{1}{15}$		Sale of $\frac{1}{15}$

	£	£
C is therefore in debit for £1,000 — £800	200	
A is therefore in debit for £480 + £200 — £600 . . .	80	
B is therefore in credit for £400 + £200 — £320 . . .		280

(See page 473)

The adjustment as between A and B is in respect of Goodwill unsold, i.e. £3,000, £1,000 (being ¼ of Goodwill of £4,000) having been dealt with.

The second Journal entry requires no correction as A and B are debited in their correct ratios.

61.　　TRADING AND PROFIT AND LOSS ACCOUNT FOR THE YEAR
ENDED 31ST DECEMBER, 19.7

		£			£
Stock (Opening) . . .		1,500	Sales		30,000
Purchases . . .		18,000	Stock (Closing) . . .		1,000
Gross Profit . . . c/d		11,500			
		£31,000			£31,000
Office Salaries . . .		4,000	Gross Profit . . b/d		11,500
General Expenses . . .		660			
Depreciation . . .		100			
Balance . . . c/d		6,740			
		£11,500			£11,500

		8 mths. ended 31 Aug., 19.7 £	4 mths. ended 31 Dec., 19.7 £			8 mths. ended 31 Aug., 19.7 £	4 mths. ended 31 Dec., 19.7 £
Repairs		151	17	Balance . . . b/d		4,493	2,247
Bad Debts . . .		20		Bad Debts Provision			
Decorating . . .		219		written back . . .		200	
Net Profit . . . c/d		4,723	2,230	Stock Reserve written back		420	
		£5,113	£2,247			£5,113	£2,247
Interest on Capital—				Net Profit . . . b/d		4,723	2,230
A		93	1				
B		73					
Salaries—							
A		1,800	900				
B		1,600					
Interest on Loan—B			30				
Net Profit—							
A: ⅗ . . .	£694		1,300				
B: ⅖ . . .	463						
		1,157					
		£4,723	£2,230			£4,723	£2,230

BALANCE SHEET AS AT 31ST DECEMBER, 19.7

		£			£
Creditors		750	*Current Assets—*		
Loan—B		666	Cash at Bank . .	£ 806	
Capital—A		2,787	Debtors . . .	1,697	
			Stock . . .	1,000	
					3,503
			Fixed Assets—		
			Fixtures, etc. . .	£800	
			Less Depreciation .	100	
					700
		£4,203			£4,203

[1] As A is sole proprietor, there is no purpose in continuing the charge for interest on capital.

Dr.			CAPITALS		Cr.	
	A £	B £			A £	B £
Drawings		1,600	1,300	Balance . . . b/d	2,800	2,200
Salary overpaid . . .			800	Interest on Capital . .	93	73
Goodwill . . .		500		Goodwill		500
Transfer to Loan . .			1,136	Profit (to 31st August, 19.7)	694	463
Balance . . . c/d		2,787		Profit (to 31st Dec., 19.7) .	1,300	
		£4,887	£3,236		£4,887	£3,236
				Balance . . . b/d	2,787	

Dr.		B LOAN		Cr.	
		£			£
Cash		500	Capital		1,136
Balance . . . . c/d		666	Interest—4 months thereon at 8% per annum		30
		£1,166			£1,166
			Balance . . . . b/d		666

62. (a)   JOURNAL

19..		£	£
Oct. 1	Folkestone Office . . . . . Dr.	2,600	
	To Willett—Capital		2,600
	Introduction of Willett's Capital as partner at this date.		
	Capitals—		
	Towns $\frac{2}{3}$ . . . . . . Dr.	40	
	Field $\frac{1}{3}$ . . . . . . Dr.	20	
	To Furniture		60
	Agreed adjustment in value of furniture at this date.		
	Accruals (or Expense Creditor) . . . Dr.	300	
	To Willett—Capital		300
	Commission due to Willett by London firm at this date.		
	Willett Capital . . . . . Dr.	1,200	
	To Capitals—		
	Towns $\frac{5}{8}$		750
	Field $\frac{3}{8}$		450
	Purchase by Willett of one-fifth share of goodwill of London firm.		
	Capitals—		
	Towns $\frac{3}{5}$ . . . . . . Dr.	1,080	
	Field $\frac{2}{5}$ . . . . . . Dr.	720	
	To Willett Capital		1,800
	Purchase by Towns and Field of half-share of goodwill of Folkestone business.		

[No adjustment being required as between Towns and Field (as stated in question), the adjustments for goodwill have been made in the new profit-sharing ratio.]

(b)   PROFIT AND LOSS ACCOUNT FOR THE YEAR ENDED
30TH SEPTEMBER, 19..

	London	Folke-stone	Total		London	Folke-stone	Total
	£	£	£		£	£	£
Staff Salaries and Office Expenses .	5,820	3,540	9,360	Commissions and Fees . .	9,477	5,265	14,742
Balances . c/d	3,657	1,725	5,382				
	£9,477	£5,265	£14,742		£9,477	£5,265	£14,742
Interest on Capitals:				Balances . b/d	3,657	1,725	5,382
Towns . .	171½						
Field . .	115½						
Willett . .		175	462				
Salaries—							
Towns . .	800						
Field . .	600						
Willett . .		600	2,000				
Balance of Net Divisible Profit—							
London:							
Towns: ½ £985							
Field: ³⁄₁₀ 591							
Willett: ⅕ 394							
	1,970						
Folkestone:							
Towns: ³⁄₁₀ 285							
Field: ⅕ 190							
Willett: ½ 475							
		950	2,920				
	£3,657	£1,725	£5,382		£3,657	£1,725	£5,382

BALANCE SHEET AS AT 30TH SEPTEMBER, 19..

	London	Folkestone	Total		London	Folkestone	Total
	£	£	£		£	£	£ £
Capitals—				Furniture . .	60	50	11
Towns £3,430				Cash in hand .	50	40	9
Field 2,310				Cash at Bank—			
Willett 3,500				Office A/cs £4,367		£1,960	
	9,240		9,240	"C" A/cs 2,190		1,660	
Current A/cs—					6,557	3,620	10,17
Towns 1,041½							
Field 496½				Debtors . .	3,710	1,685	5,39
Willett 964				*Folkestone Office*			
	2,502		2,502	*Account* . .	3,645		
Creditors—							
Clients 1,830		£1,520					
Expenses 450		230					
	2,280	1,750	4,030				
London Office Account		3,645					
	£14,022	£5,395	£15,772		£14,022	£5,395	£15,77

(c) *Dr.*   *Cr.*

CAPITALS

Dr.

19..		Towns £	Field £	Willett £
Oct. 1	To Furniture	40	20	
	,, Willett, re Goodwill	1,080	720	
	,, Towns and Field, re Goodwill			1,200
				3,500
Sept. 30	,, Balances · · c/d	3,430	2,310	3,500
		£4,550	£3,050	£4,700

Cr.

19..		Towns £	Field £	Willett £
Oct. 1	By Balances · b/d	3,800	2,600	2,600
	,, Folkestone Office ·			300
	,, Creditors · ·	750	450	
	,, Willett · ·			
	,, Towns and Field ·			1,800
		£4,550	£3,050	£4,700
Oct. 1	By Balances · · b/d	3,430	2,310	3,500

CURRENT ACCOUNTS

Dr.

19..		Towns £	Field £	Willett £
Sept. 30	To Drawings ·	1,200	1,000	1,300
	,, Folkestone Office ·			
	,, Balances · · c/d	1,041½	496½	964
		£2,241½	£1,496½	£2,264

Cr.

19..		Towns £	Field £	Willett £
Sept. 30	By Commission and Fees (pre-amalgamation)	171½	115½	620
				175
	,, Interest on Capital	800	600	600
	,, Profit— London ·	985	591	394
	Folkestone ·	285	190	475
		£2,241½	£1,496½	£2,264
Oct. 1	By Balances · · b/d	1,041½	496½	964

Dr.			FOLKESTONE OFFICE			Cr.
19..		£	19..			£
Oct. 1	To Willett—Capital . .	2,600	Sept. 30	By Willett—Current Account:		
Sept. 30	„ Profit and Loss Account—			Drawings . . .		1,300
	Folkestone Profit for year	1,725		„ Balance . . c/d		3,645
	„ Willett— Current Account:					
	Commissions and Fees .	620				
	(pre-amalgamation)					
		£4,945				£4,945

Notes. (1) The credit to Willett for Commissions is dealt with per question, but it would have been to Willett's advantage to have had the Commissions brought in as debtors at 1st October 19.., thus increasing his Capital, and, in consequence, Interest on Capital.

(2) In the Folkestone books there would be a London Office Account with entries similar to those appearing in Folkestone Office Account in London books, on reverse sides.

If there had been a complete accounting merger involving the opening of a new set of books, the opening entries would have been—

JOURNAL

		Towns & Field	Willett	Total (*Dr.*)	Total (*Cr.*)
19..		£	£	£	£
Oct. 1	Furniture	60	50	110	
	Debtors	3,850	820	4,670	
	Bank	2,780	1,600	4,380	
	Bank "C"	2,500	1,940	4,440	
	Cash	50	40	90	
	Commission . . .		300	300	
	Folkestone Fees, etc. . .		620	620	
		£9,240	£5,370		
	To Clients	2,200	1,600		3,800
	„ Sundry Expenses . .	700	250		950
	„ Suspense . . .		620		620
	„ Towns . . .	3,760			3,760
	„ Field . . .	2,580			2,580
	„ Willett . . .		2,900		2,900
		£9,240	£5,370		
	Assets and Liabilities brought into partnership on this date.				
	Towns Capital . . . . . . *Dr.*			330	
	Field Capital . . . . . . *Dr.*			270	
	To Willett				600
	Adjustment of Goodwill at this date.				

		Towns	Field	Willett
Goodwill Adjustment—		£	£	£
Cr. Towns and Field £6,000 . . (A)		⅝ 3,750	(A) ⅜ 2,250	
Cr. Willett . . £3,600 . .				3,600(B)
Reversal—				
Dr. London . . £6,000 . .		5/10 3,000	3/10 1,800	2/10 1,200
Dr. Folkestone . £3,600 . .		3/10 1,080	2/10 720	5/10 1,800
	(B)	£4,080	(B) £2,520	£3,000(A)
Adjustment (B)–(A) . . .		*Dr.* £330	*Dr.* £270	*Cr.* £600

After giving effect to the above opening and adjusting entries the Capitals are—

Towns: £3,760 — £330 = £3,430; Field: £2,580 — £270 = £2,310; Willett: £2,900 + £600 = £3,500.

Notes. (i) As the question states that no adjustment is required as between Towns and Field, it is assumed that either (*a*) it has been mutually agreed to dispense with it or (*b*) it has been dealt with prior to the extraction of the balances shown in the Balance Sheet or (*c*) dealt with as between Towns and Field privately. This adjustment would be *Dr.* Field, £250, and *Cr.* Towns, £250, arrived at as follows—

Goodwill Adjustment

	Towns	Field
Old Ratios	$\frac{2}{3}$	$\frac{1}{3}$
New Ratios (London)	$\frac{5}{8}$	$\frac{3}{8}$

Difference: Sale of $\frac{1}{24}$ ($\frac{16}{24} - \frac{15}{24}$); purchase of $\frac{1}{24}(\frac{8}{24} - \frac{9}{24})$.
Towns sells, and Field buys $\frac{1}{24}$ of the London Goodwill of £6,000 = £250.

(ii) The debit for Commission representing an asset belonging to Willett will be transferred to the debit of Creditors as it is already included in the Creditors brought into the firm by Towns and Field.

(iii) The Folkestone Commissions and Fees, due at 1st October, 19.., have been debited to Folkestone Fees Account and credited to Suspense: therefore the item shown in the Folkestone balances £620 will be compensated by the opening entry: the Suspense Account will then be transferred to Willett's Current Account. The entry is made as directed by the question, but the normal way would have been to place the amount to Willett's credit on 1st October, 19.., so that Interest on Capital would be increased.

63.   ALLOCATION OF PROFIT YEAR TO 31ST DECEMBER, 19.7

	Todd	Bond	Total
	£	£	£
Interest on Capital	500	550	1,050
Salaries [$\frac{1}{4}$ × (£1,395 — £1,050)]	57$\frac{1}{2}$	57$\frac{1}{2}$	115
Surplus	115	115	230
	£672$\frac{1}{2}$	£722$\frac{1}{2}$	£1,395

ALLOCATION OF PROFIT YEAR TO 31ST DECEMBER, 19.8

	£	£	£
Interest on Capital	520	560	1,080
Salaries	—	—	—
Less Loss	241	2	243
	£279	£558	£837

Notes. (1) No salaries are payable in the year to 31st December, 19.8, as there is no surplus remaining after interest on capital.

(2) Todd bears either—

(*a*) the whole loss, £243; or
(*b*) such lesser amount as will give him one-third of the profit available for allocation, i.e. $\frac{1}{3}$ of £837 = £279.

The maximum amount [subject to being not less than one-half of the net loss ($\frac{1}{2}$ of £243 = £121$\frac{1}{2}$)] to be borne by Todd is therefore £520 — £279 = £241, the balance of £2 being borne by Bond.

64. *Dr.* REALIZATION ACCOUNT *Cr.*

	£		£
Sundry Fixed Assets . . .	500	Discount Provision [£390 — £15] .	375
Stocks on hand . . .	3,575	A: Purchase consideration . .	12,000
Debtors [£7,800 — £300] . .	7,500		
Profit on Realization—			
A: $\frac{27}{50}$ £432			
B: $\frac{18}{50}$ 288			
C: $\frac{5}{50}$ 80			
	800		
	£12,375		£12,375

Dr. CAPITALS *Cr.*

	A	B	C		A	B	C
	£	£	£		£	£	£
Assets misappropri-ated—				Balances . . b/d	7,020	450	70
Stock . . .		600		Stock (*contra*)[1] .	330	220	50
Debts . . .		300		Discount on £300			
Realization Account:				Debtors[2] . .	9	6	
Purchase considera-tion . . .	12,000			Realization Account			
Cash . . .		64	200	Profit . .	432	288	80
				Cash . . .	4,209		
	£12,000	£964	£200		£12,000	£964	£200

Dr. CASH *Cr.*

		£		£
Balance . . . b/d		155	Bank Overdraft . . .	200
A: Settlement . . .		4,209	Creditors . . .	3,900
			B . . .	64
			C . . .	200
		£4,364		£4,364

[1] The stock at 30th June, 19.7, was inflated by £500; the opening stock for the year to June. 19.8, is therefore £500 too much, reducing the profit correspondingly. Assuming that the stock is regarded as having been sold for £600 prior to 30th June, 19.7, B must be debited with £600 and the partners credited as follows—

	A	B	C
	£	£	£
£100 profit (£600 — £500) in year to 30th June, 19.7, in ratio 3:2 .	60	40	—
£500 extra profit in year to 30th June, 19.8, due to overstatement of opening stock in ratio 27:18:5	270	180	50
	£330	£220	£50

If the stock valuation agreed on the change in the profit-sharing ratio on 1st July, 19.7, is to remain, the "sale" of the stock takes place in the year to 30th June, 19.8, and the correcting entries are—

Dr. B, £600; *Cr.* A, B, C, £600 in ratio 27:18:5.

[2] The unrequired provision is written back to the old partners, assuming that a 5 per cent provision on debtors existed at 1st July, 19.7.

65.

PROFIT AND LOSS ACCOUNT FOR THE YEAR ENDED 31ST DECEMBER, 19..

| | LIMITED COMPANY | | | | | | LIMITED COMPANY | | | | |
	A and B, 30th June	A, B, C, 30th Sept.	Pre-incorporation 30th Nov.	Post-incorporation 31st Dec.	Total		A and B, 30th June	A, B, C, 30th Sept.	Pre-incorporation 30th Nov.	Post-incorporation 31st Dec.	Total
	£	£	£	£	£		£	£	£	£	£
Expenses (time basis)	300	150	100	50	600	Gross Profit	2,477	1,239	723	361	4,800
Expenses (others)	300	360	180	100	940						
Net Profit	1,877	729	443	211	3,260						
	£2,477	£1,239	£723	£361	£4,800		£2,477	£1,239	£723	£361	£4,800

(Skeleton) BALANCE SHEET AS AT 31ST DECEMBER, 19..

	£	£		£
Issued Share Capital—			Goodwill	4,594
15,000 Shares of £1 each, fully paid		15,000	Sundry Assets	4,800
Capital Reserve—			Stock	4,380
Pre-incorporation Profit		443	Debtor: A	749
Profit and Loss Account		211	Cash at Bank and on hand	2,300
		15,654	Preliminary Expenses	120
Creditors—				
Trade	£780			
B	272			
C	237	1,289		
		£16,943		£16,943

481

Dr. **CAPITALS** **Cr.**

19..		A £	B £	C £	19..		A £	B £	C £
June 30	To Drawings .	300	240		Jan. 1	By Balances b/d	4,200	3,000	
	,, Balances c/d	4,839	3,698		June 30	,, Profit .	(½) 939	(½) 938	
		£5,139	£3,938				£5,139	£3,938	
Sept. 30	To Drawings .	150	120	90	July 1	By Balances b/d	4,839	3,698	
	,, Balances c/d	6,054	4,821	2,531		,, Goodwill .	1,000	1,000	
						,, Cash .			2,500
					Sept. 30	,, Profit .	(½) 365	(½) 243	(⅙) 121
		£6,204	£4,941	£2,621			£6,204	£4,941	£2,621
Sept. 30	To Share Capital	7,500	5,000	2,500	Sept. 30	By Balances b/d	6,054	4,821	2,531
	,, Current A/cs		352	297		,, Goodwill .	(½) 797	(½) 531	(⅙) 266
						,, CurrentA/cs	649		
		£7,500	£5,352	£2,797			£7,500	£5,352	£2,797

Dr. **CURRENT ACCOUNTS** **Cr.**

19..		A £	B £	C £	19..		A £	B £	C £
Sept. 30	To Capital .	649			Sept. 30	By Capitals .		352	297
	,, Drawings .	100	80	60		,, Balance c/d	749		
	,, Balances c/d		272	237					
Oct. 1	To Balance b/d	749			Oct. 1	By Balances b/d		272	237

Dr. **GOODWILL** **Cr.**

19..		£	19..			£
Jan. 1	To Balance . . .	1,000	Sept. 30	By Balance . . c/d		4,594
July 1	,, A and B . . .	2,000				
Sept. 30	,, A, B, and C . .	1,594				
		£4,594				£4,594
Oct. 1	To Balance . . b/d	4,594				

I. Adjusting entries—

(1) As C pays £500 for one-sixth share, the goodwill of the partnership at the date of C's admission is £3,000 against a book value of £1,000, so that the increase, viz. £2,000, is to be credited to A, £1,000; B, £1,000; and Goodwill debited £2,000.

(2) The gross profit to 30th September is evenly earned per question. [The term "period" therein must be related to this date, as otherwise if the gross profit were evenly earned throughout the whole year the aggregate gross profit to 30th September would not agree with the known gross profit to this date as per next paragraph.]

(3) The net profit for the nine months ended 30th September is—

CAPITALS

Closing	£	Opening	£
Goodwill .	3,000	Goodwill .	3,000
Stock .	3,500	Other Assets	
Cash and other		less Creditors	6,200
Assets .	7,276		
	13,776		
Creditors .	370		
	£13,406		£9,200 [i.e. A £5,200; B £4,000]

[*Note:* It is immaterial whether this statement is built up on the original capital or adjusted capital, as the Goodwill item would be compensating, i.e. Closing Capital, £11,406; Opening Capital, £7,200: increase £4,206.]

		£
Increase of Capital—		
Closing		13,406
Opening		9,200
		4,206
Add Drawings		900
		5,106
Less C: Cash paid in		2,500
Net Profit		£2,606
Gross Profit is—		
Net Profit		2,606
Add Expenses—		
¾ × £600 (even)	£450	
Jan. 1–June 30	300	
July 1–Sept. 30	360	
		1,110
		£3,716
½ year to 30th June: ⅔		2,477
¼ year to 30th Sept.: ⅓		1,239
		£3,716

The capitals at 30th September are (per Accounts)—

	£
A	6,054
B	4,821
C	2,531
	£13,406

This total is reconciled as follows—

		£
Opening Capitals (including adjusted Goodwill)		9,200
Add C		2,500
,, Profit		2,606
		14,306
Less Drawings—		
A	£450	
B	360	
C	90	
		900
		£13,406

(4) As the profit for the two months ended 30th November must be ascertained (not being divisible), separation of gross profit is necessary, and is apportioned evenly in the absence of information in question.

(5) If the cash adjustments *re* Share Capital had been dealt with before 31st December, items in Balance Sheet—A (*Dr.*), £749; B (*Cr.*), £272; C (*Cr.*), £237—would be: A (*Dr.*), £100; B (*Dr.*), £80; and *C* (*Dr.*), £60 for their drawings; these will not affect the Balance Sheet agreement, as the former net debit is £240, i.e. £749 − £509, and the latter £240, i.e. £100 + £80 + £60.

II. Note *re* premium charged to C on entry into partnership. Other alternatives are—

(1) To write off the whole Goodwill of £3,000 instead of retaining it in the books. The effect of this would be—

	A	B	C
	£	£	£
Increase	(½) 1,000	(½) 1,000	
Decrease	(½) 1,500	(⅓) 1,000	(⅙) 500
	Dr. £500	—	*Dr.* £500

Thus, by writing back £3,000 and debiting A, B, and C respectively with £1,500, £1,000 and £500 (crediting Goodwill with £3,000), the net result is a debit to A and C of £500 each, and the elimination of the original amount of Goodwill of £1,000.

(2) To write off only the increased Goodwill of £2,000. The effect of this would be—

	A	B	C
	£	£	£
Increase	½ 1,000	½ 1,000	—
Decrease	½ 1,000	⅓ 667	⅙ 333
	—	*Cr.* £333	*Dr.* £333

Thus, the book value of Goodwill would remain at £1,000, and the net result is a debit to C of £333 and a credit to B of £333.

In view of the words of the question, the second alternative does not appear to be the one intended; but, whichever of these two methods is adopted, the final credits to capitals on transfer to the new company as the excess of purchase price over assets will be *pro tanto* higher, and such profit will be credited to A, B, and C in the ratio of 3 : 2 : 1.

66. *Dr.*   REALIZATION ACCOUNT   *Cr.*

19.7		£	19.7			£
June 30	To Buildings . . .	2,000	June 30	By Creditors . . £ ?		
	,, Plant	800		*Less* Stock . ?		
	,, Profit—			Debtors ?		
	Hill: ½ . . £540			—— ?		
	Fell: ¼ . . 270					2,200
	Mount: ¼ . . 270					
	——	1,080		,, Shares in Peaks Ltd.—		
				800 Preference . £900		
				2,600 Ordinary . 780		
				——		1,680
		£3,880				£3,880

Dr.   PLANT   *Cr.*

19.7		£	19.7		£
Jan. 1	To Balance	1,000	June 30	By Depreciation (P. & L.) .	200
				,, Realization Account	800
		£1,000			£1,000

Dr.   PROFIT AND LOSS ACCOUNT   *Cr.*

19.7		£	19.7		£
June 30	To Depreciation . . .	200	June 30	By "Gross" Profit . .	660
	,, Bad Debts . . .	300			
	,, Profit—				
	Hill: ½ . . £80				
	Fell: ¼ . . 40				
	Mount: ¼ . . 40				
	——	160			
		£660			£660

Dr.   CASH AND BANK   *Cr.*

19.7		£	19.7		£
Jan. 1	To Balance	920	June 30	By Capitals (Drawings)—	
June 30	,, Suspense . . .	940		Hill	520
				Fell	930
				Mount . . .	250
				Mount . . .	160
		£1,860			£1,860

Dr.   SUSPENSE   *Cr.*

19.7		£	19.7		£
Jan. 1	To Debtors . . .	750	Jan. 1	By Creditors . . .	2,970
	,, Stock . . .	600	June 30	,, Bad Debts (P. & L.) .	300
June 30	,, Profit and Loss Account—			,, Cash	940
	"Gross" Profit .	660			
	,, Realization Account .	2,200			
		£4,210			£4,210

CAPITALS

Dr.

Date	Particulars	Hill £	Fell £	Mount £
19.7 June 30	To Drawings	520	930	250
	" Cash			160
	" Balances c/d	1,500		500
		£2,020	£930	£910
June 30	To Balance b/d		320	
	" Fell	240·00		80·00
	" Shares in Peaks Ltd.—			
	Ordinary	519·90		260·10
	Preference	741·375		158·625
	" Cash from Hill			1·275
		£1,501·275	£320	£500·00

Cr.

Date	Particulars	Hill £	Fell £	Mount £
19.7 Jan. 1 June 30	By Balances b/d	1,400	300	600
	" Profit	80	40	40
	" Profit on Realization	540	270	270
	" Balance c/d		320	
		£2,020	£930	£910
June 30	By Balances b/d	1,500·00	240	500
	" Hill		80	
	" Mount			
	" Cash to Mount	1·275		
		£1,501·275	£320	£500

SHARES IN PEAKS LTD.

Dr.

Date	Particulars	Preference No.	Preference £	Ordinary No.	Ordinary £
19.7 June 30	To Realization Account	800	900	2,600	780
		800	£900	2,600	£780

Cr.

Date	Particulars	Preference No.	Preference £	Ordinary No.	Ordinary £
19.7 June 30	By Capitals—				
	Hill	659	741·375	1,733	519·90
	Mount	141	158·625	867	260·10
		800	£900·00	2,600	£780·00

Notes. (1) It is assumed that the partners have not agreed to any particular form of division of Shares in Peaks Ltd. (which are not stated to be fully paid).

(2) The debit balance of Fell has been apportioned to Hill and Mount in the ratio of their balances at 30th June, 19.7, per *Garner* v. *Murray* (but see further notes below for students' guidance), and for sake of clarity the Capitals have been balanced off at this point.

(3) The question gives no details of the creditors, debtors, and stock at 30th June, 19.7, so they must be taken collectively in the Realization Account.

(4) The Ordinary Shares have been allocated to Hill and Mount in their profit ratios, and the Preference Shares to balance their accounts, the difference being adjusted in cash.

(5) The partners would probably agree to take shares in "round numbers" with cash adjustment (e.g. Hill, 1,700 Ordinary and 650 Preference; and Mount, 900 Ordinary and 150 Preference).

(6) No figure is given for Realization Expenses.

Further notes for students.

There are several alternative solutions to this problem, as Fell's debit balance (depending on the meaning of partners' last agreed capitals) may be written off *before* crediting the solvent partners with their share of profit on realization. The proportions would be £960 (£1,500 — £540) to £230 (£500 — £270) or, if the cash paid to Mount is ignored, £960 to £390, i.e. (£500 — £270 + £160; or £600 + £40 — £250).

If there had been a *loss* on realization, the capital ratios for the purpose of the write-off of Fell's debit balance would have to be *before* the loss was debited.

A further alternative solution arises by allocating not only the Ordinary, but the Preference Shares, in profit ratios with a cash adjustment.

Students find it difficult to work this type of problem. The best approach is to write up such parts of the problem as are straightforward; then open a Suspense Account for the Debtors, Creditors, and Stock. The Profit and Loss Account will be debited with (*a*) Depreciation (and Plant credited), (*b*) Bad Debts (and Suspense Account credited), and (*c*) Profit (credited to partners). The next step is to balance off the Profit and Loss Account for "Gross" Profit [i.e. Profit before writing off Depreciation and Bad Debts (and Suspense Account credited)].

The cash account should then be completed (the opening balance of £920) and the drawing of £1,700 having been entered (the latter being debited to the respective capitals) by crediting the known cash balance of £160 and debiting Mount. At this stage there will be a credit balance on cash of £940, but after the payment to Mount it is known that the cash account is clear, hence this sum must be reflected in the increase of the credit balance of Suspense, so that a clearing entry (viz. debit Cash and credit Suspense) is required. The resulting balance is then debited to Suspense and credited to Realization Account.

Another way of looking at the Suspense Account is to take the opening balances collectively, viz. £2,970 — £600 — £750 equals £1,620, from which will be deducted £360 (i.e. net profit after depreciation of £200). This would reduce the credit balance to £1,260, but as £940 is cash received, the credit balance will be the sum of the two latter items, equals £2,200.

Alternatively, as the profit before providing for depreciation of £200 is £660, of which £300 is used to write off Bad Debts, and £940 is received in Cash, the excess of creditors (£2,970) over stock and debtors (£1,350), i.e. £1,620, is actually increased by £580 (£940 + £300 — £660), giving £2,200.

It should be noted that the Cash and Bank Account is not complete in detail, as the £940 merely reflects the net sum paid in.

[For the benefit of students who wish to practise this type of problem, the cash adjustment payment by Mount to Hill would be 7½p if Fell's deficiency of £320 was debited to Hill and Mount in the ratio of 96 : 39.

If the ratio of this deficiency were taken as per the solution (3 : 1) and the Preference Shares were also allocated in profit ratios, Hill would receive 533 (£599·625) and Mount 267 (£300·375), and Mount would pay to Hill £140·475. The calculations may be made mentally, because the amounts in money should be £600 and £300 on the basis of 533⅓ and 266⅔ shares, so that by having to allocate 533 and 267, Hill is receiving shares to money value of ⅓ × £1·125 less and Mount ⅓ × £1·125 more, i.e. £0·375.]

67. Dr. CAPITALS Cr.

19.7		Salmon £	Rose £	White £	19.7		Salmon £	Rose £	White £
?	To Creditors			(a) 360	Sept. 30	By Balances . b/d	9,240	3,860	
?	,, Bad Debts Provision			20	?	,, Increase in Goodwill	(⅓) 550	(⅓) 550	
?	,, Balances c/d	9,790	4,410	7,500	?	,, Debtors . . .			(a) 910
					?	,, Cash . . .			(a) (b) 140
					?	,, Goodwill . .			1,240
					?	,, Furniture . .			630
					?	,, Motors . .			920
					?	,, Stock . .			4,040
		£9,790	£4,410	£7,880			£9,790	£4,410	£7,880
						By Balances . b/d	9,790	4,410	7,500

(a) Items marked (a) represent the balance of White's account after making the entries put through by the book-keeper.

(b) The item of £140 represents the cash introduced in order to bring the balance up to £7,500.

The adjustment suggested in paragraph (4) does not appear to be required. As Salmon and Rose have been credited with the full value of goodwill (£3,100) in the old profit-sharing ratio (equally), Salmon has already been credited with £310 more and Rose with £310 less than they would have been under the new arrangement viz.—

	Salmon £	Rose £
£3,100 divided equally	1,550	1,550
£3,100 divided 2 : 3 .	1,240	1,860
	£310	£310

68. It is assumed that any liability for taxation of the partners in respect of the firm's profit will be met out of their personal resources, and that the cash introduced by Ingleton is to be regarded as part of his capital and not as a loan.

(*a*) In consequence of the partners' agreement to revise the profit ratio, an adjustment is required to their capitals to give effect to the revaluation of the assets. Goodwill may be introduced into the books of the new company at its agreed value or may be entirely eliminated; it is suggested that the latter course be followed.

The capitals (including the £2,000 introduced by Ingleton) will therefore be—

	Radman		Ingleton	
	£		£	
Balances at 30th April		9,100		5,700
Cash introduced.		—		2,000
Profit on revaluation of machinery—				
(£5,000 — £3,800) = £1,200	¾	900	¼	300
Goodwill . . . £5,600	¾	4,200	¼	1,400
		14,200		9,400
Less elimination of goodwill in new ratio . . .	4/7	3,200	3/7	2,400
Adjusted capitals		£11,000		£7,000

In dealing with the capital of the new company, due regard should be had to the fact that Radman's surplus capital, taking Ingleton's as the basis figure, is £1,667, arrived at as follows—

	Radman		Ingleton	
	£		£	
Capitals as above		11,000		7,000
Less capitals in profit ratio	4/7	9,333	3/7	7,000
		£1,667		—

This surplus, which, subject to any agreement to the contrary, has priority on the partnership dissolution over any repayment of capital to Ingleton, should carry a similar right of priority in the event of the winding up of the new company. £1,667 of Preference Capital should therefore be allotted to Radman ranking for capital repayment in priority to any other class of share but without participating rights in profits or surplus.

The remaining capital—£9,333 and £7,000 to Radman and Ingleton respectively—should be allotted in the form of ordinary shares and, as the holdings will be in the same ratio as that in which profits were to be shared in the partnership, the rights of the partners to participate in the profits will remain undisturbed.

If the partnership had continued, the partners would have received in respect of salary and interest—

	Radman	Ingleton
	£	£
Salary	2,800	2,700
Interest on capital as adjusted	550	350
	£3,350	£3,050

and the balance of profits would have been divided in the ratio of 4:3. Salary and interest and share of profits would represent earned income and, subject to the maximum limit, would be available for income tax relief and for sur-tax relief. It will probably be thought desirable, therefore, in order that the partners may continue to obtain the maximum earned income relief,[1] that appropriate sums should be drawn from the new company in the form of directors' remuneration rather than as dividend, having regard to the standard distribution requirements relative to close companies.

[1] Earned Income Relief is—⅔ of the first £4,005 of earned income and 15 per cent of the remainder of earned income.

(b) Dr.   REALIZATION ACCOUNT   Cr.

	£		£
To Assets (per question) . . .	21,400	By Trade Creditors	4,600
„ Profit on realization transferred to Capitals—		„ New Company	18,000
Radman: ¾ . . . £900			
Ingleton: ¼ . . . 300			
	1,200		
	£22,600		£22,600

Dr.   CAPITALS   Cr.

	Radman	Ingleton		Radman	Ingleton
	£	£		£	£
To Goodwill written back .	3,200	2,400	By Balances . . b/d	9,100	5,700
„ Shares in New Company—			„ Realization Account—		
Preference . .	1,667	—	Profit . . .	900	300
Ordinary . .	9,333	7,000	„ Goodwill introduced .	4,200	1,400
			„ Bank	—	2,000
	£14,200	£9,400		£14,200	£9,400

Dr.   NEW COMPANY   Cr.

	£		£
To Realization Account Purchase consideration . .	18,000	By Capitals— Radman:	
		Preference Shares . .	1,667
		Ordinary Shares . .	9,333
		Ingleton:	
		Ordinary Shares . .	7,000
	£18,000		£18,000

Dr.   BANK   Cr.

	£		£
To Balance . . . b/d	2,900	By Realization Account . .	2,900
„ Ingleton	2,000	„ Loan Creditors . . .	2,000
	£4,900		£4,900

(c)   NEW COMPANY LIMITED

BALANCE SHEET AS AT 1ST MAY, 19..

	£			£
Share Capital—		Fixed Assets at cost—		
Authorized	£ ?	Machinery		5,000
		Fixtures		800
Issued and fully paid[1]:				5,800
1,667 Preference Shares of £1 each	1,667			
16,333 Ordinary Shares of £1 each	16,333	Current Assets—		
	18,000	Stocks . . .	7,400	
Current Liabilities—		Trade Debtors . .	6,500	
Trade Creditors . . .	4,600	Bank . . .	2,900	16,800
	£22,600			£22,600

[1] The "rounding off" of the share capital might be considered by Radman and Ingleton.

69. *Dr.*   CASH AND BANK   *Cr.*

19..			£	19..			£
Apr. 30	To Balance . .	b/d	1,150	May–	By Hamer and Grace—		
May–				July 31	Expenses . . .		4,000
July 31	,, Debtors . . .		12,800		,, Creditors . . .		9,000
	,, Hamer and Grace .		12,650		,, Capital Account (Brydon)		1,000
				July 31	,, Capital Account (Brydon)		12,600
			£26,600				£26,600

Dr.   TRADE DEBTORS   *Cr.*

19..			£	19..			£
Apr. 30	To Balances . .	b/d	6,150	May–			
May–				July 31	By Cash		12,800
July 31	,, Sales		10,100		,, Debtors' Suspense—		
					Discounts . .		350
				July 31	,, Balances . .	c/d	3,100
			£16,250				£16,250

Dr.   DEBTORS' SUSPENSE   *Cr.*

19..			£	19..			£
May–	To Debtors: Discounts .		350	Apr. 30	By Hamer and Grace .		6,150
July 31	,, Hamer and Grace—			May–			
	Collections .		12,800	July 31	,, Debtors: Sales . .		10,100
July 31	,, Trade Debtors: Balances						
		c/d	3,100				
			£16,250				£16,250

Dr.   TRADE CREDITORS   *Cr.*

19..			£	19..			£
May–				Apr. 30	By Balances . .	b/d	3,250
July 31	To Cash		9,000	May–			
July 31	,, Creditors' Suspense—			July 31	,, Purchases . . .		8,900
	Discounts . .		270				
	Balances . .	c/d	2,880				
			£12,150				£12,150

Dr.   CREDITORS' SUSPENSE   *Cr.*

19..			£	19..			£
Apr. 30	To Hamer and Grace .		3,250	May–			
May–				July 31	By Creditors: Discounts .		270
July 31	,, Creditors: Purchases .		8,900		,, Hamer and Grace—		
					Payments . .		9,000
				July 31	,, Trade Creditors: Balances		
						c/d	2,880
			£12,150				£12,150

| Dr. | | | HAMER AND GRACE | | | Cr. |

19..			£	19..			£
Apr. 30	To Fixed Assets . .		2,100	Apr. 30	By Creditors' Suspense .		3,250
	,, Stocks . . .		4,850		,, *Balance* . . *c/d*		*12,000*
	,, Debtors' Suspense .		6,150				
	,, Capital: Goodwill .		2,150				
			£15,250				£15,250
May 1	*To Balance* . . *b/d*		*12,000*	May—			
May—				July 31	By Debtors' Suspense—		
July 31	,, Expenses . .		4,000		Collections . .		12,800
July 31	,, Creditors' Suspense—			July 31	C ash . . .		12,650
	Payments . .		9,000				
	,, Capital (Brydon)—						
	Salary . .		300				
	Interest (3 months) .		150				
			£25,450				£25,450

| Dr. | | | CAPITAL—BRYDON | | | Cr. |

19..			£	19..			£
May—				Apr. 30	By Balance . . *b/d*		11,000
July 31	To Cash . . .		1,000		,, Hamer and Grace[1]—		
July 31	,, Cash: Balance .		12,600		Goodwill[1] . .		2,150
				July 31	Salary . .		300
					Interest . .		150
			£13,600				£13,600

Goodwill is arrived at as follows—

						£	£
Purchase Price	.	.	.	.	.		12,000
Less Net Assets .	.	.	.	.	11,000	
Less Cash and Bank	.	.	.	.	1,150	
							9,850
							£2,150

Note. Students in working through this question should realize that the *circumstances* therein differ from those in the ordinary way as the VENDOR is collecting the debts for the PURCHASERS, but the same *principles* apply as in the case of a purchaser collecting for a vendor.

CHAPTER XXIII

1.   THE COMPANIES ACT, 1948

No. of Company............

REPORT pursuant to Sect. 130 of the Companies Act, 1948, of.......................................
Company Limited.

(*a*) The total number of shares allotted is 50,000 shares, upon each of which the sum of[1]............?............ has been paid in cash.

(*b*) The total amount of cash received by the company in respect of the shares allotted wholly for cash is £137,000.

(*c*) The Receipts and Payments of the company to the...day of.......................19.... are as follows—

Particulars of Receipts	£	Particulars of Payments	£
To Amounts received on Application and Allotment of—		By Preliminary Expenses . .	2,471
50,000 Shares . . .	137,000	,, Purchase of Freehold . .	205,000
£100,000 Debentures . .	75,000	,, Builders on Account . .	12,600
,, Sale of Building Material .	1,742	,, Trading Payments . . .	24,744
,, Advance on Mortgage . .	47,000	,, Balance at Bank . . .	15,927
,, Trading Receipts . . .	*nil*		
	£260,742		£260,742

The following is an account (or estimate) of the Preliminary Expenses of the company.......................£

(*d*) Names, addresses, and descriptions of the directors, auditors (if any), managers (if any), and secretary of the company.

(*e*) Particulars of any contract, the modification of which is to be submitted to the meeting for its approval, together with the particulars of the modification or the proposed modification

....

....

We hereby certify this Report

.... ⎫
                                       ⎬   *Directors.*
.... ⎭

We hereby certify that so much of this Report as relates to the shares allotted by the company and to the cash received in respect of such shares and to the receipts and payments of the company on Capital Account is correct.

....*Auditors.*

Dated this......................day of.......................19....

---

[1] The cash received corresponds with a sum payable of £2·74 per share. It is probable that the amount called for was £2·75 per share in which case there would be a call in arrear of £500.

2.

REGISTER OF MEMBERS AND SHARE LEDGER

Name .... *Hope, Walter* ....
Address .... *"Yarborough,"* ....
.... *Wynott Avenue,* ....
.... *Deal* ....

Date of entry as a member. ....
Date of ceasing to be a member. ....

Dr.								Dr.				Cr.											Cr.	
SHARES ACQUIRED								**CASH PAYABLE ON SHARES**				**CASH PAID ON SHARES**				**SHARES TRANSFERRED**							**BALANCE**	
Number of Allotment	Number of Transfer	Date of Allotment or Entry of Transfer	Number of Shares Allotted or Transferred	Distinctive Numbers (inclusive) From	To	Transferor's Folio (if so Acquired)	Total Value of Shares Held	Date when Called	Description of Payment or No. of Call	Amount per Share	Total Amount	Date when Due	Date of Payment	Cash Book Folio	Amount	Number of Transfer	Date of Entry of Transfer	Number of Shares Transferred	Distinctive Numbers (Inclusive) From	To	Transferee's Folio	Total Value of Shares Transferred	Number of Shares	Value
18		19.. Jan. 8	800	7,021	7,820		£100	19..		12½ d	£100	19.. Jan. 5	Jan. 5		£100							£	800	£100
							300	Jan. 11		37½	300	Jan. 11	Jan. 12		300								800	400
	33	Mar. 25	700	651	1,350		350																1,500	750

It is assumed that the allotment was made on 8th January, 19.., and that the transfer was registered by the company on 25th March, 19...

3.   **THE COMPANIES ACT, 1948**

No. of Company........................

REPORT pursuant to Sect. 130 of the Companies Act, 1948, of.....................................
Limited.

(a) The total number of shares allotted is 41,044, of which 33,000 are allotted as fully paid in consideration of part of the purchase price of sundry assets acquired by the company and upon each of 5,500 of the remaining 8,044 shares the sum of One Pound has been paid in cash.

(b) The total amount of cash received by the company in respect of the shares allotted wholly for cash is £5,500 and on the shares allotted otherwise than for cash is £........................Nil........................

(c) The Receipts and Payments of the company to the[1]..............................day of October, 19...., are as follows—

Particulars of Receipts	£	Particulars of Payments	£
To Amount received on Application, Allotment and Calls in respect of 8,044 Shares	5,500	By Preliminary Expenses . .	200
,, Trading Receipts	nil	,, Vendor	1,000
		,, Plant Purchased . . .	750
		,, Fittings and Fixtures Purchased .	80
		,, Trading Payments . . .	390
		,, Balance at Bank . . .	3,080
	£5,500		£5,500

The following is an account (or estimate) of the Preliminary Expenses of the company—

Contract Stamps, Solicitors' Fees, etc.	£

(d) Names, addresses, and descriptions of the directors, auditors (if any), managers (if any), and secretary of the company—

Surname	Christian Name	Address	Description

(e) Particulars of any contract the modification of which is to be submitted to the Meeting for its approval, together with particulars of the modification or proposed modification—

....

....

We hereby certify this Report

....
                           } *Directors.*
....

We hereby certify that so much of this Report as relates to the shares allotted by the company and to the cash received in respect of such shares and to the receipts and payments of the company on Capital Account is correct.

....*Auditors.*

Dated this............*Thirteenth*............ day of...........*October*............19....

[1] Made up to a date WITHIN seven days of the date of the Report. The date of the Report is, on the facts submitted, correct, as the meeting will be held on the twenty-eighth day of October, 19.., (fourteen days' notice), and such date is not less than one, and not more than three, months from the third day of August, 19.., the latter being the date the company is entitled to commence business. [It is assumed that this date given in the question is meant to indicate that the certificate entitling the company to commence trading is dated 3rd August, 19...]

4. JOURNAL

19..		£	£

May 1	Share Capital . . . . *Dr.*
	    To Forfeited Shares . . . . . .
	    Being forfeiture of 2,000 shares of £1 each, 75p paid
	    and £1 called in respect of non-payment of Final Call of
	    25p per share, as per directors' resolution of this date
	    ....*vide* Minute Book, p.........
		2,000	2,000

	Forfeited Shares . . . . . . *Dr.*
	    To Final Call . . . .
	    Being transfer of unpaid Final Call in the foregoing
	    forfeiture.
		500	500

June 10	Cash . . . . *Dr.*
	Forfeited Shares . . . . . . *Dr.*
	    To Share Capital . . . . . .
	    Being the reissue of 1,000 shares credited as fully paid
	    for £600 as per directors' resolution of this date........
	    vide Minute Book, p.........
		600
		400
			1,000

	Forfeited Shares . . . . . . *Dr.*
	    To Profit on Shares Reissued . . .
	    Being transfer of profit on the foregoing reissue.
		350	350

Forfeited Shares Account now has a credit balance of £750 (75p received in respect of 1,000 shares forfeited but not reissued).

The Profit on Shares Reissued Account is the profit made by the company on the 1,000 shares forfeited and reissued of 35p a share, thus—

	£
Amount paid by original allottee 75p on 1,000 . . .	750
Amount paid by new holder 60p on 1,000 . . .	600
	1,350
Against the par value of £1 on 1,000	1,000
Profit	£350

Note. It is assumed that the shares were issued at par.

5. *Dr.*   APPLICATION AND ALLOTMENT   *Cr.*

	£			£
To Share Capital— 25p per Share on 10,000 Shares allotted	2,500	By Cash—Application Moneys . . ,, Cash—Allotment Moneys . .		1,250 1,250

Dr.   FIRST CALL   *Cr.*

	£			£
To Share Capital— 25p per Share on 10,000 Shares. .	2,500	By Cash—Call Moneys[1] . .		2,500
,, Calls in Advance— 50p per Share on 50 Shares paid in advance	25	,, Balance . . .	c/d	25
	£2,525			£2,525
To Balance[2] . . . . b/d	25			

[1] 9,850 at 25p per share (£2,462·50) plus 50 at 75p per share (£37·50).
[2] This balance may be transferred to Calls in Arrear Account.

Dr. CALLS IN ADVANCE *Cr.*

		£
	By First Call	25

Dr. BANK *Cr.*

	£
To Application and Allotment—	
12½p on 10,000 Shares . .	1,250
,, Application and Allotment—	
12½p on 10,000 due on Allotment	1,250
,, First Call	2,500
	5,000

BALANCE SHEET AS AT.....................

	£		£
Authorized Share Capital—		Cash at Bank	5,000
20,000 Shares of £1 each . .	20,000		
Issued Share Capital—			
10,000 Shares of £1 each, 50p			
called . . .	£5,000		
Less Calls in Arrear .	25		
	4,975		
Add Calls in Advance .	25		
	5,000		

Note. It is assumed that entries are not required in the statutory books.

6. *Dr.* APPLICATION AND ALLOTMENT *Cr.*

	£		£
To Share Capital—		By Cash—Application Moneys . .	27,500
25p per Share on 200,000 Shares al-		,, Cash—Allotment Moneys . .	22,500
lotted	50,000		

Dr. CALLS *Cr.*

	1st Call	2nd Call		1st Call	2nd Call
				£	£
To Share Capital—			By Cash—Call Moneys .	72,500	
37½p per Share on 200,000 Shares . .	75,000		,, Cash—Call Moneys .		72,000
37½p per Share on 200,000 Shares . .		75,000	,, Balances . . c/d	2,500	3,000
To Balances. . . b/d	2,500	3,000			

Dr. SHARE CAPITAL *Cr.*

	£		£
To Balance . . . . c/d	220,000	By Application and Allotment (25p) .	50,000
		,, First Call (37½p)	75,000
		,, Second Call (37½p) . . .	75,000
		,, Vendor (£1)	20,000
	£220,000		£220,000
		By Balance . . . . b/d	220,000

Dr.		VENDOR				Cr.	
		£					£
To Share Capital	. . . .	20,000	By Land and Buildings	.	.	.	60,000
„ Bank	. . . .	140,000	„ Plant	.	.	.	35,000
			„ Stock	.	.	.	45,000
			„ Goodwill	.	.	.	20,000
		£160,000					£160,000

Dr.		BANK				Cr.	
		£					£
To Application and Allotment—			By Vendor	.	.	.	140,000
12½p on 220,000 Shares	. .	27,500	„ Balance	.	.	c/d	54,500
„ Application and Allotment—							
Balance due on Allotment of							
200,000 Shares	. .	22,500					
„ First Call	. . .	72,500					
„ Second Call	. . .	72,000					
		£194,500					£194,500
To Balance	. . . b/d	54,500					

Note. Assumed that the over-subscription moneys are carried forward to allotment and that no forfeitures take place.

7.

APPLICATION AND ALLOTMENT LIST

No. of Application	Date of Receipt	Name	Address	No. of Shares Applied for	ALLOTMENT				Amount Paid on Application	Total Amount Payable on Application and Allotment [1]	ALLOTMENT PAYMENTS				Calls Paid in Advance	Amount Returnable	Share Ledger Folio	Remarks
					Date	No. of Shares Allotted	Distinctive No. of Shares (inclusive) From / To	No. of Allotment Letter			Now Due	Date Paid	Cash Book Folio	Amount Paid				
1		East, John	Southampton	100		100	1 – 100		£ 5	£ 30	£ 25			£[2] 25				
2		West, William	Cardiff	500		500	101 – 600		25	150	125			125				
3		Right, Robert	Leeds	2,000		500	601 – 1,100		100	150	50			50				
4		Left, Thomas	London	5,000		500	1,101 – 1,600		250	150					100			
5		Centre, Henry	Liverpool	6,000		600	1,601 – 2,200		300	180					120			
6		Radius, Richard	Manchester	50		50	2,201 – 2,250		2½	15	12½			12½				

[1] Assumed 25p per share is payable on allotment.
[2] Assumed allotment moneys are duly paid.

498

8.   BALANCE SHEET (*includes*)

		£
(1) Reserve—		
Premium on Debentures		150
(2) ? % Debentures (? secured)		10,000
(3) Bank Loan (secured by issue of £10,000 ? % Debentures by way		
of collateral)		6,000

9. *Dr.*   PROFIT AND LOSS APPROPRIATION ACCOUNT   *Cr.*

19..		£	19..			£
Jan. 1	To Reserve . . .	16,000	Jan. 1	By Balance . .	b/d	27,000
	,, Balance . . c/d	11,000				
		£27,000				£27,000
			19..			
			Jan. 1	By Balance		11,000

Dr.   BANK   *Cr.*

19..			£	19..			£
Jan. 1	To Balance . .	b/d	22,000	Jan. 1	By Debenture Stock . .		16,000

Dr.   RESERVE   *Cr.*

19..			£	19..			£
Jan. 1	To Balance . . .	c/d	17,391	Jan. 1	By Debenture Stock . .		1,391
					,, Profit and Loss Appropria- tion Account . .		16,000
			£17,391				£17,391
				19..			
				Jan. 1	By Balance . . .	b/d	17,391

Dr.   DEBENTURE STOCK   *Cr.*

19..		£	19..			£
Jan. 1	To Bank—		Jan. 1	By Balance . .	b/d	43,000

	Purchase and cancellation
	  of £17,391 Debenture
	  Stock at 92% . .
		16,000				

	,, Profit and Loss on cancella-
	  tion of Debenture Stock
	  Account . . c/d
		¹1,391				

	,, Balance . . . c/d	25,609				
		£43,000				£43,000
			19..			
			Jan. 1	By Balance . .	b/d	25,609

Interest ignored and calculation to the nearest £.

¹ As the amount would probably be transferred from the Cancellation Account to Reserve, the profit has been posted direct to the latter account. A transfer of £16,000 has been made to Reserve in view of the power to "apply profits in purchase of Debenture Stock."

10. *Dr.*   DEBENTURES   *Cr.*

19..		£	19..			£
Jan. ?	To Bank—		Dec. 31	By Balance . .	b/d	25,000
	Purchase and cancellation of 125 Debentures of £50 each at £48 each . .	6,000				
	„ Profit and Loss on cancellation of Debentures Account	¹250				
	„ Balance [375 Debentures of £50] c/d	18,750				
		£25,000				£25,000
			19..			
			Jan. ?	By Balance . . .	b/d	18,750

Dr.   DEBENTURE REDEMPTION RESERVE   *Cr.*

19..		£	19..			£
Jan. ?	To Reserve	6,000	Dec. 31	By Balance . . .	b/d	6,000

Dr.   RESERVE   *Cr.*

19..			£	19..			£
Jan. ?	To Balance . . .	c/d	6,250	Jan. ?	By Debenture Redemption Reserve		6,000
					„ Debentures . . .		250
			£6,250				£6,250
				19..			
				Jan. ?	By Balance . . .	b/d	6,250

¹ See Note to Answer 9 on page 499.

11. Debentures issued at a premium are those issued for subscription at a price higher than par value, having the effect of reducing the rate of yield as regards the amount invested. On the other hand, debentures at a discount are those issued for subscription at a price lower than par value, having the effect of increasing the rate of yield as regards the amount invested.

UNIVERSAL STORES LTD.

PROFIT AND LOSS ACCOUNT FOR THE YEAR ENDED
Dr.   31ST DECEMBER, 19..   *Cr.*

	£	
To Debenture Interest . . .	¹ 5,500	
„ Debenture Discount written off .	² 3,000	

BALANCE SHEET AS AT 31ST DECEMBER, 19.. (*includes*)

		£				£
1,000 7% Debentures of £100 each [Redeemable? Secured?]	.	100,000	Debenture Discount . .	£6,000		
			Less written off this year .	3,000		
						3,000

Notes. (i) If the debentures have security a statement should be shown on the Balance Sheet that the liability is secured.

(ii) In the normal course any other expenses of issue would be shown as an asset and written off in the same way as the debenture discount.

(iii) It is assumed that the sentence "The issue was fully taken up" means paid up.

(iv) Income tax ignored.

¹ £2,000 + £3,500.
² Usually written off to Profit and Loss Appropriation Account.

12. (*a*) *Dr.*   SINKING FUND   *Cr.*

		£
Year 6		
Dec. 31	By Profit and Loss Appropriation Account .	1,590·00
Year 7		
Dec. 31	,, Bank—Interest . .	79·50
	,, Profit and Loss Appropriation Account .	1,590·00
		3,259·50
Year 8		
Dec. 31	,, Bank—Interest . .	162·98
	,, Profit and Loss Appropriation Account .	1,590·00
		5,012·48
Year 9		
Dec. 31	,, Bank—Interest . .	250·62
	,, Profit and Loss Appropriation Account .	1,590·00
		6,853·10
Year 10		
Dec. 31	,, Bank—Interest . .	342·66
	,, Profit and Loss Appropriation Account .	1,590·00
		8,785·76

Dr.   SINKING FUND INVESTMENTS   *Cr.*

		£
Year 6		
Dec. 31	To Bank . . .	1,590·00
Year 7		
Dec. 31	,, Bank . . .	1,669·50
Year 8		
Dec. 31	,, Bank . . .	1,752·98
Year 9		
Dec. 31	,, Bank . . .	1,840·62
Year 10		
Dec. 31	,, Bank . . .	1,932·66
		8,785·76

BALANCE SHEET AS AT 31ST DECEMBER, YEAR 10 (*includes*)

	£		£
5% Debentures [Redeemable on?		Sinking Fund Investments at Cost .	8,785·76
Secured?]	20,000·00	Debenture Discount . . .	1,000·00
Sinking Fund	8,785·76		

(*b*) Assuming the debentures repayable at par the cash required will be brought in from the Investment Account (Debit Bank and Credit Sinking Fund Investments Account); any profit or loss transferred either to Profit or Loss on Realization of Investments Account or direct to Sinking Fund.

Upon repayment, Debentures Account will be debited and Bank credited. The Debenture Discount Account will be closed off to the Sinking Fund, and the balance of the latter account transferred to general reserve. If the profit or loss on realization of Investments has been shown in a separate account, this will be transferred to Capital Reserve in case of profit; or to General Reserve in case of loss, to the extent that there is not a Capital Reserve in existence sufficiently large to absorb it.

13. (a) Dr.   DEBENTURE STOCK   *Cr.*

Date		Nominal £	£	Date		Nominal £	£
19.4 Sept. 30	To Cash—			19.2 Sept. 30	By Cash . . .	10,000·00	10,000·00
	Debentures Redeemed .	365·59	283·33				
	,, Reserve . . .		82·26				
	,, Balance . . c/d	9,634·41	9,634·41				
		£10,000·00	£10,000·00			£10,000·00	£10,000·00
19.5 Sept. 30	To Cash—			19.4 Oct. 1	By Balance . . b/d	9,634·41	9,634·41
	Debentures Redeemed .	562·50	450·00				
	,, Reserve . . .		112·50				
	,, Balance . . c/d	9,071·91	9,071·91				
		£9,634·41	£9,634·41			£9,634·41	£9,634·41
19.6 Sept. 30	To Cash—			19.5 Oct. 1	By Balance . . b/d	9,071·91	9,071·91
	Debentures Redeemed .	372·55	316·67				
	,, Reserve . . .		55·88				
	,, Balance . . c/d	8,699·36	8,699·36				
		£9,071·91	£9,071·91			£9,071·91	£9,071·91
19.7 Sept. 30	To Cash—			19.6 Oct. 1	By Balance . . b/d	8,699·36	8,699·36
	Debentures Redeemed .	472·22	425·00				
	,, Reserve . . .		47·22				
	,, Balance . . c/d	8,227·14	8,227·14				
		£8,699·36	£8,699·36			£8,699·36	£8,699·36
				19.7 Oct. 1	By Balance . . ¹b/d	8,227·14	8,227·14

¹ *Note.* Debentures amounting to £1,772·86 redeemed at a cost of £1,475. The reduction in Debenture debt of £297·86 is reflected in the Reserve Account on page 503.

(b) *Dr.*   DEBENTURE STOCK REDEMPTION   *Cr.*

		£
19.3		
Sept. 30	By Profit and Loss Appropriation Account	283·33
19.4		
Sept. 30	„ Profit and Loss Appropriation Account	450·00
19.5		
Sept. 30	, Profit and Loss Appropriation Account	316·67
19.6		
Sept. 30	„ Profit and Loss Appropriation Account	425·00
		1,475·00

(c) *Dr.*   RESERVE   *Cr.*

		£
19.4		
Sept. 30	By Debenture Stock .	82·26
19.5		
Sept. 30	„ Debenture Stock .	112·50
19.6		
Sept. 30	„ Debenture Stock .	55·88
19 7		
Sept. 30	„ Debenture Stock .	47·22
		297·86

The profit on redemption for the first year is £82·26, arrived at as follows—

	£
Amount applied to redemption—$\frac{1}{3}$ of £850 . .	283·33
Amount redeemed $\frac{100}{77\frac{1}{2}} \times$ £283·33 . . .	365·59
Profit . .	£82·26

Notes. (i) It is assumed that the Reserve is to be applied as a Profit and Loss on Redemption Account.

(ii) It is assumed that the redemption takes place annually, after payment of the current year's debenture interest.

(d)   BALANCE SHEET AS AT 30TH SEPTEMBER, 19.7 (*includes*)

	£	
Authorized Share Capital—		
50,000 Shares of £1 each . .	50,000·00	
Issued Share Capital . . .	?	
Debenture Stock Redemption Account	1,475·00	
Reserve	297·86	
Profit and Loss Account[1] . .	2,950·00	
First Mortgage Debenture Stock—	£	
Balance at 1st October, 19.6	8,699·36	
Less Redeemed . .	472·22	
	8,227·14	

[1] The total profits for the four years ended 30th September, 19.6, are £4,425, one-third of which has been transferred to Debenture Stock Redemption Account. Actually, there would be included the profit for the year ended 30th September, 19.7, less the one-third appropriation. The question does not indicate the price received for the Debentures upon issue, but if they were issued at a discount the directors would probably utilize the Reserve against such discount.

14.   JOURNAL

19.2		£	£
Mar. 31	Profit and Loss Appropriation Account . . *Dr.*	4,000	
	To Debenture Redemption Fund . . .		4,000
	Being one-quarter of the balance of Profit and Loss Account applied towards redemption of Second Debentures, as per Debenture Deed dated.........................		
	Redeemed Debentures Account . . . . *Dr.*[1]	4,000	
	To Second Debenture-holders' Trustees . .		4,000
	Being investment of foregoing Debenture Redemption Fund through the Trustees for Second Debenture-holders.		

The 19.2 Balance Sheet will contain the following items—

	£		£
?% First Debentures [secured?] . .	?	Debenture Redemption Fund Investments	
5½% Second Debentures [secured?] .	100,000	(see notes 2 and 3)	4,000
Debenture Redemption Fund . .	4,000		
Trustees for Second Debenture-holders	4,000		
Profit and Loss Account— £			
Balance at 1st April, 19.1 1,500			
Add Profit for year ended			
31st March, 19.2 . 14,500			
─────			
16,000			
Less Debenture Redemption			
Fund 4,000			
─────			
12,000			

[1] The actual payment to the Trustees will take place some time after 31st March, 19.2, so that the Trustees at that date have become creditors. (When paid there will be a debit to the Trustees and a Credit to cash.)

[2] It is assumed that an appropriation is to be made annually to Debenture Redemption Account and to remain intact until the whole of the Second Debentures have been redeemed. The annual appropriation to the Debenture Redemption Account would, taking into account an annual rate of interest, be somewhat less than annual redemptions, but this is a matter for actuarial computation. When in due course the Debentures are completely redeemed the Debenture Redemption Fund will normally become "free" and transferred back to Profit and Loss Account (to be shown separately) or to General Reserve.

[3] If it is intended to repay the Second Debenture Holders and to apply the funds for actual reduction of the Debentures as distinct from holding such redeemed debentures as assets, the annual debit of such sum as is available will be debited direct to the Second Debentures instead of Redeemed Debentures Account, thus reducing the outstanding liability in respect of the Second Debentures.

15.   PROFIT AND LOSS ACCOUNT FOR THE YEAR ENDED. . . .

	£			£
Provision for		Balance	b/d	8,200
Depletion	4,000			
Balance, being Net Profit for year c/d	4,200			
	£8,200			£8,200
Debenture Redemption Fund .	2,000	Balance	b/d	4,200
Balance . . . . c/d	2,200			
	£4,200			£4,200
		Balance	b/d	2,200

BALANCE SHEET AS AT. . . . . . . (*includes*)

	£		£	£
?% Debentures [secured ?] . .	25.000	Mine at Cost . . .	40,000	
Debenture Redemption Fund .	2,000	*Less* Provision for Depletion	4,000	
Profit and Loss Account . .	2,200			36,000
		Depletion Fund Investments .	4,000	
		Debenture Redemption Fund		
		Investments . . .	2,000	
				6,000

16. *Dr.* 4% FIRST MORTGAGE DEBENTURE STOCK *Cr.*

19..		£	19..			£
June 30	To Debenture-holders .	100,000	June 30	By Balance .	. b/d	100,000

Dr. DEBENTURE REDEMPTION FUND *Cr.*

19..		£	19..			£
June 30	To Debenture-holders .	5,000	June 30	By Balance .	. b/d	106,540
	,, General Reserve .	101,540				
		£106,540				£106,540

Dr. DEBENTURE REDEMPTION FUND INVESTMENTS *Cr.*

19..			£	19..			£
June 30	To Balance—	b/d		June 30	By Bank—Sale of:		
	£35,000 3% Elec. Stock		32,130		£35,000 3% Elec. Stock		
	£40,000 5% Exchequer				at 90 . .	31,500	
	Loan . .		32,034		£40,000 5% Exchequer		
	£30,000 4% Consoli-				Loan at 91 .	36,400	
	dated Loan .		11,055		£30,000 4% Consoli-		
	£8,000 3½% Conver-				dated Loan at 43 ,	12,900	
	sion Loan . .		2,821		£8,000 3½% Conver-		
			78,040		sion Loan at 38 .	3,040	
	,, Profit on Realization of						
	Investments: Transfer						
	to General Reserve .		5,800				
			£83,840				£83,840

Dr. DEBENTURE-HOLDERS *Cr.*

19..		£	19..		£
June 30	To Bank	105,000	June 30	By 4% First Mortgage De-	
				benture Stock . .	100,000
				,, Debenture Redemption	
				Fund—	
				Premium of 5% on	
				Redemption . .	5,000
		£105,000			£105,000

Dr. GENERAL RESERVE *Cr.*

		19..		£
		June 30	By Debenture Redemption	
			Fund . . .	101,540
			,, Debenture Redemption	
			Fund Investments—	
			Profit on Realization	5,800
				107,340

£107,340 will appear amongst the Company's Reserves; subject to the articles the amount of £101,540 is distributable and will be shown as a Revenue Reserve, but the amount of £5,800 being profit on the sale of assets will not be, unless a surplus remains on a revaluation of the remaining assets and the articles do not forbid distribution of this kind of profit (*Lubbock* v. *British Bank of South America* and *Foster* v. *The New Trinidad Lake Asphalt Co. Ltd.*). The latter may therefore be transferred to Capital Reserve.

The Debenture Stock will be shown on the liabilities side of the Balance Sheet thus—

	£
4% First Debenture Stock . . .	100,000
Less redeemed	100,000
	....

The balance of cash remaining £14,400 [i.e. £119,400 less £105,000] will be incorporated in the Bank balance.

It is assumed that the Debentures are not to be kept alive for reissue and that interest is paid to date.

Alternatively, £100,000 may be transferred to General Reserve, the remaining balances being merged in Profit and Loss Account (subject to their availability for distribution).

17. JOURNAL

19..				£	£
Jan. 1	Plant and Machinery . . . . . Dr.			5,000	
	Stock-in-trade . . . . . Dr.			2,500	
	Patent Rights . . . . . Dr.			3,000	
	To Vendors				10,500
	Being assets taken over in pursuance of purchase agreement dated................				
10	Vendors . . . . . . Dr.			10,500	
	To Ordinary Share Capital . . .				8,000
	,, Mortgage Debentures . . .				2,500
	Being discharge of consideration by issue of 800 ordinary shares of £10 each fully paid and 25 debentures of £100 each.				
15	Application and Allotment . . . . Dr.			2,000	
	To Share Capital . . . . [1]				2,000
	Being £2 per share application and allotment money on 1,000 ordinary shares as per minute dated ....vide Minute Book, p.				
Feb. 15	First Call . . . . Dr.			2,000	
	To Share Capital				2,000
	Being £2 per share first call on 1,000 ordinary shares as per minute dated ....vide Minute Book, p.				
20	Cash . . . . Dr.			2,000	
	To First Call				2,000
	Being £2 per share first call money on 1,000 ordinary shares.				
Mar. 1	Cash . . . . Dr.			2,500	
	To Vendors				2,500
	Being debts collected on behalf of Vendors.				
1	Vendors . . . . Dr.			2,500	
	Discount on Issue of Mortgage				
	Debentures . . . . . Dr.			500	
	To Mortgage Debentures . . .				3,000
	Being discharge of liability to Vendors by issue of 30 Debentures at £83⅓ per cent.				
Apr. 1	Cash . . . . Dr.			3,000	
	To Calls in Advance				3,000
	Being money paid in advance pending further calls.				
Apr. 15	Debentures . . . . . . Dr.			2,000	
	Premium on Redemption of Debentures . Dr.			200	
	Interest on Debentures. . . . Dr.			100	
	To Cash				2,260
	,, Income Tax				40
	Being redemption of 20 debentures of £100 each at a premium of 10% and £100 interest less tax (40%) to date of redemption.				

[1] The cash entries are not required.

Entries recording the above transactions will be found in the following books—

Directors' Minute Book. Records will be found in this book of the directors' resolutions authorizing (1) the allotment of shares to vendors in discharge of purchase agreement, (2) issue of shares to public and their allotment, and (3) making calls and accepting calls paid for in advance.

Register of Members. Vendors and sundry persons acquiring shares in the company will become members of the company on the date of the entry into the register.

Register of Debentures and Charges. Vendors will be entered in this register together with other "statutory" information. On redemption of debentures details will be entered as to the satisfaction of debentures.

[Application Sheets and Calls Register will record the respective information.]

Plant Register. Plant and machinery purchased from vendor will be entered in this register.

Patent Register. Patents will be recorded in this register.

18. *Dr.*   ORDINARY SHARE CAPITAL (£10)   *Cr.*

19..		£	19..				£
?	To Ordinary Share Capital (£1) . . .	200,000	Jan. 1	By Balance . .	b/d	200,000

Dr.   ORDINARY SHARE CAPITAL (£1)   *Cr.*

19..			£	19..			£
Dec. 31	To Balance . .	c/d	300,000		By Ordinary Share Capital (£10) . . .	200,000
					,, Bonus Share Dividend .	100,000
			£300,000			£300,000
				19..		
				Jan. 1	By Balance . . b/d	300,000

Dr.   BONUS SHARE DIVIDEND   *Cr.*

19..		£	19..			£
?	To Ordinary Share Capital .	100,000	?	By Reserve . . .	100,000

Dr.   RESERVE   *Cr.*

19..			£	19..			£
?	To Bonus Share Dividend .		100,000	Jan. 1	By Balance . . b/d	150,000
Dec. 31	,, Balance . .	c/d	50,000			
			£150,000			£150,000
				Jan. 1	By Balance . . b/d	50,000

		£	£
Ordinary Share Capital (£10) . . . *Dr.*		200,000	
To Ordinary Share Capital (£1) . . .			200,000
Being the conversion of 20,000 fully-paid ordinary shares of £10 each into 200,000 ordinary shares of £1 each per resolution [described]............*vide* Minute Book, p.			
Reserve . . . . *Dr.*		100,000	
To Bonus Share Dividend . . .			100,000
Being bonus dividend of 50% sanctioned by special resolution[1] of the company in general meeting held [Date]...............			
Bonus Share Dividend . . . *Dr.*		100,000	
To Ordinary Share Capital . . .			100,000
Being utilization of bonus dividend in increasing the issued share capital as sanctioned by the company in general meeting held [Date]...........			

[1] Ordinary resolution, if Articles permit issue of Bonus Shares by way of dividend.

BALANCE SHEET AS AT 31ST DECEMBER, 19.. (*includes*)

	£
Authorized Share Capital—	
300,000 Shares of £1 each . .	300,000
Issued Share Capital—	
300,000 Shares of £1 each, fully paid	300,000
General Reserve	50,000

Note. The usual 50p per cent stamp duty and expenses would have to be paid in connection with the issue of £100,000 new capital.

19. Dr.   REDEEMABLE PREFERENCE SHARE CAPITAL   **Cr.**

19..		£	19..		£
June 30	To Sundry Members' Account	50,000	June 30	By Balance . . . b/d	50,000

Dr.   PROFIT AND LOSS ACCOUNT   **Cr.**

19..		£	19..		£
June 30	To Sundry Members' Account—		June 30	By Balance . . . b/d	60,000
	Premium on Redemption of Redeemable Preference Shares . .	5,000			
,,	Capital Redemption Reserve Fund . .	50,000			
,,	Balance . . c/d	5,000			
		£60,000			£60,000
			July 1	By Balance . . . b/d	5,000

Dr.   SUNDRY MEMBERS (REDEEMABLE PREFERENCE SHARES)   **Cr.**

19..		£	19..		£
June 30	To Bank . . .	55,000	June 30	By Redeemable Preference Share Capital . .	50,000
			,,	Profit and Loss Account: Premium of 10p per Share on Redemption .	5,000
		£55,000			£55,000

Dr.   CAPITAL REDEMPTION RESERVE FUND   **Cr.**

			19..		£
			June 30	By Profit and Loss Account: Amount transferred in respect of redemption of Redeemable Preference Shares . .	50,000

(SUMMARY) BALANCE SHEET AS AT 30TH JUNE, 19..

	£			£
Authorized Share Capital . . .	?	Sundry Assets		200,000
		Bank Balance [£85,000 − £55,000]		30,000
Capital Issued and fully paid—				
100,000 Ordinary Shares of £1 each	100,000			
50,000 Redeemable Preference Shares of £1 each £50,000				
Less Redeemed . 50,000	.....			
Capital Redemption Reserve Fund .	50,000			
Profit and Loss Account . . .	5,000			
Sundry Creditors . . .	75,000			
	£230,000			£230,000

20. (*a*) A company limited by shares about to issue redeemable preference shares must have the necessary authority in its articles. If the latter do not contain such authority it will be necessary to pass a special resolution of the company. For this purpose it will be necessary to call a general meeting giving at least 21 days' notice of the intention to pass such resolution as a special resolution.

The proposed resolution must be passed by a majority of not less than three-fourths of such members as, being entitled so to do, vote in person, or, where proxies are allowed, by proxy.

To become effective a copy of such special resolution must be filed with the Registrar of Companies within fifteen days of its being passed.

Upon this preliminary formality being complied with, arrangements will be made to raise the capital privately or by public subscription. In the latter case, a prospectus must be prepared and forwarded to the Registrar of Companies, and if a Stock Exchange quotation be desired, to the Secretary of the Share and Loan Department of the Stock Exchange, in order to comply with the formalities laid down by the Council of the Stock Exchange.

Even if it is not intended to make a public issue, a public company must forward to the Registrar of Companies a Statement in lieu of Prospectus.

(*b*) The entries in the books will depend upon the manner in which the capital is being raised, but assuming the usual application, allotment, and (say) one call, the entries in the *financial* books will be given in Journal form, thus—

Application and Allotment . . . . *Dr.*	
To Redeemable Preference Share Capital	
Cash . . . . *Dr.*	
To Application and Allotment	
Call . . . . *Dr.*	
To Redeemable Preference Share Capital . . .	
Cash . . . . *Dr.*	
To Call	

There will be suitable entries in the Register of Members, Annual Return and notification to the Registrar of Companies within one month of allotment.

The Balance Sheet will contain (*inter alia*)—

	£
Authorized Share Capital . .	**?**
Issued Share Capital—	
........% Redeemable Preference	
Share Capital . . .	
Redeemable at a premium of 10p	
per Share on 31st December,	
19..	

(*c*) The redemption which may be at the company's option or at or within a specified time (according to the terms of issue) can only be made either (*a*) out of profits of the company otherwise available for dividends, or (*b*) out of the proceeds of a new issue of shares made for the purpose of this redemption, but the law provides that no redemption can be made unless the shares are **fully** paid.

In any case, if the preference shares are redeemed at a *premium*, the amount thereof must have been provided for out of profits, or out of Share Premium Account before redemption.

(*d*) Where the redemption (wholly or in part) takes place out of profits, an amount equal to the *nominal* amount of the shares so redeemed must be transferred to a Capital Redemption Reserve Fund, and for the purposes of a reduction of share capital it is the equivalent of share capital. Such Capital Redemption Reserve Fund may, however, be applied in paying up unissued shares for issue as fully paid bonus shares.

The item of Redeemable Preference Shares will, after redemption, cease to be a constituent part of the Balance Sheet, but the Capital Redemption Reserve Fund will, in the circumstances calling for its creation, be shown as a Capital Reserve, unless it is used for bonus shares, when the appropriate amount will appear as Issued Share Capital.

(e) Where the foregoing new issue is made, provided that the redemption takes place within one month of the new issue, no additional stamp duty is payable.

21. It is assumed that the partners desire to have, so far as is possible, the same interests—both as to earnings and as to capital rights—as they possessed as partners. It is also assumed that the partners did not receive any share of profits, e.g. salaries, interest on capital, etc., other than their proportions indicated in the question.

As the basis of the division of profits in a limited company is a capital one, it is advisable to bring the partners' shareholdings into the proportions of 4:3:2. Alternatively, the partners may adjust any disproportion of share-holding by giving a salary to each of the two partners, with a higher proportionate capital to the third, but this will not ensure due preservation of priorities of capital in view of the fact that one class of share is to be issued.

The division of the share capital is suggested, therefore, as—

		A		B		C
		£		£		£
Capitals		8,350		7,000		5,900
Profit on Sale of Business[1] . .		555		417		278
Amount Due to Partners . .		8,905		7,417		6,178
Shares at £1·25 each in Profit Ratios	[8,000]	10,000	[6,000]	7,500	[4,000]	5,000
Cash Due to (+) or by (−) Partner		− £1,095		− £83		+ £1,178

[1][18,000 Shares at £1·25 per Share £22,500
Less Net Assets (Capital) 21,250

£1,250]

[Alternatively, these amounts may be retained in the books as loans to or by the parties, but this procedure is open to objection.]

Where the above suggested basis is not acceptable, the procedure will be to dispose of the shares so as to avoid calling A to provide cash. The excess of the capital held over that divided in profit ratio will be paid out to B and C.

	Shares	A	Shares	B	Shares	C
		£		£		£
The present Capitals are . .		8,905		7,417		6,178
The shares representative of the revised Capitals on the basis of A's being ⁴⁄₉ths of the total— valued at £1·25 each . .	7,124	8,905	5,343	6,679	3,562	4,452
Amount due to partners . .		Nil		£738		£1,726

The remaining shares are 1,971 (18,000 − **16,029** as shown in the preceding statement), which will be disposed of. At £1·25 per share the sale will produce £2,463, which will be paid to the partners B and C as follows—

B, £738; C, £1,726.

When the capitals are "brought into line" with profit ratios all the profits virtually become divisible in the ratio of 4:3:2, so that having regard to their other income, A, B, and C will probably approximate in the above ratio the profits by way of Directors' Remuneration so as to obtain the maximum benefit of the Earned Income Allowance for Income Tax purposes, and the Earned Income Allowance and Relief for Sur-tax.

Other alternatives are available if the shares are to be divided into different classes.

The partners might consider it desirable to divide out the shares in **capital** ratios, which will merely involve trivial differences arising by reason of the non-divisibility of a share, thus—

	Shares	A	Shares	B	Shares	C
		£		£		£
Capitals . . .		8,905		7,417		6,178
Shares at £1·25 . .	7,125	8,906	5,933	7,416	4,942	6,178
Amount due to (+) or by (−) . . .		−£1		+£1		Nil

The *profit* position (i.e. old ratio) can be secured—although it might be considered too complicated—by adjusting the dividends (or salaries as a substitute, as already mentioned) by the difference between the capital ratios and the profit ratios.

22. *Dr.* REALIZATION ACCOUNT *Cr.*

19..			£	19..			£
Apr. 1	To Assets . . .		98,238	Apr. 1	By Creditors . . .		7,973
,,	Cash Balance . .		1,235		,, Purchase Consideration:		
,,	Expenses of Realization		?		(a) £15,000 5%		
	Profit—				Debentures £15,000		
	A, $\frac{5}{10}$.	£4,250			(b) 36,500 7%		
	B, $\frac{3}{10}$.	2,550			Preference		
	C, $\frac{2}{10}$.	1,700			Shares . 36,500		
			8,500		(c) 48,500 Ord-		
					inary Shares 48,500		
							100,000
			£107,973				£107,973

The 7 per cent Preference Shares, £36,500, are divided in the ratio of 30:25:18, arrived at as follows—

					Original Capitals		
					A	B	C
					£	£	£
Per Accounts .	.	.	.	.	40,000	30,000	18,000
Less Debentures	.	.	.	.	10,000	5,000	
					£30,000	£25,000	£18,000

Notes. (i) Assets posted direct to Partners' Capital Accounts.
(ii) Assumed that the shares are of £1 each, fully paid and worth par.

CAPITALS

Dr.		A	B	C		Cr.	A	B	C
		£	£	£			£	£	£
19.. Apr. 1	To 5% Debentures	10,000	5,000	(a)	19.. Apr. 1	By Balances . . b/d	40,000	30,000	18,000
	,, 7% Preference Shares	15,000	12,500	9,000 (b)		,, Transfer from Current Accounts	2,000	1,000	500
	,, Ordinary Shares	21,250	16,050	11,200 (c)		,, Realization Account—Profit on Sale .	4,250	2,550	1,700
		£46,250	£33,550	£20,200			£46,250	£33,550	£20,200

CURRENT ACCOUNTS

Dr.		A	B	C		Cr.	A	B	C
		£	£	£			£	£	£
19.. Apr. 1	To Cash .	1,190	173	341	19.. Apr. 1	By Balances . . b/d	3,190	1,173	841
	,, Transfer to Capitals	2,000	1,000	500					
		£3,190	£1,173	£841			£3,190	£1,173	£841

CASH

Dr.		£		Cr.	£	£
19.. Apr. 1	To Balance . . b/d	2,939	19.. Apr. 1	By Current Accounts—		
				A.	1,190	
				B.	173	
				C.	341	
						1,704
				,, Realization Account—Balance Payable to Purchasing Company		1,235
		£2,939				£2,939

23.   JOURNAL

		£	£
Cash	*Dr.*	100	
Investments	*Dr.*	10,500	
Debtors	*Dr.*	35,000	
Stock	*Dr.*	33,000	
Patterns	*Dr.*	900	
Patents and Trade Marks . . .	*Dr.*	1,200	
Fixtures and Fittings	*Dr.*	750	
Motor Vehicles	*Dr.*	3,740	
Loose Tools	*Dr.*	8,840	
Plant and Machinery	*Dr.*	64,375	
Leasehold Property	*Dr.*	7,000	
Freehold Land and Buildings . . .	*Dr.*	58,000	
To Creditors			34,500
,, Bank			18,050
,, Loan			20,000
,, Bills Payable			6,350
,, Superannuation Fund . . .			4,000
,, Provision for Depreciation of Investments .			1,500
,, Liquidator of John Thynne & Co. Ltd. .			139,005
		£223,405	£223,405
[Usual narrative]			
Liquidator of John Thynne & Co. Ltd. . .	*Dr.*	139,005	
To Ordinary Share Capital . . .			50,000
,, 5% Debentures			25,000
,, Share Premium Account . . .			25,000
,, Cash			39,005
[Usual narrative]			

Cash entered for sake of completeness. Actually there would in the meantime be arrangements made to obtain the cash to pay the liquidator, e.g. a further issue of shares.

Assumed debentures issued at par.

24.   TRADING AND PROFIT AND LOSS ACCOUNT FOR THE YEAR
ENDED 31ST DECEMBER, 19..

	£		£
Stock (Opening)	7,000	Sales	49,000
Purchases	37,500	Stock (Closing)	12,400
Gross Profit . . . . c/d	16,900		
	£61,400		£61,400
Wages	3,700	Gross Profit . . . . b/d	16,900
Salaries	1,000	Discounts Received . . .	475
Trade Expenses	1,300		
Rent	600		
Rates	250		
Directors' Fees . . .	400		
Discounts Allowed . . .	765		
Bad Debts	500		
Advertising	2,500		
Depreciation of Leasehold . .	400		
Net Profit . . . c/d	5,960		
	£17,375		£17,375
Interim Dividend	1,850	By Balance . . . . b/d	5,960
Balance . . . . c/f	4,110		
	£5,960		£5,960

BALANCE SHEET AS AT 31ST DECEMBER, 19..

	£			£
Authorized Capital—		Fixed Assets—		
100,000 Shares of £1 each . .	100,000	Goodwill		25,000
		Leasehold Land and Premises:		
Issued Share Capital—		at cost . . .	£20,000	
74,850 Shares of £1 each, fully paid[1]	74,850	*Less* Depreciation .	400	
Forfeited Shares Account . .	75			19,600
Profit and Loss Account . .	4,110	Machinery at cost . . .		10,000
	79,035			54,600
Trade Creditors . . .	6,000	Current Assets—		
		Stock . . .	£12,400	
		Trade Debtors .	13,150	
		Vendor—Guarantee .	485	
		[£135 + £350]		
		Cash in hand . .	4,400	
				30,435
	£85,035			£85,035

	£	£
[1] Issued Share Capital—		
Shares issued to public	23,500	
Less Shares Forfeited . . .	150	
		23,350
Shares allotted to Vendor—		
Purchase consideration	60,000	
Less Cash	8,500	
		51,500
		£74,850

25. From the information given, the following observations may be made—

(1) *Land and Buildings.* It appears that depreciation has only been provided in respect of Plant and Machinery. In normal circumstances land is not subject to depreciation, but buildings are; this would therefore require examination. A rate of, say, 2 per cent per annum on the original cost might be suggested. If necessary, the original cost may be apportioned between land and buildings.

(2) *Stock.* The cost of the original stock as far as the limited company is concerned is £2,000. In the absence of detailed information, it may be assumed that the cost to the company of the half remaining at the year-end is £1,000 and that it is being brought into the accounts at £1,500. There can be little or no justification for such treatment,

which results in the year's profits being inflated by an unrealized book profit of £500, nor can such a profit be available for distribution as dividend. In the circumstances it is difficult to see how the auditors can report that the accounts give a true and fair view of the profit of the year.

Further information might be sought as to the basis of valuation of the original £2,000 stock. If this was an under-valuation, then the profits of the year may have been above normal on the half of the stock sold, which, among other things, would result in a higher tax liability on profits than necessary.

In the case of both the old and the new stock, the valuation should be at, say, the lower of cost and net realisable value.

26. JOURNAL

19..		£	£
Jan. 1	**Goodwill** . . . . *Dr.*	10,674	
	Stock . . . . *Dr.*	10,845	
	Debtors. . . . . . . *Dr.*	16,050	
	Bills Receivable . . . . . *Dr.*	4,746	
	Bank . . . . *Dr.*	2,685	
	To Creditors		9,000
	,, Bills Payable		6,000
	,, H. Jones		30,000
	Being assets and liabilities taken over from H. Jones, as per agreement dated.............., *vide* Minute Book, p.		
	Goodwill . . . . . . *Dr.*	14,232	
	Stock . . . . *Dr.*	14,593	
	Debtors. . . . . . . *Dr.*	27,740	
	Bills Receivable . . . . *Dr.*	4,750	
	To Creditors		17,445
	,, Bank		3,870
	,, J. Baird		40,000
	Being assets and liabilities taken over from J. Baird, as per agreement dated.............., *vide* Minute Book, p.		
	Goodwill . . . . . . *Dr.*	17,790	
	Stock . . . . *Dr.*	24,000	
	Debtors. . . . . . . *Dr.*	53,282	
	Bank . . . . *Dr.*	18,630	
	To Creditors		46,146
	,, Bills Payable		17,556
	,, R. Woods		50,000
	Being assets and liabilities taken over from R. Woods, as per agreement dated.............., *vide* Minute Book, p.		
	H. Jones . . . . . . *Dr.*	30,000	
	J. Baird . . . . . . *Dr.*	40,000	
	R. Woods . . . . . . *Dr.*	50,000	
	To Share Capital		120,000
	Being allotment of shares of £1 each, fully paid in discharge of purchase agreement dated.............., *vide* Minute Book, p.		
	Preliminary Expenses . . . . *Dr.*	1,500	
	To Bank		1,500
	Being payment of preliminary expenses of Company.		

BALANCE SHEET AS AT 1ST JANUARY, 19..

	£					£
Authorized Share Capital—		Goodwill	.	.	.	42,696
120,000 Shares of £1 each . .	120,000	Current Assets—				
		Stock .	.	.	.	49,438
Issued Capital—		Debtors	.	.	.	97,072
120,000 Shares of £1 each, fully paid	120,000	Bills Receivable	.	.	.	9,496
Creditors	72,591	Bank	.	.	.	15,945
Bills Payable	23,556	Preliminary Expenses	.	.	.	1,500
	£216,147					£216,147

The goodwill figure is arrived at as follows—

			Total	Jones	Baird	Woods
			£	£	£	£
(1) Net Assets acquired (per question)	.	.	77,304	19,326	25,768	32,210
(2) Goodwill [(3) − (1)] . . .	.	.	42,696	10,674	14,232	17,790
(3) Shares allotted proportionate to (1)	.	.	£120,000 $\frac{1}{4}$	£30,000 $\frac{1}{3}$	£40,000 $\frac{5}{12}$	£50,000

Notes. (i) It is assumed that the Bank overdraft is paid off.

(ii) The proportions above are simple ones and can be cancelled out at sight, e.g. $\frac{19,326}{77,304}$ is obviously $\frac{1}{4}$.

27. JOURNAL

		£	£
Goodwill . . . . *Dr.*		16,000	
Stock . . . . *Dr.*		12,000	
Debtors . . . . *Dr.*		20,000	
Machinery and Plant . . . . *Dr.*		6,000	
To Vendor			54,000
Application and Allotment— *Dr.*			
Ordinary Shares		4,500	
5% Preference Shares		75,000	
To Share Capital—			
Ordinary			3,000
5% Preference			75,000
„ Share Premium Account . . .			1,500
Cash (or Bank) . . . . . *Dr.*		26,500	
To Application and Allotment—			
Ordinary Shares			1,500
5% Preference Shares . . .			25,000
Cash (or Bank)— *Dr.*		53,000	
To Application and Allotment—			
Ordinary Shares			3,000
5% Preference Shares . . .			50,000
Underwriters . . . . . . *Dr.*		19,600	
Underwriting Commission [see Note (iii)] . . *Dr.*		400	
To 6% Debentures			20,000
Cash (or Bank) . . . . . *Dr.*		19,600	
To Underwriters			19,600
Vendor . . . . *Dr.*		8,000	
To Cash (or Bank)			8,000
Being payment of creditors for the Vendor in part discharge of purchase consideration.			

Notes. (i) Narratives (where omitted) follow the usual lines.

(ii) Assumed that the underwriters fully discharge their obligations.

(iii) It is not clear from the question whether the 2 per cent rebate on debentures is discount or underwriting commission. In view of no statement as to commission, it is probable that the latter is intended.

(iv) The Application and Allotment Accounts are combined, effecting a saving of time.

(v) No details are given of the preliminary expenses and the manner of discharging the debt due to vendor. Note that the liabilities are not taken over.

28. On the facts given it would appear that the preference dividend for the half-year to 30th June, 19.., was debited gross (£300), and that for the half-year to 31st December, 19.., net (£300 less tax of £120 = £180).

In published accounts dividends, paid and proposed, are shown gross. The normal accounting practice in respect of dividends proposed (dividends cannot be PAID until they are sanctioned either by the directors or, in the case of ordinary dividends, by the company in general meeting) is to debit Profit and Loss Appropriation Account and credit (Ordinary or Preference, whichever is appropriate) Dividend Payable Account with the gross amount of the dividend.

The net amount of the dividend is payable to the shareholders and the income tax, on the gross dividend, is payable to the Inland Revenue under Income Tax Schedule F. When the dividend is paid, the net amount is debited to Dividend Payable Account and credited to Bank Account, and the income tax is debited to Dividend Payable Account and credited to Income Tax Account (Schedule F). It is worthy of note that a dividend which is merely PROPOSED is not due and payable and consequently no liability for Income Tax Schedule F has yet arisen.

Income Tax Schedule F liability should be paid to the Collector of Taxes within 14 days after the end of the Income Tax month (5th day) in which a dividend is paid.

In the case of the half-year dividend to 30th June, 19.. the gross amount of £300 is in order on the assumption that the net dividend of £180 was paid to the shareholders and the £120 was remitted to the Collector of Taxes. However, in the case of the half-year dividend to 31st December, 19.. it would appear that a correcting entry is required, and this should be: debit Preference Dividend Account with £120 and credit Income Tax Account (Schedule F) with £120 to account for the Schedule F liability. As a result the final debit to Preference Dividend Account will be £600 which is 6 per cent on £10,000.

At 31st December, 19.. Income Tax Schedule F of £120 might still be outstanding but it is impossible to tell, in this instance, because a full trial balance is not given.

29.   STATEMENT OF ALLOCATION OF PROFIT

	Before In-corporation		After Incorporation		Total	
	£		£	£	£	£
Gross Profit	(¾)	3,000	(¾)	12,000		15,000
Less Expenditure	(⅕)	2,400	(⅘)	7,200	9,600	
Directors' Fees . . .				300	300	
				7,500		9,900
Net Profit		£600		£4,500		£5,100

Note. The allocable expenditure apportioned, in absence of actual facts, on a time basis.

30.

A B C Ltd.

Balance Sheet as at 31st December, Year 6

	£				£
Authorized Capital—			Shares in and Loan to Subsidiary Company—		
200,000 Ordinary Shares of £1 each	200,000		Shares at cost	£49,500	
120,000 5% Redeemable Preference Shares of £1 each	120,000		Loan	15,000	
	£320,000				64,500
Issued Share Capital—			Investments (quoted) at cost (Market value £155,000)		175,000
200,000 Ordinary Shares of £1 each, fully paid	200,000		Other Assets (net)		372,000
120,000 5% Redeemable Preference Shares of £1 each, fully paid	£120,000				
Less Redeemed during year	10,000				
		110,000			
The Preference Shares are redeemable by annual drawings at a premium of 25 p per share on 30th November each year, to be completed on 30th November, Year 17.					
Capital Redemption Reserve Fund	10,000				
General Reserve (? Revenue)	82,000		} Directors		
Profit and Loss Account—					
Balance at 1st January, Year 6	£150,000				
Add Profit for year	60,000				
	210,000				
Less Preference Dividend	£6,000				
Premium on Redemption of Preference Shares	2,500				
Capital Redemption Reserve Fund	10,000				
Provision (below)	2,000				
	20,500				
		189,500			
		591,500			
(Any provision (if made) for diminution in value of Investments would have to be shown in the Balance Sheet.)					
Profit on Sale of Investments	£18,000				
Profit and Loss Account	2,000				
		20,000			
Note. There is a contingent liability in respect of uncalled share capital of subsidiary company.					
		£611,500			£611,500

Notes. (i) There will be the Directors' Report and the Auditors' Report, together with Group Accounts as required by the Companies Acts 1948 and 1967.

(ii) The item "Other Assets" would require setting out in accordance with the Companies Acts 1948 and 1967.

(iii) Income tax ignored.

(iv) In regard to the note on Redeemable Preference Shares, the Companies Act 1967 requires to be stated the earliest and latest dates on which the company has power to redeem the shares and whether such redemption is optional or mandatory and the premium, if any, payable on redemption. In the circumstances the wording shown is considered suitable.

(v) All the details of transfers to Reserves and Provisions would normally be shown in the Profit and Loss Account.

(vi) Corresponding figures would be required for the preceding year.

31.

ALPHA BETA MINING CO. LTD.

TRADING AND PROFIT AND LOSS ACCOUNT FOR THE YEAR ENDED 30TH JUNE, 19..

		£				£
Wages	. . . .	263,647	Cost of Production	. . .	c/d	428,798
Wood, Stores, etc.	. . .	52,044				
Power Expenses	. . .	19,752				
Wagon Hire, etc.	. . .	56,224				
Rents and Royalties	. .	35,791				
Surface Damage	. . .	1,340				
		£428,798				£428,798
Opening Stock	. . .	1,749	Sales	. . . .		524,004
Cost of Ore	. . . b/d	428,798	Closing Stock	. . .		2,531
Gross Profit	. . . c/d	95,988				
		£526,535				£526,535
Salaries	. . . .	5,499	Gross Profit	. . .	b/d	95,988
Discounts and Allowances	. .	13,396				
Directors' and Auditors' Fees and Law						
charges	. . .	3,954				
Rates and Insurance	. .	8,051				
General Office Expenses	.	3,741				
Subscriptions and Donations	. .	1,790				
Balance—Net Profit for year	. c/d	59,557				
		£95,988				£95,988
Interim Dividend, 1st January, 19..	.	45,000	Balance, 1st July, 19..	. .	b/f	18,078
Balance	. . . . c/f	32,635	Net Profit for current year	.	b/d	59,557
		£77,635				£77,635

BALANCE SHEET AS AT 30TH JUNE, 19..

		£			£	£
Capital and Surplus—			Fixed Assets at Cost—			
Authorized Capital:			Leasehold Mine, Plant,			
600,000 Shares of £1 each	.	600,000	Machinery, etc.	.	600,000	
			New Works Expenditure		11,416	
Issued Share Capital:						611,416
600,000 Shares of £1 each, fully			Current Assets—			
paid	. . . .	600,000	Stock of Ore	.	2,531	
Reserve Fund (? Revenue)	.	24,314	Sundry Debtors	.	77,970	
Profit and Loss Account	.	32,635	Bills Receivable	.	7,404	
			Investments (at cost?)	.	15,480	
		656,949	[Market value ?]			
Current Liabilities—			Cash at Bank and in hand		15,358	
Sundry Creditors	. .	73,210				118,743
		£730,159				£730,159

Notes. (i) Investments should be shown as quoted, unquoted, or in subsidiaries.

(ii) There would doubtless be a Stock of Wood, Stores, etc.

(iii) No mention is made of Depreciation; Leasehold Amortization.

(iv) The nature of the investments, cost, dividends (if any), not disclosed in question.

(v) The amount, and the basis of charge, of UK corporation tax should be shown.

(vi) ? Proposed final dividend.

(vii) Directors' fees and other emoluments should be shown separately. In addition, certain information regarding emoluments of the chairman and of the other directors should be shown in the accounts or by way of note to the accounts. However, because the total amount in this instance does not exceed £10,000 these particulars need not be given. If the company is either a holding company or a subsidiary company exemption from such disclosure is not allowed.

(viii) Auditors' remuneration should be shown separately and any sums paid in respect of auditors' expenses are regarded, for published accounts purposes, as remuneration.

(ix) Where the company is not a wholly owned subsidiary the Directors' Report should include the amount of contributions (if exceeding £50) given for political and/or charitable purposes, and the name of political party recipients should be stated.

(x) The fact that no provision is made for depreciation should be stated.

(xi) Corresponding figures for the previous year are required.

---

32.   SQUARE DEALS LTD.

TRIAL BALANCE

			Dr. £	Cr. £
Balances as per List		£2,166,954		
Less Credit items—				
Creditors . . .	£14,748			
Leasehold Redemption Fund	34,720			
Vans Sold . .	423			
Bank . . .	12,371			
Sales, *less* Returns .	590,105			
Discounts . . .	2,332			
Bad Debts Provision .	1,750			
Transfer Fees . .	34			
Corporation Tax .	150			
		656,633		
			1,510,321	656,633
Items not included in List—				
Share Capital—Preference fully paid . . .				200,000
Share Capital—Ordinary fully paid				400,000
Share Capital—Ordinary partly paid . . .				75,000
Share Capital—Deferred fully paid . . .				50,000
Interest on Calls in arrear				10
General Reserve				150,000
Profit and Loss Account Balance . . .				3,678[1]
Dividends paid—Preference			6,000	
Dividends paid—Ordinary, fully paid . . .			16,000	
Dividends paid—Ordinary, partly paid . . .			3,000	
			£1,535,321	£1,535,321

---

1   PROFIT AND LOSS ACCOUNT

	£		£	
To General Reserve .	25,000	By Balance .	68,178	
„ Final Dividends (gross)				
Preference . .	6,000			
Ordinary, fully paid	24,000			
„ partly paid	4,500			
Deferred . .	5,000			
„ Balance . .	3,678			

[Note to Student. With regard to the Calls in arrear, it must be observed that in the question all Calls in arrear were discharged on 1st December, 19.6. Therefore, there is only eight months' interest at 10 per cent per annum on £150 to be taken into account.]

SQUARE DEALS LTD.

MANUFACTURING AND PROFIT AND LOSS ACCOUNT FOR THE YEAR
ENDED 31ST MARCH, 19.7

	£	£			£
Stock of Raw Materials (Opening)	£242,393		Sales, *less* Returns		590,105
Add Purchases, *less* Returns	326,623				
	569,016				
Less Stock of Raw Materials (Closing)	238,689				
		330,327			
Factory Salaries and Wages		132,769			
Factory Power and Expenses		15,663			
Factory Heating and Lighting		1,712			
Depreciation—					
Machinery and Plant	12,732				
Loose Tools	367				
		13,099			
Gross Profit c/d		96,535			
		£590,105			£590,105

		£			£
Office and Showroom Expenses		3,592	Gross Profit b/d		96,535
Salaries and Wages (Office, etc.)		6,375	Discounts		2,332
Travellers' Salaries and Commission		10,974	Transfer Fee		34
Heating and Lighting (Office, etc.)		428	Interest on Calls in arrear		10
Advertising		8,597			
Legal Expenses		112			
Bad Debts		250			
Auditors' Remuneration		500			
Leasehold Redemption Fund		4,500			
Depreciation—					
Vans, Lorries, Cars		940			
Loss on Sale of Van		157			
Directors' Emoluments—					
Salaries	£15,000				
Managing Director's Commission	2,374				
		17,374			
Net Profit c/d		45,112			
		£98,911			£98,911

	£		£
Corporation Tax	8,000	Balance b/d	45,112
Interim Dividends paid (gross)—		Balance £3,678	
Preference	6,000	*Add* Corporation Tax over-provided in previous year 150	
Ordinary, fully paid	16,000		
„ partly paid	3,000		3,828
Final Dividends proposed (gross)—		General Reserve	20,000
Preference	6,000		
Ordinary, fully paid	16,000		
„ partly paid	3,000		
Deferred	5,000		
Balance c/f	5,940		
	£68,940		£68,940

SQUARE DEALS LTD.

PROFIT AND LOSS ACCOUNT
FOR THE YEAR ENDED 31ST MARCH, 19.7

TURNOVER FOR YEAR		£590,105	£
Trading Profit for the Year			68,573
Add Interest on Calls in Arrear			10
			68,583
Deduct Depreciation		£940	
Directors' Remuneration—			
Fees	£900		
Other Emoluments.	16,474		
		17,374	
Auditors' Remuneration		500	
Leasehold Redemption Fund		4,500	
Loss on Sale of Van		157	
			23,471
Net Profit for Year before Corporation Tax			45,112
Deduct Corporation Tax on Current Year's Profit . . .			8,000
Net Profit for Year after Corporation Tax			37,112
Add Balance brought forward		£3,678	
Corporation Tax over-provided for previous			
year now written back		150	
			3,828
Transfer from General Reserve			20,000
Distributable Profit			60,940
Deduct Appropriations:			
Interim Dividends Paid—			
Preference—half year to 30th			
September, 19.6 (gross)		£6,000	
Income Tax Schedule F	£2,400		
Net Dividend Paid	3,600		
	£6,000		
Ordinary, fully paid (gross)		16,000	
Income Tax Schedule F	£6,400		
Net Dividend Paid	9,600		
	£16,000		
Ordinary, partly paid (gross)		3,000	
Income Tax Schedule F	£1,200		
Net Dividend Paid	1,800		
	£3,000		
Final Dividends Proposed—			
Preference—half year to 31st			
March, 19.7 (gross)		£6,000	
Ordinary, fully paid (gross)		16,000	
Ordinary, partly paid (gross)		3,000	
Deferred (gross)		5,000	
			55,000
Balance carried forward			£5,940

Notes. (i) No details of work in progress given.

(ii) Salaries and wages should be shown separately.

(iii) Commission to the managing director is 5 per cent of £47,486 = £2,374.

(iv) No information is given as to the amount of bank overdraft interest paid. Such amount should be separately disclosed in the published Profit and Loss Account.

(v) The question of Income Tax on the interest on calls in arrear has been disregarded.

(vi) Corresponding figures for the previous year should be shown both in the published Profit and Loss Account and Balance Sheet.

SQUARE DEALS LTD.

BALANCE SHEET

AS AT 31ST DECEMBER, 19.7

	£	£
CAPITAL EMPLOYED		
Share Capital—		
Authorized:		
250,000 6% Cumulative Preference Shares of £1 each	250,000	
700,000 Ordinary Shares of £1 each	700,000	
200,000 Deferred Shares of 25p each	50,000	
	£1,000,000	
Issued:		
200,000 6% Cumulative Preference Shares of £1 each, fully paid		200,000
400,000 Ordinary Shares of £1 each fully paid		400,000
150,000 Ordinary Shares of £1 each, 50p called and paid		75,000
200,000 Deferred Shares of 25p each, fully paid		50,000
		725,000
Reserves and Surplus—		
General Reserve	130,000	
Profit and Loss Account	5,940	
		135,940
Leasehold Redemption Fund—		
Balance at 31st March, 19.6.		39,521
		£900,461

EMPLOYMENT OF CAPITAL

	Cost or Valuation	Depreciation	
Fixed Assets—	£	£	£
Leasehold Property at Cost . . .	240,150	—	240,150
Machinery and Plant at Cost . . .	196,300	77,932	118,368
Vans, Lorries and Cars at Cost . .	9,000	3,270	5,730
Patents and Trade-marks at Cost . .	230,000	—	230,000
Loose Tools as valued at 31st March, 19.7.	1,375	—	1,375
	£676,825	£81,202	595,623
Leasehold Redemption Fund Policy			39,521
Deferred Revenue Expenditure—Advertising			750
Current Assets—			
Stock-in-Trade		238,689	
Trade Debtors less Provision (£2,000) . . .		93,347	
Cash in Hand		419	
		£332,455	
Current Liabilities and Provisions—			
Trade Creditors		14,748	
Accrued Expenses—			
Wages	£123		
Heating and Lighting . . .	272		
Managing Director's Commission .	2,374		
		2,769	
Bank Overdraft		12,371	
Corporation Tax—Accounting			
Year ended 31st March, 19.7		8,000	
Proposed Dividends (gross)		30,000	
		£67,888	
Working Capital			264,567
			£900,461

....
                        } Directors
....

NOTES ON PROFIT AND LOSS ACCOUNT (Part of Published Accounts)

1. TURNOVER[1]:

Turnover for the year is stated at the total amount received and receivable by the Company in respect of its products sold for credit and for cash during the year.

2. PARTICULARS OF DIRECTORS' EMOLUMENTS AS REQUIRED BY THE COMPANIES ACT 1967, SECTION 6[1]

Description	Number
Chairman's Emoluments: £7,500	1
Emoluments of Directors:	
Exceeding £2,500 but not more than £5,000 a year	1
Exceeding £5,000 but not more than £7,500 a year	2

[1] Where a company is neither a holding company nor a subsidiary, it is exempted from showing in its accounts—
(a) particulars of turnover where the value does not exceed £50,000 [Sch. 2 Para. 13 (A)(5)];
(b) details of directors' emoluments where the total emoluments does not exceed £7,500 [Sec. 6(6)].
Further Note. By Statutory Instrument 1971 No. 2044, The Companies (Accounts) Regulations 1971, the amount specified in (a) has been increased to £250,000, and in (b) to £15,000.

NOTES ON BALANCE SHEET (Part of Published Accounts)

1. Movement in Reserves—

	General Reserve	Leasehold Redemption Fund
	£	£
Balance at 31st March, 19.6 . . .	150,000	34,720
Add Contributions during year to 31st March, 19.7		4,500
Increase in Surrender Value of Policy at 31st March, 19.7		301
Deduct Transfer to Profit and Loss Account	20,000	
Balance at 31st March, 19.7 . . .	£130,000	£39,521

2. Leasehold Property—

The leasehold property is occupied under a lease which has less than 50 years to run.

3. Stock-in-Trade—

Stock is valued at the lower of cost and net realizable value on a basis and method applied consistently over many years (this has been assumed for illustrative purposes).

4. Proposed Dividends—

The proposed dividends are subject to confirmation by the company's shareholders.

ADJUSTMENT SCHEDULE

Factory Wages		Heating and Lighting		Advertising	
	£		£		£
Balance per Trial Balance	132,646	Balance per Trial Balance	1,868	Balance per Trial Balance	9,347
Accrual	123	Accrual	272	Less Forward	750
			2,140	Profit & Loss	£8,597
Manufacturing Account	£132,769	Manufacturing £1,712			
		Profit & Loss 428			
			£2,140		

Loose Tools		Vans, etc.	Total	Retained		Sold	
	£		£	£			£
Balance per Trial Balance	1,742	Balance per Trial Balance	7,250	6,670			580
Closing Value	1,375	Less Closing Value		5,730	Sale		423
Manufacturing Account	£367	Profit & Loss		£940	Profit & Loss		£157

Computation of Trading Profit for Published Profit and Loss Account:

Net Profit	. . . . . .	£45,112
Add Directors' Remuneration	. . .	17,374
Loss on Sale of Van	. . .	157
Depreciation	. . . .	940
Leasehold Redemption Fund	. .	4,500
Auditors' Remuneration	. .	500
		68,583
Deduct Interest on Calls in Arrear	. .	10
		£68,573

33.   GIVORTAKE LTD.

BALANCE SHEET AS AT 31ST DECEMBER, 19.4

	£	£
CAPITAL EMPLOYED—		
Share Capital—		
Authorized:		
400,000 6% Cumulative Preference Shares of £1 each .	400,000	
400,000 Ordinary Shares of £1 each . . .	400,000	
25,000 Deferred Shares of £1 each . . .	25,000	
	£825,000	
Issued and Fully Paid:		
300,000 6% Cumulative Preference Shares of £1 each .		300,000
300,000 Ordinary Shares of £1 each . . .		300,000
25,000 Deferred Shares of £1 each . . .		25,000
		625,000
Revenue Reserves—		
Profit and Loss Account		16,714
Corporation Tax—		
Accounting Year ended 31st December, 19.4		38,000
Provision for diminution in value of Investments . . .		1,000
		£680,714

EMPLOYMENT OF CAPITAL—

	£	£
Fixed Assets—		
Freehold Properties at cost	500,000	
Less Depreciation	70,000	
		430,000
Plant and Machinery at cost	300,000	
Less Depreciation	100,000	
		200,000
		630,000
Less Long-term Liabilities 5% Debentures		200,000
		430,000
Unquoted Investment—		
Shares in Associated Co at cost		5,000
		435,000
Interests in Subsidiary—		
Shares at cost	50,000	
Debentures at cost	20,000	
Current Account	6,500	76,500
		511,500
Current Assets—		
Stock	81,650	
Debtors	105,800	
Investment at cost (Market Value £4,000) . .	5,000	
Tax Reserve Certificates	12,500	
Cash at Bank	88,250	
	£293,200	
Current Liabilities—		
Creditors	47,336[1]	
Debenture Interest (gross)	5,000	
Corporation Tax—Accounting Year ended 31st December, 19.3	32,650	
Proposed Dividends (gross)	39,000	
	£123,986	
Working Capital		169,214
		£680,714

........................⎫
........................⎭ Directors

[Auditors' Report and Directors' Report.]
Group Accounts and previous year's corresponding figures, both in Balance Sheet and Profit and Loss Account, are also required.

[1] Trade Creditors £40,500 plus Directors' Emoluments £5,931 plus Auditors' Remuneration £905.

Notes on Balance Sheet (Part of Published Accounts)

1. CAPITAL COMMITMENT

Contracts for capital expenditure, not provided for in the foregoing Balance Sheet, amounted to £25,000.

2. CONTINGENT LIABILITY

There is a contingent liability of £2,500 in respect of uncalled Share Capital of the Associated Company, Extras Ltd.

3. INTEREST IN SUBSIDIARY

Subsidiary's Name	Class of Shares held	Proportion of nominal value of shares Issued of that Class	Country in which Registered
Ayardorto Ltd.	Ordinary Shares of £1 each	60%	England

4. INTEREST IN ASSOCIATED COMPANY

Associated Company's Name	Class of Shares held	Proportion of nominal value of the shares Issued of that Class	Country in which Registered
Extras Ltd.	Ordinary Shares of £1 each	12½%	England

5. QUOTED INVESTMENT

The company's quoted investment is in Imports Ltd. for which permission has been granted to deal on the Stock Exchange.

6. STOCK

Trading Stocks are valued at the lower of cost and net realizable value on bases and methods consistently applied over many years.

7. PROPOSED DIVIDENDS

The proposed dividends are subject to the shareholders' confirmation.

GIVORTAKE LTD.

PROFIT AND LOSS ACCOUNT
FOR THE YEAR ENDED 31ST DECEMBER, 19.4

	£	£
TURNOVER FOR YEAR	£628,550	
	£	£
Trading Profit for Year		150,000
Add Investment Income (gross)—		
Quoted	500	
Unquoted	500	
Subsidiary Co. Debentures	1,000	
		2,000
		152,000
Deduct Depreciation	50,000	
Directors' Remuneration—		
Fees	3,258[1]	
Other Emoluments	2,673[2]	
Debenture Interest (gross)	10,000	
Auditors' Remuneration	905	
		66,836
Profit for Year before Taxation		85,164
Deduct Corporation Tax on Profits for Year . . .	38,000	
Income Tax suffered on Investment Income now written off	800	
		38,800
Profit for Year after Taxation		46,364
Add Balance brought forward	45,000	
Deduct Corporation Tax under-provided for previous year	650	
		44,350
Distributable Profit		90,714
Deduct Appropriations:		
Provision for diminution in value of investments . .	1,000[3]	
Cancellation of rights against company discharged in Deferred Shares	25,000	
Dividends (gross)—		
Paid:		
Preference Shares for half-year to 30th June, 19.4	9,000	
Proposed:		
Preference Shares for half-year to 31st December, 19.4	£9,000	
Ordinary Shares for the year at 10% .	30,000	
	39,000	
		74,000
Balance carried forward		£16,714

		£	£
[1] Trading Profit			150,000
Less Debenture Interest		10,000	
Depreciation . . .		50,000	
Managing Director's Commission .		2,673	
Preference Dividend (gross) . . .		18,000	
Auditors' Remuneration . . .		905	
			81,578
			68,422
Less Directors' Fees [$\frac{8}{105} \times$ £68,422] . . .			3,258
			£65,164 [5% = £3,258]

[2] 3 per cent of (£150,000 − £10,000 − £50,000) − £905).
[3] 20p per share on 5,000 shares.

NOTES ON PROFIT AND LOSS ACCOUNT (Part of Published Accounts)

1. TURNOVER

Turnover for the year is stated at the total amount received and receivable by the company in respect of products sold for credit and for cash during the year.

2. PARTICULARS OF DIRECTORS' EMOLUMENTS

Description	Number
Chairman's Fees: £1,466 . . .	1
Emoluments of Directors: Not more than £2,500 a year . .	2
More than £2,500 but not more than £5,000 a year . .	1

34. Criticism, it is assumed, is merely to be directed to questions of form, layout, and conformity to legal and accounting requirements.

The Balance Sheet is not drawn up in conformity either with the requirements of the Companies Acts 1948 and 1967, or with established accounting practice. Items should be grouped under appropriate headings of Capital and Reserves, Long Term Liabilities, Current Liabilities, and Fixed and Current Assets.

(1) *Share Capital.* There is no mention of Issued Capital. The information given in the Balance Sheet against Authorized Capital might refer to Issued Capital, as the former cannot be properly described as "fully paid."

(2) *Reserves.* (a) These could to advantage be divided into Capital and Revenue although there is no legal obligation to do so.

(b) The transfer from Share Premium Account is difficult to understand in view of Sect. 56, Companies Act 1948.

(3) *Loans from Subsidiary Companies.* Loans from subsidiaries must be separately stated (as has been done with Loans *to* subsidiaries).

(4) *Profit and Loss Account.* (a) The detail should appear in a separate Profit and Loss Account, the balance of which may be grouped with Revenue Reserves.

(b) The detailed items are considered below.

(5) *Investments.* (a) Shares in subsidiaries must be separately stated.

(b) Other Industrial Investments must be grouped as Quoted and Unquoted; market value should be given.

(6) *Sundry Debtors.* In certain circumstances Income Tax suffered on Franked Investment Income may be reclaimed from the Inland Revenue in which case the inclusion of the repayable amount with Sundry Debtors is not incorrect. Normally, however, a Schedule F debit balance is carried forward for set off against Income Tax due on dividends paid at a later date. Nevertheless, it is common accounting practice to write off such debit balances to Profit and Loss Account in order to reflect the true year-end position. When the amount is eventually set off against Income Tax due on dividends paid a note should be appended to the relevant year-end Balance Sheet regarding the relief obtained.

(7) *Office Furniture.* This must be shown as required by the Companies Act 1967, Schedule 2, e.g. at cost (or valuation) less accumulated depreciation.

(8) *General.* (a) If the Balance Sheet is to be laid before the company in General Meeting it must be signed by two directors; the Auditors' Report and Directors' Report must be annexed and Group Accounts will be required.

(b) The year of the Balance Sheet is not given.

(c) Corresponding figures of the last Balance Sheet are required unless, as is possible (in view of the fact that there is no Profit and Loss Account balance brought forward), this is the first Balance Sheet of the Company.

(d) Certain of the notes on the Balance Sheet are not intelligible.

The details appearing in the Profit and Loss Account section of the Balance Sheet call for the following criticism—

(a) *Preference Dividend.* The amount of £561 is not a full half-year's dividend on the issued capital at 31st December, 19...

(*b*) *Final Dividends*. Proposed final dividends (gross) should be shown in the Profit and Loss Account, in which case the total will appear under Current Liabilities.

The Company appears from the Balance Sheet to be merely a holding company, so that any information as to its financial strength would depend on the Group Accounts. From the figures given, however, it would appear that unless some part of the loans can be called upon, there is a deficiency of current assets over current liabilities if final dividends are to be included in the latter figure.

35. At the same time as the transfer from the General Bank to the Dividend Banking Account is made there will be the usual entries for raising the Dividend Account, viz.—

(1) Debit Profit and Loss Appropriation Account with gross dividend.
Credit Dividend Account with net dividend.
Credit Income Tax Account (Schedule F) with Income Tax on gross dividend.

(2) [The entry referred to in the first paragraph.]
Debit Dividend Banking Account ⎫
Credit General Bank Account   ⎬ with *net* dividend.

As mentioned in the question, after a period of six months, the following entry is made—

Debit Deposit Account.
Credit Dividend Banking Account.

In the meantime, all the dividend warrants duly presented will have been paid out of the Dividend Banking Account and debited to the Dividend Account, so that the balance of the latter equals the balance of the Dividend Banking Account, and (after the transfer to Deposit Account) will be equal to the Deposit Account.

When (after the aforesaid six months) a dividend warrant is presented and confirmed by the company, a retransfer from Deposit to Dividend Banking Account is made, and the amount paid debited to Dividend Account. Thus the Dividend Account is always reconciled with the balance in the Dividend Banking Account and the Deposit Account.

Frequently, when the transfer (to close temporarily the Dividend Banking Account) from Dividend Banking Account to Deposit is made, a similar transfer is made from Dividend Account to Unclaimed Dividend Account, so that in this case the Deposit Account is the counterpart to the Unclaimed Dividend Account. Consistently with this method, when a retransfer is made from Deposit to Dividend Banking Account, a similar retransfer will be made from Unclaimed Dividend Account to Dividend Account (and the cash paid from the reopened Dividend Banking Account debited thereto), thus always leaving the Deposit Account equal to the Unclaimed Dividend Account.

STALE WARRANTS SCHEDULE (DIVIDEND No............)

Name of Payee	Address	Warrant Number	£	Date Presented	Date Paid	C.B. Folio	£	Balance	Remarks

Each dividend should be numbered and a separate set of accounts identified by the appropriate number—opened.

As there will usually be comparatively few warrants outstanding at the end of six months, a "Stale Warrant" Schedule—agreeing in total with the Deposit Account—will be prepared with essential details and, as the warrants are presented and confirmed, they will be entered into a separate column, thus giving the balance outstanding and keying up with the transfers from Deposit to Dividend Banking Account.

As the banker will decline to pay a stale warrant (it is customary to state on the warrant that after a certain period the warrant will not be paid without confirmation), it will be necessary for the payee to send it back to the company, either for confirmation or for a new warrant. The question of forfeiture of a dividend does not appear to require treatment in this problem.

36. The Profit and Loss Appropriation Account will be as follows—

PROFIT AND LOSS APPROPRIATION ACCOUNT

	£
Net Profit for the year	19,784
Add Balance brought forward	3,745
	23,529
Less Proposed Transfer to Reserve	5,000
	18,529

Less Dividends (gross)—

Paid: Preference Dividend for half-year to 30th June, 19..	£1,750	
Proposed: Preference Dividend for half-year to 31st December, 19..	1,750	
Ordinary Dividend at 10%	10,000	
		13,500
Balance carried forward		£5,029

If no separate Banking Account (to deal with the dividends) has been opened there will be a credit balance on the Ordinary Dividend Account of £36 (£60 less tax at 40 per cent), representing unclaimed dividends.

If a Dividend Banking Account in respect of each dividend has been opened there will be a transfer of £36 from Dividend Banking Account to a Deposit Account; and a similar transfer from the Ordinary Dividend Account to Unclaimed Ordinary Dividend Account, viz.—

Debit Deposit Account, £36. Credit Dividend Banking Account, £36.
Debit Ordinary Dividend Account, £36. Credit Unclaimed Ordinary. Dividend Account, £36.

If and when forfeiture takes place, the following entry will be made—

Debit Unclaimed Ordinary Dividend Account, £36. Credit Reserve, £36.
Debit General Bank Account, £36. Credit Deposit Account, £36.

37. It is assumed that warrants are stale at the expiry of the six months, and that a transfer to a Dividend Banking Account has been made.

The following transfers are required—

JOURNAL

		£	£
Deposit Account (No........) . . . . . *Dr.*		0·99	
To Dividend Banking Account (No.........) . . .			0·99
Interim Dividend Account (No.........) . . *Dr.*		0·99	
To Unclaimed Dividend Account (No.....) . . .			0·99

The "Stale" Warrants are—

	Gross	Tax	Net
	£	£	£
W. Jones (Warrant No. ......)—50 at 6% per annum for half-year	1·50	0·60	0·90
J. Brown (,,)— 5 ,, ,, ,,	0·15	0·06	0·09
	£1·65	£0·66	£0·99

[For guidance, *rough* Accounts are appended—

DIVIDEND BANK

	£		£
To General Bank .	1,800·00	By Sundry Warrants. . . .	1,799·01
		,, Deposit Account . . .	0·99

INTERIM DIVIDEND

	£		£
To Dividend Bank Account . .	1,799·01	By Profit and Loss Appropriation	
,, Unclaimed Dividend Account .	0·99	Account	1,800·00

DEPOSIT

	£	
To Dividend Bank Account . .	0·99	

UNCLAIMED DIVIDEND

		£
	By Interim Dividend Account . .	0·99

Items in heavy type are the postings from the foregoing Journal entries.

It is assumed that the items in ordinary type have been already dealt with at 31st March, 19...]

38. JOURNAL

	£	£
5% Preference Share Capital (£5) . . . *Dr.*	25,000	
To 5% Preference Share Capital (£1) . .		25,000
Being the subdivision of 5,000 5% Preference Shares of £5 each fully paid into 25,000 5% Preference Shares of £1 each fully paid per resolution (described) ...., *vide* Minute Book, p.		
Reserve Fund . . . . . . *Dr.*	6,000	
Profit and Loss Account . . . . . *Dr.*	4,000	
To Bonus Share (Ordinary) Dividend . .		10,000
Being bonus dividend of 20% sanctioned by resolution of the company made................, *vide* Minute Book, p.		
Bonus Share (Ordinary) Dividend . . . *Dr.*	10,000	
To Ordinary Share Capital		10,000
Being utilization of bonus dividend in increasing the issued ordinary share capital as sanctioned by the company in general meeting held [Date].		

BALANCE SHEET AS AT 31ST DECEMBER, 19..

	£	£
Authorized Capital—		
50,000 5% Preference Shares of £1 each . . .	50,000	
100,000 Ordinary Shares of £1 each . . .	100,000	
	£150,000	
Issued Capital—		
25,000 5% Preference Shares of £1 each fully paid . .	25,000	
60,000 Ordinary Shares of £1 each fully paid . . .	60,000	
		85,000
Reserve Fund		14,000
Profit and Loss Account		8,000

Notes. (i) Assumed that the Articles already permit the Bonus Share Dividend.
(ii) Fractions of shares would probably have to be dealt with.

39. (1) The directors, under Clause 115 of Table A (1948), may from time to time pay the members such interim dividends as appear to the directors to be *justified by the profits of the company*. If the clause has been eliminated, the power of the directors in this respect depends on whether—and with what restrictions—the Articles confer it.

In any case, there must be (*a*) profits of the same nature and kind as would enable a final dividend to be paid, that is, profits legally capable of distribution, and (*b*) such as to justify the payments. The directors would doubtless ordinarily obtain reasonably reliable interim accounts in order to afford them a guide in determining the foregoing essentials. In the absence of accounts the legality of the payment is emphatically open to question, unless the business is such that profits can be easily arrived at, e.g. in a purely cash business.

The directors should view the year as a whole, as a busy seasonal profit is not a fair guide to the whole year's profit.

(2) The wisdom of the interim payment depends upon a variety of circumstances. The auditor will obviously be acquainted with the actual facts obtaining, so that it is impossible to lay down an abstract rule. In general, the following points would be likely to arise in consideration of this question—

(i) The previous practice of the company (particularly in the case of a company with a Stock Exchange quotation).

(ii) The financial position of the company, taking into account the development, extension of markets or products manufactured or dealt in, re-financing requirements, e.g. redemption of high-rated debentures or loans. The question of execution of important repairs, renewals, and the like which may have been postponed, as well as the replenishing of stocks.

(iii) The particular conditions and prospects of the company, as well as the general conditions and prospects, will require careful examination.

(iv) If the profit (though legally divisible) or part thereof is due to ephemeral causes, e.g. benefit of exchange and artificial restriction, a cautious policy will be required.

(v) The psychological effect of the payment of an interim dividend (or its passing if it has been usual to pay an interim) is important, as the rate of the dividend paid is often taken as a rough guide to the final dividend.

(3) The rate of dividend to be declared depends on the answer to paragraph (ii), but in view of uncertainties existing under present conditions, a generous allocation to reserve, an adequate deduction for depreciation and provision for re-equipment and modernization should certainly be provided for and a conservative estimate made of debtors, especially foreign debtors.

In brief, the real points in the question are—

(1) *Are* there justifiable profits?
(2) Will the finances "stand" the interim?
(3) Even so, can the best interest of the members be promoted by retaining profits in the business until at all events the normal year-end?

(4) What adverse repercussions are likely to ensue if the payment of the interim is followed by the passing of the final dividend (even if due to circumstances quite beyond the control of the business).

Note. It is assumed that the problem relates to a cash dividend, and that no question of arrears of cumulative preference dividends arises.

40. TRIAL BALANCE, 31ST MARCH, 19.8

	£	Dr. £	Cr. £
Balances per List		476,648	
Less Credits—			
Gross Trading Profit	£109,357		
Machinery sold	600		
Creditors	22,989		
Bad Debts Provision	275		
		133,221	
		343,427	133,221
Balances not shown in List—			
Preference Shares			50,000
Premium on 25,000 Preference Shares			1,875
Ordinary Shares			150,000
Deferred Shares			20,000
Profit and Loss—Balance forward			6,159
Goodwill		20,000	
General Reserve			2,172
		£363,427	£363,427

GAY AND PERKINS LTD.

PROFIT AND LOSS ACCOUNT
FOR THE YEAR ENDED 31ST MARCH, 19.8

Turnover for Year		£343,720	
			£
Trading Profit for Year after charging all expenses other than those deducted in this Account.			88,528
Deduct Depreciation		£15,732	
Directors' Remuneration—			
Fees	£500		
Other Emoluments	7,000		
		7,500	
Loss on Sale of Machinery		240	
Auditors' Remuneration		900	
			24,372
Profit for Year before Taxation			64,156
Deduct Corporation Tax on profit of year to 31st March, 19.8			25,600
Profit for Year after Taxation			38,556
Add Balance brought forward		£6,159	
Less Corporation Tax under-provided previous year		565	
			5,594
			44,150
Deduct Appropriations—			
Amount written off Goodwill		£5,000	
Transfer to General Reserve		3,500	
Dividends Paid (Gross)—			
On £25,000 6% Preference Shares for half-year to 30th September, 19.7.		750	
Dividends Proposed (Gross)—			
On £50,000 6% Preference Shares for half-year to 31st March, 19.8	£1,500		
On Ordinary Shares for the year at 12% .	18,000		
On Deferred Shares for the year at 15% .	3,000		
		22,500	
			31,750
Balance carried forward			£12,400

GAY AND PERKINS LTD.

BALANCE SHEET
AS AT 31ST MARCH, 19.8

CAPITAL EMPLOYED

Share Capital—
Authorized

	£
100,000 6% Preference Shares of £1 each	100,000
150,000 Ordinary Shares of £1 each	150,000
200,000 Deferred Shares of 10p each	20,000
	£270,000

Issued and Fully Paid

		£
50,000 6% Preference Shares of £1 each		£50,000
150,000 Ordinary Shares of £1 each		150,000
200,000 Deferred Shares of 10p each		20,000
		220,000
Reserves and Surplus		
Share Premium Account	£1,875	
General Reserve	5,672	
Profit and Loss Account	12,400	
		19,947
		£239,947

EMPLOYMENT OF CAPITAL

	£	£
Fixed Assets—		
Freehold Land and Factory at cost		87,000
Machinery at cost	149,000	
Less Depreciation	60,056	
		88,944
Office Furniture at cost	1,000	
Less Depreciation	316	
		684
Goodwill *less* amounts written off		15,000
		191,628
Current Assets—		
Stock	27,156	
Work-in-Progress	34,237	
	61,393	
Debtors *less* Provision (£1,327)	31,848	
Cash at Bank and in Hand	27,367	
	£120,608	
Current Liabilities—		
Creditors	23,289	
Audit Fee	900	
Corporation Tax—Accounting Year ended		
31st March, 19.8	25,600	
Proposed Dividends (Gross)	22,500	
	£72,289	
Working Capital		48,319
		£239,947

.........................⎫
                          ⎬ Directors
.........................⎭

[Auditors' Report and Directors' Report]

NOTES ON PROFIT AND LOSS ACCOUNT (Part of Published Accounts)

1. TURNOVER

Turnover for the year is stated as the total amount received and receivable by the company in respect of its products sold for credit and for cash during the year.

NOTES ON BALANCE SHEET (Part of Published Accounts)

1. STOCK AND WORK IN PROGRESS

The company's stocks of raw materials, work in progress, and finished goods have been valued at cost. This method of valuation has been consistently applied by the directors over many years.

2. FREEHOLD LAND AND FACTORY

Provision has not been made for depreciation of freehold land and factory.

3. PROPOSED DIVIDENDS

The proposed dividends are subject to confirmation by the shareholders.

WORKING NOTES

1. The Trading Profit is computed thus:

		£	£
Gross Trading Profit for the year			£109,357
Less Office Salaries	£10,365		
Office Rent and Rates	2,507		
Office Expenses	1,731		
Travellers' Salaries and Commission . . .	5,174		
Bad Debts	1,052		
			20,829
			£88,528

2. Because the company is neither a holding company nor a subsidiary, and because the aggregate does not exceed £15,000, particulars of the emoluments of individual directors need not be shown.

3. It would appear that Income Tax of £300 due on the Preference Dividend paid on 30th September, 19.7 was not remitted to the Inland Revenue. This liability has been included with Creditors in the Balance Sheet.

4. Corresponding figures for 19.7 should be shown in both the Profit and Loss Account and the Balance Sheet.

41.   JOURNAL

		£	£
Stock . . . . Dr.		8,500	
Income Tax . . . . . . Dr.		5,000	
Machinery . . . . . . Dr.		55,000	
Motor Vans . . . . . . Dr.		1,500	
To Dividend Equalization Reserve . . .			70,000
Being sundry adjustments of previous overcharges against Revenue.			
Investments . . . . . . Dr.		10,000	
To Pension Fund			10,000
Being restoration of correct value of Investments.			
Pension Fund Investment . . . . Dr.		10,000	
To Bank			10,000
Being investment of amount of Pension Fund.			

These adjustments would have to be fully disclosed in the next accounts. The question of income tax and corporation tax arises in connection with the stock revaluation.

As to the effect upon the costing calculations the adjustments for income tax, investments, and pensions will not call for revision of such calculations. As to the remaining items, on the assumption that the balances appearing in the accounts as shown in the question coincide with those appearing in the costing records, the charge-up for materials and depreciation will be increased. If, however, the secret reserve created has not altered the figures appearing in the costing records, the costing calculations will continue to be made as before. As the creation of the secret reserve is a matter of finance, it would have no bearing upon the costings, the purpose of the latter being to charge up true cost unaffected by the creation and subsequent reversal of a secret reserve.

42. JOURNAL

		£	£
Profit and Loss Appropriation Account . . *Dr.*		5,275	
To Ordinary Dividend			[1] 275
,, Bonus Share Dividend			5,000
Being dividend of 55% sanctioned by resolution of the company in general meeting as to 50% in bonus shares and 5% in cash......., *vide* Minute Book, p........			
Bonus Share Dividend . . . . . *Dr.*		5,000	
To 5% Preference Share Capital . . .			5,000
Being issue of 5% Preference Shares in discharge of Bonus Share Dividend.			

The usual alterations (Register of Members, Balance Sheet, etc.) will be made.

43. JOURNAL

		£	£
Ordinary Share Capital (£5) . . . . *Dr.*		50,000	
To Ordinary Share Capital (25p) . . .			50,000
Being the subdivision of 10,000 Ordinary Shares of £5 each fully paid into 200,000 shares of 25p each fully paid, per special resolution dated...............duly filed..............., *vide* Minute Book, p.			

[1] £500 less tax at 45%.

44.   JOURNAL

		£	£
Share Capital (£5) . . . . . Dr.		500,000	
To Ordinary Share Capital (£1) . . .			150,000
„ 5% Preference Share Capital (£1) .			100,000
„ Capital Reduction Account . . .			250,000
Being exchange of 100,000 shares of £5 each fully paid into 200,000 Preference Shares of £1 each, and 300,000 Ordinary Shares of £1 each, all credited as 50p paid, per special resolution duly filed................, *vide* Minute Book, p.			
Call (Ordinary Shares) . . . . Dr.		150,000	
Call (Preference Shares) . . . . Dr.		100,000	
To Ordinary Share Capital (£1) . . .			150,000
„ 5% Preference Share Capital (£1) . .			100,000
Being call of 50p on the Ordinary and Preference Shares.			
Reserve . . . . Dr.		125,000	
Cash . . . . Dr.		125,000	
To Call (Ordinary Shares) . . .			150,000
„ Call (Preference Shares) . . .			100,000
Being discharge of call on the Ordinary and Preference Shares, 25p in cash and 25p by the utilization of Reserve.			
Capital Reduction Account . . . . Dr.		250,000	
To Capital Reserve			250,000
Being transfer to Reserve.			

Costs ignored.

As the shares are virtually reduced by 25p per share, the procedure in respect of the above should follow that laid down in s. 66 of the Companies Act 1948.

The usual alterations (Register of Members, Balance Sheet, etc.) will be made.

45.   JOURNAL

			£	£
Shares in Bain, Pearson & Co. Ltd. . .	(i) Dr.		60,000	
To Birmingham Banch . . .				50,000
„ Reserve	(ii)			10,000
Creditors	(v) Dr.		45,000	
To Shares in Bain, Pearson & Co. Ltd. . .				30,000
„ Investment Reserve . . .				15,000

Notes. (i) Alternatively, the purchasing company may be debited and Birmingham Branch credited, whereupon Shares in Bain, Pearson & Co. Ltd. debited and the purchasing company credited.

(ii) Subject to the "Lubbock" and "Foster" rules, this will be credited to Capital Reserve or transferred to Investment Reserve.

(iii) As there is probably a debit balance on Profit and Loss Account, the profit on sale might be used to reduce the adverse balance.

(iv) It is advisable in any case not to take profit for sale of shares until the original sum invested in the Branch is recouped.

(v) The question does not state that the creditors take the shares in *full settlement*, but this is assumed in the question. Otherwise, the debit to Creditors would be £30,000 assuming the shares were worth par, leaving a credit balance in favour of creditors of £15,000.

(vi) If the creditors take the shares in full settlement, a natural (but not necessarily the only) inference is that the shares taken by the creditors are worth £45,000, i.e. £1·50 each but the first Journal entry will not be affected as the question clearly indicates the shares are worth par, as the purchase consideration is £60,000 discharged in 60,000 shares. If after a period [the question employs the word "ultimately"] the shares have appreciated in value, enabling Forsyth & Co. Ltd. to settle their indebtness of £45,000 by a transfer of 30,000 shares, it would indicate that the remaining 30,000 shares are worth £45,000. Although it is inadvisable to write up the shares left, the book value of £30,000 may be increased to £45,000 and a further £15,000 credited to Investment Reserve.

As a result the investment will stand at £45,000, investment reserve at £30,000, leaving a net debit of £15,000, which is reflected in the original cost of the shares (£60,000) less transfer of 30,000 shares (£45,000).

46.   JOURNAL

19.8			£	£
Apr. 1	Sports Ground and Pavilion ?⎫ . . . . *Dr.*		5,338	
	Equipment ?⎭			
	Stocks . . . . . . *Dr.*		80	
	To Loan on Mortgage . . .			4,000
	,, Mortgage Interest			50
	,, Wages			48
	,, Sundry Creditors			200
	,, Liquidator of X Ltd. . . .			1,120
	Being assets and liabilities taken over as per agreement dated......................			
	Liquidator of X Ltd. . . . . *Dr.*		1,120	
	To 10% Preference Share Capital . . .			1,000
	,, Deferred Share Capital . . .			120
	Being allotment of 200 10% Preference Shares of £5 each and 480 Deferred Shares of 25p each, all fully paid, in discharge of purchase consideration................., *vide* Minute Book, p.			
	Bank . . . . . . *Dr.*		1,500	
	To 5% Debentures			1,500
	Being amount received in respect of 150 5% Debentures of £10 each, issued at par for cash.			
	Loan on Mortgage . . . . . *Dr.*		500	
	Mortgage Interest . . . . *Dr.*		50	
	To Bank			530
	,, Income Tax (40%)			20
	Being payment of Mortgage Interest to date and part repayment of Principal.			

The rent owing by N Sports Club is an asset of X Ltd., and in the acquiring company's books the asset and the liability cancel out.

The valuation of the Sports Ground, etc., is taken according to the net cost to the new company.

Assumed that the liability for interest to the debenture-holders of X Ltd. is not taken over.

47. (a)   JOURNAL

		£	£
10% Debenture Stock . . . . . *Dr.*		20,000	
15% Preference Share Capital . . . *Dr.*		40,000	
Deferred Share Capital . . . . *Dr.*		100,000	
To 12% Debenture Stock			10,000
„ 20% Preference Share Capital (25p) .			13,000
„ Deferred Share Capital (new) (25p) . .			37,000
„ Capital Reduction Account . . .			100,000
Being reduction of capital passed by Special Resolution dated......................, confirmed by Court Order dated................, *vide* Minute Book, p. ...., carried out as follows—			
1. For each £1 of 10% Mortgage Debenture Stock—			
50p of new Debenture Stock.			
One new 20% Preference Share of 25p.			
One new Deferred Share of 25p.			
2. Reduction of each 15% Preference Share from £1 to 37½p, and exchange of four new Preference Shares of 25p for five old Preference Shares and seven new Deferred Shares for ten old Preference Shares.			
3. Reduction of each old Deferred Share from £1 to 25p.			
Capital Reduction Account . . . . *Dr.*		100,000	
Reserves . . . . *Dr.*		45,350	
To Profit and Loss Account . .			55,650
„ Stock			56,961
„ Land, Buildings, and Plant . . .			32,739
Being amounts written off in pursuance of scheme of reconstruction.			
20% Preference Share Capital (25p) . . *Dr.*		13,000	
Deferred Share Capital (25p) . . . *Dr.*		37,000	
To 20% Preference Share Capital (£1) .			13,000
„ Deferred Share Capital (£1) . .			37,000
Being consideration of Preference and Deferred Shares of 25p each fully paid into Preference and Deferred Shares of £1 each, fully paid respectively.			

(b)   THE STAFFORDSHIRE CAR CO. LTD.
                  BALANCE SHEET AS AT 30TH SEPTEMBER, 19..

	£		£
Share Capital—		Fixed Assets—	
Authorized, issued and fully paid,		Land, Buildings and Plant . .	13,961[2]
and as reduced with Court sanc-		Current Assets—	
tion:		Stock . . . £24,289[1]	
20% Preference Shares of £1 each	13,000	Debtors . . . 46,750	
Deferred Shares of £1 each .	37,000	Cash at Bank . . 2,450	
			73,489
	50,000		
12% Debenture Stock . . .	10,000		
Creditors	27,450		
	£87,450		£87,450

Note. All costs of reorganization scheme ignored.

The following statement would be very useful in examination work for the purpose of arriving at the new Balance Sheet figures—

Old Balance Sheet Items	Total	New Debenture Stock	New Preference Shares	New Deferred Shares	Profit
	£	£	£	£	£
Preference Shares	40,000		8,000	7,000	25,000
Deferred Shares	100,000			25,000	75,000
Debenture Stock	20,000	10,000	5,000	5,000	
Reserves	45,350				45,350
Total.	£205,350	£10,000	£13,000	£37,000	£145,350
Elimination of—					
Profit and Loss	55,650				
Stock	56,961[1]				
Land, etc.	32,739[2]				£145,350

Details of new Share Capital—

Allotted to	New Preference		New Deferred	
	No.	£	No.	£
Old Debenture-holders . . .	20,000	5,000	20,000	5,000
Old Preference Shareholders . .	32,000	8,000	28,000	7,000
Old Deferred Shareholders . . .			100,000	25,000
	52,000	£13,000	148,000	£37,000
After consolidation of 25p into £1 shares	13,000	£13,000	37,000	£37,000

Preference shares as reduced are 40,000 × 37½p = £15,000 represented by—

            32,000 Preference Shares of 25p each (a).
            28,000 Deferred Shares of 25p each (b).

(a) This involves an exchange of four new Preference Shares for five old.
(b) This involves an exchange of seven new Deferred Shares for ten old Preference Shares.

[1] Calculation as follows: $\frac{81,250}{127,950}$ × £89,700 = £56,961.

∴ Net amount on Balance Sheet is £81,250 − £56,961 = £24,289.

[2] Calculation as follows: $\frac{46,700}{127,950}$ × £89,700 = £32,739.

∴ Net amount on Balance Sheet is £46,700 − £32,739 = £13,961.

48.

BLANK CO. LTD.

Dr.   REALIZATION ACCOUNT   Cr.

19..		£	19..		£
Nov. 30	To Patents . . .	12,000	Nov. 30	By Creditors . . .	14,000
	„ Plant and Machinery	4,000		„ Blank Co. (19..) Ltd.	
	„ Stock . . .	3,000		Purchase Consideration	6,050
	„ Debtors . . .	5,000		„ Sundry Members—	
	„ Expenses of Liquidation .	175		Loss on Realization .	4,125
		£24,175			£24,175

The remaining accounts (not required as part of answer) are dealt with as follows—

Dr.   CASH   Cr.

19..		£	19..		£
Nov. 30	To Balance . . .	125	Nov. 30	By Realization Account—	
	„ Blank Co. (19..) Ltd. .	50		Expenses of Liquidation	175

Dr.   CREDITORS   Cr.

19..		£	19..		£
Nov. 30	To Realization Account	14,000	Nov. 30	By Balances . . . b/d	14,000

Dr.   BLANK CO. (19..) LTD.   Cr.

19..		£	19..		£
Nov. 30	To Realization Account	6,050	Nov. 30	By Shares (Sundry Members) .	6,000
				„ Cash	50

Dr.   SUNDRY MEMBERS   Cr.

19..		£	19..		£
Nov. 30	To Preliminary Expenses	725	Nov. 30	By Share Capital . . .	12,000
	„ Profit and Loss Account .	1,150			
	„ Loss on Realization .	4,125			
	„ Shares in Blank Co. (19..)				
	Ltd. . . .	6,000			
		£12,000			£12,000

The purchase consideration—apart from the discharge of liabilities—is as follows—

	£
Shares	6,000
Defrayment of Costs of Liquidation	175
	6,175
Less Cash retained by Vendor [as would be done in practice] . .	125
	£6,050

Books of Blank Co. (19. .) Ltd.—

JOURNAL

19..		£	£
Nov. 30	Patents . . . . *Dr.*	4,600	
	Plant and Machinery . . . . *Dr.*	4,000	
	Stock . . . . *Dr.*	3,000	
	Debtors. . . . . . . *Dr.*	5,000	
	To Blank Co. Ltd.		6,050
	,, Creditors (£14,000 − £3,450) . .		10,550
	Being assets and liabilities taken over as per agreement dated........................		
	Blank Co. Ltd. . . . . . *Dr.*	6,050	
	To Share Capital		6,000
	,, Cash		50
	Being allotment of 12,000 shares of £1 each 50p paid and balance of cash to pay vendors' liquidation expenses.		
	Creditors . . . . . . *Dr.*	10,550	
	To 6% Debentures		6,900
	,, Cash		3,650
	Being issue of £6,900 Debentures and cash payment to creditors £200 in full, and 25p in £ on £13,800 in full settlement.		
	Allotment . . . . . . *Dr.*	6,000	
	To Share Capital		6,000
	Being 50p a share payable on allotment of 12,000 shares issued to vendors.		
	Cash . . . . *Dr.*	6,000	
	To Allotment		6,000
	Being 50p a share allotment money received on 12,000 shares.		

Dr.		CASH		*Cr.*	
19..		£	19..		£
Nov. 30	To Allotment . . .	6,000	Nov. 30	By Creditors . . .	3,650
				,, Liquidator of Blank Co.	
				,, (19..) Ltd. . .	50
				,, Balance . . . c/d	2,300
		£6,000			£6,000
Dec. 1	To Balance . . . b/d	2,300			

BLANK CO. (19. .) LTD.

BALANCE SHEET AT.................................

	£			£
Share Capital—		Fixed Assets—		
Authorized, Issued, and fully paid:		Patents	.	4,600
12,000 Shares of £1 each .	12,000	Plant and Machinery . .	.	4,000
6% Debentures . . .	6,900			
				8,600
		Current Assets—		
		Stock . . . £3,000		
		Debtors . . . 5,000		
		Cash at Bank . . 2,300		
				10,300
	£18,900			£18,900

[Alternatively, the Realization, Cash, Creditors and Blank Co. (19..) Ltd. accounts may be dealt with as follows—

Dr.	REALIZATION ACCOUNT				Cr.	
19..		£	19..			£
Nov. 30	To Patents	12,000	Nov. 30	By Blank Co. (19..) Ltd.—		
	„ Plant and Machinery	4,000		Purchase Consideration		16,725
	„ Stock	3,000		„ Creditors—		
	„ Debtors	5,000		Rebate of 25p in £ on		
	„ Cash	125		£13,800		3,450
	„ Expenses of Liquidation	175		„ Sundry Members—		
				Loss on Realization		4,125
		£24,300				£24,300

Dr.	CASH					Cr.	
19..		£	19..				£
Nov. 30	To Blank Co. (19..) Ltd.	3,825	Nov. 30	By Realization Account—			
				Expenses			175
				„ Creditors—	£		
				Full	200		
				25p in £ on			
				£13,800	3,450	3,650	
		£3,825					£3,825

Dr.	CREDITORS				Cr.	
19..		£	19..			£
Nov. 30	To Realization Account	3,450	Nov. 30	By Balances	b/d	14,000
	„ Cash	3,650				
	„ 6% Debentures	6,900				
		£14,000				£14,000

Dr.	BLANK CO. (19..) LTD.					Cr.
19..		£	19..			£
Nov. 30	To Realization Account	16,725	Nov. 30	By Shares		6,000
				„ Cash		3,825
				„ 6% Debentures[1]		6,900
		£16,725				£16,725

[1] Posted direct to Creditors.

The opening Journal entries of Blank Co. (19..) Ltd., would then be (ignoring narratives)—

JOURNAL

19..			£	£
Nov. 30	Sundry Assets (per previous Journal entry)	Dr.	16,600	
	Cash	Dr.	125	
	To Blank Co. Ltd.			16,725
	Blank Co. Ltd.	Dr.	12,900	
	To 6% Debentures			6,900
	„ Share Capital			6,000
	Allotment	Dr.	6,000	
	To Share Capital			6,000
	Cash		6,000	
	To Allotment			6,000
	Blank Co. Ltd.	Dr.	3,825	
	To Cash			3,825

49.   .... LTD. *(and reduced)*[1]

BALANCE SHEET AS AT...............................

		£	£
Authorized Capital—			
100,000 6% Cumulative Preference Shares of £1 each	£100,000		
100,000 10% Preferred Ordinary Shares of £1 each	100,000		
1,200,000 Ordinary Shares of 25p each	[2]300,000		
	£500,000		
Issued Share Capital—			
300,000 8% Cumulative Preference Shares of £1 each, fully paid	£300,000		
200,000 Ordinary Shares of £1 each, fully paid	200,000		
	£500,000		
Reduced by Order of the Court to—			
100,000 6% Cumulative Preference Shares of £1 each, fully paid	£100,000		
100,000 10% Preferred Ordinary Shares of £1 each, fully paid	100,000		
348,000 Ordinary Shares of 25p each fully paid	87,000		
	287,000		
Profit and Loss Account	£114,000		
Less Amount written off by Order of Court	114,000	—	
Sundry Creditors		100,000	
		£387,000	

	£	£	£
Fixed Assets—			
Buildings at cost, *less* Depreciation	£100,000		
Less Amount written off by Order of Court	10,000	90,000	
Plant at cost, *less* Depreciation	£80,000		
Less Amount written off by Order of Court	8,000	72,000	
			162,000
Current Assets—			
Stock		65,000	
Investments at Cost £170,000			
Less Amount written off by Order of Court	81,000	89,000	
Sundry Debtors		70,500	
Bank and Cash		500	225,000
			£387,000

[1] If the Court so orders, the words "and reduced" must be shown.
[2] Assumed Authorized Capital rearranged as above. Costs ignored.

JOURNAL

Date		£	£
	8% Cumulative Preference Share Capital (£1). *Dr.*	300,000	
	To 6% Cumulative Preference Share Capital (£1)		100,000
	„ 10% Preferred Ordinary Share Capital (£1)		100,000
	„ Ordinary Share Capital (25p) . . .		25,000
	„ Reduction of Capital Account[1] . .		75,000
	Being cancellation of 8% Cumulative Preference Share Capital under reduction of capital scheme and issue of shares in exchange per special resolution dated.............................. Court Order dated ...., *vide* Minute Book, p.		
	Ordinary Share Capital (£1) . . . *Dr.*	200,000	
	To Ordinary Share Capital (25p) . . .		50,000
	„ Reduction of Capital Account[1] . .		150,000
	Being cancellation of Ordinary Share Capital (£1) under reduction of capital scheme and issue of Ordinary Shares of 25p each, fully paid, in exchange per special resolution dated....................... Court Order dated................, *vide* Minute Book, p.		
	Reduction of Capital Account . . . *Dr.*	12,000	
	To Ordinary Share Capital (25p) . . .		12,000
	Being issue of 48,000 Ordinary Shares of 25p each, fully paid, in settlement of arrears of preference dividend of £48,000 per special resolution dated .... Court Order dated............, *vide* Minute Book, p.		
	Reduction of Capital Account . . . *Dr.*	157,500	
	To Profit and Loss Account . . .		114,000
	„ Buildings (10%)		10,000
	„ Plant (10%)		8,000
	„ Investments (15%)		25,500
	Being amounts written off assets under reduction of capital scheme per special resolution dated........ Court Order dated......................... *vide* Minute Book, p.		
	Reduction of Capital Account . . . *Dr.*	55,500	
	To Investments		55,500
	Being balance remaining on Reduction of Capital Account utilized to reduce further the value of investments.		

[1] Or Capital Reduction Account.

50. (*a*) Amalgamated Balance Sheet of A B Ltd.

			£					£
Share Capital	.	.	16,300	Sundry Assets	.	.	.	16,300

(*b*) Let A = Total value of assets of A Ltd.; and B = total value of assets of B Ltd.

$$A = 11,300 + \tfrac{1}{16} B$$
$$B = 5,000 + \tfrac{1}{10} A$$
$$\therefore \quad 10 B = 50,000 + 11,300 + \tfrac{1}{16} B$$
$$= 61,300 + \tfrac{1}{16} B$$
$$\therefore \quad 160 B = 980,800 + B$$
$$\therefore \quad 159 B = 980,800$$
$$\therefore \quad B = 6,168$$

As the sundry assets of B Ltd. amount to £5,000, the value attributable to its shareholding in A Ltd. is £1,168. The position therefore is—

				A Ltd. £						B Ltd, £
Sundry Assets	.	.	.	11,300	Sundry Assets	.	.	.	.	5,000
Add Liquidator of B Ltd.			.	385	*Add Liquidator of A Ltd.*	.	.			1,168
[$\tfrac{1}{16}$ *of B Ltd.*]					[$\tfrac{1}{10}$ *of A Ltd.*]					
				11,685						6,168
Less Liquidator of B Ltd.	.	.		1,168	*Less Liquidator of A Ltd.*	.	.			385
[$\tfrac{1}{10}$ *of A Ltd.*]					[$\tfrac{1}{16}$ *of B Ltd.*]					
				£10,517						£5,783

The Share Capital of the new company will be allocated (after eliminating intercompany holdings)—

A Ltd. . . . 10,517 to holders of 10,000 − 1,000 = 9,000 shares
B Ltd. . . . 5,783 to holders of 8,000 − 500 = 7,500 shares

Apart from the probable cash adjustment to bring A Shares down to 10,500, and B Shares up to 5,800, a schedule of individual share holdings would have to be prepared to deal with fractions. Subject to the above adjustment the exchange will be—
To A shareholders other than B Ltd., 105 A B Ltd. shares for 90 A Ltd. shares (i.e. 7 for 6).
To B shareholders other than A Ltd. 58 A B Ltd. shares for 75 B Ltd. shares.

51. (i) H LTD.

Dr. REALIZATION ACCOUNT *Cr.*

			£					£
To Assets per Question	.	.	220,000	By J Ltd.	.	.	.	155,000
„ Profit and Loss Account	.	.	30,000	„ Creditors	.	.	.	20,000
				„ Loss to Sundry Shareholders				
				(ordinary)	.	.	.	75,000
			£250,000					£250,000

Dr. SUNDRY SHAREHOLDERS *Cr.*

	Preference	Ordinary		Preference	Ordinary
	£	£		£	£
To Loss on Realization .		75,000	By Transfer from Share Capital . . .	50,000	150,000
„ Shares in J Ltd. (ordinary) . .	50,000	75,000			
	£50,000	£150,000		£50,000	£150,000

Dr.	DEBENTURE-HOLDERS		Cr.
	£		£
To Ordinary Shares in J Ltd. .	30,000	By Transfer from Debentures .	. 30,000

(ii)

J LTD.

JOURNAL

	£	£
Goodwill . . . . Dr.	45,000	
Sundry Assets . . . . . . Dr.	129,500	
Cash . . . . Dr.	500	
To Creditors		20,000
„ Liquidator H Ltd.		155,000
Assets and Creditors taken over as per agreement dated........................		
Liquidator H Ltd. . . . . Dr.	155,000	
To Ordinary Share Capital		
50p per share paid		125,000
„ Ordinary Share Capital fully paid .		30,000
Satisfaction of purchase consideration by allotment of 250,000 shares 50p paid and 30,000 shares fully paid as per minute dated....................................		
Cash . . . . Dr.	45,000	
To Ordinary Share Capital . . .		45,000
Subscription for cash by Directors for 45,000 shares fully paid.		
Creditors of H Ltd. . . . . Dr.	20,000	
To Cash		20,000
Cash paid in settlement of Creditors taken over.		

(iii)

BALANCE SHEET

	£		£
Authorized Capital—		Goodwill	45,000
325,000 Ordinary Shares of £1 each	325,000	Sundry Assets	129,500
		Cash (£500 + £45,000 − £20,000) .	25,500
Issued Share Capital—			
250,000 Shares of £1·50 paid . . £125,000			
75,000 Shares of £1 each, fully paid . . 75,000			
	200,000		
	£200,000		£200,000

Note. The purchase consideration is—

	£	
150,000 shares at 50p . .	75,000	for the Ordinary shareholders
100,000 shares at 50p . .	50,000	for the Preference shareholders
30,000 shares at £1 . .	30,000	for the Debenture-holders
	£155,000	

The net assets are valued at—

		£
Sundry Assets	. . . . .	129,500
Cash	. . . . . .	500
		130,000
Less Creditors	. . . . .	20,000
		110,000
Goodwill to Balance	. . . .	45,000
		£155,000

52.   OLD COMPANY BALANCE SHEET

	£		£
4% Debentures	10,000	Net Assets	7,000
		Revenue Account (Deficiency) . .	2,595
		Preliminary Expenses . . .	405
	£10,000		£10,000

The debentures of the old company are dealt with thus—

	£
Elected to be repaid	3,000
Elected to convert into shares of new company	2,500
Elected to convert into debentures of new company . . .	4,000
Balance to be repaid (in respect of "no replies") . . .	500
	£10,000

Issue by new company—

	Shares	Debentures
	£	£
Conversion	2,500	4,000
Subscription . . .	3,600	3,000
	£6,100	£7,000

NEW COMPANY BALANCE SHEET (*in skeleton form*)

	£	£		£
Issued Share Capital—			Net Assets (as taken over) . .	7,000
6,100 Shares of £1 each .	£6,100		Cash	2,900[1]
Less Calls in arrear .	200		Goodwill	3,000[2]
		5,900		
5% Debentures		7,000		
		£12,900		£12,900

[1] Cash being Shares paid for £3,400 plus Debentures subscribed and paid for £3,000, less repayment of Debentures of old Company, £3,500 = £2,900.

[2] The new Company discharges the old Debentures (and members' guarantees), involving a payment of £3,500, and the assumption of a liability of £6,500, equal to £10,000 against net assets acquired of £7,000, leaving £3,000 for Goodwill.

In addition, there will be the liability for three months' interest at 4 per cent per annum on the old Debentures of £10,000 (= £100), which could be added to Goodwill and brought in as a liability, or debited to Profit (or Loss) prior to incorporation.

The nature of the company's business is not stated and the use of the word "Revenue" Account is not conclusive, but probably the activities are those of a non-trading company.

53.   TRADING AND PROFIT AND LOSS ACCOUNT FOR THE YEAR
ENDED 31ST MARCH, 19.6

	£		£
Stock (Opening) . . .	2,720	Sales	39,110
Purchases	29,120	Stock (Closing)	6,590
Gross Profit . . . c/d	13,860		
	£45,700		£45,700
Wages and Salaries . .	4,100	Gross Profit . . . b/d	13,860
Other Expenses . . .	3,820	Profit on Consignment . .	135
Bad Debts Provision . .	2,160	Investment Income (gross) .	1,033
H.P. Interest . . .	345	Interest on Calls in arrear (gross)	12
Depreciation—			
Own Plant . . £647			
H.P. Plant . . 52			
	699		
Manager's Commission . .	261		
Net Profit to Appropriation A/c c/d	3,655		
	£15,040		£15,040

PROFIT AND LOSS APPROPRIATION ACCOUNT

	£			£
Transfer to General Reserve .	5,000	Net Profit . . . b/d		3,655
Taxation on Profit of Current Year	3.005	Balance . . b/f	£8,050	
Income Tax suffered on Franked Invest-		*Add* Taxation		
ment Income now written off .	413	Overprovision written back	900	
Proposed Dividend of 10% .	2,950			8,950
Balance . . . c/f	1,237			
	£12,605			£12,605

(*Draft*) BALANCE SHEET AS AT 31ST MARCH, 19.6

	£		£
Capital and Reserves—		Fixed Assets—	
Authorized Share Capital:		Plant at 1st April, 19.5 £6,467	
50,000 Shares of £1 each .	50,000	*Less* Depreciation 647	
			£5,820
Issued Capital:		H.P. Plant at cost . £1,040	
40,000 Shares of £1 each,		*Less* Depreciation 52	
75p called . £30,000			
Less Calls in arrear . 500			988
	29,500	*Deduct* present value	
General Reserve . . .	15,000	of remaining instal-	
Profit and Loss Account . .	1,237	ments . . 852	
	45,737		136
			5,956
		Investments at cost—	
		Quoted . . . £8,000	
Current Liabilities and Provisions—		Unquoted . . 1,000	
Trade Creditors, including Ac-			9,000
cruals . . £1,091		Current Assets—	
Provision for Taxation . 3,000		Stock on Hand . . £6,590	
Proposed Dividend (gross) 2,950		Debtors *less* Bad Debts Pro-	
	7,041	vision . . 9,502	
		Cash at Bank . . 21,730	
			37,822
	£52,778		£52,778

Notes (i). The rate charged on Hire Purchase is fantastically high.
(ii) No amount is shown for Directors' Fees, and if the item has been merged in "Other Expenses"
it should be deleted therefrom and shown as a separate item.
(iii) As Table A is adopted, the 10 per cent dividend is based on the paid-up Capital of £29,500.
(iv) Stock £6,590 (see page 558).

WORKING ACCOUNTS
GOODS ON CONSIGNMENT

	£			£
Per Trial Balance	720	Sales	.	900
Commission	45			
Profit and Loss . . .	135			

DEBTORS

		£			£
Per Trial Balance . . .	.	14,200	Hire-purchase Creditors . .	.	200
			Balance . . . c/d		14,000
Balance . . . . b/d		14,000			

SALES

		£			£
Goods on Sale or Return .	c/d	3,200	Per Trial Balance . . .	.	42,310
Trading Account . . .		39,110			
			Goods on Sale or Return . b/d		3,200

BAD DEBTS PROVISION

		£			£
Provision	c/d	2,160	Profit and Loss (20% of £10,800) .		2,160
			Provision . . . . b/d		2,160

TAXATION PROVISION

	£		£
Per Trial Balance . . .	9,100	Per Trial Balance . . .	10,000
Investment Income . . .	413	Profit and Loss Appropriation—	
Interest on Calls .	5	Income Tax on Investment	
Profit and Loss Appropriation—		Income written off . .	413
Overprovision written back .	900	Provision on current profits .	3,005
Balance	3,000		
	£13,418		£13,418
		Balance	£3,000

INVESTMENT INCOME

	£		£
Profit and Loss	1,033	Per Trial Balance . . .	620
		Taxation (40% on £1,033). .	413

INTEREST ON CALLS IN ARREAR

	£		£
Profit and Loss	12	Interest	12

DEBTORS RE INTEREST ON CALLS

	£			£
		Taxation (say) . . .	.	5
Interest on Calls in arrear . .	12	Balance	c/d	7
Balance . . . . b/d	7			

GENERAL RESERVE

		£		£
Balance	c/d	15,000	Per Trial Balance . . .	10,000
			Profit and Loss Appropriation .	5,000
			Balance . . . . b/d	15,000

CONSIGNEE

	£			£
Consignment Sales	900	Commission		45
		Balance	c/d	855
Balance	b/d 855			

CREDITORS

	£			£
Hire-purchase Creditor . . .	1,200	Per Trial Balance		2,030
Balance	c/d 830			
		Balance	b/d	830

H. P. CREDITOR

	£			£
Ex Debtors	200	Ex Creditors		1,200
Balance	c/d 1,000			
		Balance	b/d	1 000

PLANT

	£			£
Per Trial Balance	8,000	Hire-purchase Plant . .		1,533[1]
		Profit and Loss (10% of £6,467) .		647
		Balance	c/d	5,820
Balance	b/d 5,820			

H. P. PLANT

	£			£
Ex Plant	1,533	Hire-purchase Interest . . .		493
		Profit and Loss (5% of £1,040) .		52
		Balance	c/d	988
Balance	b/d 988			

H. P. INTEREST[2]

	£			£
Ex Hire-purchase Plant . . .	493	Profit and Loss		345
		Balance	c/d	148
Balance	b/d 148			

[1] It is assumed that the *whole* sum due had been debited to Plant.
[2] As the rate of interest is not given, the distribution of the interest may be made over the four quarters ended 30th September, 19.6, in the ratio of 4 : 3 : 2 : 1, i.e.—

					£
Quarter ended 31st December, 19.5:	$\frac{4}{10} \times £493$	.	.	.	197
Quarter ended 31st March, 19.6:	$\frac{3}{10} \times £493$	.	.	.	148
Quarter ended 30th June, 19.6:	$\frac{2}{10} \times £493$	.	.	.	99
Quarter ended 30th September, 19.6:	$\frac{1}{10} \times £493$	.	.	.	49
	(See below)	.	.	.	£493

Therefore £345 (£197 + £148) is the amount of H.P. Interest to be charged up in the accounts to 31st March, 19.6.

The total interest is the excess of £1,533 (i.e. the sum of the payments to be made under the H.P. contract) over £1,040 (i.e. the cash value).

The item of £1,533 is arrived at by reference to the account of the H.P. Creditor, which is £1,000 (after the transfer thereto of the deposit of £200). One instalment will have been paid (1st January, 19.6), so that three remain, hence each instalment is £333 and the total instalments £1,333. The liability under the H.P. contract is therefore £1,333 + £200 = £1,533.

A rough memo, H.P. Creditor Account could be built up, although in the examination time probably would not permit—

	H.P. Creditor 31st Dec., 19.5 £	31st Mar., 19.6 £	30th June, 19.6 £	30th Sept., 19.6 £	31st Dec. 19.6 £
Cost/Balance	1,040	1,037	852	618	334
Deposit/Instalment . . .	200	(1st) 333	(2nd) 333	(3rd) 333	(4th) 334
	840	704	519	285	—
Interest[1]	197	148	99	49	—
Balance forward . . .	£1,037	£852	£618	£334	—

The item boxed is shown in the Accounts, thus—

	£
Cr. H.P. Creditor	1,000
Dr. H.P. Interest Suspense	148
	£ 852

SCHEDULE OF DEBTORS

	£
General	14,000
Consignee	855
Interest on Calls . . .	7
	14,862
Less Goods on S. or R. . .	3,200
	11,662
Deduct Provision . . .	2,160
	£9,502

STATEMENT OF STOCK

	£
On hand	4,090
On S. or R.. . . .	2,500
	£6,590

CALCULATION OF MANAGER'S COMMISSION

	£			£
Profit	3,655	or Gross Profit	.	13,860
Add Manager's Commission . .	261	Profit on Consignment . .	.	135
	3,916			13,995

	£			£
Less Investment Income . .	1,033		Less Expenses, etc.—	
Interest on Calls in Arrear .	12		First five items in P. and L.:	
	1,045		[£4,100 + £3,820 + £2,160	
Profit for purpose of Commission and			+ £345 + £699] . . .	11,124
subject thereto . . .	£2,871			£2,871

Commission $\frac{10}{110}$ × £2,871 = £261

Excluding the Investment Income and Interest on Calls in Arrear, the net profit *after* charging Manager's Commission is £2,612 (£3,655 − £1,045), so that the Manager's Commission is 10 per cent thereof = £261.

[1] If calculated mathematically, the interest at 21½ per cent per quarter is allocated £182, £148, £106, and £57 for the four successive quarters.

54.   SUMMARY

Shares Applied for	Amount Paid	Shares Allotted	Amount Due on Application and Allotment	Cash Due and Paid	Amount Due on Call	Cash Due and Paid	Cash Repayable
	£		£	£	£	£	£
600	600	300	225	—	75	—	300
23,050	5,762½	11,200	8,400	2,637½	2,800	2,800	—
64,000	16,000	8,500	6,375	—	2,125	—	7,500
87,650	£22,362½	20,000	£15,000	£2,637½	£5,000	£2,800	£7,800

Dr.   CASH   *Cr.*

	£		£
To Application and Allotment—		By Application and Allotment—	
Application Moneys	22,362½	Application Moneys returned	7,800
Allotment Moneys	2,637½	,, Balance c/d	20,000
,, Call Moneys	2,800		
	£27,800		£27,800

Dr.   APPLICATION AND ALLOTMENT   *Cr.*

	£		£
To Call Account—		By Cash—	
Calls in advance	2,200	Application	22,362½
,, Cash returned	7,800	Allotment	2,637½
,, Share Capital	15,000		
	£25,000		£25,000

Dr.   CALL   *Cr.*

	£		£
To Share Capital	5,000	By Application and Allotment	2,200
		,, Cash	2,800
	£5,000		£5,000

Dr.   SHARE CAPITAL   *Cr.*

	£		£
To Balance c/d	20,000	By Application and Allotment (75p)	15,000
		,, Call (25p)	5,000
	£20,000		£20,000

55. (i)   JOURNAL

Date		£	£
	Capitals—		
	Penn . . . . *Dr.*	10,000	
	Mass	8,000	
	To Vendors		18,000
	Elimination of vendors' capital accounts. . .		
	Vendors . . . . *Dr.*	10,000	
	To Share Capital (Ordinary)		10,000
	Transfer to Share Capital Account of amounts subscribed.		
	Creditors' Suspense . . . . . *Dr.*	6,100	
	Provision for Bad Debts	500	
	Bank	3,679[1]	
	Goodwill	8,921[2]	
	To Debtors' Suspense		7,200
	„ Vendors		12,000
	Elimination of items appertaining to Vendors and introduction of Goodwill arising out of purchase agreement dated....................		
	Vendors . . . . *Dr.*	20,000	
	To Share Capital—		
	Ordinary		10,000
	5% Preference		10,000
	Discharge of purchase consideration by allotment of 10,000 5% Preference Shares of £1 each and 20,000 Ordinary Shares of 50p each, all fully paid.		
	Debtors' Suspense . . . . . *Dr.*	610	
	To Discounts Allowed		450
	„ Bad Debts		160
	Discounts Received . . . . . *Dr.*	280	
	To Creditors' Suspense		280
	Transfer of Discounts and Bad Debts relating to Vendors' Debtors and Creditors.		
	Vendors . . . . *Dr.*	960[3]	
	Debtors' Suspense	4,860[3]	
	To Creditors' Suspense		5,820[3]
	Vendors' Creditors paid off out of amounts received from Vendors' Debtors and balance debited to Vendors.		
	Directors' Fees . . . . . *Dr.*	1,333	
	To Drawings Account—		
	Penn		667
	Mass		666
	Fees for the seven months from incorporation credited to Drawings Accounts.		

[1] The position at 31st December, 19.4 was—

		Dr. £	Cr. £
Capital: Penn . . .			5,000
Mass . . .			3,000
Debtors and Creditors .		7,200	6,100
Bad Debts Provision .			500
Plant		2,000	
Furniture . . .		1,100	
Stock		7,979	
Bank Overdraft . .			3,679
		£18,279	£18,279

[3] See note on page 562.

[2] Purchase consideration . .		£ . 20,000
Less Assets taken over—		
Stock . . .	£7,979	
Plant . . .	2,000	
Furniture . .	1,100	
		11,079
Goodwill . . .		£8,921

(ii) *Dr.* VENDORS *Cr.*

	£		£
To Share Capital—		By Transfer from Capitals . .	18,000
20,000 Ordinary Shares of 50p		,, Creditors' Suspense . .	6,100[2]
subscribed in cash at par .	10,000	,, Bad Debts Provision . .	500
20,000 Ordinary Shares of 50p		,, Bank (overdraft) . . .	3,679
issued as fully paid for purchase		,, Goodwill	8,921
consideration . .	10,000		
10,000 5% Preference Shares of			
£1 issued as fully paid for pur-			
chase consideration .	10,000		
,, Debtors' Suspense . (1) .	7,200		
	£37,200		£37,200
To Creditors' Suspense . (2) .	5,820	By Debtors' Suspense . .	4,860[1]
		,, Balance . . . c/d	960
	£5,820		£5,820
To Balance . . . . b/d	960		

(iii) ALLOCATION OF SHARES

			Penn	Mass	Total
			£	£	£
Capitals at 31st December, 19.4 . .			5,000	3,000	8,000
Profit on Sale—					
Goodwill . . .	£8,921				
Bad Debts Provision .	£500				
Less Bad Debts incurred .	160				
		340			
		9,261			
Less Discounts allowed .	£450				
Less Discounts received .	280				
		170			
		£9,091	4,546	4,545	9,091
			9,546	7,545	17,091
Allocation of Shares in Penn and Mass Ltd.—					
5% Preference			⅝£6,250	⅜£3,750	£10,000
Ordinary			½ 5,000 11,250	½ 5,000 8,750	10,000 20,000
Balances (debit) (see page 562) . .			£1,704	£1,205	£2,909

(1) *Dr.* DEBTORS' SUSPENSE *Cr.*

		£		£
To Discounts allowed		450	By Vendors	7,200
,, Bad Debts		160		
,, Vendors		4,860		
,, Balance . . . c/d		1,730		
		£7,200		£7,200
			By Balance . . . b/d	1,730

(2) *Dr.* CREDITORS' SUSPENSE *Cr.*

	£		£
To Vendors	6,100	By Discounts received . . .	280
		,, Vendors	5,820
	£6,100		£6,100

The partnership position at 31st December, 19.5, is—

	£	£
Penn and Mass (as on page 561)	2,909	
Debtors still outstanding (per Debtors' Suspense on page 561).	1,730	
Penn and Mass Ltd. (per Vendors' Account in (ii) on page 561)		960
Bank overdraft		3,679
	£4,639	£4,639

Assuming that the remaining debts are collected intact (i.e. no bad debts and discounts), the company will pay the partners £770 (£1,730 − £960) which, with £1,704 from Penn and £1,205 from Mass, will discharge the overdraft (interest thereon being ignored).

Debit side — Trading and Profit and Loss Account

	Pre-incorporation £	Post-incorporation £	Total £
Stock (Opening)			7,979
Purchases			27,118
Gross Profit c/d			13,717
			£48,814
Wages and Salaries	963[1]	1,927	2,890
General Expenses	210[1]	421	631
Rent and Rates	128[1]	256	384
Depreciation of Plant	67[1]	133	200
Discounts allowed [£674 — £450]	112[2]	112	224
Bad Debts written off or provided for [£624 — £160 + £1,422]	943[2]	943	1,886
Advertising	500[2]	499	999
Directors' Fees		1,333[3]	1,333
Net Profit	4,158	1,456	5,614
	£7,081	£7,080	£14,161

Credit side

	Pre-incorporation £	Post-incorporation £	Total £
Sales			29,161
Stock (Closing)			19,653
			£48,814
Gross Profit	6,859[2]	6,358	13,717
Discounts received [£724 — £280]	222[2]	222	444
	£7,081	£7,080	£14,161

[1] Apportioned on time basis 1:2.   [2] Apportioned on weighted average per question 2 × 1:2.   [3] Wholly post-incorporation.

BALANCE SHEET AT 31ST DECEMBER, 19.5

	£	£
Share Capital—Authorized and Issued:		
10,000 5% Preference Shares of £1 each, fully paid	10,000	
40,000 Ordinary Shares of 50p each, fully paid	20,000	
		30,000
Capital Reserve—Pre-incorporation Profit		4,158
Profit and Loss Account		1,456
		35,614
Current Liabilities—		
Creditors		8,364
		£43,978

	£	£
Fixed Assets at Cost—		
Goodwill		8,921
Plant and Machinery	2,000	
Less Depreciation	200	1,800
Furniture and Fixtures		1,100
		11,821
Current Assets—		
Stock		19,653
Debtors (less Bad Debts Provision, £1,422)		8,058
Directors' Drawings Account:		
Drawings	£1,900	
Less Fees	1,333	567
Vendors (Debt Settlement)[1]		960
Cash at Bank and in hand		2,519
		31,757
Preliminary Expenses		400
		£43,978

[1] See page 561 for Vendors' Account.

56. TRIAL BALANCE AT 30TH SEPTEMBER, 19.8

	Profit and Loss		Balance Sheet	
	Dr. £	Cr. £	Assets £	Liabilities £
Share Capital—				
Preference				100,000
Ordinary				25,000
Calls in arrears			150	
Share Premium Account . . .				12,500
Freehold Premises			96,200	
Plant and Machinery . . .			28,350	
Plant and Machinery sold—				
Written down Value				1,440
Proceeds (Debtor)			1,750	
Profit thereon		310		
Rent and Rates (Office)	1,627			
Office Salaries	5,340			
Stock, September, 19.8			62,835	
Directors' Emoluments paid . . .	8,250			
Directors' Fees due	250			250
Travellers' Salaries, etc.	4,863			
Cash on Hand			124	
Balance at Bank			10,777	
Insurance	426			
Sundry Debtors			22,950	
Bad Debts	750			750
Bad Debts Provision . . .	1,110	600		1,110
Goodwill			10,000	
General Reserve				15,000
Sundry Creditors				8,786
Motor Lorries			3,100	
Motor Lorries, Depreciation . . .	400			
Motor Lorries, Running Expenses . .	2,372			
Office Furniture			800	
Loose Tools			1,246	
Profit and Loss Balance . . .				6,352
Manufacturing Account . . .		43,172		
Preference Dividend	6,000			
Income Tax on Preference Dividend .				2,400
Corporation Tax	4,700			4,700 (Future) 5,500 (Current)
Debentures				48,000
Discounts on Debentures . . .	1,500			
Debenture Interest	1,250			750
Income Tax on Debenture Interest . .				500
	38,838	44,082	238,282	233,038
Balance (Profit)	5,244			5,244
	£44,082	£44,082	£238,282	£238,282

Notes. (1) In the absence of further information, Motor Lorries have been written down by £400 to £3,100 (their value at 30th September, 19.8). Normal depreciation should be written off.

(2) A transfer from Profit and Loss to General Reserve, representing the redemption of £2,000 Debentures, is advisable, but in the absence of covenant in the Debenture deed, is not legally necessary

(3) The profit on Sale of Plant is £1,750, less written-down value of Plant sold (£1,600 less £160 depreciation), £1,440. It is not clear from the question whether cash has been received from the sale of this Plant, and so the amount is treated as a debtor.

(4) It is assumed that the balance of Manufacturing Account means balance of that account *and* Trading Account.

(5) The Bad Debts Provision is 5 per cent of £22,200 (£22,950 — £750), ignoring debtor for sale of Plant.

57.   TRIAL BALANCE, 30TH JUNE, 19.4

	Dr.	Cr.
Goodwill	500	
Land and Buildings	5,000	
Plant and Machinery	4,500	
Fixtures and Fittings	700	
Stock-in-trade	1,800	
Preference Share Capital—		
4,000 Shares fully paid		4,000
10,000 Shares, 75p called		7,500
Ordinary Share Capital—7,500 shares fully paid		7,500
Calls in Advance		250
Calls in Arrears	62½	
Share Premium Account		1,250
Underwriting Commission	500	
Purchases and Sales	24,000	56,000
Wages	17,000	
Discounts		450
Preliminary Expenses	250	
Commission		71¼
Miscellaneous Expenses	4,000	
Debtors, new	3,400	
Debtors, old	600	
Debtors Suspense		600
Creditors		2,100
Cash at Bank	16,508¾	
	£79,271¼	£79,271¼

Dr.		CASH		Cr.	
	£				£
To Preference Share Capital (Allotment and Calls)	8,687½	By Vendor			5,000
„ Calls in advance	250	„ Creditors			21,900
„ Debts collected for Vendor	2,850	„ Wages			17,000
„ Vendor re Ordinary Shares	721¼	„ Miscellaneous Expenses			4,000
„ Debtors	52,150	„ Preliminary Expenses			250
		„ Balance		c/d	16,508¾
	£64,658¾				£64,658¾
To Balance	b/d 16,508¾				

Dr.		VENDORS (PURCHASE OF BUSINESS)		Cr.	
	£				£
To Cash, etc.	1,000	By Balance			14,900
„ Debtors	3,600	„ Goodwill			500
„ Balance to Settlement Account	12,500	„ Creditors			1,700
	£17,100				£17,100

Dr.		VENDORS (SETTLEMENT)		Cr.	
	£				£
To Cash	5,000	By Balance from Purchase of Business			12,500
„ Share Capital—		„ Cash			721¼
(Ordinary)	3,500	„ Debtors			3,000
(Preference)	4,000				
(Ordinary)	3,500				
„ Collecting Commission	71¼				
„ Discount	150				
	£16,221¼				£16,221¼

58. (i) The Balance Sheet and accounts may be considered from the point of view of accounting principles and legal requirements (as contained in the Companies Acts 1948 and 1967) as follows—

Liabilities Side of Balance Sheet—

(1) Layout unsatisfactory and not in accordance with modern practice and law. The items should be grouped under appropriate heading, e.g. Capital and Reserves long- and short-term liabilities.

(2) Authorized and issued capital must be shown (under separate headings) with details of the various classes and denomination of the shares, the called-up capital and calls in advance and in arrear; also details relating to redeemable preference shares if any giving earliest and latest dates for redemption and stating whether such redemption is optional or mandatory and the premium, if any, payable on redemption.

(3) The debenture figure should be shown as £65,000; and £6,500 shown separately as an "asset" until written off.

(4) If the debentures are secured on any of the assets, the fact must be disclosed.

(5) If any debentures have been redeemed and may be reissued, details must be disclosed.

(6) If the Bank loan is secured the fact must be stated. If the loan is a current liability—as appears very likely—the amount must be grouped as such. No Bank Interest appears in the Profit and Loss account.

(7) As no item for debenture interest appears in the Profit and Loss Account and the amount in the Balance Sheet is in respect of a half-year's interest, gross (£65,000 at 10 per cent per annum for half-year), it can only be guessed that the first half-year's interest has been paid and debited to some account other than Debenture Interest (unless the debentures were raised during the year). The gross amount should appear in the Profit and Loss Account.

(8) The half-year debenture interest gross of £3,250 shown in the Balance Sheet is arithmetically correct but strictly the net amount due of £1,950 should be included with Creditors and the Taxes Act Sect. 53 liability shown separately as a Current Liability. The provision for taxes appears inadequate. Without details of past losses and profits the taxation position cannot be ascertained, but in any case a minimum "Sect. 53 liability" will be required of £6,500 at, say, 40 per cent = £1,300 representing the liability in the current year in respect of Income Tax deducted from debenture interest. The liability for Corporation Tax would, as regards 19.8–9 and 19.0–1, be based on the adjusted profit of the year ended 31st December, 19.7 and 19.0–1 (subject to the business acquired on 1st January being treated as a new business). In every case where a business is converted into a limited company it must be assessed as if discontinued and recommenced on the date of succession; there is no option. The profits of the company, in this instance, for the accounting period 1st January, 19.7 (commencement date) to 31st December, 19.7 (the end of the company's first financial year) are liable to Corporation Tax computed on the basis of the relative proportions falling within two taxation Financial Years (for Corporation Tax purposes a financial year is the 1st April in one year to 31st March in the following year, e.g. the financial year 19.6 means the year commencing 1st April, 19.6 and ending 31st March, 19.7). Corporation Tax rates are determined for each financial year. Therefore the total profits of year ended 31st December, 19.7 are liable to Corporation Tax, as follows:

Financial Year 19.6 ($\frac{3}{12}$ths × Total taxable profits)

at Financial Year 19.6 C.T. Rate

Financial Year 19.7 ($\frac{9}{12}$ths × Total taxable profits)

at Financial Year 19.7 C.T. Rate

In the case of companies commencing trading on or after 1st April, 1965 Corporation Tax is payable within nine months from the end of the accounting period for which it is assessed. Corporation Tax on the profits of the accounting year ended 31st December, 19.7 is payable on or before 30th September, 19.8 (it being assumed that 19.7 is after 1st April, 1965). Since the Corporation Tax is due and payable not later than one year after Balance Sheet date the normal practice is to include the liability separately under Current Liabilities.

(9) The item for proposed dividend deducted from the Profit and Loss Account is correctly shown gross but preferably should be stated as such and should be shown separately under Current Liabilities. Since a *proposed* dividend is not yet due and payable no Income Tax Schedule F liability arises thereon until it is *declared*.

(10) If left as a reserve its revenue or capital nature need not be distinguished. The fact that capital reserves and revenue reserves need not be distinguished does not affect what is legally distributable or not legally distributable, or what the directors determine is distributable or not distributable. Generally the aggregate amount of reserves, where substantial, should be classified under headings appropriate to the business of the company. Share Premium Account, and special reserve accounts such as Capital Redemption Reserve Fund and Debenture Redemption Reserve should, however, be shown separately.

(11) The item of Reserve appears to be the provision for Bad Debts. (See Assets, para. (6).) If left as a reserve its revenue or capital need not be disclosed.

(12) Corresponding figures of the previous Balance Sheet (and Profit and Loss Account) are not required since this is the first year of the company.

Assets Side of Balance Sheet—

(1) Layout is unsatisfactory and not in accordance with modern practice and law.

(2) Fixed, Current and neither Fixed nor Current Assets must be separated, and the items grouped under appropriate headings.

(3) The method of valuing the fixed assets, e.g. less accumulated depreciation, which must be separately shown, is not stated.

(4) Division of investments is required into (*a*) Subsidiaries (there appears to be at least one subsidiary); (*b*) quoted investments with note as to market value; and (*c*) unquoted investments.

(5) The fact and amount of the write-up of investments must be disclosed. The sum shown as appreciation seems unjustified, although the mere absence of dividends will not be incompatible with an appreciation in the value of the investments. The appreciation should be identified with each class of holding (see para. (4)).

(6) Debtors should be shown net after deduction of Bad Debts Provision, and the latter does not appear in the Balance Sheet as an identifiable item. In any case, the amount of debtors in relation to the actual sales is exceptionally large, suggesting the existence of non-trading or old unpaid debts, thus throwing doubt on the adequacy of the Bad Debts Provision (see Liabilities, para. (10)).

(7) Calls in arrear should be deducted from Share Capital. The question of interest thereon should be examined.

(8) In view of the trading figures the Stock item is excessive, whilst nothing is shown for Raw Materials and the amount of Work in Progress does not appear in the Profit and Loss Account. There is an unexplained difference of £10,000 between the Balance Sheet and Profit and Loss stock figures.

(9) The manner in which stock and work in progress is computed should be stated.

(10) Loans to Directors should be shown thus—

						£	
Amount advanced during year	.	.	.	£2,900			
Less repaid	.	.	.	.	.	1,200	
						———	1,700

The legality of the loan should be examined in the light of sect. 190, Companies Act 1948.

(11) The item of Suspense requires examination—with a company preparing such accounts it might even indicate an "out of balance" item.

(12) The cash on hand appears high compared with the Bank figure; the two items may have been "crossed."

Balance Sheet—General

The Balance Sheet should be signed by two directors of the company or one if there is only one.

Profit and Loss Account—Credit Side—

(1) Sales are extremely small.

(2) The credits for the appreciation of Goodwill and Investments do not form part of the trading profit. The full circumstances require examination. Such credits *may* form part of the divisible profits (*Stapley* v. *Read Bros.*), but the *Lubbock* and *Foster* rules must also be considered, particularly as it does not seem that these are realized profits.

(3) The item of forfeited shares if "final," i.e. remaining after the forfeited shares have been reissued and fully paid, may be considered as part of the distributable profit (unless the Articles forbid), but it does not form part of the trading profit.

(4) If the company was formed to take over the business of K. Watt as from 1st January, 19.7, the question of profit or loss prior to incorporation might arise. Any such profit should be shown as a Capital Reserve, unless it has been used to write off Preliminary Expenses or write down Goodwill.

Profit and Loss Account—Debit Side—

(1) The arrangement and order are unsatisfactory.

(2) Since the accounts are intended for presentation to the shareholders only the *legal* Profit and Loss Account is required. That is the detailed Manufacturing and Trading items need not be disclosed. The Profit and Loss Account can commence with the trading profit for the year after adjusting for all debit and credit items which require to be shown and have been debited and credited in arriving at the trading profit. "To" and "By" prefixes are no longer shown in final accounts.

(3) Details of Directors' Fees must be given, showing the amounts received from Subsidiary Companies and details of fees, other emoluments, etc., e.g.—

Directors' Emoluments:

Fees	£2,300	
Salaries	2,200	
	£4,500	
Less paid by subsidiary company . .	1,300	
		£3,200

An adjustment of £1,300 may now be necessary either to Suspense or Subsidiary Company Current Account.

(4) There is no mention of Bank or Debenture interest, ground rent, Taxation, auditors' remuneration, or depreciation.

(5) There is a charge for rent, which is not consistent with the ownership of the property indicated in the Balance Sheet, although there may also be rented premises.

(6) The opening Stock plus Purchases, Carriage, Wages (even if all the latter apply to manufacture) do not amount to the closing stock, so that the stock is over-rated, yet the Balance Sheet contains the item of Work in Progress (which may be a collection of Raw Material, Work in Progress, and Finished Goods). The item for Stock on the credit side of the Profit and Loss Account differs from that in the Balance Sheet by £10,000.

Notes on the Accounts (forming part of the Published Accounts) are required as follows:

(*a*) Balance Sheet—

(1) The number, description and amount of any shares which anyone has an option to subscribe for with the following particulars—

(i) the period during which it is exercisable;

(ii) the price to be paid for those shares.

(2) Particulars of any charge on the company's assets to secure the liabilities of any other person, including, where practicable, the amount secured.

(3) The general nature of any material contingent liabilities and their aggregated amount or estimated amount.

(4) The aggregate amount or estimated amount, where material, of contracts for capital expenditure and the aggregate amount or estimated amount, where material, of capital expenditure authorized by the directors.

(5) If fixed assets (other than unquoted investments) have been valued during the year, the amount and basis of valuation should be stated together with the names or qualifications of the valuers.

(6) The aggregate amount of fixed assets acquired during the year and of assets disposed of or destroyed during the year.

(7) Land and Buildings should be classified and quantified as to freehold and lease-hold and the leasehold should be further classified and quantified as to that held on long lease (over 50 years) and that held on short lease.

(8) Any current assets which, in the opinion of the directors, have a realizable value, in the ordinary course of business, which is less than the amount at which they are stated.

(9) The basis on which Corporation Tax is computed.

(b) Profit and Loss Account—

(1) The turnover of the year and the method by which it is computed.

(2) The fact that depreciation has not been provided in respect of fixed assets.

(3) The emoluments of the company chairman during his period as chairman, unless his duties as chairman were wholly or mainly discharged outside the United Kingdom. If more than one person has been chairman during the year the emoluments of each should be shown.

(4) The number of directors in any of the following bands:

(i) up to £2,500 a year;

(ii) over £2,500 but not over £5,000 a year.

(iii) Emoluments of the highest paid director where he is not also the chairman.

(These requirements do not apply to any director whose duties, as such, were discharged wholly or mainly outside the United Kingdom.)

(5) The number of directors who have waived rights to receive emoluments and the aggregate amount so waived.

(ii) *Comment on the Company's Position—*

(1) As stated in para. (6) above, the stock is obviously over-valued, and the Company's trading position as a whole requires careful examination.

(2) No estimate can be made of the working capital without the true Stock figures, but assuming the debtors are good, apart from the provision, the liquid position is—

		£
Debtors (£29,039 − £620)	. . . .	28,419
Cash .	. . . . .	2,200
Directors' Loans .	. . . . .	1,700
		£32,319

To this might be added those investments that are readily realizable (investments in subsidiaries must be excluded).

Against such liquid creditors are £20,450 plus proposed dividend £5,000, plus proper provision for Corporation Tax.

Apart from the question of whether there are profits available for distribution (this being dependent on the various matters referred to above), the liquid position hardly warrants the payment of a dividend. The cost to the Company of the proposed dividend of 2 per cent will be £5,000. (The dividend is being calculated on £250,000 of Share Capital, although an unspecified number of shares are not fully paid.)

(3) The company's position appears to be thoroughly unsatisfactory, and there is a complete failure to present proper accounts from which some reliable interpretation can be made.

(4) The item of Land and Buildings might provide (if it is fairly valued) possibilities for long-term finance, assuming that the asset is not already charged. The premises may be too large and the possibility of the company's selling the property and either renting or acquiring more modest premises might be important.

(5) The Reports of the Directors and Auditors (the latter likely to be qualified) and a Consolidated Balance Sheet and Profit and Loss Account are required by the Companies Acts 1948 and 1967 (unless exempted in special circumstances), and would probably help to throw more light on the position.

59. *Books of Drie Ltd.—*

Dr.   SUNDRY SHAREHOLDERS   *Cr.*

	£		£
To Profit and Loss Account . .	7,000	By Share Capital . . .	30,000
,, Cash	29,200	,, Realization Account . .	6,200
	£36,200		£36,200

Dr.   REALIZATION ACCOUNT   *Cr.*

	£		£
To Fixed Assets	37,000	By Leasehold Redemption Fund . .	3,000
,, Current Assets . . .	5,000	,, Gonnedrie Ltd.—	
,, Sundry Shareholders: Profit .	6,200	Net Purchase consideration .	45,000
		,, Profit on Discharge of Creditors	200
	£48,200		£48,200

Dr.   CREDITORS   *Cr.*

	£		£
To Cash	15,800	By Balances	16,000
,, Realization Account . .	200		

Dr.   GONNEDRIE LTD.   *Cr.*

	£		£
To Realization Account . .	45,000	By Cash	45,000

Dr.   CASH   *Cr.*

	£		£
To Gonnedrie Ltd. . . .	45,000	By Creditors	15,800
		,, Sundry Shareholders . .	29,200

ANALYSIS OF PAYMENTS TO SUNDRY SHAREHOLDERS

		Shares	£
(1) Gonne Ltd.		3,000	2,920
(2) Remainder		27,000	26,280
		30,000	£29,200

Books of Gonne Ltd.—

Dr.   SUNDRY SHAREHOLDERS   *Cr.*

	£		£
To Cash	89,420	By Share Capital . . .	50,000
		,, Debenture Redemption Fund .	5,000
		,, Profit and Loss Account . .	9,000
		,, Realization Account . .	25,420
	£89,420		£89,420

Dr.   REALIZATION ACCOUNT   *Cr.*

	£		£
To Fixed Assets	51,000	By Gonnedrie Ltd.—	
,, Current Assets . . .	33,400	Gross Purchase consideration	110,000
,, Shares in Drie Ltd. . .	3,600	,, Profit on Discharge of Creditors	500
,, Sundry Shareholders: Profit. .	25,420	,, Liquidator of Gonne Ltd., *re* Payment on 3,000 Shares . .	2,920
	£113,420		£113,420

Dr.   5 PER CENT DEBENTURES   *Cr.*

	£		£
To Gonnedrie Ltd.	10,000	By Balance	10,000

Dr.   CREDITORS   *Cr.*

	£		£
To Cash	13,500	By Balances	14,000
„ Realization Account . .	500		

Dr.   GONNEDRIE LTD.   *Cr.*

	£		£
To Realization Account . .	110,000	By Debentures	10,000
		„ Cash	100,000

Dr.   CASH   *Cr.*

	£		£
To Gonnedrie Ltd. . . .	100,000	By Creditors	13,500
„ Liquidator of Drie Ltd. .	2,920	„ Sundry Shareholders . .	89,420
	£102,920		£102,920

Notes. (i) Costs ignored.
(ii) Assumed no Debenture Interest or Taxation outstanding.
(iii) Assumed that all formalities and consents in order.
(iv) It is noted that the method of amalgamation is unusual and the question of the new capital of the amalgamated company is ignored.

60. *Dr.*   4½ PER CENT DEBENTURES   *Dr.*

19.4		£	19.4		£
Apr. 1	To Debentures Redemption Account . .	168,000	Jan. 1	By Balance . . b/d	259,000
June 30	Debentures Redemption Account . .	91,000			

Dr.   OWN DEBENTURES   *Cr.*

		Nominal				Nominal	
19.4		£	£	19.4		£	£
Jan. 1	To Balance b/d	141,000	126,900	Apr. 1	By Debentures Redemption Account	50,000	52,500
Apr. 1	„ Reserve: Profit on 50,000 Debentures redeemed of 15p each .		7,500	June 30	„ Debentures Redemption Account	91,000	91,000
June 30	„ Reserve: Profit on 91,000 Debentures redeemed of 10p each		9,100				
		£141,000	£143,500			£141,000	£143,500

Dr.   DEBENTURES REDEMPTION ACCOUNT   *Cr.*

19.4		£	19.4		£
Apr. 1	To Own Debentures— 50,000 Debentures redeemed ex own holding at £1·05 . . .	52,500	Apr. 1	By 4½% Debentures— 168,000 Debentures cancelled . . .	168,000
	„ Cash: 118,000 Debentures redeemed at £1·10 .	129,800		„ Reserve: Premium on Debentures cancelled: 50,000 at 5p . 118,000 at 10p .	2,500 11,800
		£182,300			£182,300
June 30	To Own Debentures— 91,000 Debentures redeemed ex own holding	£91,000	June 30	By 4½% Debentures— 91,000 Debentures cancelled . . .	£91,000

Dr.   DEBENTURE INTEREST   *Cr.*

19.4		£	19.4		£
Apr. 1	To Cash— Three months' Interest on £118,000 Debentures held by persons other than the company .	1,327½	Apr. 1	By Profit and Loss Account .	1,327½

Dr.   RESERVE   *Cr.*

19.4			£	19.4			£
Apr. 1	To Debentures Redemption Account— Premium on Debentures cancelled:			Apr. 1	By Own Debentures— Profit . . (*a*).		7,500
	(*a*) 50,000 at 5p .		2,500		„ Profit and Loss Account: Net Cost of redeeming 50,000 Debentures .		45,000
	(*b*) 118,000 at 10p .		11,800		„ Cost of 118,000 Debentures purchased for Redemption .		129,800
June 30	„ Balance . . c/d		259,000	June 30	„ Own Debentures— Profit . . (*a*)		9,100
					„ Profit and Loss Account: Net cost of redeeming 91,000 Debentures .		81,900
			£273,300				£273,300
				19.4 July 1	By Balance . . b/d		259,000

The average cost of the Debentures held by the company is $\frac{126,900}{141,000} \times £1 = 90\text{p}$, so that the profit shown in Own Debentures Account is—

    (*a*) Redemption of 50,000 at £52,500 at £1·05, as against cost of 90p.
    (*b*) Redemption of 91,000 at £1, as against cost of 90p.

The above amount of £52,500 is ¼ × £210,000 per (2) in Deed.

The company discharged its Debenture Debt by—

		£			£			£
(*a*) Purchasing	141,000 Debentures at 90p =	126,900	Profit	.	.	14,100		
(*b*) Paying to outsiders	118,000 Debentures at £1·10 =	129,800	Loss	.	.	11,800		
		£259,000						
	Total effective Cost . . .	£256,700	Profit	.	.	£2,300		

The amount of the Reserve equalling the nominal amount of Debentures redeemed is £259,000 and is made up of—

    Charges to Profit and Loss, £256,700 (£45,000 + £129,800 + £81,900).
    Profit on Redemption, £2,300 (£7,500 + £9,100 − £2,500 − £11,800).

61. *Dr.*   VENDOR'S DEBTORS   *Cr.*

				£						£
To Balances	.	.	b/d	4,000	By Cash (Note (a))	.	.	.		400
					,, Discount (Note (b))		.	.		21
					,, Balances	.	.	.	c/d	3,579
				£4,000						£4,000
To Balances	.	.	b/d	3,579						

Dr.   VENDOR'S DEBTORS SUSPENSE   *Cr.*

				£					£
To Discount	.	.	.	21	By Purchase of Business Account	.	.		4,000
,, Vendor	.	.	.	400					
,, Balances	.	.	c/d	3,579					
				£4,000					£4,000
					By Balances	.	.	b/d	3,579

Dr.   VENDOR'S CREDITORS   *Cr.*

			£					£
To Cash (Note (c))	.	.	400	By Balances	.	.	b/d	2,200
,, Discount (Note (c))	.	.	11					
,, Balances	.	.	1,789					
			£2,200					£2,200
				By Balances	.	.	b/d	1,789

Dr.   VENDOR'S CREDITORS SUSPENSE   *Cr.*

			£					£
To Purchase of Business Account	.	.	2,200	By Discount	.	.	.	11
				,, Vendor	.	.	.	400
				,, Balances	.	.	c/d	1,789
			£2,200					£2,200
To Balances	.	.	b/d	1,789				

Dr.   Y LTD. (NEW) DEBTORS   *Cr.*

				£					£
To Sales	.	.	.	30,000	By Cash (Note (d))	.	.		20,500
					,, Discount (Note (d))	.	.		1,079
					,, Balances	.	.	c/d	8,421
				£30,000					£30,000
To Balances	.	.	b/d	8,421					

Dr.   Y LTD. (NEW) CREDITORS   *Cr.*

				£					£
To Discount	.	.	.	200	By Purchases	.	.		17,000
,, Cash (Note (e))	.	.	.	7,800					
,, Balances	.	.	c/d	9,000					
				£17,000					£17,000
					By Balances	.	.	b/d	9,000

Dr.   CASH   *Cr.*

			£				£
To Y Ltd. (New) Debtors	.	.	20,500	By Y Ltd. (New) Creditors	.	.	7,800
,, Vendor's Debtors	.	.	400	,, Vendor's Creditors	.	.	400

Dr.		DISCOUNT		Cr.	
		£			£
To Y Ltd. (New) Debtors	. . .	1,079	By Y Ltd. (New) Creditors	. . .	200

Notes. (a) This is the minimum amount which must have been received in order to pay off £400 creditors (per note (c)).
(b) $\frac{1}{10}$ of £400 or $\frac{1}{20}$ (5 per cent) of £421.
(c) Cash and Discount £411, of which discount is $2\frac{1}{2}$ per cent or $\frac{1}{40}$.
(d) Cash and Discount £21,579, of which discount is 5 per cent or $\frac{1}{20}$.
(e) As discount is $2\frac{1}{2}$ per cent, cash must be thirty-nine times the discount, i.e. 39 × £200.

62. (1) The basis for amalgamation—

(a) It is suggested that provision should be made for—

(i) the maintenance, as between individual partners, of their present profit-sharing ratio and rights in the respective firms;

(ii) the relative profit and super-profit earning capacity of the two businesses.

(b) The average trading profits for the last three years are—

		A & B	C & D
		£	£
19.4	. . . . . .	8,270	6,580
19.5	. . . . . .	10,100	7,250
19.6	. . . . . .	9,950	7,782
		3)28,320	3)21,612
		£9,440	£7,204

(c) Assuming that no revaluation of assets and liabilities is required, that the average capital over the three years has been in the case of A & B £30,000, and in the case of C & D £24,000 (in the latter case current accounts are assumed to have been merged with capitals) and that $12\frac{1}{2}$ per cent is a fair yield on capital employed in this type of business, goodwill may be valued as follows—

(i)		A & B	C & D
		£	£
Average trading profits	. . . . .	9,440	7,204
Less interest on capital—			
A & B—$12\frac{1}{2}$% on £30,000	. . .	3,750	
C & D—$12\frac{1}{2}$% on £24,000	. . .		3,000
		5,690	4,204
Less reasonable remuneration (say)	. .	4,000	3,000
Estimated super-profits	. . . . .	£1,690	£1,204
Value at (say) five years' purchase	. .	£8,450	£6,020

Alternatively—

		£	£
(ii) Average trading profits	. . . .	9,440	7,204
Less reasonable remuneration (say)	. .	4,000	3,000
		£5,440	£4,204
Capitalized at $12\frac{1}{2}$%	. . . .	43,520	33,632
Less net tangible assets (as above)	. .	30,000	24,000
Value of goodwill	. . . . .	£13,520	£9,632

(*d*) Further information would be required before the value of goodwill could be finally computed—it is, for instance, noted that, whereas the profits of C & D show a steady upward trend, those of A & B are more erratic, with profit for 19.6 below that for 19.5. For present purposes, therefore, the goodwill of the two firms will be taken at an approximate average of the values in (*c*) (i) and (ii) above, i.e. say £12,000 and £8,000 respectively.

(*e*) Before dealing with the issue of shares, it is suggested that the capitals of the two firms be rounded off—in the case of A and B by withdrawal of the amounts standing to the credit of their current accounts, and in the case of C and D by the former withdrawing £500 and the latter paying in £150. The capitals of the partners will then be—

	A £	B £	C £	D £	Total £
Net tangible assets	16,000	14,000	15,000	10,000	55,000
Goodwill	6,400[1]	5,600[1]	4,800[2]	3,200[2]	20,000
	£22,400	£19,600	£19,800	£13,200	£75,000

[1] £12,000 in ratio of 8 : 7.
[2] £8,000 in ratio of 3 : 2.

(*f*) It is noted that in both partnerships profits are shared in capital ratios, so that no difficulty arises in the maintenance of profit allocation between the individual partners in the two firms.

(2) Capitalization of the company—

(*a*) It is suggested that the capital of the company should consist of cumulative preference shares and ordinary shares, the former being issued in consideration of net tangible assets acquired, and the latter in consideration of goodwill, as follows—

(i) £55,000 in 12½ per cent Cumulative Preference Shares of £1 each to be allotted to the old partners in their old capital ratio, i.e. 16:14:15:10. These preference shares would have priority for return of capital in a winding-up, but without participation rights in surplus assets.

(ii) £20,000 in Ordinary Shares of £1 each to be allotted to the partners in their respective shares in the goodwill of their respective firms, i.e. 64:56:48:32, or 16:14:12:8.

(*b*) The Balance Sheet of the company would then be—

BALANCE SHEET AS AT 1ST JANUARY, 19.7

	£			£
Share Capital—		Fixed Assets—		
Preference	55,000	A and B	£16,178	
Ordinary	20,000	C and D	15,480	
Current Liabilities—				31,658
A and B	£6,722	Goodwill		20,000
C and D	5,433	Current Assets—		
	12,155	A and B	£21,794	
		Less Cash withdrawn	1,250	
				20,544
		C and D	£15,303	
		Less Net Cash withdrawn	350[1]	
				14,953
	£87,155			£87,155

[1] Withdrawn by C, £500, less paid in by D, £150

(c) The effect of the allocation of shares suggested above would be to give almost the same share of profits in the company (assumed all distributed) as in the two partnerships, on the basis of profits approximately equal to the average of the past three years—£9,500 and £7,000 respectively, viz.—

	A	B	C	D	Total
	£	£	£	£	£
Partnerships—					
Ratio 8:7	5,067	4,433			9,500
3:2			4,200	2,800	7,000
	£5,067	£4,433	£4,200	£2,800	£16,500
Company—					
Preference	2,000	1,750	1,875	1,250	6,875
Ordinary	3,080	2,695	2,310	1,540	9,625
	£5,080	£4,445	£4,185	£2,790	£16,500

(d) Profits in excess of this average will, on this basis, be divided in the Ordinary Share ratio (i.e. 3:2 as regards the old firms). It may be argued that some of these additional profits are due to economies arising out of the amalgamation, and that, to that extent, they should be divided equally. To provide for this, a small number of deferred ordinary shares might be allocated in the proportion of 8:7:9:6 (i.e. 15:15 by firms), eligible for dividend only after a certain percentage had been paid on the ordinary shares (this percentage depending on the proportion of profits it is intended to appropriate to reserve).

(e) It will be advisable for profits to be distributed as directors' remuneration in order to obtain the maximum advantage of earned income relief for income tax and surtax (this will also reduce to some extent the company's corporation tax liability). The amount distributed as ordinary dividend may therefore be reduced and paid in remuneration; alternatively, the rate of preference dividend may be reduced to say 5 or 6 per cent. In either case the amount distributed in remuneration should be in the same proportion as indicated for dividends. The maximum amount which could be distributed as directors' remuneration would be determined by (i) the amount which would satisfy the Inland Revenue as being payment wholly and exclusively for the purposes of the trade, and (ii) the standard distribution computed in accordance with the rules applicable to close companies.

(f) In order to save capital duty on the nominal capital, the ordinary shares could be issued at a premium, or a small number might be issued (in the same ratio) covering a reduced book value of goodwill (which might even be left out of account entirely, thus saving transfer duty thereon).

(h) It is suggested that any attempt to issue further classes of shares to safeguard the partnership capital position would make the grading of shares too cumbersome.

63.   BLACK & CO. LTD., BALANCE SHEET AS AT 1ST APRIL, 19..

	£	£		£	£
Share Capital—			Fixed Assets at Cost—		
Authorized and Issued:			Goodwill	5,000	
720 7% Preference Shares			Land and Buildings	18,650	
of £1 each fully paid	720		Fixtures	500	
29,530 Ordinary Shares of £1					24,150
each fully paid	29,530		Current Assets—		
		30,250	Stock-in-trade	23,000	
Mortgage on Land and Build-			Debtors	6,400	
ings		10,000	Cash	1,100	
Creditors		15,400			30,500
			Costs of Mortgage		350
			Preliminary Expenses		650
		£55,650			£55,650

WHITE & CO. LTD., BALANCE SHEET AS AT 1ST APRIL, 19..

	£	£		£	£
Share Capital—			Goodwill at Cost		4,000
Authorized and Issued:			Current Assets—		
480 7% Preference Shares			Stock-in-trade	11,250	
of £1 each fully paid	480		Debtors	10,800	
24,470 Ordinary Shares of			Cash	1,100	
£1 each fully paid	24,470				23,150
		24,950	Preliminary Expenses		400
Creditors		2,600			
		£27,550			£27,550

The Capital Accounts of Black and White after the sale to the new limited companies are—

					£
Black, Balance					26,300
Plus ½ of Goodwill, £9,000.					4,500
					£30,800
White, Balance					16,200
Plus ½ of Goodwill, £9,000.					4,500
					£20,700

The closing accounts of Black and White are—

Dr.			REALIZATION ACCOUNT			Cr.
		£				£
To Sundry Assets		70,650	By Creditors			28,150
,, Profit—			,, Black & Co. Ltd.			28,530
Black	£4,500		,, White & Co. Ltd.			22,970
White	4,500					
		9,000				
		£79,650				£79,650

Dr.			CAPITALS			Cr.	
	Black £	White £				Black £	White £
To Shares—							
Black & Co. Ltd.	23,750	4,780	By Balances	b/d		26,300	16,200
White & Co. Ltd.	7,050	15,920	Profit on Realization			4,500	4,500
	£30,800	£20,700				£30,800	£20,700

Schedule of Purchase Considerations

		Black & Co. Ltd.			White & Co. Ltd.		
Purchase Consideration—		£	£			£	£
Land, etc. . . .			18,650				
Fixtures . . .			500				
Stock	A Dept.		23,000	B Dept.			11,250
Debtors . . .	A Dept.		6,400	B Dept.			10,800
Cash			50				
Goodwill . . .			5,000				4,000
			53,600				26,050
Less Creditors . .	A Dept.	15,400		B Dept.	2,600		
Loans . .		720			480		
Bank . .		8,950					
			25,070				3,080
Total (per Realization Account) . . .			£28,530				£22,970

Division of Share Capitals

		Black & Co. Ltd. £	White & Co. Ltd. £
Ordinary—			
Black	[£30,800]	23,750	7,050
White	[£20,700]	4,780	15,920
Employees		1,000	1,500
		29,530	24,470
Preference—			
Allotted to Loan Holders		720	480
Per Balance Sheets		£30,250	£24,950

The opening entries will be—

Journals

		Black & Co. Ltd.		White & Co. Ltd.	
		Dr. £	Cr. £	Dr. £	Cr. £
Sundry Assets . . . Dr.		53,600		26,050	
To Liabilities—					
Creditors			15,400		2,600
Loans			720		480
Bank			8,950		
			25,070		3,080
„ Vendors			28,530		22,970
		£53,600	£53,600	£26,050	£26,050

The rough Cash Accounts of Black & Co. Ltd., and White & Co. Ltd., will be—

Dr.		BLACK & CO. LTD., CASH		Cr.	
	£				£
To Sundries	50	By Bank			8,950
„ Shares Issued	1,000	„ Costs of Mortgage			350
„ Mortgage	10,000	„ Preliminary Expenses			650
		„ Balance		c/d	1,100
	£11,050				£11,050
To Balance	b/d	1,100			

Dr.		WHITE & CO. LTD., CASH		Cr.	
	£				£
To Shares Issued	1,500	By Preliminary Expenses			400
		„ Balance		c/d	1,100
	£1,500				£1,500
To Balance	b/d	1,100			

It is important to note that the profit on realization must be divided equally, irrespective of what amount of profit is made on the sale of either department.

64. Although it is clear that a reconstruction is desirable, it is not possible to go beyond generalization in the absence of material facts. It is, for instance, not possible to say if the opportune moment has arrived to carry out the operation, hence the following suggestions must be regarded broadly and tentatively.

The main matters requiring consideration in devising a scheme are—

(1) Whether the company has "turned the corner" and the profit of £5,000 can, in the absence of unforeseen circumstances, be maintained.

(2) The need for building up reserves, so that some portion of the £5,000 should be appropriated for that purpose (assuming that the annual profit of £5,000 is before any appropriation), thus reducing the amount of profit available for dividend.

(3) The nature and composition of the item "Net Tangible Assets"; its division into fixed and current assets and liabilities. Inquiry will be directed to the effect on future profits of the write down of Plant and the need for large-scale replacement. In particular, careful examination of the present and future working capital will be required.

(4) The reasons for the past losses, e.g. as to whether they have arisen fortuitously or steadily over a long period (the arrears period seems to indicate several years); whether the reasons are fundamental, such as inefficient management whether in buying, selling, financing, lack of organization, or indiscriminate diversifying; and to what extent such causes are capable of eradication.

(5) Where practicable, consultation with influential shareholders on the proposed scheme should take place so as to anticipate objections of sufficient weight as would reject the scheme, so that although the proposals should aim at balancing fairly competing claims of the different classes of shareholders, yet practical experience shows that a certain amount of compromising takes place to placate powerful interests.

(6) In the present case, the matter is reasonably simple, because the loss of capital falls entirely on the ordinary shareholders; they do not suffer dividend diminution nor is their position affected in a winding-up, unless the preference shareholders are, under the scheme, given some portion of the "equity."

(7) No occasion arises to curtail the preference rights, but the preference shareholders will be reluctant to acquiesce in a scheme which does not, in some form or another, offer some compensation for the sacrifice of the four years' dividend arrears, knowing that normally these would have to be paid to them before the ordinary shareholders could receive any dividend. An important point is not stated in the question, i.e. whether the preference dividends (declared or not) are preferential in a winding-up. This answer assumes they are *not* preferential.

(8) This question of compensation will require careful consideration and numerous alternatives exist for dealing with it, e.g.—

(*a*) Giving the preference shareholders income debentures or notes (to carry interest and be repaid by annual drawings or in total at a comparatively early date) for the arrears (or more likely a part only); but this would most likely entail a building up of a Sinking Fund. In any case, this, together with the interest thereon, would reduce the profit available, whilst the redemption would weaken the liquid position.

(*b*) Notwithstanding the accepted principle in reconstruction of avoiding change of status, it is probable that the preference shareholders would be willing to agree to taking some ordinary shares under the scheme, either—

(i) By splitting up the Preference Capital into Preference and Ordinary, leaving their *total* Capital intact and without asking the Ordinary shareholders to surrender some of their shares to the Preference shareholders; or

(ii) By leaving quite intact the Preference Capital (in that form) and adding to the holdings of the Preference shareholders some Ordinary shares by a surrender from the existing Ordinary shareholders.

(9) The voting power should be left undisturbed and, in consequence (depending on the exact details of the scheme), provision should be made to ensure the *status quo*, e.g. by keeping the *number* of ordinary shares with a corresponding reduction in the denomination corresponding with the loss of capital suffered.

(10) Resolutions required, including that to reduce and simultaneously increase the authorized capital, will be drafted by the solicitors of the company in consultation with the company's accountants.

Elements of the preliminary draft scheme—

	Original	Loss	Balance
	£	£	£
(1) LOSS OF CAPITAL—			
Net Tangible Assets	76,000	8,000	68,000
Goodwill	15,000	15,000	—
Profit and Loss	34,000	34,000	—
	£125,000	£57,000	£68,000

(2) DISTRIBUTION OF LOSS—	
ORDINARY SHAREHOLDERS	£57,000

(3) RECONSTITUTED CAPITAL—

	£	£		Prefer-ence £	Ordin-ary £
Preference . .		50,000	To Preference Share-		
Ordinary . . 75,000			holders . .	45,000	5,000
Less Loss, as above 57,000			„ Existing Ordinary		
		18,000	Shareholders .		18,000
Total: Net Tangible Assets	£68,000			£45,000	£23,000

The above represents the position on the footing that the preference shareholders agree to a complete cancellation of the arrears of preference dividends, but in all probability *some* compensation will be insisted upon. Tentatively, it is suggested that this be compounded at £5,000. This would involve writing down the preference shares to 90p fully paid, leaving the preference shareholders with the same *number* as before, i.e. 50,000 of 90p fully paid, totalling £45,000, and allotting ordinary shares equivalent to £5,000, which would probably carry no voting rights; and if in £1 form would be allotted to the preference shareholders in the ratio of one ordinary for ten preference; or if in 20p form, in the ratio of one ordinary for two preference. (The question of "fractions" might arise.)

[An alternative would be to keep the Preference Share Capital completely unchanged and to "lift" from the ordinary shareholders, say, £3,000, without voting rights, of their reduced capital of £18,000, leaving them with £15,000, probably in the form of 75,000 shares of 20p each fully paid, thus keeping the number of their shares intact.]

REFRAMED BALANCE SHEET

	£		£
Authorized Capital—		Net Tangible Assets . . .	68,000
50,000 6% Cumulative Preference Shares of 90p each . .	50,000		
25,000 "A" Ordinary Shares of 20p each	5,000		
350,000 Ordinary Shares of 20p each	70,000		
	£125,000		
Issued Capital—			
50,000 6% Cumulative Preference Shares of 90p each, fully paid .	45,000		
25,000 "A" Ordinary Shares of 20p each, fully paid[1] . . .	5,000		
90,000 Ordinary Shares of 20p each fully paid[1]	18,000		
	£68,000		£68,000

[1] These would be held by (1) Preference shareholders 25,000
(2) Present Ordinary shareholders . . 90,000

The "A" Ordinary and the Ordinary would rank equally for dividends (the former without voting rights), but the former ranking in priority to the latter as to Capital, so as to put the existing Preference shareholders in the same position in a winding-up as if no scheme had been carried out.

Assuming that the whole £5,000 is distributed (although, as mentioned, it would be imprudent to do so), the comparative position is—

DIVIDENDS RECEIVABLE

If No Scheme	£	After Scheme		£
Preference—		Preference—		
6% on 50,000 Shares (£1) . .	3,000	6% on 50,000 Preference Shares (90p) £2,700		
		10% on 25,000 "A" Ordinary Shares (20p) . . 500		
				3,200
Ordinary—		Ordinary—		
2⅔% on 75,000 Shares (1) . .	2,000	10% on 90,000 Ordinary Shares (20p)		1,800
	£5,000			£5,000

The Preference shareholders lose £300 "priority" dividend and gain £500 "equity" dividend, an increase of £200, which is only a little over 1½ per cent on the "lost" Preference dividends of the past four years (£12,000), and, in consequence, might not acquiesce in the scheme, unless their share in the profit is increased by holding more ordinaries (at the expense of the existing Ordinary shareholders) and keeping intact their Preference Capital. (See page 580, para. 8b (ii).)

Assuming, to satisfy their objections, £3,000 of Ordinary Capital is "diverted" and the existing Preference Capital is kept intact, then the Ordinary Share Capital would be £18,000, which, together with the Preference Capital £50,000, amounts to £68,000, divided thus—

	£
Preference Shareholders—	
15,000 shares of 20p each, fully paid	3,000
Existing Ordinary Shareholders—	
75,000 shares of 20p each, fully paid	15,000
	£18,000

The Dividends receivable would be—

		£	£
Preference—			
6% on 50,000 Preference Share (£1) . . .		3,000	
$11\frac{1}{10}$% on 15,000 "A" Ordinary Shares (20p) . .		333	
			3,333
Existing Ordinary—			
$11\frac{1}{10}$% on 75,000 Ordinary Shares (20p) . . .			1,667
			£5,000

[It should be observed that, in this alternative, the "A" Ordinary Shares should not be preferential in a winding-up, as the Preference Capital is intact; even without priority, the Preference shareholders are placed to advantage, because in the original constitution their rights of repayment did not extend beyond their Capital, whereas now they rank, in addition to their Preference share priority, for $\frac{15}{00}$, i.e. $\frac{1}{8}$ of the remaining assets (at the expense of the existing Ordinary shareholders).]

There are many other alternatives in addition to those indicated in the above answer, e.g. reducing the rate of Preference dividend and compensating by increasing the share of equity of the Preference shareholders (or creating an intermediate class of share, say, Preferred Ordinary ranking after the Preference, but before the Ordinary, although generally this alternative is rarely adopted). To this type of question there is no "MODEL" answer; all that an examiner expects is an answer setting out clearly and concisely the essential principles and applying those principles to the facts of the question, always with due regard to the time reasonably expected to be devoted to it.

65. *Dr.*   DEBENTURES   *Cr.*

19..		£	19..		£
Dec. 31	*To Transfer from own Debentures* . . .	*20,000*	Jan. 1	By Balance . . .	20,000

Dr.   OWN DEBENTURES   *Cr.*

19..		Nominal £	£	19..		£
Mar. 1	To Cash . .	2,000	2,050	Mar. 1	By Debenture Interest—	
Apr. 1	,, ,, . .	8,000	8,320		2 months on £2,000 at	
Dec. 1	,, ,, .	10,000	9,950		6% per annum . .	20
	,, Debenture Interest—			Apr. 1	,, Debenture Interest—	
	1 month on £10,000				3 months on £8,000 at	
	at 6 per cent per				6% per annum . .	120
	annum. . .		50	Dec. 31	,, *Transfer to Debentures* .	*20,000*
					,, Loss on own Debentures	
					purchases . .	230
			£20,370			£20,370

Dr.   DEBENTURE INTEREST   *Cr.*

19..		£	19..		£
Mar. 1	To Transfer	20	June 30	By Profit and Loss Account* .	440
Apr. 1	,, ,, . . .	120			
June 30	,, Cash—half year on £10,000 at				
	6% per annum . .	300			
		£440			£440

Proof—

Taking own Debentures as an investment, the interest is—

	£
£2,000 at 6 per cent per annum for 4 months (1st March to 30th June) .	40
£8,000 at 6 per cent per annum for 4 months (1st April to 30th June) .	120
	£160

The interest on Debentures of £20,000 at 6 per cent per annum for six
months ended 30th June   = £600

* Net charge, therefore, is £600 — £160   = £440

As regards the purchase of 1st December, the seller is entitled to the full half-year's interest of £300. The true price is too little by the interest of the intervening month of June (i.e. £50), and therefore the real cost is par.

If the Debenture had been still quoted (assuming real price of par) cum interest it would have been £100 + accruing Interest thereon at 6 per cent per annum for five months, i.e. £102½; but when the quotation goes x.d. it is "ex" the full period interest, i.e. 6 months = £3, deflating the price to 99½, hence the adjustment to cover the month's interest, as the buyer owns the Debenture for one month prior to 31st December.

Dr.				DEBENTURE INTEREST			*Cr.*
19..			£	19..			£
Dec. 31	To Cash—half year on £10,000 at			Dec. 1	By Transfer . . .		50
	6% per annum . .		300	31	,, Profit and Loss Account .		250
							£300

The loss on Debentures purchased is—

	Cost	Accrued Interest	Par	Loss
19..	£	£	£	£
Mar. 1 . . .	2,050	20	2,000	30
Apr. 1 . . .	8,320	120	8,000	200
	£10,370	£140	£10,000	£230

If the Debentures purchased by the company are regarded as a diminution of total debenture liability, i.e. set-off, the chargeable Debenture Interest is—

Half-year ended 30th June, on outstanding Debentures—

	£
£20,000 for 2 months: Interest thereon at 6 per cent per annum .	200
£18,000 for 1 month: Interest thereon at 6 per cent per annum .	90
£10,000 for 3 months: Interest thereon at 6 per cent per annum .	150
	£440

Half-year ended 31st December, on outstanding Debentures—

	£
£10,000 for 5 months	250
Nil for 1 month	—
	£250

An alternative method of proof of profit on Debentures purchased (assuming the real price (allowing for accruing interest) is par) is—

Purchase	Par as adjusted		Purchase Price	Debentures Purchased at premium	Profit Loss
	£			£	£
	100				
Mar. 1. *Add* 2 months' accruing interest .	1				
	—	101%	102½%	2,000 @ 1½% [102½ — 101]	30
	100				
Apr. 1. *Add* 3 months' accruing interest .	1½				
	—	101½%	104%	8,000 @ 2½% [104 — 101½]	200
	100				
					£230

66.   JOURNAL

	£	£
4% Debenture Stock . . . . *Dr.*	500,000	
Premium on Redemption . . . *Dr.*	10,000	
To Debenture Stock Redemption Account.		(*a*) 510,000
Being redemption of 4% Debenture Stock at 102.		
Debenture Stock Redemption Account *Dr.*	191,862	
To 7% Cumulative Preference Share. . (*b*)		
Capital (£1)		170,544
,, Share Premium Account (12½p) . .		21,318
Being acceptance of alternative (*a*) by holders of £188,100 4% Debenture Stock and allotment of 7% Cumulative Preference Shares per Minute Book, p.		
Debenture Stock Redemption Account (96%) *Dr.*	204,000	
Discount on 5% Debenture Stock (4%) . (*c*) *Dr.*	8,500	
To 5% Debenture Stock . . .		212,500
Being acceptance of alternative (*b*) by holders of £200,000 4% Debenture Stock and allotment of 5% Debenture Stock, per Minute Book, p.		
Debenture Stock Redemption Account . *Dr.*	114,138	
To Cash . . . . . . (*d*)		114,138
Being repayment to holders of £111,900 4% Debenture Stock at 102%, per Minute Book, p.		

$(a = b + c + d)$

		£
payable as to—		
4% Debenture Stock . . .		500,000
Less Par Value—alternative (*a*)	£188,100	
,, ,, ,. (*b*)	200,000	
		388,100
Balance at Par for repayment . . .		111,900
Add Premium 2%		2,238
		£114,138

67. (a)   JOURNAL

		£	£
Shops Fittings . . . . *Dr.*		1,000	
Goodwill . . . . *Dr.*		1,800	
To Ivor Pill—Capital			2,800
Ivor Pill—Capital . . . . . . *Dr.*		9,550	
To Freehold Shop			9,550
Sales . . . . *Dr.*		4,650	
Stock (new) . . . . *Dr.*		3,600	
To Purchases			3,000
,, Wages and Salaries			375
,, Rates			100
,, Sundry Expenses			450
,, Audit			25
,, Stock (old)			3,450
,, Ivor Pill—Capital (Profit) . . .			850
(See page 587)			
Ivor Pill—Capital . . . . . *Dr.*		60	
To Trade Debtors			60
Ivor Pill—Capital . . . . . *Dr.*		9,240	
To Drawings			1,600
,, Ivor Pill—Vendor Account . . .			7,640
Ivor Pill—Vendor Account . . . . *Dr.*		6,500	
To Share Capital.			6,500
Ivor Pill—Vendor Suspense Account . . . *Dr.*		100	
Trade Creditors . . . . . *Dr.*		260	
To Bank Suspense Account			360

(b)

SOCCERBALLS LTD.
TRADING AND PROFIT AND LOSS ACCOUNT
FOR THE NINE MONTHS ENDED 31ST DECEMBER, 19.8

	£		£
Stock, 1st April, 19.8	3,600	Sales	13,950
Purchases	9,000	Stock 31st December, 19.8	4,050
Gross Profit c/d	5,400		
	£18,000		£18,000

	Pre-incorpn.	Post-incorpn.		Pre-incorpn.	Post-incorpn.
	£	£		£	£
Wages and Salaries .	375	750	Gross Profit .	1,800	3,600
Rates	100	200			
Rent	210	420			
Sundry Expenses	450	900			
Directors' Remuneration .		660			
Audit	25	50			
Depreciation .	75	150			
Net Profit c/d .	565	470			
	£1,800	£3,600		£1,800	£3,600
Profit Prior to Incorporation Account	565		Net Profit b/d	565	470
Balance forward		470			
	£565	£470		£565	£470

BALANCE SHEET AS AT 31ST DECEMBER, 19.8

		£			£
Authorized Share Capital 10,000 Shares of £1 each		10,000	Fixed Assets— Shop Fittings and Furniture:		
			Cost .	£3,000	
Issued Share Capital—			Less Depreciation .	225	
6,500 Shares of £1 each fully paid		6,500			2,775
Profit and Loss Account		470	Goodwill, at cost		1,800
Profit Prior to Incorporation		565	Current Assets—		
Current Liabilities—			Trade Debtors	£2,040	
Vendor .	£1,040		Stock .	4,050	
Trade Creditors .	700				6,090
Expenses Creditors[1] .	1,390	3,130			
		£10,665			£10,665

[1] Directors' Remuneration £660 + Rent £630 + Audit £100.

The detailed Journal entry on page 585 and the transfers may be avoided by breaking up the Trading and Profit and Loss items into three parts, the first appertaining to Pill and the other two to Soccerballs Ltd., thus—

Trading and Profit for the Year Ended 31st December, 19.8

	Pill 1st Jan. to 31st Mar., 19.8	Soccerballs Ltd. 1st Apr. to 30th June, 19.8	Soccerballs Ltd. 1st July to 31st Dec., 19.8		Pill 1st Jan. to 31st Mar., 19.8	Soccerballs Ltd. 1st Apr. to 30th June, 19.8	Soccerballs Ltd. 1st of July to 31st Dec., 19.8
	£	£	£		£	£	£
Stock	3,450	3,600	3,750	Sales	4,650	4,650	9,300
Purchases	3,000	3,000	6,000	Stock	3,600	3,750	4,050
Gross Profit c/d	1,800	1,800	3,600				
	£8,250	£8,400	£13,350		£8,250	£8,400	£13,350
Wages and Salaries	375	375	750	Gross Profit	1,800	1,800	3,600
Rates	100	100	200				
Rent		210	420				
Sundry Expenses	450	450	900				
Directors' Remuneration			660				
Audit	25	25	50				
Depreciation		75	150				
Net Profit[1]	850	565	470				
	£1,800	£1,800	£3,600		£1,800	£1,800	£3,600
Profit Prior to Incorporation Account		565		Net Profit . b/d		565	470
Balance forward			470				
		£565	£470			£565	£470

[1] This item will be journalized as follows—

	£	£
Profit and Loss Account . Dr.	850	
To Ivor Pill—Capital .		850

587

68. (a)   STORM LTD.

SUMMARY OF CASH ACCOUNT FOR THE
Dr.   YEAR ENDED 31ST MARCH, 19.9   Cr.

	£		£
Share Capital . . .	160,000	Debenture Interest for year, *net* . .	1,740
5 per cent Debentures . .	60,000	Preliminary Expenses . .	3,000
Cloud Ltd., Dividend net . .	1,440	Purchase of Fixed Assets . .	120,000
Liquidator—Thunder Ltd. . .	80,000	Own Debentures (£4,000) . .	3,970
		Shares in Thunder Ltd. . .	75,000
		Fixed Assets—Thunder Ltd. . .	30,000
		Goodwill . . .	18,000
		Trading payments (*less* receipts) (see Schedule, pages 590–1)	12,260
		Balance	37,470
	£301,440		£301,440

(b)   PROFIT AND LOSS ACCOUNT
FOR THE YEAR ENDED 31ST MARCH, 19.9

	£		£
Directors' Fees . . .	6,500[1]	Gross Profit	5,300[1]
Depreciation of Fixed Assets . .	9,000[1]	Dividend from Subsidiary . .	1,800
Debenture Interest . . .	2,950	Balance, Loss . . . c/d	11,350
	£18,450		£18,450
Balance . . . . b/d	11,350	Balance . . . . . c/d	14,350
Preliminary Expenses . .	3,000		
	£14,350		£14,350
Balance . . . . b/d	14,350		

[1] Trading Loss £15,500 − £5,300 = £10,200.

BALANCE SHEET AS AT 31ST MARCH, 19.9

	£		£	£
Authorized and Issued Share Capital—		Fixed Assets—		
200 000 Shares of £1 each fully paid	200,000	Goodwill at cost . . .		18,000
Capital Reserve . . .	5,350	Fixed Assets at cost . 150,000		
	205,350	*Less* Depreciation Provision 9,000		141,000
Less Profit and Loss Account—adverse balance. . .	14,350	Share in Subsidiary Company at cost		39,670
	191,000	Current Assets—		
5 per cent Debentures . £60,000		Cash at Bank . .	37,470	
Less Redeemed and available for reissue .	4,000	Debtors . . .	8,480	
	56,000	Stock . . .	10,430	56,380
Current Liabilities—				
Trade Creditors . £7,350				
Accruals . . . 500				
Income Tax . . . 200				
	8,050	...............} Directors		
	£255,050			£255,050

Computation of excess of Trading Payments over Trading Receipts—

	"Receipts,' i.e. not *paid*	"Payments," i.e. not *received*
	£	£
Depreciation	9,000	
Directors' Fees unpaid	500	
Creditors (Goods)	7,350	
Debtors (Goods)		8,480
Stock on hand		10,430
	16,850	18,910
Trading Loss		10,200
Balance, net **payments** (per Cash Summary) (see page 590).	12,260	
	£29,110	£29,110

Rough Working Accounts—

Dr.   SHARES IN CLOUD LTD.   **Cr.**

	£		£
To Share Capital . . .	40,000	By Dividend, net:	
		3 months to acquisition .	360
		,, Balance	39,640
	£40,000		£40,000

Dr.   ADJUSTMENT ACCOUNT   **Cr.**

	£		£
To Capital Reserve	260	By Income Tax:	
		Pre-acquisition Dividend £360, net .	240
		,, Income Tax:	
		Interest on Debentures redeemed (£30, net)	20
	£260		£260

Dr.   INVESTMENT INCOME   **Cr.**

	£		£
To Investment Account . . .	360	By Dividend *net* (Cloud Ltd.) . .	1,440
,, Adjustment Account:		,, Income Tax on £1,440, net . .	960
Tax on £360, net . . .	240		
,, Profit and Loss . . .	1,800		
	£2,400		£2,400

Dr.   CAPITAL RESERVE   **Cr.**

	£		£
To Balance	5,260	By Profit on Sale of Shares in Thunder Ltd. (£80,000 — £75,000) . .	5,000
		,, Adjustment Account . . .	260
	£5,260		£5,260

Dr.   DEBENTURES REDEEMED   **Cr.**

	£		£
To Cash	3,970	By Debentures	4,000
,, Capital Reserve	60	,, Interest net for 3 months .	30
	£4,030		£4,030

Dr.	DEBENTURE INTEREST		*Dr.*
	£		£
To Cash—½ year to 30.9.19.8 on £60,000 *net*	900	By Profit and Loss Account . . .	2,950
,, Debentures Redeemed . . .	30		
,, Cash—½ year to 31.3.19.9 on £56,000 *net*	840		
	1,770		
,, Income Tax on £1,740 net . .	1,160		
,, Adjustment—Income Tax on £30 net	20		
	£2,950		£2,950

Dr.	INCOME TAX		*Cr.*
	£		£
To Investment Income (Sch. F) . .	960	By Debenture Interest (Sect. 53) . .	1,160
,, Provision	200		
	£1,160		£1,160

The Company is liable to tax for the year ended 31st March, 19.9 on its total profit, or the amount of Taxed Charges for that year, whichever is the **greater,** with the right to carry forward the amount on which it is assessed (s. 53, Taxes Act 1970). Hence it is liable cn £500 at 40% = £200.

£

The £500 is made up of—
Debenture Interest from which tax deducted . . . 1,500 (net £900)
,, ,, ,, ,, ,, ,, . . . 1,400 (net £840)

2,900
Less Dividend from Cloud Ltd. 2,400

£500

The transfer to adjustments are £240 and £20, because the dividend credited to Cost of Shares is "net" only instead of being credited with the gross of £600, whilst the cost of Debentures is shown at the net of £30 instead of £50, so that both sums represent a technical, but not a real, profit.

If the above transfers were not made, the Income Tax Account would be—

Dr.	INCOME TAX		*Cr.*
	£		£
To Investment Income— Tax on £1,800 . . .	720	By Debenture Interest (including own) Tax on £2,950 (i.e. £1,770 grossed)	1,180
,, Balance to Capital Reserve . .	260		
,, Provision	200		
	£1,180		£1,180

The excess of cash paid out over that paid in is made up of—

	£	£
Trading Transactions: Debtors	8,480	
Stock	10,430	
	18,910	
Less Creditors	7,350	
	11,560	
Less Trading Profit . .	5,300	
(See page 591)		6,260
Directors' Fees paid (Profit and Loss Account £6,500, of which £500 is accruing) (see page 589) . . .		6,000
		£12,260

The construction of the Trading Account is—

Dr.			£	Cr.			£
To Excess of Purchases over Sales (see below)	.	.	5,130	By Stock	. . . .	.	10,430
,, Gross Profit	. . .	.	5,300				
			£10,430				£10,430

DEBTORS AND CREDITORS

			£				£
[1]To Cash net (See Cash Summary, pages 588 and 590)	. . .	.	6,260	By Debtors	. . .	.	8,480
,, Creditors	. . .	.	7,350	,, Trading Account (see above)		.	5,130
			£13,610				£13,610

[1] The difference of £6,000 (see item of £17,260 on page 589) is the item of Directors' Remuneration paid.

Students may find it easier to put the appropriate entries relating to the cash build-up and merely copy the items into the final accounts, starting with the loss as stated in question, viz. £10,200 after charging £15,500 (i.e. a *Trading* Profit of £5,300).

		£	£
Loss, after charging Trading Profit on the £15,500	. . .	10,200	
Debtors	. . . .	8,480	
Stock	. . . .	10,430	
Creditors	. . . . .		7,350
Directors' Fees accrual	. . . .		500
Depreciation (either as a separate Fund or to the credit of Fixed Assets)	. . . .		9,000
∴ [2]Cash, *add* difference—balancing figure	. . . .		12,260
		£29,110	£29,110

[2] As all the essential details are available to prepare the final accounts except the £12,260, the balancing cash book figure of £37,470 can be inserted in the Balance Sheet, and in order to get this balance in the Cash Summary the item of £12,260 on the credit side is required.

69. *X and Y's Books*—

Dr.				X Y LTD.		Cr.	
			£				£
To Cash, *re* Shares	.	.	8,000	By Sales	. . .	.	37,000
,, Goodwill	. .	.	7,000	,, Shares in XY Ltd.	. .	.	43,000
,, Sundry Fixed Assets	.	.	25,000	,, Creditors	. .	.	5,700
,, Stock	. .	.	3,000	,, Sundry Fixed Assets	.	.	1,200
,, Debtors	. .	.	5,500				
,, General Expenses	.	.	4,000				
,, Loss on Sale of Fixed Assets		.	1,000				
,, Purchases	. .	.	19,500				
,, Balance	. .	c/d	13,900				
			£86,900				£86,900
				By Balance	. . .	b/d	13,900

Dr.				REALIZATION ACCOUNT		Cr.	
			£				£
To Sundry Fixed Assets	.	.	23,200	By XY Ltd.—Purchase consideration:			
,, Stock	. .	.	3,000	,, Goodwill	. .	.	7,000
Profit—				,, Sundry Fixed Assets	.	.	25,000
X$\frac{11}{20}$	. .	£4,840		,, Stock	. . .	.	3,000
Y$\frac{9}{20}$	. .	3,960					
			8,800				
			£35,000				£35,000

Dr.   SUNDRY FIXED ASSETS   Cr.

	£		£
To Balance	23,200	By Sale	200
„ XY Ltd.	1,200	„ Loss on Sale . . .	1,000
		„ Realization Account . .	23,200
	£24,400		£24,400

Dr.   DEBTORS   Cr.

	£		£
To Balance	7,500	By XY Ltd.	5,500
		„ Balance . . . c/d	2,000
	£7,500		£7,500
To Balance . . . . b/d	2,000		

Dr.   CREDITORS   Cr.

	£		£
To XY Ltd.	5,700	By Balance . . . b/d	8,000
„ Balance . . . . c/d	2,300		
	£8,000		£8,000
		By Balance . . . b/d	2,300

Dr.   CAPITALS   Cr.

		X £	Y £			X £	Y £
To Balances . .	c/d	16,840	13,960	By Balances . . b/d		12,000	10,000
				„ Profit on Realization .		4,840	3,960
		£16,840	£13,960			£16,840	£13,960
To Shares in XY Ltd. . .		23,650	19,350	By Balances . . b/d		16,840	13,960
„ Loss on Debtors . .		110	90	„ XY Ltd., Loan . .		7,645	6,255
„ Cash . .		725	775				
		£24,485	£20,215			£24,485	£20,215

BALANCE SHEET AS AT 30TH APRIL, 19.6

	£		£
Capital A	£16,840	Shares in XY Ltd. . . .	43,000
„ B	13,960	Cash at Bank	2,000
	30,800	Debtors	2,000
Creditors	2,300		
XY Ltd.	13,900		
	£47,000		£47,000

Dr.   CASH   Cr.

	£		£
To Balance . . . b/d	2,000	By Creditors . . .	2,300
„ Debtors	1,800	„ X	725
		„ Y	775
	£3,800		£3,800

JOURNAL

		£	£
Cash . . . . *Dr.*		8,000	
Goodwill . . . . *Dr.*		7,000	
Sundry Fixed Assets . . . . *Dr.*		25,000	
Debtors . . . . *Dr.*		5,500	
Stock . . . . *Dr.*		3,000	
General Expenses . . . . . *Dr.*		4,000	
Purchases . . . . *Dr.*		19,500	
To Creditors			5,700
,, Sales			37,000
,, X and Y			29,300
		£72,000	£72,000
X and Y . . . . *Dr.*		43,000	
To Share Capital			43,000
Loss on Sales of Fixed Assets . . . . *Dr.*		1,500	
X and Y — Cash retained *re* Sale . . . *Dr.*		200	
To Sundry Fixed Assets			1,700

Dr.		BANK		*Cr.*
	£			£
To X and Y	8,000	By Preliminary Expenses . . .		700
		,, Bank Charges . . .		20
		,, Balance	c/d	7,280
	£8,000			£8,000
To Balance . . . b/d	7,280			

Dr.		X AND Y		*Cr.*
	£			£
To Share Capital . . .	43,000	By Sundries		29,300
,, Cash	200	,, Balance . . .	c/d	13,900
	£43,200			£43,200
To Balance . . . b/d	13,900			

TRADING AND PROFIT AND LOSS ACCOUNT
FOR FOUR MONTHS ENDED 30TH APRIL, 19.6

	£		£
Stock	3,000	Sales	37,000
Purchases	19,500	Stock	2,100
Gross Profit . . c/d	16,600		
	£39,100		£39,100

	Pre-acquisition £	Post-acquisition £		Pre-acquisition £	Post-acquisition £
General Expenses .	3,000	1,000	Gross Profit b/d	13,280	3,320
Bank Charges .		20			
Loss on Sale of Fixed Assets . .		1,500			
Net Profit to Profit prior to Incorporation Account .	10,280				
Net Profit . c/f		800			
	£13,280	£3,320		£13,280	£3,320

BALANCE SHEET AS AT 30TH APRIL, 19.6

	£			£	£
Authorized Share Capital—			Fixed Assets at Cost		
50,000 Shares of £1 each . .	50,000		Sundries (£25,000 — £1,700)		23,300
			Goodwill at cost . .		7,000
Issued Share Capital:			Current Assets—		
43,000 Shares of £1 each fully paid .	43,000		Bank	7,280	
Profit and Loss Account . . .	800		Debtors . . .	5,500	
Profit prior to Incorporation . .	10,280		Stock	2,100	
Current Liabilities . . .	5,700				14,880
			Preliminary Expenses . .		700
			X and Y—Vendors . .		13,900
	£59,780				£59,780

70. *Dr.*   A—VENDOR   *Cr.*

	£			£
To Cash	9,100	By Balance (Capital, 1st Jan.) . .		6,400
		„ Balance (per Trial Balance) . c/d		2,700
	£9,100			£9,100
To Balance . . . b/d	2,700	By Fixtures—increase in value . .		350
„ Bad Debt Provision for reduced valuation of Debtors . .	150	„ Preliminary Expenses payments made by A, £80, *plus* Salary £20 . .		100
„ Share Capital—Balance of Purchase Consideration . . .	2,000	„ Transfer—Director's Fee . .		1,000
		„ Goodwill		3,400
	£4,850			£4,850

Dr.   PRELIMINARY EXPENSES   *Cr.*

	£		£
To Balance per Trial Balance . .	320	By Balance	420
„ Vendor	100		
	£420		£420

Dr.   BAD DEBT PROVISION   *Cr.*

	£		£
To Bad Debt written off . .	110	By A	150
„ Capital Reserve . . .	40		
	£150		£150

Dr.   DIRECTOR'S FEE   *Cr.*

	£		£
To Transfer from Vendor—£1,000 paid on account	1,000	By Profit and Loss Account . . .	2,250
„ Provision	1,250		
	£2,250		£2,250

TRADING AND PROFIT AND LOSS ACCOUNT
FOR THE YEAR ENDED 31ST DECEMBER

	£			£
Stock-Opening	1,300	Sales		22,450
Purchases	18,000	Stock-Closing		2,550
Gross Profit c/d	5,700			
	£25,000			£25,000
General Expenses	1,600	Gross Profit b/d		5,700
Director's Remuneration	2,250			
Bad Debts	35			
Net Profit c/d	1,815			
	£5,700			£5,700

	£		£
Interest on £10,000 at 6% per annum for two months	[1]100	Net Profit b/d—Prior to Incorporation—2 months[2]	678
Net Profit prior to Incorporation (£678 − £100)	578	Post Incorporation—10 months[2]	1,137
Balance forward	1,137		
	£1,815		£1,815

[1] Tax ignored.
[2] Division of profit—

		£
Prior to incorporation	$= \frac{1}{3}$(£1,815 + £2,250)	678
Post incorporation	$= \frac{8}{8}$(£1,815 + £2,250) − £2,250	1,137
		£1,815

BALANCE SHEET AS AT 31ST DECEMBER

	£			£	
Share Capital—			Fixed Assets—		
10,000 Shares of £1 each fully paid	10,000		Fixtures and Fittings at cost		1,050
Revenue Reserves—			Goodwill		2,782
Profit and Loss	1,137		Current Assets—		
Current Liabilities—			Cash at Bank	£5,085	
Trade Creditors	£2,750		Debtors	3,350	
A (Interest and balance of			Stock	2,550	
Director's Remuneration)					10,985
(£100 + £1,250)	1,350		Preliminary Expenses		420
		4,100			
		£15,237			£15,237

Notes. The amount of reimbursement for Preliminary Expenses in cash is £100 only, as £320 is shown as a separate debit (and not charged to A's Capital), so that A is already covered on this amount inasmuch as the item is taken over by A Ltd., as an asset and A's Capital has not been reduced by £320. If the amount had been charged against A's Capital there would have been a correcting entry by crediting him with £420 (instead of £100 only as shown in his account) and a debit to Preliminary Expenses £420. This adjusting credit would thus adjust A's Capital back to the same figure as shown in the Trial Balance. The cash paid for reimbursement would be £420 instead of £100, but it will be the same result as shown in A's account, as the capital part and the payment to A is £320 less than shown in A's Account.

The Bad Debt to A Ltd. is only £35, as £110 is charged against the opening Bad Debt Provision.

The amount of purchase consideration is made up of—

	£	£
Net Tangible Assets, per Capital Account . .		6,400
Increase in Value of Fixtures. . . .	350	
Less decrease in value of Debtors . . .	150	
		200
Goodwill		3,400
		£10,000

Discharged by—

	£	£	£
Cash		9,100	
Less Reimbursement of Preliminary Expenses .	100		
Director's Fee paid on account . .	1,000		
		1,100	
			8,000
Shares			2,000
			£10,000

If the item of £320 has been debited to A's Capital, the account would be—

Dr.		£		Cr.			£
To Preliminary Expenses paid	. .	320	By Balance (1st Jan.)				6,400
,, Cash	.	9,100	,, Balance (as would appear in Trial Balance) . . .	c/d			3,020
		£9,420					£9,420
To Balance . . .	b/d	3,020	By Fixtures		.		350
,, Bad Debt Provision . .	.	150	,, Preliminary Expenses . .		.		420
,, Share Capital . .	.	2,000	,, Director's Fee . .		.		1,000
			,, Goodwill . . .		.		3,400
		£5,170					£5,170

71. Dr.   5 PER CENT DEBENTURES   Cr.

19.7			£	19.7				£
July	1	To Stock redeemed—cost .	2,450	Jan.	1	By Balance . .	b/d	55,000
		,, Debenture Redemption Fund—Profit on Redemption . . .	50					
Dec.	31	,, Balance . . c/d	52,500					
			£55,000					£55,000
19.8			£	19.8				£
Mar.	31	To Stock redeemed—cost .	1,492	Jan.	1	By Balance . .	b/d	52,500
		,, Debenture Redemption Fund—Profit on Redemption . . .	8					
Dec.	31	,, Stock repaid by Drawings	2,000					
		,, Balance . . c/d	49,000					
			£52,500					£52,500
				19.9				£
				Jan.	1	By Balance . .	b/d	49,000

Dr. TRUSTEES FOR 5 PER CENT DEBENTURES—CASH ACCOUNT *Cr.*

19.7				£	19.7			£
Jan.	1	To Balance . . b/d		97	July	1	By Redemption £2,500 Debenture Stock . .	2,450
		,, Cash—General . .		3,000			,, Purchase of 3% Funding Stock . . .	658
Feb.	1	,, Interest, net—½ yr. (£1,800)		27			,, Balance . . . c/d	43
Aug.	1	,, ,, ,, ,, ,,		27				
				£3,151				£3,151
19.8					19.8			
Jan.	1	To Balance . . b/d		43	Mar. 31		By Redemption £1,500 Debenture Stock . .	1,492
		,, Cash—General . .		3,000			,, Purchase of 3% Funding Stock . . .	1,520
Feb.	1	,, Interest, net—½ yr. (£2,500)		38			,, Repayment by Drawing of £2,000 Debenture Stock	2,000
Aug.	1	,, ,, ,, ,, (£4,100)		62			,, Balance . . . c/d	51
Nov.	10	,, Proceeds of Sale of £2,000 3% Funding Stock .		1,920				
				£5,063				£5,063
19.9								
Jan.	1	To Balance . b/d		51				

TRUSTEES FOR 5 PER CENT DEBENTURES—INVESTMENT ACCOUNT
Dr. (3 PER CENT FUNDING STOCK) *Cr.*

				Nominal £	£					Nominal £	£
19.7						19.7					
Jan.	1	To Balance .		1,800	1,675	Dec. 31	By Balance . c/d			2,500	2,333
Sept. 30		,, Purchase at 94 .		700	658						
				£2,500	£2,333					£2,500	£2,333
19.8						19.8					
Jan.	1	To Balance . b/d		2,500	2,333	Nov. 10	By Sale at 96 .	.		2,000	1,920
Apr. 30		,, Purchase at 95 .		1,600	1,520		,, Balance . c/d			2,100	1,933
				£4,100	£3,853					£4,100	£3,853
19.9											
Jan.	1	To Balance . b/d		2,100	1,933						

72.   Bowmen Ltd.
(a)   Journal

19.4		£	£
May 1	Realization Account . . . . . Dr.	233,800	
	To Land		5,100
	„ Buildings		22,850
	„ Plant		45,050
	„ Stocks		85,800
	„ Debtors		45,000
	„ Investments		10,000
	„ Goodwill		20,000
	Creditors . . . . . . Dr.	17,800	
	To Realization Account. . . .		17,800
	Debentures (Liability) . . . . Dr.	45,000	
	Realization Account (Premium on Redemption) .	4,000	
	To Debentures held (Asset) . . .		4,800
	„ Sundry Members		200
	„ Debenture Holders		44,000
	Archers Ltd. . . . . . . Dr.	263,995	
	To Realization Account (Purchase considera-tion)		263,995
	Realization Account (Expenses) . . . Dr.	750	
	To Cash		750
	Share Capital . . . . . . Dr.	120,000	
	General Reserve . . . . . Dr.	75,000	
	Profit and Loss . . . . . Dr.	21,550	
	Insurance Fund . . . . . Dr.	10,000	
	Realization Account . . . . Dr.	43,245	
	To Sundry Members		269,795
	(See rough supporting Ledger Account.)		
	Sundry Members (Shares in Archers Ltd.) . Dr.	139,983	
	Debenture Holders (Debentures of Archers Ltd.) Dr.	44,000	
	Cash . . . . Dr.	80,012	
	To Archers Ltd. (Discharge of Purchase Consideration)		263,995
	Sundry Members (81½p per share) . . Dr.	130,000	
	Sundry Members (*re* fractions) . . . Dr.	12	
	To Cash (see below)		130,012

Summary of Cash receivable from Archers Ltd.—

		£
The members whose shares "divide out" receive cash (in addition to shares in Archers Ltd.) on 159,980 at 81½p. . .		129,983·75
The members whose shares involve fractions receive cash—		
20 at 81¼ (in lieu of shares)	£16·25	
[1]20 at 60p (i.e. 12 at £1)	12·00	
		28·25
Total as above		£130,012·00

[1] For the 20 now exchangeable shares the members receive (⅔ + ⅓), i.e. ⅔ of £1 = £12

SCHEDULES

SHARES EXCHANGEABLE
(1) 160,000 − 310 (As below) = 159,690
(2) 310 − 20 (See (a) below)   290

See (x) below 159,980
Shares not exchanged
(See (b) below)   20

ORDINARY SHARES IN ARCHERS LTD.
63,876
116 (See (c) below)
$\frac{5}{8}$ = 63,992 at £1·62½ = £103,987 (See (d) below)
$\frac{7}{8}$ = 8 at £1 = 8

(d) £103,995

(1) As above (1) 159,690 divided by 5
(2) ,, ,, (2) 290 ,, ,, 5

As above (x) 159,980
See (b) below   20

PREFERENCE SHARES IN ARCHERS LTD.
31,938
58 (See (f) below)
$\frac{1}{2}$ = 31,996 at £1·12½ = £35,995½ (See (e) below)
$\frac{2}{5}$ = 4 at £1 = 4

£35,999½

Schedule of Fractions—

Holdings of Shares	Total exchangeable	Exchangeable into Ordinary	Exchangeable into Preference	Not exchangeable
114	110	44	22	4
92	90	36	18	2
72	70	28	14	2
22	20	8	—	2
10	—	—	4	10
= (a) + (b) above 310	(a) 290	(c) 116	(f) 58	(b) 20

(See above)(See above)

Purchase Consideration—

Shares—	£
Ordinary = 63,992 at £1·62½ (d) above . . .	103,987
4½ per cent Cumulative Preference £31,996 at £1·12½ = £35,995½ (e) above	35,996 (to nearest £)
Cash	80,000
Cash (fractions)	12
£44,000 4½ per cent Debentures	44,000
	£263,995

(b)

ARCHERS LTD.

JOURNAL

19.4		£	£
May 1	Land . . . . Dr.	5,100	
	Buildings . . . . Dr.	22,850	
	Plant . . . . Dr.	45,050	
	Stock . . . . Dr.	81,510	
	Debtors . . . . Dr.	45,000	
	Investments . . . . . . Dr.	10,000	
	Goodwill . . . . Dr.	73,410	
	To Creditors		17,800
	,, Doubtful Debt Provision . . .		1,125
	,, Liquidator of Bowmen Ltd. . .		263,995
		£282,920	£282,920
	Liquidator of Bowmen Ltd. . . . . Dr.	263,995	
	To Ordinary Share Capital . .		63,992
	,, 4½ per cent Preference Share Capital .		31,996
	,, Share Premium—		
	Ordinary (63,992 at 62½p) . .		39,995
	Preference (31,996 at 12½p) . .		4,000
	,, Cash		80,012
	,, 4½ per cent Debentures . . .		44,000
		£263,995	£263,995

It is assumed that the cash payment of 50p per share is payable to *all* members including those who are paid cash for fractions.

There are 20 shares not capable of exchange, i.e. into 8 ordinary shares and 4 Preference Shares of Archers Ltd., and it is assumed that the £1 per share is meant to cover "compensation for 12 shares."

Sctudents will usually find it necessary to build up from the Journal rough supporting acounts to assist in the final entries. The three most important ones are—

Dr.			REALIZATION ACCOUNT			Cr.
		£				£
To Sundries		233,800	By Creditors	.	.	17,800
,, Expenses		750	,, Purchase Consideration	.	.	263,995
,, Debentures (Premium) .	.	4,000				
,, Sundry Members .	.	43,245				
		£281,795				£281,795

Dr.			CASH			Cr.
		£				£
To Balance (per B.S.) .	.	50,750	By Realization Account—			0
,, Archers Ltd. .	.	80,012	Expenses .	.	.	75
			,, Sundry Members	.	.	130,00
			,, ,, ,,	.	.	1
		£130,762				£130,762

Dr.			SUNDRY MEMBERS			Cr.
	£	£				£
To Shares in Archers Ltd.			By Debentures held .	.	.	200
Ordinary .	103,987		,, Realization Account .	.		43,245
Preference .	35,996		,, Transfers . .	.		226,550
		139,983	(per Journal			
,, Cash . . .	.	130,000	Composite entry)			
,, ,, (fractions) .	.	12				
		£269,995				£269,995

73.   TRADING AND PROFIT AND LOSS ACCOUNT
FOR THE YEAR ENDED 31ST DECEMBER, YEAR 19..

		£				£
Opening Stock . . .		120	Sales		91,931
General Expenses (detailed) .		78,035	Closing Stock		160
Manager's Fixed Remuneration . . .	£1,800					
,, Commission .	460					
		2,260				
Royalties . . .		4,638				
Hire Purchase Interest . .		550				
Depreciation—						
Plant and Machinery .	£1,425					
Motor Lorries .	743					
Lease amortization .	773					
		2,941				
Net Profit . . . c/d		3,547				
		£92,091				£92,091
Balance forward . . .		6,094	Balance forward . . .			2,547
			Net Profit . . . b/d			3,547
		£6,094				£6,094

BALANCE SHEET AS AT 31ST DECEMBER, YEAR 19..

	£			£	£	£
Share Capital—			Fixed Assets			
Authorized—			Plant and Machinery	19,000	9,975	9,025
50,000 Shares of 25p each .	12,500					
			Motor Lorries .	3,000	2,500	500
Issued—			Premium on Lease .	10,000	4,673	5,327
40,000 Shares of 25p each fully paid	10,000					
Profit and Loss Account . . .	6,094			32,000	17,148	14,852
	16,094		Motor Lorries acquired on Hire Purchase			
Hire Purchase liability . . .	2,925		(Cash price) .	5,400	743	4,657
				£37,400	£17,891	£19,509
Current Liabilities—						
Creditors and accruals .	£2,100					
Bank overdraft . .	5,600		Current Assets—			
Hire Purchase Interest .	550		Cash		£50	
Minimum Rent .	625		Debtors . . .		5,723	
Manager's Commission .	460		Stock of Gravel . .		160	
		9,335				5,933
			Hire Purchase Interest Suspense .			650
			Contingent Assets—			
			Short Workings Account . .			2,262
		£28,354				£28,354

WORKING SCHEDULES AND ACCOUNTS

Dr.   Cr.

T.B. = Total £230,206 − [items marked * viz. £5,600   £   £
+ £2,100 + £2,547 + £91,931 + £10,000 + £2,925] = 115,103   115,103

Gravel output—		
Sales	61,600	cubic yards
Closing Stock	150	,, ,,
	61,750	
Less Opening Stock . . .	110	cubic yards
	61,640	
Add Yardage unaccounted for .	200	cubic yards
Total Output . . .	61,840	,, ,,
Royalties 61,840 cub. yd. at 7½p .	£4,638	

ROYALTIES

	£		£
To Lessor	4,638	By P. & L.	4,638

SHORT WORKINGS

	£		£
To Balance	4,400	By Lessor	2,138
		" Balance, per B.S.	2,262
	£4,400		£4,400

LESSOR

	£		£
To Short Workings	2,138	By Royalties	4,638
" Cash	1,875		
" Balance, per B.S.	625		
	£4,638		£4,638

NEW LORRIES

	£			£
To Cash	5,400			

VEHICLE SUPPLIERS LTD.

	£			£
To Cash—Deposits . . .	1,200	By New Lorries	5,400
„ „ —11 Instalments of £225 .	2,475	„ H.P. Interest Suspense . .	1,200
„ Balance—13 Instalments of £255	2,925		
	£6,600		£6,600
		By Balance	2,925

HIRE PURCHASE INTEREST SUSPENSE

	£		£
To Vehicle Suppliers Ltd. . .	1,200	By Profit and Loss Account—	
		11 at £50	550
		„ Balance—	
		13 at £50	650
	£1,200		£1,200
To Balance	650		

ANNUAL DEPRECIATION ON H.P. LORRIES

Y—Cost £5,400—R.V. £200 . . . £5,200

$\frac{1}{7}$ thereof £743

Depreciation—

	Asset at cost (a)	Previous Depn. (b)	Balance of Asset per T.B. (a) − (b)	Current Depn. (c)	Depn. to date [(b) + (c)] (d)	Balance of Asset (a) − (d)
	£	£	£	£	£	£
Premium on Lease . . .	10,000	3,900	(6,100) ▲	773	4,673	5,327
Plant	19,000	8,550	(10,450)	1,425	9,975	9,025
Motor Lorries	3,000	2,500	(500)		2,500	5,327
Hire Purchase	5,400			743	743	4,657
	£37,400	£14,950		£2,941	£17,891	£19,509
	B.S.			P. & L.	B.S.	B.S.

Lease (Amortization based on depletion)

$$\frac{\text{Current output}}{\text{Total content}} = \frac{61,840}{800,000} \times £10,000$$

$$= \tfrac{1}{80} \times £61,840 = £773$$

Manager's Commission—

		£
Net Profit *after* Commission		3,547
Commission		460
Profit, subject to and forming the basis of Commission . .		£4,007

	Total £		Manager £	Balance £
Commission on profit . .	1,000			1,000
„ „ „ . .	550	$\frac{1}{11} \times 550$	50	500
		i.e. $(\tfrac{1}{10} \times 500)$		
„ „ „ . .	2,457	$\frac{1}{6} \times 2,457$	410	2,047
		i.e. $(\tfrac{1}{6} \times 2,047)$		
	£4,007		£460	£3,547

74.

Purchase Consideration—

		£
8,000 Shares at £3 each		24,000
£3,300 Debentures (discharging the Debenture debt of £3,000 at 110 per cent)		3,300
		£27,300

S Ltd., by purchasing £1,000 (costing £960) of its own Debentures has to that extent extinguished its debenture indebtedness, leaving £3,000 still outstanding.

JOURNAL

		£	£
Realization Account . . . . . *Dr.*		19,040	
Creditors . . . . *Dr.*		2,000	
To Sundry Assets			21,040
Debentures . . . . *Dr.*		4,000	
Realization Account (Premium on Debentures) . *Dr.*		300	
To Debenture-holders			3,300
„ Realization (Profit on purchased £1,000 own Debentures)			40
„ Own Debentures			960
B Ltd. . . . . *Dr.*		27,300	
To Realization Account			27,300
Share in B Ltd. . . . . . . *Dr.*		24,000	
Debentures in B Ltd. . . . . . *Dr.*		3,300	
To B Ltd.			27,300
Share Capital . . . . . . *Dr.*		10,000	
Reserves . . . . *Dr.*		6,000	
Realization Account . . . . . *Dr.*		8,000	
To Sundry Members			24,000
Debenture Holders . . . . . *Dr.*		3,300	
To Debentures in B Ltd.			3,300
Sundry Members . . . . . *Dr.*		24,000	
To Shares in B Ltd.			24,000
Goodwill . . . . . . *Dr.*		8,260	
Sundry Assets [As valued—per Balance Sheet of S Ltd.] . . . . . . *Dr.*		21,040	
To Creditors			2,000
„ Liquidator of S Ltd.			27,300
Liquidator of S Ltd. . . . . *Dr.*		27,300	
To Share Capital (£1 fully paid) . .			8,000
„ Share Premium (£2 per share) . .			16,000
„ Debentures			3,300

CHAPTER XXIV

1. [It is advisable to prepare in draft form the Balance Sheet of Craigmount Trust Ltd. before proceeding with the main part of the question.]

CRAIGMOUNT TRUST LTD.

BALANCE SHEET AS AT 31ST DECEMBER, 19.4

	£			£
Share Capital	200,000	Goodwill		10,000
Profit and Loss Account: Dividends (19.4)—		Investments in Subsidiaries—		
R. R. Ltd. . . £1,800		R. R. Ltd. . . £25,000		
S. S. Ltd. . . 7,500		*Less* Dividend . . (a) 1,600		
				23,400
_____ (c) 9,300		S. S. Ltd. . . £56,000		
T. T. Ltd. 3,000		*Less* Dividend . . (b) 4,166⅔		
				51,833⅓
		T. T. Ltd.		69,000
		R. R. Ltd.		2,000
		Cash		15,066⅔
		Sundry Net Assets . . .		41,000
	£212,300			£212,300

CAPITAL RESERVE ARISING ON PURCHASE

	R. R. Ltd.	S. S. Ltd.	T. T. Ltd.
	£	£	£
Purchase Price of Shares	25,000	56,000	69,000
Less Par Value of Shares	20,000	50,000	80,000
Excess (+) or Deficiency (−) . . .	+ 5,000	+ 6,000	− 11,000
Reserve and Profit and Loss Account [see below]	4,800	9,166⅔	10,400
Goodwill	£200		
Capital Reserve		£3,166⅔	£21,400 } = £24,366⅔

¹ Dividends received made up of items (a), (b), and (c).

RESERVES AND PROFIT AND LOSS ACCOUNTS AS AT
DATE OF PURCHASE OF SHARES

	R. R. Ltd.	S. S. Ltd.	T.T. Ltd.
	£	£	£
Reserve	4,000		17,000
Profit and Loss Account	2,000	5,000	−4,000
	6,000	5,000	13,000
Add Buildings written up		6,000	
	£6,000	£11,000	£13,000
Proportions—			
Craigmount Trust Ltd.	⅘ 4,800	⅚ 9,166⅔	⅘ 10,400
Minority Shareholders	⅕ 1,200	⅙ 1,833⅓	⅕ 2,600

PROFITS AND LOSSES ARISING DURING 19.4

	R.R. Ltd.	S.S. Ltd.	T.T. Ltd.	Total
	£	£	£	£
Profits and Losses *after* Current Dividend . .	+5,000	+10,000	− *2,000*	+13,000
Plant written off			−*10,000*	−*10,000*
	+£5,000	+£10,000	−£12,000	+£3,000
Proportions—	£	£	£	£
Craigmount Trust Ltd.	⅘ 4,000	⅚ 8,333⅓	⅘ −*9,600*	[1]2,733⅓
Minority Shareholders (see below) . .	⅕ 1,000	⅙ 1,666⅔	⅕ −*2,400*	266⅔
MINORITY SHAREHOLDERS	£	£	£	£
Share Capital	5,000	10,000	20,000	35,000
Profit and Reserve (31st Dec., 19.3) . . .	1,200	1,833⅓	2,600	5,633⅓
Profit and Loss (19.4) *after* Current Dividend .	1,000	1,666⅔	−*2,400*	266⅔
	7,200	13,500	20,200	40,900
Less (19.3) Dividend (⅕ × £2,000) . . .	400			
„ „ (⅙ × £5,000) . . .		833⅓		1,233⅓
	£6,800	£12,666⅔	£20,200	[1]£39,666⅔

[1] Per Consolidated Balance Sheet

Draft Consolidated Balance Sheet of Craigmount Trust Ltd. and its Subsidiaries as at 31st December, 19.4

	£	£		£	£	£
Share Capital of Craigmount Trust Ltd., Authorized and Issued—			Goodwill—			
200,000 Shares of £1 each, fully paid		200,000	S. S. Ltd.		10,000	
Capital Reserve		24,366⅔	T. T. Ltd.		25,000	
Profit and Loss Account—			Craigmount Trust Ltd.		10,000	45,000
Subsidiary Companies (per Schedule)	2,733⅓		Sundry Assets—			
Craigmount Trust Ltd.	9,300	12,033⅓	Craigmount Trust Ltd.			41,000
6% Debentures		10,000	Land and Buildings—			
Minority Shareholders (per Schedule)		39,666⅔	R. R. Ltd.		9,000	
Creditors—			S. S. Ltd.	20,000		
R. R. Ltd. [£6,000 — £2,000]	4,000		Add Appreciation	6,000	26,000	
S. S. Ltd. [£16,000 — £1,000]	15,000		T. T. Ltd.		11,000	46,000
T. T. Ltd.	28,000	47,000	Plant—			
			R. R. Ltd.		10,000	
			S. S. Ltd.		40,000	
			T. T. Ltd.	65,000		
			Less written off	10,000	55,000	105,000
			Stock—			
			R. R. Ltd.		7,000	
			S. S. Ltd.		12,000	
			T. T. Ltd.		23,000	42,000
			Debtors—			
			R. R. Ltd. [£10,000 — £1,000]		9,000	
			S. S. Ltd.		13,000	
			T. T. Ltd. [£14,000 — £3,000]		11,000	33,000
			Cash—			
			R. R. Ltd.		4,000	
			S. S. Ltd.		1,000	
			T. T. Ltd.		1,000	
			Craigmount Trust Ltd.		15,066⅔	21,066⅔
		£333,066⅔				£333,066⅔

[The Balance Sheet is shown in detail solely to assist the student in following its compilation.]

607

Notes. (i) Plant written off against current earnings.
(ii) Capital Reserve may be set off against Goodwill.
(iii) It is assumed that Craigmount Trust Ltd. has paid no dividend.

SCHEDULE OF PROFIT AND LOSS

	R. R. Ltd.	Proportion		S. S. Ltd.	Proportion		T. T. Ltd.	Proportion	
		Craig-mount	Min-ority		Craig-mount	Min-ority		Craig-mount	Min-ority
	£	£	£	£	£	£	£	£	£
Profit (or Loss)	‡ 7,250	5,800	1,450	‡ 19,000	15,833⅓	3,166⅔	‡ −12,000	−9,600	−2,400
Less Dividend	2,250	† 1,800	¶ 450	9,000	† 7,500	¶ 1,500			
Net Balance per Accounts	£5,000	*£4,000	£1,000	£10,000	*£8,333⅓	£1,666⅔	−£12,000	*−£9,600	−£2,400

		£
Items marked † amount to	. . . .	9,300
Items marked * amount to	. . . .	2,733⅓
Total (per C.B.S.)	. . . .	£12,033⅓

‡ [It will be observed that the total net profits are £14,250, *all* of which are retained in the organization, except for the items marked ¶, representing dividends paid to Minority shareholders, viz. £1,950, leaving a balance of £12,300, which is made up of—
   (a) £12,033⅓ for the group.
   (b) £266⅔ for the minority shareholders (the items in heavy type and italics: £1,000 + £1,666⅔ −£2,400).]

Note to Students. The adverse result (as shown by the accounts) representing T.T. Ltd. is £6,000, but this has been increased by the write-off *re* Plant, £10,000, making £16,000, of which £4,000 was already in debit at the commencement of the year 19.4.

2. *Draft* Consolidated Balance Sheet of H Ltd. and its Subsidiary, S Ltd., as at 31st December, 19..

	£	£			£	£
Share of Capital of H Ltd.		20,000	Sundry Assets, H Ltd.	£13,250		
Revenue Reserves—			Less Depreciation	1,800	11,450	
H Ltd.	1,800		Sundry Assets, S Ltd.	£13,820		
S Ltd. £500			Less Depreciation	620	13,200	
Less Minority Shareholders 50	450				24,650	
		2,250	Goodwill[1]		4,210	
Profit and Loss Account—						
H Ltd., Profit for year £750						
Less Depreciation 1,800						
£1,050						
Loss (*deducted below*) £1,050						
Profit and Loss Account—Credit Balance £1,700						
Less Loss (*above*) 1,050	650					
S Ltd., Profit for year £700						
Less Depreciation 620						
£80						
Less Minority Shareholders 8	72					
		722				
Minority Shareholders of S Ltd.—						
Share Capital: 1,000 Ordinary Shares of £1 each fully paid	1,000					
Reserves of S Ltd. (see above)	50					
Capital Reserve, 10% of £3,100[1]	310					
Profit and Loss Account (see above)	8					
		1,368				
Creditors—						
H Ltd.	3,000					
S Ltd.	1,520					
		4,520				
		£28,860				£28,860

[1] For footnote, see foot of next page.

3.   CONSOLIDATED BALANCE SHEET OF BISHOP & CO. LTD., AND ITS
SUBSIDIARY COMPANY, WEBSTER & CO. LTD., AS AT
31ST DECEMBER, 19..

	£			£		£
Share Capital of Bishop & Co. Ltd.— Authorized, issued, and fully paid: 100,000 Shares of £1 each		100,000	Fixed Assets— Freehold Property: At Cost	£ ?		
Reserves and Surplus, *less* amounts attributable to outside Shareholders:			*Less* Depreciation	?		95,000
Capital Reserve arising on consolidation	£4,500		Plant and Machinery: At Cost	£ ?		
Revenue Reserve (general)	50,000		*Less* Depreciation	?		14,000
Profit and Loss Account	10,000					109,000
		64,500				
		164,500	Current Assets— Stocks		£35,000	
Minority Interest in Capital and Surplus		2,500	Debtors		27,000	
Current Liabilities—			Investments at Cost		2,000	
Creditors		32,000	Cash at Bank		26,000	90,000
		£199,000				£199,000

Note. It is assumed that the Balance Sheets are those made up as at the date of
purchase of the shares by Bishop & Co. Ltd., since the question does not indicate the
date of such purchase.

If the whole of the profit of Webster & Co. Ltd. has been earned since the acquisition of the shares by Bishop & Co. Ltd., the latter company for the expenditure of
£18,000 acquired $\frac{9}{10} \times$ £15,000 fewer assets, i.e. £13,500, thus converting the Capital
Reserve of £4,500 into Goodwill, £9,000. This may be proved by the fact that the
cost of shares in Webster & Co. Ltd. was £18,000, and the net assets acquired, reflected
in the Share Capital Account, were £9,000 [$\frac{9}{10} \times$ £10,000].

(Footnote to page 609)

	£	£	£
Computation of Goodwill—			
Goodwill, S Ltd.			2,000
Excess of Cost of Share over Equity purchased			
Cost of Shares		14,000	
Less Nominal Value		9,000	
		5,000	
Less Reserve	1,500		
Profit and Loss Account	1,600		
	£3,100		
90 % thereof		2,790	
			*2,210
			£4,210

	£	£
Or		
* Cost of Share in S Ltd.		14,000
Less 90 % of Equity in S Ltd.		11,790
[i.e. Share Capital	10,000	
Reserve	1,500	
Profit and Loss	1,600	
	£13,100]	
		£2,210

4. CONSOLIDATED BALANCE SHEET OF GENERAL MANUFACTURING CO.
LTD. AND ITS SUBSIDIARY COMPANY, COMPONENT CO. LTD.,
AS AT 30TH JUNE, 19.8

	£				£
Share Capital of General Manufacturing Co. Ltd.—		Fixed Assets—			
Authorized and Issued:		Goodwill			32,000
15,000 Shares of £10 each, fully		Freehold Premises—		£	
paid	150,000	General . .		103,000	
Revenue Reserves—		Component . .		30,000	
General . . £95 000					133,000
Profit and Loss Accounts 87,250		Machinery—			
———	182,250	General . . .		30,000	
		Component . .		27,100	
Creditors—					57,100
General . . . £9,000		Current Assets—			
Component . . 16,100		Stock—			
———	25,100	General . .		33,250	
		Component . .		20,200	
					53,450
		Debtors—			
		General . .		28,000	
		Component . .		9,800	
					37,800
		Cash—			
		General . .		33,000	
		Component . .		11,000	
					44,000
	£357,350				£357,350

Notes. (i) It is assumed that the interim dividend was paid out of current profits;
if paid out of profits undistributed on 1st July, 19.7, the dividends should not have
been credited to Profit and Loss Account, but to the investment.

(ii) Goodwill is £(112,000 − 50,000 − 2,000 − 28,000)   = £32,000

(iii) Profit and Loss Account is £(80,000 + 8,000)   = £88,000

Less Internal Unrealized Profit[1] . . .   750

——— = £87,250

(iv) Unrealized Profit on internal transactions eliminated.
(v) Internal Debit and Credit items eliminated.

[1] Unsold Stock in books at £3,000, cost £2,250 (part of £6,000, cost £4,500).

5. (1) The relevant provisions of the Companies Acts 1948 and 1967 are as follows—

(*a*) A parent/subsidiary relationship exists only if one company is a member of
another and controls the composition of its board of directors, or holds more than half
in nominal value of its equity share capital (C.A. 1948, Sect. 154 (1)). From the facts
given it would seem that A Ltd. is not a subsidiary of X & Co. Ltd., but that B Ltd.
and C Ltd. are.

(*b*) When at the end of its financial year a company has subsidiaries, group accounts
must be laid before the company in general meeting, together with the company's own
Balance Sheet and Profit and Loss Account (C.A. 1948, Sect. 150). The various forms
of group accounts are dealt with in the following section.

(*c*) A holding company's directors shall secure that, except where in their opinion
there are good reasons against it, the financial year of each subsidiary shall coincide
with the company's own financial year (C.A. 1948, Sect. 153). In this case, assuming
that there are good reasons for not altering the financial year of the subsidiaries, the
group accounts will incorporate the subsidiaries' Balance Sheets and accounts at the
various year-ends in 19.9 (C.A. 1948, Sect. 152 (2)).

(*d*) The aggregates respectively of shares in and amounts owing to and from
subsidiaries must be separately stated in the Balance Sheet of the parent company
(C.A. 1967, Sch. 2, Sect. 15 (2)).

(2) X & Co. Ltd. Balance Sheet as at 31st December, 19.9 (*includes*)—

Assets	£
Investment at cost (? Quoted)	50,000
Investments in Subsidiary Companies at cost, *less* Provision[1]	159,000
Loan to Subsidiary Company	3,000

PROFIT AND LOSS ACCOUNT FOR THE YEAR ENDED 31ST DECEMBER,
19.9 (*includes*)

Debit side—   £
   To Provision for loss incurred by Subsidiary Company . . 1,000
      [*See above.*]

Credit side—
   By Dividend Receivable from Subsidiary Company (gross) . 8,125

The following further information should be given—

(1) Group Accounts as indicated above.
(2) A statement giving—
   (*a*) the reasons why the directors consider that the subsidiaries' financial years should not end with that of the company;
   (*b*) the dates on whicht he subsidiaries' financial years ending last before 31st December, 19.9 ended.

(3) The various qualifications in the auditors' report of B Ltd. and C Ltd. will be dealt with in the auditors' report of X & Co. Ltd., covering the group accounts.

(4) The group accounts, as well as the accounts of X & Co. Ltd., must give all the information required by Schedule 2 to the Companies Act 1967. Sufficient details are not given in the question to permit this to be dealt with.

Note. In view of the loss incurred by A Ltd., a provision in respect of diminution in value of the investment may be made.

[1] £150,000 (B Ltd.) + £10,000 (C Ltd.) − (⅔ × £1,500 [C Ltd.'s Loss]) = £160,000 − £1,000 [*see above*].

6. CONSOLIDATED BALANCE SHEET OF PARENT CO. LTD. AND ITS SUBSIDIARIES, AS AT 31ST MARCH, 19..

	£	£	£
Share Capital of Parent Co. Ltd.—			
Authorized and Issued:			
250,000 Shares of £1 each, fully paid	£250,000		
Less Shares held by B Subsidiary Ltd.	47,000		203,000
Reserves and Surplus, *less* amounts applicable to outside Shareholders—			
Debenture Stock Reserve		£400	
Revenue Reserves:			
General		£75,000	
Profit and Loss Accounts—			
Parent Co. Ltd.		£23,192	
B Subsidiary Ltd.	£37,429		
Less Minority Share-holders: 6%	2,246	35,183	
C Subsidiary Ltd.		11,656	
		70,031	
		19,602	
Less A Subsidiary Ltd. (Loss)		50,429	125,829
			328,829
Minority Shareholders—			
A Subsidiary Ltd.:			
Share Capital		£1,240	
B Subsidiary Ltd.:			
Share Capital	£12,000		
Profit and Loss Account	2,246[1]	14,246	
			15,486
Debentures—			
4½% First Mortgage Debenture Stock: issued	£50,000		
Less Purchased and Cancelled	44,600	£5,400	
4% Debenture Stock (A Subsidiary Ltd.)	£20,000		
Less held by Parent Co. Ltd.	1,900	18,100	
			23,500
Current Liabilities—			
Trade Creditors		42,252	
Current Taxation		77,166	
			£487,233

	£
Goodwill	21,060
Sundry Assets (detailed)	396,173
Investments at cost—3½% War Stock (MARKET value?)	70,000
	£487,233

[1] $\frac{13}{200}$ or 6% of B Ltd. = 6% of £37,429

Internal Loans [eliminated] are—

Liabilities		£	Assets			£
Parent Co. Ltd. (from B Ltd.)	.	19,600	Parent Co. Ltd. (to A Ltd.)	.	£620	
A Ltd. (from Group Co.'s)	.	34,165	,, ,, (to B Ltd.)	.	47	
B Ltd. (from Parent Co. Ltd.)	. .	47				667
			B Ltd. (to Parent Co. Ltd.)	. .		19,600
			C Ltd. (to Group Co.) .	. .		33,545
		£53,812				£53,812

Goodwill—

	SHARES IN—					
	A Ltd.		B Ltd.		C Ltd.	Parent Co. Ltd.
	Pref- erence	Ordinary	Pref- erence	Ordinary	Ordinary	Ordinary
	£	£	£	£	£	£
Cost of Shares . .	2,820	10,000	50,000	200,000	54,000	53,000
Par Value of Shares .	3,760	10,000	50,000	188,000	50,000	47,000
Goodwill . . .				12,000	4,000	6,000 = 22,000
Capital Reserve . .	940					940

Net Cost of Goodwill (per C.B.S.) £21,060

Notes. (i) It is assumed that all the profits and reserves have been earned since the date of the share purchases.

(ii) The Preference Shares are assumed to be preferential as to capital, and all "priorities" (debenture interest and preference dividends) met.

(iii) For examination purposes, a candidate may ignore the actual working of the calculation required to throw back the loss arising in A Subsidiary Ltd. to Parent Co. Ltd., and thence to B Subsidiary Ltd. through its shareholding in Parent Co. Ltd. The question has been worked accordingly, but it is advisable to show the *basis* of the calculation.

For further information both the foregoing calculation and the result are appended.

SCHEDULE OF PROFIT AND LOSS ACCOUNTS

		Parent Company Ltd.	A Subsidiary Ltd.	B Subsidiary Ltd.	C Subsidiary Ltd.
		£	£	£	£
Balances per Accounts		23,192	−19,602	37,429	11,656
Add B Ltd.	94%	46,010		$\frac{47}{250}$ 11,517	
C Ltd.	100%	11,656			
		80,858			
Less A Ltd.	100%	19,602			
		61,256	−19,602	48,946	11,656
Less B Ltd.	$\frac{47}{250}$	11,517			
		49,739			
Less Parent Company Ltd. . .	100%		−19,602		11,656
Parent Company Ltd. . .	94%			46,010	
Minority Shareholders—6% of £48,946 . .				£2,936	
		£49,739			

(See page 615)

Formula:

$$H = 23,192 + 11,656 - 19,602 + B \tfrac{94}{100}$$
$$B = 37,429 + \tfrac{47}{250} H.$$

The two results may be compared—

	As on page 614			Per Solution on page 613		
	£	£	£	£	£	£
Minority Shareholders—						
A Ltd., Share Capital		1,240			1,240	
B Ltd., Share Capital	12,000			12,000		
Profit	2,936			2,246		
		14,936			14,246	
			16,176			15,486
Profit and Loss Accounts			49,739			50,429
			£65,915			£65,915

7.   CONSOLIDATED BALANCE SHEET OF HOLDING LTD. AND ITS
         SUBSIDIARIES AS AT 31ST DECEMBER, 19.9

	£			£
Share Capital of Holding Ltd.—		Fixed Assets at Cost—		
Authorized and Issued:		Goodwill (a)		30,750
100,000 Ordinary Shares of £1 each		Land, Buildings, Plant and Ma-		
fully paid	100,000	chinery		75,000
Share Premium Account	10,000			105,750
Profit and Loss Accounts (b)	21,250			
	131,250	Current Assets—		
Minority Shareholders—		Stocks	£21,000	
Share Capital £10,000		Sundry Debtors	19,000	
Less Loss (c) 1,500		Cash at Bank	31,000	
	8,500			71,000
Current Liabilities—				
Sundry Creditors £27,000				
Bills Payable 10,000				
	37,000			
	£176,750			£176,750

Notes.

		£
(a) Goodwill—		
Debit balance of A Ltd.		1,000
Less proportion attributable to Minority Shareholders—¼		250
		750
Excess of purchase price of Shares in B Ltd., over par value		
[£60,000 — £30,000]	£30,000	
Less credit balance of Profit and Loss Account at the		
date of purchase of Shares	6,000	
		24,000
Goodwill in A Ltd.		6,000
Goodwill		£30,750

(b)   SCHEDULE OF PROFIT AND LOSS ACCOUNTS

	Holding Ltd.	A Ltd.	B Ltd.
	£	£	£
Balances per Accounts	23,000	−6,000	3,000
Add ⅔ of B's Profit	2,000		
⅓ of B's Profit		1,000	
	25,000		
Less ¾ of A's Loss	3,750		
	21,250	−5,000	3,000
Less due to Holding [¾]		3,750	
,, ,, ,, [⅔]			2,000
,, ,, A [⅓]			1,000
Holding Ltd.'s Interest therein (per C.B.S.) . .	£21,250		
Proportion attributable to Minority Shareholders .		−£1,250	

(c) Minority Shareholders of A Ltd.—

	£	£
Debit balance of Profit and Loss Account (since acquisition), per statement	1,250	
Add debit balance of Profit and Loss Account (at date of acquisition) per statement	250	
		£1,500

8.   CONSOLIDATED PROFIT AND LOSS ACCOUNT OF HOLDINGS LTD.,
AND ITS SUBSIDIARY COMPANIES FOR THE YEAR ENDED 31ST MARCH, 19.8

	£	£
Trading Profits of the Group (subject to the items stated below)		486,501
Interest on Government Securities		35,000
		521,501
Less Depreciation .	17,000	
Emoluments of the Directors of Holdings Ltd.:		
As Directors £ ?		
As Executives ?		
	13,000	
Corporation Tax on profits of the year	178,100	
Income Tax on Government Securities	14,000	
		222,100
Net Profit of the Group		299,401
Less Proportion of Profits attributable to outside Ordinary Stockholders of Subsidiaries.		31,823
Less **Proportion of Profits retained in the accounts of Subsidiaries attributable to Holdings Ltd. [see page 618 (2) and (4)]**		1,944
Net Profit of Holdings Ltd. for the year (see page 619)		265,634
Add Balance brought forward from previous year		51,430
		317,064
Less Dividends (gross)—		
Paid: Preference—for the year	30,000	
Ordinary—8 % interim	80,000	
	110,000	
Proposed: Ordinary—17 % final	170,000	
		280,000
Balance carried to Consolidated Balance Sheet[1]		£37,064

[1] This will equal the amount in the Balance Sheet of Holdings Ltd. (see pages 619, 620 and 624).

CONSOLIDATED BALANCE SHEET AT 31ST MARCH, 19.8 (*includes*)

	Author-ized	Issued and Converted into Stock	
	£	£	£
Capital, Reserves, and Surplus—			
Share Capital of Holdings Ltd.:			
5 % Cumulative Preference .	?	600,000	
Ordinary .	?	1,000,000	
	£ ?		1,600,000
Revenue Reserves and Surplus applicable to the Members of Holdings Ltd.			
Holdings Ltd.: Reserves (*y*)	300,000		
Profit and Loss Account (see above) (*x*)	37,064		
		337,064	
Subsidiaries: Reserves (*y*)	132,800		
Profit and Loss Accounts (*x*)	38,548		
		171,348	508,412(*z*)
			2,108,412
Proportion of Share Capital, Reserves and undistributed Profits of Subsidiaries applicable to outside Ordinary Stockholders .			225,719
Current Liabilities (*include*)—			
Corporation Tax—Accounting Year ended 31st March, 19.8		178,100	
Proposed Dividend (gross) to Members of Holdings Ltd. (see note page 619)		170,000	
			348,100
			£2,682,231

WORKING SCHEDULES

£

(1) Corporation Tax on Profits of the year—
Amount to be provided £64,000 + £45,000 + £69,100 178,100

(2) Profits retained in accounts of Subsidiaries—

		A Ltd.	B Ltd.
		£	£
Trading Profits		122,352	206,515
Interest on Government Securities, *less* Tax		4,800	1,200
		127,152	207,715

	£	£		
Less Directors' Emoluments and Depreciation	5,000	13,500		
Corporation Tax on current profits	45,000	69,100		
Preference Dividend (gross)	10,000	6,000		
Ordinary Dividend (gross): Interim	40,000	50,000		
Final	50,000	67,500		206,100
		150,000		
Less Dividends (gross) from B Ltd.				
(20 per cent + 27 per cent on £50,000) Ordinary Stock	23,500			
		126,500		
				1,615
Less Proportion applicable to outside Ordinary Stockholders—⅕				323
		£652	£1,292	

£1,944

(3) Proportion of Profits applicable to outside Stockholders—
Preference Dividends (gross):

	£	£
A Ltd.—5% on £100,000		5,000
B Ltd.—6% on £50,000		3,000
Ordinary Stock in B Ltd.:		
Profit for year retained in accounts (per (2))	1,615	
Add Ordinary Dividends (gross)	117,500	
Profit for year available for Ordinary Stockholders	£119,115	
50,000/250,000 thereof (see page 619)		23,823
		£31,823

(4) Revenue Reserves and Surplus of Subsidiaries—

	£	£
Reserves of A Ltd. and B Ltd.	141,000	
Less ⅕ of B Ltd. to outside Stockholders (see below)	8,200	
		£132,800
Profit and Loss Accounts of A Ltd. and B Ltd.:		
Balances at 1st April, 19.7	40,300	
Less ⅕ of B Ltd. to outside Stockholders (see below)	3,696	
	36,604	
Add Balance of Profit of year (per (2))[1]	1,944	
		£38,548

(5) Minority Interest—

	£	£
Share Capital: A Ltd., Preference	100,000	
B Ltd,, Preference	50,000	
Ordinary	50,000	
		200,000
Reserves: B Ltd. (per (4))		8,200
Profit and Loss Account Balance, 1st April, 19.7: B Ltd. (per (4))		3,696
Profit for the year: B Ltd. (per (3))	23,823	
Less Interim Ordinary Dividend—⅕ × £50,000	10,000	
		13,823[2]
		£225,719

[1] Reflected in the deduction of £1,944 shown in bold type on page 617.
[2] See note, page 622.

The item of £23,823 shown on p. 618 (3) may be proved as follows—

		£
B Ltd., Trading Profit.		206,515
Interest on Government Securities		2,000
		208,515
Less Directors' Emoluments (£6,000) and Depreciation (£7,500)		13,500
		195,015

Deduct—

		£	
Corporation Tax on profits of the year	. .	£69,100	
Income Tax on Government Securities		800	
			69,900
			125,115
Less Preference Dividends (gross)			6,000
			£119,115

Proportion attributable to outside Ordinary Stockholders—

$\frac{50,000}{250,000}$, i.e. $\frac{1}{5}$, ... £23,823

The net profit of Holdings Ltd. (£265,634), as shown on page 617, being the net profit of the group attributable to Holdings Ltd., less retentions in the books of the subsidiaries, will be the same as that shown in the books of Holdings Ltd. Therefore, if the Profit and Loss Account of **Holdings Ltd.** is shown in consolidated form (as in the answer given on page 617), it should correspond with that which would be submitted as a "straight" Profit and Loss Account. This would be as follows—

PROFIT AND LOSS ACCOUNT OF HOLDINGS LTD. FOR THE YEAR
ENDED 31ST MARCH, 19.8

				£
Trading Profit			.	157,634
Interest on Government Securities (gross) (*a*) .	.	.	.	25,000
				182,634
Less Depreciation and Directors' Emoluments	.	.	.	11,500
				171,134
Dividends from Subsidiaries—				
Dividends, Ordinary and Preference received (gross)	(*b*)	£78,000		
Dividend, Final Ordinary proposed . .	(*c*)	90,500		
				168,500
				339,634
Less Income Tax on Interest and Dividends.	.	.	(*a*)	10,000
				329,634
Less Corporation Tax on current profits	.	.	.	64,000
Agreeing with relevant figures on page 617 .	.	.	.	265,634[1]
Balance of Profit and Loss Account of previous year, forward	.			51,430
				317,064
Deduct Dividends paid and proposed to Members of Holdings				
Ltd. (See page 617)		.	.	280,000[2]
Balance to Balance Sheet of Holdings Ltd. .	.	.	.	£37,064

[1] For footnotes [1] and [2] see foot of next page.

The Balance Sheet of Holdings Ltd. (*not* the Consolidated Balance Sheet of the Group) will be—

	£
Sundry Net Assets	1,380,564
Holdings in Subsidiary Companies (£500,000 plus £200,000)	700,000
Dividends Receivable from Subsidiary Companies (gross)	90,500
	2,171,064
Less Corporation Tax on current profits . . .	64,000
	2,107,064
Proposed Final Dividend to Shareholders of Holdings Ltd. (net)	170,000
	£1,937,064

	£
Represented by—	
Ordinary Stock	1,000,000
Cumulative Preference Stock	600,000
Revenue Reserves	300,000
Profit and Loss Account, per page 617 . . .	37,064
	£1,937,064

As previously stated. the amount standing to the credit of Profit and Loss Account of Holdings Ltd. is the same as that shown by the Consolidated Balance Sheet of the group (see page 617). This is because in the Consolidated Profit and Loss Account of the **group** a deduction is made in respect of the profits of the subsidiaries appropriate to the stockholders of Holdings Ltd. (i.e. after deduction of the amount appropriate to the outside Ordinary Stockholders of B Ltd.) of a sum representing the profits of the subsidiaries *still available for distribution*, viz. £1,944. Since this sum represents the group profit applicable to Holdings Ltd., as shown by the Consolidated Profit and Loss Account of the group, *less* that part that has been brought in the books of Holdings Ltd., it must be equal to the profit earned by Holdings Ltd. itself.

Footnotes to page 619—

[1] The draft Profit and Loss Account (see page 623) requires amending as follows to complete the items introduced since preparation of the draft—

	£
Net Profit (before appropriation of Dividend paid and payable by Holdings Ltd.)	239,134
Less Corporation Tax	64,000
	175,134

Add Dividends (Final) receivable from Subsidiaries—

	A Ltd. £	B Ltd. £	Total £
Gross	(i) 50,000	(ii) 40,500	90,500
			90,500
			£265,634

(i) 12½ per cent on £400,000 Ordinary Stock
(ii) 27 ,, ,, ,, £150,000 ,, ,,

[2] £110,000 paid (per draft Profit and Loss) plus £170,000 proposed (i.e. 17 per cent on £1,000,000 Ordinary Stock, £170,000).

Some readers may experience difficulty with the item of inter-company dividends, and therefore the examination rough working accounts are appended.

DIVIDENDS RECEIVABLE (D.R.)

	£			£
To D.P. (d) . . .	5,000	By Bal. per Q. (Holdings Ltd.) .		78,000
„ „ (e) . . .	3,000	„ „ „ (A Ltd.) . .		10,000
„ „ (f) . . .	80,000			
	£88,000			£88,000

DIVIDENDS PAYABLE (D.P.)

		£				£
To Bal. per Q.—			By M.S. (a)	(See below)		5,000
Inter. Pref. £10,000			„ „ (b)	(„ „)		3,000
plus £6,000 .	.	16,000	„ „ (c)	(„ „)		10,000
„ Bal. per Q.—			„ „ (d)	. . .		5,000
Inter. Ordy £40,000			„ „ (e)	. . .		3,000
plus £50,000 .	.	90,000	„ „ (f)	. . .		80,000
		£106,000				£106,000

OUTSIDE ORDINARY STOCKHOLDERS (M.S.) *includes*)

	£	
To Dividends (a)	5,000	*The account will be credited with the Preference*
„ „ (b)	3,000	*Dividends £8,000 plus their proportion of the Net*
„ „ (c)	10,000	*Profit of B Ltd., £23,823*

(a) Dividend on £100,000 Preference Stock (A Ltd.) at 5 per cent, £5,000 held by M.S.

(b) Dividend on £50,000 Preference Stock (B. Ltd.) at 6 per cent, £3,000 (see page 618).

(d) Similar holding by Holdings Ltd. as in (a).

(e) „ „ „ „ „ as in (b).

(f) Dividends: Interim Ordinary—

		£
(i) £400,000 Ordinary Stock in A Ltd. held by Holdings Ltd., at 10 per cent		40,000
(ii) £150,000 Ordinary Stock in B Ltd., held by Holdings Ltd., at 20 per cent		30,000
(iii) £50,000 Ordinary Stock in B Ltd. held by A Ltd., at 20 per cent		10,000
		£80,000

In order to prepare Consolidated Accounts, the proposed final dividends payable by the subsidiaries must be brought into account (seeing that the parent Company has brought them into the accounts) by the subsidiaries. These will cancel out in the consolidation, except that the gross final dividend of B Ltd. payable to the Minority Shareholders against their credit balance of their share of the net profit of B Ltd., viz. £13,500 (£50,000 Ordinary Stock at 27 per cent) now becomes a *current* liability (as distinct from the long-term liability if this portion of the net profit attributable to them had not been released), and therefore should appear either as a current liability or the Minority Stockholders' balance split between the present proposed final dividend and the balance not yet released by way of dividend, thus—

Minority Stockholders (B Ltd.)—

	£
Proposed Final Dividend (gross)	13,500
Balance retained in B Ltd. (see page 618 (2)) . .	323
	£13,823

Although the final dividends payable by B Ltd. to Holdings Ltd. and A Ltd., and by A Ltd. to Holdings Ltd., cancel out in the consolidation (except that the amount payable to the outside Ordinary Stockholders should be disclosed) and thus do not affect the aggregate group position relating to the assets and liabilities, yet they do affect the position of the individual companies in so far as such dividends will reduce the current assets and so diminish the sum available for payment to the creditors, and the aggregate group assets are not of importance to the creditors of the *subsidiary companies*. Therefore it should be made quite clear to all that there are proposed final dividends payable by the subsidiary companies.

If the subsidiaries do not make the entries necessary to show the proposed final dividends then the holding company will not bring into account such proposed final dividends receivable from the subsidiaries.

The net profit of the holding company will be less by the amount of the proposed gross final dividends from the subsidiaries should it not take into account such dividends, so that although the *group* result is unaffected, the reduction essential (where the Profit and Loss Account of **Holdings Ltd.** is shown in *consolidated* form) will be correspondingly *increased*, and the Consolidated Balance Sheet will show the corresponding figure as a retention. In the problem the original figure of £1,944 (see page 618) will be increased by £90,500, i.e a total of £92,444, as shown on pages 620 and 625.

NOTES

In the absence of "proof" being available through the question not supplying the details of assets and liabilities or the cost of acquisitions of shares, readers may find it difficult to be satisfied about the accuracy of the Profit and Loss figures.

Therefore, by taking the figures supplied by the question and ignoring the actual cost of the share acquisitions, the "balancing figures" necessary to build up the Consolidated Balance Sheet are—

PROFIT AND LOSS ACCOUNTS FOR THE YEAR ENDED 31ST MARCH, 19.8

	Holdings Ltd.	A Ltd.	B Ltd.		Holdings Ltd.	A Ltd.	B Ltd.
	£	£	£		£	£	£
Depreciation and Directors' Fees	11,500	5,000	13,500	Trading Profit	157,634	122,352	206,515
Income Tax	10,000	3,200	800	Inter-company Dividends	78,000	10,000	
Net Profit c/d	239,134	132,152	194,215	Interest on Government Securities	25,000	8,000	2,000
	£260,634	£140,352	£208,515		£260,634	£140,352	£208,515
Dividends (gross):				Profit Forward b/d	51,430	21,820	18,480
Preference	30,000	10,000	6,000	Net Profit	239,134	132,152	194,215
Ordinary	80,000	40,000	50,000				
Balance (per Balance Sheets)	180,564	103,972	156,695				
	£290,564	£153,972	£212,695		£290,564	£153,972	£212,695

BALANCE SHEETS AT 31ST MARCH, 19.8

	Holdings Ltd.	A Ltd.	B Ltd.		Holdings Ltd.	A Ltd.	B Ltd.
	£	£	£		£	£	£
Share Capital	1,600,000	600,000	350,000	Stock held by Holdings Ltd. in			
Reserves	300,000	100,000	41,000	A Ltd.	500,000		
Profit and Loss	180,564	103,972	156,695	B Ltd.	200,000		
				Held by A Ltd. in B Ltd.		50,000	
				Sundry Net Assets	1,380,564	753,972	547,695
				(Total £2,682,231)			
	£2,080,564	£803,972	£547,695		£2,080,564	£803,972	£547,695

623

CONSOLIDATED BALANCE SHEET OF HOLDINGS LTD. AND ITS SUBSIDIARY COMPANIES AS AT 31ST MARCH, 19.8

	£	£	?
Authorized Share Capital—			
Holdings Ltd.			?
Issued Share Capital—			
Ordinary Stock . .		1,000,000	
Cumulative Preference Stock . .		600,000	
			1,600,000
Revenue Reserves and Surplus—			
Reserves:			
Holdings Ltd. . .	£300,000		
Subsidiaries (see page 617)	37,064		
		337,064	
Profit and Loss Account:			
Holdings Ltd. (see page 618 (4))	£132,800		
[1]Subsidiaries [£36,604 + £1,944]	38,548		
		171,348	
			508,412
			2,108,412
Outside Ordinary Stockholders . .			225,719[2]
(For details see summary on other side)			
Total Capital employed by Group . .			2,334,131
Current Liabilities:			
Corporation Tax—Accounting			
Year ended 31st March, 19.8	£178,100		
Proposed Final Ordinary Dividend (gross)	170,000		
			348,100
			£2,682,231

	£
Sundry Net Assets	2,682,231
	£2,682,231

OUTSIDE ORDINARY STOCKHOLDERS

	£
A Ltd. Preference . . .	100,000
B Ltd.	50,000
Ordinary	50,000
	200,000
Proportion [20%]—	
Balance of Profit and Loss B Ltd. .	3,696
Revenue Reserve B Ltd. . .	8,200
Current Profit and Loss B Ltd. . £23,823	
Less Interim Ordinary Dividend paid (net). 10,000	13,823
	£225,719

[1] See pages 617 and 618 (2) and (4).
[2] See Consolidated Balance Sheet on p. 617.

624

The Profit and Loss Account of Holdings Ltd., framed in consolidated form where, as mentioned on page 622, the proposed final dividends payable by subsidiaries is ignored, will be—

CONSOLIDATED PROFIT AND LOSS ACCOUNT OF HOLDINGS LTD.
AND ITS SUBSIDIARY COMPANIES FOR THE YEAR ENDED 31ST MARCH, 19.8

	£
Net Profit of the Group	299,401
Less retained by Subsidiaries (£1,944 + £90,500) (*see* below) . .	92,444
	206,957
Less Minority Shareholders (as shown on page 618) . . .	31,823
	175,134
Add Balance of Holdings Ltd., Profit forward	51,430
	226,564
Less Dividends gross	280,000
Balance to Balance Sheet of Holdings Ltd.. . . . . *Dr.*	£53,436

[Also agreeing with Consolidated Balance Sheet, as indicated below.]

Profit and Loss Account of Holdings Ltd., as per Profit and Loss Account (see p. 617) excluding proposed dividends gross from Subsidiaries, viz.—	37,064
£90,500 (see page 620)	90,500
(Per above and Consolidated Balance Sheet) . . . . *Dr.*	£53,436

	£
The relevant part of the Consolidated Balance Sheet will now be—	
Subsidiaries £38,548 (item (*x*) per page 617) + £90,500 (see note below)	129,048
Add Reserves (items (*y*) page 617)	432,800
	561,848
Deduct Holdings Ltd. *Dr.* balance	53,436
Per Consolidated Balance Sheet (item (*z*) page 617)	£508,412

The difference between the Profit and Loss items as shown on page 617 and those above is reconciled as follows—

	£		£
Profit and Loss—H Ltd. on page 617	37,064		
„ „ „ —Subsidiaries on			
page 618	38,548		
Profit and Loss H Ltd. (as above) .	53,436	Profit and Loss Sub-sidiaries (see below)	129,048
	£129,048		£129,048

	£
The item *debited* on page 618(2) in respect of retained profit . .	1,944
Add Increase	90,500
	£92,444
The item *credited* on page 618(4) in respect of retained profit . .	1,944
Add Increase	90,500
	£92,444
This revised figure brings the item on page 617(4) of . . .	36,604
by	92,444
Profit retained in subsidiaries (as above)	£129,048

9. The £50,000 falls to be subdivided into—

(*a*) pre-acquisition profits attributable to the Group which will be credited against the Cost of Shares acquired, i.e. reducing Goodwill or increasing Capital Reserve.

(*b*) post-acquisition profits attributable to the Group which will be shown in the Consolidated Balance Sheet.

(*c*) The profits, both "pre" and "post" attributable to the Minority Shareholders, which will be shown in the Consolidated Balance Sheet.

The problem is: How much arises under each heading?

In this type of problem the difficulty lies in the treatment of the "derived" profit accruing to a subsidiary from another subsidiary; which, in the example above, is Y Ltd.

Y Ltd. has two sets of profit, viz. the "straight" profit of £40,000 and a "derived" profit because of its shareholding in Z Ltd. Therefore all the profit attributable to it **since** acquisition could normally be considered "free" profit (after allowing for Minority Interests), provided that the Parent Company (X Ltd.) either acquired its shares in Y Ltd. on the **same** date or **before** Y Ltd. acquired its shares in Z Ltd.

If, however, X Ltd. acquires shares in Y Ltd. at a **later** date, then part of the "derived" profits (that otherwise would be "free") of Y Ltd. are, as regards X Ltd., pre-acquisition profits. The profits are, therefore, dealt with as follows—

(1) *Profit of Y Ltd.* (excluding "derived" profit)—

	Total	80% Parent		20% Minority
		Pre	*Post*	
	£	£	£	£
Profit . .	40,000	24,000	8,000	8,000

(2) *Profits of Z Ltd.*

These profits are attributable to three parties, i.e. X Ltd., Y Ltd., and Minority Shareholders, thus—

Shares		Total	X Ltd.		Y Ltd.		Minority
			Pre	*Post*	*Pre*	*Post*	
		£	£	£	£	£	£
5,000	12½% to Minority . .	1,250					1,250
5,000	12½% to Y Ltd. . .	1,250			(*a*) 625	(*b*) 625	
30,000	75% to X Ltd. . .	7,500	(*c*) 5,250	(*d*) 2,250			
		10,000	5,250	2,250	625	625	1,250
Adjustment (3)					+300	−625 +200	+125
Total . . .		£10,000	£5,250	£2,250	£925	£200	£1,375

(*a*) 12½% of £5,000 Reserve at acquisition.
(*b*) 12½% of £5,000 Profits earned (since acquisition) by Z Ltd.
(*c*) 75% of £7,000 Reserve at acquisition.
(*d*) 75% of £3,000 Profit earned since acquisition.

(3) Derived Profit of Y Ltd., through its shareholding in Z Ltd., is £625.
This is analysed—

	£
Minority Interest 20%	125

Profit attributable to Y Ltd. at the date X Ltd. acquired its stake in Y Ltd.—
£3,000 (£8,000 − £5,000, i.e. the Revenue Reserves of Z Ltd. at this date had grown by £3,000)

			£
	12½% of £3,000 .	. £375	
Less Minority Interest 20% thereof	.	75	
			300

Profit attributable to Y Ltd. since X Ltd. acquired its stake in Z Ltd.
£2,000 (£10,000 − £8,000, i.e. in the meantime the Revenue Reserves had grown by a further £2,000)

			£
	12½% of £2,000 .	. £250	
Less Minority Interest: 20% thereof	.	50	
			200
			£625

For the student fully familiar with consolidation work a quick "short cut" method is readily available, as follows—

The profit increase of Z Ltd. is £5,000 (since the acquisition of shares therein by Y Ltd.) made up in two stages—

		£
(a) Before X Ltd. entered on the scene	. . .	3,000
(b) Since „ „ „ „ „ „	. . .	2,000
		£5,000

As X Ltd. in effect takes one-tenth (x) of the profit of Z Ltd., via its holding of shares in Y Ltd., it is clear that the profits attributable to X Ltd. are—

		£
(a) Pre-acquisition: $\frac{1}{10}$ of £3,000	. . . .	300
(b) Post-acquisition: $\frac{1}{10}$ of £2,000	. . . .	200
		£500

(x) This fraction is obtained from the fact that—

Y Ltd. owns $\frac{1}{8}$ of Z Ltd., and X Ltd., $\frac{4}{5}$ of Y Ltd.;

hence X Ltd. owns $\frac{4}{5} \times \frac{1}{8}$ ($\frac{4}{40}$ or $\frac{1}{10}$)

The final disposal of the profits of the subsidiaries is, therefore—

	Total	Parent				Minority
		Pre	*Post*	*Pre*	*Post*	
	£	£	£	£	£	£
(1)	40,000	24,000	8,000			8,000
(2)	10,000	5,250	2,250	925	200	1,375
	£50,000	(a) £29,250	(c) £10,250	(b)£925	(c) £200	(d) £9,375

(a) credited to Cost of Shares in Y Ltd. acquired by X Ltd.
(b)   „   „   „   „   „   „ Z „   „   „   „   „
(c) carried forward in Consolidated Balance Sheet.
(d) credited to Minority Interest.

10. *Goodwill*—

	X Ltd. in Y Ltd. £	X Ltd. in Z Ltd. £	Y Ltd. in Z Ltd. £	Total £
Cost	160,000	36,000	4,500	200,500
Share Capital acquired . .	80,000	30,000	5,000	115,000
	80,000	6,000	500	85,500
$\frac{3}{4}$ of £7,000		5,250		
$\frac{4}{5}$ of £30,000 . . .	£24,000			
$\frac{1}{8}$ of £5,000 . . .			625	30,175
$\frac{1}{10}$ of £3,000 . . .	300			
	24,300			
	£55,700	£750	£1,125	£55,325
$\frac{3}{4}$ of £3,000		2,250		
$\frac{4}{5}$ of £10,000	8,000			
$\frac{1}{10}$ of £2,000	200			
	£8,200	£2,250		£10,450
	£	£		
Share Capital	20,000	5,000		
Profit 20% of £40,000 . . .	8,000			
12½% of £10,000 . . .		1,250		
20% of £625 . . .	125			
	£28,125	£6,250		£34,375

The total profit growth since Y Ltd. acquired its shares in Z Ltd. is (as before) £5,000, i.e. closing figure of £10,000 *less* opening figure of £5,000, so that the derived profit ($\frac{1}{8}$) is £625, as in the preceding problem, the Minority Interest being £125.

The profit attributable to X Ltd. is (as before) £500, but the pre- and post-acquisition division is obviously different. The disposal is as follows—

		£	*Disposed of by*
inority Interest 20%		+125	Credit to Minority Interest

Loss attributable to Y Ltd. at the date X Ltd. acquired its stake in Y Ltd., £1,600 (£5,000 — £3,400), i.e. the Revenue Reserves of Z Ltd. at this date had diminished by £1,600) 12$\frac{1}{2}$% of £1,600 . . . . . . £200

        Less Minority Interest 20% thereof . 40

        ———   −160   Debit to Cost of Shares

Profit attributable to Y Ltd. since X Ltd. acquired its stake in Y Ltd., £6,600 (£10,000 — £3,400), i.e. in the meantime the Revenue Reserves of Z Ltd. had grown by £6,600) 12$\frac{1}{2}$% of £6,600 £825

        Less Minority Interest: 20% thereof . 165

        ———   +660   Profit forward to consolidated Balance Sheet

Total £660 + £125 − £160 equals . . .   £625

CONSOLIDATED BALANCE SHEET OF X LTD. AND ITS SUBSIDIARIES
AT 31ST DECEMBER, 19.9

	£		£
Share Capital	200,000	Sundry Assets	189,500
Revenue Reserves . . .	10,450	Goodwill	55,325
Minority Shareholders . .	34,375		
	£244,825		£244,825

The short cut ascertainment of the pre- and post-acquisition figures of £160 and £660 is—

			£
Pre-acquisition loss of Z Ltd.	£1,600 (x) 10% thereof	. .	160
Post-acquisition profit of Z Ltd.	£6,600 (x) 10% thereof	. .	660

(x) See above.

	H Ltd. £	S Ltd. £	T Ltd. £	Total £
Balance per Profit and Loss Account	12,000	6,000	Dr. 2,000	16,000
Profit from T Ltd.	1,200 (b)	1,800 (a)		
,, S Ltd.	5,310 (c)			
Minority Shareholders				380

H Ltd. £
```
12,000
 1,200 (b)
 5,310 (c)
———
18,510
```
9/10 × £500 = £450 (d)
9/10 × £1,400 = 1,260
9/10 × £5,500 = £4,950 (c)
9/10 × £400 = 360
```
18,510
£18,510
```

S Ltd. £
```
6,000
1,800 (a)
———
7,800
  780
———
7,020
1,710
———
5,310
5,310
———
  —
```
1/8 × £11,000 = £2,200
3/5 × £4,000 = £2,400
1/8 × £9,000 = £1,800 (a)
3/5 × £2,000 = £1,200 (b)

T Ltd. £   (Dr. 2,000)
```
2,000
  400
———
1,600
4,600
———
3,000
3,000
———
  —
```
```
         £
       1,800
Pre-acquisition  1,400
Post-acquisition  £400
```

Total £
```
16,000
   380
———
15,620
 2,890
———
18,510
18,510
———
£18,510
```
```
         £
       1,620
Pre-acquisition  1,260
Post-acquisition  £360
```
(1/10)

As regards the item of £1,800, since T Ltd.'s debit balance on Profit and Loss at the date when S Ltd. acquired its shares was £11,000 (reduced to £4,000 when H Ltd. acquired its shares in T Ltd.), and the present debit balance is down to £2,000, it must have made in the meantime £9,000 profit, dealt with as follows—

(i) £9,000 ("derived" profit to S Ltd.) since S Ltd.'s acquisition (£11,000 − £2,000) but this profit attributable to S Ltd. because such part of it was earned before H Ltd. got hold of the shares in S Ltd. When this happened the adverse balance of T Ltd. had come down to £4,000, therefore £11,000 − £4,000 was earned before H Ltd. acquired its shares in S Ltd., i.e. £7,000.

Therefore ⅛ × £9,000 attributable to S Ltd. is divisible

⅛ × £7,000 thereof had been earned for S Ltd. *before* H Ltd. "came in"
⅛ × £2,000 thereof since H Ltd. "came in".

(ii) £6,000 "direct" profit to S Ltd. is divided—

```
                                            £        £
Pre-acquisition                           2,500
  Less Dividend out of pre-acquisition profit  2,000
                                          ——       500 (d) 9/10  450
Post-acquisition                         15,500
  Less Dividends out of post-acquisition profit 10,000
                                          ——     5,500 (c) 9/10 4,950
                                         £6,000            £5,400
```

Goodwill—

		Shares in S Ltd.	Shares in T Ltd. (H Ltd. Holding)	Shares in T Ltd. (S Ltd. Holding)	Total
		£	£	£	£
Cost of Shares	. .	38,000	8,000	3,200	49,200
Less Nominal Value	. .	36,000	12,000	3,000	51,000
		Dr. 2,000	*Cr.* 4,000	*Dr.* 200	*Cr.* 1,800
Pre-acquisition Profit (*Loss*) .		450	2,400	2,200 ⎫	
Pre-acquisition of "derived" Profits of S Ltd. (from T Ltd.)			1,260	⎬	2,890
		Dr. £1,550	*Cr.* £2,860	*Dr.* £2,400	*Dr.* £1,090

CONSOLIDATED BALANCE SHEET OF H LTD.
AND ITS SUBSIDIARIES AS AT 31ST DECEMBER

	£				£
Share Capital H Ltd. . . .	50,000	Sundry Fixed Assets . . .			70,000
Revenue Reserves—		Goodwill. . . .			1,090
General (£14,000 − £400) . .	13,600	Cash at Bank . .	.	£8,300	
Profit and Loss Accounts . .	18,510	Cash in Transit .	(*x*)	100	
					8,400
Minority Shareholders . . .	9,780	Debtors . . .	.		15,300
Creditors	21,500	Stocks on hand .	.	£18,000	
		Stock in Transit .	(*x*)	600	
					18,600
	£113,390				£113,390

				S Ltd.		T Ltd.
				£		£
Minority Shareholders—						
Share Capital				4,000		5,000
Reserve ($\frac{1}{10}$ of £4,000) . . .				400		
Profit/*Loss*		. (Profit)		780	(*Loss*)	400
				£5,180		£4,600
					£9,780	

(*x*) The Inter-company balances will cancel out after dealing with the above (as with Current Accounts of Branches and Head Office in Branch Accounts).

12.   DRAFT SCHEDULE

	A Ltd. £	B Ltd. £		C Ltd. £	Total £
Profit/Loss for year .	800	1,800		−480	2,120
Internal Profit or *Loss*		128			
Transfer from C Ltd.—*Loss*		1,672			
Minority Interests .		¼ 418		$\frac{1}{10}$ −48	370
	800	1,254		−432	1,750
Pre-acquisition Profit			A Ltd. 8 months £256	300	+300
			B Ltd. 11 months 44		
				132	
			A Ltd. 4 months £128	128	
	£800	£1,254		−£4	£2,050
	£	£		£	£
31st Dec., 19.7 Balances	1,500	−800		1,920	2,620
Minority Interests .		−200		−192	8
	1,500	−600		1,728	2,628
		7 months −350			350
	£1,500	−£250		£1,728	£2,978

				Minority Interests	

Cost of Shares—

		£			£	£
Pre-acquisition Loss of B Ltd.	Dr.	300	19.7 Profit of B Ltd.	. 418		
,, ,, ,, *C Ltd.*	Dr.	350	*Loss of C Ltd.* .	. 48		
				——	370	
			19.7 Profit of C Ltd.	. 192		
			Loss of B Ltd.	. 200		
				——	8	
	Dr. £650				£362	

Summary—

	£	£	£
Consolidated Profit and Loss current year . . .		2,050	
,, ,, ,, ,, forward . . .		2,978	
		——	5,028
Minority Interests			362
			——
			5,390
Less Cost of Shares			650

Accounting for (as shown in individual Company Balance
Sheets) = £2,300 + £1,000 + £1,440) . . . . | £4,740

Proof of current year profit attributable to A Ltd.—

A Ltd. acquired shares in C Ltd. on 1st December, 19.7, so that it suffers one-twelfth of the loss attributable to its holdings, i.e.—

				£
10 per cent = $\frac{1}{12} \times \frac{1}{10} \times$ £480	*Dr.* 4
(*C Ltd. lost £40 every month, thus A Ltd.'s share = £4*)	

A Ltd. held its 75 per cent interest in B Ltd. throughout the whole of the year, thus its share does not contain any element of pre-acquisition profit, but B Ltd. through its holding of 80 per cent in C Ltd. as and from 1st September, 19.7, must bring into account this loss from that date. Therefore the position of A Ltd. is—

		£
B Ltd. current profit	.	1,800
"Derived" loss through C Ltd.—		
$\frac{4}{12} \times \frac{80}{100} \times$ £480 = $\frac{4}{15} \times$ £480	.	128
		——
		£1,672

(C Ltd. lost £40 every month, or £160 in four months, thus B Ltd.'s share is 80 per cent of £160, or as B Ltd. holds ⅘ of C Ltd. its share of the monthly loss is £32, that is £128 for four months)

75 per cent of £1,672	*Cr.*	1,254
Add Profit of A Ltd. (own trading) . . .	*Cr.*	800
		——
Per Schedule (and as below)	.	£2,054

The Consolidated Profit and Loss is—

		£
Profit (set out in the usual detail) for year . . .	.	2,120
Less Minority Interests	.	370
		——
		1,750
Add the pre-acquisition loss attributable to B Ltd. . .	300
		——
(as above)	.	2,050
Add Balance forward	.	2,978
		——
		£5,028

If instead of the above, the Profit and Loss Account of A Ltd., framed as a consolidated statement, is published, this will be—

		£
Profit of Group for year	. . . . . .	2,120
Less Minority Interest	. . . . . .	370
		1,750
Add pre-acquisition loss attributable to A Ltd.	. . .	300
		2,050

Less undistributed profit attributable to A Ltd.—			
B Ltd.	. . . . . .	(*a*) £1,254	
Less C Ltd. Loss	. . . . .	(*a*) 4	
		1,250	
		800	
Add Balance forward A Ltd.	. . . . .	1,500	
Per Profit and Loss Account of A Ltd.	. . . .	£2,300	

(*a*) The details will probably not be shown in the published accounts.

The above figures can be proved as follows—	£	£
Total Group Profit figure		5,028
Less undistributed profit for year (as above) . . .	1,250	

Less undistributed profit for previous years—		
A Ltd. Profit	£1,728	
Less B Ltd. Loss . . . . . (*b*)	250	
	1,478	
		2,728
		£2,300

	£
(*b*) The Profit and Loss forward of the Group attributable to A Ltd. .	2,978
The common element is the Profit and Loss of A Ltd. (this is part of the £2,978 forward, and is part of the total Profit and Loss of A Ltd. as per A's books)	1,500
Therefore, undistributed past profit of subsidiaries attributable to A Ltd.	£1,478

13.

Workings—

	£	£			£
Profit, H Ltd. . . .	£1,510			Profit H Ltd.	1,510
Less Dividend (*a*) to cost of shares . . .	1,500	10		*Less* Dividend Receivable (*b*) .	1,500
					10
S Ltd.		9,600		S Ltd.	9,600
		9,610			9,610
H Ltd. Balance forward . .		10		H Ltd. Balance forward . . .	10
		£9,620			£9,620

Capital Reserve—		£	Capital Reserve—		£
Cost of Shares		11,000	Cost of Shares		11,000
Less Nominal Value of Shares in S Ltd.		10,000	Less Nominal value of Shares in S Ltd.		10,000
		1,000			1,000
Less Transfer of Dividend incorrectly credited to Profit and Loss Account of A Ltd. (a). . . .		1,500			
Credit . . .		500			
Add Balance of Profit and Loss Account S Ltd. . .	2,500		Less Balance of Profit and Loss Account S Ltd. . . .		2,500
Deduct Dividend . .	1,500	1,000			
		£1,500			£1,500

		£
Dividend Receivable	(c) . .	1,500
Less Dividend Payable	(c) . .	1,500
		—

CONSOLIDATED BALANCE SHEET OF H LTD. AND S LTD.
AS AT 31ST DECEMBER, 19.9
(both 1 and 2)

		£					£
Share Capital		20,000	Sundry Assets				31,120
Reserves—							
Revenue . . .	£9,620						
Capital . . .	1,500						
		11,120					
		£31,120					£31,120

Notes—

(i) The Capital Reserve (the fact that the dividend of £1,500 is to be regarded as paid out of the Profit and Loss Account of 19.8 or 19.9 is immaterial) is the excess of net assets of S Ltd. acquired over the cost of shares, i.e.—

	£
Net Assets of S Ltd. at 31st December, 19.8, i.e.—	
Share Capital of S Ltd..	10,000
Profit and Loss Account Balance of S Ltd. . .	2,500
	12,500
Less Cost of Shares in S Ltd.	11,000
	£1,500

(ii) In dealing with first part of the question, the item of £1,500 credited to Profit and Loss Account of H Ltd. must be transferred to Capital Reserve, as such dividend is a release of part of the accumulated profit of S Ltd. existing at 31st December, 19.8.

The old profit remaining in the books of S Ltd. is now £1,500, leaving the balance not dealt with at £1,000, i.e. the Profit and Loss Account of S Ltd. as per its Balance Sheet is now—

	£
Profit and Loss forward 31st December, 19.8 . .	2,500
Less Dividend paid thereout	1,500
Balance (to be credited in consolidation to Capital Reserve) .	1,000
Profit for 19.9	9,620
Per Balance Sheet of S Ltd.	£10,620

(iii) As regards the second part of the question, the item of £1,500 is properly included in the Profit and Loss Account of H Ltd., and is cancelled in the consolidation by the dividend paid out of 19.9 profit of S Ltd., leaving undisturbed the balance forward of S Ltd. at £2,500 (to be taken to credit of Cost of Shares).

14. CONSOLIDATED BALANCE SHEET OF H LTD. AND S LTD.,
AS AT 31ST DECEMBER, 19.9
(both 1 and 2)

	£		£
Share Capital	20,000	Sundry Assets	31,120
Revenue Reserve—		Goodwill	1,000
Profit and Loss Account . .	8,000		
Minority Shareholders . .	4,120		
	£32,120		£32,120

Workings—

		£			£
Profit, H Ltd. . . .		1,510	Profit, H Ltd. . . .		1,510
Less Dividend to Cost of Shares	(a)	1,200	*Less* Dividend Receivable .	(a)	1,200
		310			310
Add S Ltd. ⅘ × £9,600 . .		7,680	*Add* S Ltd. ⅘ × £9,600 .		7,680
		7,990			7,990
„ H Ltd. Balance forward .		10	H Ltd. Balance forward .		10
		£8,000			£8,000

		£			£
Goodwill—			Goodwill—		
Cost of Shares		11,000	Cost of Shares . . .		11,000
Less Nominal Value of Shares in S Ltd. acquired		8,000	*Less* Nominal Value of Shares in S Ltd. acquired . .		8,000
		3,000			3,000
Less Transfer of Dividend incorrectly credited to Profit and Loss Account of H. Ltd. (a) . . .		1,200	*Deduct* balance of Profit and Loss Account of S Ltd. (£2,500) ⅘ thereof		2,000
		1,800			
Deduct balance of Profit and Loss Account of S Ltd. £2,500					
Less Dividend . . 1,500					
		£1,000			
⅘ thereof		800			
		£1,000			£1,000

		£			£
Minority Shareholders—			Minority Shareholders—		
Share Capital of S Ltd. ⅕ . .		2,000	Share Capital ⅕ . . .		2,000
Profit and Loss of S. Ltd.—			Profit and Loss of S Ltd.		
Forward . . . £2,500			Forward . . . £2,500		
Less Dividend . . 1,500			Current . . . 9,600		
		1,000			£12,100
Profit and Loss of S Ltd. for year . . .		9,600	⅕ thereof		2,420
		10,600			4,420
			Less Dividend Receivable .	(b)	300
⅕ thereof		2,120			
		£4,120			£4,120
			Dividend paid to H Ltd. . .	(a)	1,200
			„ „ „ Minority Shareholders . . .		300
					1,500
			Dividend Payable by S Ltd. . .		1,500

Goodwill—   £

   Cost of Shares 11,000

     Less Equity of H Ltd. (£10,000 + £2,500) = £12,500 ⅘ thereof . 10,000

                                                   £1,000

The difference between the item of £1,500 Capital Reserve as shown in preceding question and Goodwill of £1,000 as above is explained by the fact that the cost of shares acquired was the same in each case, but in the latter the Minority Shareholders retain an interest in one-fifth of the equity of £12,500, i.e. £2,500.

The difference between the Profit and Loss Accounts of £9,620 in the Consolidated Balance Sheet in the preceding question and £8,000 in that shown in this question is explained as follows

                                                          £

(1) H Ltd. is entitled to ⅘ of profit of £9,600—instead of the whole of £9,600; therefore, the diminution is £9,600 − £7,680; or ⅕ of £9,600 1,920

(2) The Profit of H Ltd., as shown in both cases for the current year, is £1,510, made up of dividend from S Ltd. of £1,500 plus £10 in the preceding example, but in the present question the profit is *still* £1,510, although the dividend received being £1,200 instead of £1,500, its own profit being more by the sum of . . . 300

∴ Net diminution = £1,620

CHAPTER XXV

1. (1)   BALANCE SHEET AS AT 30TH JUNE, 19.4

	£		£
Share Capital—		Fixed Assets—	
Authorized	300,000	Land	12,000
		Buildings:	
Issued	260,000	At 1st July, 19.3 . £13,000	
Reserve	15,000	Additions . . 10,000	
Profit and Loss Account . .	16,000		23,000
		Shafting, etc.	
	291,000	At 1st July, 19.3 . £135,000	
5% Debentures	40,000	Additions . . 25,000	
Provision for Renewals . .	25,000		160,000
Current Liabilities—		Machinery:	
Trade Creditors . . .	16,000	At 1st July, 19.3 . £40,000	
		Additions . . 25,000	
			65,000
			260,000
		Current Assets—	
		Stock £24,000	
		Trade Debtors . . 38,000	
		Investments . . 15,000	
		Cash at Bank and in hand 35,000	
			112,000
	£372,000		£372,000

(2) *Dr.*   CAPITAL ACCOUNT FOR THE YEAR TO 30TH JUNE, 19.4   *Cr.*

Expenditure	Amount Expended to 30th June, 19.3	Amount Expended during Year	Total	Receipts	Amount Received to 30th June, 19.3	Amount Received during Year	Total
	£	£	£		£	£	£
Land . . .	12,000		12,000	5% Debentures .	40,000	—	40,000
Shafting, etc. .	135,000	25,000	160,000	Share Capital .	260,000	—	260,000
Machinery . .	40,000	25,000	65,000				
Buildings . .	13,000	10,000	23,000				
	£200,000	£60,000	260,000		£300,000	—	300,000
Balance per General Balance Sheet .			40,000				
			£300,000				£300,000

GENERAL BALANCE SHEET AS AT 30TH JUNE, 19.4

	£		£
Balance of Capital Account in Credit	40,000	Cash in hand and at Bank . .	35,000
Trade Creditors . . .	16,000	Trade Debtors . . .	38,000
Renewals Fund . . .	25,000	Stock	24,000
Reserve	15,000	Investments (Reserve) . .	15,000
Profit and Loss Account . .	16,000		
	£112,000		£112,000

The advantages of the Double Account System are—

(1) A clear statement is presented as to the capital raised and its utilization in the acquisition of permanent assets.

(2) A clear-cut separation of the fixed and floating capital of the organization is effected.

(3) The assets acquired during the past year are shown, and such assets remain at cost.

(4) Capital profits, e.g. profit on redemption of Debentures and the like, must remain in the business, as distribution of a profit of this nature is illegal (*Wall* v. *London Provincial Trust*).

The disadvantages are—

(1) That inasmuch as assets remain at *cost* in the Capital Account, the Balance Sheet does not show the true position.

(2) The Capital Account includes short-term assets, and indeed fictitious assets, e.g. preliminary expenses.

(3) The principle of the Renewals System of depreciation is considered unsound and complicated, giving rise to lack of uniformity in carrying out this system.

(4) The lack of comprehension of the significance of the accounts by the general public.

The capital raised and sunk under the Double Account System is shown on page 636. Depreciation has been provided for by means of a Renewals Fund.

[In regard to Renewals, it was, prior to nationalization, the practice of English Railways (with one exception) to estimate for renewals yearly, so that each year bore its proper charge. The other railway provided for the expenditure on renewals only as and when the necessity arose. The first procedure is known as the Maintenance basis, the second as the Expenditure basis. The deferment of the charges of the burden in the latter method causes the profits (other things being equal) to rise more slowly than in the former during a period of industrial recovery.]

2. Dr.   No. 4. Receipts and Expenditure on Capital Account   **Cr.**

Expenditure	Amount Expended to 31st Dec., 19..	Amount Expended during Year	Total	Receipts	Amount Received to 31st Dec., 19..	Amount Received during Year	Total
	£	£	£		£	£	£
To Lines Open for Traffic			2,990,000	By Stocks and Shares			3,000,000
,, Rolling Stock			890,000	,, Debenture Stock			1,000,000
,, Balance			120,000				
			£4,000,000				£4,000,000

No. 18. General Balance Sheet

	£		£
Capital Account—		Cash at Bank	80,000
Balance on Credit thereof per Account No. 4	120,000	Stores, Fuel, and Supplies in hand	110,000
Sundry Creditors	100,000	Sundry Debtors	90,000
Revenue Account	60,000		
	£280,000		£280,000

3. It is assumed that the present cost of constructing a new main similar in type and quality to the old is £30,000 plus 25 per cent thereof = £37,500; $\frac{1}{4}$ for auxiliary and $\frac{3}{4}$ for renewal.

The cost of the auxiliary main is chargeable to Capital and made up of the following items—

	£
Cash cost, $\frac{1}{4}$ of £37,500	9,375
Old Materials used	100
	£9,475

The treatment of the renewal is capable of several alternatives—

(1) To charge the whole cost of renewal, less receipts for sale of old asset, any portion of the latter re-used being transferred to the new asset account; any improvement will be ignored.

(2) Where no improvement has been effected, either to maintain at its original figure the book value of the replaced asset or to charge to revenue the increased cost of the renewal (conversely for decrease).

(3) Where an improvement has been effected, to charge to revenue so much of the renewal cost as represents the original book value of old asset and to capitalize the balance.

(4) To write up the books as on the Single Account System.

The Journal entries (ignoring narratives) will appear as follows—

JOURNAL

(1)		£	£
Renewals . . . . *Dr.*		28,125	
To Cash			28,125
Cash . . . . *Dr.*		500	
Auxiliary Main . . . . . . *Dr.*		100	
To Renewals			600
New Main . . . . *Dr.*		150	
To Old Main			150

The balance of renewals, £27,525, will be transferred to the debit of Revenue Account.

JOURNAL

(2) (a)		£	£
Cash . . . . *Dr.*		500	
Auxiliary Main . . . . . . *Dr.*		100	
To Old Main . . . . . (c)			600
Renewals . . . . *Dr.*		21,750	
New Main . . . . . . (a) *Dr.*		150	
To Old Main . . . . . (c)			21,900
New Main . . . . . . (b) *Dr.*		28,125	
To Cash			28,125
(b)			
Renewals . . . . . . [1]*Dr.*		5,775	
To New Main			5,775

[1] (a) + (b) − (c): i.e. £150 + £28,125 − (£650 + £21,900) = £5,775.

The entries in (2) have been made on the assumption that no improvement has been effected or, alternatively, that the question of the value of the improvement is to be ignored, but actually the cost of the replacement of the identical object is £22,500 + 15 % of £22,500 = £28,125.

The entries will be as in (2 (a)) and instead of (2 (b)) will be—

JOURNAL

		£	£
(3)			
Renewals . . . . Dr.	¹	5,625	
To New Main			5,625

The cost of the new main as shown in (2 (a)) was £28,275, but the cost of the main (identical with the old) is £28,125, so that the difference represents improved value, viz. £150. The new main now stands at £28,275 as in (2(a)) less transfer above, £5,625, i.e. £22,650. This is the original cost £22,500, plus improvement cost £150.

(4) The entries here follow the usual lines applicable to the Single Account System.

¹ In 2(b) it was necessary to transfer the whole of the excess cost on the footing that no improvement took place (or alternatively, that the value of the improvement is to be ignored), but as £150 out of £5,775 (as shown in 2 (b)) is attributable to improvement, a further charge against Revenue of £5,625 only (as compared with £5,775) is necessary.

CHAPTER XXVI

1. It is taken as a general assumption that the purchasing company has already been supplied with a comprehensive report covering the history of the client company, its ownership and management, past and current trading, the present position in regard to outstanding orders, raw materials, export and home sales, government controls, etc., details of the assets and liabilities (it is probable that a recent valuation of fixed assets will have been obtained, showing current values in excess of book values), etc. On this basis the letter now required will be confined to the valuation of the company's shares, as follows—

Address
Date

The Directors,

.... Company

DEAR SIRS,

Re..COMPANY LTD.

In accordance with instructions given to me by the Directors of the above company, I have prepared a basis on which the shares of that company might be acquired, and have pleasure in submitting the necessary figures for your consideration, together with supporting computations.

I. *Preference Shares.*

(1) As regards capital.

The net tangible assets of the two companies, based on the Balance Sheets as at 31st December, 19.9, amount to £577,555, as follows—

	£	£
Main Company:		
Assets (detailed) (excluding Shares in Subsidiary Company)		576,283
Less Creditors		56,286
		519,997
Subsidiary Company:		
Assets (detailed) (excluding Goodwill)	71,876	
Less Creditors	14,318	
		57,558
Net Assets excluding Goodwill, at 31st December, 19.9		£577,555

Representing:

	£	£	£
Share Capital:			
Main Company	400,000		
Less Investment in Subsidiary Company	50,000		
		350,000	
Subsidiary Company		50,000	
			400,000
Reserves: Main Company			100,000
Profit and Loss Accounts:			
Main Company		69,997	
Subsidiary Company		7,559	
			77,556
			577,556
Deduct Goodwill of Subsidiary Company			1
			£577,555

(It is assumed that the subsidiary company is wholly owned.)

The preference shares carry a preferential right to repayment of capital in a winding up, without the right of participation in surplus assets. On the basis of the book value of the net assets of the two companies, as set out above, the £100,000 of issued Preference Share Capital is covered more than 5½ times (assumed no premium on repayment).

(2) As regards dividend.

The average annual profits of the two companies for the six years ended 31st December, 19.9, as shown by the accounts, have been—

	£
Main Company	45,833
Subsidiary Company	6,417
	£52,250

From this figure there falls to be deducted the estimated annual provision for depreciation of freehold and leasehold properties (assumed that no other adjustments are required) say .	5,000
	£47,250

Profits of £47,250 are sufficient to cover the annual preference dividend—which is cumulative—of £6,000 almost 8 times.[1]

On the same basis, the profits for 19.9 only amount to £44,100, which is sufficient to cover the dividend more than seven times.

(3) Valuation.

Assuming that the market yield for shares in this class of business and carrying equal rights is 4½ per cent, the estimated fair value of the company's preference shares is £1·33⅓ x.d. per share $\left(\text{i.e.} \ \frac{6}{4\frac{1}{2}} \times £1 \right)$.

II. *Ordinary Shares.*

(1) As regards dividend.

As indicated above, the average annual profits of the six years to 31st December, 19.9, were £47,250, and for the year 19.9 £44,100. On the basis of the latter figure, the profits available for the ordinary shareholders may be computed thus—

	£
Adjusted profits of the two companies	44,100
Less amount transferred to Reserve for retention in the businesses[2] say	6,100
Net profit available for dividends	38,000
Deduct preference dividend	6,000
Amount available for ordinary dividend	£32,000

(2) Valuation based on dividend yield.

In view of the fact that ordinary shares of companies of a similar type currently

---

[1] In practice, when taxation has to be taken into account, the following might be substituted—
After deducting corporation tax at say, 40%, there would remain average annual profits of £28,350, which are sufficient to cover the gross preference dividend over 4½ times.

[2] The question does not state out of what earnings 7 per cent was paid by a similar company. The figures taken here for the purpose of illustration are less than would probably be necessary in practice in present circumstances.

yield 7 per cent, the estimated value of each ordinary share of this company is £1·52½ arrived at as follows—

$$\text{Yield per ordinary share} = \frac{32,000}{300,000} \times 100 = x$$

∴ Estimated value of one ordinary share, x.d. $= \frac{x}{7} = £1·52½$ approx.

The capital required to produce £32,000 on

a 7 per cent basis is £32,000 $\times \dfrac{100}{7}$ $= £457,143.$

(3) As regards capital.[1]

The net tangible assets of the two companies based on the Balance Sheets at 31st December, 19.9, as shown in paragraph I (1), amount to £577,555, so that after deducting the nominal amount of the Preference Share Capital there would remain, excluding Goodwill, £477,555 for the Ordinary Shareholders.

III. *Capitalization of the Company.*

The capitalization of the company is, therefore, computed as follows—

	£
100,000 Preference Shares at £1·33⅓ each . . .	133,333
300,000 Ordinary Shares at £1·52½ each (approx.) . .	457,143 (as above)
	£590,476

The Goodwill is, therefore, £47,921 computed as follows—

	£	£
Capitalization of the Company		590,476
Less Net Tangible Assets as per Balance Sheets .	577,555	
Deduct Depreciation on Leasehold and Freehold Properties . . . . . . (say)	35,000	
		542,555
Goodwill		£47,921

This is approximately one year's purchase of the adjusted profit (after estimated depreciation of properties), either on the basis of the *average* profits for the six years ended 31st December, 19.9, or of the 19.9 profits.

In the above calculations the assumption has been made that it is intended to take over both classes of shares.

Yours faithfully,

Note to Students.

Much more information would be required by the purchasing company, most of which would be available to the auditor. Full use must be made of the permission given in the question to insert any necessary figures and make relevant assumptions. Such assumptions must, of necessity, be made and noted, e.g. that the profits of the Main Company, as set out in the question, do not include dividends from the Subsidiary Company; that no adjustments (other than for depreciation of properties) are required to the profits given in the question, e.g. profits used to write down or write off goodwill and other assets, abnormal income or expenditure, basis and amount of depreciation of plant, etc.; that the Directors' Fees are not abnormal or highly variable; that profits have been consistently computed; that there are no secret reserves.

---

[1] In present circumstances, the value of ordinary shares depends almost entirely on dividend yield. The capital cover for the ordinary shares would not therefore be likely materially to affect the valuation. In calculating the net tangible assets, a deduction could be made for the estimated cumulative depreciation of freehold and leasehold properties on the basis of the adjustment made in arriving at net profits.

A statement as to current trading and prospects, as well as other information, will be required from the Directors.

Although the question is an important one, time conditions will not permit of dealing with statistical matter, e.g. coefficient of dispersion, but this, together with the vital effect of a *whole* as distinct from a *part* purchase of shares should be noted.

2.

(The question set is designed to do no more than test the student's knowledge of general principles of share valuation, as a considerable number of essential points are missing. They are probably omitted so that the student may be afforded a reasonable opportunity of showing a knowledge of the subject without the necessity for dealing with detail, and at the same time being required to indicate in general what other considerations would be called for.)

It is assumed that the current profits earned are sufficient to cover the proposed dividends; that reasonable limitations are placed in the articles on the amount of Directors' Emoluments; that there is no immediate intention to issue further capital; that there are no options of underwriters or other persons on any part or all of the unissued capital; that income is "normal"; that net assets are worth book values; that there are no secret reserves.

No indication is given of priority rights in winding up, or of participating rights of the Preferred Ordinary Shares, and it is assumed that they have no rights beyond a 6 per cent dividend.

In estimating the required yield the following matters would call for consideration—

(1) Business trend generally.

(2) Business trend in the particular industry.

(3) Business trend of the particular company (the chairman's speech, even after dilution of an optimistic speech, often being of guidance).

(4) Share valuations of similar companies.

(5) Share gearing. (In the company given, the deferred capital is small compared with the preference and preferred ordinary—tending to low yield in times of depression.)

(6) Comparison of earnings and dividends.

(7) Market capitalization in relation to tangible assets. Actually, different considerations will apply in each class of share, e.g. stability and cover for Preference Shares and possibility of loss of premium on redemption, whilst in regard to Deferred Shares the past history may form no guide as to potentialities and prospects of the near future.

(8) Demand and supply in the investment market.

(9) Political factors, where necessary.

(10) Ratio of profits to capital.

The cover for the Preference Shares—assuming priority of capital repayment in a winding-up—is as follows—

	£	£
Net Assets		105,300
Less Liabilities:		
Debentures	5,000	
Creditors	6,500	
		11,500
		93,800
As against Issued Capital of		32,000
Surplus		£61,800

Approximate cover three times.

The cover for the Preferred Ordinary Shares—assuming priority of capital repayment in a winding-up (after payment of the Preference Shares)—is as follows—

	£
Surplus as above	61,800
As against issued Capital of	20,000
Surplus	£41,800

Approximate cover three times.

The cover for the Deferred Shares, therefore, is—

			£
Surplus as above	. . . . . .	.	41,800
As against issued Capital of	. . . .	.	5,000
			36,800

Approximate cover eight times.

From a purely break-up viewpoint, the valuations, assuming—

(1) That no participation rights in the surplus are possessed by the Preference and the Preferred Ordinary Shares, and
(2) That no premium is payable on repayment of the Preference and Preferred Ordinary Shares, are—

			Per Share
	£		£
(a) Preference Shares			1
(b) Preferred Ordinary Shares . .			1
(c) Deferred Shares:			
Net Assets . . .	[1]93,800		
Less amount required for (a) and (b) . . .	52,000		
Surplus . . .	£41,800 $= £\frac{41,800}{5,000}$		8·36

[If all the shares are of equal standing in a winding-up, the share valuation is $\frac{93,000}{57,000} = £1·63$ per share.

As there are ample assets to pay all the shareholders £1 per share, the result in this case is the same as if the preference and preferred ordinary shares had a priority as to repayment of capital, with participating rights *pari passu* with the deferred shares in surplus.]

As the shares are apparently well covered, there will be little or no tendency to require an abnormally high yield, and for the purposes of valuation on a yield basis the expected return may be taken at, say, 5, 6½, and 8 per cent respectively.

The approximate values on a yield basis will, therefore, be as follows—

Preference Shares . . . . . . $\frac{5}{5} \times £1 = $ par

Preferred Ordinary Shares . . . $\frac{6}{6\frac{1}{2}} \times £1 = £0·92\frac{1}{8}$

Deferred Shares . . . . . $\frac{50}{8} \times £1 = £6·25$

The latter basis in the circumstances given would be preferable to the break-up basis, although it is possible that the Preferred Ordinary Share yield required would be higher than 6½ per cent, as these shares rank second for dividends, and yet apparently have no equity rights. It is assumed that, on present indications, the company will be able to continue the payment of a dividend on the deferred shares. The year's profit figure is not given, but the Profit and Loss Account balance is small compared with the proposed dividends.

---

[1] Strictly, if the break-up aspect is taken, goodwill will realize nothing, and probably other assets will realize amounts less than the book values; hence the viewpoint might more properly have been described as "from a viewpoint of sale as a going concern," so distinguishing the position from that arising from the "earnings" viewpoint.

The capitalization of the Deferred Shares is 5,000 × £6·25 = £31,250 as against net tangible assets of—

	£	£
Per Balance Sheet		93,800
Less Goodwill		5,000
		88,800
Deduct Preference Shares	32,000	
Preferred Ordinary Shares . . .	20,000	
		52,000
		£36,800

Note to Student. All the above factors would appear to indicate that the deferred shares are not overvalued, but the combination of unknown factors makes it impossible to appraise the value with reasonable certainty. This note is not part of the formal answer, as the student is supposed to have been appointed Auditor and the internal factors are assumed to be known by him.

3. The usual practice of Trust Investment companies is to ignore fluctuations in the value of investments; and where a part of a holding is sold, to credit the Investment Account with the net realized sum. Most companies carrying on a Trust Investment business frequently state in the Directors' Report the percentage of increase or decrease of value (as compared with cost) of shares comprised in their portfolios.

Where there are a series of purchases and sales of one class of shares, the method adopted in ascertainment of profits or losses is—

(*a*) To take the average cost per share on the occasion of each sale; or
(*b*) To take the sale as appertaining to the earliest purchase.

The question as to the comparative methods of ascertainment of profit or loss is largely one of expediency, and as the first-named method is simple it is usually adopted.

Theoretically, it is the more prudent course to take the several parts of the holdings (of each class) in one company as a *whole* where a profit has arisen and *separately* in the case of a loss. On the other hand, it is equally important to adopt one method consistently.

In addition, as the cost as a whole is frequently required for the purpose of computing average yield, the "average" method will usually be employed.

Ignoring dividends, costs, etc., the two methods are shown below—

(*a*) Where each sale is compared with the average cost, the result will be—

Cost Price		Sale Price (a)		Average Cost (b)		Profit (a − b)
	£		£			£
£50 at 101	50·50					
£50 at 95	47·50					
	98·00					
£100 at 102	102·00	£25 at 99 . .	24·75	$\frac{25}{100}$ × 98 . .	24·50	0·25
	£200·00					
		£150 at 105 . .	157·50	$\frac{150}{175}$ × 175½ .	150·43	7·07
		(*a*) £182·25		(*b*) £174·93		£7·32

	£
The amount realized is . . .	182·25 (*a*)
The cost of shares realized is . .	174·93 (*b*)
Net Profit as above . . .	£7·32

The average cost of the holding should be recomputed after each purchase or sale, so that, at the time of the last sale, the holding is £175 stock at a book value of £200 − £24·50, i.e. £175·50.

(*b*) Where the first shares bought are "cleared" by the first sold and each subsequent purchase dealt with likewise, the result will be—

		Cost				Sale		Loss	Profit
		£						£	£
£50 at 101	. . .	50·50	(a)	50·50	(a)	£25 at 101 − £25 at 99 =		0·50	
£50 at 95	. . .	47·50	(b)	47·50	(a)	£25 at 101 − £25 at 105 =			1·00
					(b)	£50 at 95 − £50 at 105 =			5·00
£100 at 102	. . .	102·00	(c)	102·00	(c)	£75 at 102 − £75 at 105 =			2·25
						Balance, Profit		7·75	
		£200·00							
								£8·25	£8·25

	£	£
The amount realized is . .		182·25
The cost of shares realized is as above . . .	200·00	
Less £25 at 102[1] . .	25·50	
		174·50
Net Profit (as above) .		£7·75

[1] Balance on hand at latest price.

4. In almost every examination question of this type, information on very many vital matters is lacking, but the omissions and ambiguities are often deliberate in order to test the candidate's grip on essential accounting matters. Yet, even when these difficulties are resolved, other factors of fundamental importance are unknown to the candidate. The most satisfactory procedure is to make the valuation on all the factors known or reasonably implied, leaving to comment those factors likely to disturb the accuracy of the valuation.

The solution should proceed on these lines—

Further information would be required as to (i) the number of shares to be disposed of; (ii) possibility of diminution of goodwill by reason of the sale of shares—assuming that the seller is the dominant personality of the business; (iii) reasons for the sale (although it is noted from the phraseology of the question that the initiative arose not from the largest shareholder but from P, this factor alone being important as affecting future control and policy); (iv) the nature and capacity of the business, and whether results fluctuate violently and at present may be approaching or have passed their cyclical peak; (v) general prospects of the business; (vi) existence of reserves; (vii) examination of the special factors underlying the recent profits; (viii) technical factors, e.g. unmarketability of shares in private companies, rights of shareholders as to voting, as to position in a winding up, etc. (It will be observed that it is not known whether P is to become a director or not, nor is it known who holds the Debentures.)

Subject to these general factors the following assumptions are made—

(1) There has been no alteration in the amount of share capital or debentures during the last three years.

(2) The contribution to the Debenture Redemption Fund is obligatory under the terms of the Debenture Trust Deed.

(3) The profits available means "*now* available" (see *re Long Acre Press*), so that the annual contribution of £250 must be deducted from the profits notwithstanding that at a later date the Debenture Redemption Fund, after the redemption of the Debenture Stock, will become a "free" Reserve. As the yearly contributions are £250 and a further £8,000 is required, it will take thirty-two years to complete (ignoring interest, see (4)).

(4) It appears that the interest on the Funds has been credited to Profit and Loss Account. It makes no difference to the position of the Leasehold Amortization Fund in the *long* run how the £14,000 required at the date of the expiry of the lease is built up, i.e. by crediting interest to the Fund or to Profit and Loss Account, but in the latter case the annual contributions will be larger and, if they are equal, the net debit, with the increasing benefit to Profit and Loss Account of the interest on the growing fund, will decrease annually.

The same principle is applicable to the Debenture Redemption Fund. The fact that the interest has been credited to the Profit and Loss Account instead of to the

Profit and Loss Appropriation Account is immaterial because the annaul contribution, although debited to the Appropriation Account, has to be deducted from profits to arrive at the figure available for dividends.

(5) No adjustment of Goodwill arising from inflated profit (arising by reason of interest under (4) being credited to Profit and Loss) is possible on the information.

(6) It is not stated whether the goods delivered on 31st December, 19.6, were sold on that date or taken into stock. It is assumed that they were taken into stock and form part of the stock figure of £6,000.

(7) The term "book values" is taken to mean the effective book figures after deducting appropriate provisions from the relevant assets, so that the Leasehold Amortization Fund (provision for depreciation of the leasehold), Depreciation Fund and Bad Debts Provision are taken as deductions from asset figures.

Computation of Goodwill

	19.4		19.5		19.6
	£		£		£
Profit per Question . . .	3,600		5,900		5,700
Less Debenture Interest . . . £500		£500		£500	
Transfer to Debenture Redemption Fund . . . 250		250		250	
Preference Dividend . . 600		600		600	
	1,350 ——		1,350 ——		1,350
	2,250		4,550		4,350
Deduct omitted Creditor . .					350
	£2,250		£4,550		£4,000

Summary

	£
Adjusted profits—19.4	2,250
Adjusted profits—19.5	4,550
Adjusted profits—19.6	4,000
Total profits available . . .	£10,800

$$\text{Goodwill: } 2 \times \frac{10,800}{3} = £7,200.$$

A "short cut" computation is—

		£
Average profits based on figures in question—		
i.e. ⅓ (£3,600 + £5,900 + £5,700)		5,066
	£	
Less Debenture Interest	500	
Transfer to Debenture Redemption Fund . .	250	
Preference Dividend	600	
		1,350
		3,716
Deduct omitted creditor	£350	
⅓ thereof		116
Average "profits available"		£3,600
Goodwill: 2 years' purchase, i.e. £3,600 × 2 =		£7,200

Goodwill Adjustment

	£
Revalued Goodwill	7,200
Less Goodwill per Balance Sheet . . .	6,000
Increase of Goodwill	£1,200

Computation of Value of Ordinary Shares on "Assets" Basis

	£
Ordinary Shares	12,000
Profit and Loss Account	9,100
Debenture Redemption Fund	2,000
	23,100
Add Appreciation in Goodwill	1,200
	24,300
Deduct Creditor omitted	350
Equity of Ordinary Shares	£23,950

Alternatively, this may be shown as follows—

	£	£
Assets per Balance Sheet		56,600
Add Appreciation of Goodwill		1,200
		57,800
Less Depreciation Fund	1,500	
Leasehold Amortization Fund	4,000	
		5,500
		52,300
Deduct Debenture Stock	10,000	
Creditors per Balance Sheet	£8,000	
Add omission	350	
	8,350	
Preference Share Capital	10,000	
		28,350
Equity of Ordinary Shares		£23,950

Each ordinary share is worth $£\dfrac{23,950}{1,200} = £19 \cdot 95\frac{5}{6}$ cum div., say £20 cum div.

Note. From the profit for the year figure in the Balance Sheet, it appears that preference dividends are paid to date.

If the seller and buyer agree that the former retains the forthcoming dividend, the price will be ex div. and less by the dividend per share. Theoretically, profits will be increasing between 1st January, 19.7 and the actual transfer, but in practice this is usually ignored unless such transfer takes place at a date well advanced in the year following the end of the datum year (19.6 in this instance) or special factors exist. (Usually, such profits are not known at the transfer date, although the agreement of sale could provide for the payment by the purchaser to the vendor of a proportion of the year's profit (adjusted on the above lines) when known.)

If the Annuity method be chosen for the share valuation, the computation will be based on the adjusted average profit of £3,600 (regard being had to trend of interest rates) as compared with the accepted standard of return on similar companies (ascertained from Stock Exchange quotations of similar companies but adjusted up by reason of the fact that the company under review is a *private* company). Assuming 5 per cent to be a fair return for risk in a similar *public* company, a return of (say) 8 per cent would be required from this private company.

Annual Profits available (per average) £3,600.

Giving an earnings rate of 30 per cent $\left(\dfrac{3,600}{12,000} \times 100 \text{ per cent}\right)$, out of which the dividend might be, say, 15 or 20 per cent.

Yield required 8 per cent.

Value of each ordinary share, assuming a 20 per cent dividend, is $\frac{20}{8} \times £10 = £25$ ex div.

It should be noted that the valuation is ex div. If the share were a quoted security the price towards the date the dividend would be declared would tend to move upwards by the market estimate of the forthcoming dividend, falling back after declaration of the dividend to the "true yield" price ex div., and the computation made is that to arrive at such "true yield" price.

The fact that, owing to the various market factors, e.g. faulty estimate of likely dividend, a quoted share may actually fall during the period before, or rise after, declaration of the dividend (and even after the quotation becomes ex div. when it would theoretically fall) obscures but does not affect the foregoing principle.

It should be observed that the whole equity is capitalized at £30,000, arrived at as follows—

$$\tfrac{100}{12}^1 \times £3,600 = £30,000$$

The price of each ordinary share is £25, i.e. $£\dfrac{30,000}{1,200}$

The Goodwill based on Capitalization is—

		£
Capitalized Value of Earnings		30,000
Equity (per page 649)	23,950	
Less Goodwill included therein—original . . £6,000		
appreciation . . 1,200		
	7,200	
		16,750
Goodwill		£13,250

12 per cent will be the standard earnings yield assuming that one-third of the profits are put to reserve, leaving a standard dividend yield of 8 per cent.

5. A unit trust is a trust set up and run by a management company and supervised by trustees (normally a bank or an insurance company) in accordance with a trust deed duly approved by the Department of Trade and Industry. The object of a unit trust is to acquire a portfolio of securities and to receive subscriptions from the public for units the value of which are pooled, and flexibility related to the portfolio. To the investor the major advantage of a unit trust is that he, with a small investment only, can obtain the advantages of diversification, although the range of diversification varies among the various unit trust funds now available. To illustrate the foregoing a unit trust fund with a portfolio of £1m comprising say 100 different holdings could be pooled and divided into 4 million units of 25p each. If units were offered for public subscription with say a minimum investment of £50 an investor holding £50 worth of units in effect acquired an interest in a portfolio of 100 securities and thereby obtained a high degree of diversification for a small cash outlay.

Whilst the management company is responsible for the investment policy of the trust the trustees are responsible for ensuring that the managers adhere to the terms of the trust deed, particularly to ensure that no investments of a type not authorised by the deed are acquired. The portfolio investments are held in the name of the trustees. The managers deal with the selling of units to and purchasing of units from members of the public either direct or through agents such as banks, stockbrokers, solicitors, accountants.

The managers' market prices for selling or buying units are regulated by the Department of Trade and Industry under the Prevention of Fraud (Investments) Act 1958. The daily prices are fixed by the managers by reference to the current market quotations of the underlying securities after adjustments have been made for stamp duties, brokers' commissions, and the selling expenses, including a service charge to cover trustees' remuneration and management expenses. The charges levied on unit holders in respect of trust management fees are restricted by the Department of Trade and Industry to 13¼ per cent over the life of the trust.

There is a considerable number and variety of unit trusts covering a wide field of investment ranging from specialist portfolios of bank, insurance and investment trust shares to those designed for pension funds, charities and trustees. The majority, however, comprise a varying number of mainly British equities with a selection of North American and Commonwealth equities. A list of active trusts, under management company headings, giving current buying and selling prices and yields appears in the *Financial Times* and most of the daily papers.

Unit-linked life assurance is growing in popularity and new types of unit-linked policy are continually coming on to the market.

The main advantages of unit trusts may be summarised as follows:

(1) The selection and supervision of a diversified portfolio of investments by experienced investment managers.

(2) Readily marketable sub-units on a basis prescribed by the Department of Trade and Industry for ascertaining the buying and selling prices, with modest charges for the amount and responsibility of the work involved.

(3) Protection of unit holders by a trust deed approved by the Department of Trade and Industry, and adequate security arrangements against fraud and embezzlement.

(4) Regular distribution of income by half-yearly instalments when unit holders are given details of the distribution and an Income Tax deduction certificate. Some trusts provide for the accumulation of dividends and these are re-invested in further units. In such cases the undistributed dividends must still be "returned" to the tax authorities by the unit holders.

(5) The encouragement of small savings, sometimes accepted in small sums on savings account for investment in due course in sub-units.

(6) The added attraction of life cover in the case of the linked life assurance unit trust.

1. Statement of Claim against........................ Insurance Company in respect of Fire Loss—

		£
Stock—Opening		23,600
Purchases		84,000
		107,600
Less Sales	£128,000	
Deduct 35% Gross Profit	44,800	
		83,200
Estimated Stock at date of Fire		24,400
Less Salvaged Stock		3,000
Amount of Claim		£21,400

2. Statement of Claim against........................ Insurance Company in respect of Fire Loss—

		£
Stock—Opening		3,675
Purchases		10,494
		14,169
Less Sales	£15,650	
Deduct 36% Gross Profit	5,634	
		10,016
Estimated Stock at date of Fire		4,153
Less Stock Salvaged		450
Amount of Claim		£3,703

3. Statement of Claim against........................ Insurance Company in respect of Fire Loss—

		£
Stock—Opening		4,000
Purchases		6,900
		10,900
Less Sales	£10,200	
Deduct 30% Gross Profit	3,060	
		7,140
Estimated Stock at date of Fire		3,760
Less Stock Salvaged		900
Amount of Claim		£2,860

[*Note to Questions* 1–3. Before the claim will be admitted, the insurance company may appoint an assessor to verify such claim. In any case, the claim must conform to the conditions and terms of the policy, e.g. as to average clause.]

4. Draft Statement of Claim for compensation for compulsory removal—

	£
Loss on Stock	300
Loss on Fittings	500
Estimated value of Lease	?
Estimated value of Goodwill as per computation .	3,270
Add Interest at ?%	?
	£

	19.4		19.5		19.6	
	£	£	£	£	£	£
Profits per Accounts . . .		2,300		3,000		2,100
Less Salary	1,400		1,400		1,400	
Interest on Capital . .	300		325		400	
Depreciation . . .	100		90		81	
		800		815		881
		£1,500		£2,185		£1,219

	£
Average profits: 19.4 . . .	1,500
19.5 . .	2,185
19.6 . . .	1,219
	3 ⟌ 4,904
	£1,635

Two years' purchase of average profits £1,635 × 2 = £3,270.

The foregoing claim is prepared in draft form in the absence of further data, viz.—

(1) Details as to terms and cost of lease; whether there was an option available to Lessee to renew; as to whether all fixtures belong to Lessor.

(2) It is advisable that the relevant Balance Sheets be inspected.

(3) The original cost of goodwill cannot be claimed for, but the present worth of an annuity of profits, after allowing for reasonable management remuneration, and interest to the proprietor upon his capital outlay, may be included. The marked decline in earnings in 19.6 may preclude an average being taken, whilst it may not be possible to claim in this class of business *two* years' purchase. In any case the proprietor may have been able to obtain similar or better premises.

(4) Income Tax not being an expense of the business is not deducted from profits.

5.

JOURNAL

		£	£
Stock Destroyed . . . . . . *Dr.*		4,000	
,, Damaged . . . . . . *Dr.*		1,000	
To Trading Account			5,000
Insurance Co. Ltd. . . . . . . *Dr.*		8,185	
To Machinery			3,000
,, ,, ...			350
,, Stock Destroyed			4,500
,, ,, Damaged			300
,, Fire Expenses			35
Profit and Loss Account . . . . . *Dr.*		700	
To Stock Damaged			700
Machinery . . . . . . [1]*Dr.*		50	
Stock Destroyed . . . . . . *Dr.*		500	
To Profit and Loss Account			550
Salvaged Stock . . . . *Dr.*		?	
To Profit and Loss Account			?

Cash received will be credited to the insurance company, and that paid for Fire Expenses and Repairs to Machinery debited to the respective accounts.

[1] Alternatively, the profit on machinery may be transferred to reserve.

6. The first calculation will be to find the percentage of Gross Profit (i.e. Net Profit plus Insured Standing Charges) on Turnover; ascertained from the accounts of the **last complete financial period,** i.e. 30th September, 19.7 (and not based on the turnover of the period immediately preceding the fire), because it is the only practical way of ascertaining the required percentage. This calculation is—

	£
Net Profit for the last complete financial year	6,000
Insured Standing Charges complete financial year . . .	14,000
	£20,000
Turnover for the last complete financial year	£80,000

$$\text{Percentage} = \frac{20,000}{80,000} \times 100 \qquad = \underline{\underline{25}}$$

	£
Rate of Gross Profit applied to reduced Turnover—	
25 per cent of (£26,000 − £9,000) i.e. of £17,000 . . .	4,250
Cost of Working	1,760
	£6,010

Average proviso—

Rate of Gross Profit applied to Annual Turnover—

25 per cent of £60,000 = £15,000

and this exceeds the amount **insured** (£12,000); the average proviso applied thus—

$$\frac{12,000}{15,000} = \frac{4}{5} \text{ or 80 per cent of £6,010} \qquad . \qquad . \qquad . \qquad . \qquad £4,808$$

The full period of loss through the dislocation is available (five months), as the period of indemnity insured is seven months, i.e. in official language the period of indemnity is adequate.

It will be observed that the expenditure of £1,760 is accepted by the insurer without limitation. A reduction of this figure may be required in certain circumstances.

7. The rate of Gross Profit $= \dfrac{\text{Net Profit} + \text{INSURED Standing Charges}}{\text{Turnover}}$

$= \dfrac{6,000 + 14,000}{80,000} = 25$ per cent.

	£	£
Rate of Gross Profit, 25 per cent of £14,000 applied to Reduced Turnover of		3,500
Increase in Cost of Working	2,000	

Apportioned to cover Insurable Standing Charges not included in the insurance—

$\dfrac{\text{Net Profit} + \text{Insured Standing Charges}}{\text{Net Profit} + ALL \text{ Standing Charges}}$

$= \dfrac{6,000 + 14,000}{6,000 + 15,000} = 98 \cdot 67$ per cent of £2,000 . . . 1,973

Amount payable limited to the sum produced by applying rate of Gross Profit to the amount of the reduction in turnover avoided by such cost of working.
25 per cent of actual turnover of £6,000.

(Potential Loss £20,000 less actual reduction of £14,000) . .	1,500
	5,000
Less Savings in Insured Standing Charges (not apportioned) .	200
	£4,800

Average—

Rate of Gross Profit applied to Annual Turnover (i.e. twelve months ended 31st March) £80,600.
∴ 25 per cent of £80,600 = £20,150.
The amount insured being only £18,000, the amount payable under the policy is limited to—

$\dfrac{18,000}{20,150} \times £4,800$ £4,288

Note that basis of ascertaining Gross Profit is Net Profit + *Insured* (not insurable) Standing Charges.

8. Rate of Gross Profit (based on year to 31st March, 19.9)—

		£
Stock, 1st April, 19.8		8,860
Purchases		20,770
		29,630
Less Stock, 31st March, 19.9—		
Per Balance Sheet	£7,510	
Add amount written off	160	
		7,670
		21,960
Profit (= 28 % on Sales)		8,540
Sales		£30,500

Estimated value of Stock, 2nd August, 19.9—

		£
Stock, 1st April, 19.9, at cost	£7,670	
Less abnormal stock	360	
		7,310
Purchases		7,470
		14,780
Less Sales	£11,800	
Less abnormal line sold	350	
		11,450
Less Gross Profit thereon—28 % . . .	3,206	
		8,244
Estimated Stock		£6,536

CLAIM

		£
Estimated Stock (as above)		6,536
Less Salvage		1,021
		£5,515

9. (a)

	Sweets	Stationery	Fancy Goods	
			Old	New
	£	£	£	£
Year ended 31st December, 19.7—				
Stock at Cost, 1st January, 19.7 .	90	940	240	1,270
Purchases	2,251	3,710	—	1,960
	2,341	4,650	240	3,230
Less Stock at Cost, 31st December, 19.7	220	1,230	120	1,410
Cost of Sales	2,121	3,420	120	1,820
Sales	3,030	4,560	70	2,800
Gross Profit . . .	£ 909	£1,140	*Loss* £50	£980
Rate of Gross Profit on Turnover .	30%	25%	—	35%
	£	£	£	£
1st January to 30th April, 19.8—				
Sales	1,040	1,720	33	1,240
Gross Profit thereon . .	312	430	—	434
Cost of Sales . . .	728	1,290	60	806
Stock at Cost, 1st January, 19.8 .	£220	£1,230	£120	£1,410
Purchases	835	1,110	—	650
	1,055	2,340	120	2,060
Stock at Cost, 30th April, 19.8	£327	£1,050	£60	£1,254

VALUE OF STOCK DESTROYED BY FIRE, 30TH APRIL, 19.8

	Stock at Cost	Salvage	Less Depreciation	Net Value of Stock Destroyed
	£	£	£	£
Sweets	327	72	—	255
Stationery . . .	1,050	—	—	1,050
Fancy Goods—				
Old Shop-soiled Stock .	60	—	30[1]	30
New Stock . .	1,254	370	—	884
				£2,219

(b) Dr.   PROVISION FOR DEPRECIATION OF SHOP-SOILED STOCK   **Cr.**

19.7		£	19.7			£
Dec. 31	To Trading Account—		Jan. 1	By Provision . . b/d		
	Loss on Sale of Shop-soiled Stock (£120 − £70) . .	50		(50% on £240) . .		120
	„ Profit and Loss Account—					
	Over-provision written back	10				
	„ Balance (50% on £120) c/d	60				
		£120				£120
19.8		£	19.8			£
Apr. 30	To Trading Account—		Jan. 1	By Balance . . b/d		60
	Loss on Sale of Shop-soiled Stock (£60 − £33) . .	27				
	„ Profit and Loss Account—					
	Over-provision written back	3				
	„ Insurance Claim Account .	30				
		£60				£60

[1] Even assuming that the 50 per cent provision was a fair estimate at the end of December, 19.6, it is probable that at 30th April, 19.8, there was further deterioration in the stock value.

10.   Z LTD.

JOURNAL

19.5		£	£
Sept. 30	Insurance Company . . . . . *Dr.*	55,800	
	To Insurance Claim		55,800
	Being claim admitted arising from destruction by		
	fire of factory— £		
	Factory Buildings 28,000		
	Plant 15,000		
	Stock $= \dfrac{16,000}{30,000} \times$ £24,000 . . 12,800		
	£55,800		
19.6			
Mar. 31	Freehold Land . . . . . . *Dr.*	4,000	
	Insurance Claim . . . . . . *Dr.*	28,000	
	To Freehold Factory		25,000
	„ Capital Reserve		7,000
	Being transfer of cost of land (per directors' esti-		
	mate) and surplus of insurance admitted claim over		
	book value of Freehold Factory, exclusive of the		
	land, transferred to Capital Reserve.		
	Provision for Depreciation of Plant . . . *Dr.*	4,000	
	Insurance Claim . . . . . . *Dr.*	15,000	
	To Plant		14,000
	„ Capital Reserve		1,000
	„ General Reserve		4,000
	Being surplus of insurance admitted claim over		
	original cost of plant (transferred to Capital Reserve)		
	and provision for depreciation released (to General		
	Reserve).		
	Profit and Loss Account . . . . . *Dr.*	12,800	
	Insurance Claim . . . . . . *Dr.*	11,200	
	To Trading Account		24,000
	Being total value of Stock *at cost* destroyed by fire		
	transferred to Trading Account; and further loss		
	arising from operation of average clause owing to		
	inadequate insurance cover transferred to Profit and		
	Loss Account.		

As the claims were paid on 30th September, 19.5, it is almost certain that at 31st March, 19.6, they will have been agreed and admitted. On this assumption the accounts for the year ended 31st March, 19.6, laid before the Members of Z Ltd. will show the following information—

	£
(1) Capital Reserve, being surplus of insurance claim paid over book value.	
Factory .	7,000
Plant .	1,000
At Credit .	£8,000

(2) General Reserve (or as a separate item in the Profit and Loss Account), being provision for depreciation of Plant destroyed by fire (in respect of which insurance claim paid) no longer required.

At Credit .	£4,000

(3) Profit and Loss for loss of Stock destroyed by fire and not covered by insurance.

At Debit .	£11,200
The Stock lost is .	30,000
Less Salvage .	6,000
Net Cost of Stock .	£24,000

Average—

$$\frac{\text{Amount Insured}}{\text{Total Stock}} \times \text{Net Loss, i.e.—}$$

$\frac{16,000}{30,000} \times £24,000$	=	12,800
Leaving amount uncovered of .		11,200
		£24,000

The debit against the insurance company of £55,800 in the first entry in the Journal will be dealt with on receipt of that sum from the Insurance Company, i.e. Debit Cash £55,800; Credit Insurance Company £55,800.

If no account had been opened for Salvaged Stock, the Sales of £3,500 would be credited to Trading Account, followed by a transfer entry, viz.—

Debit Profit and Loss Account £2,500;
Credit Trading Account £2,500.

Some students find the entries troublesome, but if, broadly, the item of £24,000 (Stock destroyed after taking into account salvage) be regarded as a "special" Sale (resulting in a "special" loss) and credited to Trading Account at £12,800, with a further *credit* thereto of £11,200 and *debit* to Trading of £11,200 for loss. This ends the matter, and Trading Account for the year ended 31st March, 19.6, will be debited with £18,500, the opening Stock, and credited with the closing Stock in the ordinary way.

In the answer above reference has been made to Trading Account and Sales, but to be strictly correct, the stock destroyed is better dealt with, not as a sale, but as a *reduction of purchases*; and similarly for the disposal of Salvage (unless its condition is such that it can be sold in the ordinary way). This is because there is no disposal strictly comparable with a true Sale, as there is no element of profit, and by crediting the amounts to Sales might, unless clearly kept separate from normal Sales, vitiate profit ratios.

Note. It is assumed that the salvaged Stock has been sold and entered in Sales during the year.

It is probable, however, that it might have had to be sold as remnants or soiled goods at less than cost. When salvaged its condition would be such as to enable the management to judge whether or not it could be sold in the ordinary way. If it is unlikely, the accounts should deal with it separately.

The position may be dealt with by amending the last Journal entry as follows: a debit to Salvaged Stock Account £6,000 and a credit to Trading Account £6,000 (or by increasing the £24,000 item to £30,000).

The disposal of the goods would be reflected in a debit to Cash (or Debtors) and credit to Salvaged Stock Account, and the balance written off to Profit and Loss Account.

Alternatively, the original Journal entry may be left undisturbed, and the Sales of the salvage goods credited to Trading Account, and a final entry as follows—

Debit Profit and Loss Account.
Credit Trading Account.

in respect of the loss (similar to the loss involved by reason of the under-cover for insurance).

If, for example, the salvaged stock was sold for £3,500 this would be credited to the Salvaged Stock Account, if opened, as above, and the latter account closed by a credit thereto £2,500, and a debit to Profit and Loss Account.

CHAPTER XXVIII

1.   *re AB*

STATEMENT OF AFFAIRS AS AT.........................

Gross Lia-bilities	Liabilities	Ex-pected to Rank	Assets	Esti-mated to Pro-duce
£		£		£
3,388	Unsecured Creditors . . (i)	3,388	Cash in Hand . . .	14
300	Creditor fully secured . £300		Plant and Tools . . .	120
	Estimated Value of Security 425		Stock-in-trade (Cost £1,370) . (iv)	770
			Furniture, Fittings, and Fixtures .	273
	Balance to *Contra* . . £125		Motor Vehicles	130
			Household Furniture . . .	400
2,137	Creditors partly secured £2,137 (ii)			
	Less Estimated Value			1,707
	of Security . . 1,900(iii)		Book Debts—	
		237	Good	1,800
	Creditor for Rent Recoverable		Doubtful . . . £250	
	by Distress . . . £125		Bad 96	
	Preferential Creditors—			
	Rates 65			£346
	Income Tax . . . 87			
			Estimated to Produce . .	60
277	Deducted *Contra* . £277		Surplus from Creditor fully secured	125
				3,692
			Deduct Preferential Creditors .	277
				3,415
			Deficiency explained in Statement(K)	210
£6,102		£3,625		£3,625

LIST "K" DEFICIENCY (OR SURPLUS) ACCOUNT

	£			£
Excess of Assets over Liabilities on the		*Net Loss of Business*		1,783
31st day of December, 19.. —		Bad Debts		286
Business	2,430	Depreciation of—		
Private [£1,650 + £478 + £425] .	2,553	Stock-in-trade (iv) . . . £350		
Deficiency as per Statement of Affairs .	210	Plant and Tools . . . 315		
		Motor Vehicles . . 196		
		Household Furniture . . 78		
				939
		Drawings		2,185
	£5,193			£5,193

In addition to the information given in the question, the following assumptions are made: (1) Plant and Tools are worth £120, (2) Motor Vehicles are worth £130, (3) Stock has depreciated by £350, £250 of such Stock at depreciated value being in the hands of a Trade Creditor under lien for debt of £300, (4) Book Debts are divided into (*a*) Good £1,800, (*b*) Doubtful £250 (estimated worth £60), (*c*) Bad £96, (5) Household Furniture is worth £400. (6) Income Tax is not more than one year's assessment ended prior to the previous 6th April.

Notes to Students—

    (i) Unsecured creditors are £3,688, less partly secured creditor (see Note ii), £300.
    (ii) Partly secured creditors: (*a*) Bank, £1,837; (*b*) Trade Creditor with Lien £300.
    (iii) Security for partly secured creditors comprises (*a*) £1,650, Private House; and (*b*) Stock, £250.
    (iv) The item of Stock in Balance Sheet is disposed of by inclusion (*a*) as a free asset, £770; (*b*) as part security, £250; and (*c*) depreciation, £350.
    (v) Items in italics account for the item of £1,538 overdrawn Capital in Balance Sheet.

2. *re Wright & Johnson*

STATEMENT OF AFFAIRS AS AT 1ST NOVEMBER, 19.8

Gross Lia- bilities	Liabilities		Ex- pected to Rank	Assets		Esti- mated to Produce
£			£			£
12,000	Unsecured Creditors . . .		12,000	Cash at Bankers . . .		145
2.300	Creditors partly secured	£2,300		,, in hand		55
	Less Estimated			Stock-in-trade (Cost £1,000) .		850
	Value of Security	2,000		Fixtures		100
			300			
140	Preferential Creditors—			Book Debts—		1,150
	Deducted *contra* .	£140		Good . . .		450
				Doubtful . . . £23		
				Bad . . . 34		
					£57	
				Estimated to Produce .		*nil*
						1,600
				Deduct Preferential Creditors (*per contra*) . . .		140
						1,460
				Deficiency explained in Statement (K)		10,840
£14,440			£12,300			£12,300

LIST "K" DEFICIENCY (OR SURPLUS) ACCOUNT

	£			£
To Excess of Assets over Liabilities on 1st day of January, 19.6 . .	2,160	By Net Loss of Business . . .		9,180
,, Deferred Creditor . . .	1,000	,, Bad Debts		57
,, Deficiency as per Statement of Affairs	10,840	,, Depreciation of—		
		Stock-in-trade . . £150		
		Trade Fixtures . . 100		
				250
		,, Partners' Drawings . .		4,513
	£14,000			£14,000

Notes. (i) Williams being a deferred creditor for £1,000 (loan at a rate of interest varying with profits) cannot prove against the estate until the unsecured creditors have been paid in full.

(ii) Johnson is liable to the creditors for any withdrawal of his capital.

(iii) No information is given as to private assets of Wright and his own creditors.

3.   *re A and B*

JOINT STATEMENT OF AFFAIRS AS AT 31ST MARCH, 19..

Gross Lia-bilities	Liabilities		Ex-pected to Rank	Assets	Esti-mated to Produce
£			£		£
6,050	Unsecured Creditors[1]	. .	6,050	Property—	
				Cash	100
				Stock-in-trade (Cost £3,100)	2,000
				Machinery . . .	1,090
				Buildings . . .	500
					3,690
	Preferential Creditors— . £			Book Debts— £	
	Rent 50			Good . . .	1,000
	Salaries . . . 100			Doubtful . . . 500	
150	Deducted *contra* . . £150			Bad 500	
				£1,000	
				Estimated to Produce .	300
					4,990
				Deduct Preferential Creditors (*per contra*) . . .	150
					4,840
				Deficiency explained in Statement (K)	1,210
£6,200			£6,050		£6,050

LIST (K) JOINT DEFICIENCY (OR SURPLUS) ACCOUNT

	£			£
Excess of Assets over Liabilities on the .... day of............, 19.. . . .	2,000	Bad Debts		700
Deficiency as per Statement of Affairs .	1,210	Depreciation of—		
		Stock-in-trade .	£1,100	
		Machinery . .	910	
		Buildings . .	500	
				2,510
	£3,210			£3,210

re A

STATEMENT OF AFFAIRS AS AT 31ST MARCH, 19..

Gross Lia-bilities	Liabilities		Ex-pected to Rank	Assets	Esti-mated to Produce
£			£		£
6,900	Unsecured Creditors .	. .	6,900	Furniture . . .	350
				Estimated Surplus from Securities in the hand of Bank (*re* Firm)[2]	5,750
					6,100
				Deficiency explained in Statement (K)	800
£6,900			£6,900		£6,900

[1] £2,000 + £2,500 + £1,500 + £50.
[2] See note (i) on page 664.

LIST (K) DEFICIENCY (OR SURPLUS) ACCOUNT

	£			£
Estimated Surplus from Securities (Policy and House) in the hands of Bank	5,750	Loss in Business (Capital)		1,000
Appreciation in value of House	1,000	Depreciation of Life Policy[1] . £50		
Deficiency as per Statement of Affairs	800	,, ,, Furniture . 450		
				500
		Loss—Security utilized by Bank:		
		Life Policy* £50		
		House 6,000		
				6,050
	£7,550			£7,550

re B

STATEMENT OF AFFAIRS AS AT 31ST MARCH, 19..

Gross Lia-bilities	Liabilities	Ex-pected to Rank	Assets	Esti-mated to Produce
£ 2,300	Unsecured Creditors .	£ 2,300	Furniture . . .	£ 500
			Life Policy . . .	150
				650
			Deficiency explained in Statement (K)	1,650
£2,300		£2,300		£2,300

LIST (K) DEFICIENCY (OR SURPLUS) ACCOUNT

	£			£
Deficiency as per Statement of Affairs .	1,650	Loss in Business (Capital) .		1,000
		Depreciation of Life Policy .	. £150	
		,, ,, Furniture .	. 500	
				650
	£1,650			£1,650

Notes (i). The estimated surplus of £5,750 in A's statement is arrived at as follows—

Estimated Dividend in Joint Estate $\frac{4840}{6050}$ = 80p in £

∴ ,, ,, receivable by Bank—	£	
As unsecured Creditor in Joint Estate—£1,500 at 80p in £ =	1,200	[See Note (v) to
Balance made up out of Security lodged by A =	300	Question 5 on page 667]
Total . . .	£1,500	
Security lodged by A—	£	
Life Policy valued at . . .	50	
House valued at . .	6,000	
	6,050	
Less utilized by Bank .	300	
Surplus to separate estate of A .	£5,750	

(ii) There are no details to connect the present capital with the past.

(iii) The separate estates of A and B have, at the above date, neither capital nor deficiency (before depreciation, etc.), as the assets equal the liabilities, e.g. B's liabilities £2,300, assets £2,300. [Business Capital £1,000, Life Policy £300, Furniture £1,000.]

---

* Policy taken as worth £100 on an investment basis and revalued at £50.

4.

Re Victor Mont

STATEMENT OF AFFAIRS

IN BANKRUPTCY   No.   of 19..

Gross Lia-bilities	Liabilities (as stated and estimated by Debtor)	Ex-pected to Rank	Assets (as stated and estimated by Debtor)	Esti-mated to Pro-duce
£		£		£
26,120	Unsecured Creditors as per List (A)[1]	26,075	Property as per List (H), viz.—	
800	Creditors fully secured, as		(b) Cash in Hand . .	5
	per List (B) . . £ 800		(d) Stock-in-trade (Cost £8,000)	6,500
	Estimated Value of securities 1,600		(e) Machinery and Plant . .	450
			(i) Office Furniture . .	250
	Balance thereof to *contra* £800		(m) Private Furniture . .	220
14,000	Creditors partly secured as		Total as per List (H) . .	7,425
	per List (C) . . £14,000		Book Debts as per List (I), viz.—	
	Less Estimated Value of		Good . . .	4,800
	Securities . . 8,500		Doubtful . . £2,100	
		5,500	Bad . . . 450	
	Creditors for Rent, etc., re-			£2,550
	coverable by Distress, as			
	per List (F) . . £250		Estimated to Produce . .	980
	Creditors for Rates, Taxes,			
	Wages, etc., payable in			13,205
	full, as per List (G) . 200		Bills of Exchange on hand,	
450	Deducted *contra* £450		as per List (J) . . £	
			Estimated to Produce . .	1,450
			Surplus from Securities in the hands	
			of Creditors fully secured (*per*	
			contra)	800
				15,455
			Deduct Creditors for distrainable	
			Rent, and for preferential Rates,	
			Taxes, Wages, and Sheriff's	
			Charges, etc. (*per contra*) .	450
				15,005
			Deficiency explained in Statement (K)	16,570
£41,370		£31,575		£31,575

[Followed by List (K) and schedules, particulars of Trading, and duly sworn by Debtor.]

[1] £24,000, plus wife £2,000, plus loan interest £75 (5 per cent on £2,000 only for nine months) rank-ing for dividend, i.e. £45 (3 per cent on £2,000 for nine months) excluded, but included in gross liabilities. The availability of the loan and interest (£2,075) presupposes that the loan is a private one and not for the husband's use in his business. Assumed that there is no tax liability.

5.   *re A B & Co.*

Rough preparatory Balance Sheet.

[The letters in parenthesis connect with those shown in the Statement of Affairs on page 667.]

BALANCE SHEET, 4TH FEBRUARY, 19.4

	£	£		£	£
Unsecured Creditors	36,800		Cash		130 (*e*)
Trade Creditors .	7,000		Debtors		42,260 (*i*)
Income Tax, 19.3–19.4 .	600		Stock		2,420 (*f*)
		44,400 (*a*)	Motors, etc. . . .		1,000 (*g*)
,, ,, 19.4–19.5 .		400¹	Furniture		300 (*h*)
Rates and Wages .		510 (*d*)	Premises (Security) . .	12,300	
Mortgage and Interest .	10,180		Stock (,,) . .	18,000	
Midland Bank Ltd. .	15,000				30,300 (*c*)
		25,180 (*b*)			
Balance . .		5,920			
		£76,410			£76,410

DEFICIENCY OR SURPLUS ACCOUNT

	£			£
Undisclosed Income	25,500	Deficiency at 30th June, 19.3 (*m*)		1,500 (*j*)
		Loss		5,920 (*k*)
		Bad Debts . . .		10,160 (*k*)
		Drawings . .	£1,600 (*b*)	
		Plus Income Tax,		
		19.4–19.5 . .	400¹	
				2,000
		Balance . .		5,920
	£25,500			£25,500

¹ The items £400 will cancel themselves, the drawings remaining at £1,600 and the liability disappearing.

If the item of Bad Debts £25,500 had been dealt with, the debtors would be £25,500 less, and the undisclosed income item £25,000 would disappear—but this result is not compatible with the existence of £10,160 Bad Debts.

re A B & Co.

STATEMENT OF AFFAIRS AS AT 4TH FEBRUARY, 19.4

Gross Lia-bilities	Liabilities	Ex-pected to Rank	Assets	Estimated to Produce
£		£		£
44,400	Unsecured Creditors . (a)	44,400	Cash in Hand . . .	130 (e)
25,180	Creditors fully se-cured . (b)£25,180		Stock (Cost £...........) . .	2,420 (f)
			Motor Vehicles . . .	600 (g)
	Estimated Value of Securities . . (c) 30,300		Office Furniture, Fixtures, etc.	150 (h)
			Surplus from A's separate Estate . . .	200
	Surplus to *contra* . £5,120			
				3,500
1,200	Liabilities on Bills Dis-counted . . £1,200		Book Debts—	
			Good . . .	14,460 (i)
			Doubtful and Bad £27,800	
	of which it is expected to rank	nil		
			Estimated to Produce .	2,300 (i)
510	Preferential Creditors—		Surplus from Creditors fully secured . . .	5,120
	Deducted *contra* (d) £510			
				25,380
			Deduct Preferential Creditors (*per contra*) . . .	510
				24,870
			Deficiency, explained in State-ment (K) . . .	19,530
£71,290		£44,400		£44,400

LIST (K) DEFICIENCY (OR SURPLUS) ACCOUNT

	£		£
Surplus from A's separate Estate .	200	Excess of Liabilities over Assets on the 30th day of June, 19.3 . .	1,500 (j)
Discrepancy in Books . (m) .	25,500		
[Unexplained Income] . .		Net Loss from the 30th day of June, 19.3 to the 4th day of February,	
Deficiency as per Statement of Affairs . . .	19,530	19.4	16,080 (k)
		Bad Debts . . .	25,500 (c)
		Depreciation of Motor £400 (g)	
		„ Furniture 150 (h)	
			550
		Drawings	1,600 (h)
	£45,230		£45,230

Although the question states the *book* value of debts at £27,800 (estimated value £2,300) it would appear that the estimated loss of £25,500 had already been written off, in which case the discrepancy of £25,500 and Bad Debts £25,500 disappear, but as the question also states that the Bad Debts were £10,160 [only] the above assumption has been ignored.

Notes. (i) Income Tax is not preferential for 19.3–19.4 as this charge is preferential only for a year's assessment up to the 5th April *preceding* the date of the Receiving Order [i.e. 5th April, 19.3 = 19.2–19.3].

(ii) The business is not in existence in 19.4–19.5, hence the assessment must be cancelled.

(iii) A claim under s. 168, Income and Corporation Taxes Act 1970, is available, but as the question gives no information as to other income, allocation of liability and tax paid, the amount repayable cannot be ascertained, the figure being retained in the solution as an unsecured creditor. In any case, the tax deducted on the mortgage interest is accountable to the Inland Revenue.

(iv) It is assumed that the Rates are actually due.

(v) Trade creditors holding separate security are not *secured* creditors of the Joint Estate. (See s. 167, Bankruptcy Act, 1914; *In re* West Riding Bank, 1881; *Dutton Massey* v. *Manchester and Liverpool Banking Co.*, 1924.) Consequently, such creditors prove in the Joint Estate as unsecured creditors.

CHAPTER XXIX

1. STATEMENT AS TO THE AFFAIRS OF HORNER AND MUDD LIMITED
ON THE................. DAY OF........ 19..

	Esti- mated rea- lizable values £
Assets not specifically pledged—	
Cash in hand	10
Marketable Securities	300
Debtors	650
Stock-in-trade	1,680
Goods out on Consignment	30
Plant and Machinery	900
Fixtures and Fittings	120
Goodwill	*nil*
Assets specifically pledged—	
Estimated realizable value £8,000	
Due to Secured Creditors 5,075	
	2,925
Estimated Total Assets available for Preferential Creditors and Unsecured Creditors, carried forward	£6,615
Summary of Gross Assets—	
Gross realizable value of assets specifically pledged £8,000	
Other assets 3,690	
Gross Assets £11,690	

LIABILITIES

Gross Lia- bilities £		£
	Estimated Total Assets available for Preferential Creditors and Unsecured Creditors, brought forward	6,615
5,075	*Less* Secured Creditors	—
320	Preferential Creditors	320
		6,295
25,090	Unsecured Creditors	25,090
	Estimated Deficiency as regards creditors, being the difference between—	
£30,485	Gross Liabilities £30,485	
	and	
	Gross Assets 11,690	
		18,795
	Issued and Called up Capital—	
	8,000 Ordinary Shares of £1 each, fully paid 8,000	
	10,000 Deferred Shares of 5p each, fully paid 500	
		8,500
	Estimated Deficiency as regards Members	£27,295

Note (1) Assumed that the shares are fully paid.
(2) Goodwill taken as being worthless.
(3) Assumed that the investments are marketable securities.
(4) See also next page.

[A Deficiency Account is not required, nor is sufficient information given for one to be prepared, A rough account may, however, be built up on the basis of the information given, thus—

ROUGH BALANCE SHEET

	£		£
Capital	8,500	Assets (first 9 items in list in question) .	17,310
Liabilities (last 5 items in list in question)	30,485	Deficiency [*see below*] . . .	21,675
	£38,985		£38,985

Assets are estimated to produce £11,690, as shown in the summary on the Statement of Affairs.

ROUGH DEFICIENCY ACCOUNT

	£
Excess of Capital and Liabilities over Assets (*see above*) . .	21,675
Losses now written off (£17,310 − £11,690) . . .	5,620
Deficiency per Statement of Affairs	£27,295]

2. *Dr.*　　　　LIQUIDATOR'S DISTRIBUTION ACCOUNT　　　*Cr.*

	£		£
To Balance	40,521	By Dividend at 5% per annum on 25,000 Preference Shares of £1 each . . . . .[1]	1,146
		„ Repayment of Share Capital—	
		25,000 Preference Shares (£1) .	25,000
		25,000 Deferred Shares (5p) .	1,250
		„ Distribution to Members of Surplus—	
		(*a*) Preference Shareholders (50p) . . .[2]	12,500
		(*b*) Deferred Shareholders (2½p) . . .[2]	625
	£40,521		£40,521

Notes. (i) Assumed that all the shares are fully paid.
(ii) It is evident that the examiner intends Income Tax to be ignored.

[1] £25,000 at 5 per cent per annum for 11 months.

[2] (*a*) $\frac{25,000}{26,250} \times £13,125$; (*b*) $\frac{1,250}{26,250} \times £13,125$, or $\frac{1,250}{25,000}\left(\frac{1}{20}\right) \times £12,500$.

3. *Dr.*　　　　LIQUIDATOR'S DISTRIBUTION ACCOUNT　　　*Cr.*

	£		£
To Balance	215,809	By "Interest" on £125,000 at 5% per annum for eleven months . .	5,729
		„ Balance—Payment to Shareholders rateably to Nominal Value of Shares—	
		Preference $\frac{100}{101} \times £210,080$.	208,000
		Ordinary $\frac{1}{101} \times £210,080$.	2,080
	£215,809		£215,809

4. The following are the steps to be taken by a liquidator in a voluntary winding up. [Assumed Members' Voluntary Winding up.]—

1. Advertisement in *London Gazette* within fourteen days of resolution.
2. Advertisement in local press.
3. Copy of resolution to be sent to Registrar within fifteen days.
4. Notice to Registrar of appointment of liquidator within twenty-one days.
5. Notification to Bank.
6. Notification by advertisement to creditors and meeting arranged.
7. Sale of assets by auction or otherwise.
8. Calls on contributories, if necessary.
9. Payments to creditors.
10. Payment of dividends to contributories.
11. Distribution of any capital or other surplus to contributories.

[In addition, accounts in prescribed form will, if the proceedings continue for more than one year, be prepared, verified by affidavit, and sent to the Department of Trade and Industry. There will also be the first meeting of creditors, annual and final meeting of the members of the company.]

LIQUIDATOR'S CASH ACCOUNT

Dr. Receipts	£	£	Cr. Payments	?	£
To Balance		?	By Auctioneer's Charges	?	
,, Sale of Assets		200,000	,, Incidental Expenses	?	
,, Contributories—			,, Liquidator's Remuneration	?	
Preference	£24,000				2,000
Ordinary	4,000		,, Preferential Creditors		?
		28,000	,, Unsecured Creditors—		
,, Calls Collected		2,000	Dividend of £ in £		32,000
			,, Return to Contributories—		
			Preference	£70,000	
			Anticipatory Calls	24,000	
					94,000
			Ordinary	£90,000	
			Anticipatory Calls	4,000	
					94,000
			,, Surplus Distributed *pari passu*—		
			Preference	£4,000	
			Ordinary	4,000	
					8,000
		£230,000			£230,000

Notes. (i) It is assumed that the calls in arrear were received. Had they not been recovered, the contributories concerned would have no right of repayment. The position in this case cannot be shown, as the question does not give the share holdings of the defaulters.

(ii) It is assumed that the surplus is one of capital and that there is no contrary stipulation in the Memorandum and Articles regarding the distribution of the surplus.

5. *Dr.*   LIQUIDATOR'S FINAL STATEMENT OF ACCOUNT   *Cr.*

Receipts	£	*Payments*	£
To Assets Realized . . .	25,750	By Liquidation Costs . . .	250
„ Proceeds of Calls—		„ Creditors—£1 in £ . . .	7,500
5,000 Ordinary Shares of 25p		„ Repayment to Preference Share-	
per Share . . . £1,250		holders	5,000
4,000 Deferred Shares of		„ Repayment to Ordinary Share-	
12½p per share . . 500		holders	10,000
	1,750	„ Surplus Divided equally—	
		i.e. 25p per Share:	
		Preference Shareholders	
		(5,000) . . £1,250	
		Ordinary Shareholders	
		(10,000) . . 2,500	
		Deferred Shareholders	
		(4,000) . . 1,000	
			4,750
	£27,500		**£27,500**

Notes. (i) The holder of 1,000 deferred shares receives no return of surplus by reason of his default.

(ii) The question of preference dividends is ignored.

(iii) The surplus is divisible *equally*, that is, each share attracts the same cash repayment per share. As there is a surplus of £4,750 divisible amongst 19,000 shares it is equivalent to a return of 25p in £.

6.   STATEMENT OF AFFAIRS OF LOAMSHIRE FARMING CO. LIMITED
ON THE 1ST JANUARY, 19..

	Esti- mated rea- lizable Values £	Due to Secured Credi- tors £	Defi- ciency ranking as un- secured £	Surplus carried to last Column £	Esti- mated rea- lizable values £
Assets not specifically pledged—					
Cash in hand					10
Bills receivable					1,500
Debtors					1,350
Stock-in-trade					4,000
Land and Buildings					10,000
Machinery, Tools, etc.					200
Assets specifically pledged—					
Sundry Assets	3,500	3,000	—	500	
do.	1,000	2,000	1,000	—	
	£4,500	£5,000	£1,000	£500	
Estimated surplus from Assets specifically pledged					500
Estimated Total Assets available for Preferential Creditors, Debenture holders secured by a Floating Charge, and Unsecured Creditors, carried forward .					£17,560
Summary of Gross Assets—					
Gross realizable value of assets specifically pledged					£4,500
Other Assets					17,060
Gross Assets					£21,560

Gross Lia-bilities			£
	Estimated Total Assets available for Preferential Creditors, etc., brought forward		17,560
£	*Less—*		
4,000	Second Creditors to extent covered by pledged assets . . .		—
600	Preferential Creditors		600
			16,960
15,000	Debenture-holders with floating charge		15,000
	Estimated surplus as regards Debenture-holders		1,960
	Unsecured Creditors—		
1,000	Unsecured balance of partly secured creditors	£1,000	
7,000	Sundry	7,000	
1,000	Bank Overdraft	1,000	
10,000	Bills payable	10,000	
1,000	Contingent liability on bills discounted	1,000	
			20,000
	Estimated deficiency as regards creditors, being—		
	Gross Assets	21,560	
£39,600	*Less* Gross Liabilities	39,600	¹18,040
	Issued and called up capital—		
	20,000 6% Preference Shares of £1 each, fully paid . . .	20,000	
	20,000 Ordinary Shares of £1 each, 50p called up . . .	10,000	
			30,000
	Estimated Deficiency as regards Members		£48,040

¹ The nominal amount of unpaid capital liable to be called up is £10,000, estimated to produce £?, which is not charged in favour of Debenture holders.

7.   LIQUIDATOR'S FINAL STATEMENT OF RECEIPTS AND PAYMENTS

Dr.   *Cr.*

Receipts	£	Payments	£
To Balance	25	By Cash—	
Realization of Assets—		Costs of Liquidation . .	300
New Company—for Payment of Creditors and Costs of Liquidation . . . . ¹	4,400	Preferential Creditors . . £500	
		Unsecured Creditors:	
		50p in £ on £7,250 . . 3,625	
New Company—for Payment to Dissentient Shareholders:			4,125
1,500 Shares at 33⅓p per Share	500	„ Cash—	
		Dissentient Shareholders:	
		1,500 Shares at 33⅓p per Share .	500
	4,925		4,925
„ 7½% Debentures in New Company .	7,250	„ Unsecured Creditors of £7,250—	
„ 20,000 Shares of £1 each, 50p paid in New Company . .	10,000	Issue of 7½% Debentures in New Company . .	7,250
		„ Assenting Shareholders—	
		20,000 Shares of £1 each, 50p paid [one new share for one old share] . . .	10,000
	£22,175		£22,175

¹ Costs and Creditors £4,425, *less* Cash Balance £25.
[Detailed statement of scheme will follow the above.]

Note. The company being in *voluntary* liquidation no *statutory* form of Liquidator's Final Account is required.

The details of the call to provide the cash funds do not appear above, but in the books of the new company.

8. *Dr.*   RECEIVER'S RECEIPTS AND PAYMENTS ACCOUNT   *Cr.*

	£		£
To Freehold Property . . .	190,000	By Costs £400	
		„ Receivers' Remuneration . 3,500	
			3,900
		„ Preferential Creditors . .	4,108¹
		„ Debenture-holders for Principal and Interest . .	70,000
		„ Liquidator . . .	111,992
	£190,000		£190,000

¹ See next page.

Dr.   LIQUIDATOR'S RECEIPTS AND PAYMENTS ACCOUNT   *Cr.*

		£			£
To Receiver	. . . .	111,992	By Costs £850		
,, Realizations—			,, Liquidator's Remuneration 2,250		
Stocks	. . .	15,000			3,100
Debtors (other than W Ltd.)		4,120	,, Unsecured Creditors . .		41,892[1]
P Ltd. (damages for breach of			,, Balance available for Contribu-		
contract) . . .		170	tories . . . . c/d		109,000
W Ltd. . . . £300					
Less Damages set-off . 90		210			
Fixed Plant . . £ ?					
Loose Tools . . ?					
Leasehold Property . ?					
		22,500[2]			
		£153,992			£153,992
To Balance . . . . b/d		109,000	By Preference Shareholders—		
			80,000 Shares at £1·12½ each .		90,000
			,, Ordinary Shareholders—		
			95,000 Shares at 20p each .		19,000
			5,000 Shares at *nil* each .		—
			[20p *less* Call in arrear]		
		£109,000			£109,000

	Un- secured £	Pre- ferential £
[1] Creditors (excluding Debentures)—		
Directors *re* Bank Loan	7,000	
Bank Loan	3,000	
Landlord (satisfied by transfer of Plant, £5,500) . . .	—	—
Managing Director for Accountant's Salary	—	200
National Insurance Contributions		180
Inland Revenue:		
Accounting year ended 19.6	1,600	
,, ,, ,, 19.7		3,728
,, ,, ,, 19.8	400	
Sundry Creditors [£30,272 − £200 − £180]	29,892	
	£41,892	£4,108

[2]Leasehold Property		£25,000
Fixed Plant and Machinery £20,000		
Less taken by Landlord 5,500		
		14,500
Loose Plant and Tools		4,000
		43,500
Loss on Realization per question		21,000
		£22,500

Note. The loss of 80p a share on Ordinary Shares is made up as follows—

	Balance Sheet £	Realized £	Loss £	
Freehold Property . . .	202,500	190,000	12,500	
Leasehold Property ⎱				(including £5,500 Plant
Fixed Plant ⎰	49,000	22,500	26,500	handed over to
Loose Plant				Landlord)
Stock	25,000	15,000	10,000	
Debtors	6,000	4,420	1,580	
Profit and Loss . . .	15,000	—	15,000	
			65,580	
Add—				
Claims			90	
Costs, etc.: Receiver . .			3,900	
Costs, etc.: Liquidator . .			3,100	
			72,670	
Less—				
Claims		£ 170		
Release of Landlord's Claim .		2,500		
			2,670	
			70,000	
Add Premium on Preference Shares			10,000	
			£80,000	

Loss per Ordinary Share $\frac{80,000}{100,000} \times £1 = 80$p, leaving a repayment of 20p a share.

9.   STATEMENT AS TO THE AFFAIRS OF X LIMITED
ON THE 28TH DAY OF FEBRUARY, 19..

Gross Liabilities £		Estimated realizable values £
	Assets not specifically pledged—	
	Cash in hand	50
	Debtors	7,700
	Unpaid calls	350
	Stock-in-trade	31,000
	Plant	6,000
	Fixtures	100
	Goodwill	500
	Assets specifically pledged—	
	Leasehold Premises £10,000	
	Less due to Secured Creditors 5,000	
		5,000
	Estimated Total Assets available for Preferential Creditors, Debenture-holders secured by a floating charge, and Unsecured Creditors carried forward	£50,700
	Summary of Gross Assets—	
	Gross realizable value of assets specifically pledged 10,000	
	Other assets 45,700	
	Gross Assets	£55,700
	Estimated total assets available for Preferential Creditors, Debenture-holders secured by a floating charge, and Unsecured Creditors, brought forward	50,700
5,000	*Less* Secured Creditors	
700	Preferential Creditors	700[1]
		50,000
61,000	Debenture-holders secured by a floating charge	61,000
	Estimated Deficiency as regards Debenture holders	11,000
	Add Unsecured creditors—	
	Trade Accounts £22,100	
33,150	Bills Payable 1,200	
	Outstanding Expenses 4,350	
	Contingent Liabilities on contracts 5,500	
		33,150[2]
	Estimated Deficiency as regards Creditors, being the difference between—	
£99,850	Gross Liabilities 99,850	
	and	
	Gross Assets 55,700	
		44,150
	Issued and Called-up Capital—	
	100,000 Shares of £1 each, 50p called up 50,000	
	Add Calls in advance 500	
		50,500
	Less Calls in arrear, irrecoverable 150	
		50,350
	Estimated Deficiency as regards Members	£94,500

Note. The nominal amount of unpaid capital liable to be called up is £49,500, estimated to produce £? which is charged in favour of the Debenture-holders.

[1] See schedule of creditors on page 675.
[2] Per schedule on page 675, £27,650, plus contingent liabilities on contracts £5,500.

DEFICIENCY ACCOUNT

	£
Items contributing to Deficiency—	
Excess of Capital and Liabilities over Assets on the (three years ago)........19....	
as shown by Balance Sheet	35,089
Net dividends and bonuses declared (during the three years) . . .	—
Net trading losses (after charging of the items shown below) . . .	16,684
Estimated losses now written off or provided for in the Statement of Affairs—	
Bad Debts	1,100
Depreciation of:	
Stock	1,250
Plant	9,000
Fixtures	400
Leasehold Premises	1,000
Goodwill	24,500
Other losses:	
Contingent liabilities on contracts	5,500
	94,523
Items reducing Deficiency—	
Profits and Income (other than Trading Profits) (during the three years)—	
Transfer Fees	23
	£94,500
Deficiency as shown by Statement	

	£
Note as to Net Trading Losses—	
Provision for depreciation	£5,000
Charges for United Kingdom Taxation	?
Interest on debentures	9,000
Directors' Fees	3,000
	17,000
Less other Trading Profits and Losses	316
Net Trading Losses as shown above	£16,684

Creditors	Un-secured £	Pre-ferential £
Trade	22,100	
Bills Payable	1,200	
Wages		100 (see note (ii))
Rent	450	(see note (i))
Income Tax: preceding year . . .		600
Income Tax: current year . . .	700	(see note (iii))
Miscellaneous*	2,660	
Telephone	40	
Directors' Fees . . .	500	
Total [£28,350] . . .	£27,650	£700

	£
* Expense Creditors per Balance Sheet . . .	5,050
Less detailed in question	
[£100 + £450 + £600 + £700 + £40 + £500]	2,390
	£2,660

Notes. (i) The Landlord is unsecured and cannot proceed to distrain without leave of Court. As in this instance there is no competition with the unsecured creditors (*all* the assets being charged to secured creditor and debenture-holders), he will probably be allowed to distrain for arrears of rent.

(ii) Insufficient details are given as to wages of 5 men (£100), but on the facts the amount is almost certain to be preferential, as the limit is £200 or four months' wages, whichever is the less.

(iii) Income Tax is preferential only for a year ended before 6th April preceding the date of winding up. The current year's tax cannot therefore be preferential.

10.

X LTD., IN LIQUIDATION

Dr.		LIQUIDATOR'S CASH ACCOUNT		Cr.

	£			£
To Assets realized	2,436	By Preferential Creditors . . .		736
,, ,, ...	4,924	,, Bank on account . . .		1,200
		,, Bank—balance discharged .		3,070
		,, First Dividend of 66⅔p in the £ on		
		£2,694		1,796
(Balance of Cash at this stage £558)	7,360			6,802
Calls on Ordinary Shares—		,, Costs of Liquidation . .		485
24,000 "A" at 6¼p per share .	1,500	,, Final Dividend of 33⅓p in the £ on		
6,000 "B" 26¼p ,, ,, .	1,575	£2,694		898
		,, Preference Shares, 2,000 at £1·12½		
		per share		2,250
	£10,435			£10,435

The Calls due, assuming all paid, would produce—

		£
"A" Ordinary Shares 24,000 at 10p per share		2,400
"B" Ordinary Shares 6,000 at 30p per share		1,800
		£4,200

	£	£
Total cash after receipt of call moneys of £4,200 = £558 + £4,200		4,758
Available to meet—		
Cost of Liquidation	485	
Unsecured Creditors 33⅓p in the £ . . .	898	
Preference Shareholders, at £1·12½ on 2,000 Shares	2,250	
		3,633
Surplus		£1,125

Amount repayable to each Ordinary Shareholder (per Share)—

$$\frac{1,125}{30,000} = 3\frac{3}{4}p, \text{ thus involving a loss per ordinary share of } £1\cdot03\frac{3}{4} = 96\frac{1}{4}p.$$

Therefore, to avoid making an unnecessarily large call, the Liquidator will make a call on—

"A" Shareholders 6¼p, to make the 90p already paid and lost into a final loss of 96¼p.

"B" Shareholders 26¼p, to make the 70p already paid and lost into a final loss of 96¼p.

This may be computed by the "short cut" method as follows—

			£
Costs of Liquidation, etc. (as above)			3,633
"A" Ordinary Share Capital per Balance Sheet .	£21,600		
"B" ,, ,, ,, ,, ,, ,,	4,200		
			25,800
			29,433
Less Cash balance			558
Deficiency			£28,875

Therefore loss per ordinary shareholder—

$$\frac{\text{Deficiency}}{\text{Notionally fully paid Ordinary Share Capital}} = \frac{28,875}{30,000} \times £1 \quad = 96\frac{1}{4}p$$

CHAPTER XXX

1.

PRODUCTION ACCOUNT—COMMODITY A

SIX MONTHS ENDED 30TH JUNE, 19..

	£	£			£
Raw Materials Consumed:			Cost of Production . . c/d		64,000
Opening Stock . .	5,000				
Purchases . . .	30,000				
	35,000				
Less Closing Stock .	5,560				
		29,440 (*a*)			
Carriage Inwards . .		360			
Direct Wages . .		25,000			
		54,800			
Deduct Increase in Work in Progress—					
Balance at 30th June, 19.. . .	4,000				
Less Balance at 1st Jan. 19.. . .	1,200				
		2,800			
PRIME COST		52,000			
Rent, Rates, Insurance, and Works Overhead . .		10,000			
Factory Supervision . . .		2,000			
WORKS COST		64,000			
Administration Charges . . .		?			
		£64,000			£64,000

	Tons	£		Tons	£
Stock of Finished Goods	1,000	4,000	By Sales	15,000	75,000
Cost of Production of Finished Goods. b/d	16,000	64,000 (*b*)	,, Stock of Finished Goods	2,000	8,000
Advertising, Discounts, and Selling Costs		3,750 (*x*)			
Distribution Expenses					
Net Profit . . .		11,250 (*d*)			
	17,000	£83,000		17,000	£83,000

(*a*) As above.   (*b*) As above.

(*c*) £63,750 [£4,000 + £64,000 + £3,750 − £8,000].

(*d*) As above.   (*e*) 75p per ton, i.e. $\dfrac{11,250}{15,000} \times £1$.

(*x*) Sales, 15,000 tons at 25p = £3,750

[The profit per ton sold is Selling Price £5 less £4·25. (Cost of Production £4 + Selling Costs 25p) = 75p, i.e. 15,000 at 75p = £11,250.]

Work in Progress has been valued at Prime Cost in absence of data. Much more information is required, e.g. Cost of Power, Depreciation.

2.   MANUFACTURING, TRADING AND PROFIT AND LOSS ACCOUNT FOR THE MONTH ENDED 31ST MARCH, 19.3

		£				£
Raw Materials Consumed—			Prime Cost	c/d		20,196
[£300 + £8,726 — £200] . .		8,826				
Carriage Inwards [See Note (i)] .		341				
Direct Wages and Salaries . .		11,029				
		£20,196				£20,196
Prime Cost . . .	b/d	20,196	Works Cost of Manufactured			
Depreciation of Plant and			Goods	c/d		24,596
Machinery . . .		1,300				
Coal [and Power ?] . .		579				
Indirect Wages and Salaries .		?				
Repairs to Plant and Machinery .		250				
Factory Rent and Rates .		2,271				
Factory Charges . .		?				
		£24,596				£24,596
Works Cost . . .	b/d	24,596	Transfer to Trading Section .	c/d		27,150
Gross Profit on Manufactured						
Goods . . .	c/d	2,554				
		£27,150				£27,150
Opening Stock		974	Sales			29,942
Purchases—			Closing Stock			2,794
Transfer from Manufacturing						
Section . . .		27,150				
Outside . . .		1,274				
Carriage Inwards [See Note (i)] .		50				
Gross Profit on Sales . .		3,288				
		£32,736				£32,736
Office Salaries . . .		940	Gross Profit—		£	
„ Rent and Rates . .		650	Manufacturing . .		2,554	
General Expenses . .		317	Trading . . .		3,288	5,842
Carriage Outwards . .		233				
Printing and Stationery . .		93				
Travelling Expenses . .		279				
Discounts Allowed . .		374				
Provision for unrealized Profit on						
Closing Stock [See Note (ii)] .		263				
Net Profit = 8.99% of Sales .		2,693				
		£5,842				£5,842

Notes. (i) Carriage Inwards apportioned in absence of other data on the basis of purchases, i.e. $\frac{8726}{10000}$ and $\frac{1274}{10000}$ of £391 to Manufacturing and Trading sections respectively.

(ii) In the absence of information, it has been assumed that—

    (a) as no opening provision for unrealized profit on stock is given in the question (and the accounts are in balance), the opening stock of manufactured goods consisted entirely of "outside" goods;

    (b) the closing stock of manufactured goods consisted entirely of "own" goods, the opening stock and all "outside" purchases having been sold.

The provision required is then $\frac{2794}{27150}$ × £2,554 = £263.

(iii) Assumed no Work in Progress.

(iv) Since the foregoing accounts are in respect of one month only it may be assumed that they are intended for management purposes in which case it would be normal to prepare them in columnar form and to show, for comparison purposes, the corresponding figures for the month ended 31st March 19.2. If March were not the first month of the business's financial year the cumulative figures to date for current year and previous year could also be shown, together with the current month and current cumulative budgeted figures.

444

444

	£	£
Sales, *less* Returns		121,770
Raw Materials Consumed—		
Opening Stock	5,163	
Purchases, less Returns	39,207	
	44,370	
Less Closing Stock (*a*)	7,369	
		37,001
Carriage Inwards		1,332
Direct Wages and Salaries		35,372
Depreciation of Plant and Machinery		9,180
Factory Power and Expenses		2,370
Factory Rates, Heating, Lighting and Insurance		1,942
„ Rent [$\frac{9}{10} \times$ (£4,220 + £800)]		4,518
Production Cost of Manufactured Goods		91,715
Deduct Increase in Stock of Manufactured Goods		7,792
		£83,923
Trading Profit for Year		£37,847
Add Discount (*b*)		512
Interest on Calls in Arrear		25
Bank Interest		146
		£38,530
Office Wages and Salaries		£12,146
Office Rates, Heating, Lighting and Insurance		1,227
Office Rent [$\frac{1}{10} \times$ (£4,220 + £800)]		502
Carriage Outwards		1,519
Travellers' Salaries and Commission [£6,530 + £346]		6,876
Advertising		2,370
Postage, Stationery and Office Expenses [£510 − £19]		491
Legal Expenses and Audit Fee		1,325
Directors' Remuneration		9,000
Depreciation—Office Machinery and Equipment	£1,000	
Office Furniture and Fittings	50	
		1,050
		£36,506

Net Profit for Year before Taxation		£2,024

(a) No amount is shown for Work in Progress.
(b) The discount being net, the discounts allowed and received cannot be ascertained.

Net Profit for Year before Taxation		£2,024
Deduct Corporation Tax on Current Profits		875
Net Profit for Year after Taxation		1,149
Add Balance brought forward		19,202
Profit available for Appropriation		£20,351

Appropriations for Year—

Amount Written Off Preliminary Expenses . . .		£1,050

Dividends (Gross):
Paid—

Preference Dividend of 7% for the year . .	£2,100	
Interim Ordinary Dividend of 10% on Called Up Capital for the Year	5,250	
		7,350

Proposed—

Final Ordinary Dividend of 6% on Called Up Capital for the year	3,150	
Deferred Dividend of 12% for the year . .	1,200	
		4,350
		£12,750
Balance Carried Forward		£7,601

BALANCE SHEET AS AT 31ST JANUARY, 19..

CAPITAL EMPLOYED—

	£	£
Authorized:		
50,000 7% Preference Shares of £1 each . .	50,000	
100,000 Ordinary Shares of £1 each . . .	100,000	
10,000 Deferred Shares of £1 each . .	10,000	
	£160,000	

	£	£
Issued:		
30,000 7% Preference Shares of £1 each, fully paid		30,000
70,000 Ordinary Shares of £1 each		
75p called	52,500	
Less Calls in arrear	250	
		52,250
10,000 Deferred Shares of £1 each, fully paid . . .		10,000
		92,250
Reserves:		
General	5,000	
Profit and Loss Account	7,601	
		12,601
		£104,851

EMPLOYMENT OF CAPITAL—

	£	£
Fixed Assets:		
Machinery and Plant at cost	100,000	
Less Aggregate depreciation . . .	47,980[1]	
		52,020
Office Machinery and Equipment . . .	10,000	
Less Aggregate depreciation	5,200[2]	
		4,800
Office Furniture and Fittings	1,000	
Less Aggregate depreciation	430[3]	
		570
		57,390
Preliminary Expenses—		
Balance at 1st February, 19.. . . .	2,100	
Less written off during year . . .	1,050	
		1,050
		58,440
Current Assets—		
Stocks:		
Raw Materials	7,369	
Work in Progress	?	
Manufactured Goods	29,310	
	36,679	
Stationery, etc.	19	
	36,698	
Debtors	11,592	
Cash at Bank	8,146	
Cash in Hand	225	
	£56,661	
Current Liabilities—		
Trade Creditors	3,738[4]	
Accrued Expenses:		
Rent £800		
Travellers' Commission . . 346		
	1,146	
Corporation Tax Accounting		
Year ended 31st January 19.. . . .	875	
Unclaimed Dividends	141	
Proposed Dividends (gross)	4,350	
	£10,250	
Working Capital		46,411
		£104,851

---

1 At 1st February, 19.. £97,000 plus £3,000 less £58,200 plus £3,000 = £38,800, plus 15% on £61,200, i.e. £9,180 = £47,980.
2 At 1st February, 19.. £10,000 less £5,800 = £4,200 plus 10% on £10,000, i.e. £1,000 = £5,200.
3 At 1st February, 19.., £1,000 less £620 = £380 plus 5% on £1,000, i.e. £50 = £430.
4 £3,595 + £143.

4. *Dr.* MILL MANUFACTURING ACCOUNT *Cr.*

	£		£
To Cost	66,636	By Transfer to Factory Manufacturing	
,, General Profit and Loss Account .	6,664	Account	73,300
	£73,300		£73,300

Dr. FACTORY MANUFACTURING ACCOUNT *Cr.*

	£	£		£
To Paper—			By Transfer to Selling Department .	124,300
Stock (Opening) .	18,700			
Purchases (from Mill)	73,300			
	92,000			
Less Stock (Closing)	24,200	67,800		
,, Other Purchases and Expenses—				
Stock (Opening) .	14,800			
Purchases . .	43,900			
	58,700			
Less Stock (Closing)	13,500	45,200		
Factory Cost		113,000		
,, General Profit and Loss Account .		11,300		
		£124,300		£124,300

Dr. SELLING DEPARTMENT *Cr.*

	£		£
To Stock (Opening) at "Cost" .	27,400	By Sales	148,000
,, Purchases (from Factory) .	124,300	,, Stock (Closing) at "Cost" .	37,300
,, Selling Department Expenses .	16,400		
,, General Profit and Loss Account .	17,200		
	£185,300		£185,300

Dr. GENERAL PROFIT AND LOSS ACCOUNT *Cr.*

	£		£
To Provision for Increase of Mill Stock in Factory—		By Profit—	
$\frac{1}{11}$ × £5,500 [£24,200 − £18,700] .	500	Mill	6,664
,, Provision for Increase of Factory Stock in Selling Department:		Factory	11,300
$\frac{1}{11}$ × £9,900 [£37,300 − £27,400] .	900	Selling Department . .	17,200
,, Provision for Increase of Mill Stock in Selling Department (a) . .	491		
,, Balance—Profit . . .	33,273		
	£35,164		£35,164

(*a*) The computation is as follows—

The true cost of increase of Factory Goods (for which a provision has been created) is £9,900 *less* £900 thereof = £9,000. But the true cost of Factory Goods is made up of the following—

Mill Goods £67,800 *plus* Other Goods, etc., £45,200 = £113,000.

This shows a ratio of 3 : 2; thus for £1 of Factory Cost, three-fifths represents Mill Goods at loaded price; hence $\frac{3}{5}$ × £9,000 is attributable to Mill Goods at the cost to the Factory, that is, at loaded price. This amounts to £5,400. As this figure includes Mill profit, it is necessary to create a provision for its elimination, viz. $\frac{1}{11}$ of £5,400 = £491.

[Alternatively, this Provision is—

$$\frac{\text{Increase of goods}}{\text{Transfer value from factory}} \times \text{Mill loading in factory, i.e.} \quad \frac{\overset{9}{\cancel{9,900}}}{\cancel{124,300}} \times \frac{67,800}{\underset{1}{\cancel{11}}} = \frac{9}{1,243} \times 67,800$$

$$= \text{£491.]}$$

5. It is assumed that—

(1) Opening stocks carried the same loading as the transfers during the current year.
(2) Selling expenses are wholly attributable to sales to outside customers.

	A	B	C
	£	£	£
Cost of Current Year's Production	31,200	29,500	33,600
Less Increase in Closing Stocks of Finished Goods	5,000	4,500	6,500
Cost of Sales	26,200	25,000	27,100
Sales	36,100	34,300	37,700
Gross Profit	£9,900	£9,300	£10,600
Loadings are therefore			
On Cost	$\frac{99}{262}$	$\frac{93}{250}$	$\frac{106}{271}$
On Sales	$\frac{99}{361}$	$\frac{93}{343}$	$\frac{106}{377}$

STATEMENT OF COST VALUE OF STOCKS AT HEAD OFFICE AT 31ST DECEMBER, 19..

	A		B		C	
		£		£		£
Commencing Stocks at Cost[1]		2,450		1,725		2,100
Add Branch Profit	($\frac{99}{262}$)	926	($\frac{93}{250}$)	642	($\frac{106}{271}$)	821
Commencing Stocks at Loaded Price		3,376		2,367		2,921
Purchases from Branch at Loaded Price . .		12,200		10,800		14,500
Goods for Sale at Loaded Price . . .		15,576		13,167		17,421
Goods Sold (75%)		11,682		9,875		13,066
Closing Stocks at Loaded Price		3,894		3,292		4,355
Less Branch Profit	($\frac{99}{361}$)	1,068	($\frac{93}{343}$)	893	($\frac{106}{377}$)	1,225
Closing Stocks at Cost[1]		£2,826		£2,399		£3,130

Total £8,355

[1] Assumed that branch cost is the basis of valuation for Balance Sheet purposes.

6.   KEEP FIT LTD.

MANUFACTURING, TRADING AND PROFIT AND LOSS ACCOUNT FOR
THE YEAR ENDED 31ST DECEMBER, 19..

	£			£
Ingredients used—			Cost of Production of 750,000 tins	
Stock, 1st Jan., 19.. . . £500			(= 2½p per tin) . . . c/d	18,750
Less Unsuitable . . . 140				
	360			
Purchases 6,190				
	6,550			
Less Stock, 31st Dec.,				
19.. . . £370				
Less Unsuitable 70				
	300			
		6,250		
Tins, Labels, etc., used—				
Stock, 1st Jan., 19.. . . 350				
Purchases 3,200				
	3,550			
Less Stock, 31st Dec., 19.. 425				
		3,125		
Freight and Carriage Inwards . .		781		
Manufacturing Wages . . .		4,688		
Prime Cost		14,844		
Factory Expenses . . .		2,344		
Factory Rent		1,562		
		£18,750		£18,750
Stock of Tinned Salts, 1st Jan., 19..		1,800	Sales	28,950
Transfer—Cost of Production .		18,750	Goods out on Consignment . .	500
Gross Profit . . . . c/d		10,150	Stock of Tinned Salts on hand at 31st	
			Dec., 19..	1,250
		£30,700		£30,700
Distribution Charges . . .		1,500	Gross Profit . . . b/d	10,150
Selling Expenses . . .		3,290		
Advertising		1,875		
Directors' Fees		1,000		
Loss on Unsuitable Ingredients .		35		
Net Profit		2,450		
		£10,150		£10,150

Rough working accounts—

Unsuitable Ingredients

	£		£
Opening Stock at Cost (£1·40) 140		Sales . . .	50
		Closing Stock at £1·10 .	55
		P. & L.. . .	35
	£140		£140

Sales

	£		£
Unsuitable Ingredients .	50	Sundries . . .	30,000
Consignment . . c/d	1,000		
P. & L. . . .	28,950		
	£30,000		£30,000
		Consignment[1] . b/d	1,000

[1] The Stock out on consignment is incorporated into the accounts at cost (i.e. £500), and the £1,000 balance on Sales Account will be deducted from Debtors, as the consignments have been treated as sales.

7.   MANFAC LTD.

MANUFACTURING AND TRADING AND PROFIT AND LOSS ACCOUNT
FOR THE YEAR ENDED 30TH SEPTEMBER 19.6

MANUFACTURING ACCOUNT	£	£
Raw Materials: Stock, 1st November 19.5 . .	37,412	
Purchases, *less* returns . .	194,672	
	232,084	
Stock, 30th September 19.6 .	40,572	
COST OF MATERIALS CONSUMED		191,512
Manufacturing Wages		36,480
PRIME COST		227,992
Factory Expenses		31,364
Depreciation Plant and Machinery		23,325
COST OF FINISHED GOODS		£282,681

TRADING ACCOUNT		
Stock of finished goods 1st November 19.5 . .	15,840	
Factory Cost of Production . . .	282,681	
	298,521	
Stock of finished goods 30th September 19.6 .	19,634	
COST OF SALES		278,887
GROSS PROFIT ON SALES		251,373
SALES *less* returns		£530,260

PROFIT AND LOSS ACCOUNT		
Gross Profit on Sales			£251,373
Investment Income			12,000
Office Salaries and Administration Expenses .		25,610	
Directors' Emoluments—			
Salaries	25,000		
Fees	3,000		
		28,000	
Advertising	4,800		
Selling Expenses,			
Commissions, etc.	35,478		
		40,278	
Auditors' Remuneration		1,550	
Interest on Loan (gross)		1,500	
			96,938
NET PROFIT FOR YEAR			£166,435

PROFIT AND LOSS APPROPRIATION ACCOUNT	£	£
Balance brought forward	95,250	
Add: Overprovision for Corporation Tax—		
Accounting year to 30th Sept. 19.5 . .	1,850	
	97,100	
Profit for Year	166,435	
	263,535	
Less:		
General Reserve	50,000	
Income Tax Schedule F	200	
Corporation Tax—		
Accounting year to 30th Sept. 19.6 . .	67,600	
Ordinary Dividend 5% (Paid 1st March 19.6) .	10,000	
Proposed Dividend 20% (gross)		
(subject to confirmation by shareholders) .	40,000	
		167,800
BALANCE CARRIED FORWARD		£95,735

Manfac Ltd.

Profit and Loss Account
for the Year Ended 30th September 19.6

Turnover for Year		£530,260

	£	£
Profit for Year before Taxation		166,435
After Crediting:		
Franked Investment Income (gross)—		
Unquoted Investment	12,000	
And after Charging:		
Directors' Remuneration—		
Fees	3,000	
Other Emoluments	25,000	
Auditors' Remuneration	1,550	
Depreciation—		
Plant and Machinery	23,325	
Interest on Loans—		
Maturing within five years . . .	1,500	
	£54,375	
Corporation Tax at 40% based on Profit for the year, payable 1st January 19.8 . . .	£67,600	
Balance on Income Tax Schedule F Account now written off	200	
		67,800
Profit for Year after Taxation		98,635
Balance brought forward	£95,250	
Add: Overprovision for Corporation Tax in previous year	1,850	
		97,100
Total Available for Appropriation		£195,735
Less: Appropriations:		
Ordinary Dividend 5% (Paid 1/3/19.6) .	10,000	
General Reserve	50,000	
Proposed Dividend 20%		
(subject to confirmation by shareholders)	40,000	
		100,000
Balance Carried Forward		£95,735

Notes on Profit and Loss Account (part of submitted set of accounts):

1. Turnover is stated at the total amount received and receivable by the Company in respect of all goods sold during the year.
2. Particulars of Directors' Emoluments:

        Chairman's Emoluments . . . £15,000

        Emoluments of Directors:

Exceeding	Not Exceeding	Number
£5,000	£7,500	1
£7,500	£10,000	Nil
£10,000	£12,500	Nil
£12,500	£15,000	1

BALANCE SHEET
AS AT 30TH SEPT., 19.6

CAPITAL EMPLOYED—	Authorized	Issued and Paid Up	
ORDINARY CAPITAL:	£	£	£
200,000 Shares of £1 each	200,000	200,000	200,000
RESERVES AND SURPLUS:			
General Revenue Reserve		130,000	
Profit and Loss Account		95,735	
			225,735
CORPORATION TAX—Accounting Year to 30th Sept. Year 15 . . .			67,600
			£493,335

EMPLOYMENT OF CAPITAL—		Cost or Valuation	Depre- ciation	
FIXED ASSETS:		£	£	£
Freehold Land and Buildings at cost . .		96,550	—	96,550
Leasehold Land and Buildings at cost . .		48,220	—	48,220
Plant and Machinery at cost . .	£385,000			
Additions during year . . .	80,000			
		465,000	241,725	223,275
		£609,770	£241,725	£368,045

INVESTMENTS:			
Unquoted Investment at Directors' Valuation			100,000
CURRENT ASSETS:			
Stocks—Raw Materials . . .	£40,572		
Finished Goods . .	19,634		
		60,206	
Trade Debtors		39,220	
Balance at Bank		59,534	
			158,960
CURRENT LIABILITIES:			
Trade Creditors		15,520	
Corporation Tax—Accounting year to 30th Sept. 19.5		58,150	
Proposed Dividend of 20% (gross) (Subject to Confirmation) . . .		40,000	
Loan from Frendnede Ltd. . . .		20,000	
			133,670
WORKING CAPITAL			25,290
			£493,335

Notes on Balance Sheet (part of submitted set of accounts):

1. Trading Stocks—These are valued at the lower of cost and net realizable value on bases and methods which have been consistently applied over a number of years.
2. Land and Buildings—The Company's land and buildings which are held leasehold consist of the following:

Land and Buildings held on leases with more than 50 years to run	£38,220
Land and Buildings held on leases with less than 50 years to run .	10,000
	£48,220

3. Loans—The company has a loan amounting to £20,000 outstanding from Frendnede Ltd. The rate of interest on this loan is 7½ per cent per annum. The loan is repayable within five years and is unsecured.

4. Fixed Assets Acquired during year—The following are particulars of fixed assets acquired by the Company during 19.6—

	Plant and Machinery £
Balance at beginning of year at cost . . .	385,000
Additions at cost (purchased 30th June 19.6) .	80,000
	305,000
Deduct: Disposals at cost	Nil
Total as in Balance Sheet at cost . . .	£305,000
Depreciation at 30th Sept. 19.5	£218,400
Depreciation charge for 19.6	23,325
Aggregate Depreciation as in Balance Sheet . .	£241,725

5. Statement of identities and places of incorporation of companies not Subsidiaries whose shares the Company holds and particulars of these shares:

Name of Associate Company	Class of Share held	Proportion of Nominal Value of Shares Issued of that Class	Country in which Registered
Intake Ltd.	Ordinary Shares of £1 each	6·66%	Scotland

WORKING NOTES—Profit and Loss Account:

(i) Depreciation of Plant and Machinery—This is calculated as follows:

Plant and Machinery at Cost	£385,000
Aggregate Depreciation as at 30th Sept. 19.5 . .	218,400 (a)
Written-down value at 1st Oct. 19.6 . . .	166,600
Depreciation thereon at 12½%	20,825 (b)
Written-down value at 30th Sept. 19.6 . . .	£145,775
Additions purchased 30th June 19.6 . . .	£80,000
Depreciation thereon at 12½% (12½% of ¼ × £80,000) .	2,500 (c)
Written-down value of additions to Plant and Machinery at 30th Sept. 19.6 . .	£77,500
Plant and Machinery at Cost	£385,000
Additions	80,000
	£465,000
Aggregate Depreciation [(a) + (b) + (c)]. . .	241,725
Written-down value at 30th Sept. 19.6 . . .	£223,275

(ii) Treatment of Income Tax Schedule F and Income Tax Section 53—The relevant accounting entries in respect of Franked Investment Income received by Manfac Ltd. (£12,000 gross), dividends paid (£10,000 gross) and Loan Interest paid (£1,500 gross) are given below to explain how the £200 debit balance of Income Tax Schedule F is arrived at.

INCOME TAX ACCOUNT

	Sch. F £	Sect. 53 £			Sch. F £	Sect. 53 £
19.6			19.6			
Jan. 31 To Dividend Received A/c.	4,800		Mar. 1 By Ordinary Dividend A/c. (Income Tax on Interim Dividend paid) . . .		4,000	
Sept. 30 ,, Transfer to Sch. F —set off		600	Aug. 31 ,, Loan Interest A/c (Income Tax deducted)			600
			Sept. 30 ,, Transfer from Sect. 53		600	
			,, ,, ,, Profit and Loss A/c .		200	
	£4,800	£600			£4,800	£600

Companies are required to send to the Collector of Taxes a return of all payments of dividends and other distributions, yearly interest, annuities, etc., in respect of any fiscal month (commencing on the 6th day of a month and ending on the 5th day of the succeeding month). The return should be made within 14 days after the end of the fiscal month, i.e. the 19th day, and any Income Tax due remitted forthwith. To arrive at a Schedule F liability Income Tax suffered on dividend income and other distribution received, i.e. on franked investment income, may be deducted from Income Tax retained on payment of dividends and other distributions. To arrive at a Taxes Act, Section 53 liability Income Tax suffered on yearly interest, annuities, etc., received may be deducted from Income Tax retained on payments of yearly interest, annuities, etc. However, for monthly settlement purposes Income Tax suffered on the total taxed income received may be set off against Income Tax retained on the total taxed payments made without differentiating between Schedule F and Section 53 liabilities. Note particularly that whereas Corporation Tax liability is assessed on the trading profits of the accounting year the final liability or otherwise to account for Income Tax under Schedule F or Section 53 is determined at the close of the fiscal year, i.e. 5th April.

In this particular instance although the £200 debit Schedule F balance at 30th September 19.6 (the end of Manfac Ltd.'s accounting year) is an asset which can ultimately be set off against Income Tax retained on future dividends paid it is common accounting practice at the year end to write off such balances to Profit and Loss Account in order to reflect the true position at the end of the company financial year. When, probably during the accounting year ended 30th September 19.6, the £200 is set off against Income Tax retained from dividends paid by Manfac Ltd. the amount of relief obtained should be disclosed in the year end published accounts by way of note.

(iii) Corresponding figures for the preceding year should be shown.

Notes to Students:

(i) The question states that the directors of Manfac Ltd. estimate the value of the unquoted investment in Intake Ltd. to be £100,000. This estimated value is indicated in the Balance Sheet and consequently it is unnecessary in this case to include a note giving the extensive information which would otherwise have been required to comply with Paragraph 5(a) of Schedule 2 to the Companies Act 1967 (company's share of the aggregate profits of Intake Ltd. before and after taxation, company's accumulated share of the aggregate undistributed profits of Intake Ltd. since the investment was acquired, etc.).

(ii) The question also states that (a) the investment of Manfac Ltd. in Intake Ltd. consists of 100,000 Ordinary Shares of £1 each; (b) the issued Ordinary Share Capital of Intake Ltd. is 7,500,000 Ordinary Shares of £1 each. This investment does not exceed in value, one-tenth of the nominal value of the issued Ordinary Share Capital of Intake Ltd. but it does exceed one-tenth in value of the assets of Intake Ltd. and accordingly it is necessary to show the information given in Note 5, which forms part of the published Balance Sheet, in order to comply with Section 4 of the Companies Act 1967.

CHAPTER XXXI

1. 19·5 Sales at 19·4 prices $\qquad$ = £120,960 × $\frac{5}{6}$ $\qquad$ = £100,800

Increase in sales volume of 19.5 over 19.4 $\qquad$ = £100,800 − £90,000 = £10,800

Percentage increase in sales volume of 19.5 over 19.4

$$= £\frac{10,800}{90,000} \times 100 \qquad = 12\%$$

(A) Assuming all overheads are variable

STATEMENT OF VARIANCES

	19.4 £	Variances due to 12% increase in volume £	112% of 19.4 Volume £	19.5 Actual £	Other Variances £
Sales	90,000	10,800	100,800	120,960	20,160
Direct Labour Cost and Direct Materials Cost	60,000	7,200	67,200	65,000	2,200
	30,000	3,600	33,600	55,960	22,360
Overheads	40,000	4,800	44,800	44,000	800
Profit (Loss)	(£10,000)	(£1,200)	(£11,200)	£11,960	£23,160

SUMMARY OF VARIANCES

		£
19.4 Loss	. . . .	10,000
Add Additional loss due to increased volume	. . .	1,200

		£
		11,200
Less Increase in Sales prices	20,160	
Reduction in expenditure £2,200 + £800	3,000	
		23,160
19.5 Profit		£11,960

(B) Assuming all overheads are fixed

STATEMENT OF VARIANCES

	19.4 £	Variances due to 12% increase in volume £	112% of 19.4 Volume £	19.5 Actual £	Other Variances £
Sales	90,000	10,800	100,800	120,960	20,160
Direct Labour Cost and Direct Materials Cost	60,000	7,200	67,200	65,000	2,200
	30,000	3,600	33,600	55,960	22,360
Overheads	40,000	—	40,000	44,000	4,000
Profit (Loss)	(£10,000)	£3,600	(£6,400)	£11,960	£18,360

SUMMARY OF VARIANCES

	£	£
19.4 Loss		10,000
Less Gain due to increased volume	3,600	
Increase in Sales Prices	20,160	
Reduction in Labour and Materials . . .	2,200	
	25,960	
Less Increase in Overheads	4,000	
		21,960
19.4 Profit		£11,960

Management would require further detailed information concerning the effectiveness of the new production methods to ascertain whether the proportionate reduction in costs is, in fact, due to greater efficiency or to reduced prices or a mixture of both.

2.

ADEPT LTD.

The year's trading results may be presented as follows:

Dept	Sales	Variable Cost	Gross Margin	Fixed Cost	Net Margin
	£	£	£	£	£
A	60,000	32,000	28,000	16,000	12,000
B	30,000	22,000	8,000	14,000	(6,000)
C	24,000	19,000	5,000	3,000	2,000
D	54,000	32,000	22,000	12,000	10,000
	£168,000	£105,000	£63,000	£45,000	£18,000

Each department is contributing to its proportion of the total fixed costs of the company's business and consequently if one department were closed down and that part of the premises sublet the business as a whole would benefit only if the rental exceeded the amount of that department's gross margin.

The relevant figures for each department are as follows: (amounts in parentheses represent losses).

Dept	Rental	Gross Margin	Gain or Loss
	£	£	£
A	7,000	28,000	(21,000)
B	7,000	8,000	(1,000)
C	7,000	5,000	2,000
D	7,000	22,000	(15,000)

Although Department C earned a book profit of 2,000 during the year the business as a whole would gain if this department were closed down. On the other hand, although Department B made a book loss of £6,000 its contribution towards the fixed costs is such that a greater loss would be incurred if the department were closed down and the premises sublet.

In order to maximize profits, the directors should be advised to consider closing down Department C. On the basis of the results of the previous year the earnings would then be:

			£
Dept A—Gross Margin	.	.	28,000
Dept B— „ „	.	.	8,000
Dept D— „ „	.	.	22,000
Total Gross Margin .	.	.	58,000
Less Fixed Costs .	.	.	45,000
Net Margin . .	.	.	13,000
Add Rent Receivable	.	.	7,000
New Net Profit .	.	.	20,000
Old Net Profit . .	.	.	18,000
Increase in Net Profit .	.	.	£2,000

Note. In practice, many other factors would be considered before coming to such an important decision, e.g. the possibility of improvement in trade, the duration of the sub-tenancy, the nature of the sub-tenant's trade, dilapidations, the possibility of carrying on the trade of Department C within the premises of the other departments, the effect of closure of Department C on the trade of Department A, B and D, the nature of the fixed costs, and the spread of Department C's proportion of £3,000 over the other three departments.

3.

PROFIT OR LOSS AT VARIOUS
LEVELS OF OUTPUT

	30 Units		40 Units		60 Units	
	Per Unit	Total	Per Unit	Total	Per Unit	Total
	£	£	£	£	£	£
Sales	1·50	45	1·50	60	1·50	90
Less Variable Cost	0·60	18	0·60	24	0·60	36
Gross Margin	0·90	27	0·90	36	0·90	54
Less Fixed Cost	1·00	30	0·75	30	0·50	30
Profit/(Loss)	(£0·10)	(£3)	£0·15	£6	£0·40	£24

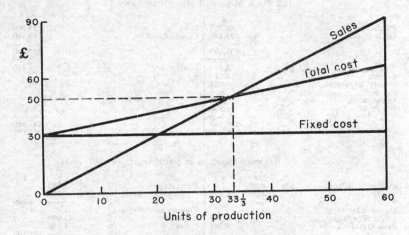

$$\text{The number of units of output required to break even} = \frac{\text{Fixed Cost}}{\text{Gross Margin per Unit}}$$

$$= \frac{\text{£}30}{\text{£}0·90}$$

$$= 33\tfrac{1}{3} \text{ units}$$

∴ Sales Value of Break-even Point $= 33\tfrac{1}{3} \times \text{£}1·50$

$= \text{£}50$

Alternatively $\text{£}30 \div \dfrac{\text{£}0·90}{\text{£}1·50} = \text{£}50$

4. (1) Additional Working Capital—

	Weeks	Purchases	Wages	Salaries	General Expenses	Rent	Total Payments	Receipts re Sales	Over-draft
		£	£	£	£	£	£	£	£
January	4	—	975	448	—	—	1,423	—	1,423
		4,000							
February	4	1,761	1,560	512	206	—	8,039	—	9,462
March	5	5,871	1,950	640	206	600	9,267	6,000	12,729
April	4	4,697	1,560	512	206	—	6,975	10,000	9,704
	17	£16,329	£6,045	£2,112	£618	£600	£25,704 —	£16,000 =	£9,704
Outstandings (*see below*)		7,631	585	64	206	200	(£8,686)	18,000	
		£23,960	£6,630	£2,176	£824	£800	£34,390	£34,000	

(Items in italics are shown in the Balance Sheet.)

(2)

TRADING AND PROFIT AND LOSS ACCOUNT
FOR FOUR MONTHS ENDED 30TH APRIL

		£			£
Purchases		23,960	Sales		34,000
Gross Profit	c/d	13,140	Closing Stock		3,100
		£37,100			£37,100
Wages		6,630	Gross Profit	b/d	13,140
Salaries		2,176			
General Expenses		824			
Rents		800			
Depreciation		720			
Net Profit		1,990			
		£13,140			£13,140

BALANCE SHEET AS AT 30TH APRIL

		£	£			£	£
Capital Introduced		5,000		Fixed Assets		5,000	
Add Profit		1,990	6,990	*Less* Depreciation		720	
							4,280
Current Liabilities (per Schedule)			8,686	Current Assets—			
Bank Overdraft			9,704	Debtors		18,000	
				Stock		3,100	
							21,100
			£25,380				£25,380

SCHEDULE OF OUTSTANDINGS (*see above*)

	Weekly (a)	Period Outstanding (b)	Amounts Outstanding (a) × (b)
	£		£
Purchases $\frac{19960}{17}$ [1]	1,174	6½ weeks	7,631
Wages $\frac{6630}{17}$	390	1½ ,,	585
Salaries $\frac{2176}{17}$	128	½ week	64
	Monthly		
General Expenses	206	1 month	206
Rent	200	1 ,,	200
			£8,686

[1] Total per Schedule (£23,960 — £4,000, original outlay for goods purchased).

Sales (March £9,000 + April £9,000) £18,000

5.

COMPUTATION OF WORKING CAPITAL REQUIRED

Month	Materials	Wages	Power	Insurance	Rent	General Admin. Charges	Commission	Total	Cash Receipts re Sales	Balance, Working Capital Required	Cumulative Figures
	£	£	£	£	£	£	£	£	£	£	£
Jan.	—	5,250	—	480	375	—	—	6,105	—	6,105	6,105
Feb.	—	6,000	—	—	—	600	200	6,800	—	6,800	12,905
Mar.	18,000	6,000	600	—	—	1,200	200	25,400	4,000	21,400	34,305
Apr.	3,000	6,000	—	—	375	1,200	200	11,375	4,000	7,375	41,680
May	3,000	6,000	—	—	—	1,200	200	10,400	4,000	6,400	48,080
June	3,000	6,000	600	—	—	1,200	200	11,375	4,000	7,375	54,480
July	3,000	6,000	—	—	375	1,200	200	10,400	4,000	6,400	61,855
Aug.	3,000	6,000	—	—	—	1,200	200	10,400	4,000	6,400	68,255
Sept.	3,000	6,000	600	—	—	1,200	200	11,375	4,000	7,375	74,655
Oct.	3,000	6,000	—	—	375	1,200	200	11,375	4,000	7,375	82,030
Nov.	3,000	6,000	—	—	—	1,200	1,500	11,700	4,000	7,700	89,730
	£42,000	£65,250	£1,800	£480	£1,500	£11,400	£3,300	£125,730	£36,000	£89,730	

STATEMENT OF CURRENT ASSETS AND LIABILITIES
AT 30TH NOVEMBER, 19.9

		£	£
Current Assets—			
Stocks: Raw Materials		15,000	
Finished Goods . . . . . (x)		32,625	
			47,625
Debtors (Oct. £30,000, Nov. £34,000) . . .			64,000
Prepayments: Insurance ($\frac{1}{12} \times$ £480) . . .		40	
Rent ($\frac{1}{12} \times$ £1,500)		125	
			165
			111,790
Current Liabilities—			
Raw Materials ($\frac{2}{12} \times$ £36,000)		6,000	
Wages ($\frac{1}{8} \times \frac{1}{12} \times$ £72,000)		750	
Power ($\frac{2}{12} \times$ £2,400)		400	
General Administrative Charges ($\frac{3}{24} \times$ £14,400) . .		1,800	
Travellers' Commission (5% of £34,000) . . .		1,700	
			10,650
Excess of Current Assets over Current Liabilities . .			£101,140

		£
Represented by—		
Working Capital provided		89,730
Provision for depreciation ($\frac{11}{12} \times$ £3,720) . . .		3,410
Profit $\frac{100000}{150000} \times$ £12,000		8,000
		£101,140

(x) Value of Stock of Finished Goods at 30th November, 19.9, is computed as follows—

	£
Total Expenditure on production to date (less Travellers' Commission) $\frac{11}{12} \times$ (£138,000 − £7,500)	119,625
Selling price of production to date $\frac{11}{12} \times$ £150,000	137,500
Actual Sales to date	100,000
Selling price of stock	£37,500
Cost price thereof $= \frac{37500}{137500} \times$ £119,625 [$\frac{3}{11} \times$ £119,625] . . .	£32,625

In order to present a complete representation of the *whole* year, the figures for December, 19.9, are shown below—

	Matls.	Wages	Power	Insce.	Rent	General Admin. Charges	Commn.	TOTAL	Cash Recd.	Working Capital	Cumu- lative Figures
	£	£	£	£	£	£	£	£	£	£	£
Fwd.	42,000	65,250	1,800	480	1,500	11,400	3,300	125,730	36,000	89,730	89,730[2]
Dec.	3,000	6,000	—	—	—	1,200	1,700	11,900	30,000	−18,100	71,630
	£45,000	£71,250	£1,800	£480	£1,500	£12,600	[1]£5,000	£137,630	£66,000		£71,630

[1] 5 per cent on Sales for year £150,000, *less* December Sales £50,000 not payable till January following, i.e. 5 per cent on receipts from Debtors of £100,000.
[2] See page 695.

Current Assets— £
  Stock: Raw Materials 15,000
  Debtors 84,000
                                                  99,000

Current Liabilities— £
  Raw Materials ($\frac{2}{12}$ × £36,000) 6,000
  Wages ($\frac{1}{8}$ × $\frac{1}{12}$ × £72,000) 750
  Power ($\frac{3}{12}$ × £2,800) 600
  General Charges ($\frac{3}{24}$ × £14,400) 1,800
  Travellers' Commission (5 % × £50,000). . . 2,500
                                            11,650

                                            £87,350

Represented by £ £
  Working Capital provided 71,630
  Provision for Depreciation (£3,410 + £310) . 3,720
  Profit—11 months to Nov., 19.9 . . . 8,000
          1 month to Dec., 19.9 . . . 4,000
                                  12,000(per
                                            question)
                                         £87,350

Proof— £
Excess of Assets over Liabilities at 30th Nov., 19.9 . . 101,140
  ,,   ,,   ,,   ,,   ,,   ,, 31st Dec., 19.9 . . . 87,350

             Decrease £13,790

Represented by— £ £
  Decrease in Working Capital 18,100
    Less Provision for Depreciation 310
        Profit 4,000
                                    4,310

                                          £13,790

6.

BETA LIMITED

RECONCILIATION OF WORKING CAPITAL

AT 31ST MARCH, 19.7, WITH THAT AT 31ST MARCH, 19.6

	£	£
Working Capital at 31st March, 19.6—		
Current Assets	125,800	
Less Current Liabilities	108,000	
		17,800
Add (1) Cash received on issue of Ordinary Shares at a premium	60,000	
(2) Cash received on sale of Leasehold Property	7,500	
		67,500
(3) Profit retentions—		
Depreciation of Fixed Assets . . .	21,000	
Transfer to General Reserve . . .	5,000	
Increase in carry forward of Profit and Loss Account	500	
Amount written off Preliminary Expenses .	200	
		26,700
		112,000
Deduct: Expenditure on Fixed Assets—		
Freehold Property	40,000	
Plant and Machinery	30,000	
Loan to the Associated Company . .	6,400	
Repayment of Debentures . . .	9,600	
		86,000
		£26,000

Working Capital at 31st March, 19.7, as per Balance Sheet—		
Current Assets	136,400	
Less Current Liabilities	110,400	
		£26,000

	31st March, 19.6	31st March, 19.7
	£	£
Computation of Working Capital—		
Current Assets	125,800	136,400
Less Current Liabilities . . .	108,000	110,400
	£17,800	£26,000

RECONCILIATION OF OPENING AND CLOSING WORKING CAPITALS,
YEAR TO 31ST MARCH, 19.7

	£	£
As at 31st March, 19.6		17,800
Add: Increase in Share Capital	50,000	
Premiums thereon	10,000	
Sale of Leasehold Property (a) . . .	7,500	
Increase in General Reserve	5,000	
Increase in Profit and Loss Account Balance . .	500	
Preliminary Expenses written off . . .	200	
Depreciation	21,000	
		94,200 (c)
		112,000
Less: Repayment of Debentures (b)	9,600	
Additions to Freeholds	40,000	
Additions to Plant, etc.	30,000	
Loan to Associated Company . .	6,400	
		86,000
Working Capital—31st March, 19.7		£26,000

Notes. (a) Profit on Sale (£2,500) *plus* cost at 31st March, 19.6 (£5,000).
   (b) Reduction in Debentures £10,000 *less* profit on redemption £400.
   (c) The additions may alternatively be subdivided into cash receipts and
       profit retentions.

7. CALCULATIONS OF FIGURES FOR PLOTTING ON BREAK-EVEN CHART

Turnover of Department				Commissions earned for Department					Variable Expenses
A	B	C	Total	A	B	C	Total		
£	£	£	£	£	£	£	£		£
2,000	3,000	5,000	10,000	200	600	1,500	2,300	½ × £2,300	1,150
4,000	6,000	10,000	20,000	400	1,200	3,000	4,600	½ × £4,600	2,300
10,000	15,000	25,000	50,000	1,000	3,000	7,500	11,500	½ × £8,000 £4,000	
								1/10 × £3,500 £350	4,350
12,000	18,000	30,000	60,000	1,200	3,600	9,000	13,800	½ × £8,000 £4,000	
								1/10 × £5,800 £580	4,580

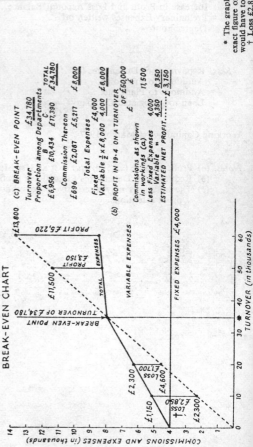

BREAK-EVEN CHART

(b) PROFIT IN 19-4 ON A TURNOVER OF £50,000

	£	£
Commissions as shown in workings (a)		11,500
Less Fixed Expenses	4,000	
Variable Expenses	4,350	8,350
ESTIMATED NET PROFIT.........		£3,150

(c) BREAK-EVEN POINT

Turnover £34,780
Proportion among Departments

	A	B	C	TOTAL
	£6,956	£10,434	£17,390	£34,780
Commission Thereon	£696	£2,087	£5,217	£8,000

Fixed Total Expenses £4,000
Variable ½ × £8,000 4,000 £8,000
£8,000

* The graph, being compiled on too small a scale to enable the exact figure of Sales at Break-even point (£34,780) to be shown would have to be grossed up, i.e. enlarged.

† Loss £2,850 = £1,150 + £4,000 − £2,300.

8.   CALCULATIONS OF FIGURES FOR PLOTTING
                                      ON BREAK-EVEN CHART

| Weekly | Weekly Operating Cost | | | Weekly Revenue | | |
Mileage	Fixed	Running	Total	Fixed	Running	Total
0	£8	—	£8	£6		£6
100	£8	100 × 1p = £1	£9	£6	100 × 2p = £2	£8
200	£8	200 × 1p = £2	£10	£6	200 × 2p = £4	£10
400	£8	400 × 1p = £4	£12	£6	400 × 2p = £8	£14
600	£8	600 × 1p = £6	£14	£6	600 × 2p = £12	£18

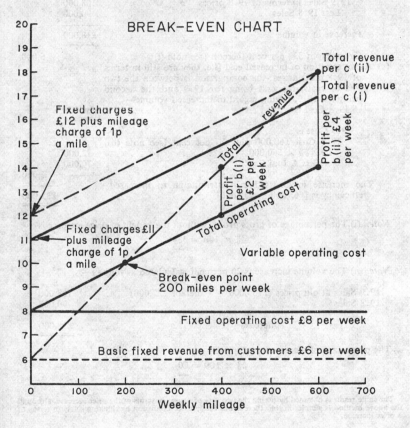

BREAK-EVEN CHART

Total revenue per c (ii)

Total revenue per c (i)

Fixed charges £12 plus mileage charge of 1p a mile

Total revenue

Profit per c (ii) £4 per week

Profit per b (ii) £2 per week

Total operating cost

Fixed charges £11 plus mileage charge of 1p a mile

Variable operating cost

Break-even point 200 miles per week

Fixed operating cost £8 per week

Basic fixed revenue from customers £6 per week

Weekly mileage

9.   £   £

(a) The amount of £135,000 if there had been no increase, would have been $\frac{100}{125} \times$ £135,000 = £108,000

The increase in Gross Profit attributable to the price increase (solely) is—

		£	£
19.9 Sales	. . . .	135,000	
Less Sales equivalent at 19.8 prices	. . .	108,000	
			27,000

(b) As the price factor has been eliminated the comparison now is the relative Sales at "old" prices.
The increase in Gross Profit attributable to volume (solely) is—

		£
19.9 Sales in terms of 19.8 prices	. . .	108,000
Less 19.8 Sales	. . . . .	90,000
Increase in volume	. . . . . .	£18,000

Gross Profit 33⅓ per cent thereon [see note (i)]   .   6,000

(c) As no question of increased cost (i.e. they are still in terms of 19.8 cost) arises, the comparison is between the two sets of costs, the first being for 19.8 and the second being for 19.9, having regard to increased volume—

19.8 Cost is £60,000

19.9 Cost is
19.8 Cost £60,000 plus 20 per cent [see note (ii)]

		£	£
i.e. $\frac{120}{100} \times$ £60,000	. . . . .	72,000	
Less Actual Cost	. . . . .	70,000	
			2,000

The increase in Gross Profit attributable to increased efficiency is [£65,000 − £30,000]   £35,000

Note. (i) The percentage of gross profit, without the benefit of price increase is—

$$\tfrac{30}{90} \times 100 = \underline{33\tfrac{1}{3}}$$

Note. (ii) The volume increase is 20 per cent, calculated as follows—

		£
19.9 Sales at old prices (£135,000 − ⅕ thereof £27,000)	. .	108,000
19.8 Sales	. . . .	90,000
Increase	. . . .	£18,000

The percentage of increase in volume is—

$$\tfrac{18}{90} \times 100 = \underline{20}$$

The same result is obtained by taking the two sets of figures in terms of the price increase, although the above method is simpler in that there is not likely to be confusion by thinking solely in terms of a price increase.

		£
19.9 Sales .	. . . . .	135,000
19.8 Sales if made at 19.9 prices, i.e.—		
$\frac{125}{100} \times$ £90,000	.	112,500
		£22,500

The percentage of increase in volume is—

$$\frac{225}{1,125} \times 100 = \underline{20}$$

For the benefit of readers who find difficulty in understanding the answer, the explanation of the increase in gross profit is shown in the form below—

TRADING ACCOUNT

	19.8 £	19.9 Based solely on increased volume £	Increase £		19.8 £	19.9 Based solely on increased volume £	Increase £
Cost of Sales . (33⅓%)	60,000	72,000	12,000	Sales . . .	90,000	108,000	18,000
Gross Profit . (Tentative) c/d	30,000	36,000	6,000				
	£90,000	£108,000	£18,000		£90,000	£108,000	£18,000

Actual increased Gross Profit for Trading account 19.9 . . .	65,000	Gross Profit (Tentative) . . b/d	6,000
		Further profit by reason of—	
		(a) Increased price, viz. what would have been sold at £108,000 is sold at an increased price of 25%, i.e.	
		$\frac{125}{100} \times £108,000 - £135,000$	
		∴ £135,000 − £108,000.. .	27,000
		Comparative decrease of cost of Sales 19.8—	
		£60,000	
		Add 20% . . . 12,000	
		Comparative Cost . . 72,000	
		Actual only . . . 70,000	
		Benefit of lower cost per unit sold Increase over 19.8 . . .	2,000
			35,000
		To which is added the gross profit of 19.8	30,000
	£65,000		£65,000

10. (1)   STATEMENT OF INCREASES IN 19.6 OVER 19.5

	19.5 £	% of Sales		19.6 £	% of Sales	Increase £	% of increased Sales
Sales 80,000 at 50p .	40,000		160,000 at 47½p	76,000		36,000	
Gross Profit 25% .	£10,000		22½% . .	17,100	19·72%	7,100	
Advertising . .	800	2·00		3,800	5·00	3,000	8·33
Travellers' Commissions (3% on Sales)	1,200	3·00	3½% on Sales .	2,660	3·50	1,460	4·05[1]
	2,000	5·00		6,460	8·50	4,460	12·38
Travellers' Salaries .	1,500	3·75		1,640	2·15	140	39
Sales Department Expenses . .	1,700	4·25		1,700	2·24	—	
	5,200	13·00		9,800	12·89	4,600	12·77
General Expenses .	1,800	4·50		1,800	2·37		
[See below]	£7,000(a)	17·50(a)	[See below]	£11,600(c)	15·26	£4,600(e)	12·77
Net Profit . .	3,000(b)	7·50(b)		£5,500(d)	7·24	£2,500(f)	6·95

(a) + (b) = 25 per cent Gross Profit as above.
(c) + (d) = 22½ per cent Gross Profit as above.
(e) + (f) = 19·72 per cent Gross Profit as above.

[1] The reason for the increase from 3½ per cent to 4·05 per cent is that on the increase of Sales of £36,000 which could involve (at 3½ per cent) £1,260, there is to be accounted for the increase of ½ per cent on the basic turnover of £40,000 (£200) the respective percentages being 3·50 and 0·55.

£

Sales increase—
Volume 80,000 at 50p each 40,000
Less price decrease 160,000 at 2½p each 4,000

£36,000

£

(2) (*a*) Break-even Sales: Expenses to be recovered—
Advertising Expenses 3,800
Travellers' Salaries and Expenses 1,640
Fixed Charges: £1,700 + £1,800 3,500

£8,940

%

Gross Profit on Sales 22½
Less Travellers' Commission thereon 3½

Gross Margin percentage 19

Sales required to absorb £8,940: $\frac{100}{19}$ × £8,940 . . . £47,052

If Sales reached exactly the "Break-even" figure the position would be—

	£	% on Sales
Sales	47,052	
Gross Profit 22½ per cent	£10,586	
Advertising	3,800	8·08
Travellers' Commissions 3½ per cent . . .	[1]1,646	3·50
	5,446	11·58
Travellers' Salaries and Expenses	[1]1,640	3·50
Sales Department Expenses	1,700	3·60
	8,786	18·68
General Expenses	1,800	3·82
	10,586	22·50
Net Profit	—	—
Gross Profit	£10,586	22·50

£

(*b*) Break-even "extra" Sales: Extra expenses to be covered—
Advertising £3,800 − £800 3,000
Travellers' Salaries and Expenses 140

£3,140

Extra expenses shown on page 702, excluding Travellers' Commissions [£4,600 − £1,460 = £3,140; or £11,600 − £7,000 − £1,460].
Extra Sales required to recover the above $\frac{100}{19}$ × £3,140 = £16,526

[1] If the percentage calculations were made beyond two decimal places the above figures would be precisely the same (both being 3·5 per cent).

	£	% on Sales
This figure is absorbed as follows—		
Sales	16,526	
Gross Profit—22½ per cent	3,717	
Advertising (increase: £3,800 — £800)	3,000	18·16
Travellers' Commissions 3½ per cent	577	3·50
Travellers' Salaries and Expenses (increase: £1,640 — £1,500)	140	0·84
	3,717	22·50
Extra Net Profit	—	—
Gross Profit	£3,717	22·50

Note. In addition to, or by way of substitute for, the column of Percentage on Sales, it is desirable to have a similar percentage column based on *Gross Profit*.

Other percentages may be required, e.g. the gross and net profit in terms of (*a*) Issued Share Capital and (*b*) the "real" Capital employed, i.e. the "net" assets of the business.

(3) [Notes prior to compiling statement.]

As the gross profit is 22½ per cent on Sales, the latter have amounted to—

$$\frac{100}{22\frac{1}{2}} \times £17,100 = £76,000$$

As the Sales have reached £76,000 after reducing prices by 5 per cent, i.e. 47½p from 50p, the Sales would (at the old price) have been—

$$\frac{20}{19} \times £76,000 = £80,000$$

At the price of 50p the number of units sold to produce £80,000 is 160,000; that is, the volume has exactly doubled.

If there had been no alteration in price, and assuming that the Cost of Sales (i.e. net purchases, being Purchases *plus* Opening Stock *less* Closing Stock) had moved rateably with Sales (without any alteration in price) the comparative Trading Accounts would be—

	19.4 £	19.5 £	Increase £			19.4 £	19.5 £	Increase £
Cost of Sales	30,000	60,000	30,000	Sales		40,000	80,000	40,000
Gross Profit	10,000	20,000	10,000					
	£40,000	£80,000	£40,000			£40,000	£80,000	£40,000

The Trading Account, in fact, for 19.5 is—

		£				£
Cost of Sales	(*b*)	58,900	Sales		(*a*)	76,000
Gross Profit (22½%)	(*a*)	17,100				
		£76,000				£76,000

(*a*) The known or ascertainable sum, therefore (*b*) is the balancing sum. The reconciliation between the Gross Profit that would arise consequent solely on increase of volume, and that Gross Profit actually earned, is as shown below—

STATEMENT OF PROFIT AND VARIATIONS
BY REASON OF VOLUME INCREASE AND PRICE REDUCTION FOR 19.5

		£
Increase in Gross Profit attributable to Volume . . .		10,000
Less Decrease through reduction in Selling Price of 2½p:		
160,000 units at 2½p		4,000
		6,000
Add Saving in Cost of Sales—		
Notional Cost	£60,000	
Less Actual	58,900	
	———	1,100
		7,100

[This is G.P. 19.5 £17,100 − G.P. 19.4 £10,000.]

Deduct Increase of expenses—			
Advertising		£3,000	
Travellers' Salaries		140	
Travellers' Commissions—			
3% on Sales increase of £36,000	(*a*) £1,080		
½% on *Total* Sales £76,000 . .	380		
	———	1,460	
			4,600
Increase of Net Profit			£2,500

(*a*) [or 3 per cent on Sales increase at old price £40,000 . .	£1,200	
Less 3 per cent on reduced price of all Sales units 160,000 at 2½p,		
i.e. 3 per cent of £4,000]	120	
	———	
	£1,080	

	£
Net Profit for 19.5—	
Profit for 19.4	3,000
Add Increase for 19.5	2,500
Total as per Profit and Loss Account	£5,500

The answer is capable of further elaboration, but it is doubtful whether under normal examination conditions this would be possible.

The further matters for consideration are—

(1) The "break-down" of the Saving in Cost of Sales into volume and price, which cannot be done in this problem as the basic information is not given.

(2) *Advertising*. The "break-down" could be made in different ways, but the management would be chiefly interested in the pull of individual advertising media, and in the absence of this information the net Sale (and/or Gross Profit) increase per £ of increased advertising expenditure.

[This part of the problem is certainly too lengthy to be dealt with completely as part of a general problem such as this.]

(3) *General (and normally non-fluctuating) Expenses*. This item has no "saving" in the narrow sense, as the expenses remain the same as before, but can be dealt with on the lines adopted in Standard Costing.

Taking these expenses at £3,500 [£1,700 + £1,800] they represent a change on the 19.4 turnover of 8¾ per cent of £40,000.

Therefore 8¾ per cent of £76,000 is £6,650, and would be the expense if related to turnover, so that the increased turnover has been able to absorb £3,150 of the General Expenses [this can be seen by comparing the increased turnover of £36,000 = $\frac{9}{10}$ × £40,000; therefore a "saving" of $\frac{9}{10}$ × £3,500 = £3,150].

This is a "net" sum, that is, the actual "saving" despite the fact that there might have been an increased cost of parts of the general expenses, in which case there would be a higher "gross" saving diminished by a loss for extra expenditure.

11.   AIRTON & CO. LTD.

TRADING AND PROFIT AND LOSS ACCOUNT FOR THE YEAR ENDED
31ST MARCH, 19.9

		£			£
Gross Profit	c/d	3,100	Cash Sales .		100
			Excess of Credit Sales over Purchases (b)		200
			Closing Stock		2,800
		£3,100			£3,100
General Expenses		1,435	Gross Profit[1]	(d) b/d	·3,100
Directors' Fees[2]	(a)	850			
Depreciation	(d)	415			
Net Profit	c/f	400			
		£3,100			£3,100

Draft BALANCE SHEET AS AT 31ST MARCH, 19.9

	£	£		£	£
Share Capital [details] .		10,000	Fixed Assets at cost .		4,600
Revenue Reserve (Profit and Loss			Current Assets—		
Account)		400	Cash on hand (see below)	2,365	
Depreciation Provision		415	Debtors	6,000	
Creditors—			Stock on hand	2,800	
Goods	4,800				11,165
Directors' Fees	150				
		4,950			
		£15,765			£15,765

Dr.   CASH (BANK) ACCOUNT   **Cr.**

		£			£
To Share Capital		10,000	By Fixed Assets (£4,000 + £600) .		4,600
,, Cash Sales .		100	,, General Expenses .		1,435
			,, Directors' Fees	(a)	600
			,, Excess of payments to Creditors over receipts from Debtors .	(c)	1,100
			,, Balance (see above)	c/d	2,365
		£10,100			£10,100

Dr.   PURCHASES AND CREDIT SALES   **Cr.**

		£			£
To Cash, being excess of payments over receipts	(c)	1,100	By Transfer to Directors' Fees		100
,, *Trading Account*		200	,, Debtors outstanding	c/d	6,000
,, Creditors outstanding	c/d	4,800			
		£6,100			£6,100

The excess of £1,100 can be reconciled in several ways, and one "sample" is given
below—

Statement of Excess of Payments to Creditors over Receipts from Debtors

		£	£
Gross Profit (after depreciation)	(d)	2,685	
Depreciation	(d)	415	
Creditors and Debtors .		4,800	6,000
Stock on hand			2,800
Transfer *re* Goods to Directors			100
Cash Sales .			100
Excess of payments over receipts	(c)	1,100	
		£9,000	£9,000

[1] Gross Profit as shown in the accounts is £3,100, i.e. £2,685 + £415.
[2] Directors' Fees—Cash paid £600, *plus* goods taken out £100, *plus* accrual £150 = £850.

12. (*a*)

QUARTERLY CASH BUDGET
FOR THE YEAR ENDING 31ST DECEMBER, 19.4

	3 mos. ended 31/3/19.4	3 mos. ended 30/6/19.4	3 mos. ended 30/9/19.4	3 mos. ended 31/12/19.4
	£'000	£'000	£'000	£'000
Opening balance . . .	35	25	45	60
Cash from debtors . . .	140	150	145	160
„ „ debentures . .				25
„ „ sale of old plant and equipment . .				
	£175	£175	£190	£250
Cash Payments:				
Creditors, etc. . . .	87	109	75	109
Administrative, selling and distributive, expenses and interest .	23	21	25	23
Dividends . . .	40			
Corporation Tax . . .			30	
Capital items				88
	150	130	130	220
Closing balance . . .	25	45	60	30
	£175	£175	£190	£250

(*b*)

BUDGETED SOURCE AND DISPOSAL OF FUNDS STATEMENT
FOR THE YEAR ENDING 31ST DECEMBER 19.4

	£'000	£'000	£'000
Opening Cash—1/1/19.4 . .			35
Source of Funds—			
Debtors		595	
Debentures . . .		25	
Sale of Old Plant and Equipment		5	
		625	
Disposal of Funds—			
Creditors	380		
Administration, etc. . .	92		
Dividends	40		
Corporation Tax . . .	30		
Capital Items . . .	88		
		630	
Excess Disposal		£5	
Deduct Excess disposal . .			5
Closing Cash—31/12/19.4 . .			£30

Workings:

	3 mos. ended 31/3/19.4	3 mos. ended 30/6/19.4	3 mos. ended 30/9/19.4	3 mos. ended 31/12/19.4
	£'000	£'000	£'000	£'000
Opening debtors	50	60	45	65
Sales	150	135	165	150
	200	195	210	215
Less Closing debtors	60	45	65	55
Cash from debtors	£140	£150	£145	£160
Cost of Sales	102	94	110	102
Less Depreciation	5	5	5	5
	97	89	105	97
Closing Stock	65	75	60	65
	162	164	165	162
Less Opening Stock	65	65	75	60
Purchases, etc.	97	99	90	102
Opening creditors	40	50	40	55
	137	149	130	157
Less Closing creditors	50	40	55	48
Payments	£87	£109	£75	£109

Notes for Students:

(1) Since corporation tax is to be paid during the three months ended 30th September 19.4 it may be assumed that this will be the due date for payment in which case it should be noted that the company must have commenced trading on or after 1st April 1965. The point worthy of note here is that companies already trading at 1st April 1965 continue to be liable to pay corporation tax on 1st January (2nd January in Scotland) of the fiscal year in respect of which the profits would have been assessed under the normal basis of Schedule D Case I. However, in the case of companies commencing trading on or after 1st April 1965 corporation tax is payable within nine months from the end of the accounting period for which it is assessed.

(2) Had details of the quarterly debtors and creditors figures not been given a Funds Statement could still have been prepared as follows:

	£'000	£'000	£'000
Opening Cash .			35
Cash Flow—			
Net Profit .		100	
Depreciation .		20	
		120	
Source of Funds—			
Debentures		25	
Sale of Plant .		5	
		150	
Application of Funds—			
Dividend .	40		
Corporation Tax .	30		
Capital Items .	88		
		158	
Net decrease in working capital .			8
			27

Change in form of Working Capital—

	Source £'000	Application £'000
Debtors .		5
Creditors .	8	
	8	5

Add excess of source .	3
Closing cash .	£30

NET DECREASE IN WORKING CAPITAL

	1st January 19.4 £'000	31st December 19.4 £'000
Stock .	65	65
Debtors .	50	55
Cash .	35	30
	150	150
Less Creditors .	40	48
	£110	102
Net decrease .		8
		£110

13. The steps involved and matters to be considered in the feasibility study prior to the introduction of a computer are:

(1) A detailed examination of relevant existing systems and procedures must be carried out. This involves an intensive investigation by the systems analyst and his staff of the existing systems and procedures to assess their value. By means of preparation of flow charts in respect of all relevant processes amendments will doubtless be required to streamline the flow procedure for computerization purposes. Of course a computer system is viable only where the runs for each process are sufficiently lengthy because the frequent stopping and changing of the sequence of operations could be uneconomic.

(2) The cost of effecting the relevant existing systems and procedures should be ascertained and for comparison purposes the estimated cost of computerizing these systems and procedures, amended as appropriate, should also be ascertained. Much consideration and care must be given to this most important aspect of the feasibility study. With regard to a proposed computer installation scientifically prepared details are required under the following broad headings:

(i) Initial capital cost of the computer and peripheral equipment;

(ii) Estimated useful working life of the computer and peripheral equipment;

(iii) Staffing and Maintenance Costs. Existing suitable personnel can generally be readily trained to undertake a great proportion of the computerized work but certain work requiring specialized knowledge and experience will necessitate the engagement of new staff, e.g. computer programmers.

(iv) The estimated cost of redesigning systems and procedures;

(v) The costs involved in the preparatory entire systems study, i.e. the feasibility study and the detailed systems study which follows therefrom.

(3) Selecting the computer—If the detailed examination mentioned in (1) shows that the complexities involved in producing necessary information would be best served and much sooner and more economically produced by computer the problem then is to find the most suitable and most economic computer.

In determining the most suitable computer regard must be had not only to the immediate requirements of the business but also to the short term and long term potential rate of business growth. Consideration should be given to the following matters also:

(i) The type of input media, e.g. whether punched cards or paper tape;

(ii) The extent of the basic records to be maintained and stored and whether storage is to be by magnetic disc or by magnetic tape;

(iii) The quantity of data to be processed and arising therefrom the machine capacity required;

(iv) The type and amount of peripheral equipment required;

(v) The character and layout of output documents;

(vi) The accommodation required to house and operate the data processing plant and equipment, staff, and records.

It should, of course, be remembered that all proposals are subject to ratification by the board of directors (or owners, if not a limited company) before implementation.

(4) Staff Preparation. The introduction of an electronic computer into a business will have a profound effect on existing personnel. Immediately it is known by staff that a computer is to be installed speculation will run high and fear and uncertainty will ensue. Consequently staff preparation must begin timeously and should cover both the psychological and the practical effects of the proposed new systems and procedures. The following points might be appropriate:

(i) Soon after the decision is made by the Board to carry out a feasibility study all managerial staff must be informed;

(ii) All appropriate staff should formally be informed of the eventual outcome of the feasibility study. In this instance it is assumed that the feasibility study has determined that it is both practical and economic to install a computer and consequently a detailed systems study must ensue.

(iii) A systems study team headed by the Systems analyst must be officially set up and because a detailed specification of existing systems and procedures suitably adjusted to meet the new demands must be prepared to enable the computer programs to be written it follows that specially selected personnel from existing staff should form part of the team. Other members of the team will be specialists from the organization supplying the computer and peripheral equipment who will, of course, be involved temporarily only, and specially recruited full-time staff such as experienced pro-grammers.

(iv) Introductory courses should be held and these normally will be conducted by senior staff of the computer supply organization.

(v) Maximum participation from the business' executive and managerial staff should be encouraged in all aspects of the systems study and views and comments should be welcomed.

(vi) All appropriate levels of staff should be kept informed of progress and relevant proposals, plans and decisions. In particular it should frequently be stressed that the object of computerization is to cope with growth and development of business and not to create redundancies. In-service staff training courses should be inaugurated to fit members of staff for the new systems and procedures and for the challenging and progressive opportunities which will be open to them. By so doing, uncertainty, dissatisfaction and resentment would be allayed and resignations of key personnel should be minimized.

14.

TRADING ACCOUNT
FOR THE YEAR ENDED 31ST MARCH, 19.5

	£			£
Opening Stock	21,000	Sales		90,000
Purchases	66,000	Cash	30,000	
		Credit	60,000	
	87,000			
Less Closing Stock	15,000			
	72,000			
Cost of Goods sold	72,000			
Profit & Loss Account				
Gross Profit	18,000			
	£90,000			£90,000

PROFIT AND LOSS ACCOUNT
FOR THE YEAR ENDED 31ST MARCH, 19.5

	£		£
Depreciation	1,310	Trading Account	
Other Expenses	2,090	Gross Profit	18,000
Manager's Salary	2,920		
Capital Account			
Net Profit	11,680		
	£18,000		£18,000

BALANCE SHEET
AS AT 31ST MARCH, 19.5

	19.4 £	19.5 £		19.4 £	19.5 £
Capital Account	37,200	36,200	Fixed Assets:		
Add Profit for Year	1,000	11,680	At Cost	35,740	35,740
			Less Depreciation	5,240	6,550
	38,200	47,880		30,500	29,190
Less Drawings	2,000	2,000			
	36,200	45,880	Current Assets:		
Current Liabilities:			Stock	21,000	15,000
Bank Overdraft	17,300	18,310	Debtors	16,000	30,000
Trade Creditors	14,000	10,000			
	£67,500	£74,190		£67,500	£74,190

The Balance Sheet as at 31st March, 19.5, shows a number of improvements over that for the previous year:

	19.4	19.5
(a) Acid Test . . .	$\dfrac{16,000}{31,300} = 0.512:1$	$\dfrac{30,000}{28,310} = 1.06:1$
(b) Working Capital Ratio	$\dfrac{37,000}{31,300} = 1.18:1$	$\dfrac{45,000}{28,310} = 1.58:1$
(c) Primary Ratio . .	$\dfrac{1,000}{67,500} = 1.48\%$	$\dfrac{11,680}{74,190} = 15.7\%$
(d) Fixed Assets to Current Assets . . .	$\dfrac{30,500}{37,000} = 0.824:1$	$\dfrac{29,190}{45,000} = 0.648:1$
(e) Stock to Debtors .	$\dfrac{21,000}{16,000} = 1.31:1$	$\dfrac{15,000}{30,000} = 0.5:1$

The proportion of total funds invested in fixed assets decreased and also the current assets are held in a more liquid form. This greater liquidity contributes to a better working capital ratio and to a very much better liquidity ratio.

Bank overdraft has had to be increased but if the improvement in the trading position can be maintained a substantial repayment ought to be possible during the year ended 31st March, 19.6.

The amounts for 19.5, arising out of points (a) to (e) are arrived at as follows:

(a) *Stock Turnover:*

$$19.4, \quad \pounds\frac{(13,000 + 42,000 - 21,000)}{\frac{1}{2}(13,000 + 21,000)} = 2 \text{ times}$$

$$\therefore 19.5, \text{ being double} = 4 \text{ times}$$

$$\text{Average stock, } 19.5 = \frac{\pounds21,000 + 15,000}{2} = \pounds18,000$$

$$\therefore \text{ Cost of Goods Sold, } 19.5 = \pounds72,000$$

(b) *Rate of Gross Profit to Sales:*

$$19.4, \quad \frac{\pounds6,000}{\pounds40,000} = 15\%$$

$$\therefore 19.5, \text{ increase of one-third} = 20\%$$

If gross Profit = 20% of Sales, then Cost of Goods Sold = 80% of Sales, now 80% = £72,000, as above.

$$\therefore \text{ Sales for } 19.5 \ (100\%) = \pounds90,000$$
$$\text{and Gross Profit} = \pounds18,000$$

(c) *Closing Stock for 19.5:*
£21,000 less £6,000 = £15,000

(d) *Ratio of Cash to Credit Sales:*
For 19.4, £8,000:£32,000 = 1:4
∴ for 19.5, ratio doubled 1:2
19.5, Sales as above £90,000
Cash ($\frac{1}{3}$) £30,000
Credit ($\frac{2}{3}$) 60,000
_____
£90,000

(e) Net Profit before charging remuneration
= £18,000 − £3,400 = £14,600
If Remuneration is 25% × £(14,600 − remuneration) then £14,600 is 125% of Net Profit after charging remuneration. Remuneration is now $\frac{25}{125}$ × £14,600 = £2,920.

Trade Creditors to Stock
    19.4:

$$£14,000 : £21,000$$
$$= \quad 2:3$$

∴ 19.5:
2:3
$x : £15,000$

∴ $x = \frac{2}{3} \times £15,000 = £10,000 =$ Trade Creditors.

Debtors to Credit Sales
    19.4:

$$£16,000 : £32,000$$
$$= \quad 1:2$$

∴ 19.5:
1:2
$£x : £60,000$

∴ $x = \frac{1}{2} \times £60,000 = £30,000 =$ Trade Debtors.

15.   SHRAPNELL (ENGINEERING) LTD.
                    Calculation of Net Cash Inflows

	19.1	19.2	19.3, 19.4 & 19.5
SALES—NUMBER OF UNITS	192,000	264,000	300,000
	£	£	£
SALES VALUE (50p per unit)	96,000	132,000	150,000
COSTS:			
Lease of premises	7,500	7,500	7,500
Other fixed costs	18,000	21,000	22,500
Variable costs (22½p per unit)	43,200	59,400	67,500
Total (excluding depreciation) . . .	68,700	87,900	97,500
PROFIT BEFORE CHARGING DEPRECIATION . . .	27,300	44,100	52,500
Deduct: Revenue which could be obtained by selling the offcuts .	4,800	6,600	7,500
ADDITIONAL SURPLUS ACCRUING FROM THE PROJECT . .	22,500	37,500	45,000

Calculation of Writing Down Allowances

		£
Initial Cost of Plant and Machinery . . .		120,000
Less: Government grant 25% . . .		30,000
		90,000
19.1 Writing Down Allowance 20%		18,000
		72,000
19.2 ,, ,, ,, ,, ...		14,400
		57,600
19.3 ,, ,, ,, ,, ...		11,520
		46,080
19.4 ,, ,, ,, ,, ...		9,216
		36,864
19.5 ,, ,, ,, ,, ...		7,373
		£29,491

Computation of Tax Liability

Year		Surplus	Writing Down Allowances	Taxable Surplus	Tax at 40%
		£	£	£	£
19.1		22,500			
	Less: Installation Costs . . .	22,500			
		—	18,000	18,000	7,200
19.2		37,500	14,400	23,100	9,240
19.3		45,000	11,520	33,480	13,392
19.4		45,000	9,216	35,784	14,314
19.5		45,000	7,373	37,627	15,051
		£172,500	£60,509	£111,991	£44,797

Calculation of Rate of Return

Year		Cash Flows in (out)	12%[1] Index	Present Values	14%[1] Index	Present Values
		£	£	£		£
19.0	Capital Cost	(120,000)				
	Installation Cost . . .	(22,500)				
	[2]Working Capital . . .	(22,500)	(165,000)	1·00	(165,000)	1·00	(165,000)
19.1	Surplus	22,500				
	Government Grant . . .	30,000				
	[2]Working Capital . . .	(7,500)	45,000	0·89	40,050	0·88	39,600
19.2	Surplus	37,500				
	Tax—19.1	7,200	44,700	0·80	35,760	0·77	34,419
19.3	Surplus	45,000				
	Tax—19.2	(9,240)	35,760	0·71	25,390	0·68	24,317
19.4	Surplus	45,000				
	Tax—19.3	(13,392)	31,608	0·64	20,229	0·59	18,649
19.5	Surplus	45,000				
	Residual Value of Plant and Machinery	29,500				
	[2]Working Capital . . .	30,000				
	Tax—19.4	(14,314)	90,186	0·57	51,406	0·52	46,897
19.6	Tax—19.5	(15,051)	(15,051)	0·51	(7,676)	0·46	(6,923)
		TOTALS—outflow	(172,676)			(171,923)
		inflow	172,835			163,882

$$\text{Rate of Return}[3] = 12\% + \frac{172,835 - 172,676}{172,835 - 172,676 + 171,923 - 163,882} \times 2\%$$

$$= 12\!\cdot\!04\%$$

[1] Since an extract of Present Value tables is given in the question it is obviously intended that the appropriate rates should be taken from this extract. Consequently the middle rate, viz., 12 per cent, has been used for the first set of present values and from this it is simple to determine the other required rate.

[2] The initial figure of working capital £22,500 must be available at the beginning of the project and is therefore included as a 19·0 outflow. The additional £7,500 required in 19.2 must be available at the beginning of the year which is the same as saying that it must be available at the end of 19.1.

Working capital is continually circulating so that during the life of an asset this continual outflow/inflow can be ignored, but on the termination of a project, the final inflow must be included. In other words, just as the value of the fixed assets must be brought in, so must the value of the working capital.

[3] The rate of return has been found by interpolation. The general reasoning behind the calculation is as follows:

At the 12 per cent rate inflow exceeds outflow by £159.
At the 14 per cent rate outflow exceeds inflow by £8,041.
Therefore the total difference in the present values between 12 per cent and 14 per cent is £159 + £8,041 = £8,200. In other words, in this instance, 2 per cent is equivalent to £8,200. The required rate is somewhere between 12 per cent and 14 per cent and to ascertain the rate 12 per cent must be increased so as to eliminate the £159 excess inflow.

The amount of the increase is $\frac{159}{8,200}$ of 2%

therefore the rate of return $= 12\% + \dfrac{159}{8,200} \times 2\%$

$= 12\!\cdot\!04\%$ (approx.)

CHAPTER XXXII

1. REVENUE ACCOUNT FOR THE YEAR ENDED 31ST DECEMBER, 19. .

	£		£
Opening Stock	2,000	Sales	860,000
Purchases	750,000	Closing Stock	500
General Expenses	6,000		
Bad Debts	2,500		
Net Profit (= 5p a unit)	100,000		
	£860,500		£860,500

REVENUE DISTRIBUTION ACCOUNT FOR THE YEAR ENDED
Dr.   31ST DECEMBER, 19. .   *Cr.*

		Standard Output	Actual Output	(a) Profit at 5p a Unit on Actual Output	(b) Penalty on Excess Units		(a) (b) Net Share		
	%	Units	Units	£	Units	10p a Unit £10,000	£		£
A	25	500,000	600,000	30,000	100,000	£10,000	20,000	Net Profit	100,000
B	10	200,000	180,000	9,000			9,000		
C	15	300,000	300,000	15,000			15,000		
D	17½	350,000	300,000	15,000			15,000		
E	27½	550,000	500,000	25,000			25,000		
F	5	100,000	120,000	6,000	20,000	2,000	4,000		
	100	2,000,000	2,000,000	£100,000	120,000	£12,000			

Transfer to Penalty Account	12,000
	£100,000
	£100,000

Dr.   PENALTY ACCOUNT   *Cr.*

	Deficiency of Output	Fraction	Amount Receivable			Units	£
	Units		£				
B . .	20,000	2/12	2,000	Revenue Distribution			
D . .	50,000	5/12	5,000	Account . .	120,000	12,000
E . .	50,000	5/12	5,000				
	120,000		£12,000		120,000	£12,000

STATEMENT OF ACCOUNT WITH MEMBERS AT 31ST DECEMBER, 19. .

	+ Share of Profit on Actual Output	— Penalty	+ Distribution of Penalty by Deficiency of Units	Net Distribution of Revenue	Amount Due for Goods Supplied	Final Amount Due
	£	£	£	£	£	£
A .	30,000	**10,000**	—	20,000	—	20,000
B .	9,000	—	2,000	11,000	4,000	15,000
C .	15,000	—	—	15,000	—	15,000
D .	15,000	—	5,000	20,000	500	20,500
E .	25,000	—	5,000	30,000	—	30,000
F .	6,000	**2,000**	—	4,000	—	4,000
	£100,000	£12,000	£12,000	£100,000	£4,500	£104,500

2. *Books of London Firm*

EUROPEAN AGENTS

Dr.	Francs	Rate	£		Cr.	Francs	Rate	£
To Balance	60,000	12	5,000·00		By Remittance to U.S.A.	24,000	12	2,000·00
,, Profit on Exchange			50·85		,, Draft	36,000 ²	11·8	3,050·85
	60,000		£5,050·85			60,000		£5,050·85

AMERICAN FIRM

Dr.	$	Rate	£		Cr.	$	Rate	£
To Remittance (per European Agents)	6,000	3	2,000		By Loss on Exchange			?
,, Profit on Exchange			?					

BANK

Dr.	Francs	Rate	£		Cr.	Francs	Rate	£
To Foreign Currency Suspense—Delivery under Forward Exchange Contract	25,000	11·9	2,100·84					
,, Foreign Currency Suspense—Balance of Draft ¹	11,000	11·8	932·20					

¹ Assumed that 11·8 is the *actual* rate when proceeds are credited by the Bank.
² See note on page 719.

717

FOREIGN CURRENCY SUSPENSE

Dr.	Francs	Rate	£		Cr.	Francs	Rate	£
To European Agents	36,000	11·8	3,050·85		By Bank [1]	25,000	11·9	2,100·84
					„ Profit and Loss on Forward	11,000	11·8	932·20
					Exchange Account [2]			17·81
	36,000		£3,050·85			36,000		£3,050·85

[1] See page 719.

[2] Loss on Forward Exchange is $\frac{1}{118} \times £2,100·84 = £17·81$

Alternatively, 11,000 francs at 11·8 may be posted direct to bank, merely passing through the Foreign Currency Suspense Account 25,000 francs.

The latter account would then read—

Dr.				FOREIGN CURRENCY SUSPENSE			Cr.
	Francs	Rate	£		Francs	Rate	£
To European Agents .	25,000	11·8	2,118·64	By Bank . . ,, Profit and Loss on Forward Exchange Account[1]	25,000	11·9	2,100·84
							17·80
	25,000		£2,118·64		25,000		£2,118·64

[1] The difference of one new penny arises by the ignoring of fractions.

3. It is advisable to prepare a rough Trial Balance before attempting the final accounts and making the necessary adjustments. In doing so, the reader will observe that the item representing sales of "new" and "old" goods is missing, so that the balancing item (so described) can be taken as sales of new and old goods. These figures can be proved from the information given in the question.

[The accounts can be built up from the facts given in the question, but time in the examination would not usually permit.]

As a preliminary to the preparation of the Trial Balance, the opening entries (of which the debtors and creditors have already been absorbed in the accounts) should be made, thus—

OPENING ENTRIES

	Dr. £	Cr. £
Fixed Assets	6,000	
Stock	5,000	
Debtors	3,000	
Goodwill	3,000	
To Creditors		2,000
,, Vendor		15,000

TRIAL BALANCE

	Dr. £	Cr. £
Process 1: Raw Materials purchased	20,000	
Process 2: Raw Materials purchased ("other Goods") .	6,000	
General Expenses	3,600	
Vendor	10,000	*15,000*
Debtors	4,550	
Creditors		10,700
Cash at Bank	2,000	
Share Capital		20,300
Preliminary Expenses	700	
Preliminary Expenses owing		100
Sales ("old" Goods)		5,550
Goodwill	*3,000*	
Stock	*5,000*	
Fixed Assets	*6,000*	
Sales ("new" Goods)—balancing item [see Note at top of page 720].		9,200
	£60,850	£60,850

[Items in italics from opening entries.]

Note. The sales of "new" goods are proved as follows—

		£
Goods sold—50% of £14,720 (as shown in Selling Department Profit and Loss Account in respect of goods acquired from Process 2)	. . .	7,360
Add Profit—25% of £7,360 [i.e. 20% of £9,200]		1,840
Sales of "new" Goods		£9,200

The book-keeper had credited Share Capital with the cash received from share-holders, viz. £19,500 + £800 (i.e. shares re-issued), so that, to adjust, £500 must be debited to Call Account and credited to Share Capital, and £800 debited to Share Capital and credited to Forfeited Shares Re-issued. This makes the Share Capital £20,000, which is then debited with £2,000 in respect of the shares forfeited and Forfeited Shares Account credited.

Dr.   **PROCESS 1**   **Cr.**

	£			£
To Raw Materials consumed—		By Transfer to Process 2 . . .		17,600
Purchases . . £20,000				
Less Closing Stock . 5,000				
	15,000			
,, General Expenses . . .	1,000[1]			
,, Profit to Summary . . .	1,600			
	£17,600			£17,600

Dr.   **PROCESS 2**   **Cr.**

	£			£
To Raw Materials consumed—		By Transfer to Selling Department		14,720
Process 1: Goods—				
Transfer ex Process 1 £17,600				
Less Closing Stock 9,600				
	8,000			
Other Goods—				
Purchases . 6,000				
Less Closing Stock 2,000				
	4,000			
	12,000			
,, General Expenses . . .	800[1]			
,, Profit to Summary . . .	1,920			
	£14,720			£14,720

[1] See calculation on page 722.

SELLING DEPARTMENT TRADING AND PROFIT AND LOSS ACCOUNT
FOR THE YEAR ENDED 30TH JUNE, 19.8

	£			£	£
Opening Stock	5,000	Sales: "old" . . .	£5,550		
Transfer from Process 2	14,720	"new" . . .	9,200		
Gross Profit . . . c/d	2,390				14,750
[on "old" goods, £550; on "new"		Closing Stock . . .			7,360
goods (20% of £9,200), £1,840]					
	£22,110				£22,110
General Expenses . . .	1,800				
Net Profit to Summary . . .	590	Gross Profit . . . b/d			2,390
	£2,390				£2,390

PROFIT AND LOSS ACCOUNT (SUMMARY)

	£		£
Provision for Unrealized Profit on		Process 1: Profit	1,600
Unsold Stock . . .	2,197[1]	Process 2: Profit	1,920
Net Profit	1,913	Selling Dept.: Profit . . .	590
	£4,110		£4,110

Provision for unrealized profit on unsold Stock—

		£
Selling Dept. (to eliminate Process 2 profit)—$\frac{15}{115} \times$ £7,360		960
Selling Dept. (to eliminate Process 1 profit)—$\frac{1}{11} \times \frac{8000}{12800} \times$ (£7,360 − £960) . .		364
Process 2 (to eliminate Process 1 profit)—$\frac{1}{11} \times$ £9,600		873
		£2,197

(DRAFT)

BALANCE SHEET AT 30TH JUNE, 19.8

	£	£		£	£
Share Capital, £1 fully paid		24,000	Fixed Assets		6,000
Profit on Shares Re-issued (a)	.	550	Goodwill		3,000
Forfeited Shares (b) . .	.	750	Cash at Bank . . .		2,000
Profit and Loss Account .	.	1,913	Debtors		4,550
		27,213	Stocks on hand—		
Creditors—			Process 1 . .	5,000	
Trade . . .	10,700		Process 2 . .	9,600	
Preliminary Expenses .	100		Process 2 . .	2,000	
		10,800	Selling Dept. .	7,360	
				23,960	
			Less Provision for unrealized		
			profit on unsold Stock	2,197	
					21,763
			Preliminary Expenses . .	.	700
		£38,013			£38,013

(a) Profit on 1,000 shares. Amount received on each share 75p + 80p − 100p = 55p; profit, 1,000 × 55p.

(b) Amount carried forward on Forfeited Shares, pending re-issue, 1,000 × 75p.

WORKING ACCOUNTS

VENDOR

	£		£
T.B.	10,000	T.B.	15,000
S.C.	5,000		

SHARE CAPITAL

	£		£
F.S.R.	800	T.B.	20,300
F.S.	2,000	Call	500
Balance	24,000	Vendor . . .	5,000
		F.S.R. . . .	1,000

CALL

					£						£
S.C.	.	.	.	.	500	F.S.	.	.	.	.	500

FORFEITED SHARES

					£						£
Call	.	.	.	.	500	S.C.	.	.	.	.	2,000
F.S.R.	.	.	.	.	200						
P.S.R.	.	.	.	.	550						
Balance.	.	.	c/d		750						
						Balance	.	.	. b/d		750

FORFEITED SHARES RE-ISSUED

					£						£
						S.C.	.	.	.	.	800
S.C.	.	.	.	.	1,000	F.S.	.	.	.	.	200

PROFIT ON SHARES RE-ISSUED

					£
	F.S.	.	.	.	.	**550**

CALCULATION OF ALLOCATION OF GENERAL EXPENSES APPLICABLE TO PROCESS 1 AND 2

Process 1:

Let

$$A = \text{proportion}$$
$$\text{Raw Materials} = £15,000$$
$$\text{Expenses} = A \times £1,800$$
$$\text{Profit} = \tfrac{1}{10} \times (1,800A + 15,000)$$
$$\text{Cost of Product to Process 2: } \tfrac{11}{10} (1,800A + 15,000)$$

Process 2:

$$\text{Raw Materials} = \tfrac{11}{10} (1,800A + 15,000) - 9,600 \text{ [ex Process 1]} + 4,000 \text{ [other Goods]}$$
$$= 1,980A + 16,500 - 9,600 + 4,000$$
$$= 1,980A + 10,900$$

So
$$A = \frac{15,000}{1,980A + 10,900 + 15,000} \text{ i.e. } \frac{15,000}{1,980A + 25,900}$$

Hence
$$A(1,980A + 25,900) = 15,000$$
$$1,980A^2 + 25,900A - 15,000 = 0$$
$$99A^2 + 1,295A - 750 = 0$$

Then
$$(9A - 5)(11A + 150) = 0$$

so either
$$9A = 5 \quad \text{or} \quad 11A = -150$$

Therefore $A = \tfrac{5}{9}$, so that expenses in Process 1 $= \tfrac{5}{9} \times £1,800 = £1,000$
(and $\tfrac{4}{9} \times £1,800 = £800$ in Process 2.)

INDEX

Unless otherwise stated, references are to the Chapter (in Roman numerals) and to the number of the particular question and answer therein.

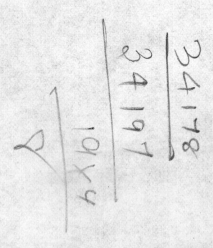

34178
34197
10 × 4